4.00

PEGGY DAVI

Kevin  Francis

Tea with Clarice Cliff
Released February
1997. **SOLD OUT**

Young Clarice
SOLD OUT
Issue Price £130.00

Persian Dancer
Issue Price £115.00
SOLD OUT

Susie Cooper
Issue Price £145.00
SOLD OUT

Pyjama Girl
Released November 1998
Issue Price £175.00

Lo La Palooza
Released June '97
SOLD OUT
Issue Price £149.00

D-Day Landings
Limited Edition 750
£147.00

Charlotte Rhead figurine
Limited Edition of 950 worldwide
SOLD OUT
Issue Price £195.00

Approximate average height is 9 inches.

PEGGY DAVIES CERAMICS

Peggy Davies Ceramics, the sole producers of Kevin Francis ware, established by the world renowned ceramic artist Peggy Davies, is at the forefront when it comes to design and quality in the world of Limited Edition, hand crafted, hand painted ceramic art.

Celebrating ten years of producing the world's most intricate pieces in 1997, the Kevin Francis range has become much sought after, so much so that there is now an investment label on these quality items. Our range is being added to approximately four times a year. To join our free register of Collectors for regular brochures, or to find out more about the thriving Kevin Francis Collectors Guild, write, phone or fax Rod Davies or Rhys Davies

Peggy Davies Ceramics
Freepost Mid 16669, Stoke-on-Trent, ST4 1BJ
Tel: 01782 848002 Fax: 01782 747651 Email: rhys@kevinfrancis.co.uk
Website: www.kevinfrancis.co.uk **www.bulldogs.co.uk**

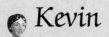

Charles knew that a pair of earrings from Grays would do the trick

MILLER'S

PRICE GUIDE

collectibles

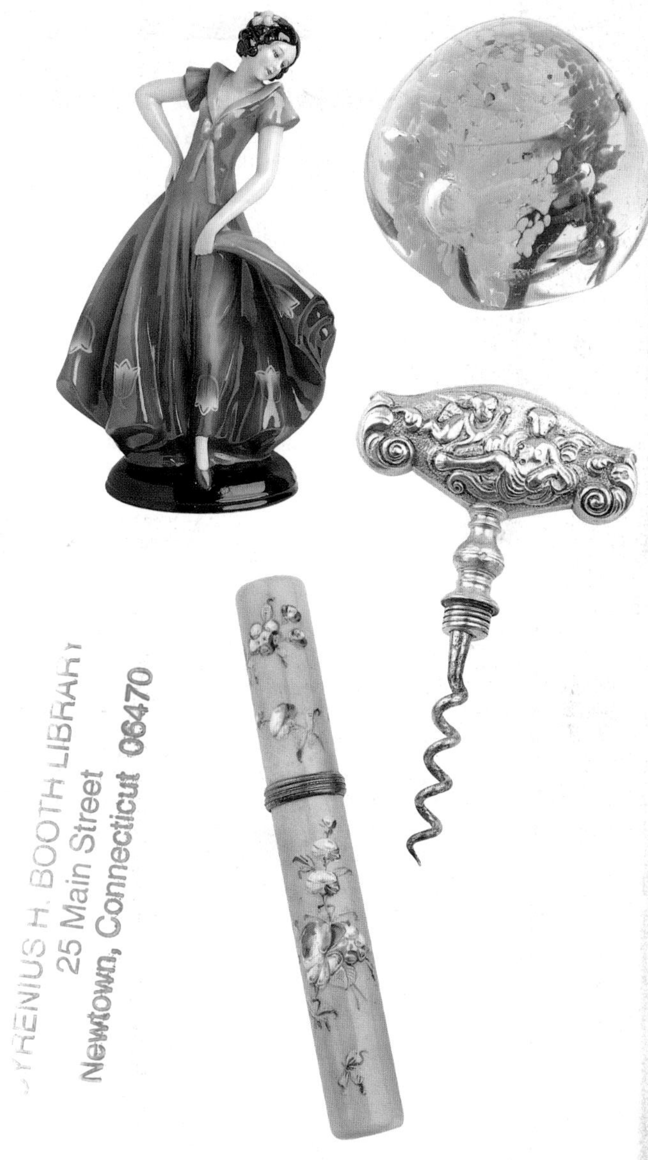

MILLER'S

PRICE GUIDE

collectibles

MADELEINE MARSH *GENERAL EDITOR*

2003/4
VOLUME XV

MILLER'S COLLECTIBLES PRICE GUIDE 2003/4

Created and designed by
Miller's
The Cellars, High Street
Tenterden, Kent, TN30 6BN
Tel: 01580 766411
Fax: 01580 766100

General Editor: Madeleine Marsh
Managing Editor: Valerie Lewis
Production Co-ordinator: Kari Reeves
Editorial Co-ordinator: Deborah Wanstall
Editorial Assistants: Caroline Bugeja, Joanna Hill, Maureen Horner
Production Assistants: Gillian Charles, Helen Clarkson, Ethne Tragett
Advertising Executive: Jill Jackson
Advertising Co-ordinator & Administrator: Melinda Williams
Advertising Assistant: Emma Gillingham
Designer: Philip Hannath
Advertisement Designer: Simon Cook
Indexer: Hilary Bird
Jacket Design: Victoria Bevan
Production: Angela Couchman
Additional Photographers: Gareth Gooch, David Mereweather, Dennis O'Reilly, Robin Saker
North American Consultants: Marilynn and Sheila Brass
US Advertising Representative: Katharine Buckley,
Buckley Pell Associates, 34 East 64th Street, New York, NY 10021
Tel: 212 223 4996 Fax: 212 223 4997 E-mail: buckley@moveworld.com

First published in Great Britain in 2003
by Miller's, a division of Mitchell Beazley,
imprint of Octopus Publishing Group Ltd,
2–4 Heron Quays, London E14 4JP

A CIP catalogue record for this book is
available from the British Library

ISBN 1-84000-697-8

Illustrations by Smart Solutions Ltd, Whitstable, Kent, England
Printed and bound by Rotolito Lombarda, Italy

Front Cover Illustrations:
A Fada plastic bullet radio, c1945, 10in (25.5cm) wide. **£650–750/$950–1,100 ⊞ EKK**
A Snoopy pop-up music box, by Mattel, c1960, 11in (28cm) high. **£75–85/$110–120 ⊞ CWo**
A *Movie Life* magazine, including a Beatles article, 1960s, 11in (28cm) high. **£4–5/$5–7 ⊞ BTC**

How To Use This Book

It is our aim to make this guide easy to use. In order to find a particular item, turn to the contents list on page 9 to find the main heading, for example, Shipping. Having located your area of interest, you will see that larger sections may be sub-divided by subject or maker. If you are looking for a particular factory, maker, or object, consult the index, which starts on page 453.

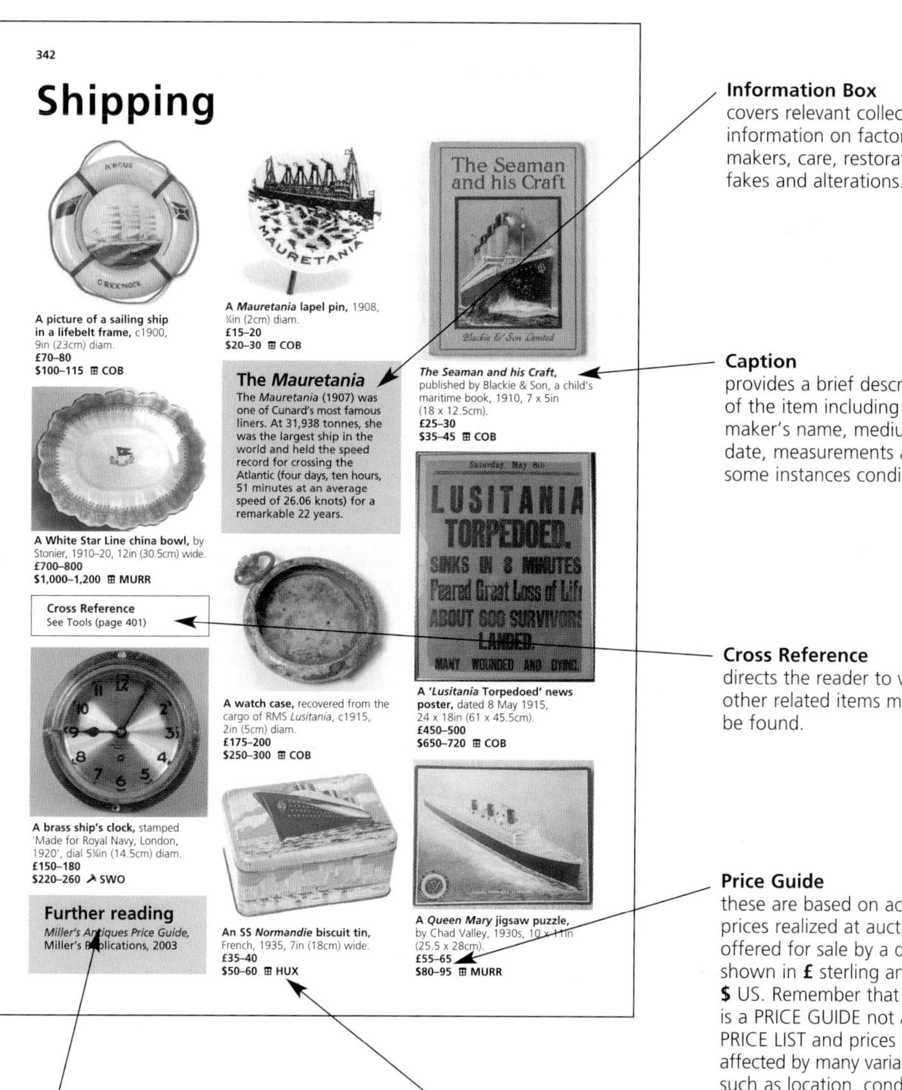

342

Shipping

A picture of a sailing ship in a lifebelt frame, c1900, 9in (23cm) diam.
£70–80
$100–115 ⊞ COB

A *Mauretania* lapel pin, 1908, ¾in (2cm) diam.
£15–20
$20–30 ⊞ COB

The Seaman and his Craft, published by Blackie & Son, a child's maritime book, 1910, 7 x 5in (18 x 12.5cm).
£25–30
$35–45 ⊞ COB

The *Mauretania*
The *Mauretania* (1907) was one of Cunard's most famous liners. At 31,938 tonnes, she was the largest ship in the world and held the speed record for crossing the Atlantic (four days, ten hours, 51 minutes at an average speed of 26.06 knots) for a remarkable 22 years.

A White Star Line china bowl, by Stonier, 1910–20, 12in (30.5cm) wide.
£700–800
$1,000–1,200 ⊞ MURR

Cross Reference
See Tools (page 401)

A watch case, recovered from the cargo of RMS *Lusitania*, c1915, 2in (5cm) diam.
£175–200
$250–300 ⊞ COB

A '*Lusitania* Torpedoed' news poster, dated 8 May 1915, 24 x 18in (61 x 45.5cm).
£450–500
$650–720 ⊞ COB

A brass ship's clock, stamped 'Made for Royal Navy, London, 1920', dial 5¾in (14.5cm) diam.
£150–180
$220–260 ⚒ SWO

Further reading
Miller's Antiques Price Guide, Miller's Publications, 2003

An SS *Normandie* biscuit tin, French, 1935, 7in (18cm) wide.
£35–40
$50–60 ⊞ HUX

A *Queen Mary* jigsaw puzzle, by Chad Valley, 1930s, 10 x 11in (25.5 x 28cm).
£55–65
$80–95 ⊞ MURR

Information Box
covers relevant collecting information on factories, makers, care, restoration, fakes and alterations.

Caption
provides a brief description of the item including the maker's name, medium, date, measurements and in some instances condition.

Cross Reference
directs the reader to where other related items may be found.

Price Guide
these are based on actual prices realized at auction or offered for sale by a dealer, shown in **£** sterling and **$** US. Remember that Miller's is a PRICE GUIDE not a PRICE LIST and prices are affected by many variables such as location, condition, desirability and so on. Don't forget that if you are selling, it is quite likely you will be offered less than the price range. Price ranges for items sold at auction tend to include the buyer's premium and VAT if applicable.

Source Code
refers to the 'Key to Illustrations' on page 443 that lists the details of where the item was sourced. The ⚒ icon indicates the item was sold at auction. The ⊞ icon indicates the item originated from a dealer.

Further Reading
directs the reader towards additional sources of information.

Acknowledgments

We would like to acknowledge the great assistance given by our consultants who are listed below. We would also like to extend our thanks to all the auction houses, their press offices, dealers and collectors who have assisted us in the production of this book.

Beverley/Beth
30 Church Street
Alfie's Antique Market
Marylebone
London NW8 8EP
(Ceramics)

Alan Blakeman
BBR Elsecar Heritage Centre
Wath Road, Elsecar, Barnsley
Yorks S74 8AF
(Advertising, Packaging, Bottles, Breweriana)

Graham Budd
Sotheby's
34–35 New Bond Street
London W1A 2AA
(Football Memorabilia)

Mike Chapman
Beanos Record Shop
Middle Street, Croydon
London CR0 1RE
(Records)

Alan Cook
Antique Photographic Company Ltd
Lincolnshire
(Magic Lanterns)

Andrew Hilton
Special Auction Services
The Coach House, Midgham Park
Reading, Berks RG7 5UG
(Commemorative Ware)

David Huxtable
S03/05 Alfies Antique Market
13–25 Church Street
London NW8 8DT
(Advertising & Packaging)

Malcolm Phillips
Comic Book Postal Auctions
40–42 Osnaburgh Street
London NW1 3ND
(Comics)

John Pym
Hope & Glory
131a Kensington Church Street
London W8 7LP
(Royal Commemorative)

Mike Reynolds
Memory Lane Records
55 Frith Street
Croydon
Surrey
(Records)

Chris Trigg
Vintage & Rare Guitars
7–8 Saville Row
Bath, Somerset BA1 2QP
(Guitars)

Tony Trowbridge
Fossil Shop
The Blue Slipper
24 St John's Road
Sandown, Isle of Wight
PO36 8ES
(Fossils)

T. Vennett-Smith
11 Nottingham Road
Gotham
Nottinghamshire NG11 0HE
(Autographs)

Dominic Winter Book Auctions
The Old School
Maxwell Street
Swindon
Wiltshire SN1 5DR
(Books)

Jamie Woollard
Offworld
142 Market Halls
Arndale Center
Luton, Bedfordshire
LU1 2TP
(Sci-Fi)

Contents

Introduction

One of the by-products of getting older is that you see your own past becoming collectable. This year's guide includes toys from the 1980s ranging from computer and video games to Transformers to My Little Pony. These objects reflect the increasing influence of TV, Film and new technology both on what we want to play with as children and what we wish to collect as adults. This is well illustrated in our Sci-Fi section which runs from 1960s *Thunderbirds* vehicles to modern *Buffy the Vampire Slayer* trading cards. These pages also include *Star Wars* material, where 'The Power of the Force' is demonstrated by the huge sums paid for merchandise that originally sold for pocket money prices.

After all this staring at TV and computer screens, it's perhaps a relief to turn to our books section. Special features this year include detective fiction, which proves, in collectable terms at least, that crime certainly does pay. Comics can also fetch seriously high prices. Illustrated in Record Breakers (page 428), is a first issue of the *Beano* (1938) that fetched a world record £7,450 ($10,800) at auction. Today's chuckouts can become tomorrow's antiques, quite literally in the case of the pot lids and bottles dug up from Victorian rubbish dumps. In Advertising & Packaging, we have a biscuit tin worth £3,000 ($4,500), while in Sport a single ticket stub from an early cup final is valued at £2,000 ($3,000). Football memorabilia illustrates perfectly that what makes an object collectable is not necessarily fine materials or craftsmanship but the passion of the purchase. To the non-enthusiast a collection of old football programmes would be worthless, but included in this section are programmes that sold at auction to football fans for hundreds of pounds.

Sometimes artistry and passion come together as in the case of vintage guitars, to which we devote a new section this year. Fine vintage guitars can fetch thousands of pounds, both because of their romantic rock and roll associations and because they are, quite simply, brilliant to play. The Rock & Pop section also includes records. Since the advent of the CD player, many music fans have relegated their vinyl to the loft, but who knows? If you're lucky, there might be a collectable classic lurking there.

Technology always moves forward, but for some enthusiasts, the designs of the past have never been bettered. Many of the objects in this book still work today such as valve radios, Bakelite telephones and magic lanterns. You might not want to use surgical instruments in our Medical section but the enema cufflinks (page 270) would certainly provide a talking point at a party.

Most women would probably prefer prettier jewellery. This year we cover Victorian sentimental jewellery, decoding its hidden messages of love, and 20th-century costume jewellery, which in certain instances can cost more than the real thing. For those who love fashion accessories, there are cosmetics and compacts, vintage handbags and wardrobes full of collectable clothes, shoes and accessories – not forgetting a special feature on corsets.

The joy of *Miller's Collectables Price Guide* is that there is something for everybody, whatever your taste and whatever your pocket. Special features this year include autographs, royal memorabilia, Portmeirion pottery and Masonic material. The oldest items in this book are fossils, ranging from a dinosaur's leg bone at £4,500–5,000 ($6,500–7,250) to a dinosaur coprolite (a ball of petrified dung) – 120 million years of history and real contact with a dinosaur for a price range of only £5–10 ($10–15).

At the end of the guide, our Collectables of the Future page suggests some modern purchases which could well become the antiques and collectables of tomorrow. Record Breakers celebrates objects that have achieved the most remarkable results at auction, while Pocket Money Collectables shows some of the collectables you can still buy for under £5 ($10). Variety is the spice of life and the essence of this Guide. If you have an interesting collection yourself or if there are further subjects you would like to see covered, please let us know. Also we invite you to join the Miller's Club. Members can nominate candidates for the BACA awards, which were started by Miller's to recognize excellence in this remarkable industry. We value your input and we look forward to receiving your suggestions. Thank you for your support, enjoy the Guide and cherish your collectables.

Madeleine Marsh

Advertising & Packaging

A Mrs S. A. Allen's Hair Restorer ceramic advertising figure, with a woman holding a bottle and leaning against a large shield inscribed in red and black lettering with gold highlighting, 19thC, 21in (53.5cm) high.
£2,600–3,000
$3,800–4,400 BBR
This is a rare and highly decorative figure, hence its high value.

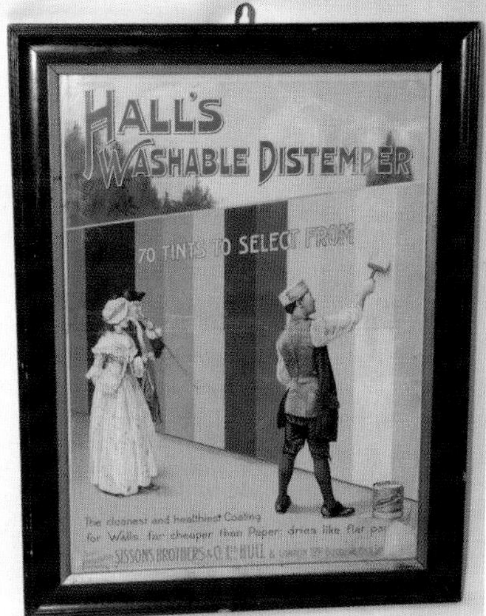

A Hall's Washable Distemper advertising card, c1900, 20 x 15in (51 x 38cm).
£80–90
$115–130 JUN

An Atkinson's Bears Grease pot lid, depicting a chained and muzzled bear, some crazing, 19thC, 2¾in (7cm) diam.
£75–85
$110–125 BBR

A Clark & Co Anchor Machine Cottons silk ball advertising globe, on a turned wooden stepped base, minor damage, c1900, 3in (7.5cm) diam.
£280–330
$410–475 TMA

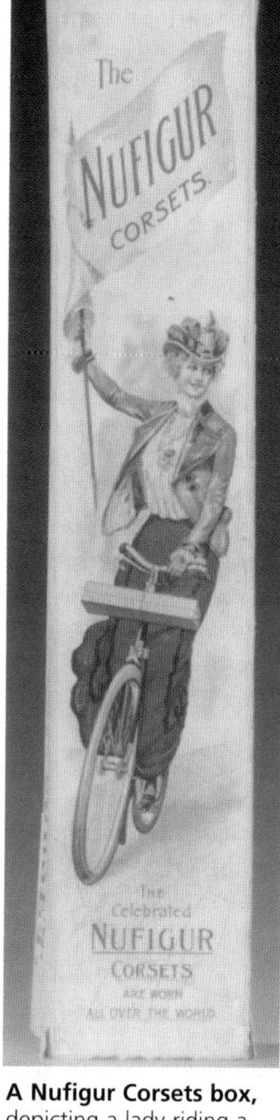

A Nufigur Corsets box, depicting a lady riding a bicycle and holding a banner, box end missing, c1900.
£180–200
$260–290 B(Kn)
The value of this box reflects the bicycling subject matter.

► **A Spratt's enamel dog bowl,** c1900, 10in (25.5cm) diam.
£60–70
$90–100 B&R

A Fry's Cocoa/Caracas chocolate giveaway folding ruler, 1905, 12in (30.5cm) wide.
£90–100
$130–145 ⊞ HUX

A Marshall's Semolina tin tray, c1900, 12 x 16in (30.5 x 40.5cm).
£40–50
$60–75 ⊞ B&R

◄ A MacFarlane, Lang & Co glass display cabinet, c1900, 36in (91.5cm) high.
£720–800
$1,000–1,150 ⊞ JUN

A Player's Navy Cut finger plate with match striker, 1910, 7¼in (18.5cm) high.
£225–275
$325–400 ⊞ HUX

◄ An Alexandra Cream Separators advertising card, c1910, 17 x 12in (43 x 30.5cm).
£200–250
$290–360 ⊞ JUN

A Schweppes advertising vesta case, c1910, 2½in (6.5cm) high.
£70–80
$100–115 ⊞ HUX

A Bovril novelty advertising kaleidoscope card, 1910–18, 6¼ x 4½in (16 x 11.5cm).
£35–45
$50–65 ⊞ MURR

A brass Oxo dispenser, used in a café, c1910, 17in (43cm) high.
£150–175
$220–255 ⊞ B&R

Meat extracts

Meat extracts became extremely popular in the late 19th century. Bovril was developed in Canada in the 1870s – its name originating from bo, Latin for ox and vril, a term meaning life force. Oxo was launched in the UK in 1900. As well as being produced for home use, these drinks were served in cafés and even pubs, hence the large Oxo urn.

◄ **A Palethorpes Sausages advertising mirror,** in original frame, c1920, 18 x 23in (45.5 x 58.5cm).
£250–300
$360–440 ⊞ SMI

► **An O.K. Sauce penknife,** 1920s, 3in (7.5cm) long.
£30–35
$45–50 ⊞ HUX

A Reliance clothes brush, c1920, 6in (15cm) long.
£8–10
$12–15 ⊞ AL

A Ruby Remedy for Worms in Puppies bottle, c1925, 5in (12.5cm) long.
£10–15
$15–20 ⊞ HUX

An Ogden's Robin Cigarettes packet, 1920s, 3in (7.5cm) high.
£10–15
$15–20 ⊞ RTT

A Scent Spray Soaps glass shop counter container, c1920, 8in (20.5cm) high.
£180–200
$260–290 ⊞ SMI
The inscription makes this jar particularly desirable. Similar glass containers were produced for Smith's crisps, before the days of individual packets. Crisp jars are more commonplace and as such cheaper than this unusual Scent Spray Soaps example.

◄ **A Cammel Laird Shipbuilders paperweight,** 1920s, 4in (10cm) high.
£75–85
$110–125 ⊞ COB

A Shell advertising mirror, c1920, 26 x 9in (66 x 23cm).
£175–200
$255–290 ⊞ JUN

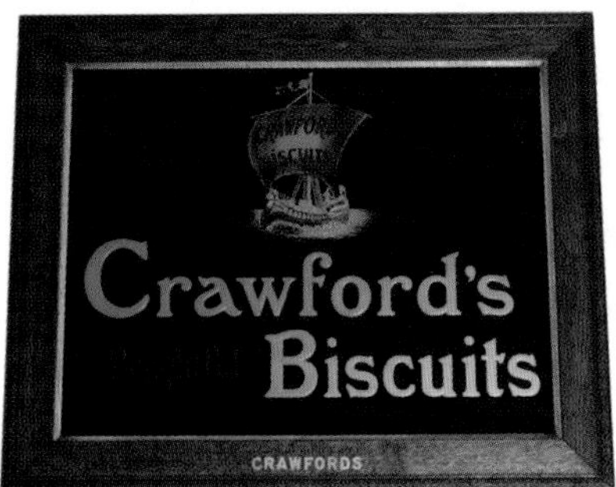

A Crawford's Biscuits advertising mirror, in original frame, c1920, 23 x 18in (58.5 x 45.5cm).
£450–500
$650–720 ⊞ SMI

◄ A Winsor & Newtons prepared canvas & artists' colour manufactory, 1920s, 4¾ x 3¾in (12 x 9.5cm).
£6–8
$8–12 ⊞ RTT

A United Dairies cream jug, c1925, 2¾in (7cm) high.
£15–20
$20–30 ⊞ HUX

Auction or dealer?

All the pictures in our price guides originate from auction houses and dealers. Look for the symbol at the end of each caption to identify the source.

When buying at auction, prices can be lower than those of a dealer, but a buyer's premium and VAT will be added to the hammer price. Equally, when selling at auction, commission, tax and photography charges must be taken into account. Dealers will often restore pieces before putting them back on the market.

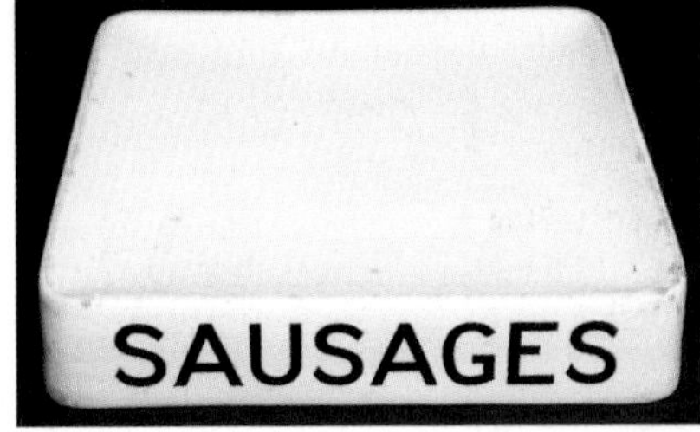

A ceramic sausage stand, 1920s, 12in (30.5cm) square.
£200–250
$290–360 ⊞ SMI

A selection of metal advertising giveaway pencil sharpeners, c1925, largest 1½in (4cm) high.
£20–40
$30–60 each ⊞ HUX

► A Huntley & Palmers Biscuits 78rpm record, 1920–30, 4in (10cm) square.
£45–55
$65–80 ⊞ RUSS

A Perrier metal menu holder, 1925–35, 3in (7.5cm) high.
£25–30
$35–45 ⊞ HUX

A Turog Bread metal menu holder, 1925–35, 4in (10cm) high.
£40–50
$60–75 ⊞ HUX

A rubber Penfold Man advertising figure, on a wooden base, 1930s, 20in (51cm) high.
£550–650
$800–950 ⊞ MSh
Penfold, a well-known British manufacturer of golf balls, was founded by Albert E. Penfold in 1927 and expanded to the USA in the 1930s. Penfold Man was the company symbol and is dressed in typical golfer's uniform of the period: large tweed cap, colourful pullover, boldly-checked jacket and plus fours. The golfing theme makes this figure particularly desirable.

A Lodge Plugs tin advertising sign, c1930, 9 x 13in (23 x 33cm).
£35–40
$50–60 ⊞ JUN

A Hinders Zix Pads ceramic advertising display, c1930, 12in (30.5cm) high.
£80–100
$115–145 ⊞ JUN

A Lanvin Chocolat au Lait tin stand-up display bar, c1930, 6½in (16.5cm) wide.
£50–55
$75–80 ⊞ MSB

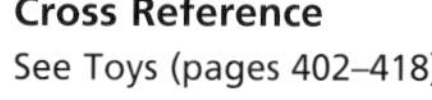
Cross Reference
See Toys (pages 402–418)

◄ **A United Dairies model railway tanker,** 1930s, 7in (18cm) wide.
£45–55
$65–80 ⊞ RTT

A St Ivel Cream sign, 1930s, 9 x 7in (23 x 18cm).
£30–50
$45–75 ⊞ MURR

A Bovril ceramic mug, c1930, 3½in (9cm) high.
£10–15
$15–20 ⊞ AL

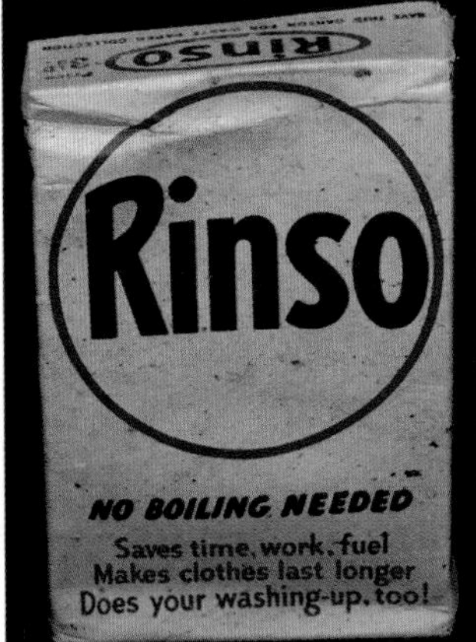

A Rinso detergent packet, with contents, 1939–45, 5in (12.5cm) high.
£10–12
$15–18 ⊞ HUX

A Fry's Five Boys chocolate bar shop dummy, 1950, 3½in (9cm) wide.
£15–20
$20–30 ⊞ HUX

Cross Reference
See Breweriana (pages 74–77)

▶ Two Cinzano promotional cloth dolls, 1950s, 12in (30.5cm) high.
£15–20
$20–30 ⚒ G(L)

A Wills's Woodbines advertising sign, c1940, 15 x 20in (38 x 51cm).
£130–150
$190–220 ⊞ JUN

A Kranebet Liquore poster, 1946, 40 x 28in (101.5 x 71cm).
£40–50
$60–75 ⊞ RTT

A Silk Cut Cigarettes packet, 1940–50, 3¼in (8.5cm) high.
£3–5
$5–7 ⊞ RTT

A Meredith & Drew glass biscuit jar, with an aluminium lid, 1950, 9in (23cm) high.
£35–40
$50–60 ⊞ AL

A Sadolins Paints advertising poster, by Stockmarr, c1950, 25 x 33in (63.5 x 84cm).
£500–600
$720–870 ⚒ VSP

An Oxo tin tray, early 1950s, 13 x 16in (33 x 40.5cm).
£30–35
$45–50 ⊞ HUX

An Ovaltine cup and saucer, 1950s, 10in (25.5cm) diam.
£25–30
$35–45 ⊞ HUX

Ovaltine was created by Swiss chemist Dr George Wander in 1904. Creative advertising contributed to the success of the brand. The Ovaltine Dairy Maid (shown on the cup) was a favourite image and in 1935 the Ovaltiney Club was launched on Radio Luxembourg. The Club's song 'We are the Ovaltineys' became one of the most famous jingles of all time and by 1939 there were five million club members.

A Dixon of Dock Green Sweet Cigarettes packet, 1960, 3½in (9cm) high.
£12–15
$18–20 ⊞ HUX

A Polo packet shop dummy, 1950s, 3½in (9cm) wide.
£6–8
$8–10 ⊞ HUX

A Raphaël apéritif glass carafe, c1955, 7in (18cm) high.
£10–12
$15–18 ⊞ HUX

A Coca-Cola bottle opener, American, 1950–60, 3in (7.5cm) high.
£28–32
$40–48 ⊞ RUSS

A Clarnico Chocolate Peppermint Creams shop dummy, c1955, 6in (15cm) wide.
£6–8
$8–10 ⊞ HUX

A Sutton & Sons glass ashtray, c1950, 5in (12.5cm) wide.
£25–30
$35–45 ⊞ JUN

A Wall's Strawberry Snocreme advertisement, 1957, 5 x 10in (12.5 x 25.5cm).
£15–18
$20–25 ⊞ RUSS

A Coca-Cola painted pine box, American, 1950–60, 10 x 16in (25.5 x 40.5cm).
£25–30
$35–45 ⊞ MIN

A full pack of Hubbly Bubbly 10 inch drinking straws, 1960s, box 3¼in (8.5cm) wide.
£8–10
$12–15 ⊞ RTT

► **A Pillsbury Poppie Fresh vinyl promotional doll,** 1972, 6in (15cm) high.
£10–12
$15–18 ⊞ RTT
Poppin Fresh, the Pillsbury Doughboy, popped out of his first can of refrigerated dough in a 1965 US TV commercial. Devised by advertising agency Leo Burnett, the Doughboy was created by artist Rude Perz. His pudgy figure and distinctive 'Hoo hoo' giggle, made him a favourite advertising character. These promotional dolls were first produced in the early 1970s. As well as Poppin and his wife Poppie there were also Granpopper, Granmommer and a Pillsbury playhouse.

► **A Campbell's Soups metal advertising truck,** 1970s, 19in (48.5cm) long.
£20–25
$30–35 ⊞ COB

Enamel Signs

A Home & Colonial Tea double-sided enamel sign, c1910, 8 x 20in (20.5 x 51cm).
£90–100
$130–145 ⊞ JUN

◄ **A W. D. & H. O. Wills Westward Ho! Smoking Mixture enamel sign,** c1910, 37 x 18in (94 x 45.5cm).
£120–140
$175–200 ⊞ HUX

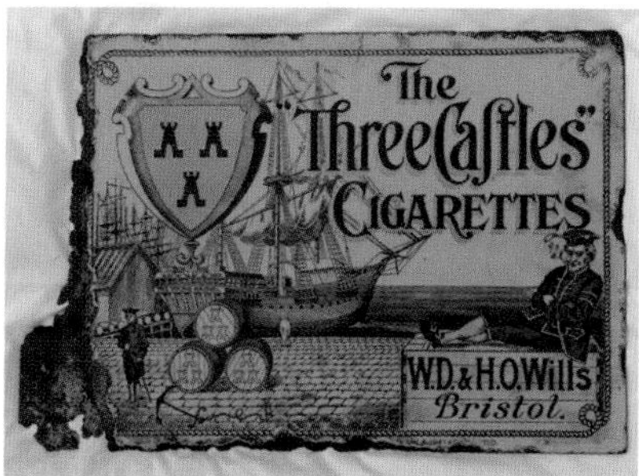

A W. D. & H. O. Wills Three Castles Cigarettes double-sided enamel sign, 1910, 11 x 15in (28 x 38cm).
£150–200
$220–290 ⊞ JUN

A Selo Film enamel cut-out sign, 1920, 18 x 14in (45.5 x 35.5cm).
£200–250
$300–350 ⊞ JUN

A Pratts enamel advertising sign, c1920, 36 x 48in (91.5 x 122cm).
£140–160
$200–230 ⊞ JUN

A Schweppes enamel advertising sign, restored, c1920, 24 x 36in (61 x 91.5cm).
£180–210
$260–300 ⊞ JUN

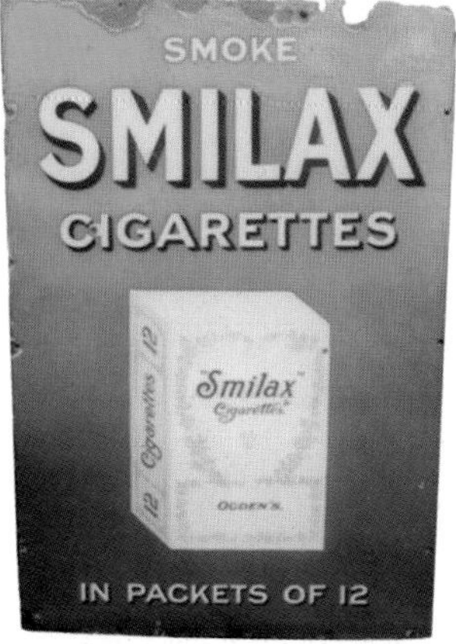

► A Smilax Cigarettes enamel advertising sign, 1920s, 36 x 21in (91.5 x 53.5cm).
£150–200
$220–300
⊞ MURR

A Mew's beer enamel advertising sign, 1930s, 38 x 25in (96.5 x 63.5cm).
£150–200
$220–300 ⊞ JUN

A Wills's Gold Flake Cigarettes enamel advertising sign, c1930, 36 x 24in (91.5 x 61cm).
£150–170
$220–250 ⊞ JUN

◄ A Coca-Cola enamel advertising sign, 1960s, 14in (35.5cm) diam.
£100–120
$145–175 ⊞ JUN

Tins

◀ **Three shop advertising tins,** Golden Assam Tea, Kangra Valley Tea and Yorkshire Perfect Baking Powder, c1880, 4in (10cm) high.
£400–450
$580–650 each ⊞ SMI

A Curtin & Harvey Brown Sporting Gunpowder tin, with original paper label, late 19thC, 8¾in (22cm) high.
£60–75
$90–110 ⚒ SWO

A Huntley & Palmer's Fire Brigade biscuit tin, c1892, 6in (15cm) high.
£550–650
$800–950 ⊞ HUX

◀ **A Gaiety Girl Cigarettes tin,** c1890, 4in (10cm) wide.
£55–65
$80–95 ⊞ TMa

A Rowntree's Toffee tin, c1900, 2in (5cm) diam.
£90–100
$130–145 ⊞ MRW

Further reading

Miller's Advertising Tins: A Collector's Guide,
Miller's Publications, 1999

A Hudson's Soap shop counter string tin, c1900, 9in (23cm) high.
£200–250
$300–350 ⊞ SMI
Before the days of self-service and pre-packaging, purchases were wrapped by the shopkeeper in paper and string. String tins were heavily weighted at the bottom and often included a string cutter on the lid. Manufacturers used these tins to advertise their products in the grocery.

Three Cakeoma curved give-away puzzle tins, c1900, 2in (5cm) wide.
£30–35
$45–50 ⊞ HUX

Three Cadbury's Bournville Cocoa sample tins, reused as vesta cases, c1905, 2in (5cm) long.
£15–45
$20–65 each ⊞ HUX

A Huntley & Palmer's biscuit tin, modelled as a stack of plates, 1908, 8in (20.5cm) diam.
£450–500
$650–720 ⊞ TMa

A Kyriazi Frères Egyptian Cigarettes tin, 1910, 4in (10cm) wide.
£130–160
$200–230 ⊞ HUX

A Garstin's Tonic Dog Soap tin, 1910–20, 8in (20.5cm) wide.
£40–50
$60–75 ⊞ MURR

A metal cachou tin/penny toy, modelled as a lute, 1910, 3½in (9cm) long.
£60–70
$90–100 ⊞ HUX

A Batger & Co Jersey Cream Toffee tin, 1910–20, 6½in (16.5cm) wide.
£40–50
$60–75 ⊞ MURR

◄ **A Paris Gourmand sweet tin/money box,** modelled as the Eiffel Tower, 1920s, 11in (28cm) high.
£85–95
$125–140 ⊞ HUX

► **A Kinema Toffee tin,** decorated with a picture of Charlie Chaplin, 1920, 5½in (14cm) wide.
£100–120
$145–175 ⊞ HUX

A Mackenzie & Mackenzie Albert biscuit tin/money box, 1910, 7½in (19cm) wide.
£550–600
$800–870 ⊞ HUX

A Rowntree's Chocolate tin, decorated with a motoring scene, c1910, 6in (15cm) wide.
£60–70
$90–100 ⊞ JUN

A Huntley & Palmer's biscuit tin, modelled as a painting on an easel, c1914, 7in (18cm) high.
£650–750
$950–1,100 ⊞ HUX

A Huntley & Palmer's biscuit tin, modelled as a Kashmiri table, 1920, 7in (18cm) high.
£225–250
$325–350 ⊞ TMa

A Huntley & Palmer's biscuit tin, lithographed with a Russian rural scene, 1920, 8in (20.5cm) wide.
£60–70
$90–100 ⚒ G(L)

A Thorne's Extra Super Crême Toffee tin, 1920s, 12in (30.5cm) diam.
£50–60
$75–90 ⊞ MURR

A golly sweet tin, 1940s, 6in (15cm) wide.
£85–95
$125–140 ⊞ HUX

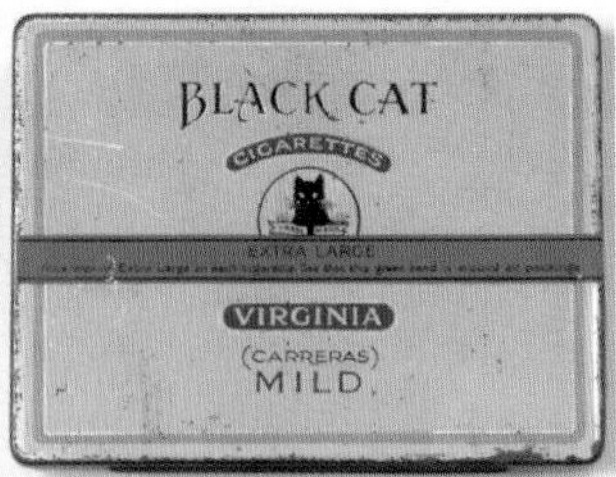

A Black Cat Cigarettes tin, 1920s, 6in (15cm) wide.
£8–10
$10–15 ⊞ COB

A Mother Christmas tin, c1925, 7½in (19cm) diam.
£60–70
$90–100 ⊞ HUX

A CWS biscuit tin, modelled as a motorcyclist and sidecar, 1925, 7in (18cm) long.
£2,700–3,000
$4,000–4,500 ⊞ HUX

The Cooperative Wholesale Society (CWS) was formed in 1863. Since they manufactured a wide variety of food and drink products, they also created a large number of tins. The 1920s saw a particular fashion for tins that could also serve as toys but as they were played with by children, the tins often became broken or damaged. Transport themes are very popular with collectors today and this is a very rare, surviving example – hence its high value.

A Kewpie Klenser tin, 1920s, 5in (12.5cm) high.
£35–40
$50–60 ⊞ HUX

A Mickey Mouse tin, French, c1935, 6¾in (17cm) diam.
£130–150
$200–220 ⊞ HUX

A Mapleton's Fru-Grains tin, c1950, 8in (20.5cm) high.
£8–10
$10–15 ⊞ RTT

Aeronautica

The Daily Mirror

THE MORNING JOURNAL WITH THE SECOND LARGEST NET SALE.

MONDAY, JULY 26, 1909.

CHANNEL CROSSED BY MONOPLANE: M. BLERIOT STARTING ON HIS WONDERFUL FLIGHT FROM LES BARAQUES.

The Daily Mirror, 26 and 27 July 1909, with coverage and photographs of Blériot's historic flight across the English Channel, and front and back pages of 28 July 1909 detailing a Mr Latham's unsuccessful attempt, 30 x 20in (76 x 51cm).
£28–32
$38–48 ⚒ SWO

A wooden box, made from an aircraft propeller, 1914–16, 11in (28cm) wide.
£60–75
$90–110 ⊞ COB

► Two cachou tins, decorated with aircraft, c1910, 2in (5cm) wide.
£65–75
$95–110 each
⊞ HUX

A silver-plated pewter inkwell, by Rumpler Taube for WMF, mounted with a Luftwaffe reconnaissance bi-plane, 1912–13, 12½in (32cm) wide.
£3,000–3,500
$4,500–5,000 ⊞ AU

WMF is short for Württembergische Metallwarenfabrik, a German foundry that was one of the principal producers of Art Nouveau metalware. This example typifies their excellent craftsmanship and quality.

A WWI RFC BE2C bi-plane propeller boss, fitted with a modern quartz clock, manufacturer's stamp, 1914–18, 12in (30.5cm) square.
£200–240
$300–350 ⊞ OLD

◄ A leather flying helmet, 1920–30.
£75–85
$110–125 ⊞ OLD

► An aluminium model of an American Mustang, c1930, 8in (20.5cm) high.
£85–95
$125–140 ⊞ HarC

A photograph of an airman, c1915, 8 x 6in (20.5 x 15cm).
£75–85
$110–125 ⊞ COB

A brass Schneider Trophy car mascot, modelled as an aeroplane, 1929, 7in (18cm) long.
£350–400
$500–580 ⊞ COB

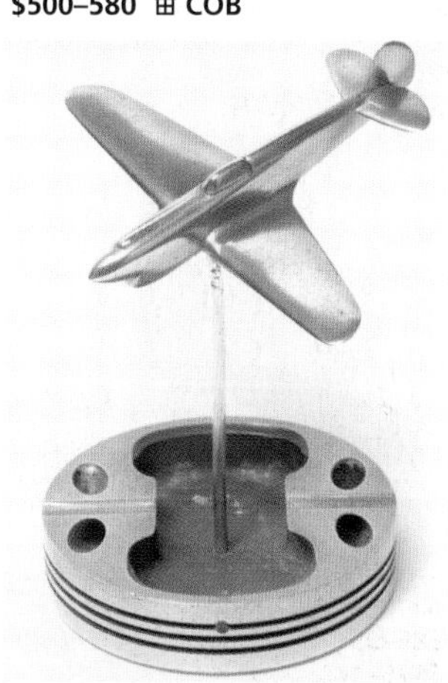

A Brooklands Aero Club membership badge, No. 268, depicting a bi-plane banking above the Brooklands racing track, minor chip, 1930s, 3¾in (9.5cm) high, display mounted.
£500–600
$720–870 ⚒ B(Kn)
Brooklands was the first purpose-built motor racing circuit in the world, constructed in 1906 at Weybridge, Surrey by wealthy landowner Hugh Locke King. Not only was it the birthplace of British motorsport but also British aviation, providing a home for aviation companies and designers and a venue for flying displays and races. The 1920s and '30s were the golden age of Brooklands, and it is to this period that this badge belongs. Frederick Gordon Crosby designed a range of badges for Brooklands Automobile, Flying and Aero clubs that are very collectable today. Beware, however, of fakes made in the Far East. These can be identified by poor quality enamel, which peels off easily, and a waisted tongue fitting as opposed to the screw-and-bolt or straight tongue fitting, found on original models.

A needle book, decorated with aircraft, 1930s, 4 x 6in (10 x 15cm).
£20–25
$30–35 ⊞ COB

A Luftwaffe leather flying helmet, with original maker's label, German, post-1936.
£175–200
$250–300 ⊞ OLD
These helmets were standard issue for bomber crews.

An RAF clock, mounted in an oak case, c1930, 14in (35.5cm) high.
£300–350
$450–500 ⊞ JUN

A WWII squadron leader's hat, 1939–45.
£35–45
$50–65 ⊞ OLD

A WWII polished laminated mahogany aircraft propeller, with brass edging, 1939–45, 32in (81.5cm) long.
£85–95
$125–140 ⊞ OLD

◄ A pair of WWII leather and suede Luftwaffe flying boots, eastern European, 1939–45, 14in (35.5cm) high.
£175–200
$250–300 ⊞ OLD

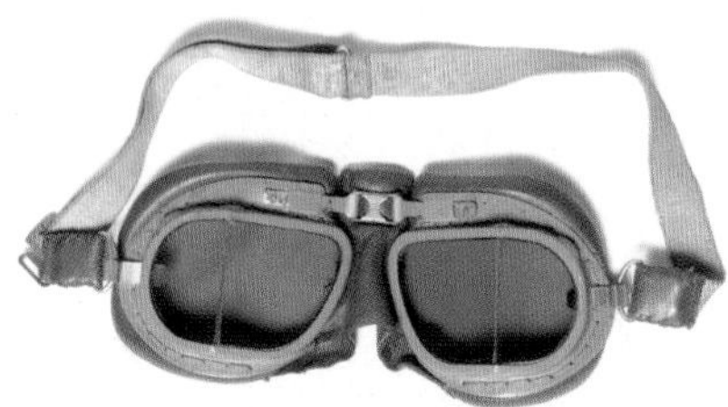

A pair of WWII RAF Mk VIII goggles, with tinted lenses, 1939–45, 3in (7.5cm) high.
£65–75
$95–110 ⊞ OLD

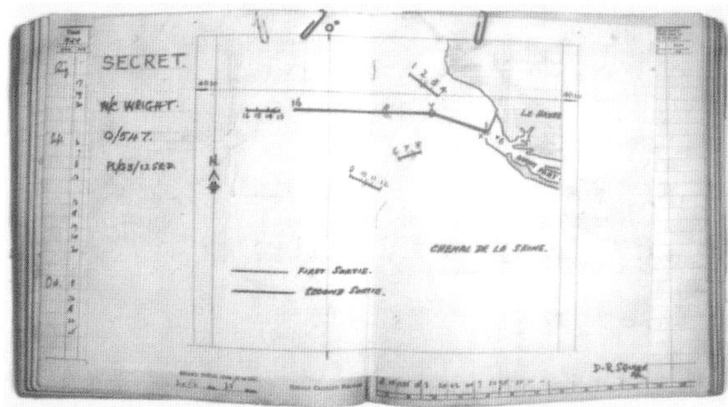

A WWII pilot's logbook, of Wing Commander C. F. C. Wright, DFC, 220 Squadron RAF, with entries covering his entire war service including details of raids etc, khaki cloth boards, 1939–59.
£700–800
$1,000–1,150 ⚒ DW
220 Squadron was part of Britain's Coastal Command and was one of the first squadrons to fly the newly-developed Hudson in the early stages of WWII. The logbook also records his service after WWII in various parts of the UK and Europe.

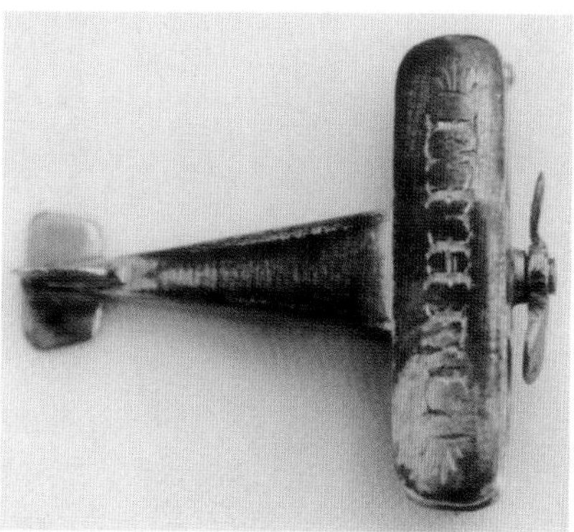

A sweetheart brooch, in the shape of an aeroplane, inscribed 'Ethel', 1940s, 1¼in (3cm) long.
£35–40
$50–60 ⊞ BCA

A cast-aluminium agent's model of a TWA Martin Skyliner, N86505, with twin engines, one propeller missing, c1945, wing span 18½in (47cm), on a display stand.
£325–365
$470–520 ⚒ SK(B)

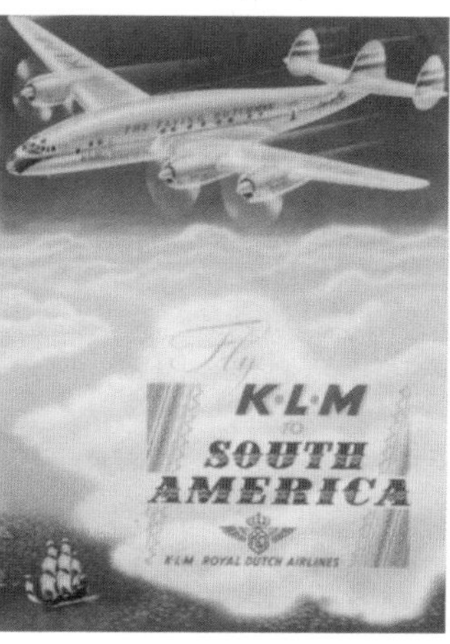

A KLM poster, 'To South America', by Paul Erkelens, on japan paper, 1946, 39¾ x 27½in (101 x 70cm).
£1,000–1,200
$1,500–1,750 ⚒ VSP

A KLM sticker, commemorating its 30-year anniversary, 1949, 4½in (11.5cm) diam.
£5–8
$8–12 ⊞ COB

A tin mechanical toy, modelled as two aeroplanes circling a control tower, c1950, 9in (23cm) high.
£80–90
$115–130 ⊞ JUN

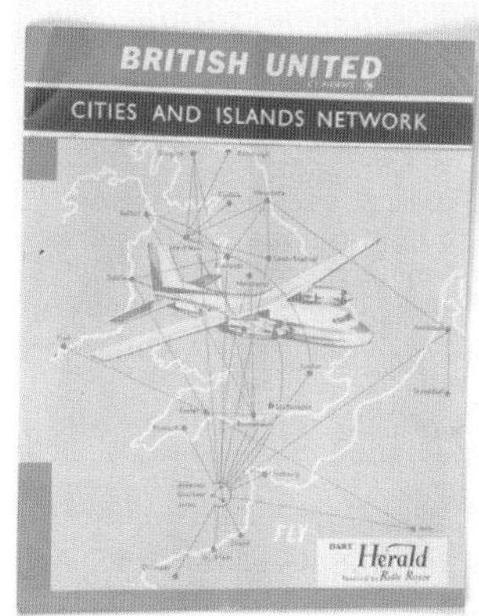

A British United Airways timetable, 1963, 8 x 7in (20.5 x 18cm).
£10–15
$15–20 ⊞ MRW

◄ **A BOAC poster,** 'Take A Longer Look At Africa', c1950, 39½ x 25¼in (100.5 x 64cm).
£100–120/$145–175 ⚒ VSP

BEA and Air France airline tickets, 1960s, 4 x 8in (10 x 20.5cm).
£5–10
$10–15 each ⊞ COB

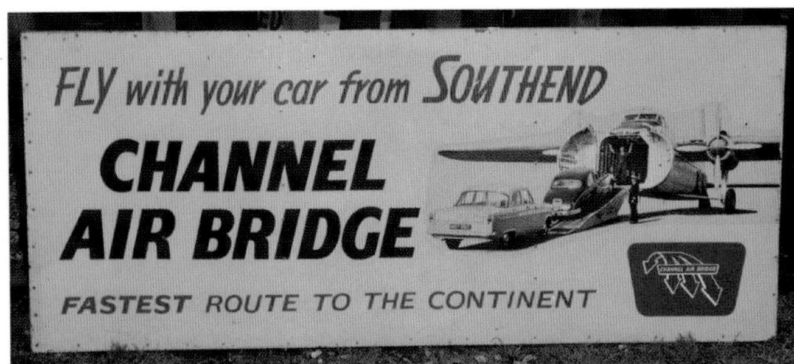

A Channel Air Bridge wooden advertising sign, 1960s, 25 x 58in (63.5 x 147.5cm).
£100–130
$145–200 ⊞ JUN

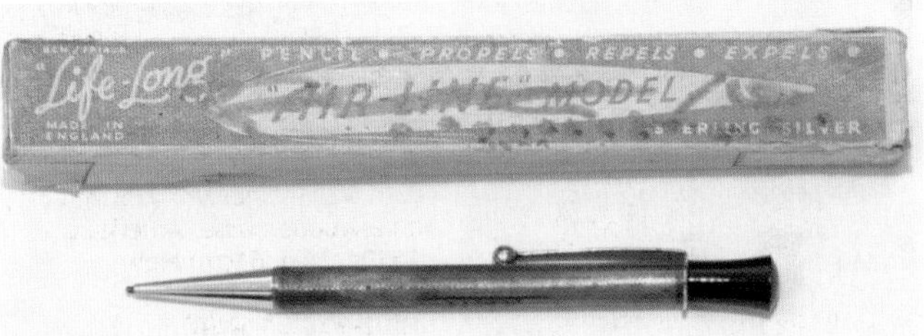

A sterling silver Life-Long Air-Line Model pencil, c1960, 6in (15cm) long, in original box.
£10–15
$15–20 ⊞ JUN

A gilt metal BEA badge, 1960s, 2in (5cm) diam.
£25–30
$35–45 ⊞ COB

◄ **An agent's model of a Concorde airliner,** by Space Models Limited, finished in TWA livery, late 1960s, wingspan 10in (25.5cm), on display stand.
£275–300
$400–450 ⚒ SK(B)

► **John Player & Sons,** History of British Aviation, set of 30 cards from Tom Thumb cigars, 1988.
£25–28
$35–40 ⊞ LCC

Airships

A photograph of an airship, c1910, 10 x 12in (25.5 x 30.5cm).
£30–35
$45–50 ⊞ HUX

A cachou tin, decorated with an airship, 1908, 2¾in (7cm) wide.
£180–200
$250–300 ⊞ HUX

A wind and course calculator, by Addison & Luard, from a British airship, c1920, 9in (23cm) diam.
£700–800
$1,000–1,150 ⊞ Cas

Amusement & Slot Machines

A National brass till, c1900, 17in (43cm) high.
£700–800
$1,000–1,150 ⊞ JUN

Insurance values

Always insure your valuable collectables for the cost of replacing them with similar items, regardless of the original price paid. Both dealers and auctioneers can provide a valuation service for a fee.

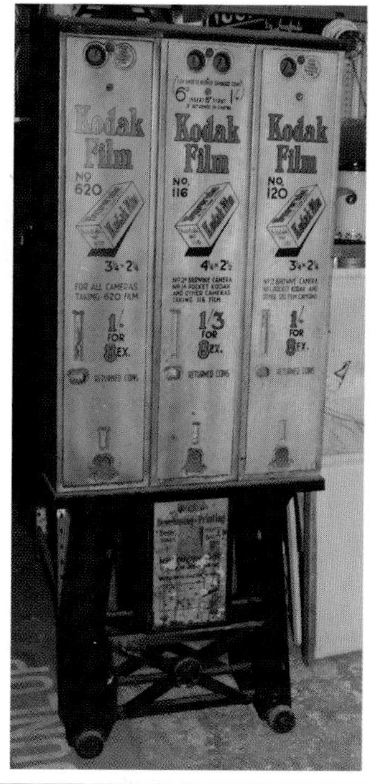

A Walting Blue Seal slot machine, with cast-aluminium front and top, on a wooden base, American, 1930s, 24in (61cm) high.
£550–650
$800–950 ⚒ SK(B)

◀ A Kodak film vending machine, c1930, 69in (175.5cm) high.
£700–800
$1,000–1,150 ⊞ JUN

A Cupid's Arrow fortune teller penny slot machine, c1930, 23in (58.5cm) high.
£350–400
$500–580 ⊞ JUN

An Allwin What's My Line? penny slot machine, c1930, 33in (84cm) high.
£500–600
$720–870 ⊞ JUN

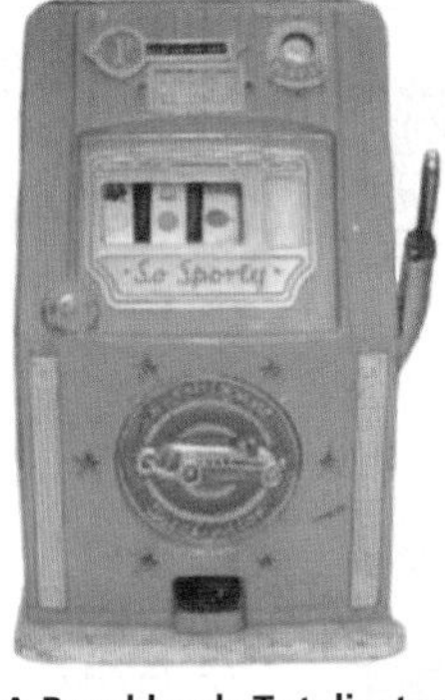

A Brooklands Totalisator one-armed bandit, with old pennies, c1937, 27in (68.5cm) high.
£500–600
$720–870 ⚒ BRIT

A KitKat slot machine, in an oak case, 1950s, 32in (81.5cm) high.
£600–700
$870–1,000 ⊞ JUN

► **A Whales Redcar Double Six slot machine,** 1950s, 32in (81.5cm) high.
£425–475
$620–700 ⊞ JUN

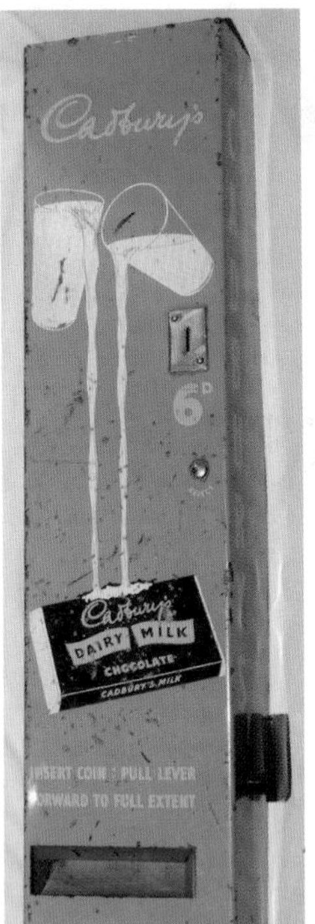

A tablet vending machine, 1960, 14in (35.5cm) high.
£75–85
$110–125 ⊞ HUX

◄ **A Cadbury's Dairy Milk vending machine,** c1960, 31in (78.5cm) high.
£200–230
$300–330 ⊞ HUX

► **A Williams Streets Defender table-top video arcade game,** 1980, 32in (81.5cm) wide.
£1,400–1,600
$2,000–2,300
⊞ WAm

A Taito Space Invaders video arcade game, Japanese, 1978, 68in (172.5cm) high.
£1,400–1,600
$2,000–2,300 ⊞ WAm

Computer games

The first known computer game was a tennis simulation game devised by Willie Higinbotham at Brookhaven National Laboratory in 1958. Computer games remained in the labs until 1971, when Norman Bushnell produced Computer Space, the first commercially-available electronic arcade game. Alhough it was not a success (the game was too difficult to play), Bushnell went on to found Atari in 1972, and electronic games were here to stay. Space Invaders, launched in 1978, was one of the most successful. It was largely responsible for bringing games out of bars and pubs, and introducing them to a wider (and younger) audience in cinemas, shops and restaurants. Today it is regarded as a golden age classic game. The Game On exhibition at London's Barbican Art Gallery, which chronicled the history of video games, also hosted a computer 'antiques roadshow', reflecting the growing interest in the field of collectable computer games.

A Gottlieb Nintendo Super Mario Brospin ball machine, American, 1990, 78in (198cm) high.
£600–700
$870–1,000 ⊞ WAm

Antiquities

A pottery cup, with lug handle and pouring spout, Jordanian, 2nd millennium BC, 5in (12.5cm) wide.
£60–70
$90–100 ⊞ HEL

A pottery cuneiform tablet, Mesopotamian, 2nd millennium BC, 1½in (4cm) long.
£125–150
$180–220 ⊞ HEL

A moulded pottery upper part of an Ushabti figure, Egyptian, late Dynastic Period, 730–332 BC, 4in (10cm) high.
£40–50
$60–75 ⊞ HEL

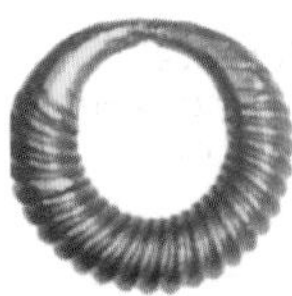

◀ A Mediterranean-style electrum pennanular striped ring, Celtic, c700 BC, ½in (1.5cm) diam.
£1,400–1,600
$2,000–2,300 ⚒ DNW
Before the introduction of struck coinage in Celtic lands, Celtic ring money was used instead of coins.

A miniature bronze jug, with wide handle and cut-away spout, dark green patina, minor damage, c7thC BC, 1¼in (3cm) high.
£65–75
$95–110 ⊞ ANG

A pottery head from a votive figurine, Phoenecian, 1st millennium BC, 4in (10cm) high.
£150–180
$220–260 ⊞ HEL

Further reading

Miller's Antiques Under £1000 Price Guide, Miller's Publications, 2003

◀ A pottery amphora, with traces of painted decoration, Cypriot, Geometric Period, 1050–650 BC, 15in (38cm) high.
£630–700
$900–1,000 ⊞ HEL

A black figure olpe, with painted decoration of Dionysus and a maenad, Greek, Athens, Leagros Group, late 5thC BC, 9½in (24cm) high.
£2,000–2,200
$3,000–3,200 ⊞ HEL

A bronze ornamental razor, with two opposed crescent blades linked by ornate openwork scrolls and loops, with a ring handle, Celtic, c4th–3rdC BC, 3½in (9cm) wide.
£600–700
$870–1,000 B(Kn)

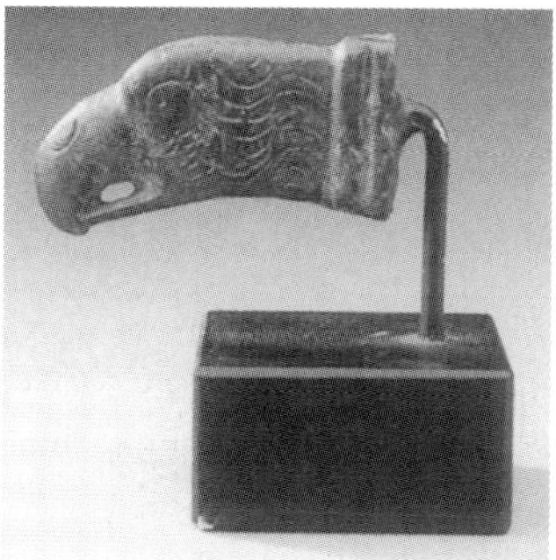

A bronze terminal, modelled as an eagle's head with hooked beak and incised details of the eyes and feathers, probably a knife handle, Roman, c2nd–3rdC AD, 1¾in (4.5cm) long, mounted.
£80–120
$115–175 B(Kn)

A bronze concave brooch, with stylized animal design, the five recesses originally set with glass, dark patina, probably Spanish, 8thC AD, 2in (5cm) diam.
£60–70
$90–100 ANG

A pair of bronze armlets, comprising vertical linked concave lozenges with hollow backs, the segments divided by a medial ridge, c3rdC BC, 2¾in (7cm) diam.
£330–360
$475–500 B(Kn)

A terracotta portrait bust of Minerva, on a wooden plinth, Hellenic, c2nd–1stC BC, 7in (18cm) high.
£450–550
$650–800 G(L)

◄ **A bronze male head,** with close-cropped hair and well-delineated facial features, possibly from a sword pommel, Roman, c2nd–3rdC AD, ¾in (2cm) high.
£250–300
$350–450 B(Kn)

Two cock metal 'Billy's and Charley's' pilgrim badges, 19thC, largest 4in (10cm) diam.
£75–90
$110–130 SWO

William Smith (Billy) and Charles Eaton (Charley) were Victorian mudlarks who searched the foreshore of the Thames for historical finds. In 1857, they decided it would be more profitable to make their own 'medieval' objects, principally pilgrim badges, which were then retailed through the shop of a well-known London antiques dealer. Although in 1858 one archaeological expert publically condemned these products as forgeries, many purchasers were fooled, and up until Charles' death in 1870, thousands of 'Billy's and Charley's' were produced. Today, these fakes are collectable in their own right.

Architectural Salvage

A decorative iron chimney crane, 18thC, 40in (101.5cm) wide.
£175–200
$200–300 ⊞ HCJ

An iron bolt, Continental, mid-18thC, 9½in (24cm) long.
£275–325
$400–470 ⊞ Penn

► A cast-iron door stop, modelled as the Duke of Wellington, with original paint, 1850, 14in (35.5cm) high.
£85–95
$125–140 ⊞ GBr

A pair of double brass door knobs, c1830, 5in (12.5cm) long.
£85–95
$125–140 ⊞ Penn

Items in the Architectural Salvage section have been arranged in date order.

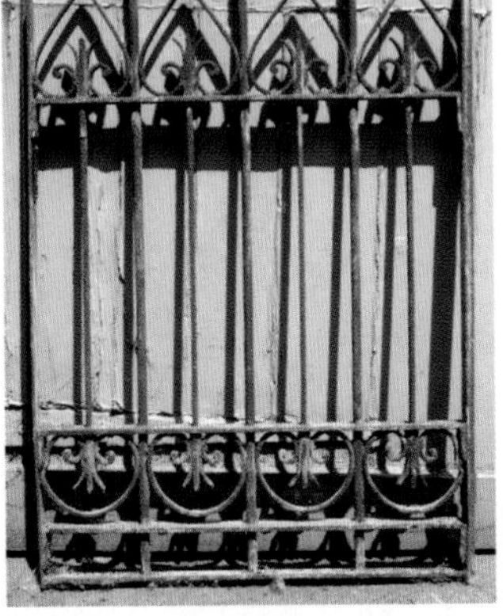

◄ A pair of iron gates, 19thC, 37in (94cm) high.
£315–350
$450–500 ⊞ PAS

A brass bear door stop, marked 'Warwick', c1870, 13¾in (35cm) high.
£225–275
$325–400 ⊞ Penn

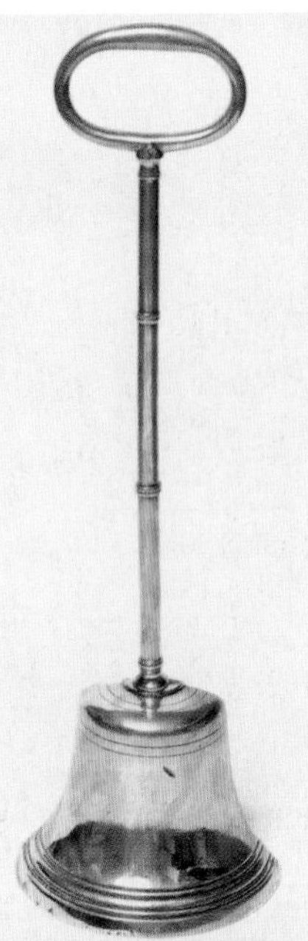

◄ A brass door stop, 1870, 19in (48.5cm) high.
£250–300
$350–450 ⊞ GBr

A cast-iron boot scraper, 1880, 9in (23cm) high.
£85–95
$125–140 ⊞ SMI

A row of three Victorian theatre seats, upholstered in red velvet, 32¾in (83cm) high.
£150–165
$220–240 ⊞ L(w)

► A pair of Gothic revival painted and ebonized curtain poles, with gilt-metal lobed rings, 19thC, 78¾in (200cm) long, with two short poles.
£550–600
$800–870 ⚒ DN

A pair of wooden shutters, 19thC, 70in (178cm) high.
£300–350
$450–500 ⊞ PAS

◄ A pair of ceramic finger plates and matching double knobs, black with gilt decoration, c1880, finger plates 11in (28cm) long.
£225–250
$325–360 ⊞ Penn

► A Victorian servants' brass and ceramic bell pull, 5in (12.5cm) long.
£100–120
$145–175
⊞ OLA

A set of five pierced brass finger plates, c1890, 13in (33cm) long.
£250–280
$350–410 ⊞ Penn

Two brass sash window locks, c1890, 2in (5cm) long.
£15–20
$20–30 each
⊞ Penn

A set of six Art Nouveau brass handles, c1890, 5½in (14cm) long.
£175–195
$255–275 ⊞ Penn

► A Hobbs iron and brass lock, with original keep, key and beehive handles, c1890, 9in (23cm) wide.
£200–225
$300–325 ⊞ Penn

A blue and white floral pedestal lavatory bowl, 'The Model', c1900, 16in (40.5cm) high.
£1,100–1,300
$1,600–2,000 ⊞ WRe

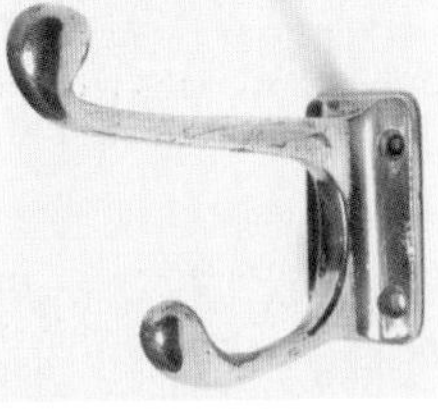

A brass coat hook, c1900, 3½in (9cm) high.
£6–8
$8–12 ⊞ Penn

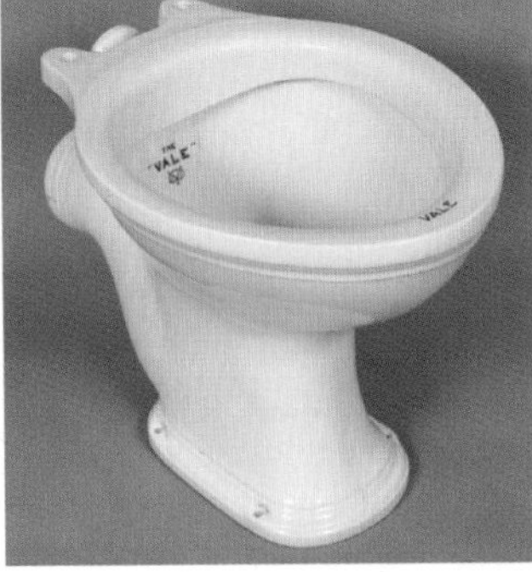

A Thomas Twyford white pedestal lavatory bowl, 'The Vale', c1900, 16in (40.5cm) high.
£750–850
$1,100–1,250 ⊞ WRe

An Arts & Crafts brass letterbox and pull handle, c1900, 12in (30.5cm) wide.
£200–250
$300–350 ⊞ Penn

A cast-iron register grate, early 20thC, 38in (96.5cm) square.
£1,100–1,300
$1,600–2,000 ⊞ WRe

◄ **A brass bell push,** c1920, 3½in (9cm) diam.
£50–60
$75–90 ⊞ Penn

Electric Fires

◄ **A Dosing-type electric fire,** with radiator lamps, c1912, 21in (53.5cm) high.
£80–90
$115–130 ⊞ JUN

An enamelled electric fire, c1920, 13in (33cm) high.
£30–40
$45–60 ⊞ JUN

An enamelled electric fire, 1920, 19in (48.5cm) high.
£40–50
$60–75 ⊞ JUN

◄ **A Bakelite electric fire,** c1950, 13in (33cm) diam.
£30–40
$45–60 ⊞ JUN

An Excel chrome electric fire, 1950s, 16in (40.5cm) high.
£85–95
$125–140 ⊞ JUN

Art Deco

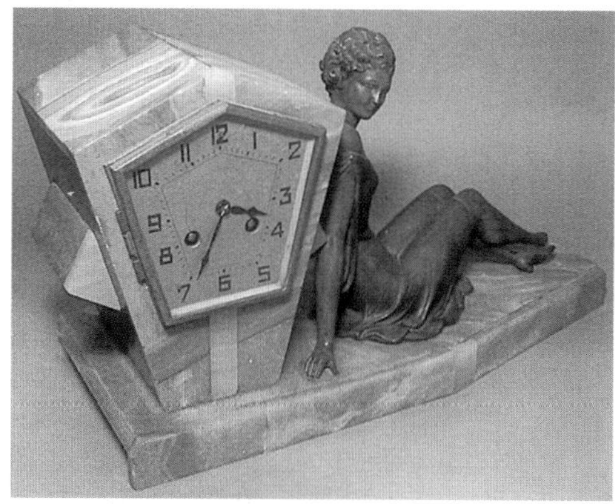

◄ **An orange marble mantel clock,** with eight-day movement striking on a bell, in a shaped case with spelter figure of a young woman to one side, c1930, 17in (43cm) wide.
£80–100
$115–145 BLH

An amber and black flash jar and cover, c1930, 4¾in (12cm) high.
£35–45
$50–65 G(L)

◄ **A Bakelite and chrome ceiling lamp,** with sunburst arms and original glass shades, 1930s.
£80–100
$115–145 JAZZ

A crackle glass and chrome cocktail set, 1930s, shaker 9in (23cm) high.
£40–45
$60–65 RTT

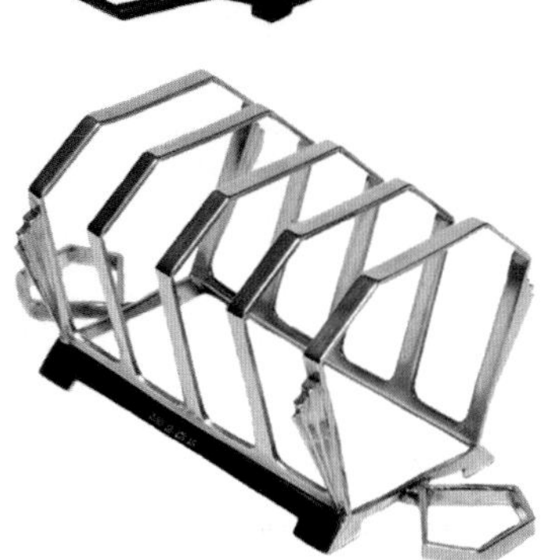

A silver toast rack, by Deakin & Francis, Birmingham 1932, 5in (12.5cm) wide.
£70–80
$100–115 WAC

A pair of Bakelite candlesticks, 1930s, 6½in (16.5cm) high.
£40–45
$60–65 LBe

► **A silver, paste and red stone brooch,** probably French, 1930s, 2in (5cm) wide.
£125–150
$180–220 RGA

A silver straight-pull corkscrew, London 1932, 4in (10cm) long.
£120–140
$175–200 CAL

Ceramics

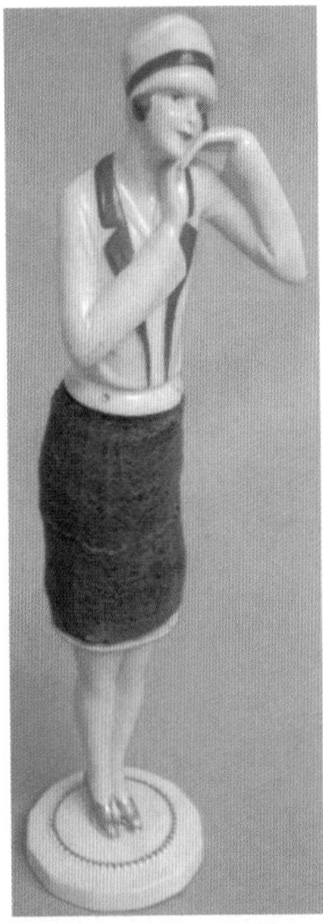

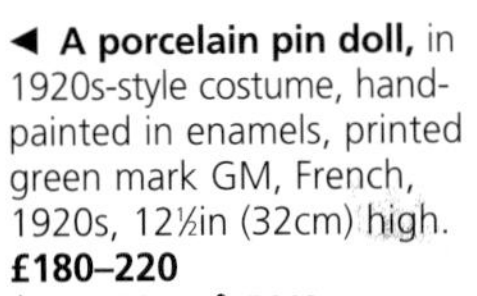

◄ **A porcelain pin doll,** in 1920s-style costume, hand-painted in enamels, printed green mark GM, French, 1920s, 12½in (32cm) high.
£180–220
$250–320 BLH

A Gibson Ceres ware fruit bowl, decorated with Sheila pattern, c1930, 8in (20.5cm) diam.
£90–100
$130–145 ⊞ CoCo

◄ **An earthenware wall plaque of a lady harlequin,** Viennese, 1920s, 10in (25.5cm) high.
£500–600
$720–870 G(L)

A Keeling & Co Losol ware ginger jar, decorated with Suntrae pattern, c1930, 10½in (26.5cm) high.
£325–375
$470–560 ⊞ DSG

A Decoro vase, with geometric decoration, 1930s, 5½in (14cm) high.
£75–85
$110–125 ⊞ CoCo

A Sadler racing car teapot, with OKT42 number plate, c1937, 9in (23cm) wide.
£650–750
$950–1,100 ⊞ BD

Sadler's racing car teapot with its famous OKT42 number plate was first made in 1937. The most common colours are green, yellow and cream; rarer glazes include black, blue, grey, pink and maroon. Up until 1939, all pots were finished in a platinum lustre and marked underneath: MADE IN ENGLAND REGISTERED No.820236. Production ceased during WWII. Post-1945, chrome plating was largely abandoned in favour of a sponged, mottled glaze that was cheaper to produce. The number plate was no longer applied and pots were backstamped with the Sadler name and mark. Production ceased in 1952. Values reflect rarity of colour.

A Sadler earthenware novelty teapot, modelled as an early coupé motor car, with goggled driver finial, c1947, 8½in (21.5cm) wide.
£85–100
$125–145 G(L)

Art Nouveau

A Thomas Foster & Son twin-handled vase, printed marks, incised signature, 1880s, 13in (33cm) high.
£380–450
$575–650 SWO

A pair of brass gas wall lights, with original etched glass shades, converted for electricity, 1890–1900, 14in (35.5cm) wide.
£225–250
$325–350 ⊞ JeH

A pair of brass and copper wall lights, c1900, 12in (30.5cm) wide.
£350–400
$500–580 ⊞ WAC

An Art Nouveau copper jardinière, embossed with stylized motifs, on three scroll legs, impressed monogram to base, c1900, 9in (23cm) high.
£35–45
$50–65 G(L)

► **A brass box,** with raised stylized trailing flowers and fairies with pewter heads, c1900, 7½in (19cm) wide.
£250–300
$350–450
SWO

A brass oval dish, with embossed rim, c1900, 12in (30.5cm) wide.
£30–35
$45–50 ⊞ CAL

A Liberty & Co Tudric pewter biscuit box, by Archibald Knox, c1900, 5½in (14cm) high.
£520–620
$750–900 G(L)

A Minton vase, with Secessionist tree decoration on a red ground, c1900, 8½in (21.5cm) high.
£380–450
$575–650 G(L)

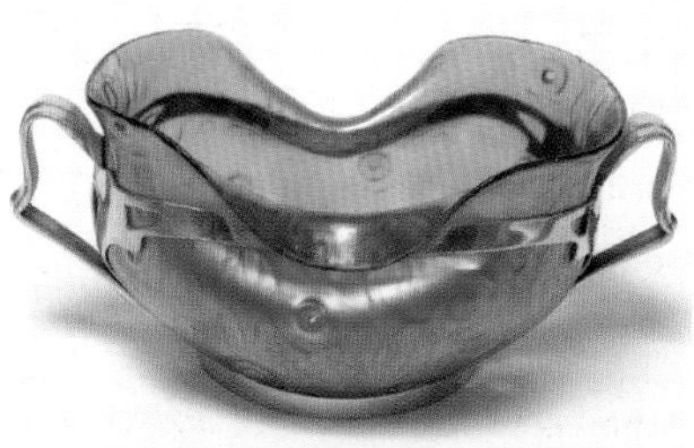

► **A Loetz iridescent glass and pewter bowl,** c1900, 11in (28cm) wide.
£500–600
$800–870 ⊞ WAC

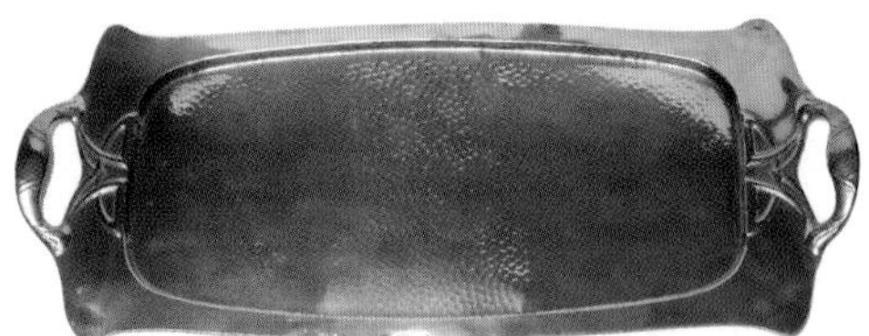

A copper tray, c1900, 25in (63.5cm) wide.
£200–225
$300–325 ⊞ WAC

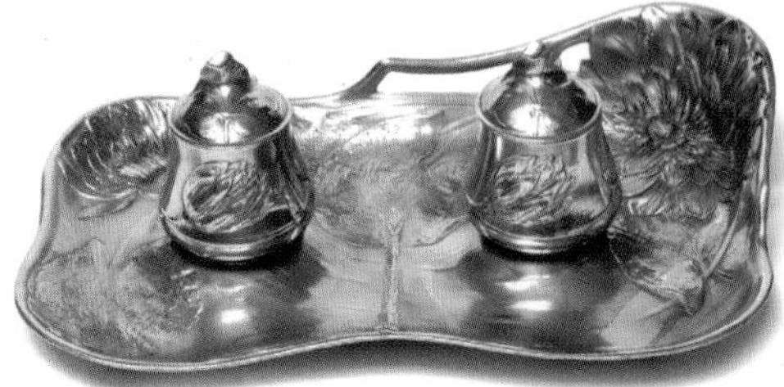

A Kayserzinn pewter inkstand, c1900, 14in (35.5cm) wide.
£300–350
$450–500 ⊞ WAC

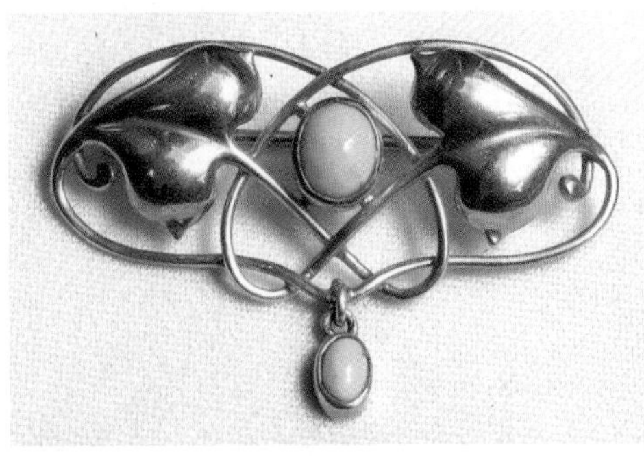

A Murrle Bennet 9ct gold brooch, set with two turquoises, c1905, 1½in (4cm) wide.
£400–450
$580–650 ⊞ RGA

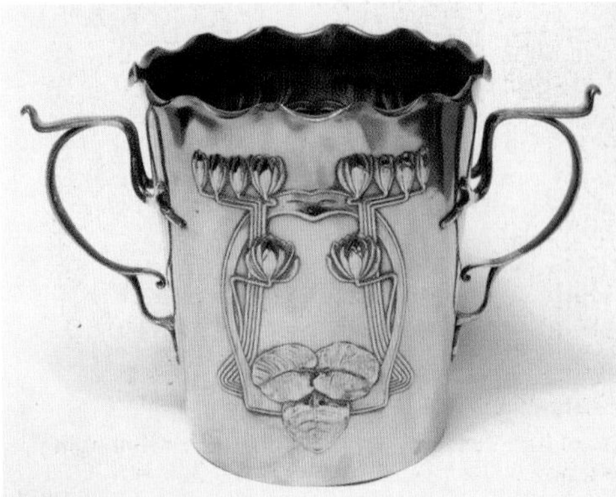

A copper and brass wine cooler, c1910, 9in (23cm) high.
£130–160
$200–230 ⊞ WAC

A Bishop & Stonier *Fwi-Yama* Korea vase, 1901, 7in (18cm) high.
£80–90
$115–130 ⊞ CoCo

A silver photograph frame, with floral embossed decoration, Birmingham 1904, 12½in (32cm) high.
£150–180
$220–260 ⚒ SWO

A WMF pewter card tray, No. 264, c1910, 7in (18cm) wide.
£200–225
$300–325 ⊞ WAC

A set of four wine glasses, with enamel decoration, c1910, 7in (18cm) high.
£250–300
$350–450 ⊞ WAC

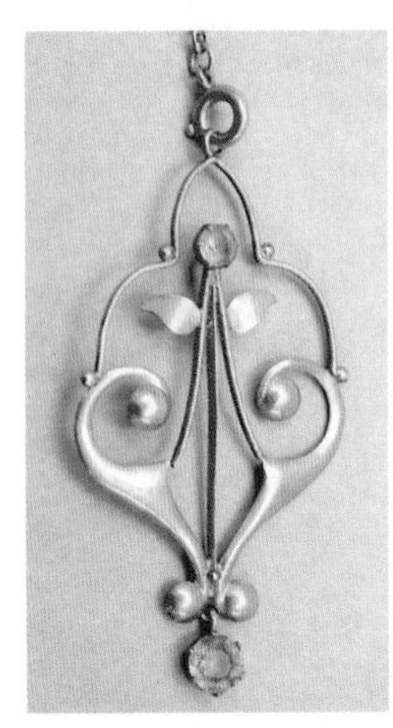

A 9ct gold openwork pendant, set with two round-cut peridots, early 20thC.
£50–60
$75–90 ⚒ G(L)

Arts & Crafts

A brass and copper wine jug, c1900, 13in (33cm) high.
£100–125
$145–175 ⊞ WAC

A hammered copper tray, c1900, 16in (40.5cm) wide.
£80–100
$115–145 ⊞ EAL

A Newlyn copper rose bowl, c1900, 7in (18cm) diam.
£400–450
$580–650 ⊞ WAC

◄ **A Newlyn copper tea tray,** the border embossed with a fish and rocaille decoration, early 20thC, 28in (71cm) wide.
£420–480
$620–700 ⚒ G(B)

A Newlyn copper wall sconce, c1900, 11in (28cm) high.
£400–450
$580–650 ⊞ WAC

A brass lantern, with vaseline glass tube, c1900, 12in (30.5cm) high.
£380–430
$575–625 ⊞ JeH

A Murrle Bennet silver matrix pendant, set with a turquoise, c1905, 1½in (4cm) high.
£400–450
$580–650 ⊞ RGA

A copper fire screen, c1910, 31in (78.5cm) high.
£75–85
$110–125 ⊞ WAC

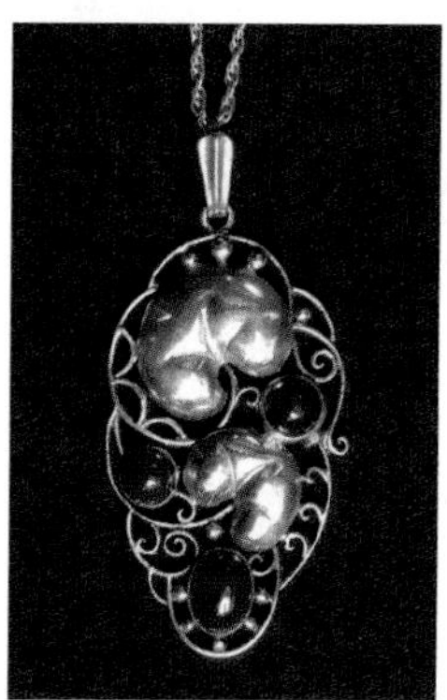

A Karl Karst silver pendant, set with a cornelian, German, c1910, 2in (5cm) high.
£300–350
$450–500 ⊞ RGA

A copper wall-hanging mirror, inset with a Ruskin ceramic heart, c1920, 17in (43cm) high.
£375–425
$550–625 ⊞ WAC

Ceramics

A Wardle & Co pottery vase, impressed marks, c1870, 10½in (26.5cm) high.
£85–100
$125–145 ⊞ RUSK

A W. L. Baron waisted vase, the blue glaze incised and painted with a fish among vegetation, rim chipped, 1875–1925, 9½in (24cm) high.
£100–120
$145–175 ⚒ G(L)

A W. L. Baron vase, for Liberty & Co, with three twisted lug handles, impressed marks, 1875–1925, 12in (30.5cm) high.
£80–100
$115–145 ⚒ G(L)

A Leeds Art Pottery jardinière, wear to rim, c1900, 9in (23cm) high.
£120–140
$175–200 ⊞ DSG

A George Cartlidge Morris ware mushroom vase, decorated with panels of poppies, printed and painted marks, early 20thC, 7in (18cm) high.
£700–800
$1,000–1,150 ⚒ Pott

◄ **A Pinder, Bourne & Co charger,** c1900, 13¼in (33.5cm) high.
£170–200
$250–300 ⊞ DSG

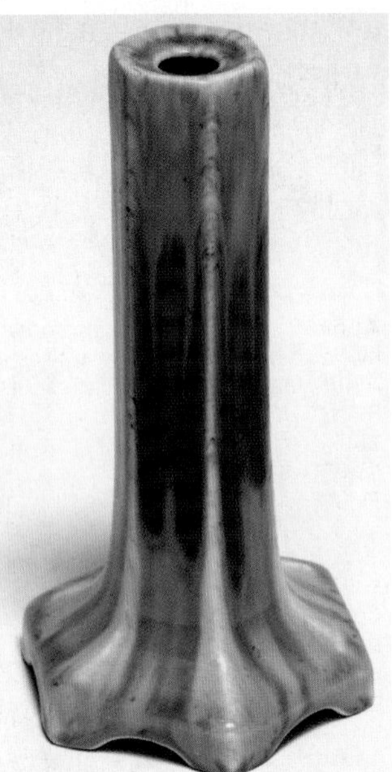

A Ruskin Pottery crystalline glaze lamp base, c1930, 8in (20.5cm) high.
£200–225
$300–325 ⊞ RUSK

Autographs

In our celebrity-obsessed culture, the values of autographs continues to escalate. 'Many prices have doubled in the last two years,' claims Mrs Vennett-Smith, whose auction house specializes in the field. Demand is strong in every area: historical figures, film stars, great explorers, sporting heroes etc. 'Royalty is always popular, although interest in specific individuals tends to be affected by the press and who is in the news at the moment.' This year for the first time we include a Camilla Parker-Bowles signature. The Jubilee celebrations stimulated interest in the Queen and Prince Philip and the death of the Queen Mother influenced demand for her autograph. 'Items relating to Princess Diana are still sought-after, particularly photographs.'

When it comes to value, medium is important. 'People like objects they can look at', explains Mrs Vennett-Smith. 'It's easier to display a signed photograph than, for example, a programme autographed on one of the inner pages.' An interesting letter can enhance the value of a signature but if the figure is significant, a simple autograph or a 'clipped signature' (removed at some time in the past from a letter or other document) can still command large sums.

It is important to beware of fakes and facsimile signatures. Such was the demand for autographs of the Apollo XI crew that many photographs were inscribed with auto-pens which automatically reproduced their signatures. Many members of the Beatles' entourage signed on behalf of the band members; secretaries would autograph for their employers and, according to Mrs Vennett-Smith, Jean Harlow's autograph was often penned by her mother. 'The safest way is to buy from a reputable dealer or auction house', she advises. 'Try to buy objects in good condition, and it is worth saving up for the best examples. Someone who is still alive might continue producing autographs for 30 or 40 years but if you go for something like a Laurel and Hardy, a Bela Lugosi or even an Elizabeth I, they're never going to produce any more signatures!'.

Apollo XI crew, a colour photograph signed by Neil Armstrong, Michael Collins and Buzz Aldrin, mounted, framed and glazed, 1969, 8 x 10in (20.5 x 25.5cm).
£6,750–7,500
$9,750–11,000
⊞ FRa

Charlie Chaplin, a signed photograph, minor damage, 1930s, 10¼ x 8in (26 x 20.5cm).
£230–260
$330–380 ⚒ B(Ch)

Sir Winston Churchill, a signed photograph, dated 1947, mounted, framed and glazed, 13 x 10in (33 x 25.5cm).
£1,200–1,400
$1,750–2,000 ⚒ CO

► **Tommy Cooper,** a signed printed caricature sketch by Bill Hall, minor damage, 1950s–60s, 9 x 6in (23 x 15cm).
£80–100
$115–145
⚒ VS

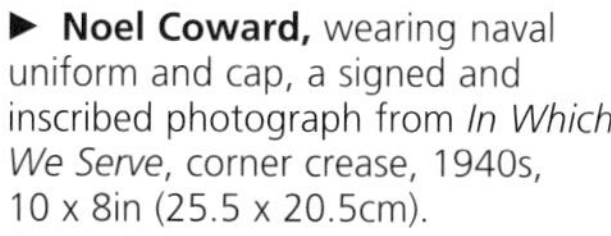

► **Noel Coward,** wearing naval uniform and cap, a signed and inscribed photograph from *In Which We Serve*, corner crease, 1940s, 10 x 8in (25.5 x 20.5cm).
£125–150
$180–220 ⚒ VS

Doris Day, wearing a buckskin suit, a signed photograph from *Calamity Jane*, 1950s, 10 x 8in (25.5 x 20.5cm).
£200–230
$300–330 ⊞ FRa

Errol Flynn, a signed hand-tinted publicity card, showing Flynn and Olivia De Havilland in *The Adventures of Robin Hood*, c1938, 9 x 7in (23 x 18cm).
£150–180
$220–260 ⚒ CO

◄ **Clark Gable,** a signed photograph, from *Gone With The Wind*, c1940, 13 x 10in (33 x 25.5cm).
£4,500–5,000
$6,500–7,250 ⊞ FRa

Stephen Fry, a signed photograph, 1980s, 6 x 4in (15 x 10cm).
£8–10
$12–15 ⊞ S&D

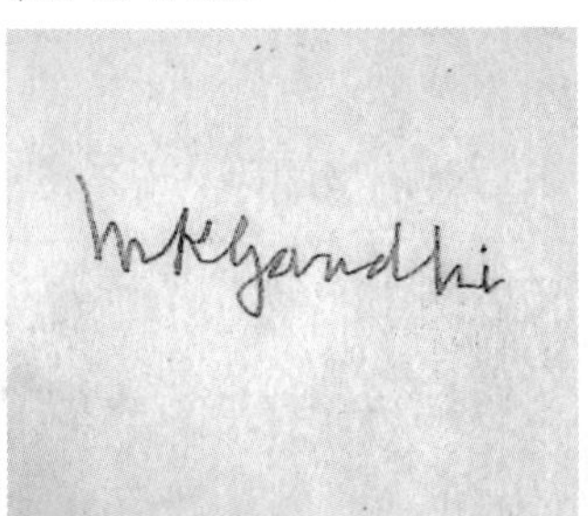

Mahatma Gandhi, a signed album page, undated, 2¾ x 4in (7 x 10cm).
£600–650
$870–950 ⚒ VS

◄ **Greta Garbo,** a signed publicity photograph, signed in pencil, with additional printed signature, mounted, framed and glazed, c1930, 13 x 11in (33 x 28cm).
£1,800–2,200
$2,600–3,200 ⚒ CO

Sarah Michelle Gellar, a signed photograph, from *Buffy The Vampire Slayer,* holding a wooden stake, framed and glazed, 2002, 10 x 8in (25.5 x 20.5cm).
£135–165
$200–250 ⊞ FRa

► **Annabeth Gish,** as agent Monica Reyes in *The X-Files*, signed Inkworks card, 2001, 2½ x 3½in (6.5 x 9in).
£30–40
$45–60 ⊞ NOS

Matt Groening, a signed paperback copy of *The Simpsons Comics Royale*, with a doodle of Bart, dated 22 July 2001.
£170–200
$250–300 CO

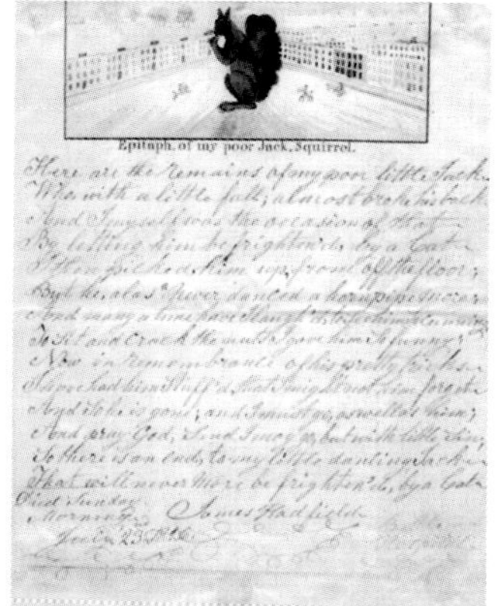

James Hadfield, a signed epitaph with a watercolour drawing of a squirrel surrounded by buildings and horsemen, dated 23 July 1826, with attached note 'I bought this of Hadfield in Bethlehem Hospital. He was the lunatic who tried to shoot George III...'.
£550–650
$800–950 F&C

Pamela Hayden, a signed Inkworks card, 2001, 3½ x 2½in (9 x 6.5cm).
£35–40
$50–60 NOS
Pamela Hayden was the voice of Millhouse Van Houten and many others.

◀ **Bill Hanna,** a signed cartoon drawing of Fred Flintstone, on white card, 1980s, 11½ x 8in (29 x 20.5cm).
£50–60
$75–90 DW

Lenny Henry, a signed photograph, 1980s, 5 x 4in (12.5 x 10cm).
£4–6
$8–10 S&D

Adolf Hitler, wearing Nazi party uniform, a signed photograph, small tear and surface creasing, c1934, 6 x 4in (15 x 10cm).
£4,500–5,000
$6,500–7,250 FRa

◀ **Sir Henry Irving,** a signed portrait photograph, 1902, 4½ x 6½in (11.5 x 16.5cm).
£80–100
$115–145 DW

Pope John Paul II, a signed photograph, 1990s, 6 x 4in (15 x 10cm).
£320–380
$450–550 VS

◀ **Tommy Lee Jones,** a signed still from *Men in Black*, 1997, 10 x 8in (25.5 x 20.5cm).
£50–60
$75–90 CO

◀ **Helen Keller,** a typed letter signed in pencil, to John D. Morris, early 20thC.
£210–250
$300–360 VS

The Kray Twins, aged 18, wearing boxing gear, a signed photograph of the twins 1994.
£600–700
$870–1,000 DW
This photograph was taken a month before the Kray twins appeared at the Royal Albert Hall, London in the early 1950s. It was signed by both twins and sent to Robin McGibbon by Ronnie Kray while in Broadmoor, in 1994 – the year before he died.

Stan Laurel and Oliver Hardy, a signed and inscribed postcard, minor damage, 1940.
£310–350
$450–500 VS

Bruce Lee, a signed album page, the reverse signed by John Saxon, 20thC, 4 x 5½in (10 x 14cm).
£600–650
$870–950 VS

◄ **Vivien Leigh,** a signed photograph, 1940s, 6 x 4½in (15 x 11.5cm).
£180–220
$260–320 VS

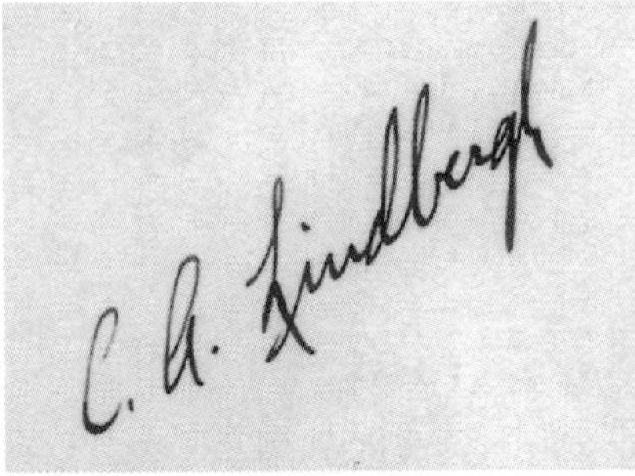

Charles Lindbergh, a signed card, 20thC.
£420–480
$620–700 VS

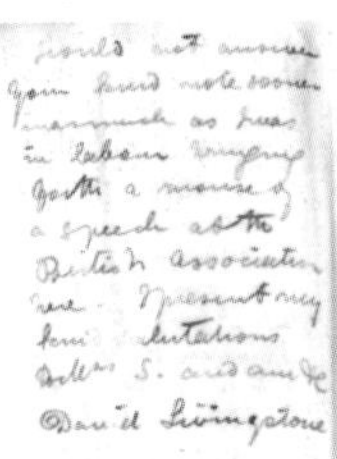

David Livingstone, a signed two-page letter to the Rev. Sidney thanking him for sending a copy of his life of Lord Hill and apologizing for not replying sooner as he was preparing a speech to the British Association, with carte-de-visite portrait by photographer King of Bath, dated 20th September 1864.
£220–250
$320–350 F&C

Jennifer Lopez, a signed promotional poster from *The Wedding Planner*, framed and glazed, 2001, 42 x 29in (106.5 x 73.5cm).
£200–240
$300–350 CO

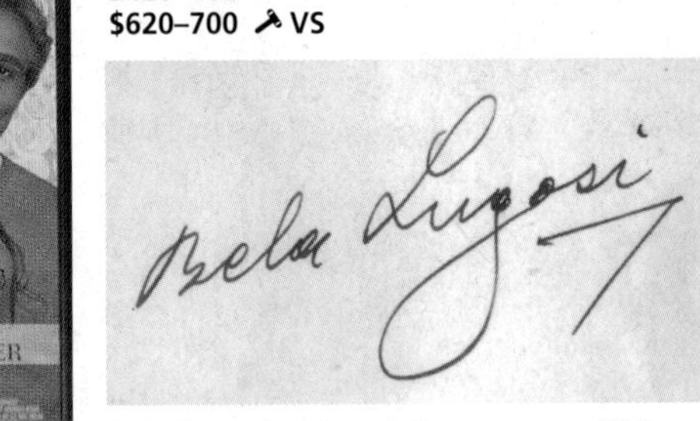

Bela Lugosi, a signed album page, red ink, c1950, 3¼ x 5in (8.5 x 12.5cm).
£230–260
$330–380 VS

◄ **John Major and Nelson Mandela,** shaking hands, a signed photograph, taken inside 10 Downing Street, 1996, 10 x 11in (25.5 x 28cm).
£330–380
$475–575 VS

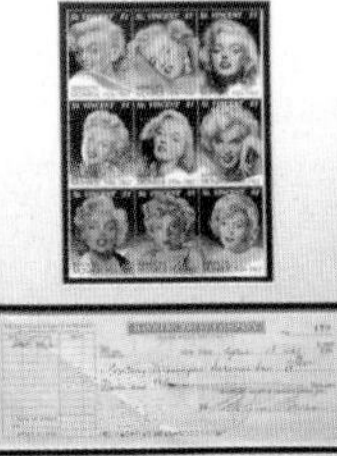

Marilyn Monroe, a signed cheque, mounted with photograph, 1961, 8 x 10in (20.5 x 25.5cm).
£4,500–5,000
$6,500–7,250 FRa

B. L. Montgomery, a signed and inscribed photographic reproduction of a painting by Oswald Birley, signed 'To Sir James and Lady Bowker, with my best wishes, Montgomery of Alamein FM, October 1954', framed and glazed in original wooden frame, 13 x 10in (33 x 25.5cm).
£270–320
$400–450 VS

Robert de Niro, a signed photograph of de Niro with a Mohican hair style, from *Taxi Driver*, 1998, 10 x 8in (25.5 x 20.5cm).
£135–165
$200–240 FRa

Christobel and Emily Pankhurst, an album page signed by Emily Pankhurst, '17th April 1918', Christobel Pankhurst 'Votes For Women 22nd Sept 1908' and Mary Gawthorpe 'Votes for Women Symbolises Chances for Women', 5 x 8in (12.5 x 20.5cm).
£420–470
$620–675 VS

To order Miller's books in the UK please ring 01903 828800 or order online
www.millers.uk.com

► **Ronald Reagan,** a signed photograph and calligraphic inscription, with matching photograph and calligraphic inscription of Nancy Reagan, 1980s, 11 x 8in (28 x 20.5cm).
£230–260
$330–380 VS

J. K. Rowling, a signed *Harry Potter* promotional postcard, depicting Harry in Snape's classroom, 2001, 10 x 8in (25.5 x 20.5cm).
£400–450
$580–650 CO

Piotr Ilyich Tchaikovsky, a signed and inscribed cabinet card with portrait photograph, 1891, 6¾ x 4½in (17 x 11.5cm).
£11,500–12,500
$16,750–18,250 FRa

◄ **Margaret Thatcher,** a signed photograph, late 20thC, 7 x 5in (18 x 12.5cm).
£30–40
$45–60 PICC

Royalty

Albert, Edward, Henry, George and Mary, a card signed by the children of King George V and Queen Mary, 1910, 6 x 4in (15 x 10cm).
£650–750
$950–1,100 ⊞ AEL

◄ **Diana, Princess of Wales,** an invitation to Prince Harry's fourth birthday party written by the Princess, with handwritten envelope together with a 'Thank you' card and handwritten envelope, dated 27 August 1988, card 5 x 6¾in (12.5 x 17cm).
£2,250–2,500
$3,300–3,600
⚒ B(Ch)

Edward VII, a signed photograph, taken in Montreal, Canada, showing the 18-year-old Prince standing in a group which includes the Duke of Newcastle and Edmund Head, Governor General of Canada, signed 'Albert Edward', mounted, framed and glazed, 1860, 7 x 6in (18 x 15cm).
£450–525
$650–775 ⚒ DW
The Prince of Wales' tour of Canada was the first ever Royal visit to the country.

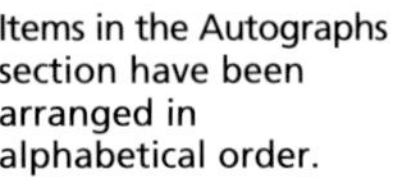

Items in the Autographs section have been arranged in alphabetical order.

Edward VII and Queen Alexandra, a signed photograph, 1910, 8 x 6in (20.5 x 15cm).
£500–550
$720–800 ⊞ AEL

Elizabeth I, a signature and a portrait, slight fading and surface creasing, mounted, framed and glazed, signature c1588, 21 x 13in (53.5 x 33cm).
£13,000–14,500
$18,500–21,000 ⊞ FRa

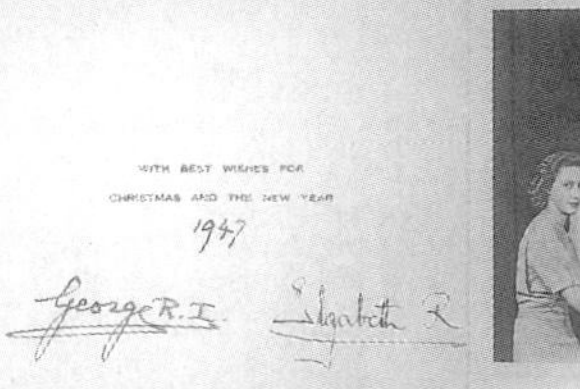

King George VI and Queen Elizabeth, a signed Christmas card, with Princesses Elizabeth and Margaret, with gold embossed crown to cover, slight foxing, 1947, 8 x 6in (20.5 x 15cm).
£450–500
$650–720 ⚒ VS

King George VI and Queen Elizabeth, a signed Christmas card, gold embossed crown to cover, minor stain, dated 1949 in the King's hand, 8 x 6in (20.5 x 15cm).
£400–450
$580–650 ⚒ VS

Queen Mary, a signed photograph, 1913, 11 x 7in (28 x 18cm).
£350–400
$500–580 ⊞ AEL

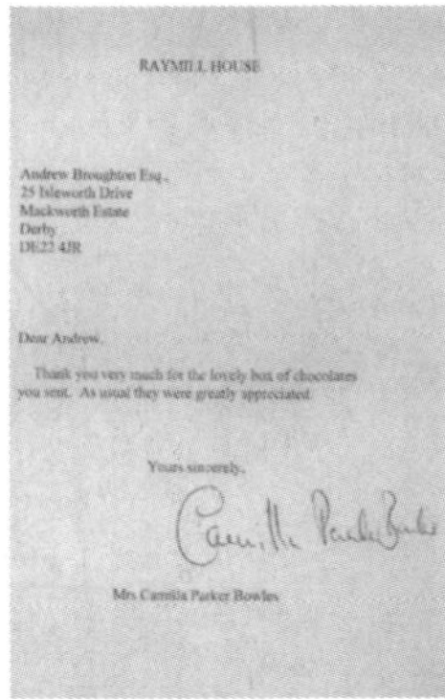

RAYMILL HOUSE

Andrew Broughton Esq.,
25 Isleworth Drive
Mackworth Estate
Derby
DE22 4JR

Dear Andrew,

Thank you very much for the lovely box of chocolates you sent. As usual they were greatly appreciated.

Yours sincerely,

Camilla Parker Bowles

Mrs Camilla Parker Bowles

Camilla Parker-Bowles, a signed typewritten letter thanking the sender for a box of chocolates, late 20thC, 8¼ x 5¾in (21 x 14cm).
£80–100
$115–145 ⚒ VS

Automobilia

A lighting-up timetable and mirror, 1899, 2 x 3in (5 x 7.5cm).
£10–12
$15–18 ⊞ COB

► An acetylene generator, for car headlamps, c1905, 13in (33cm) high.
£130–150
$200–220 ⊞ JUN

A pair of motoring goggles, in original box, 1910, 4in (10cm) wide.
£190–220
$275–325 ⊞ SSM

A pottery tobacco jar, modelled as a motorist's head, c1910, 6in (15cm) high.
£200–275
$300–400 ⊞ MURR

◄ A wooden fretwork model of a car, c1910, 15in (38cm) long.
£120–150
$175–225 ⊞ JUN

► An enamel petrol can, French, c1920, 7in (18cm) high.
£45–55
$65–80 ⊞ AL

A calorimeter, c1920, 6in (15cm) high.
£30–40
$45–60 ⊞ JUN
A calorimeter is an instrument used for measuring heat.

A Pratts forecourt petrol pump, original globe, repainted, c1925, 103in (261.5cm) high.
£750–850
$1,100–1,250 ⊞ JUN

A Junior Shell lighter fluid tin, c1930, 4in (10cm) high.
£25–30
$35–45 ⊞ JUN

A selection of Esso metal penknives, round tops c1925, square top c1955, 2¾in (7cm) high.
£35–55
$50–80 each ⊞ HUX

A Vacuum Motor Car Oils double-sided enamel sign, 1920s, 16 x 18in (40.5 x 45.5cm).
£190–220
$275–325 ⊞ JUN

► A Speedwell Grease tin, c1930, 5in (12.5cm) high.
£25–30
$35–45 ⊞ JUN

A wood and glass bead roadwork sign, c1930, 44in (112cm) wide.
£180–200
$250–300 ⊞ JUN

A Hastings RAC Rally flag, 1933, 7 x 8in (18 x 20.5cm).
£60–70
$90–100 ⊞ BiR

A BP metal funnel, c1920s, 11in (28cm) high.
£40–50
$60–75 ⊞ JUN

A Mobiloil enamel cabinet top sign, 1920s, 12 x 15in (30.5 x 38cm).
£100–130
$145–200 ⊞ JUN

A Sir Malcolm Campbell's Bluebird cardboard jigsaw puzzle, 1930s, 11 x 10in (28 x 25.5cm).
£100–150
$145–225 ⊞ MURR

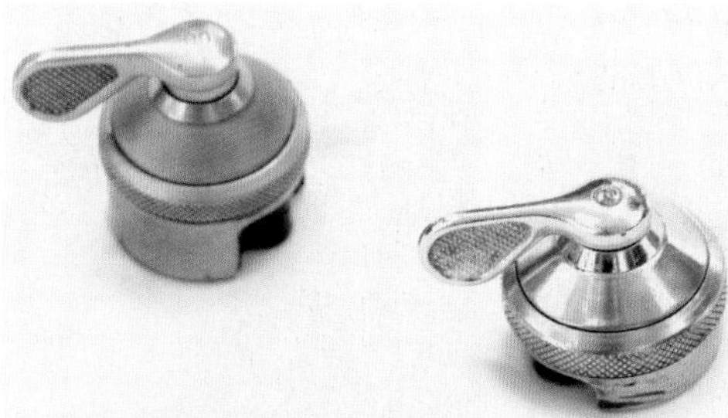

◄ **Two Bosch dashboard dimmer switches,** 1930s, 1½in (4cm) wide.
£100–125
$145–180 each ⊞ BCA

► **A Dagenite car batteries showcard,** featuring mainly pre-war Dinky Toy models, 1946–50, 23¾ x 13¾in (60.5 x 35cm).
£110–140
$160–200 ⚒ VEC

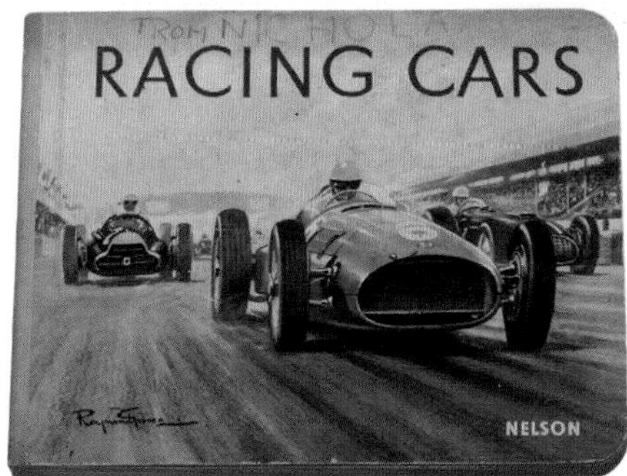

A children's board book, *Racing Cars*, published by Nelson, c1950, 7 x 6in (18 x 15cm).
£20–25
$30–35 ⊞ JUN

A Warwick & Royale School of Motoring advertising sign, 1950s, 30in (76cm) wide.
£25–35
$35–50 ⊞ COB

◄ **A Shell forecourt petrol pump,** with reproduction globe, c1958, 75in (190.5cm) high.
£700–800
$1,000–1,150 ⊞ JUN

In 1833, Marcus Samuel opened a shop in London selling seashells to natural history enthusiasts. On a visit to the Caspian Sea, his son Marcus Jnr recognized the potential for exporting oil to Asia and in 1892 he commissioned the first dedicated oil tanker to transport Russian kerosene to the Far East. The name Shell (reflecting the company origins) was first used as a trademark in 1891, and in 1897 Marcus Samuel founded the Shell Transport and Trading company. In 1904, the pecten or scallop shell (traditional emblem of the pilgrim) was adopted as the company symbol, and it remains one of the most distinctive advertising emblems of all time.

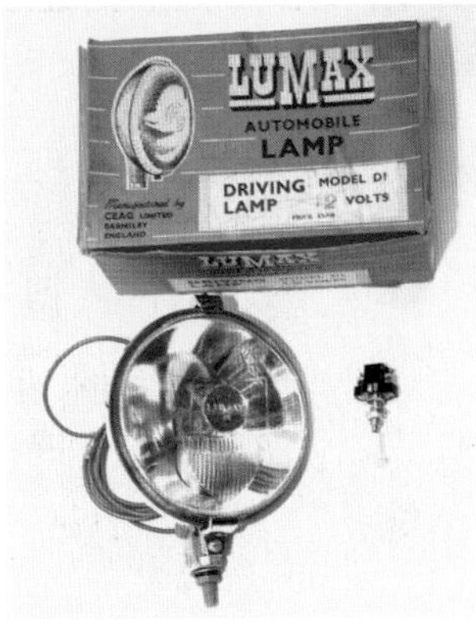

A Lumax car lamp, with original box, c1960, 6 x 9in (15 x 23cm).
£30–40
$45–60 ⊞ JUN

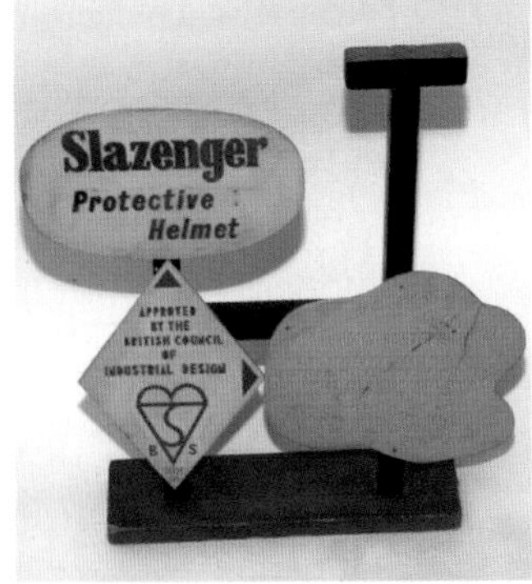

A Slazenger motorcycle helmet display stand, 1960s, 18in (45.5cm) high.
£70–80
$100–115 ⊞ JUN

An Esso plastic cigarette lighter, 1960s, 2in (5cm) high.
£40–50
$60–75 ⊞ HUX

Michelin

A Michelin cut-out card advertising sign, c1920, 30in (76cm) high.
£400–450
$580–650 ⊞ JUN

The Michelin man

The Bibendum figure was introduced by Michelin in 1898. According to legend, one of the Michelin brothers looked at a pile of their tyres and observed that if it had arms it would look like a man. An advertising executive showed them a picture of a rotund Bavarian, raising a tankard of ale and proclaiming, 'Nunc est bibendum' (now is the time to drink). Name and image came together and Bibendum, the Michelin man, became one of the most familiar and collectable advertising figures of the 20th century.

A Michelin pendant, 1920s, 1½in (4cm) high.
£70–80
$100–115 ⊞ HUX

◄ **A Michelin compressor,** c1930, 14in (35.5cm) wide.
£350–400
$500–580 ⊞ JUN

► **A rubber Michelin Man,** 1950s, 2in (5cm) high.
£8–10
$10–15 ⊞ RTT

Mascots

A bronze lion mascot, by Graf und Stift, Austrian, 1920, 7in (18cm) high.
£2,250–2,500
$3,300–3,600 ⊞ AU

A Guy Motors Native American lorry mascot, c1920, 5in (12.5cm) high.
£90–100
$130–145 ⊞ JUN

A bronze bulldog car mascot, c1920, 3½in (9cm) high.
£225–250
$325–360 ⊞ BrL

A hollow-cast white metal elephant's head mascot, by F. Bazin for Latill factory, French, mid-1920s, 9in (23cm) wide.
£1,500–1,750
$2,150–2,500 ⊞ AU

A chrome-plated and bronze Egyptian lady car mascot, with integral cap marked 'Weber & Ruhl', mid-1920s, 7in (18cm) high.
£2,250–2,500
$3,300–3,600 ⊞ AU

A silver-plated bronze car mascot, Spirit of Triumph, by F. Bazin, French, mid-1920s.
£1,350–1,500
$2,000–2,150 ⊞ AU

A metal moving bird mascot, 1920s, 11in (28cm) wide.
£450–500
$650–720 ⊞ BAJ

► A nickel-plated car mascot, The Speed Nymph, by L. Lejeune, 1930s, 7in (18cm) high.
£270–300
$400–450 ⊞ BCA

Plaques & Badges

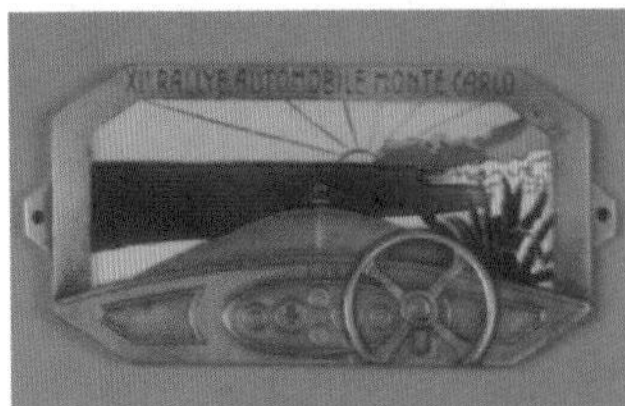

An Automobile Club Nice et Côte d'Azur plaque, 'XIe Rallye Automobile Monte Carlo', by Drago of Nice, enamelled with club badge, 1931, 3in (7.5cm) high, in original presentation case.
£230–260
$330–380 B(Kn)

A British Automobile Racing Club silver metal plaque, commemorating the International Nine-Hour Race at Goodwood, 22 August 1953, 3¾ x 2¾in (9.5 x 7cm), on a hinged wooden backboard.
£550–600
$800–870 WW

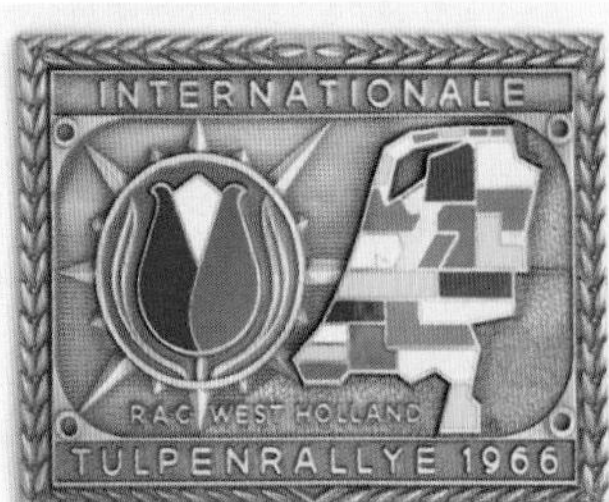

An International Tulpenrallye chrome and enamel badge, Dutch, 1966, 3in (7.5cm) high.
£55–65
$80–95 ⊞ BiR

A Nürburg-Ring car badge and lapel pin, 1930s, 4in (10cm) high.
£230–260
$330–380 ⊞ SSM

A Wallasey Rally chrome and enamel plaque, 1956, 3½ x 4in (9 x 10cm).
£30–40
$45–60 ⊞ BiR

A Playboy car badge, c1970, 3in (7.5cm) square.
£18–20
$25–30 ⊞ JUN

► A bronze Monte Carlo Rallye plaque, 1989, 3 x 4in (7.5 x 10cm).
£130–160
$200–230 ⊞ BiR

A chrome and enamel 21st Monte Carlo Rallye car badge, 1951, 3½in (9cm) wide.
£290–320
$425–475 B(Kn)

A Westland New Zealand car badge, 1950s, 5in (12.5cm) high.
£25–35
$35–50 ⊞ COB

A silvered metal Monte Carlo Rallye plaque, 1980, 3 x 4½in (7.5 x 11.5cm).
£200–230
$300–330 ⊞ BiR

Badges

A Nottinghamshire Automobile Club enamel badge, 1903, 1¼in (3cm) diam.
£225–250
$325–350 ⊞ BAJ

Three Brooklands Automobile Racing Club red enamel badges, by W. G. Lewis, Birmingham, each modelled as the front view of a racing car, mounted on a printed card in original cardboard case with printed label, 1939.
£100–120
$145–175 ⚒ WW

An SFC Dance Club badge, inscribed 'The Gay Nineties', 1930s–50s, 1in (2.5cm) high.
£5–8
$8–12 ⊞ RTT

A Mr Chip of Keiller badge, 1950s, 1¼in (3cm) diam.
£2–4
$3–7 ⊞ RTT

A Tufty Club badge, 1960s, 1¼in (3cm) diam.
£4–5
$6–8 ⊞ RTT

A Butlin's Brighton enamel badge, 1961, 1in (2.5cm) diam.
£12–15
$15–20 ⊞ RTT

► **A Buzby Club badge,** 1970s, 1¾in (4.5cm) diam.
£1–2
$2–3 ⊞ RTT

◄ **A U.K. Mods badge,** 1970s, 1in (2.5cm) diam.
£2–3
$3–5 ⊞ RTT

◄ **Two Mabel Lucie Attwell badges,** 1990, 1in (2.5cm) diam.
£5–10
$7–15 each
⊞ MEM

A Vivienne Westwood badge, inscribed 'World's End', given away free with purchases at Nostalgia of Mud shop, 1983, 2½in (6.5cm) wide.
£80–100
$115–145 ⊞ ID

Bicycles

A Staffordshire pearlware jug, transfer-printed with a stagecoach and four in full flight to one side, the other with a man riding a hobbyhorse with his girlfriend, the collar with painted decoration, c1820, 6in (15cm) high.
£1,100–1,300
$1,600–2,000 B(Ch)
Familiarly known as the hobbyhorse, the first two-wheeled vehicle was patented by the German Baron von Drais in 1817. This forerunner of the bicycle had no pedals, but was propelled by a running motion. Hobbyhorse riding and racing was popular in the Regency period. This rare jug with an attractive and unusual image, is of great interest to vintage cycle enthusiasts, hence its high price range.

A pair of earthenware plates, one decorated with a man riding a velocipede and being attacked by ducks, the other depicting a woman riding a velocipede with one hand while playing a musical instrument, c1868, 6½in (16.5cm) diam.
£300–350
$450–500 B(Ch)
Both of these plates feature a rare depiction of lamps attached to the front supports of the velocipede.

Cross Reference
For more Staffordshire see Ceramics (page 143–144)

► **An Ordinary bicycle,** with Bown bearings, hollow forks, tapered round backbone, cranked down bars, rat-trap pedals and brake lever, the wheels with radial spokes and crescent rims, repainted in matt black, c1882, rear wheel 18in (45.5cm) diam.
£2,000–2,200
$3,000–3,200 B(Ch)

A Royal Enfield gentleman's tandem, by the Enfield Cycle Co, Redditch, front chain missing, c1900.
£550–600
$800–870 B(Kn)

A lithographic print, 'Noces en Velocipede', depicting the bride and groom having departed the wedding reception, with the guests following in disarray, French, c1868, mounted and framed, 16¼ x 22¾in (41.5 x 58cm)
£900–1,100
$1,300–1,600 B(Ch)

A solid-tyred safety bicycle, nickel-plated and re-enamelled, with diamond frame and curved seat tube, c1891, frame 21in (53.5cm) long.
£2,400–2,800
$3,500–4,000 B(Ch)

A nickel-plated brass kerosene-powered bicycle lamp, by Mathews & Willard, with original patented burner, correct rear bracket and side glasses, c1899, 5½in (14cm) high.
£175–200
$250–300 B(Kn)

◄ **A Bradbury Cycles enamel advertising sign,** c1905, 18 x 12in (45.5 x 30.5cm).
£750–850
$1,100–1,250 JUN

◄ **A Nord German bicycle,** with speedometer, c1910.
£275–325
$400–470 ⊞ YEST

A Lucas Lamps advertising card, 'We make light of our work', c1910, 36 x 24in (91.5 x 61cm).
£550–650
$800–950 ⊞ JUN

Lucas & Sons was established in 1875 when Joseph Lucas began manufacturing lamps in Birmingham. Simple and strong, their first bicycle lamps were designed to hang from the axle inside the large front wheel of the Ordinary or Penny Farthing. Joseph Lucas called his quality lamps King of the Road. In 1886, the Safety Head Lamp was introduced and in 1895, Lucas launched the Silver King of the Road, priced at 16s and fitted with a patent lens reflector. This lamp gave improved light and could be opened up so that the lens could be cleaned easily. Lucas lamps are popular with collectors today.

A Triumph Light Roadster gentleman's bicycle, No. 221688, with original black enamel and yellow lined finish and nickel brightwork, with Villiers two-speed gear, eccentric bottom bracket, extended front mudguard, inverted lever brakes mounted on unusually wide bars, Raleigh pattern front stirrup brake, Triumph rear, Phillips aluminium pedals, Brooks saddle and steering lock, c1914, wheels 28in (71cm) diam.
£650–750
$950–1,100 ⚒ B(Ch)

A photographic postcard of a cyclist in uniform, c1915, 6 x 4in (15 x 10cm).
£3–4
$5–8 ⊞ S&D

► **A photographic postcard of a female cyclist,** c1920, 6 x 4in (15 x 10cm).
£6–8
$12–15 ⊞ S&D

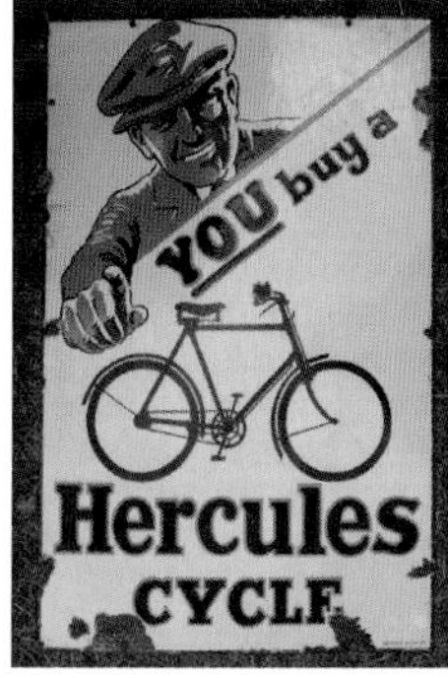

A Hercules Cycle enamel advertising sign, 1920s, 34 x 20in (86.5 x 51cm).
£180–220
$250–320 ⊞ JUN

► **A Phillips Folding military bicycle,** No. R20296, finished in original khaki, with cottered bottom bracket, central hinge tube from top tube to down tube and roller lever front brake, Cyclo three-speed Deraileur gear, Phillips WD insignia on down tube, reflector and a hint of white flash, 1920s, wheels 28in (71cm) diam.
£350–400
$500–580 ⚒ B(Ch)

◄ **A Shorter & Son Daisy Bell china lamp base,** 1920s, 10in (25.5cm) high.
£270–300
$400–440 ⊞ AU

► **A Leach Marathon touring bicycle,** with combined Derailleur and hub gears, c1947.
£400–450
$580–650 ⊞ AVT

◄ **A Paris Galibier racing bicycle,** with distinctive frame design and original components, c1948.
£700–800
$1,000–1,150
⊞ AVT

► **A Brooks bicycle seats advertising card,** 1950s, 10 x 9in (25.5 x 23cm).
£25–30
$35–45 ⊞ JUN

A Moulton Stowaway bicycle, No. 150196, collapsible, unused condition with some original Polythene wrappings, with toolbag, pump and other accessories, 1960s.
£450–550
$650–800 ⚒ B(Ch)

An Itera plastic bicycle, c1985.
£130–150
$200–220 ⚒ B(Ch)

A Sinclair C5 electric three-wheeler, unused, c1980.
£380–450
$550–650 ⚒ B(Kn)

The Sinclair C5 was an open-topped, battery-powered tricycle launched by Clive Sinclair in 1985 at a modest £399 ($580). Since changes in British law meant that electrically-assisted cycles could be ridden without road tax by anyone over the age of 14, Sinclair anticipated sales of 50,000 per annum, rising to 100,000 as everyone from housewives to students to businessmen took to the single-seater vehicle. The project, however, was an almost immediate flop. The machine had to be pedalled uphill, the engine cut out, it had no reverse gear, the semi-reclining riding position was not popular and, above all, the machine's small size made it extremely vulnerable on the road. Production ceased before the year was over and the C5 became a famous failure.

Books

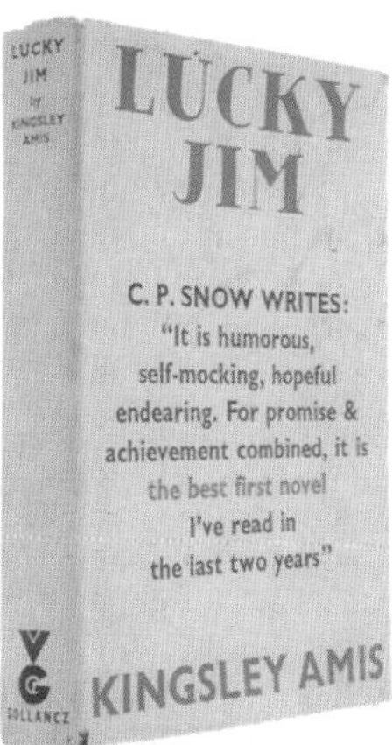

Kingsley Amis, *Lucky Jim*, first edition, published by Victor Gollancz, original green cloth in yellow dust jacket with red and black lettering, minor damage, 1953, 8°.
£2,750–3,000
$4,000–4,500 ⊞ JON

Margaret Drabble, *A Summer Bird-Cage*, first edition, published by Weidenfeld & Nicolson, dust jacket price clipped, 1962, 8°.
£200–250
$300–350 ⚒ DW

LOCATE THE SOURCE
The source of each illustration in Miller's can be found by checking the code letters below each caption with the Key to Illustrations, pages 443–451.

Martin Amis, *The Rachel Papers*, first edition, dust jacket, 1973, 8°.
£425–475
$620–700 ⚒ BBA

Maria Edgeworth, *Frank*, illustrated by F. S. Fraser, published by George Routledge & Sons, 1917, 8 x 5in (20.5 x 12.5cm).
£10–15
$15–20 ⊞ ADD

Anthony Burgess, *Time for a Tiger*, first edition, published by William Heinemann, 1956, 8 x 5in (20.5 x 12.5cm).
£500–600
$720–870 ⊞ NW

◄ Louis de Bernières, *Captain Corelli's Mandolin*, first edition, published by Secker & Warburg, London, 1994, 9 x 6in (23 x 15cm).
£400–450
$580–650 ⊞ ADD

William S. Burroughs, *Junkie*, first edition, published by Ace Books, New York, minor damage, 1953, 6½ x 4¼in (16.5 x 11.5cm).
£425–475
$620–700 ⊞ ASC
This first edition of Burroughs' first book was written under the pseudonym William Lee (his mother's maiden name), and is bound with Maurice Helbrant's *Narcotic Agent*.

T. S. Eliot, *Four Quartets*, first edition, published by Faber & Faber, 1934, 9 x 6in (23 x 15cm).
£150–200
$220–300 ⊞ BIB

Gustave Flaubert, *Madame Bovary*, first UK English translation, published by Vizetelly & Co, 1886, 8 x 5in (20.5 x 12.5cm).
£250–300
$350–450 ⊞ ADD

Bonnie Golightly, *Beat Girl*, first edition, paperback original, published by Avon, 1959, 6½ x 4in (16.5 x 10cm).
£25–30
$35–45 ⊞ ASC

Robert Graves, *Good-Bye To All That*, first edition, first issue, including portrait, poem by Siegfried Sassoon, engraving of WWI soldier on upper cover, cloth slipcase, 1929, 8°.
£450–500
$650–720 ⚒ DW

Graham Greene, *The Lawless Roads*, first edition, endpaper maps, plates, dust jacket, 1939, 8°.
£1,000–1,200
$1,500–1,750 ⚒ BBA

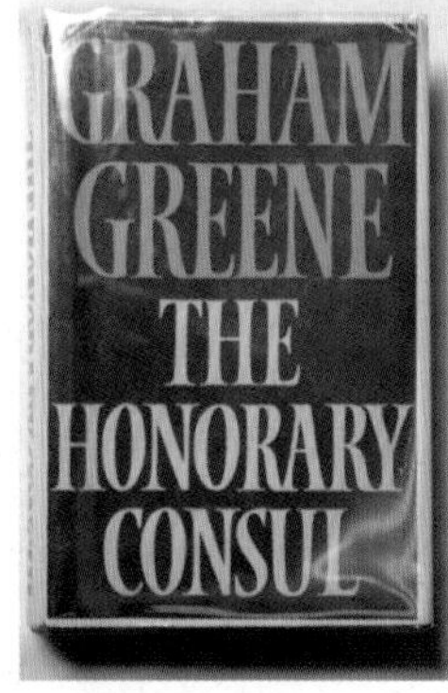

Graham Greene, *The Honorary Consul*, published by Bodley Head, 1973, 8 x 6in (20.5 x 15cm).
£30–40
$45–60 ⊞ ADD

Aldous Huxley, *Brave New World*, published by Chatto & Windus, 1932, 8 x 5in (20.5 x 12.5cm).
£400–500
$580–720 ⊞ ADD

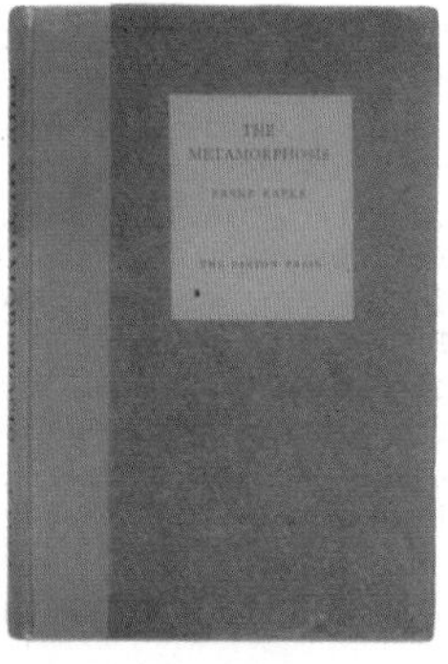

Franz Kafka, *The Metamorphosis*, first English edition, translated by A. L. Lloyd, published by Parton Press, 1937, slim 8°.
£375–425
$560–620 ⚒ DW

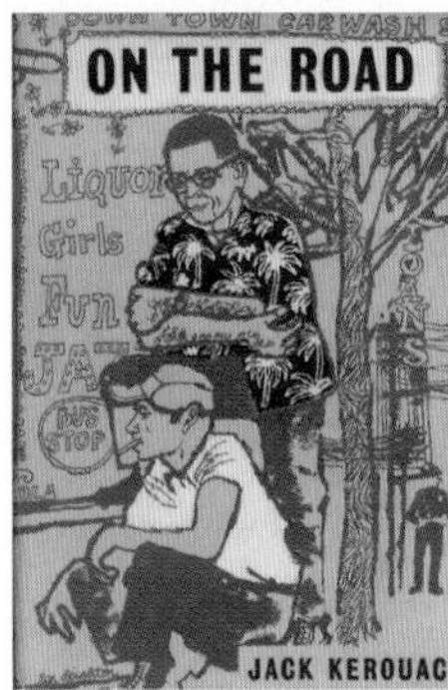

Jack Kerouac, *On The Road*, first UK edition, published by André Deutsch, dust jacket designed by Len Deighton, 1958, 7¾ x 5½in (19.5 x 14cm).
£500–575
$720–850 ⊞ ASC

Jack Kerouac, *Tristessa*, first edition, paperback original, published by Avon, 1960, 6½ x 4in (16.5 x 10cm).
£25–30
$35–45 ⊞ ASC

C. S. Lewis, *Till We Have Faces*, first edition, published by Geoffrey Bles, 1956, 7 x 5in (18 x 12.5cm).
£100–120
$145–175 ⊞ ADD

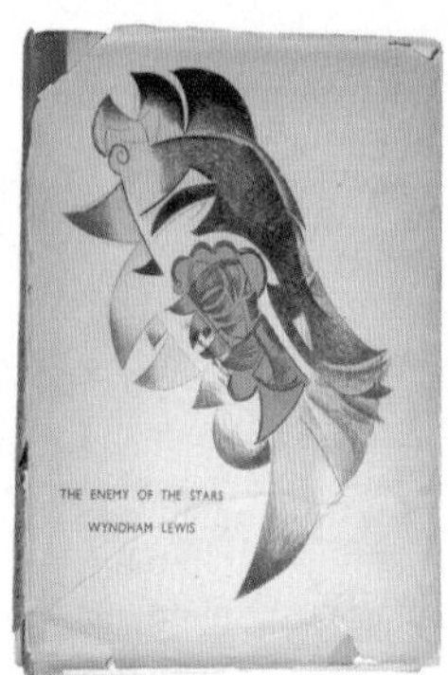

Wyndham Lewis, *Enemy of the Stars*, first edition, published by Desmond Harmsworth, 1932, 12 x 9in (30.5 x 23cm).
£125–150
$180–220 ⊞ ADD

Richard Neville, *Play Power*, first edition, published by Jonathan Cape, with Headopoly underground poster game in pocket at rear, 1970, 8 x 6in (20.5 x 15cm).
£125–150
$180–220 ⊞ ADD
Richard Neville was the founder of Oz in the 1960s, arguably the most famous of all the underground magazines of the period.

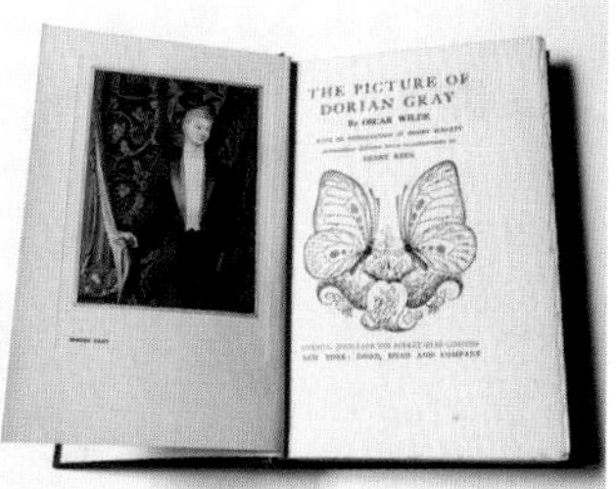

Oscar Wilde, *The Picture of Dorian Gray*, illustrated by Henry Keen, first edition, published by John Lane, The Bodley Head, 1925, 10 x 7in (25.5 x 18cm).
£100–120
$145–175 ⊞ BAY

Tom Wolfe, *The Kandy Kolored Tangerine Flake Streamline Baby*, first UK edition, published by Jonathan Cape, psychedelic 'op-art' dust jacket, 1966, 6½ x 4in (16.5 x 10cm).
£40–45
$60–65 ⊞ ASC

◀ **Frank Lloyd Wright,** *The Life-Work...*, with contributions by Frank Lloyd Wright, published by C. A. Mees, Holland, black and white illustrations and photographs throughout, 1925, 4°.
£300–350
$450–500 ⚒ DW

Children's Books

Ernest Aris, *Woodfolk Market*, 1910–20, 6 x 5in (15 x 12.5cm).
£20–30
$30–45 ⊞ J&J

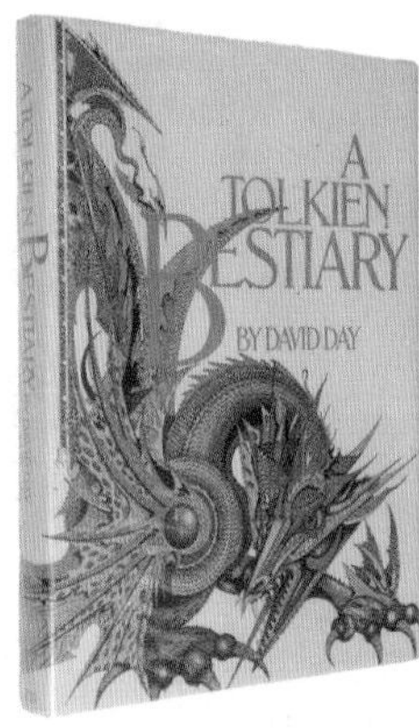

David Day, *A Tolkien Bestiary*, first edition, published by Mitchell Beazley, 1979, 11 x 9in (28 x 23cm).
£50–60
$75–90 ⊞ ADD

Mabel Lucie Attwell's Painting Book, published by Dean, 1934, 11 x 9in (28 x 23cm).
£45–55
$65–80 ⊞ J&J

Charles Lutwidge Dodgson (Lewis Carroll), *Alice's Adventures in Wonderland*, first edition, with 24 colour illustrations by Margaret Tarrant, The Sunshine Series, published by Ward Lock, c1930, 11 x 9in (28 x 23cm).
£60–70
$90–100 ⊞ BIB

◀ Captain W. E. Johns, *Biggles Flies North*, first edition, published by Oxford University Press, dust jacket, 1939, 8°.
£300–350
$450–500 ⚒ BBA

▶ Lewin and Jellico, *Tuesday at the Zoo* and *Wednesday at the Zoo*, from the *Happy Days at the Zoo Series*, published by John Swain & Sons, 1920s, 5 x 4in (20.5 x 10cm).
£15–18
$20–25 each ⊞ J&J

R. D. Blackmore, *Lorna Doone*, published by Samson Low, 1883, 7 x 5in (18 x 12.5cm).
£35–45
$50–65 ⊞ BAY

Charles Lutwidge Dodgson (Lewis Carroll), *Alice's Adventures in Wonderland*, first edition, illustrated by Helen Oxenbury, published by Walker Books, 1999, 9½ x 8in (24 x 20.5cm).
£15–20
$20–30 ⊞ BIB

Roald Dahl, *The Giraffe and the Pelly and Me*, first edition, illustrated by Quentin Blake, published by Jonathan Cape, 1985, 13 x 9¼in (33 x 23.5cm).
£65–75
$95–110 ⊞ BIB

G. A. Henty, *A March on London*, first edition, published by Blackie & Son, 1898, 7½ x 5in (19 x 12.5cm).
£125–150
$180–220 ⊞ BAY

Hugh Lofting, *Doctor Dolittle in the Moon*, first edition, with one colour plate and black and white drawings by the author, published by Jonathan Cape, original dust jacket, 1929, 8°.
£250–300
$350–450 ⊞ JON

Mrs Sherwood, *The Fairchild Family*, illustrated by Florence Rudland Wells Gardner, published by Darton & Co, 1912, 9 x 6in (23 x 15cm).
£15–20
$20–30 ⊞ ADD

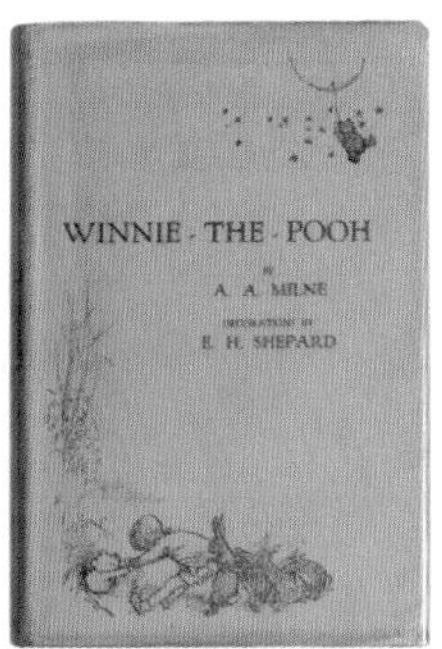

A. A. Milne, *Winnie the Pooh*, first edition, decorated by E. H. Shepard, published by Methuen, 1926, 8 x 6in (20.5 x 15cm).
£650–750
$950–1,100 ⊞ ADD

J. R. R. Tolkien, *The Hobbit*, first edition, first impression advertisements, pictorial endpapers, two maps printed in red and black, nine black and white illustrations by the author, published by Allen & Unwin, 1937, 8 x 6in (20.5 x 15cm).
£9,000–10,000
$13,000–14,500 ⊞ ADD

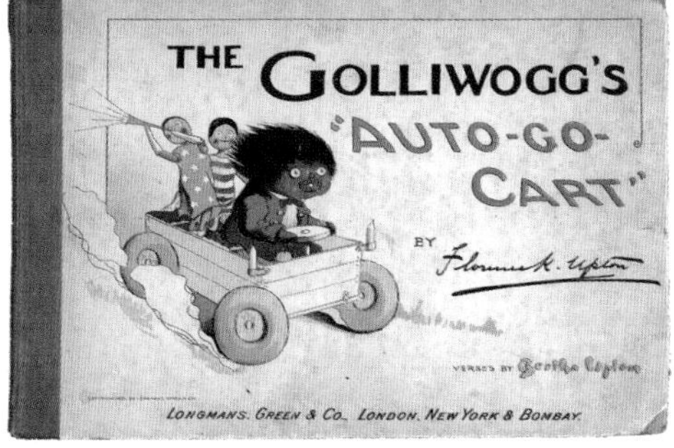

Florence and Bertha Upton, *The Golliwogg's Auto-Go-Cart*, first edition, published by Longmans, Green & Co, 1901, 9 x 11in (23 x 28cm).
£300–325
$450–470 ⊞ BIB

Mary Norton, *The Borrowers*, first edition, with pictorial endpapers, colour frontispiece and line drawings in the text by Diana Stanley, published by Dent, with pictorial dust jacket and wraparound band, 1952, 8°.
£1,000–1,250
$1,500–1,750 ⊞ JON
This is the scarce first book in the *Borrowers* sequence and winner of the Carnegie Medal for children's literature.

Louis Wain, *Pussies at Work*, Father Tuck's Little Pets Series, c1900, slim 4°.
£600–700
$870–1,000 ⚒ DW

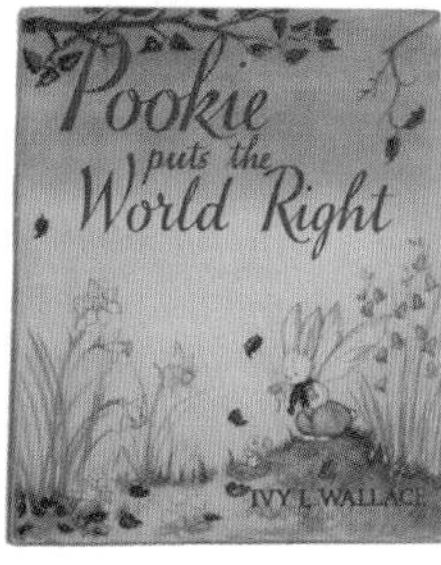

Ivy Wallace, *Pookie Puts the World Right*, published by Collins, 1952, 10¼ x 8¼in (26 x 21cm).
£15–20
$20–30 ⊞ J&J

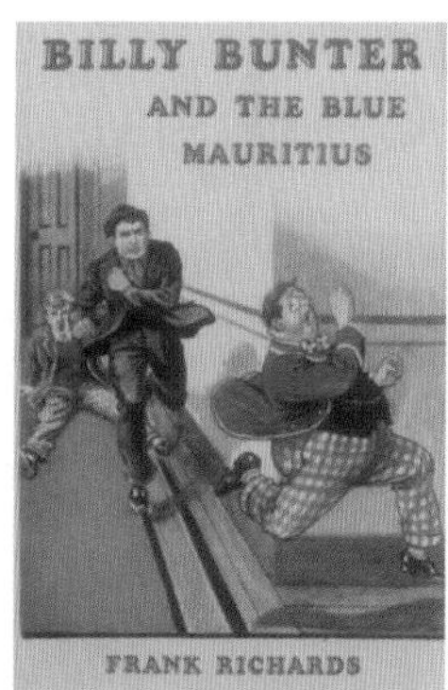

Frank Richards, *Billy Bunter and the Blue Mauritius*, first edition, published by Skilton, with dust jacket, 1952, 8°.
£125–150
$180–220 ⊞ JON

Louis Wain, *Somebody's Pussies*, published by Raphael Tuck & Sons, c1905, 10 x 7in (25.5 x 18cm).
£700–800
$1,000–1,150 ⊞ ADD

Little Redcoats, a book of nursery rhymes mounted on linen, published by Frederick Warne and Co, 1908, 11 x 8in (28 x 20.5cm).
£60–70
$90–100 ⊞ JUN

Crime Fiction & Thrillers

The founding father of crime fiction is often regarded as Edgar Allan Poe (1809–49) who, in his short stories, established many of the main principles of the detective novel. It was not until some 40 years later, however, that the genre really took off when Arthur Conan Doyle (1859–1930), a struggling young doctor, created Sherlock Holmes. The greatest detective of them all first appeared in *A Study in Scarlet* (1887) and from 1891 *The Strand Magazine* published the short stories. Sherlock Holmes became a hit on both sides of the Atlantic, creating an archetype for the infallible detective hero and inspiring a host of imitators.

The inter-war years were a golden age for detective fiction. Dame Agatha Christie (1890–1976) introduced Hercule Poirot in *The Mysterious Affair at Styles* in 1920, the first of the 66 detective novels that were to make her a contender for the most successful author of all time, with world sales in excess of 300 million. Other popular crime writers and characters of the period included Dorothy L. Sayers (Lord Peter Whimsey), G. K. Chesterton (Father Brown) and American novelist Raymond Chandler who, in *The Big Sleep* (1939), the first of his seven Philip Marlowe novels, took murder out of the drawing room and on to 'the mean streets', pioneering another favourite archetype, the hard-boiled yet honourable private eye. The Cold War ushered in a new genre of thriller, the spy novel. Ian Fleming's James Bond first appeared in *Casino Royal* (1953), while writers such as John Le Carré and Len Deighton portrayed less glamorous visions of the life of the secret agent.

Aided and abetted by television and film dramatizations, crime fiction flourished from the 1960s onwards with writers such as P. D. James, Ruth Rendell and Colin Dexter in the UK, and American authors including Carl Hiaasen and Elmore Leonard. Crime novels are popular with collectors today, particularly early or rare first editions by leading names and works that launch a celebrated sleuth or series, for example Sue Grafton's *A is for Alibi*, which kick-started an alphabet of crime novels. As the following examples show, while golden age writers such as Agatha Christie are highly collectable, first editions by more recent writers can also command large sums and would-be crime collectors should start off by investigating their own shelves for evidence of any desirable volumes. As with all books, condition, edition and the presence of a dust jacket are crucial to value.

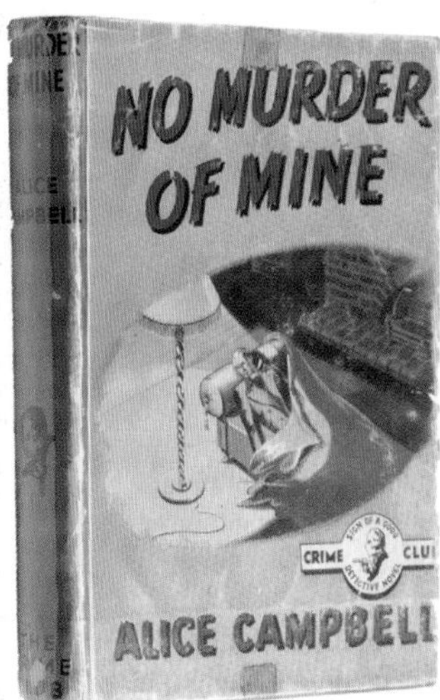

Alice Campbell, *No Murder of Mine*, first edition, published by Collins Crime Club, 1941, 8 x 5in (20.5 x 12.5cm).
£200–250
$300–350 ⊞ NW

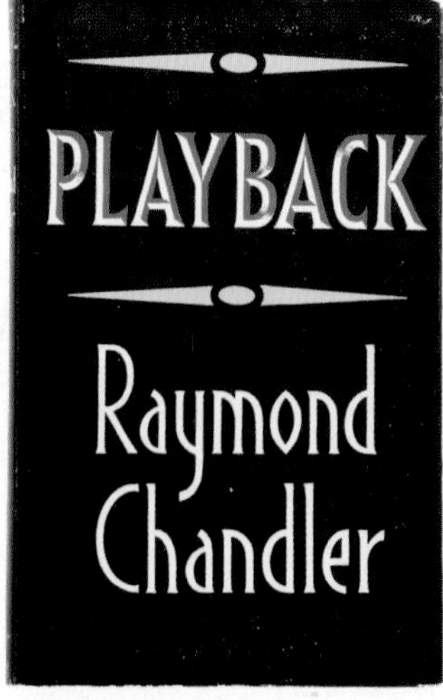

Raymond Chandler, *Playback*, first UK edition, published by Hamish Hamilton, 1958, 8 x 5in (20.5 x 12.5cm).
£175–200
$250–300 ⊞ ADD

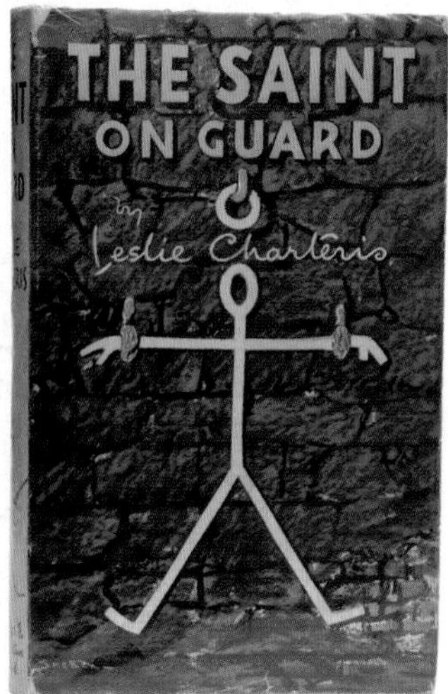

Leslie Charteris, *The Saint on Guard*, first edition, published by Hodder & Stoughton, 1945, 7½ x 5½in (19 x 14cm).
£55–65
$80–95 ⊞ BIB

Gilbert Chester, *A Date with Danger*, the Sexton Blake Library Detective Story Magazine Series No. 135, c1930, 7 x 5in (18 x 12.5cm).
£8–10
$12–15 ⊞ ADD

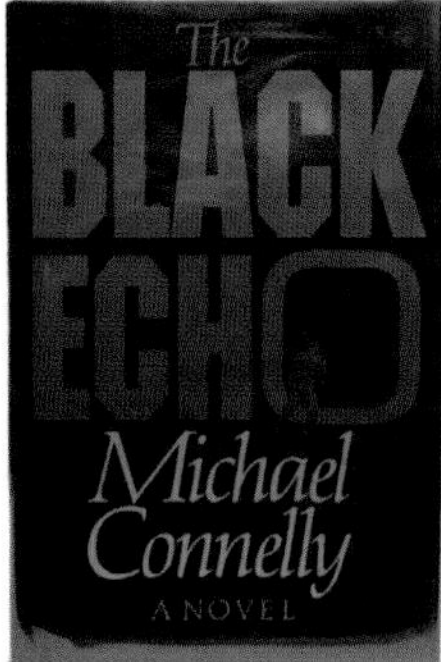

Michael Connelly, *The Black Echo*, first edition, signed by the author, published by Little, Brown & Co, 1992, 9½ x 6½in (24 x 16.5cm).
£120–140
$175–200 ⊞ BIB

Colin Dexter, *The Riddle of the Third Mile*, first edition, published by Macmillan, dust jacket, 1983, 8°.
£300–350
$450–500 ⚒ BBA

G. K. Chesterton, *The Secret of Father Brown*, first edition, published by Cassell, pictorial dust jacket, 1927, 8°.
£1,500–1,800
$2,200–2,600 ⊞ JON

Bernard Cornwell (Susannah Kells), *Coat of Arms*, first edition, signed by the author as Susannah Kells, published by Collins, dust jacket, 1986, 8°.
£80–100
$115–145 ⚒ BBA
As a young journalist, Cornwell was sitting in a Belfast pub with his fellow hacks discussing how much easier life was for novelists. After a few drinks they came up with a fictitious name and a bet, that whoever wrote a book under that name would be given a bottle of Jameson's whisky by each of the group. Years later Cornwell won the wager, and now out of print, his three novels written as 'Susannah Kells' are sought after. Cornwell is attracting a growing number of collectors.

◄ **Agatha Christie,** *A Pocket Full of Rye*, first edition, signed by the author, published by Collins, 1953, 8 x 5in (20.5 x 12.5cm).
£1,000–1,200
$1,500–1,750 ⊞ ADD

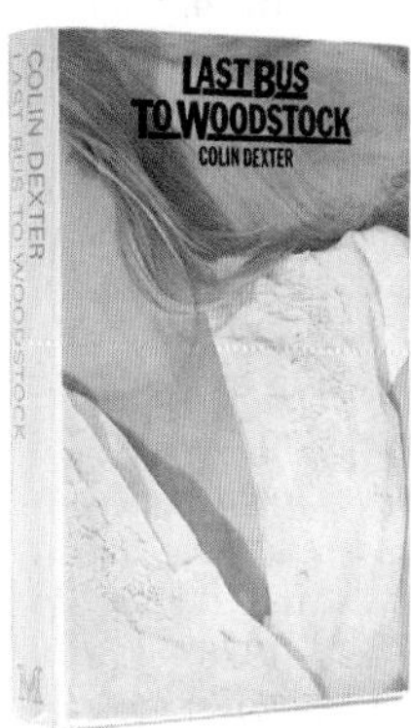

John Creasey, *Accidents for Inspector West*, first edition, published by Hodder & Stoughton, 1957, 8 x 5in (20.5 x 12.5cm).
£35–45
$50–65 ⊞ ADD

Colin Dexter, *Last Bus to Woodstock*, first edition, published by Macmillan, 1975, 8 x 5in (20.5 x 12.5cm).
£875–975
$1,250–1,400 ⊞ NW

Michael Dibdin, *The Last Sherlock Holmes Story*, first edition, published by Jonathan Cape, 1978, 8 x 5½in (20.5 x 14cm).
£225–250
$325–350 ⊞ BIB

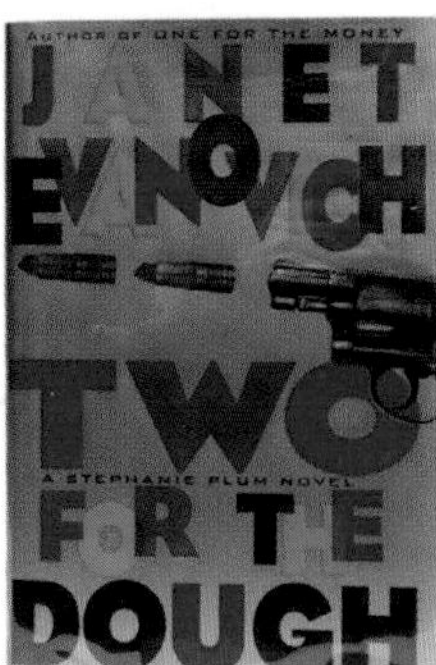

Janet Evanovich, *Two for the Dough*, first edition, signed by the author, published by Scribner, 1996, 9¾ x 6½in (25 x 16.5cm).
£35–45
$50–65 ⊞ BIB

Ian Fleming, *Casino Royale*, second impression, published by Jonathan Cape, dust jacket, 1953, 8°.
£700–800
$1,000–1,150 ⚒ DW

Ian Fleming, *From Russia with Love*, first edition, published by Jonathan Cape, 1957, 8 x 5in (20.5 x 12.5cm).
£1,500–1,750
$2,200–2,500 ⊞ NW

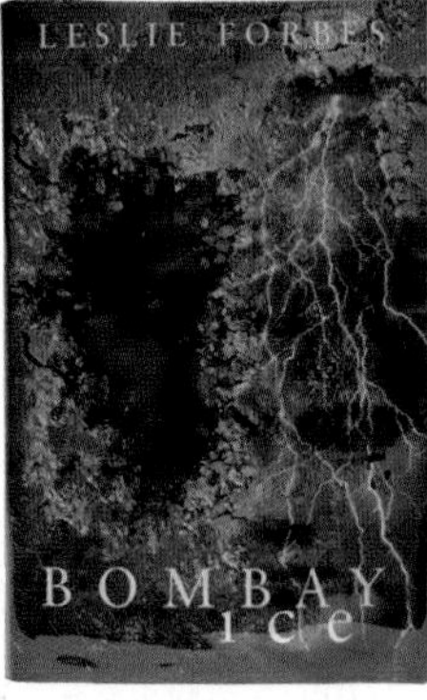

Leslie Forbes, *Bombay Ice*, first edition, signed by the author, published by Orion Publishing Group, 1998, 9 x 5¾in (23 x 14.5cm).
£100–120
$145–175 ⊞ BIB

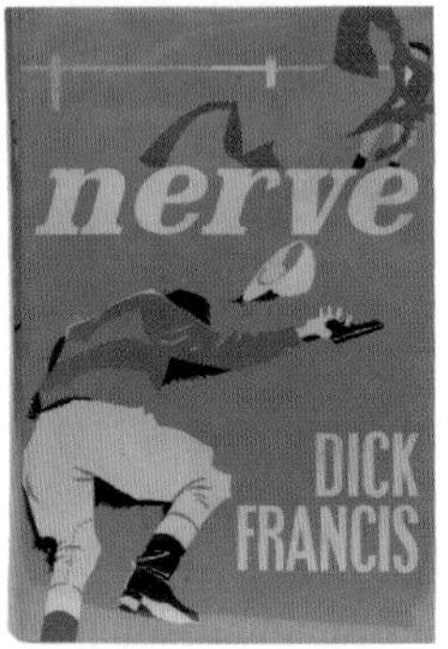

Dick Francis, *Nerve*, first edition, published by Michael Joseph, 1964, 7½ x 5¼in (19 x 13.5cm).
£625–725
$900–1,000 ⊞ BIB

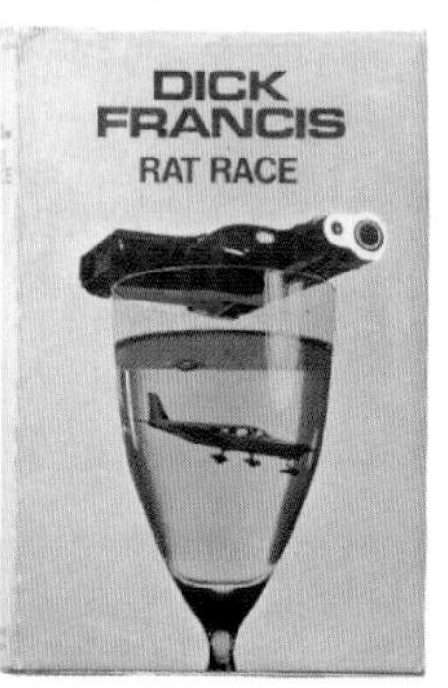

Dick Francis, *Rat Race*, first edition, signed by the author, published by Michael Joseph, 1970, 8 x 6in (20.5 x 15cm).
£200–250
$300–350 ⊞ ADD

R. Austin Freeman, *For the Defence, Dr. Thorndyke*, first edition, published by Hodder & Stoughton, 1934, 8 x 5½in (20.5 x 14cm).
£400–450
$580–650 ⊞ BIB

Jonathan Gash, *The Judas Pair*, first edition, published by Collins, 1977, 8 x 6in (20.5 x 12.5cm).
£125–150
$180–220 ⊞ ADD

Anthony Gilbert, *Death Takes a Wife*, first edition, published by Collins Crime Club, 1959, 7½ x 5in (19 x 12.5cm).
£50–60
$75–90 ⊞ BIB

Sue Grafton, *'A' is for Alibi*, first edition, signed by the author, published by Macmillan, 1982, 8¼ x 5¼in (21 x 13.5cm).
£650–750
$950–1,100 ⊞ BIB

Robert van Gulik, *The Chinese Maze Murders*, first edition, published in the Hague, dust jacket, 1956, 8°.
£400–500
$580–720 ⚒ BBA

Bruce Hamilton, *To be Hanged*, published by Collins Crime Club, 1930, 7½ x 5½in (19 x 14cm).
£75–85
$110–125 ⊞ BIB

Carl Hiaasen, *Double Whammy*, first edition, published by Century, 1987, 8½ x 6in (21.5 x 15cm).
£65–75
$95–110 ⊞ BIB

◀ **P. D. James,** *Unnatural Causes*, signed by the author, published by Faber & Faber, 1967, 7½ x 5¼in (19 x 13.5cm).
£1,400–1,600
$2,000–2,300 ⊞ BIB

Peter Lovesey, *The Detective Wore Silk Drawers*, first edition, published by Macmillan, 1971, 8 x 5in (20.5 x 12.5cm).
£40–50
$60–75 ⊞ ADD

◀ **John Le Carré,** *The Looking-Glass War*, first edition, signed by the author, published by Heinemann, 1956, 8 x 5½in (20.5 x 14cm).
£1,700–2,000
$2,500–3,000 ⊞ NW

▶ **Elmore Leonard,** *The Switch*, first English edition, published by Secker & Warburg, 1979, 8°.
£120–150
$175–225 ⚒ BBA

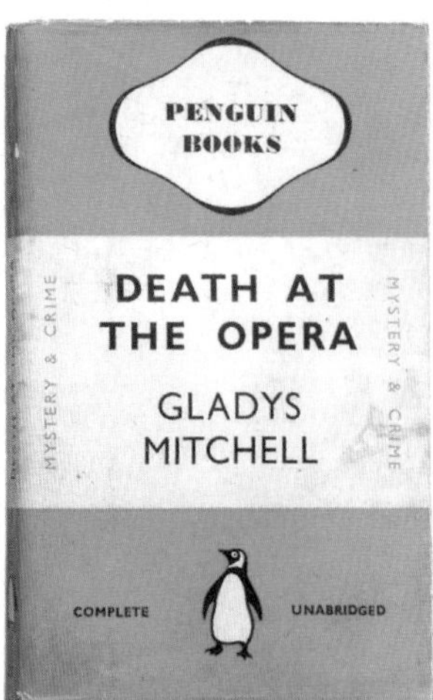

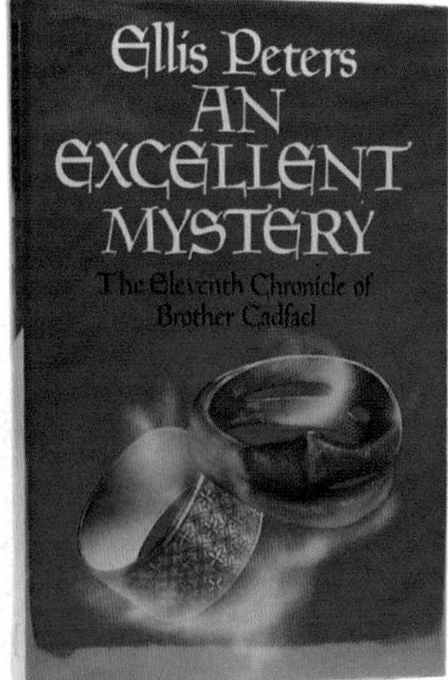

Ellis Peters, *An Excellent Mystery*, first edition, published by Macmillan, 1985, 8 x 5½in (20.5 x 14cm).
£75–85
$110–125 ⊞ BIB

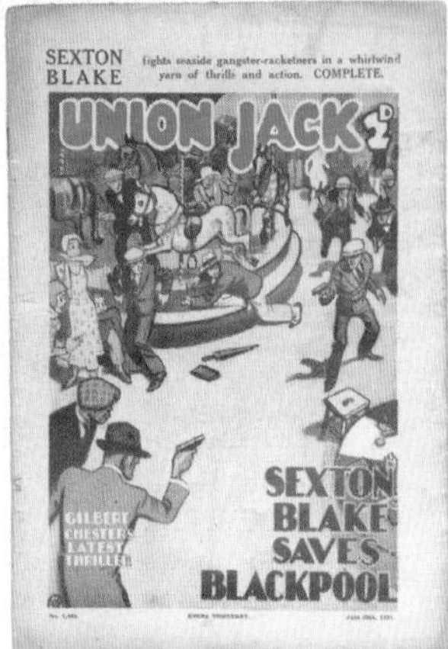

◄ **Gladys Mitchell,** *Death at the Opera*, first edition, published by Penguin Books, 1939, 7 x 5in (18 x 12.5cm).
£30–35
$45–50 ⊞ ADD

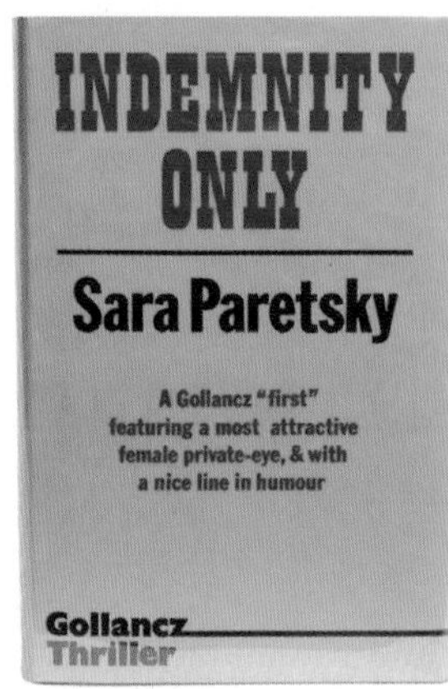

Sara Paretsky, *Indemnity Only*, first edition, signed by the author, published by Victor Gollancz, 1982, 8¼ x 5¼in (21 x 13.5cm).
£300–350
$450–500 ⊞ BIB

Ruth Rendell, *Vanity Dies Hard*, first edition, published by John Long, 1966, 8 x 5in (20.5 x 12.5cm).
£600–700
$870–1,000 ⊞ NW

◄ ***Union Jack,*** magazine No. 1444, July 1931, 11 x 7in (28 x 18cm).
£10–12
$15–18 ⊞ ADD

► **R. D. Wingfield,** *A Touch of Frost*, first edition, published by Constable, 1990, 9 x 5¾in (23 x 14.5cm).
£700–800
$1,000–1,150 ⊞ BIB

Peter O'Donnell, *Cobra Trap*, first edition, published by Souvenir Press, 1986, 8¾ x 5¾in (22 x 14.5cm).
£85–95
$125–140 ⊞ BIB

Ian Rankin, *Mortal Causes, An Inspector Rebus Novel*, first edition, published by Orion, 1994, 9 x 5in (23 x 12.5cm).
£165–195
$240–280 ⊞ BIB

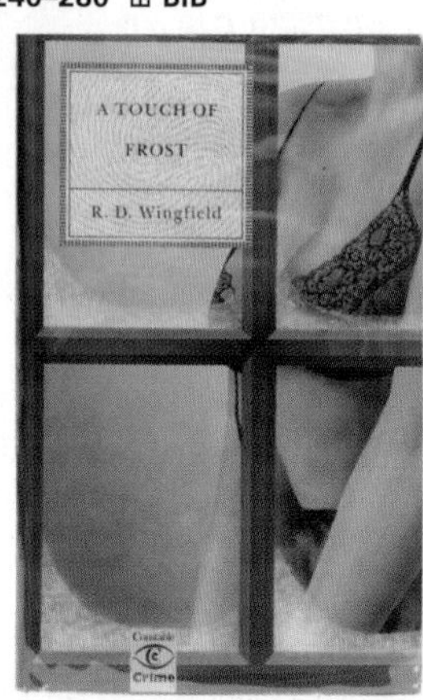

Travel

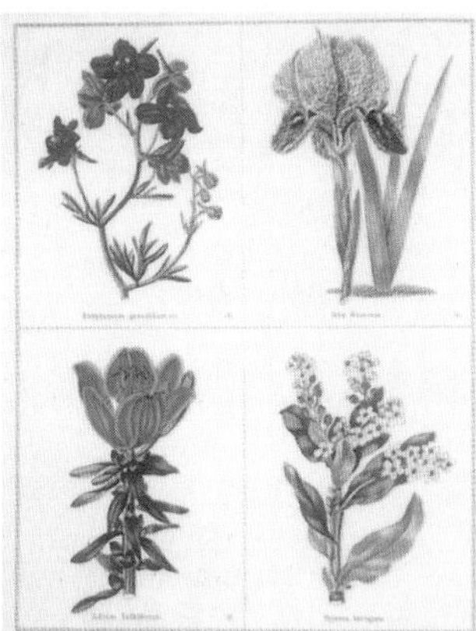

Thomas Witlam Atkinson, *Travels in the Regions of the Upper and Lower Amoor, and the Russian Acquisitions on the Confines of India and China...*, first edition 1860, 8°.
£100–120
$145–175 DW

Bruce Chatwin, *The Song Lines*, first edition, signed by the author, published by the Franklin Library, USA, 1987, 9 x 6in (23 x 15cm).
£125–150
$180–220 ADD

Fanny Bullock Workman and William Hunter Workman, *Ice-Bound Heights of the Mustagh, An Account of Two Seasons of Pioneer Exploration and High Climbing in the Baltistan Himalaya*, first edition, 1908, 8°.
£450–500
$650–720 DW

William Beattie, *The Danube: Its History, Scenery and Topography*, with portrait frontispiece, two black-and-white maps and 78 views, pp 53–60 missing, published by Virtue & Co, c1870, 4°.
£120–140
$175–200 DW

◀ **Bruce Chatwin,** *In Patagonia*, first edition, published by Jonathan Cape, 1977, 9 x 6in (23 x 15cm).
£425–475
$620–700 BIB

Capt. Sir John C. Willoughby, *East Africa and its Big Game: The Narrative of a Sporting Trip from Zanzibar to the Borders of the Masai*, first edition with 17 plates, four lithographed, folding coloured map, publisher's catalogue, 1889, 8°.
£140–160
$200–230 BBA

Karen Blixen, *Out of Africa*, first edition, minor damage, 1937, 8°.
£350–400
$500–580 DW

Also writing under the name Isak Dinesen, Karen Blixen (1885–1962) was born in Denmark. She married her cousin Baron Bron Blixen-Finecke in 1914 and went with him to manage a coffee plantation in Kenya. After their divorce in 1921, she ran the plantation herself for ten years, recording her experiences in her memoirs *Out of Africa* (1937).

Sir Henry Morton Stanley, *The Congo and the Founding of its Free State: A Story of Work and Exploration*, 2 vols, first American edition, with 44 plates, four folding maps and folding map hand-coloured in outline, 1885, 8°.
£400–450
$580–650 BBA

Value

The earliest printed form of the text is usually the most sought after, hence the value of the first edition or impression. Dust jackets were not commonly used in the US and UK until the early 1900s and were often discarded. Today they are crucial to the value of a book, as is overall condition.

Bottles

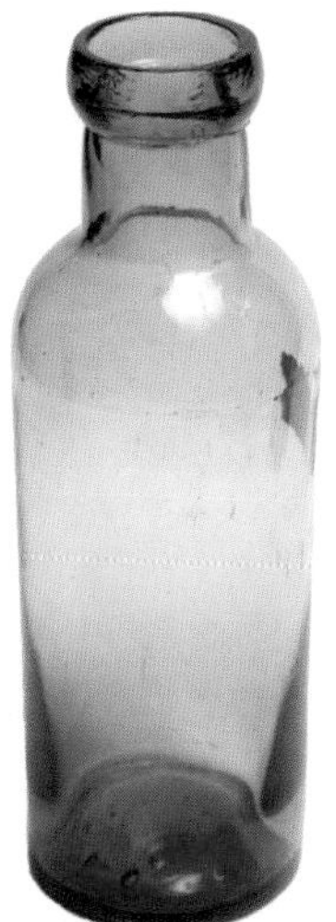

A chemist's glass bottle, 19thC, 7in (18cm) high.
£10–12
$15–18 BoC

A sealed glass Middle Temple bottle, c1840, 11in (28cm) high.
£70–80
$100–115 CAL

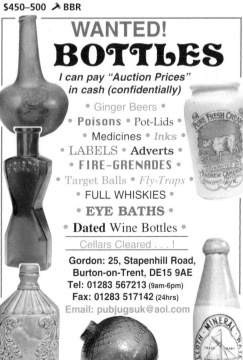

A Haynes Patent glass bottle, embossed 'The Property of Mayo & Rugg Ld, Earlsdon, Coventry', c1880, 9in (23cm) high.
£150–200
$220–280 BBR

A Wilson's Patent Poison glass bottle, embossed 'Caution, Not To Be Taken', 1880–1900, 6¾in (17cm) high.
£500–600
$720–870 BBR

A Harden's glass fire grenade, embossed 'Harden Grenade' and 'Sprinkler', 1880–1900, 17¼in (44cm) long.
£600–650
$850–950 BBR

A glass hamilton bottle, embossed 'Hamilton's Patent Aerated Waters, Prepared by Knight & Davies, Chemists, Bath', 1830–40, 7¼in (18.5cm) long.
£3,200–3,500
$4,500–5,000 BBR
This extremely rare and early hamilton bottle is in excellent condition – hence its high value.

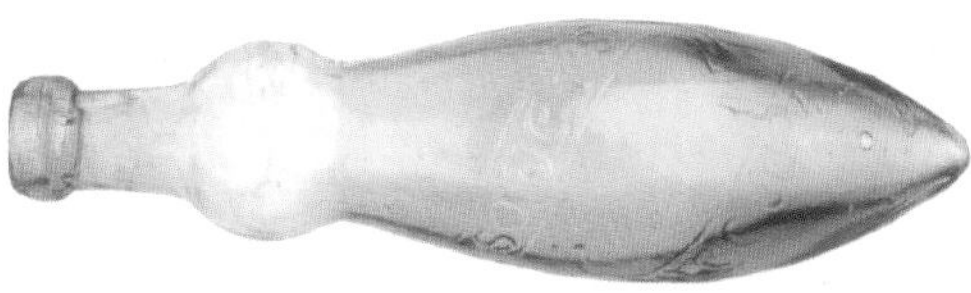

A glass hamilton bottle, embossed 'Soyer's Nectar', 1870–80, 10½in (26.5cm) long.
£320–350
$450–500 BBR

A glass poison bottle, embossed 'J.B.M./B.', 1880–1900, 3¾in (9.5cm) high.
£420–470
$600–680 BBR

◄ **A glass blood mixture bottle,** embossed 'Clarke's World Famed Blood Mixture, Lincoln, England', c1890, 11½in (29cm) high.
£25–30
$35–45 ⊞ JAM

A stoneware hot water bottle/foot warmer, 1920s, 10in (25.5cm) high.
£120–160
$175–230 ⊞ MURR

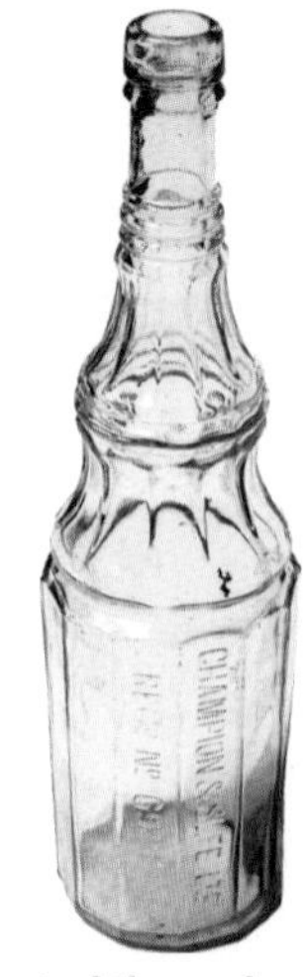

A set of three glass vinegar bottles, c1900, 16in (40.5cm) high.
£25–30
$35–45 ⊞ JAM

Ginger Beer Bottles

From the 19th century onwards, ginger beer became an extremely popular drink. As packaging expert Alan Blakeman notes, it was traditionally sold in cool, stoneware bottles, hence the term 'stone ginger'. Values of bottles depend on shape, size and the rarity and quality of the transfer-printed image. In addition to the standard, straight-sided 'stonies', there are also 'champagne' bottles – straight-sided but with a long, sloping neck – and skittle-shaped bottles, resembling the pin used in bowling. Colour is another factor that affects value. Some bottles came with coloured tops which can be particularly rare. However, the more commonplace g.bs (as they are known) were produced in vast numbers until 1928 when Mary Donoghue sued a ginger beer maker after finding a decomposed snail's shell in her drink, helping to bring to an end the tradition of the opaque, stoneware bottle.

A glass London ginger beer bottle, 19thC, 7in (18cm) high.
£10–12
$15–18 ⊞ BoC

A stoneware ginger beer bottle, 19thC, 7in (18cm) high.
£6–8
$8–10 ⊞ BoC

A stoneware ginger beer bottle, transfer-printed with a sailing ship and 'Stone Ginger, D. Kelly & Co, (Limited), Leith', 1910–20, 5¾in (14.5cm) high.
£320–370
$450–550 BBR

A stoneware ginger beer bottle, transfer-printed 'Tettenhall Rock Mineral Water Co, Wolverhampton, Prize Medal Stone Beer', c1920, 7½in (19cm) high.
£20–25
$30–35 ⊞ JAM

A stoneware ginger beer bottle, transfer-printed 'Pearson's Coventry, Stone Genuine Ginger Beer', c1920, 7in (18cm) high.
£15–20
$20–30 ⊞ JAM

A stoneware ginger beer bottle, transfer-printed 'Four-in-Hand Stone Beer Co', c1920, 7in (8cm) high.
£12–16
$18–25 ⊞ JAM

A stoneware ginger beer bottle, embossed 'Schweppes', 1920–30, 6¾in (17cm) high.
£10–12
$15–18 ⊞ JAM

A stoneware ginger beer bottle, transfer-printed 'W. Daly, Durban', South African, c1935, 9in (23cm) high.
£10–12
$15–18 ⊞ JAM

Syphons

Three glass soda syphons, acid-etched with 'Jewsbury & Brown, Manchester', 'Oasis , Southend Mineral Water Co Ltd', and 'Wm Thomson, Aberdeen', with plated metal taps, 1950s, 12in (30.5cm) high.
£20–25
$30–35 ⚒ BBR

◄ **An etched glass soda syphon,** c1920, 13in (33cm) high.
£75–85
$110–125 ⊞ JAM

Boxes

A satinwood and ebony-strung tea caddy, 18thC, 11¾in (30cm) wide.
£220–250
$320–350 ⚒ SWO

A tortoiseshell toothpick box, inset with silver neo-classical decoration, 18thC, 3in (7.5cm) wide.
£250–300
$350–450 ⚒ SWO

A mahogany jewellery box, with key, early 19thC, 9in (23cm) wide.
£225–275
$325–400 ⊞ LaF

A toleware tea caddy, surface damaged, early 19thC, 4½in (11.5cm) wide.
£90–110
$130–160 ⚒ G(L)

◄ A rosewood and sycamore Tunbridge ware cottons box, 1850, 3in (7.5cm) wide.
£80–90
$115–130 ⊞ MB

A Tunbridge ware box, c1850, 2¼in (5.5cm) wide.
£80–90
$115–130 ⊞ VB

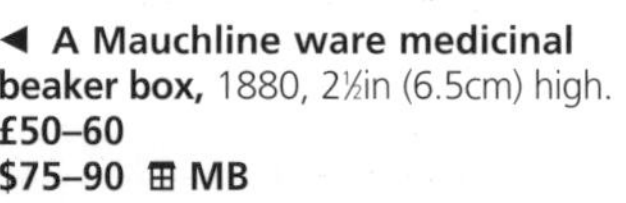

◄ A Mauchline ware medicinal beaker box, 1880, 2½in (6.5cm) high.
£50–60
$75–90 ⊞ MB

An oak table snuff box, with silver mounts, 1820, 4in (10cm) diam.
£150–175
$220–255 ⊞ MB

A Tartan ware pill box, mid-19thC, 2in (5cm) diam.
£40–50
$60–75 ⊞ VBo

A Mauchline ware box, c1880, 5in (12.5cm) wide.
£40–50
$60–75 ⊞ VBo

A miner's brass snuff box, dated 1899, 3in (7.5cm) wide.
£35–45
$50–65 ⊞ EXC

A Tunbridge ware box, for gaming counters, lid damaged, 19thC, 1¼in (3cm) high.
£10–15
$15–20 ⊞ VBo

A Chinese export octagonal box, with two handles, lined and covered with Chinese painted paper, 19thC, 11½in (29cm) wide.
£300–350
$450–500 ⚒ DN

A carved wood snuff box, in the shape of a frog, late 19thC, 3½in (9cm) long.
£270–320
$400–460 ⚒ G(L)

A late Victorian oak cigar box, with silver-plated decoration, 9in (23cm) wide.
£300–350
$450–500 ⊞ WAC

A metal jewellery box, set with rhinestones, 1930s, 8in (20.5cm) wide.
£150–200
$220–300 ⊞ LBe

Breweriana

A Saracen's Head leather tankard, 1775–1825, 6in (15cm) high.
£160–200
$230–300 ⚒ SWO

A carved wood gnome cork stopper, German, Black Forest, c1890, 4in (20cm) high.
£15–20
$20–30 ⊞ Dall

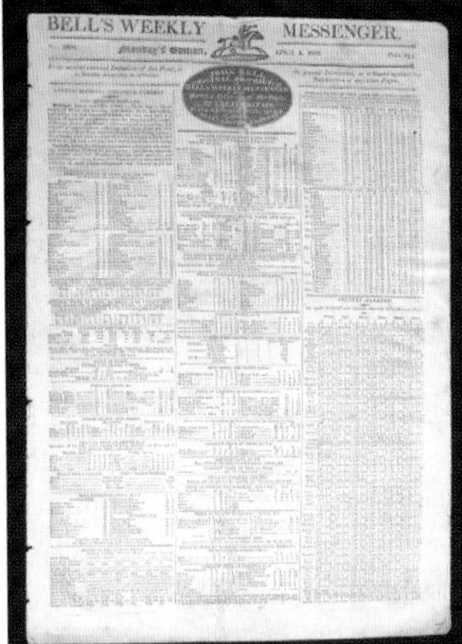
BELL'S WEEKLY MESSENGER.

Bell's Weekly Messenger, by Bell's Whisky Co, 1819, 16 x 11in (40.5 x 28cm).
£18–20
$25–30 ⊞ J&S

A Portland Whisky pottery match holder and striker, by Lovatt's Pottery, 1910–20, 8in (20.5cm) diam.
£75–90
$110–130 ⊞ MURR

◄ **A Denbac liquor flask,** French, c1920, 12in (30.5cm) high.
£225–250
$325–350 ⊞ DSG

A brass spigot, c1880, 10in (25.5cm) long.
£18–23
$25–35 ⊞ GAC

A Dunville's Whisky enamel tray, c1900, 11½in (29cm) diam.
£25–30
$35–45 ⊞ AL

◄ **A Baggs Bros Table Waters enamel tray,** c1900, 12in (30.5cm) diam.
£65–80
$95–115 ⊞ MURR

An Ellis's Ruthin Table Waters glass match striker and ashtray, c1910, 5in (12.5cm) diam.
£40–45
$60–65 ⊞ HUX

A Dewar's Whisky rubber figure of a Highlander, on a wooden plinth with red and black lettering, 1920–40, 22in (56cm) high.
£240–280
$350–400 BBR
This figure is rare in this large size.

A Dewar's White Label Whisky metal menu holder, 1925–35, 2½in (6.5cm) high.
£40–50
$60–75 ⊞ HUX

A Johnnie Walker Scotch Whisky copper tray, c1930, 13in (33cm) diam.
£25–30
$35–45 ⊞ AL

A brass corking machine, L'Incassable, c1930, 7in (18cm) long.
£35–40
$50–60 ⊞ HO

A carved wood cork stopper, modelled as a drummer, with lever mechanism, Italian, c1930, 5in (12.5cm) high.
£30–35
$45–50 ⊞ Dall

A Stella Artois poster, by Mireille Stappers, c1935, 39¼ x 24½in (99.5 x 62cm).
£240–280
$350–400 VSP

► **A ceramic musical decanter,** modelled as Oliver Hardy, Japanese, 1950, 11½in (29cm) high.
£80–90
$115–130 ⊞ MF

A carved wood articulated bottle stopper, c1950, 5in (12.5cm) high.
£40–45
$60–65 ⊞ CAL

A King William IV Scotch Whisky water jug, printed in brown on a cream ground, c1950, 3½in (9cm) high.
£140–180
$200–250 BBR

A Hook Norton Brewery enamel tray, 1955, 14in (35.5cm) wide.
£12–16
$15–20 ⊞ HUX

A corkscrew and bottle opener bar set, modelled as Andy Capp and Florrie, 1950s, 5½in (14cm) high.
£30–35
$45–50 ⊞ Dall

A Baby Bass celluloid advertising sign, 1950s, 10 x 8in (25.5 x 20.5cm) high.
£60–75
$90–110 ⊞ MURR

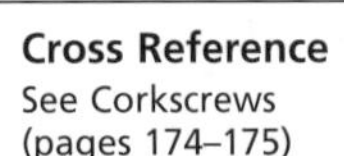

Cross Reference
See Corkscrews (pages 174–175)

The McCallum water jug, by Elisher, 1950s, 6½in (16.5cm) high.
£50–60
$75–90 ⊞ HUX

► **A Martell Brandy water jug,** 1950s, 6½in (16.5cm) high.
£45–55
$65–80 ⊞ HUX

A Schweppes Ginger Beer glass ashtray, 1950s, 6½in (16.5cm) wide.
£10–12
$15–18 ⊞ RTT

A Tia Maria plastic advertising figure, 1965, 10½in (26.5cm) high.
£45–55
$65–80 ⊞ HUX

A set of three Beswick bar figures, The Colonel, The Couple and The Rugby Players, c1970, 9½in (24cm) high.
£420–480
$600–700 ⊞ PrB

Guinness

◄ **A Carlton Ware Guinness plate,** c1948, 7½in (19cm) diam.
£75–85
$110–125 ⊞ NAW

A Carlton Ware Guinness Toucan mustard pot and spoon, c1958, pot 3in (7.5cm) high.
£10–12
$15–18 ⊞ PrB

◄ **A Guinness plastic walking penguin,** 1960s, 3½in (9cm) high.
£35–40
$50–60 ⊞ HUX

A Guinness celluloid advertising sign, 1940s, 12 x 10in (30.5 x 25.5cm).
£250–300
$350–450 ⊞ MURR

► **A Guinness ceramic model of Tweedledum and Tweedledee,** decorated in brown, green and cream, 1950–60, 3in (7.5cm) high.
£70–80
$100–115 ⚒ BBR

A Carlton Ware Guinness Toucan pepper pot, c1958, 4in (10cm) high.
£10–12
$15–18 ⊞ PrB

Buttons

A set of eight cameo buttons, early 19thC, ½in (1.25cm) diam.
£430–480
$625–700 ⊞ JBB

Thirteen metal buttons, with glass and cut-steel rivets, some with cold-painted enamel, c1860–1910, largest 2in (5cm) diam.
£3–15
$5–20 each ⊞ EV

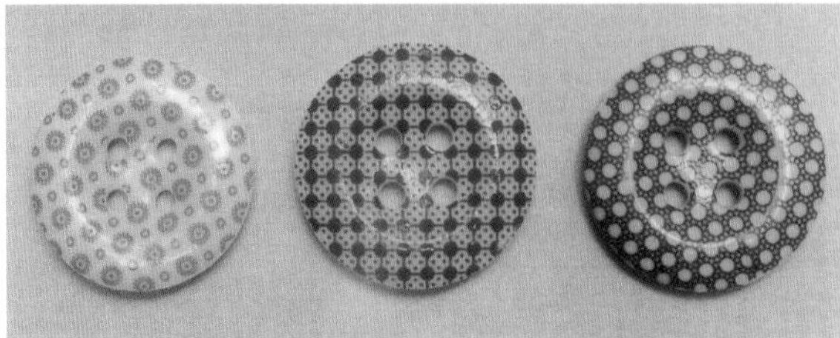

Three ceramic buttons, transfer-printed with calico designs, c1850, 1in (2.5cm) diam.
£60–85
$90–125 each ⊞ TB

A set of six mosaic buttons, Italian, c1890, ¾in (2cm) diam.
£110–125
$160–180 ⊞ JBB

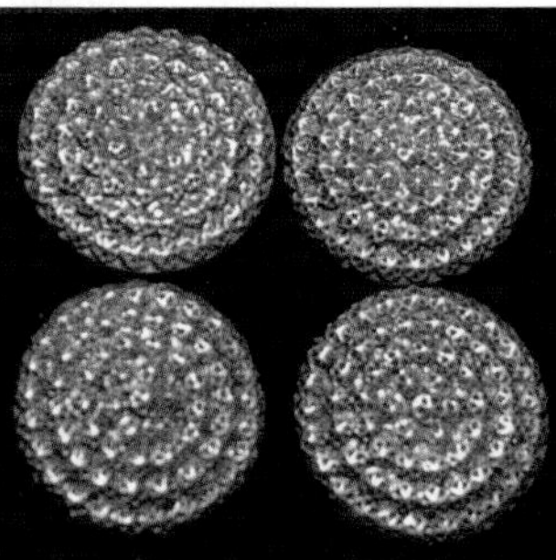

A set of four silver Charles Horner buttons, c1899, ½in (1.25cm) diam.
£65–75
$95–110 ⊞ JBB

A tortoiseshell button, inlaid with engraved abalone and silver birds, 1870–80, 1½in (4cm) diam.
£85–100
$120–150 ⊞ TB

► **A metal button,** depicting Venus and Taurus the bull, c1900, ¾in (2cm) diam.
£10–12
$15–18 ⊞ EV

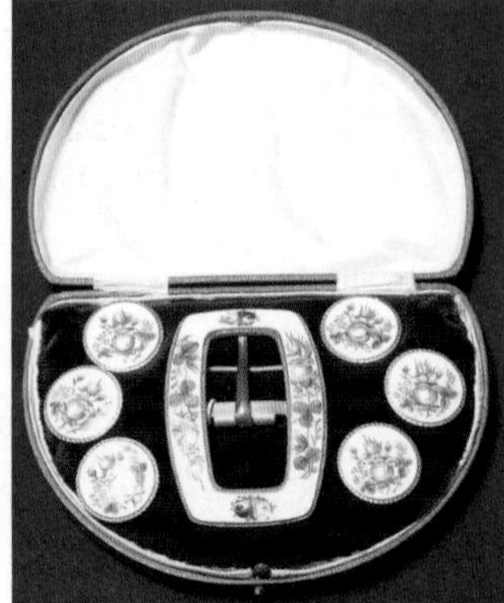

An enamel on silver button and buckle set, decorated with pink and blue flowers, 1900, in a fitted case 6in (15cm) wide.
£550–650
$800–950 ⊞ JBB

A set of six silver buttons, decorated with butterflies, French, c1900, 1in (2½cm) diam.
£100–120
$145–175 ⊞ JBB

A set of four enamel buttons, French, c1900, 1in (2.5cm) diam.
£200–240
$300–350 ⊞ JBB

A set of six clear glass buttons, set with aventurine swirls, on black glass bases, with metal loop shanks, c1900, ¼in (75mm) diam.
£25–27
$35–40 ⊞ EV

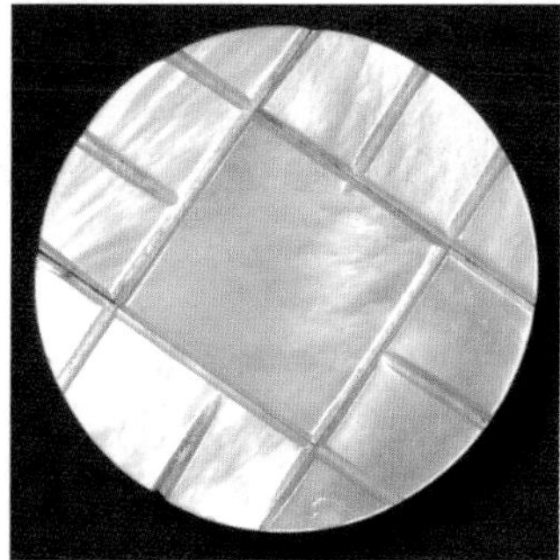

A mother-of-pearl button, c1920, 1½in (4cm) diam.
£3–5
$4–7 ⊞ FMN

A set of six silver buttons, each depicting a female head and shoulders, French, c1900, 1in (2.5cm) diam.
£125–150
$180–220 ⊞ JBB

A set of six gilding metal military buttons, by Hawkes & Co, c1900.
£100–125
$145–175 ⊞ EXC

A painted metal button, with fabric centre, c1910, 1in (2.5cm) diam.
£4–6
$5–8 ⊞ FMN

A moulded glass button, with silver coating, c1920, 1in (2.5cm) diam.
£3–4
$4–7 ⊞ FMN

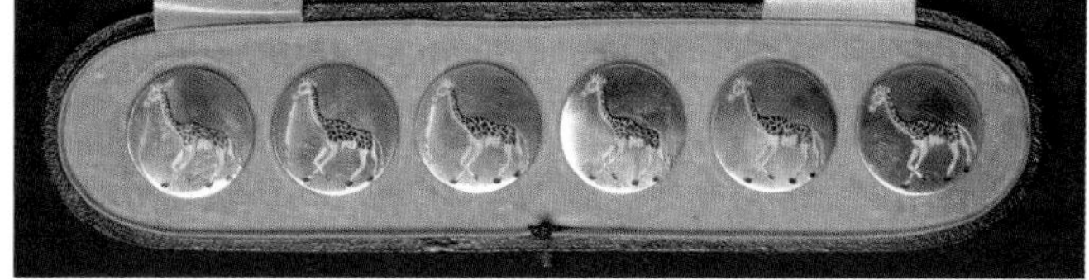

A set of six silver and enamel buttons, each depicting a giraffe, c1920, 1in (2.5cm) diam.
£225–250
$325–360 ⊞ JBB

◄ A carved tortoiseshell button, c1920, 1½in (4cm) diam.
£6–8
$8–10 ⊞ FMN

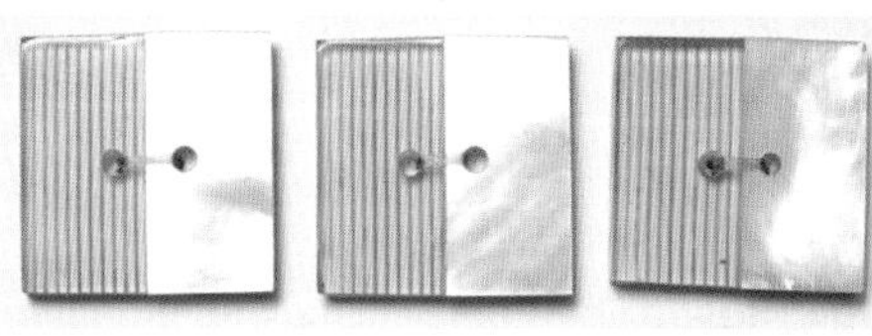

A set of three Art Deco Bakelite and pearl buttons, 1¼in (3cm) square.
£25–30
$35–45 ⊞ EV

Cameras

A Meagher Kinnear's Patent wetplate camera, c1865, 11¾in (30cm) wide.
£600–700
$870–1,000 ⊞ APC

A Meagher mahogany tailboard plate camera, with six double dark plate holders, a Ross rapid lens and a set of Waterhouse stops, c1870, in original baize-lined leather case.
£350–400
$500–580 ⚒ HOLL

A George Hare mahogany full-plate field camera, c1885, 13¾in (35cm) wide.
£350–400
$500–580 ⊞ APC

◄ A Richard Verascope oxidized brass stereo camera, with Zeiss Tessar f4.5 55mm lenses, spare magazine, yellow filters, time delay, c1890, 6in (15cm) wide, with fitted leather case.
£300–330
$440–480
⊞ WAC

An Alfred C. Kemper Chicago Kombi gilt-metal miniature box camera, 1892, 1½in (4cm) square, with presentation case.
£350–400
$500–580 ⊞ HEG

A Kodak vest pocket camera, the 127 roll film with trellis struts, introduced in 1913 with autographic feature, 1915–26, 4¾in (12cm) wide.
£20–25
$30–35 ⊞ HEG

An Ensign camera, with hood, focal plane reflex and Aldis lens, c1920, 10in (25.5cm) high.
£100–150
$125–225 ⊞ VCL

A polished mahogany and brass studio camera, with 6¼in (16cm) square focussing screen in a repeating back, fitted with a brass-barrelled Perken, Son & Rayment lens with wheel stops, early 20thC, 26in (66cm) long.
£160–180
$230–260 ⚒ B(WM)

Three Kodak Beau Brownie box cameras, with two-tone enamel front plates in blue, tan and black, 1930–33, 4in (10cm) high.
£70–80
$100–115 ⊞ HEG
This camera was also made with green- and rose-coloured cases. Rose is the rarest and costs £100–150 ($145–225).

► **A Wirgin Gewir folding plate camera,** with Trioplan f2.9 105mm lens, c1936, 5in (12.5cm) high, with a leather case.
£295–325
$440–470
⊞ WAC

A Kodak No. 1a Gift Kodak Art Deco camera, with box, c1930, 21in (53.5cm) long.
£450–500
$650–720 ⊞ APC

A Coronet Midget Bakelite camera, c1935, 7in (18cm) high.
£125–150
$180–220 ⊞ APC

◄ **A Kodak Baby Brownie Bakelite camera,** c1940, 6in (15cm) square, with original box.
£20–25
$30–35 ⊞ APC

◄ **A Zeiss Ikon camera,** 1940s.
£45–55
$65–80 ⊞ JOA

► **A Goerz Minicord TLR sub-miniature camera,** 1951, 4in (10cm) high.
£150–175
$225–255 ⊞ HEG

A Mycro IIIA 16mm sub-miniature camera, by the Sanwa Co, c1950, 2in (5cm) wide, with leather case.
£30–35
$45–50 ⊞ HEG

A Kodak Signet 35mm compact camera, 1951–58, 4in (10cm) wide.
£70–80
$100–115 ⊞ HEG

A Vredeborch Vrede metal box camera, with brown covering, German, c1953, 4in (10cm) high.
£25–30
$35–45 ⊞ HEG
This camera was produced with black, red and green coverings, black costing £10 ($15), red and green costing £25–30 ($35–45).

◀ A Bolsey sub-miniature camera, with eight still or motion pictures, 1955, 3in (7.5cm) high.
£100–120
$145–175 ⊞ HEG

A Zorki C Leica II 35mm Rangefinder camera, 1955–58, 5½in (14cm) wide.
£80–100
$115–145 ⊞ HEG
The black version is less expensive at £35–45 ($50–65).

A Kodak Brownie Twin 20 camera, 1959–64, 620 roll film, with original box.
£15–20
$20–30 ⊞ BSA

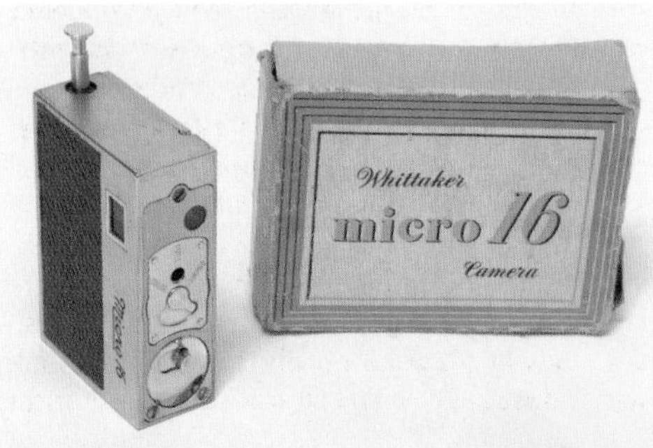

◀ A Wm R. Whittaker & Co Micro 16mm sub-miniature camera, 1950s, 3in (7.5cm) high.
£30–35
$45–50 ⊞ HEG
These are available in black, blue and green with a value of £40–60 ($60–90).

A Braun Nizo Heliomatic camera, c1960, 5in (12.5cm) wide.
£40–50
$60–75 ⊞ VCL

A Pentax SV screw mount 35mm camera, with auto Takumar f1.8 55mm lens, c1962, 5½in (14cm) wide.
£45–55
$65–80 ⊞ HEG

A Mickamatic Mickey Mouse camera, with moving ear, 1970, 8in (20.5cm) wide.
£60–70
$90–100 ⊞ APC

A Leica R4 camera, with f2 50mm lens, Portuguese, c1983, 5in (12.5cm) wide.
£400–500
$580–720 ⊞ VCL

Magic Lanterns & Optical Toys

As far back as the 16th century, experiments were being carried out to project images and in 1656 Samuel Pepys recorded the purchase of 'A lanthorn with pictures in glasse to make strange things appear on the wall.' It was in the 19th century, however, that magic lanterns became a really popular craze, and were used for both drawing room and public entertainment.

Early lanterns were lit by candles, oil lamps, gas and limelight – literally a ball of lime ignited with gas, (a mixture of oxygen and town gas). Lime produced a brilliant light and was used in magic lanterns and theatrical lights, hence the expression 'in the limelight'. Invented in the early 1820s, limelight was a dangerous means of illumination and in unskilled hands was a continual hazard until the invention of electricity.

At the end of the 19th century, many magic lanterns began to be converted for electric light. Prices started from a shilling (a dime) and designs ranged from simple magic lanterns produced for children to sophisticated machines that could project huge panoramic views. There were also double or triple magic lanterns, using multiple projectors to produce special dissolving effects and apparently moving images. Cheaper models were made from tinplate, while mahogany was used for top-of-the-range items.

Initially slides were hand-painted, but by the second half of the 19th century the development of mass-produced lithographed and photographic slides made them cheaper and more available. Popular subjects included ghosts, comic, circus, religious and educational stories as well as topical news themes. A typical show would invariably have a combination of these, culminating with dazzling chromotrope slides, creating moving kaleidoscopic effects.

The same period also saw the development of optical toys. Often ending in the letters 'trope' or 'scope', these included the zoetrope, the praxinoscope, and the phenakistoscope, which includes the extremely rare American version named the Ludoscope (page 84). When the image was rotated it created the optical illusion of movement. These early animation toys and mechanical lantern slides used the persistence of vision to create the illusion, and were the precursors of the moving image first shown in the mid-1890s and creating the basis for the cinema or 'movies'. Also shown here are stereoscopes, which use two photographs taken from slightly different positions and mounted on to a single card, to create a single 3D image when viewed through the double lenses.

According to specialist dealer, Alan Cook, the market for magic lanterns and pre-cinema optical toys is currently very buoyant. As with period cameras, British makers produced some of the finest commercial lanterns of the day, with the French excelling at optical toys and the Germans, with their tinplate skills, producing a fine range of toy magic lanterns. Rarity and condition are important to value and since many collectors use these machines, demand for magic lantern slides has also risen, with unusual subjects commanding high prices.

A Smith, Beck & Beck stereoviewer, with walnut cabinet, c1865, 19¾in (50cm) high.
£1,500–1,700
$2,200–2,500 ⊞ APC

A Goodnight mahogany mechanical magic lantern slide, c1880, 8in (20.5cm) wide.
£180–200
$250–300 ⊞ APC

◄ A Negretti and Zambra Rowsell's Patent graphoscope, 1875, 15¾in (40cm) high.
£500–600
$720–870 ⊞ APC

A Chadwick mahogany scientific magic lantern, c1880, 29½in (75cm) long.
£270–300
$400–440 ⊞ APC

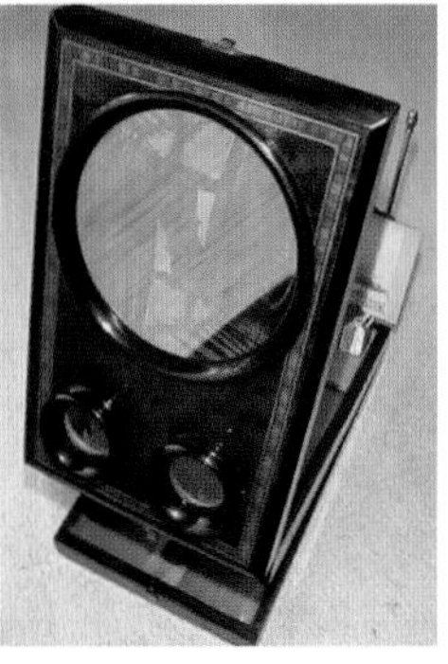

A burr-walnut and fruitwood stereo viewer, French, c1890, 9¾in (25cm) high.
£270–300
$400–440 ⊞ APC

An Ernst Planck Climax child's magic lantern, with a brass and red lacquer finish, circular and flat sides, German, c1895, 8in (20.5cm) high, boxed.
£300–350
$450–500 ⊞ APC

An anamorphic mirror, with three views, 19thC, 6in (15cm) wide.
£550–600
$800–870 ⊞ APC
Viewed with the cylindrical mirror, the distorted images become clear.

A Victorian mahogany and brass magic lantern, converted to electricity, focal length 8in (20.5cm).
£280–320
$400–460 GH

A Professor Zimmerman's Ludoscope optical toy, c1900, 8in (20.5cm) square, boxed.
£1,800–2,000
$2,500–3,000 ⊞ APC

A cardboard zoetrope, with 12 film strips, German, c1900, 9¾in (25cm) diam.
£350–400
$500–580 ⊞ APC

► **A child's magic lantern,** for glass strip slides and 35mm film, with hand-cranked oil lamp illuminant, 1910–30, 12in (30.5cm) high.
£70–80
$100–115 ⊞ HEG

A Richard Verascope stereo viewer, with glass slides, c1910, 4¾in (12cm) high.
£90–100
$130–145 ⊞ APC

Ceramics
Animals

A pottery model of Massier-style birds on a well, by Maunier, 1880, 13in (33cm) high.
£550–650
$800–950 ⊞ MLL

An Onnaing jug, modelled as a duck, 1880, 9in (23cm) high.
£300–350
$450–500 ⊞ MLL

A Théodore Haviland porcelain box and cover, after Edouard-Marcel Sandoz, modelled as a fennec, chip to rim of cover, impressed marks, early 20thC, 6in (15cm) wide.
£150–200
$220–300 ⚒ S(O)
A fennec is a small African fox-like animal with long ears.

▶ A Five-Lille vase, modelled as a fish and an eel, 1900, 13in (33cm) long.
£150–200
$220–300 ⊞ MLL

A glazed cubist-style pottery model of a dog, designed by Louis Wain, produced by Max Emmanuel & Co, inscribed 'Louis Wain', maker's mark, 1914–19, 5½in (14cm) high.
£1,000–1,200
$1,500–1,750 ⚒ DW
In 1914, celebrated cat artist Louis Wain launched a range of 'futurist' china cats and dogs. Nine registered designs were produced by Max Emmanuel & Co. They appear not to have been very successful and according to legend a ship carrying a cargo of them to the USA was torpedoed. Their rarity and the artist's popularity make these animal figures very collectable today.

A pair of Mosanic faïence models of cats, each wearing an apron, bandage and red cross, one inscribed 'Mosanic', paws and ears glued, early 20thC, 9½in (24cm) high.
£400–450
$580–650 ⚒ TEN

Items in the Ceramics section have been arranged in date order within each sub-section.

A Bing & Grøndahl model of a salmon trout, Danish, c1915, 9in (23cm) long.
£120–140
$175–200 ⊞ PSA

A pottery teapot, modelled as a rooster, 1930s, 7in (18cm) high.
£75–85
$110–125 ⊞ ML

A Rye Pottery model of a cat, by David Sharpe, 1960s, 12in (30.5cm) high.
£80–100
$115–145 ⊞ MARK

A ceramic novelty Easter vase, German, 1920, 3in (7.5cm) high.
£50–60
$75–90 ⊞ HAL

A Shorter & Son tureen, six plates and a sauce boat, 1930s, tureen 11in (28cm) wide.
£130–150
$200–220 ⊞ PrB
The fish tableware was Shorter's best known range and was produced until the early 1970s.

◄ A pottery model of a panda, Russian, 1930s–40s, 4in (10cm) high.
£40–50
$60–75 ⊞ MRW

A Hornsea model of a Pekinese, marked, 1956, 4in (10cm) high.
£90–100
$130–145 ⚒ BBR

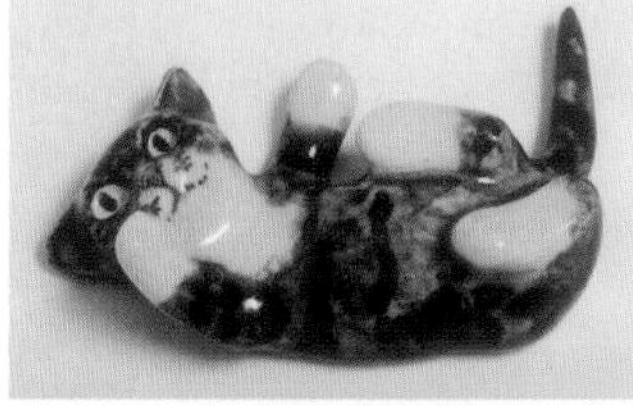

A ceramic Bonzo water jug, c1930, 6¼in (16cm) high.
£100–120
$145–175 ⊞ HUX

A SylvaC model of a rabbit, No. 1028, c1930, 10in (25.5cm) high.
£170–190
$250–275 ⊞ HarC

A Hornsea spill vase, modelled as a squirrel beside a tree, 1950s, 4in (10cm) high.
£8–10
$10–15 ⊞ PrB

◄ A Winstanley pottery model of a cat, 1998, 5in (12.5cm) long.
£15–20
$20–30 ⊞ RIA

Bargeware

A bargeware ale mug, with cartouche inscribed 'Borough Arms Dunmeer 1848', 5in (12.5cm) high.
£350–450
$500–650 ⊞ JBL

A bargeware tobacco jar and high-domed cover, cartouche inscribed 'A Pipe Lets Take for Old Times Sake', c1875, 5in (12.5cm) high.
£350–450
$500–650 ⊞ JBL

◄ A bargeware kettle-on-stand, cartouche inscribed 'Home Sweet Home', c1880, 10in (25.5cm) high.
£280–330
$410–475 ⊞ JBL
These kettles were used to top up large teapots with boiling water.

A set of three bargeware cream jugs, cartouches inscribed 'A Present from a Friend', c1880, largest 8in (20.5cm) high.
£450–500
$650–720 ⊞ JBL

A Measham Ware teapot and cover, cartouche inscribed 'Mr James Stewart Senr., Biddulph 1902', slight damage, 13in (33cm) high.
£70–80
$100–115 ⚒ FHF

Belleek

A Belleek Ring Handle and Limoges pattern plate, First Period, 1863–90, 6in (15cm) diam.
£150–180
$220–260 ⊞ MLa

► A Belleek tea service, comprising 23 pieces, green printed mark, 1946–80.
£240–280
$350–410 ⚒ L

A Belleek Thorn pattern mug, Second Period, 1891–1926, 3in (7.5cm) high.
£120–150
$175–220 ⊞ MLa

A Belleek Neptune cup and saucer, Second Period, 1891–1926, cup 2in (5cm) high.
£85–95
$125–140 ⊞ MLa

A pair of Belleek models of dogs, Sixth Period, 1965–80, 4in (10cm) wide.
£220–250
$320–360 ⊞ MLa

Beswick

A Beswick drip glaze vase, c1930, 12in (30.5cm) high.
£120–140
$175–200 ⊞ CoCo

A Beswick jester wall mask, No. MN279, small chip and firing crack, c1935, 6in (15cm) high.
£30–40
$45–60 Pott

A Beswick model of a giraffe, No. MN853, c1940, 7¼in (18.5cm) high.
£50–60
$75–90 Pott

A Beswick model of Beatrix Potter's Jemima Puddleduck, by Martyn Alcock, c1950, 4¼in (11cm) high.
£15–20
$20–30 BBR

► A Beswick model of a boxer dog, No. 1202, by Arthur Gredington, c1950, 5½in (14cm) high.
£40–50
$60–75 BBR

► A Beswick vase, decorated with Zebrette pattern, c1950, 9in (23cm) high.
£30–40
$45–60 ⊞ BEV

◄ A Beswick model of Beatrix Potter's Hunca Munca, by Arthur Gredington, stamped, c1950, 2¾in (7cm) high.
£15–20
$20–30 BBR

► A Beswick model of an Appaloosa pony, No. 1516, by Arthur Gredington, c1960, 5¼in (13.5cm) high.
£220–250
$320–360 BBR

◄ A Beswick model of an Aberdeen Angus cow, No. 1563, by Arthur Gredington, c1960, 4¼in (11cm) high.
£110–140
$160–200 BBR

A Beswick model of a Persian kitten, by Albert Hallam, c1960, 4½in (11.5cm) high.
£50–60
$75–90 BBR

A Beswick model of Beatrix Potter's Anna Maria, gold backstamp, c1965, 3in (7.5cm) high.
£180–200
$260–300 F&C

► A Beswick model of a stag, on a naturalistic base, 1970s, 14in (35.5cm) high.
£85–100
$125–145 G(L)

◄ A Beswick model of Beatrix Potter's Mr Jackson, brown backstamp, 1973–76, 2¾in (7cm) high.
£160–180
$230–260 F&C

Two Beswick models of Winnie the Pooh and Kanga, by Albert Hallam, c1970, Kanga 3¼in (8.5cm) high.
£30–40
$45–60 each BBR

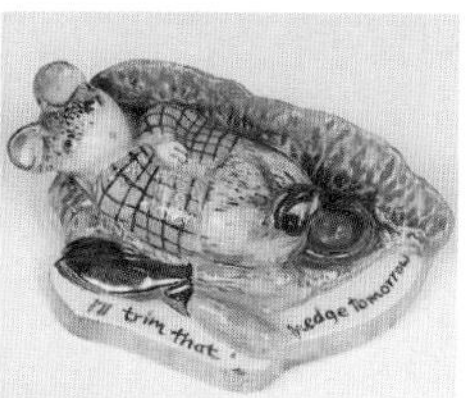

A Beswick model of Beatrix Potter's Lazybones, from the Kitty McBride series, c1975, 3½in (9cm) wide.
£60–70
$90–100 UNI

A Beswick model of Beatrix Potter's Mr Tod, by Ted Chawner, backstamp, 1988, 4¾in (12cm) high.
£60–70
$90–100 BBR

◄ Two Beswick models of Tom and Jerry, by Simon Ward, special edition of 2,000, 1995, Tom 4in (10cm) high.
£40–50
$60–75 BBR

Blue & White

A Caughley blue and white teapot and cover, transfer-printed with Pagoda pattern, with Chinese kick handle, c1785, 5in (12.5cm) high.
£130–150
$190–220 ⊞ WAC

A Davenport blue and white meat plate, decorated with Chinoiserie Bridgeless pattern, early 19thC, 13¼in (33.5cm) wide.
£150–180
$220–260 WilP

◄ **A blue and white jug,** decorated with Fishermen with Nets pattern, spout damaged, c1820, 4¼in (11cm) high.
£110–130
$160–200 SWO

► **A blue and white drainer dish,** some damage, c1830, 3½in (9cm) diam.
£70–80
$100–115 ⊞ NAW

A pair of Minton blue and white soup plates, c1810, 9½in (24cm) diam.
£170–200
$250–300 ⊞ DAN

Bretby

A Bretby owl vase/ stick stand, 19thC, 26in (66cm) high.
£1,750–2,000
$2,500–2,900 ⊞ DUK
This large piece has a rare and attractive design.

A Bretby footed bowl, c1900, 8in (20.5cm) high.
£110–130
$160–200 ⊞ DSG

A Bretby biscuit barrel, c1915, 4in (10cm) high.
£70–80
$100–115 ⊞ DSG

A Bretby jardinière, restored, c1900, 8in (20.5cm) high.
£180–200
$250–300 ⊞ DSG

► A Bretby hand-painted vase, c1915, 42in (106.5cm) high.
£30–40
$45–60 ⊞ WAC

Burleigh Ware

A Burleigh Ware bowl, by Charlotte Rhead, decorated with New Sylvan pattern No. 4123, c1929, 10in (25.5cm) diam.
£360–400
$550–580 ⊞ BDA

◄ A Burleigh Ware child's cup and saucer, by Charlotte Rhead, decorated with Gee-Gee pattern, c1930, cup 2½in (6.5cm) high.
£140–160
$200–230 ⊞ BDA

A Burleigh Ware parrot vase, with insert, c1930, 8in (20.5cm) high.
£600–700
$870–1,000 ⊞ RH

► A Burleigh Ware butterfly jug, c1930, 8in (20.5cm) high.
£300–350
$440–500 ⊞ RH

Four Burleigh Ware jugs, decorated with Primrose pattern, 1930s, largest 6in (15cm) high.
£20–65
$35–95 each ⊞ BUR

A Burleigh Ware squirrel jug, c1930, 7in (18cm) high.
£100–130
$145–2000 ⊞ RH

A Burleigh Ware bunny jug, c1930, 8in (20.5cm) high.
£120–140
$175–200 ⊞ RH

A Burleigh Ware tube-lined charger, by Harold Bennett, signed, c1930, 19in (48.5cm) diam.
£225–275
$325–400 ⊞ BUR

A Burleigh Ware Pied Piper jug, c1930, 8in (20.5cm) high.
£170–200
$250–300 ⊞ RH

A Burleigh Ware Pecksniff character jug, from the Dickens series, 1940s, 4in (10cm) high.
£50–65
$75–95 ⊞ BUR

A Burleigh Ware water jug, modelled with a swooping bird and flowers, early 20thC, 7in (18cm) high.
£170–200
$250–300 ⚒ G(L)

Burmantofts

A Burmantofts two-handled vase, c1890, 6in (15cm) high.
£130–150
$200–220 ⊞ DSG

A pair of Burmantofts majolica vases, with incised floral decoration, pattern No. 166, both chipped, c1890, 8½in (21.5cm) high.
£170–200
$250–300 ⚒ G(L)

A Burmantofts vase, impressed marks, monogram, c1890, 17in (43.5cm) high.
£100–120
$145–175 ⚒ SWO

Candle Extinguishers

A pair of Stevenson & Hancock candle extinguishers, each modelled as Sarah Gamp, both damaged, 19thC, largest 3in (7.5cm) high.
£160–190
$230–275 ⚒ SWO

A Minton candle extinguisher, modelled as Lady Teazle, c1850, 4in (10cm) high.
£780–880
$1,125–1,275 ⊞ TH

A Worcester candle extinguisher, modelled as Mr Caudle, c1880, 4in (10cm) high.
£400–450
$580–650 ⊞ TH

A Crown Staffordshire candle extinguisher, modelled as a Princess, c1930, 3½in (9cm) high.
£240–280
$350–400 ⊞ TH

► A Royal Worcester candle extinguisher, modelled as a nun, printed marks, date code for 1960, 3¾in (9.5cm) high.
£140–160
$200–230 ⚒ DD

Carlton Ware

This section on Carlton Ware includes the relief-moulded tableware that was one of the factory's best known products in the 1930s. Inspired by the colour and texture of leaves and embossed with flowers and fruit, this decorative earthenware was designed for everyday use. Some patterns such as Apple Blossom were extremely popular c1935 and were manufactured in large quantities. Other lines, for example Cherries, were less successful and only made for a limited period. These rarer pieces are sought-after by collectors today.

Condition is very important. Lids were prone to breakage and china should be checked for chips, hairline cracks and signs of restoration. Original boxed sets command a premium but, even when empty, the packaging has its own value. Boxes were clearly marked underneath with details of the original contents and collectors track down period presentation boxes in the hope that one day they will be able to fill them.

A Carlton Ware vase, decorated with Early Blush pattern, 1895, 9in (23cm) high.
£350–400
$500–580 ⊞ BEV

A Carlton Ware vase, 1900–10, 11in (28cm) high.
£200–250
$300–360 ⊞ StC

A Carlton Ware lustre vase, decorated with fish, 1920, 10in (25.5cm) high.
£430–480
$620–700 ⊞ HarC

A Carlton New Chinese vase, decorated with Bird in Cloud pattern, unfinished, 1920s–30s, 6½in (16.5cm) high.
£200–240
$300–350 ⊞ StC

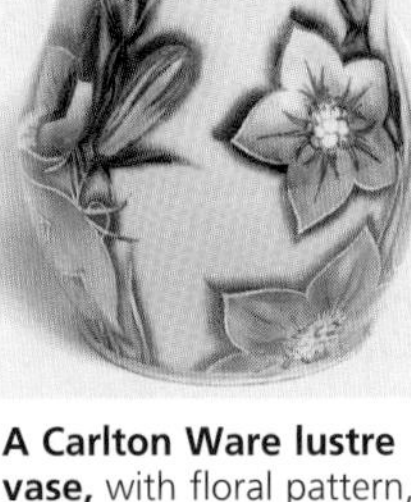

A Carlton Ware lustre vase, with floral pattern, c1930, 5in (12.5cm) high.
£80–100
$115–145 ⊞ BD

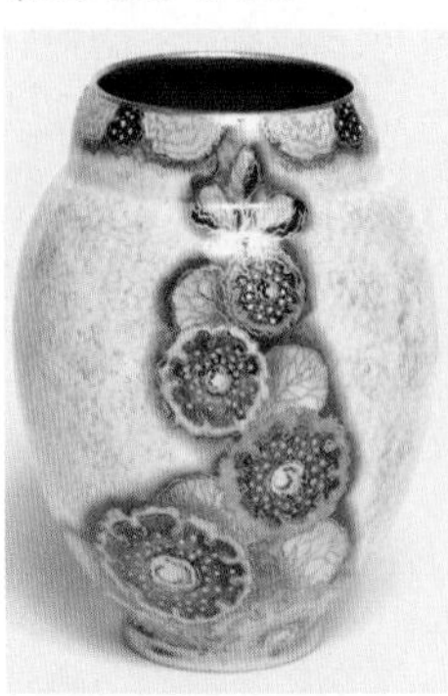

A Carlton Ware lustre vase, decorated with Hollyhocks pattern, c1930, 6in (15cm) high.
£250–300
$360–440 ⊞ BD

A Carlton Ware coffee set, decorated with trees and swallows on a pearl iridescent ground, c1930.
£140–180
$200–260 ⚒ G(L)

► **A Carlton Ware lustre serving dish,** 1930s, 12in (30.5cm) wide.
£150–180
$220–260
⊞ CoCo

A pair of Carlton Ware Handcraft bookends, hand-painted, 1930s, 5¾in (14.5cm) high.
£300–350
$440–500 ⊞ BEV

A Carlton Ware Old Stoneware jug, c1935, 5in (12.5cm) high.
£45–55
$65–80 ⊞ StC

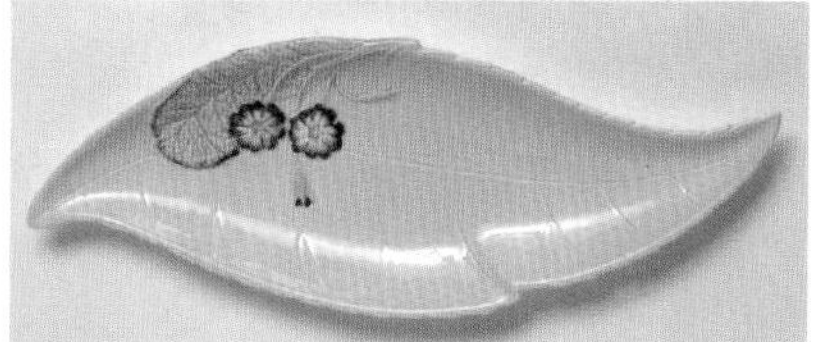

A Carlton Ware sandwich plate, decorated with Primrose pattern, 1930s, 13in (33cm) wide.
£45–55
$65–80 ⊞ CoCo

A Carlton Ware dog, with all-over ribbing, No. 2600, 1930s, 6¼in (16cm) high.
£110–130
$160–190 🔨 DA

A Carlton Ware biscuit barrel, decorated with Blackberry pattern, 1930s, 6in (15cm) high.
£130–150
$190 220 ⊞ HarC

A Carlton Ware plate, decorated with Iris pattern, 1930s, 9½in (24cm) wide.
£165–185
$240–270 ⊞ StC

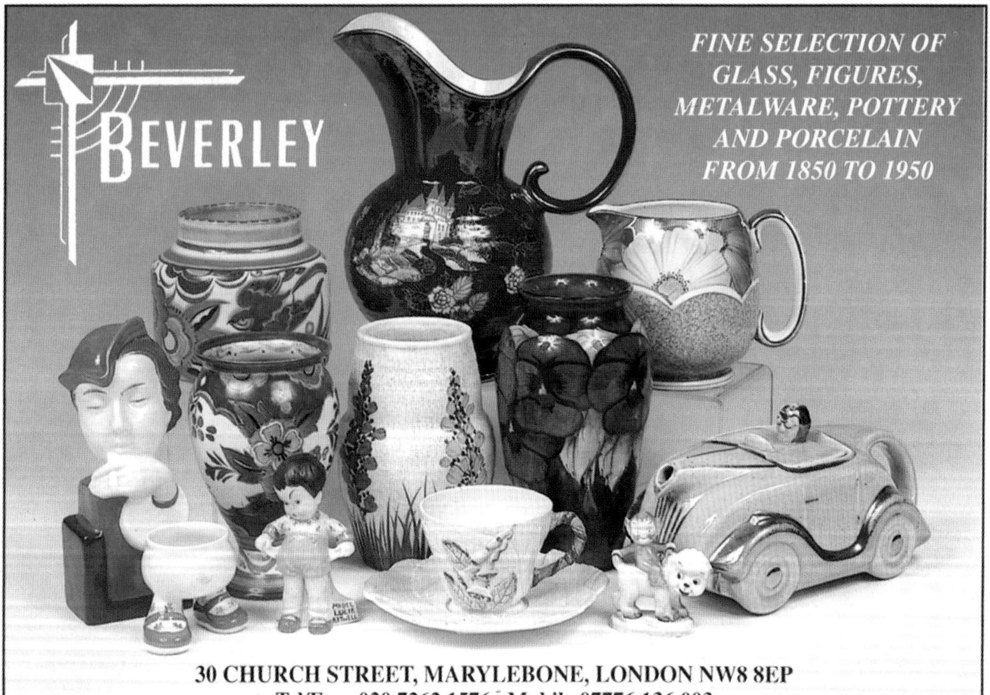

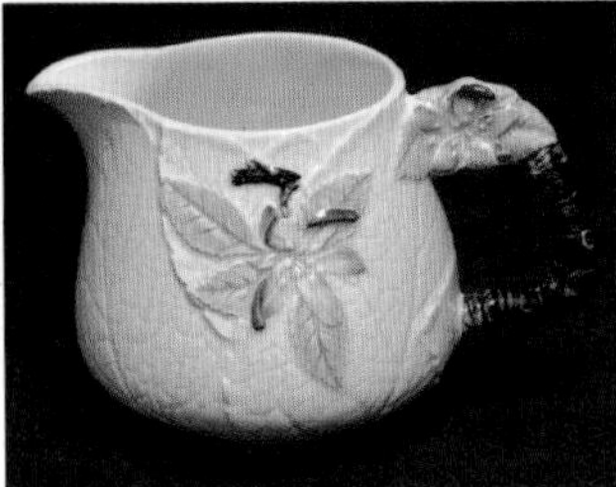

A Carlton Ware jug, decorated with Apple Blossom pattern, c1935, 4in (10cm) high.
£50–60
$75–90 ⊞ RH

A Carlton Ware cruet set, moulded with Pink Lily pattern, c1935, 2in (5cm) high.
£130–150
$190–220 ⊞ RH

A Carlton Ware teapot, decorated with Wild Rose pattern, c1935, 6in (15cm) high.
£150–170
$220–250 ⊞ RH

A Carlton Ware three-way tray, moulded with Apple Blossom pattern, late 1930s, 9½in (24cm) long.
£35–45
$50–65 ⊞ StC

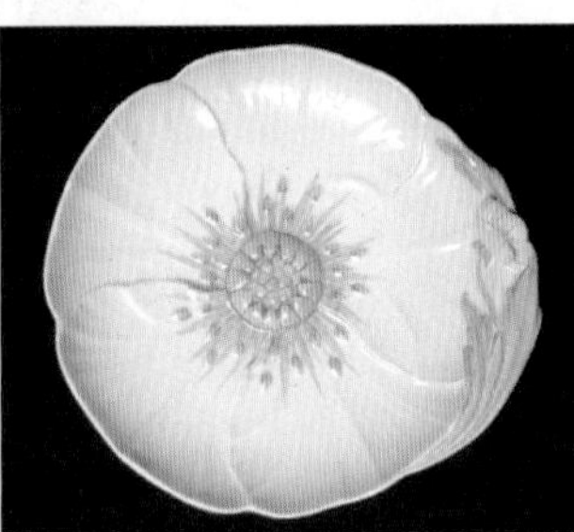

A Carlton Ware plate, moulded with Buttercup pattern, c1950, 7in (18cm) diam.
£45–50
$65–75 ⊞ HarC

A Carlton Ware pitcher, moulded with Foxglove pattern, c1940, 11in (28cm) high.
£260–300
$380–440 ⊞ AOT

A Carlton Ware trio, moulded with Convulvulus pattern, c1960, plate 8in (20.5cm) wide.
£20–25
$30–35 ⊞ PrB

◄ **A Carlton Ware lustre Dragon teapot,** c1980, 8in (20.5cm) high.
£140–180
$200–260 ⊞ AOT

A Carlton Ware bonbon dish, moulded with Primula pattern, c1945, 6in (15cm) long.
£25–30
$35–45 ⊞ StC

A Carlton Ware Walking Ware sugar basin, 1970s, 6in (15cm) high.
£60–65
$90–95 ⊞ BEV

Chintz Ware

A Royal Winton hot water jug, with lid, decorated with Sunshine pattern, 1930s, 7in (18cm) high.
£200–250
$300–360 ⊞ BEV

A Shelley trio, decorated with Summer Glory pattern, c1930, plate 5in (12.5cm) diam.
£60–70
$90–100 ⊞ HarC

A James Kent trio, decorated with Harmony pattern, c1930, cup 2½in (6.5cm) high.
£45–55
$65–80 ⊞ CoCo

Cross Reference
See Royal Winton (page 140)

► A James Kent Old Foley tea service, comprising 20 pieces, 1930s, cup 2½in (6.5cm) high.
£150–180
$220–260 ⚒ GAK

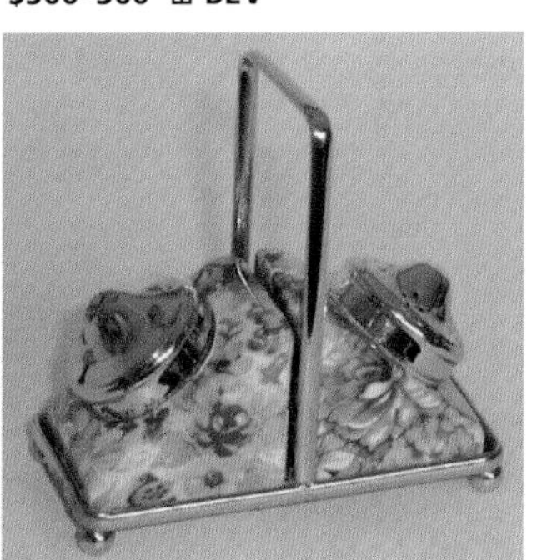

◄ A Midwinter cruet set, decorated with Springtime pattern, in a chrome stand, c1930, 4½in (11.5cm) wide.
£70–80
$100–115 ⊞ JOA

► A Royal Winton toast rack, decorated with Hazel pattern, c1940, 4½in (11.5cm) wide.
£120–140
$175–200 ⊞ RH

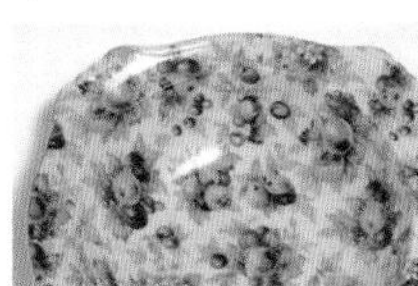

A Royal Winton dessert bowl, decorated with Evesham pattern, c1940, 7in (18cm) diam.
£40–50
$60–75 ⊞ RH

A Royal Chelsea bone china coffee can, c1950, 2½in (6.5cm) high.
£30–35
$45–50 ⊞ CoCo

Clarice Cliff

A Clarice Cliff Beehive honey pot, decorated with Autumn pattern, 1930s, 4in (10cm) high.
£180–215
$250–300 G(L)

A Clarice Cliff Beehive honey pot, decorated with Crocus pattern, c1930, 3¾in (9.5cm) high.
£190–230
$275–330 G(L)

A Clarice Cliff cream jug, cup and saucer, decorated with Gayday pattern, c1930, jug 4in (10cm) high.
£140–165
$200–245 G(L)

A Clarice Cliff posy case, 1930s, 7in (18cm) wide.
£80–90
$115–130 BrL

A Clarice Cliff conical sugar sifter, decorated with Crocus pattern, c1930, 5½in (14cm) high.
£250–300
$360–440 G(L)

A Clarice Cliff vase, decorated with Crocus pattern, c1930, 8in (20.5cm) high.
£70–85
$100–125 G(L)

A Clarice Cliff Lynton shape sugar shaker, decorated with Blue Crocus pattern, c1930, 5in (12.5cm) high.
£650–700
$950–1,100 BD

A Clarice Cliff Bonjour Shape sugar shaker, decorated with Spring Crocus pattern, c1930, 5in (12.5cm) high.
£650–750
$950–1,100 BD

◀ **A Clarice Cliff milk jug,** decorated with Spring Crocus pattern, c1930, 3¼in (8.5cm) high.
£90–110
$130–160 G(L)

▶ **A Clarice Cliff dinner plate,** decorated with Spring Crocus pattern, c1930, 9in (23cm) high.
£90–100
$130–145 RH

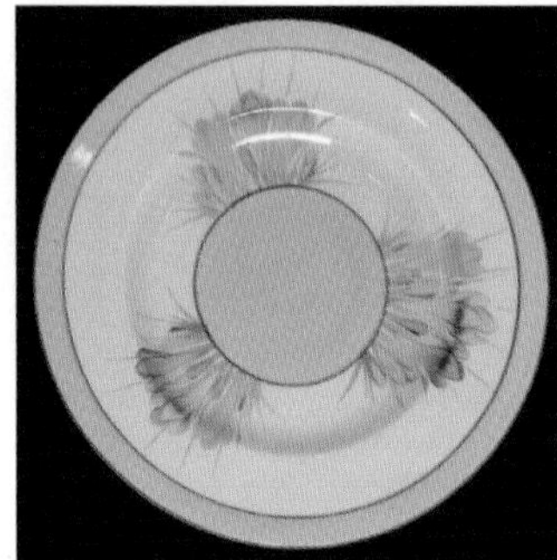

A Clarice Cliff bowl, cup, saucer and plate, decorated with Passion Fruit pattern, c1930, bowl 8in (20.5cm) diam.
£95–115
$140–170 G(L)

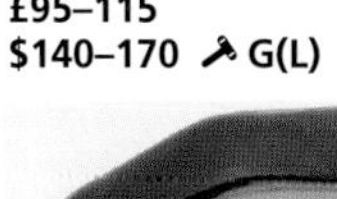

A Clarice Cliff Fantasque bowl, decorated with Broth pattern, with Lawley backstamp, c1930, 7in (18cm) diam.
£650–750
$950–1,100 ⊞ WAC

A Clarice Cliff Bizarre tea plate, decorated with Sliced Fruit pattern, 1930s, 5½in (14cm) diam.
£150–180
$220–260 SWO

A Clarice Cliff jardinière, modelled as a water lily, pattern No. 973, 1930s, 5in (12.5cm) diam.
£120–145
$175–210 G(B)

A Clarice Cliff bowl, decorated with Nasturtium pattern, c1930, 7¾in (19.5cm) diam.
£150–180
$220–260 G(L)

A Clarice Cliff bowl, decorated with Gay Day pattern, c1930, 6½in (16.5cm) diam.
£150–180
$220–260 G(L)

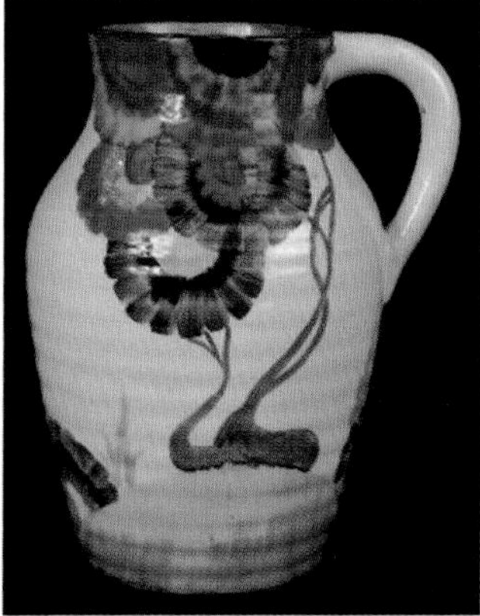

A Clarice Cliff Bizarre jug, decorated with Rodanthe pattern, base moulded 'Isis', 1930s, 9¾in (24.5cm) high.
£400–480
$580–700 SWO

A Clarice Cliff Biarritz cup and saucer, 1930s, 2¼in (6cm) high.
£140–170
$200–250 SWO

A Clarice Cliff Fantasque bowl, decorated with Melon pattern, c1930, 6in (15cm) diam.
£120–140
$175–200 G(L)

A Clarice Cliff Bizarre jug, decorated with Crocus pattern, marked, base restored, 1930s, 8in (20.5cm) high.
£130–150
$190–220 SWO

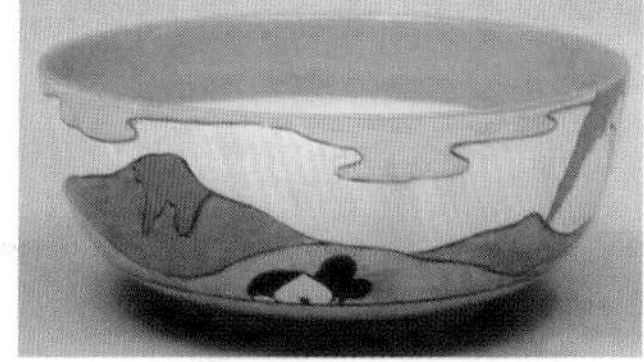

A Clarice Cliff Bizarre bowl, decorated with Mountain pattern, printed factory marks, 1930s, 9½in (24cm) diam.
£500–600
$720–870 DD

A Clarice Cliff tea cup and saucer, decorated in Delecia Citrus pattern, 1930s, 2½in (6.5cm) high.
£300–350
$440–500 ⊞ RH

Susie Cooper

A Susie Cooper coffee cup and saucer, decorated in Nosegay pattern, c1930, 2¼in (5.5cm) high.
£45–50
$65–75 ⊞ RH

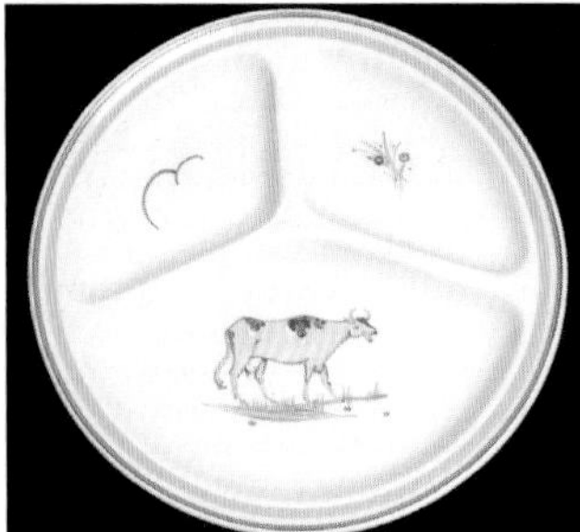

A Susie Cooper child's Nursery series feeding dish, c1930, 8in (20.5cm) diam.
£165–195
$240–280 ⊞ BD

A Susie Cooper teapot, decorated with Swansea Spray pattern, c1930, 7in (18cm) high.
£180–200
260–290 ⊞ RH

► **A Susie Cooper silver lustre floral plate,** with wide green border, 1930s, 11in (28cm) diam.
£120–150
$175–220 ⚒ G(L)

◄ **A Susie Cooper ginger jar,** hand-painted, c1930, 5in (12.5cm) high.
£250–300
$360–440 ⊞ CoCo

► **A Susie Cooper wall mask,** modelled as a Judge, restored, blue painted signature, c1933, 11¼in (28.5cm) high.
£400–500
$580–720
⚒ S(O)

◄ **A Susie Cooper part tea service,** comprising 17 pieces, decorated with Fragrance pattern, 1955–60, teapot 6½in (16.5cm) high.
£180–200
$260–300 ⊞ PrB

► **A Susie Cooper trio,** decorated with Gentian pattern, 1955–60, plate 7in (18cm) diam.
£40–45
$60–65 ⊞ PrB

Crown Devon

A Crown Devon vase, decorated with Fairy Castle pattern, c1930, 6in (15cm) high.
£550–600
$800–870 ⊞ RH

A Crown Devon hand-painted honey pot, c1930, 5in (12.5cm) high.
£80–90
$115–130 ⊞ CoCo

► A Crown Devon lustreware vase, decorated with stylized trees on a powder blue ground, gilt mark, c1930, 6in (15cm) high.
£100–130
$145–190 ⚒ WW

A Crown Devon mug, decorated with a geometric pattern, c1930, 4in (10cm) high.
£80–100
$115–145 ⊞ RH

Crown Ducal

◄ A Crown Ducal dish, decorated with Persian Rose pattern, c1925, 12in (30.5cm) wide.
£180–200
$250–300
⊞ DSG

► A Crown Ducal toast rack, decorated with Orange Tree pattern, 1930s, 6in (15cm) wide.
£120–140
$175–200 ⊞ JOA

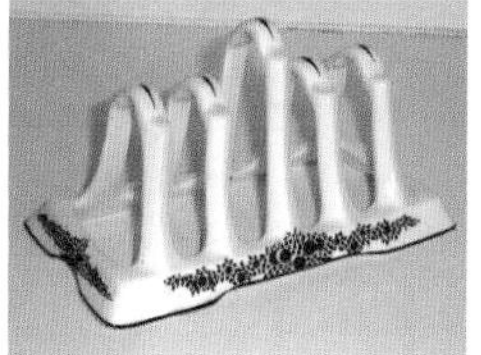

◄ A Crown Ducal mug, designed by Charlotte Rhead, tubelined with motto 'Another Little Drink Won't Do Us Any Harm', c1933, 4½in (11.5cm) high.
£40–45
$60–65 ⊞ BDA

A Crown Ducal cheese dish, decorated with Orange Tree pattern, 1930s, 8in (20.5cm) wide.
£120–140
$175–200 ⊞ JOA

Cross Reference
See Charlotte & Frederick Rhead (page 139)

A Crown Ducal wall plaque, designed by Charlotte Rhead, decorated with Manchu pattern No. 4511, c1935, 12½in (32cm) diam.
£380–420
$570–600 ⊞ BDA

A Crown Ducal vase, designed by Charlotte Rhead, shape No. 211, decorated with Foxglove pattern No. 4953, signed, c1937, 5½in (14cm) high.
£340–380
$500–570 ⊞ BDA

Cruets

A Staffordshire novelty condiment set, comprising an open salt, a pepper pot, a mustard and an oil bottle, each piece modelled as a country gentleman, wearing a hat with transfer-printed motif, yellow breeches, burnt orange top coat, purple/pink waistcoat and green cravat holding a tankard of ale, the circular bases with blue transfer-printed decoration, 19thC, largest 6¼in (16cm) high.
£200–240
$300–350 ⚒ FHF

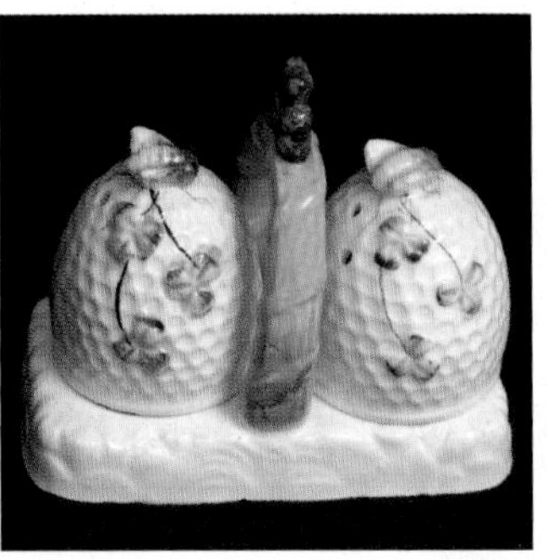

A beehive cruet set, Japanese, c1930, 3½in (9cm) high.
£35–40
$50–60 ⊞ CoCo

A cruet set, modelled as a chicken on a nest, Japanese, c1930, 3in (7.5cm) high.
£25–30
$35–45 ⊞ CoCo

A Bonzo cruet set, Japanese, 1930s, 4in (10cm) high.
£40–45
$60–65 ⊞ MURR

A pottery Pink Panther three-piece cruet set, 1998, 5in (12.5cm) wide.
£70–80
$100–115 ⊞ TAC

A dog cruet set image:

A dog cruet set, Japanese, 1930s, 3in (7.5cm) high.
£15–20
$20–30 ⊞ VB

► A pottery Pink Panther cruet set, 1998, 5in (12.5cm) high.
£60–70
$90–100 ⊞ TAC

Cups & Saucers

A New Hall tea bowl, pattern No. 241, c1790, 3½in (9cm) diam.
£40–45
$60–65 ⊞ JAY

A Coalport coffee can, decorated with Church Gresley pattern, c1810, 2½in (6.5cm) high.
£60–70
$90–100 ⊞ JAY

◄ **A Staffordshire porcelain christening mug,** inscribed 'W. M. Cumplen', c1870, 3½in (9cm) high.
£165–185
$250–275 ⊞ DAN

► **A faïence ale mug,** c1874, 5in (12.5cm) high.
£165–185
$240–270 ⊞ SER

A Derby coffee can, c1830, 2½in (6.5cm) high.
£55–65
$80–95 ⊞ JAY

A Poulson Bros pottery ale mug, with transfer-printed decoration, 1884–1927, 4in (10cm) high.
£75–85
$110–125 ⊞ CoCo

A porcelain cup, unmarked, late 19thC, 2½in (6.5cm) high.
£40–45
$60–65 ⊞ SER

A Cube Teapot Co breakfast set, produced by Foley China Works, c1930, plate 5in (12.5cm) square.
£250–300
$350–450 ⊞ HarC

A Gaudy Welsh mug, 19thC, 4in (10cm) high.
£90–110
$130–160 ⊞ WAC

A blue and white porcelain cup, decorated with a chinoiserie pattern, late 19thC, 2½in (6.5cm) high.
£50–55
$75–80 ⊞ SER

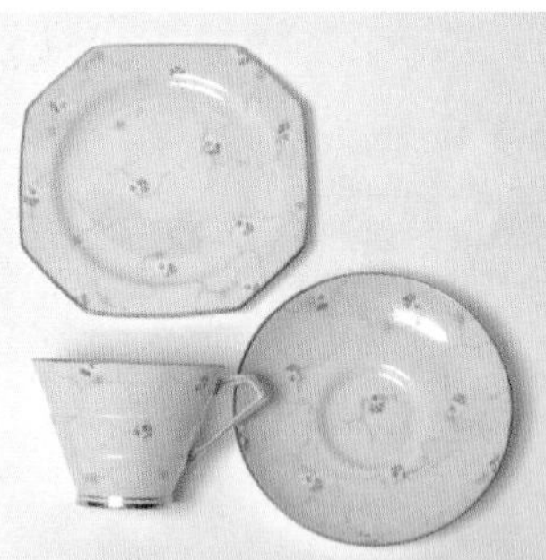

A Paragon trio, 1930s, plate 6in (15cm) wide.
£25–30
$35–45 ⊞ HarC

◄ **A Paragon trio,** 1940s, plate 6in (15cm) diam.
£30–35
$45–50 ⊞ CAL

► **A Honiton Devon ware trio,** 1950, plate 6in (15cm) diam.
£15–18
$20–25 ⊞ BrL

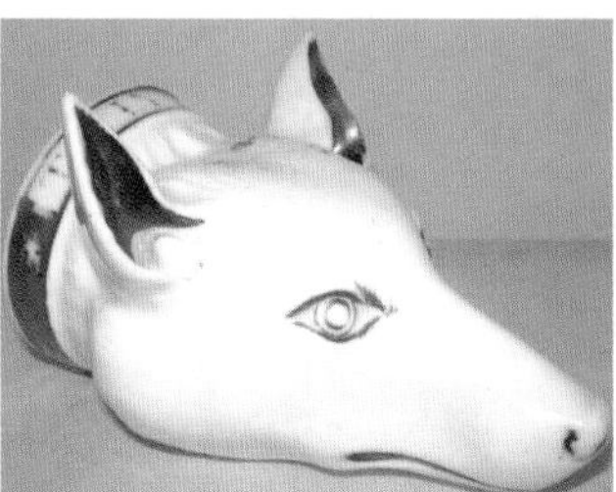

A porcelain stirrup cup, modelled as a fox's mask, the white glaze titled and gilt-enriched, inscribed 'Tally Ho' to the collar, 19thC, 4in (10cm) long.
£580–680
$850–1,000 ⚒ SJH

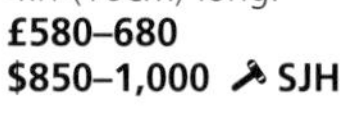

A Regal Pottery hand-painted coffee can and saucer, 1921–31, cup 2½in (6.5cm) high.
£35–40
$50–60 ⊞ CoCo

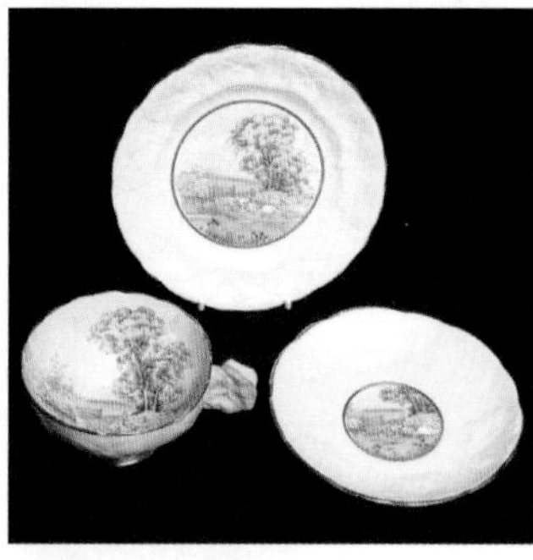

A Paragon trio, the cup handle modelled as a flower, 1930s, plate 6in (15cm) diam.
£130–150
$200–220 ⊞ BD

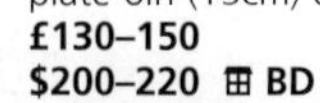

Denby

A frog Loving Cup, with greyhound handles, with applied sprigs and underglazed name and date, 1895, 5in (12.5cm) high.
£90–110
$130–160 ⊞ KES

► **A Denby carriage foot warmer,** impressed mark, c1900, 7¾in (19.5cm) long.
£250–300
$350–450 ⊞ KES

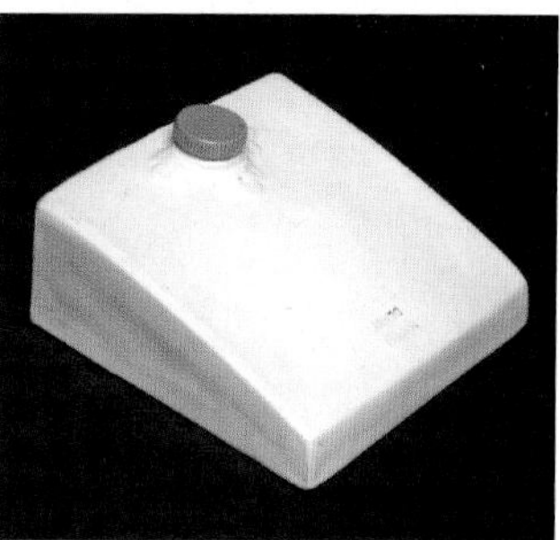

A Denby tube-lined tobacco jar, decorated with Festoon pattern, with electric blue glaze, rim damaged, presser missing, c1925, 4in (10cm) high.
£125–145
$180–200 ⊞ KES

A Denby casket tobacco jar, with pastel blue glaze, c1928, 5in (12.5cm) square.
£150–185
$220–270 ⊞ KES

◄ **A Denby Antique Green vase,** c1930, 7½in (19cm) high.
£100–125
$145–175
⊞ DSG

► **A Denby vase,** moulded with Gazelle pattern, c1935, 6½in (16.5cm) high.
£120–140
$175–200 ⊞ DSG

◄ **A Denby Peasant ware sauce tureen,** designed by Albert Colledge, c1954, 5in (12.5cm) high.
£25–30
$35–45 ⊞ CHI

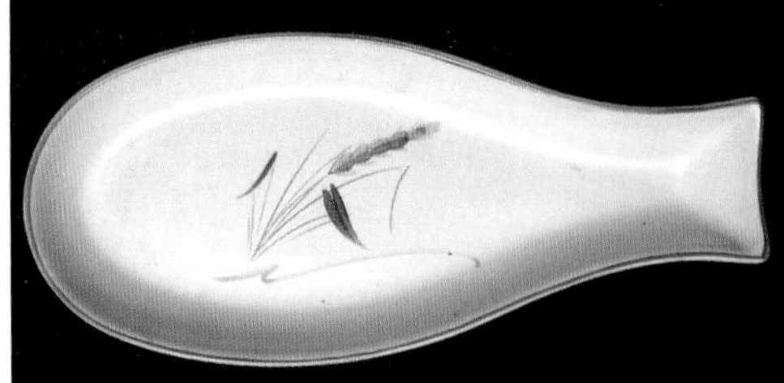

A Denby Greenwheat serving dish, designed by Albert Colledge, 1950s–70s, 13in (33cm) wide.
£35–40
$50–60 ⊞ CHI

A Denby Greenwheat sauce boat, designed by Albert Colledge, 1950s–70s, 11in (28cm) wide.
£20–25
$30–35 ⊞ CHI

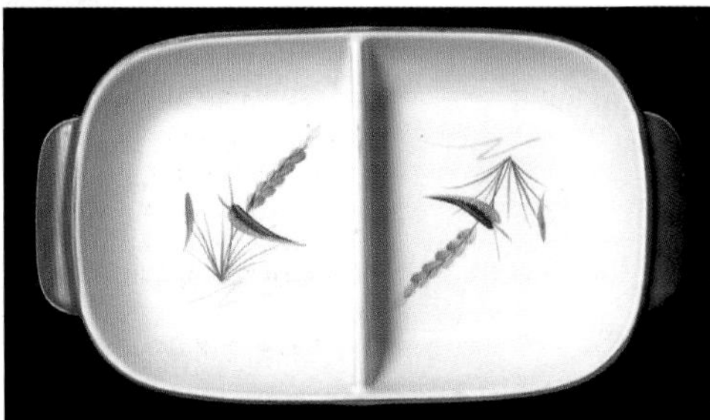

A Denby Greenwheat serving dish, designed by Albert Colledge, 1950s–70s, 12in (30.5cm) wide.
£30–35
$45–50 ⊞ CHI

► A Denby Arabesque bowl, designed by Gill Pemberton, c1965, 11in (28cm) diam.
£40–45
$60–65 ⊞ KES

A Denby Flamstead bowl, designed by Glyn Colledge, c1967, 9in (23cm) diam.
£55–65
$80–95 ⊞ KES

A Denby Langley breakfast plate and dinner plate, 1960s, larger 10in (25.5cm) diam.
£7–8
$9–12 each ⊞ HarC

A Denby Langley sauce boat and saucer, 1960s, 5in (12.5cm) diam.
£8–10
$12–15 ⊞ HarC

A Denby Chevron coffee pot, 1960s, 11in (28cm) high.
£30–40
$45–60 ⊞ CHI

A Denby Chevron tea kettle, 1960s, 8in (20.5cm) high.
£30–40
$45–60 ⊞ CHI

Doulton

A Doulton Lambeth drinking vessel, maker's mark for Harriet E. Hibbut, 1877, 5½in (14cm) high.
£40–50
$60–75 ⊞ LBr

► **A Doulton Lambeth stoneware vase,** c1900, 7¾in (19.5cm) high.
£60–75
$90–110 G(L)

► **A Doulton Lambeth jug,** 1884, 4¾in (12cm) high.
£165–185
$240–270 ⊞ BrL

A Doulton Burslem jug, c1891–1902, 10in (25.5cm) high.
£450–550
$650–800 ⊞ WAC

◄ **A Royal Doulton jug,** decorated with moulded landscape designs, below a green-glazed silver-mounted rim, Sheffield hallmarks, c1900, 8in (20.5cm) high.
£65–75
$95–110 BWL

A Royal Doulton footed bowl, c1900, 12in (30.5cm) diam.
£325–365
$470–550 ⊞ WAC

A Royal Doulton 11-piece silver-mounted tea service, including teapot, milk jug and sugar bowl, the silver mounts embossed with floral garlands, hallmarked, c1904.
£190–230
$275–330 ⚒ G(L)

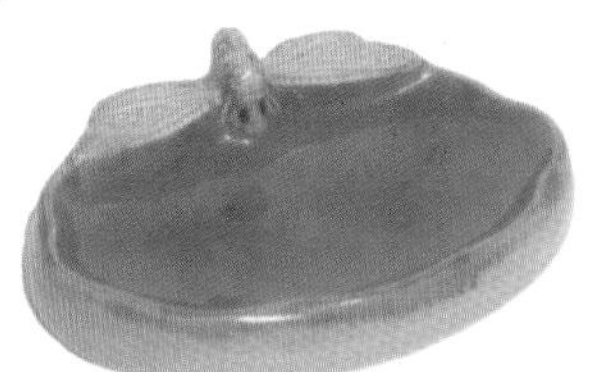

A Royal Doulton Wright's Coal Tar Soap dish, with dragonfly detail, marked, c1920, 6in (15cm) wide.
£20–30
$30–45 ⚒ BBR

A Royal Doulton six-piece part tea service, pattern No. VI289, c1920.
£75–85
$110–125 ⚒ BLH

A Royal Doulton model of a seated bulldog, Old Bill, damaged, 1918–25, 6½in (16.5cm) high.
£85–100
$125–145 ⚒ G(L)

A Royal Doulton trio, decorated with Norfolk pattern, c1920, plate 6in (15cm) wide.
£20–25
$30–35 ⊞ HarC

A Royal Doulton coffee can and saucer, decorated with Kew pattern, 1920s, cup 2in (5cm) high.
£35–40
$50–60 ⊞ CoCo

A Royal Doulton Shakespeare jug, depicting Romeo, c1930, 9in (23cm) high.
£60–65
$90–95 ⊞ HarC

A Doulton Magnella jug, c1930, 9in (23cm) high.
£90–110
$130–160 ⊞ WAC

A Royal Doulton Jarge character jug, by Harry Fenton, No. D6288, circle mark, lion and crown, 1950–60, 6½in (16.5cm) high.
£80–100
$115–145 ⚒ BBR

A Royal Doulton North American Indian character jug, designed by Max Henk, No. D6611, circle mark, lion and crown, c1967, 7¾in (19.5cm) high.
£50–60
$75–90 ⚒ BBR

A Royal Doulton model of Old Vole, by Harry Sales, No. DBH, circle mark, lion and crown, 1985–92, 13½in (34.5cm) high.
£80–100
$115–145 ⚒ BBR

► A Royal Doulton model of Jogging Bunnykins, by Harry Sales, No. DB22, circle mark, lion and crown, 1983–89, 2½in (6.5cm) high.
£50–60
$75–90 ⚒ BBR

A Royal Doulton model of Eeyore's Tail, designed by Shane Ridge, circle mark, lion and crown, 1996–present, 3¼in (8.5cm) high.
£10–15
$15–20 ⚒ BBR

◄ A Royal Doulton figure of The Auctioneer, No. HN2988, 1986, 8¾in (22cm) high.
£80–90
$115–130 ⚒ BLH

Egg Cups

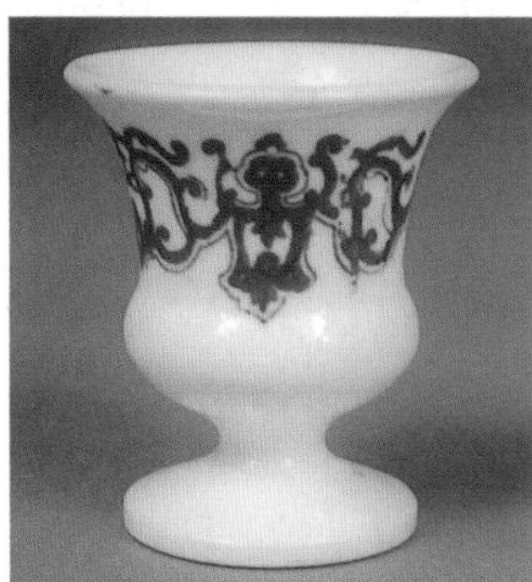

A campana-shaped egg cup, probably Spode, c1840, 2½in (6.5cm) high.
£100–120
$145–175 ⊞ AMH

A Copeland egg cup, c1850–67, 2¼in (5.5cm) high.
£90–100
$130–145 ⊞ AMH

A Minton egg cup, pattern No. A300, c1860, 2in (5cm) high.
£50–60
$75–90 ⊞ AMH

A Copeland Spode egg cup, c1891, 2in (5cm) high.
£45–50
$65–75 ⊞ AMH

A porcelain egg cup, probably by George Proctor, Longton, c1892, 2½in (6.5cm) high.
£40–45
$60–65 ⊞ AMH

A Coalport egg cup, c1870, 2in (5cm) high.
£50–60
$75–90 ⊞ AMH

► Two lustre egg cups, modelled as elephants, Japanese, c1920, 3in (7.5cm) high.
£25–30
$35–45 each ⊞ CoCo

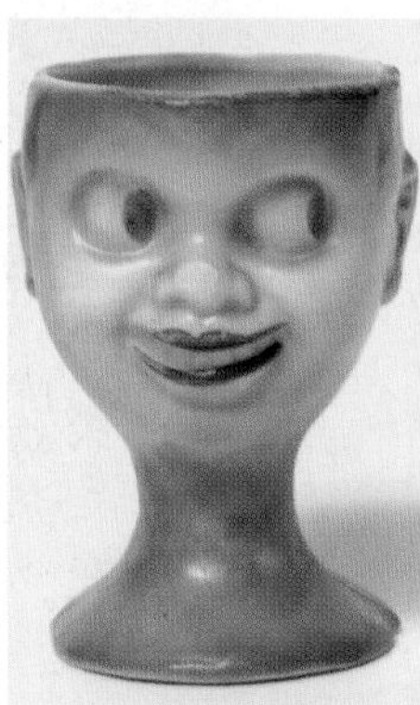

An egg cup, modelled as a smiling face, c1910, 3in (7.5cm) high.
£20–25
$30–35 ⊞ HUX

An egg cup, modelled as a cat, Japanese, 1920s, 2½in (6.5cm) high.
£15–20
$20–30 ⊞ HUX

► A pottery egg cup, modelled as a pheasant, 1930s, 3½in (9cm) high.
£15–20
$20–30
⊞ CoCo

Fairings

A fairing, entitled 'Velocipede for Stout Travellers', restored, c1870, 2¼in (5.5cm) high.
£650–750
$950–1,150 ⚒ SAS

A fairing, entitled 'To the Derby', c1870, 2¼in (5.5cm) high.
£800–1,000
$1,150–1,500 ⚒ SAS

A fairing, entitled 'Kiss Me Quick', c1870, 2¼in (5.5cm) high.
£460–500
$675–725 ⚒ SAS
Unusual bicycling subject matter is very collectable.

A fairing, entitled 'The Spoils of War', 19thC, 2¾in (7cm) high.
£100–120
$145–175 ⚒ SAS

A fairing, entitled 'Baby's First Step', 19thC, 2¼in (5.5cm) high.
£85–100
$125–145 ⚒ SAS

A fairing, entitled 'By Appointment, the First of April', c1870, 2¼in (5.5cm) high.
£220–260
$320–380 ⚒ SAS

► **A fairing,** entitled 'Return from the Ball', 19thC, 2¼in (5.5cm) high.
£200–220
$300–320 ⚒ SJH

A fairing, entitled 'The Power of Love', 19thC, 2¼in (5.5cm) high.
£60–75
$90–110 ⚒ SJH

A fairing, modelled as a shell dish with foxes wearing clothes, 19thC, 2¼in (5.5cm) high.
£85–100
$125–145 ⚒ SJH

◄ **A fairing,** entitled 'Well! What Are You Looking At?', 19thC, 2¼in (5.5cm) high.
£240–280
$350–400 ⚒ SAS

Figures

A pair of porcelain figures of a cricketer and a tennis player, each on a scroll-moulded base, Continental, impressed date 1838, 9¾in (25cm) high.
£210–250
$300–350 SJH

A Sampson figure of a boy, wearing 18thC dress, 19thC, 5in (12.5cm) high.
£110–135
$160–200 SER

A Royal Dux porcelain figure of a peasant shepherd boy, with a dog at his feet, late 19thC, 17in (43cm) high.
£360–400
$500–580 G(B)

A Gebrüder Heubach bisque figure of a skipping girl, her head with finely-painted features, moulded blond hair, wearing a pale blue dress with rosebuds and gold decoration, standing in front of a wooden stall, German, c1910, 11½in (29cm) high.
£120–140
$175–200 B(Ch)

◄ **An Ipsen bisque figure of a boy,** signed KK, c1925, 8in (20.5cm) high.
£250–300
$350–450 DSG

A porcelain half-figure of a male doll, Continental, c1920–30, 2in (5cm) high.
£40–45
$60–65 HO

A Crown Staffordshire bust, 1930s, 3in (7.5cm) high.
£110–130
$160–190 CoCo

An Arcadian figure of Miss Prudence, 1930s, 4in (10cm) high.
£150–175
$220–255 TWO

A Bing & Grøndahl group, 'Girl with Bull calf and Goose', c1948, 9in (23cm) wide.
£280–320
$400–450 PSA

► **A Hummel figure of a boy holding a basket,** c1970, 3in (7.5cm) high.
£55–65
$80–100 PrB

Goss & Crested China

An Arcadian model of a banjo, with Newmarket crest, c1903, 5in (12.5cm) long.
£15–20
$20–30 ⊞ G&CC

An Arcadian 'One Special Scotch' bottle, with St Leonards crest, c1903, 3in (7.5cm) high.
£8–10
$12–15 ⊞ G&CC

An Arcadian model of a Staffordshire bull terrier, with Broadstairs crest, c1903, 3¼in (8.5cm) high.
£17–22
$20–30 ⊞ G&CC

A Botolph model of a Red Cross van, with City of London crest, 1914–18, 3½in (9cm) long.
£40–45
$60–65 ⊞ TWO

An Arcadian model of a puppy with monocle, cigar and beer on an ashtray, with British Empire Exhibition crest, 1924–25, 3¼in (8.5cm) high.
£135–145
$200–210 ⊞ G&CC

An Arcadian model of a peacock, with Wisbech crest, 1920s, 5in (12.5cm) high.
£50–55
$75–80 ⊞ TWO

A Carlton model of a Welsh goat on a plinth, inscribed 'Ar Afr Gymreig', with Aberystwyth crest, c1900, 4¼in (11cm) high.
£85–95
$125–140 ⊞ CCC

◄ **A Carlton model of a stick telephone,** entitled 'Hello Hello', with Newton Abbot crest, c1902, 4½in (11.5cm) high.
£30–35
$45–50 ⊞ G&CC

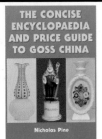

A Carlton Mother Shipton model of a British tank, with Knaresborough crest, 1914–18, 6in (15cm) long.
£50–60
$75–90 ⊞ TWO
Mother Shipton was the trademark used by Carlton for the retailer J. W. Simpson.

A Carlton model of a battleship, with three funnels and Chester crest, 1920s, 5in (12.5cm) long.
£50–55
$75–80 ⊞ TWO

◀ A Carlton model of a goose, with arms of Norwich, 1920s, 3in (7.5cm) high.
£35–40
$50–60 ⊞ TWO

▶ A Corona model of an upright piano, with open keyboard and Shirley crest, c1906, 2½in (6.5cm) high.
£18–20
$25–30 ⊞ LBe

▶ A Dainty Ware model of a coal bucket, with Anglo-American Exposition, London crest, 1914, 2¾in (7cm) long.
£15–20
$20–30
⊞ G&CC

A Goss three-handled butterfly vase, with arms of Brighton, Hove and Sussex, c1880, 4¾in (12cm) high.
£80–90
$115–130 ⊞ G&CC

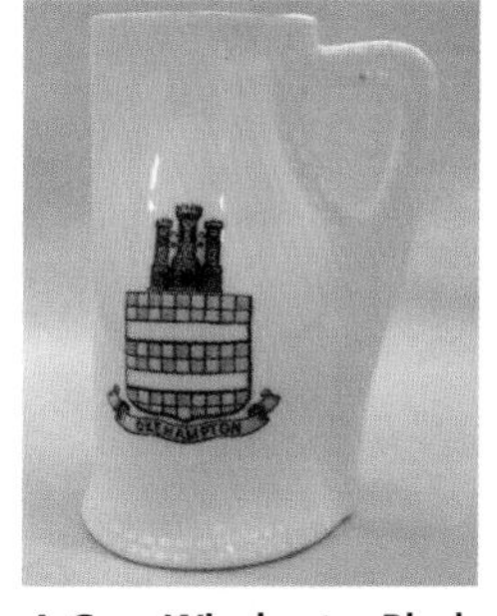

A Goss Winchester Black Jack, with Okehampton and Devon crests, c1880, 4¾in (12cm) high.
£25–30
$35–45 ⊞ G&CC

A Goss model of a Pompeiian ewer, with Walton-on-the-Naze crest, c1890, 3½in (9cm) high.
£15–20
$20–30 ⊞ G&CC

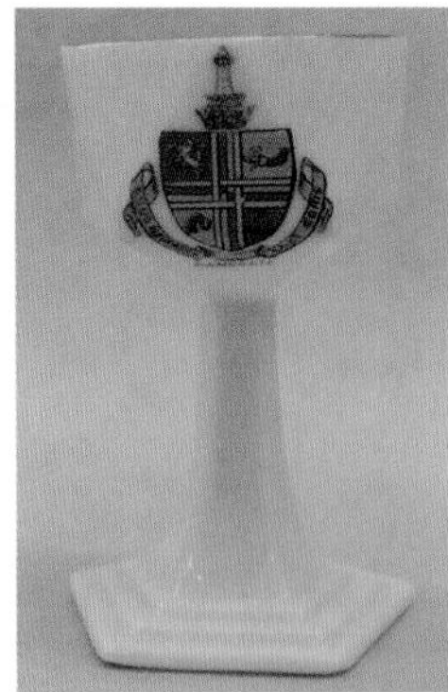

A Goss model of a Glastonbury salt cellar, with Ramsgate crest, c1890, 3¼in (8.5cm) high.
£20–25
$30–35 ⊞ G&CC

► A Grafton model of a fledgling, with Aberdeen crest, c1900, 2½in (6.5cm) high.
£25–30
$35–45 ⊞ G&CC

A collection of Goss Mabel Lucie Attwell wedding figures, mid-1930s, 4in (10cm) high.
£1,500–1,700
$2,200–2,500 ⊞ MEM
These rare wedding figures are made by a very collectable designer.

Items in the Goss & Crested China section have been arranged in alphabetical order by factory.

A Savoy model of a grotesque bird, with Paignton crest, 1920s, 4in (10cm) high.
£10–15
$15–20 ⊞ TWO

A Saxony model of a lifeboatman, with Clacton-on-Sea crest, c1910, 4½in (11.5cm) high.
£15–20
$20–30 ⊞ G&CC

A Saxony model of the Margate Lifeboat Memorial, with Margate crest, c1910, 3½in (9cm) high.
£70–80
$100–115 ⊞ G&CC

A Shelley model of a bulldog and kennel, entitled 'The Black Watch', with Prestatyn crest, c1910, 4in (10cm) high.
£25–30
$35–45 ⊞ TWO

A Shelley model of a hand grenade, with Eastbourne crest, 1914–18, 3in (7.5cm) high.
£30–35
$45–50 ⊞ TWO

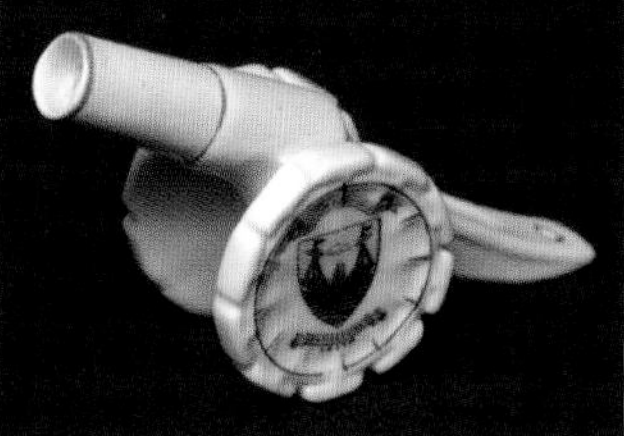

A Swan model of a howitzer, with Leith crest, 1914–18, 6in (15cm) long.
£20–25
$30–35 ⊞ TWO

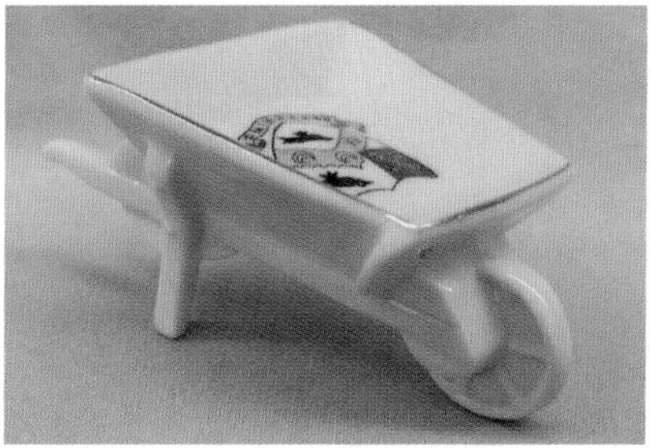

A Willow Art model of a wheelbarrow, with Kettering crest, c1905, 4¼in (11cm) long.
£20–25
$30–35 ⊞ G&CC

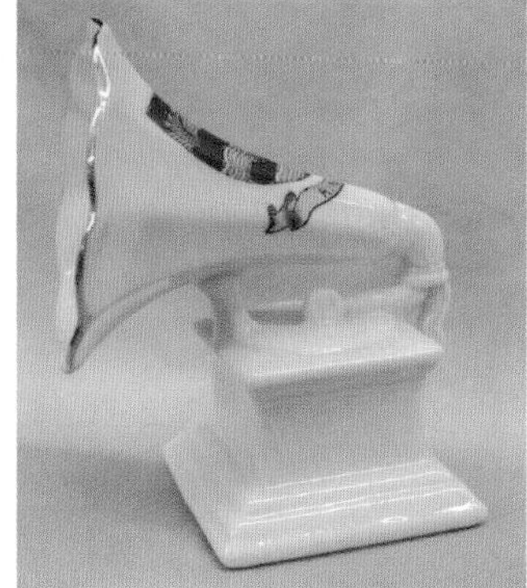

► A Willow Art model of a gramophone, with Ringwood crest, c1905, 3¼in (8.5cm) high.
£30–35
$45–50 ⊞ G&CC

A Willow Art model of a monoplane, with RAF roundels and tail markings, 1914–18, 6in (15cm) long.
£150–175
$220–255 ⊞ TWO

Gouda

A Gouda Arnhem vase, c1900, 4½in (11.5cm) wide.
£130–150
$200–220 ⊞ DSG

A Gouda Arnhem high-fired vase, c1900, 5in (12.5cm) high.
£45–50
$65–75 ⊞ DSG

◄ A pair of Gouda earthenware wall pockets, with polychrome decoration, c1930, 9½in (24cm) high.
£90–110
$130–160 ⚒ G(L)

A pair of Gouda dressing table pots, c1920, 3in (7.5cm) diam.
£25–30
$35–45 ⊞ PrB

A Gouda bowl, decorated with Rhodian pattern, c1930, 7½in (19cm) diam.
£90–110
$130–160 ⊞ PrB

T. G. Green

◄ **A T. G. Green Mochaware jug,** 1910–20, 8in (20.5cm) high.
£165–180
$240–260 ⊞ CAL

A T. G. Green blue and white globe teapot, green shield mark, c1920s, 5in (12.5cm) high.
£170–200
$250–300 ⊞ GeN

◄ **A T. G. Green Cube teapot,** decorated with Dickens' Days pattern, 1930, 4in (10cm) square.
£100–120
$145–175 ⊞ CAL

A T. G. Green Cornish Ware Table Salt storage jar, 1920s, 5in (12.5cm) high.
£225–250
$325–350 ⊞ SMI

A T. G. Green Soap Flakes storage jar, black shield mark, c1920s, 5½in (14cm) high.
£360–400
$500–580 ⊞ GeN

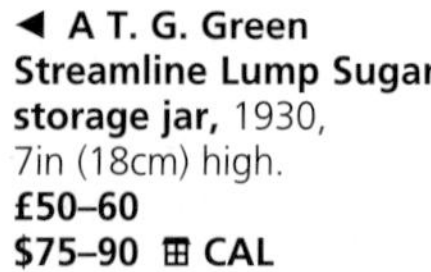

◄ **A T. G. Green Streamline Lump Sugar storage jar,** 1930, 7in (18cm) high.
£50–60
$75–90 ⊞ CAL

A T. G. Green cup and saucer, decorated with Seagull pattern, 1930s, cup 3in (7.5cm) high.
£65–75
$95–110 ⊞ CAL

A T. G. Green Polka Dot trio, 1930s, cup 3in (7.5cm) high.
£15–20
$20–30 ⊞ CAL

◄ **A T. G. Green Blue Domino cheese dish,** 1930–50, 7in (18cm) long.
£90–110
$130–160 ⊞ CAL

A T. G. Green Cornish Ware butter dish, 1950s, 6in (15cm) diam.
£80–100
$115–145 ⊞ CAL

A T. G. Green Cornish Ware oil jug, 1960s, 7½in (19cm) high.
£90–110
$130–160 ⊞ CAL

◄ **A T. G. Green Cornish Ware coffee pot,** designed by Judith Onions, 1966, 7in (18cm) high.
£65–75
$95–110 ⊞ CAL

A set of T. G. Green Church Gresley storage jars, from the Granville range, 1970–80, 5in (12.5cm) high.
£30–40
$45–60 ⊞ CAL

◄ **A T. G. Green mustard pot,** marked, 1980s, 2½in (6.5cm) high.
£35–40
$50–60 ⊞ TAC

Hancock & Sons

A Hancock & Sons porcelain vase, decorated with a portrait, c1910, 4½in (11.5cm) high.
£45–55
$65–80 ⊞ TWAC

A pair of Hancock & Sons Corona Ware vases, by Molly Hancock, decorated with Cherry Ripe pattern, signed, 1924, 5½in (14cm) high.
£175–200
$250–300 ⊞ PIC

A Hancock & Sons Morris Ware vase, by George Cartlidge, c1930, 12in (30.5cm) high.
£1,000–1,200
$1,500–1,750 ⊞ BD

Japanese Ceramics

A Sunita Gawa pottery mug, c1920, 5in (12.5cm) high.
£90–110
$130–160 ⊞ BRU

A Noritake trio, green Komaru mark, c1920, cup 4in (10cm) high.
£30–35
$45–50 ⊞ DgC

A Noritake Tennis cup and saucer, gold Komaru mark, 1920s, 7in (18cm) wide.
£30–35
$45–50 ⊞ DgC

A Noritake hand-painted lemon dish, c1930, 5½in (14cm) diam.
£35–40
$50–60 ⊞ WAC

A Maruhon ware hand-painted jam pot, 1930s, 4in (10cm) high.
£25–28
$35–40 ⊞ TAC

◄ **A pincushion,** in the form of a seated boy, c1930, 3in (7.5cm) high.
£35–40
$50–60 ⊞ CoCo

Jugs

A Jones & Walley semi-glazed jug, moulded with Gypsy pattern, 1842 mark, 8in (20.5cm) high.
£50–60
$75–90 ⊞ TAC

A Staffordshire stoneware jug, with applied decoration depicting a cow, calf, horse and fowl, 19thC, 6in (15cm) high.
£140–160
$200–230 ⚒ SWO

A Mochaware jug, 19thC, 6½in (16.5cm) high.
£160–180
$230–260 ⊞ SER

A Lambeth-style stoneware harvest jug, 19thC, 8in (20.5cm) high.
£85–95
$125–140 ⊞ ML

► A Devonware milk jug, painted with a cat and inscribed 'The Devonshire Nightingale', early 20thC, 10in (25.5cm) high.
£200–250
$300–350 ⚒ G(L)

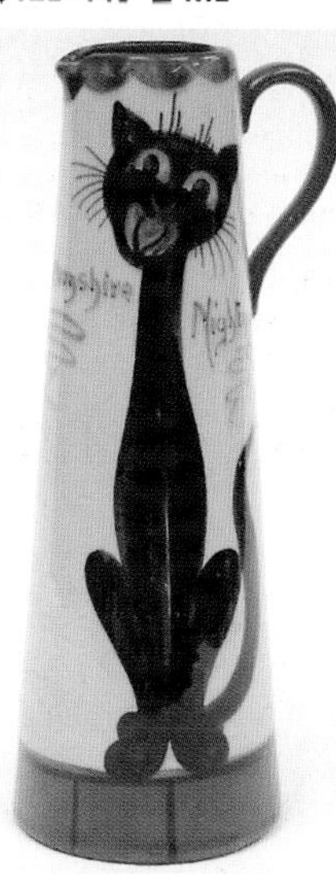

A Gaudy Welsh pitcher, 19thC, 7in (18cm) high.
£90–100
$130–145 ⊞ CoCo

A Savoie jug, 1880, 9in (23cm) high.
£145–165
$200–250 ⊞ MLL

A Honiton jug, 1950, 3in (7.5cm) high.
£12–15
$15–20 ⊞ BrL

Lustre Ware

A Sunderland lustre jug, transfer-printed with west view of the Iron Bridge over the Wear, inscribed 'Swiftly see each moment flies see and learn be timely wise...', 19thC, 8in (20.5cm) high.
£100–140
$145–200 ⚒ DA

A Tyneside pink lustre wall plaque, decorated with an unnamed sailing ship, c1850, 7½ x 8½in (19 x 21.5cm).
£300–350
$450–500 ⚒ G(L)

A Victorian silver lustre albarello vase, by Louise Powell, with floral decoration on a blue ground, monogrammed, 8in (20.5cm) high.
£300–350
$450–500 ⚒ G(L)

Majolica

A majolica jug, dated 1857, 8in (20.5cm) high.
£70–80
$100–115 ⊞ CoCo

A pair of majolica plates, late 19thC, 9in (23cm) diam.
£100–120
$145–175 ⊞ CoCo

A majolica basket/jardinière, 1890, 10in (25.5cm) wide.
£80–90
$115–130 ⊞ MLL

LOCATE THE SOURCE
The source of each illustration in Miller's can be found by checking the code letters below each caption with the Key to Illustrations, pages 443–451.

A Longchamps majolica cachepot, 1890, 8in (20.5cm) diam.
£300–350
$450–500 ⊞ MLL

A majolica slipper, decorated with flowers, late 19thC, 12in (30.5cm) long.
£130–150
$200–220 ⊞ SER

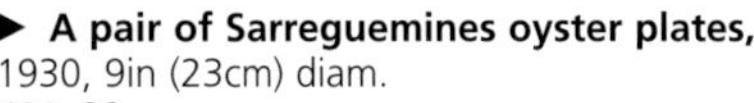

► **A pair of Sarreguemines oyster plates,** 1930, 9in (23cm) diam.
£80–90
$115–130 ⊞ MLL

Maling

A Maling toilet jug, polychrome-decorated with a stylized foral design on a white ground, printed black castle mark and pattern No. 3132, c1930, 10½in (26.5cm) high.
£120–140
$175–200 ⚒ GAK

A Maling hand-painted lustre dish, 1930s, 8in (20.5cm) wide.
£75–85
$110–125 ⊞ CoCo

► **A Maling Art Deco-style hand-painted butter dish,** with raised floral decoration, c1940, 7in (18cm) wide.
£55–65
$80–95 ⊞ CoCo

A Maling lustre fruit bowl, printed, enamelled and gilded with fruiting vines, c1930, 9½in (24cm) diam.
£170–200
$250–300 ⚒ G(L)

Midwinter

As Midwinter items from the 1950s are commanding high prices today, particularly Terence Conran designs, attention is turning to their tableware from the 1960s and '70s. 1962 saw the launch of the Fine shape, created by David, Marquis of Queensberry, which moved away from the organic curving forms of the '50s to a straighter, more streamlined look based on the traditional milk churn. Patterns reflected the rapidly changing fashions of the day. Bestsellers included Barbara Brown's Focus (1964), an Op Art design, and Jessie Tait's Spanish Garden (1968), inspired by a Liberty of London tie, but portrayed in glowing, almost psychedelic colours.

In 1972, the company introduced the Stonehenge range. Its studio pottery 'oatmeal' look captured the mood of the moment, tying in with the trend for wholefood, hand-craftsmanship and a more 'natural' lifestyle, famously portrayed in the BBC comedy series *The Good Life* (1974–78). Eve Midwinter's Sun, Moon and Earth patterns perfectly complemented the 1970s' farmhouse-style kitchen that featured in both town and country homes, and these designs are popular with enthusiasts today. In addition to specific collectors, pottery from this period is also purchased by those still using tableware originally purchased in the '60s and '70s, keen to replace broken or missing items.

A Midwinter cruet set, decorated with Red Domino pattern, 1950s, 4½in (11.5cm) wide.
£20–25
$30–40 ⊞ FLD

A Midwinter Stylecraft jug, designed by Jessie Tait, decorated with Homeware Red pattern, c1953, 6in (15cm) high.
£30–35
$45–50 ⊞ HSt

A Midwinter tea service, designed by Jessie Tait, decorated with Red Domino pattern, c1953, cup 3in (7.5cm) high.
£210–240
$300–350 ⊞ CHI

► A Midwinter Stylecraft plate, designed by Terence Conran, decorated with Saladware pattern, 1955, 12in (30.5cm) diam.
£150–170
$220–250 ⊞ HSt

A Midwinter cup and saucer, designed by Jessie Tait, decorated with Festival pattern, 1955, cup 3in (7.5cm) high.
£35–40
$50–60 ⊞ CHI
This pattern owes its name and inspiration to the 1951 Festival of Britain.

A Midwinter Stylecraft vegetable dish, designed by Jessie Tait, decorated with Primavera pattern, 1954, 10in (25.5cm) diam.
£90–100
$130–145 ⊞ CHI

◄ A Midwinter vegetable dish, designed by Terence Conran, decorated with Plant Life pattern, c1956, 10in (25.5cm) wide.
£135–150
$200–220 ⊞ CHI

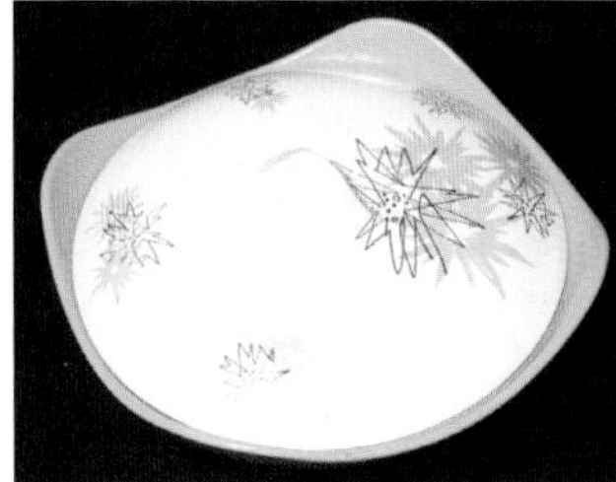

A Midwinter tureen, decorated with Quite Contrary pattern, 1957, 9in (23cm) wide.
£25–30
$35–45 ⊞ FLD

A Midwinter Stylecraft tureen, decorated with Happy Valley pattern, 1960s, 9½in (24cm) wide.
£50–60
$75–90 ⊞ FLD

A Midwinter coffee cup and saucer, decorated with Fishing Boat pattern, 1950s, cup 3in (7.5cm) high.
£14–16
$20–25 ⊞ FLD

A Midwinter sauce boat and stand, decorated with Oakley pattern, c1968, 4½in (11.5cm) diam.
£35–40
$50–60 ⊞ CHI
This design was made specially for Boots the Chemists Ltd.

A Midwinter celery vase, designed by Jessie Tait, moulded with Mosaic pattern, c1960, 7in (18cm) high.
£150–175
$225–255 ⊞ CHI

A Midwinter coffee pot, decorated with Spanish Garden pattern, c1968, 8in (20.5cm) high.
£30–35
$45–50 ⊞ CHI

Cross Reference
See Sixties & Seventies (page 355–360)

◄ **A Midwinter salt pot,** designed by Eve Midwinter, decorated with Earth pattern, 1970s, 4in (10cm) high.
£10–12
$15–18 ⊞ CHI

A Midwinter Stonehenge soup bowl and saucer and a side plate, designed by Eve Midwinter, decorated with Sun pattern, 1970s, soup bowl 5in (12.5cm) diam.
£14–18
$20–25 ⊞ CHI

Moorcroft

A pair of Moorcroft Macintyre vases, pattern No. M700, decorated with a floral Art Nouveau design, late 19thC, 8¾in (22cm) high.
£250–300
$350–450 TRM

► **A Moorcroft Macintyre Florian ware teapot and cover,** decorated with Cornflower pattern, mark to base, 1900, 4in (10cm) high.
£600–700
$870–1,000
SJH

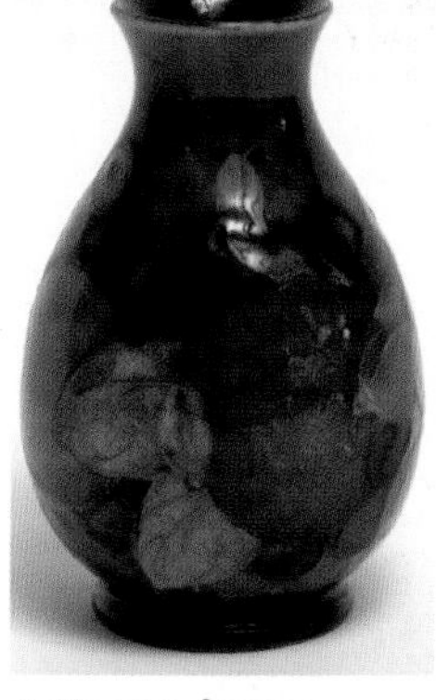

A Moorcroft vase, decorated with Pomegranate pattern, c1930, 5in (12.5cm) high.
£250–300
$350–450 MED

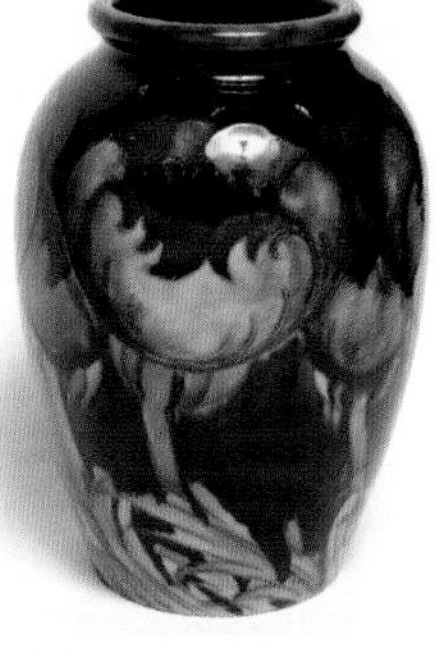

A Moorcroft vase, decorated with Poppy pattern, c1930, 10in (25.5cm) high.
£800–1,000
$1,150–1,500 BD

◄ **A Moorcroft ginger jar,** decorated with Poppy pattern, 1940s, 5in (12.5cm) high.
£320–360
$460–500 HarC

A Moorcroft vase, decorated with Orchid pattern, 1970–80, 8in (20.5cm) high.
£400–450
$580–650 DSG

A Moorcroft vase, decorated with Carousel pattern, 1995, 11in (28cm) high.
£400–450
$580–650 MPC

◄ **A Moorcroft vase,** decorated with Flame of the Forest pattern, c1997, 9in (23cm) high.
£440–480
$650–700 MPC

Myott

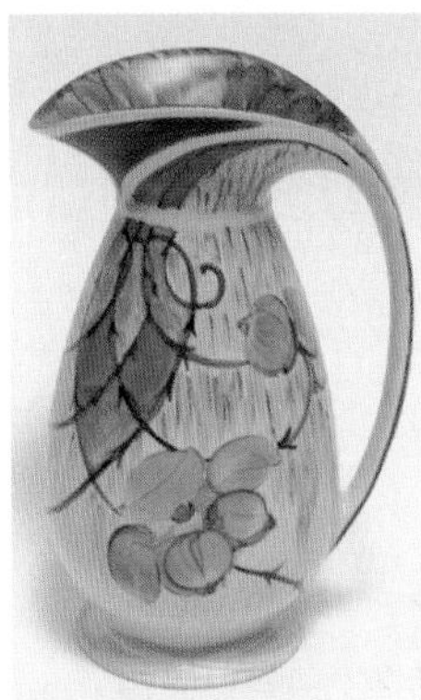

A Myott jug, c1930, 7in (18cm) high.
£90–100
$130–145 ⊞ RH

A Myott flower planter, with insert, c1930, 10in (25.5cm) wide.
£140–160
$200–230 ⊞ RH

A Myott jug, c1930, 8in (20.5cm) high.
£50–60
$75–90 ⊞ BD

A Myott star-shaped vase, c1930, 9in (23cm) high.
£180–200
$250–300 ⊞ RH

A Myott jug, c1930, 7in (18cm) high.
£180–200
$250–300 ⊞ RH

► **A Myott jug,** c1930, 8½in (21.5cm) high.
£100–120
$145–175 ⊞ RH

A Myott jug, c1930, 8in (20.5cm) high.
£80–90
$115–130 ⊞ RH

A Myott hand-painted coffee cup and saucer, 1930s, cup 2½in (6.5cm) high.
£40–45
$60–65 ⊞ CoCo

► **A pair of Myott hand-painted jugs,** c1935, 9in (23cm) high.
£90–110
$130–160 ⊞ PrB

Nursery Ware

A Yorkshire pottery child's plate, transfer-printed with a cottage among trees, early 19thC, 5in (12.5cm) diam.
£80–90
$115–130 ⊞ CoCo

A child's dish, with central cartoon design, c1910–20, 8in (20.5cm) diam.
£55–65
$80–95 ⚒ TRM

A Florence Upton child's mug, decorated with gollies, c1910–20, 5in (12.5cm) high.
£130–160
$200–230 ⊞ MURR

A Florence Upton storage jar, depicting gollies and Dutch dolls, c1910–20, 7in (18cm) high.
£150–175
$225–255 ⊞ MURR
This jar was retailed by Woolworths.

A toothbrush holder, modelled as a golly, 1920s–30s, 7in (18cm) high.
£100–150
$145–175 ⊞ MURR

► **A Crown Ducal child's mug,** designed by Charlotte Rhead, with tube-lined decoration, c1932, 2¾in (7cm) high.
£200–250
$300–350 ⊞ BDA

A Staffordshire Pinky and Perky egg cup, c1960, 4in (10cm) high.
£8–10
$12–15 ⊞ CTO

A Wedgwood Peter Rabbit table lamp, 1980s, 8in (20.5cm) high.
£30–35
$45–50 ⊞ CCH

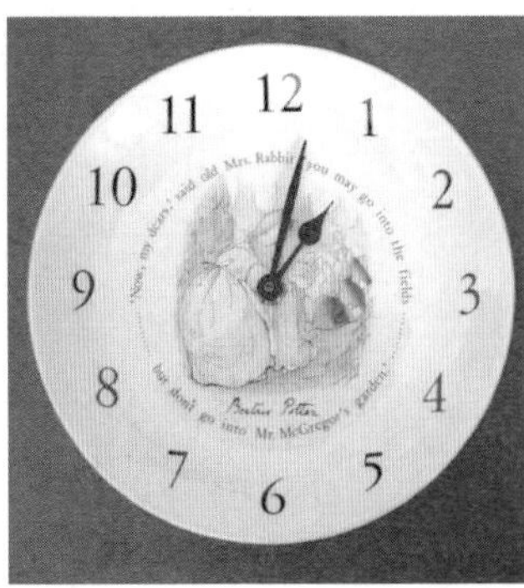

A Wedgwood Peter Rabbit clock, 1980s, 8in (20.5cm) diam.
£25–30
$35–45 ⊞ CCH

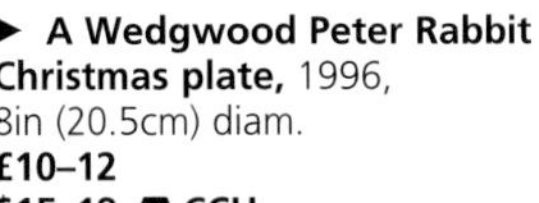

► A Wedgwood Peter Rabbit Christmas plate, 1996, 8in (20.5cm) diam.
£10–12
$15–18 ⊞ CCH

◄ A Wedgwood jasper ware Peter Rabbit miniature plate, 1980s, 4¼in (11cm) diam.
£45–50
$65–75 ⊞ CCH

A Wedgwood Peter Rabbit light switch plate, 1990s, 4¾in (12cm) high.
£20–25
$30–35 ⊞ CCH

Poole Pottery

A Carter & Co lustre charger, c1910, 11in (28cm) diam.
£450–500
$650–720 ⊞ HarC

A Carter, Stabler & Adams muffin dish and cover, painted with banded yellow and black geometric borders on a cream ground, the dish with a lilac and black dash rim, impressed mark and painted initials 'XK', 1930s, 6¼in (16cm) diam.
£40–50
$60–75 ⚒ FHF

A Poole Pottery vase, c1930, 8¼in (21cm) high.
£115–130
$170–200 ⊞ RUSK

◄ A Carter, Stabler & Adams vase, 1930s, 11in (28cm) high.
£580–650
$850–950 ⊞ BEV
Floral patterns in pastel colours on a matt ivory ground are among the most collectable pieces of Poole pottery from the 1930s. Condition is important to value – the earthenware body chips easily and is difficult to restore, and rims and handles are particularly vulnerable to damage.

Three Poole Pottery wall hanging flying birds, c1950, largest 6in (15cm) long.
£130–150
$200–220 ⊞ HarC

A Poole Pottery vase, designed by Truda Carter, decorated with CS pattern, c1950, 9½in (24cm) high.
£75–85
$110–125 ⊞ WAC

A Poole Pottery charger, designed by Anne Read, 1959, 12in (30.5cm) diam.
£345–385
$500–575 ⊞ HarC

Two Poole Pottery vases, enamelled with abstract motifs, printed dolphin marks, 1950s, 7½in (19cm) high.
£65–85
$95–125 each ⚒ G(L)

► **A Poole Pottery studio charger,** early 1960s, 10in (25.5cm) diam.
£400–450
$580–650 ⊞ CHI

Two Poole Pottery Delphis pin dishes, c1970, 4in (10cm) diam.
£30–35
$45–50 each ⊞ HarC

A Poole Pottery model of a cat, with flambé red glaze, hand-painted with blue and green decoration at the neck, 1960s, 11½in (29cm) high.
£50–60
$75–90 ⚒ BLH

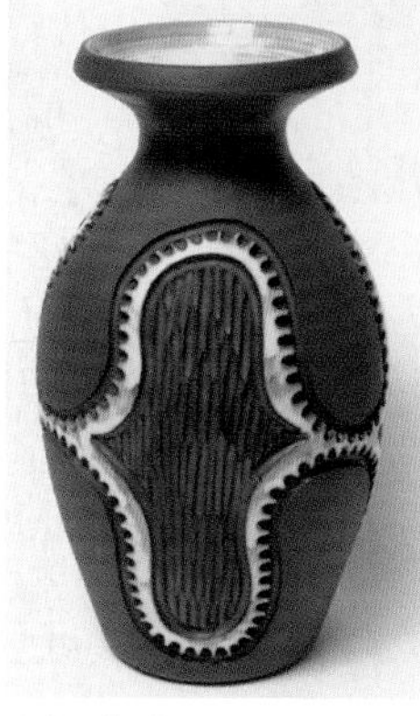

A Poole Pottery Atlantis vase, c1970, 12in (30.5cm) high.
£650–750
$950–1,100 ⊞ HarC

► **A Poole Pottery presentation plate,** by A. Bradbury and C. Davies, painted with a picture of a ship 'Poole Whaler 1783', inscribed verso, dated 1981, 8in (20.5cm) diam.
£45–55
$65–80 ⚒ G(L)

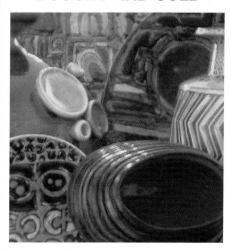

Portmeirion

The story of Portmeirion pottery begins in the late 1950s when Susan Williams-Ellis started to design individual ceramics for her gift shop in Portmeirion, the famous holiday village in Wales owned by her father, Sir Clough Williams-Ellis. Manufactured in Stoke-on-Trent, her designs were so popular that Susan and her husband took over Gray's Pottery (1960) and Kirkham's (1961), and from 1962 they traded as Portmeirion Potteries.

Portmeirion items became extremely fashionable. The tall cylindrical shape of cups and coffee pots captured the streamlined look of the 'swinging sixties' and patterns were varied and imaginative. Totem (1963), a raised decoration inspired by Victorian tiles, was an immediate bestseller, spawning other embossed lines and establishing the success of the company. In the 19th century, Kirkham's had produced pot lids and other printed wares. Susan discovered their original copper plates and used them to create black and white china that epitomized Pop Art style and the trend for Victorian revivalism. The Greek Key pattern, based on a Kirkham's border for Victorian pub barrels and grocers' jars, was translated onto coffee sets and tableware. Produced in gold from 1968, it was another major success story. Designs drew on a range of different sources from Islamic pottery to astrological drawings.

In 1971, Susan and her husband began collecting antiquarian and botanical and natural history books. In 1972, they introduced the Botanic Garden range, still in production today and now considered a design classic. Undoubtedly one of the most exciting British commercial potteries of the 1960s and '70s, Portmeirion is attracting a growing number of collectors.

A Portmeirion lidded jar, decorated with Tiger Lily pattern, c1962, 6in (15cm) high.
£170–190
$250–275 ⊞ CHI
Tiger Lily was inspired by traditional hand-painted bargeware.

A Portmeirion ashtray, decorated with Talisman pattern, c1962, 9in (23cm) square.
£150–170
$220–250 ⊞ CHI

A Portmeirion cheese dish, decorated with Totem pattern, c1963, 8in (20.5cm) diam.
£150–180
$220–260 ⊞ CHI

► A Portmeirion coffee pot, decorated with Totem pattern, c1963, 12in (30.5cm) high.
£75–90
$110–130 ⊞ CHI
Totem was produced in various colours – white and blue are rarer than the more commonplace ochre, and as such are sought-after by collectors.

A Portmeirion coffee service, comprising coffee pot, six cups and saucers, milk jug and sugar bowl, decorated with Cypher pattern, c1964, coffee pot 12½in (32cm) high.
£120–140
$175–200 ⊞ PrB

A Portmeirion mug, decorated with Variations pattern, c1964, 4in (10cm) high.
£35–40
$50–60 ⊞ CHI

◄ **A Portmeirion Tea storage jar,** decorated with Greek Key pattern, 1960s, 8in (20.5cm) high.
£65–75
$100–110 ⊞ CHI

A Portmeirion part coffee service, comprising coffee pot, six cups and saucers and milk jug, designed by Susan Williams-Ellis, decorated with Jupiter pattern, c1964, coffee pot 12½in (32cm) high.
£100–120
$145–175 ⊞ PrB

A Portmeirion jug, decorated with Greek Key pattern, 1960s, 4in (10cm) high.
£25–30
$35–45 ⊞ CHI

◄ **A Portmeirion mug,** decorated with Greek Key pattern, 1960s, 5in (12.5cm) high.
£25–30
$35–45 ⊞ CHI

A Portmeirion spice jar with wooden lid, decorated with Monte Sol pattern, c1965, 4in (10cm) high.
£25–30
$35–45 ⊞ CHI
Susan Williams-Ellis was inspired to design this pattern while breakfasting in the Monte Sol Hotel, Ibiza.

A Portmeirion rolling pin, decorated with Tivoli pattern, 1960s, 13in (33cm) long.
£85–95
$125–140 ⊞ CHI

► **A Portmeirion storage jar with wooden lid,** decorated with a picture of the *Great Republic*, c1965, 8½in (21.5cm) high.
£50–60
$75–90 ⊞ CHI

A Portmeirion storage jar, decorated with Samarkand pattern, c1965, 4in (10cm) high.
£55–65
$80–95 ⊞ CHI

A Portmeirion Sugar shaker, decorated with Dolphins pattern, c1965, 5in (12.5cm) high.
£70–80
$100–115 ⊞ CHI

◄ **A Portmeirion Tea storage jar,** decorated with Dolphins pattern, c1965, 4in (10cm) high.
£130–150
$200–220 ⊞ CHI

► **A Portmeirion Cold Cream jar,** 1960s–70s, 6in (15cm) high.
£25–30
$35–45 ⊞ CHI

A pot lid, inscribed 'Cold Cream', 19thC, 2½in (6.5cm) diam.
£10–15
$15–20 ⚒ BBR
This 19th-century pot lid is identical to the print reproduced on the Portmeirion jar (see left), and both must have come from the same Kirkham's copper plate.

A Portmeirion chicken, 1960s–70s, 7in (18cm) long.
£60–75
$90–110 ⊞ CHI

Four Portmeirion mugs, by John Caffley, from the Zodiac series, c1970, 4in (10cm) high.
£20–25
$30–35 each ⊞ CHI

A Portmeirion tea and coffee service, comprising coffee pot, teapot, six cups and saucers, milk jug and sugar bowl, decorated with Magic City pattern, c1966, coffee pot 12½in (32cm) high.
£125–140
$180–200 ⊞ PrB

A Portmeirion bottle, decorated with Red Peppers pattern, 1970s, 10in (25.5cm) diam.
£8–10
$12–15 ⊞ Law

◀ A Portmeirion duck, signed by Susan Williams-Ellis in 1975, 12in (30.5cm) long.
£85–100
$125–145 ⊞ CHI

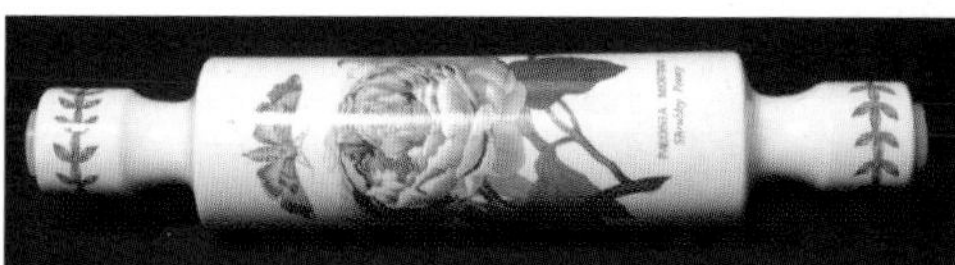

A Portmeirion rolling pin, from the Botanic Garden series, decorated with Peony pattern, 1970s, 13in (33cm) long.
£70–80
$100–115 ⊞ CHI

A Portmeirion storage jar with wooden lid, decorated with Oranges and Lemons pattern, c1975, 4½in (11.5cm) high.
£15–20
$20–30 ⊞ CHI

A Portmeirion vase, from the Botanic Garden series, c1983, 11in (28cm) high.
£35–45
$50–65 ⊞ CHI

Pot Lids

'Shooting Bears, by F. & R. Pratt, 19thC, 3in (7.5cm) diam.
£80–90
$115–130 JBL

▶ **'Our Pets',** by F. & R. Pratt, c1850, 4in (10cm) diam.
£240–280
$350–400 SAS

'Our Home', by F. & R. Pratt, c1850, 4in (10cm) diam.
£240–280
$350–400 SAS

'Dublin Industrial Exhibition 1853', by F. & R. Pratt, c1853, 4¾in (12cm) diam.
£100–120
$145–175 SAS

'War' and 'The Thirsty Soldier', by F. & R. Pratt, 19thC, 4¼in (11cm) diam, in moulded frames.
£80–100
$115–145 each SWO

Further reading

Miller's Bottles & Pot Lids: A Collector's Guide,
Miller's Publications, 2002

'Embarking for the East', by F. & R. Pratt, c1855, 4¾in (12cm) diam.
£100–120
$145–175 SAS

▶ **'Victoria Cherry Tooth Paste',** 1890–1900, 3¾in (9.5cm) wide.
£220–250
$320–360 BBR

'Wellington', by F. & R. Pratt, c1850, 4½in (11.5cm) diam.
£130–180
$200–260 JBL

'Dangerous Skating', by F. & R. Pratt, c1855, 3¼in (8.5cm) diam, with base.
£90–110
$130–160 SAS

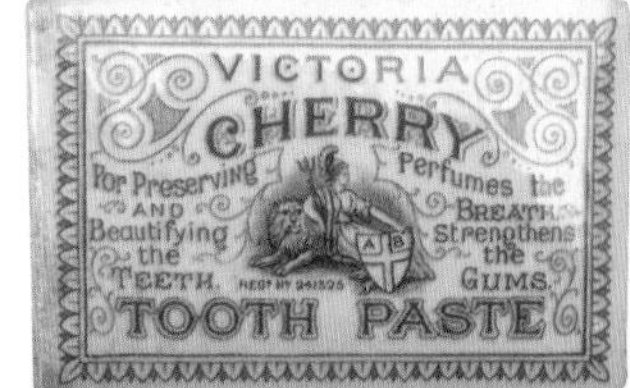

'Cucumber Winter Cream, Chave & Jackson, Chemists, Hereford', 1890–1900, 3¼in (8.5cm) diam.
£270–300
$400–440 ⚒ BBR

'Cold Cream of Roses, prepared and sold by Eugene Rimmel', 1890–1900, 3in (7.5cm) diam.
£120–140
$175–200 ⚒ BBR

'Wright's Gold Medal Shaving Compound', late 19thC, 3½in (9cm) diam.
£700–850
$1,100–1,250 ⚒ BBR

'Jules Hauel Perfumier Philadelphia', late 19thC, 3¾in (9.5cm) diam.
£400–450
$580–650 ⚒ BBR

'Ambrosial Cream for Shaving', 1890–1900, 3¼in (8.5cm) diam.
£50–60
$75–90 ⚒ BBR

'Rimmels Coral Tooth Paste', late 19thC, 3¼in (8.5cm) diam.
£250–300
$350–580 ⚒ BBR

'Worsley Wholesale Perfumer Philadelphia, late 19thC, 3½in (9cm) diam.
£700–800
$1,000–1,150 ⚒ BBR

Rare pot lids

Many of the commercial pot lids shown here are very rare pieces in terms of colour, condition and transfer quality, hence their high value.

◄ **'Rose Cold Cream, Cornell & Cornell, Ipswich',** 1900–10, 2½in (6.5cm) diam.
£50–60
$75–90 ⚒ BBR

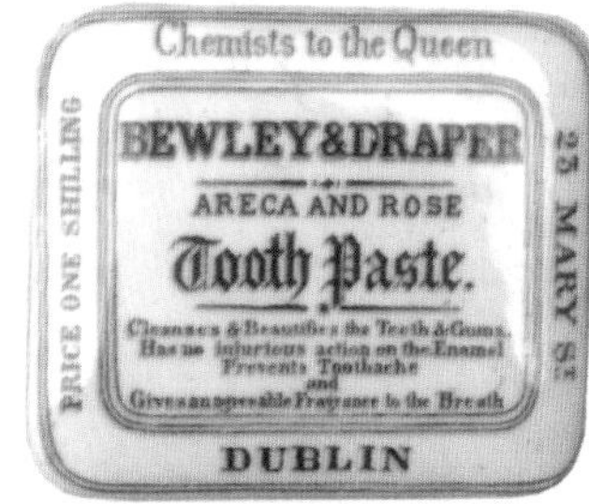

'Bewley & Draper Areca and Rose Tooth Paste', 1910–20, 2¾in (7cm) diam.
£160–190
$230–275 ⚒ BBR

◄ **'Crosse & Blackwell Anchovy Paste',** 1910–20, 3¼in (9cm) diam.
£15–20
$20–30 ⚒ BBR

Quimper

◄ **A pair of Quimper faïence bowls,** HB monogram, 19thC, 11in (28cm) diam.
£150–180
$220–260 G(L)

A Quimper dish, c1900, 12in (30.5cm) diam.
£170–200
$250–290 ⊞ MLL

A pair of Quimper two-handled bowls, early 20thC, 4½in (11cm) diam.
£30–40
$45–60 G(L)

A Quimper jug, 1920, 6in (15cm) high.
£50–60
$75–90 ⊞ MLL

A Quimper cruet, modelled as two chicks, c1920, 4in (10cm) wide.
£60–70
$90–100 ⊞ MLL

A Quimper presentation box, 1930, 5in (12.5cm) wide.
£50–60
$75–90 ⊞ MLL

A pair of Quimper dishes, 1930, 3in (7.5cm) diam.
£30–40
$45–60 ⊞ MLL

A Quimper tea service, comprising eight pieces, 1930, tray 14in (35.5cm) diam.
£400–450
$580–650 ⊞ MLL

► **A Quimper jug,** 1930, 7in (18cm) high.
£60–70
$90–100 ⊞ MLL

A Quimper puzzle jug, 1930, 5½in (14cm) high.
£145–165
$200–240 ⊞ MLL

A Quimper vase, designed by P. Fouillen, c1930, 6in (15cm) high.
£100–120
$145–175 ⊞ SER

A Quimper egg cup, c1940, 3in (7.5cm) diam.
£20–25
$30–35 ⊞ SER

A Quimper bagpipe dish, 1930, 8in (20.5cm) wide.
£70–80
$100–115 ⊞ MLL

A Quimper plate, c1940, 10in (25.5cm) diam.
£40–45
$60–65 ⊞ SER

A Quimper bagpipe dish, c1940, 6in (15cm) wide.
£25–30
$35–45 ⊞ SER

A Quimper butter dish, c1940, 8½in (21.5cm) long.
£40–45
$60–65 ⊞ SER

A Quimper wall pocket, c1940, 9in (23cm) high.
£25–30
$35–45 ⊞ SER

A Quimper figure of St Anne, c1940, 3in (7.5cm) high.
£45–50
$65–75 ⊞ SER

► **A Quimper bowl,** marked HB Quimper, 1943–68, 5½in (14cm) diam.
£80–100
$115–145 ⊞ SER

Radford

A Radford vase, decorated with flowers, c1930, 6in (15cm) high.
£90–100
$130–145 ⊞ RH

A Radford vase, decorated with flowers, c1930, 5in (12.5cm) high.
£90–100
$130–145 ⊞ RH

A Radford vase, decorated with a landscape with trees, Burslem mark, c1930, 6in (15cm) high.
£180–200
$250–300 ⊞ BEV

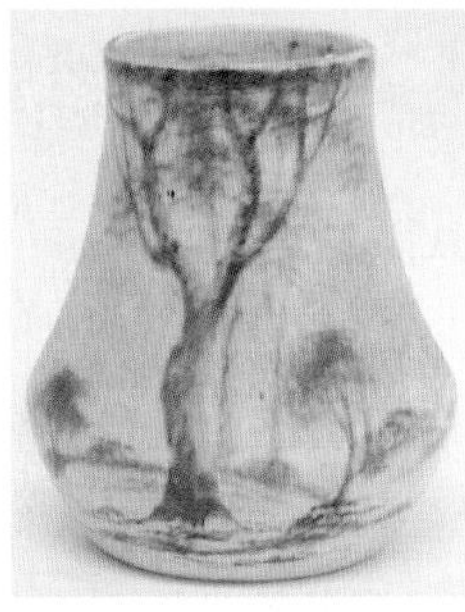

A Radford earthenware vase, for Woods, decorated with a landscape, Burslem mark, c1930, 6in (15cm) high.
£90–100
$130–145 ⚒ G(L)

A Radford hand-painted vase, with four lips, c1930, 6¾in (17cm) high.
£60–70
$90–100 ⊞ BEV

◄ **A Radford jug,** decorated with primroses, c1930, 3in (7.5cm) high.
£40–50
$60–75 ⊞ RH

A Radford vase, decorated with Broom pattern, c1930, 6in (15cm) high.
£80–110
$115–160 ⊞ RH

A Radford bowl, decorated with Broom pattern, c1930, 8in (20.5cm) diam.
£50–60
$75–90 ⊞ RH

A Radford vase, decorated with flowers, signed, c1935, 6in (15cm) high.
£25–30
$35–45 ⊞ WAC

A Radford jug, decorated with Broom pattern, 1930s, 6in (15cm) high.
£80–90
$115–130 ⊞ BEV

A Radford vase, decorated with flowers, 1930s, 5in (12.5cm) high.
£85–100
$125–145 ⊞ BEV

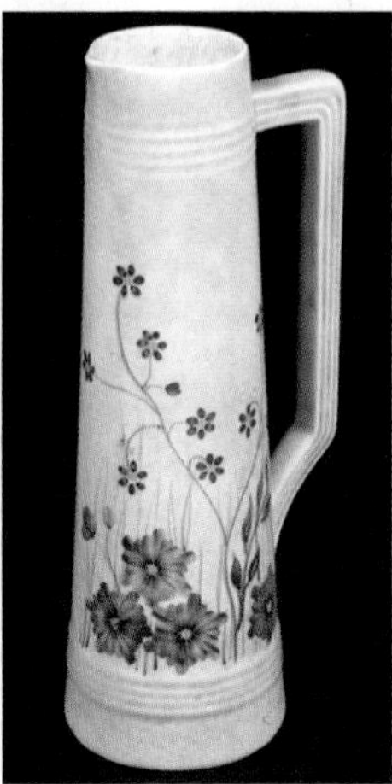

A Radford jug, decorated with flowers, 1940s, 11in (28cm) high.
£130–150
$200–220 ⊞ BEV

Charlotte & Frederick Rhead

A Frederick Rhead Cairo ware Venice/Agra vase, by Royal Cauldon, c1925, 10½in (26.5cm) high.
£180–200
$260–300 ⊞ DSG

A Frederick Rhead tankard, by Royal Cauldon, c1925, 7½in (19cm) high.
£180–200
$260–300 ⊞ DSG

A Charlotte Rhead vase, with hand-painted decoration, c1940, 4½in (11.5cm) high.
£110–130
$160–200 ⊞ PrB

A Charlotte Rhead vase, by Royal Cauldon, tube-lined with a broad band of fruit and leaves, small chip, c1930, 6½in (16.5cm) high.
£50–60
$75–90 ⚒ G(L)

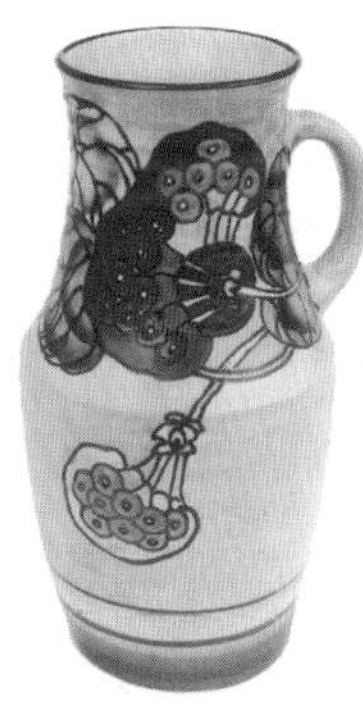

A Charlotte Rhead single-handled vase, by Bursley, with tube-lined decoration, pattern No. 1987, shape No. 125, c1930, 10½in (26.5cm) high.
£350–400
$500–580 ⊞ BDA

Facts in brief

Both talented pottery designers, Charlotte Rhead (1885–1947) was the sister of Frederick Hurten Rhead (1880–1942). Charlotte worked for a number of different factories and her works are very sought after. Early examples have a tube-lined "C. Rhead" signature. Later wares have a transfer mark of her full signature.

Royal Copenhagen

A Royal Copenhagen model of a faun, c1923, 4in (10cm) high.
£80–100
$115–145 ⊞ PSA

► A Royal Copenhagen model of a shepherd and lambs, c1968, 8in (20.5cm) high.
£300–350
$450–500 ⊞ PSA

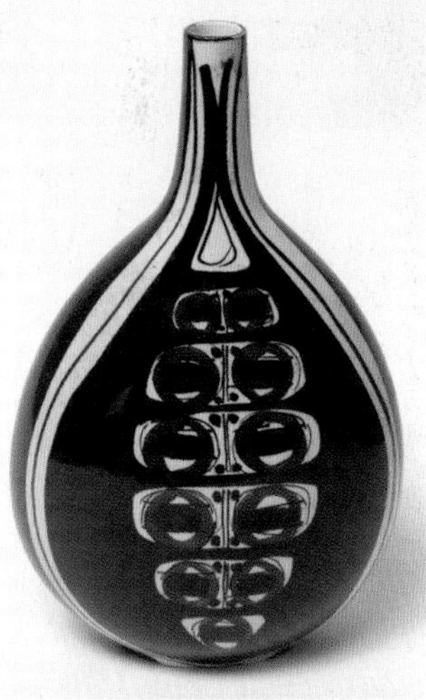

A Royal Copenhagen faïence vase, c1970, 11in (28cm) high.
£100–125
$145–180 ⊞ HarC

Royal Winton

A Royal Winton hand-painted vase, 1930, 8in (20.5cm) high.
£170–200
$250–300 ⊞ BEV

Cross Reference
See Chintz Ware (page 97)

► **A Royal Winton Olde Inne teapot,** c1930, 6in (15cm) high.
£60–70
$90–100 ⊞ RH

A Royal Winton Old England butter dish, modelled as an English country cottage, c1930, 5in (12cm) high.
£60–70
$90–100 ⊞ RH

► **A Royal Winton hand-painted lustre vase,** c1940, 13in (33cm) high.
£220–250
$320–360 ⊞ BEV

Rye

◄ **A Rye Pottery plate,** moulded with leaves and fruiting vines, c1890, 9½in (24cm) diam.
£100–120
$145–175 ⚒ G(L)

A Rye Pottery six-handled miniature bowl, c1900, 2½in (6.5cm) diam.
£100–120
$150–175 ⊞ DSG

A Rye Pottery vase, moulded with hops, 1890, 4in (10cm) high.
£110–130
$160–190 ⊞ DSG

◄ **A Rye Pottery jug,** c1950, 3½in (9cm) high.
£12–15
$18–20 ⊞ PrB

► **A Rye Pottery bottle stopper,** designed by David Sharp, in the form of a policeman's head, 1950s, 5in (12.5cm) high.
£20–25
$30–35 ⊞ PrB

Shelley

Shelley (1872–1966) produced a wide range of high-quality tableware in the 1920s and '30s. During the 1930s, the pottery experimented with the latest geometric designs. The Vogue (1930–33) and Mode (1930–31) shapes both came with solid triangular handles, but although fashionable, these made the cups difficult to hold, resulting in short production runs. As such, these shapes are both very collectable today. Probably in response to their lack of success, Shelley introduced a design with an elongated open triangular handle, the Eve shape (1932–38). Other best-selling shapes of the inter-war period include Queen Anne, introduced in 1926, and Regent (1932–39) with its circular handle. Queen Anne cups had a curving handle; their eight panels provided a perfect surface for painting and printing and some 170 patterns have been recorded in this design.

Shelley china came in a huge variety of decorations ranging from transfer-printed chintz ware to the hand-painted Harmony ware, in which colours were poured onto the shape as it turned on the wheel, creating a characteristic streaky pattern.

A Shelley jug, with a hand-painted design of monks catching butterflies, c1910, 7in (18cm) high.
£170–200
$250–300 ⊞ RH

A Shelley Vincent trio, decorated with Poppy pattern, 1924, cup 4in (10cm) high.
£50–60
$75–90 ⊞ CoCo

Two Shelley napkin rings, decorated with Pansy Chintz pattern, c1930, 2in (5cm) diam.
£50–60 each
$75–90 each ⊞ BD

◄ **A Shelley vase,** decorated with a banded design, c1930, 6½in (16.5cm) high.
£70–80
$100–115 ⊞ PrB

A Shelley Boo-Boo Mushroom House teapot, designed by Mabel Lucie Attwell, with associated lid, c1926, 5in (12.5cm) high.
£240–280
$350–400 ⊞ G(L)

A Shelley vase, decorated with a banded design, c1930, 8in (20.5cm) high.
£85–95
$125–140 ⊞ PrB

A Shelley bowl and platter, with streaked decoration, No. 8823/A, c1930, bowl 8¾in (22cm) diam.
£70–85
$100–125 ⚒ SWO

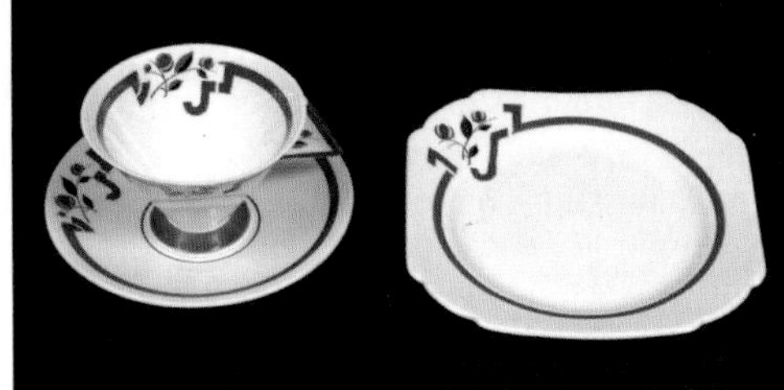

A Shelley Vogue trio, decorated with J pattern, 1930, plate 7in (18cm) square.
£300–350
$450–500 ⊞ BEV

A Shelley Harmony vase, c1930, 7in (18cm) high.
£70–80
$100–115 ⊞ PrB

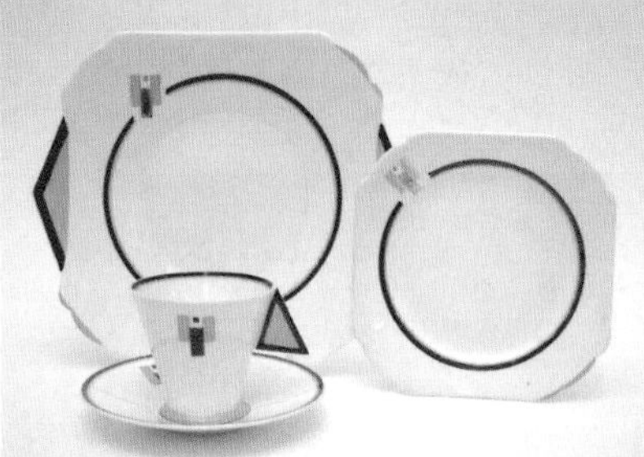

A Shelley bone china part tea service, comprising 17 pieces, printed and enamelled with abstract motifs, the cups with solid triangular handles, pattern No. 11791, 2 cups cracked, c1930.
£420–520
$620–750 ⚒ G(L)

A Shelley Queen Anne cup and saucer, decorated with Cottage pattern, c1930, cup 3in (7.5cm) high.
£65–75
$95–110 ⊞ RH

◀ **A Shelley Regent trio,** decorated with Anemone pattern, 1932–34, cup 3in (7.5cm) high.
£80–90
$115–130
⊞ BEV

A Shelley Queen Anne trio, c1930, plate 6in (15cm) square.
£100–125
$145–180 ⊞ BD

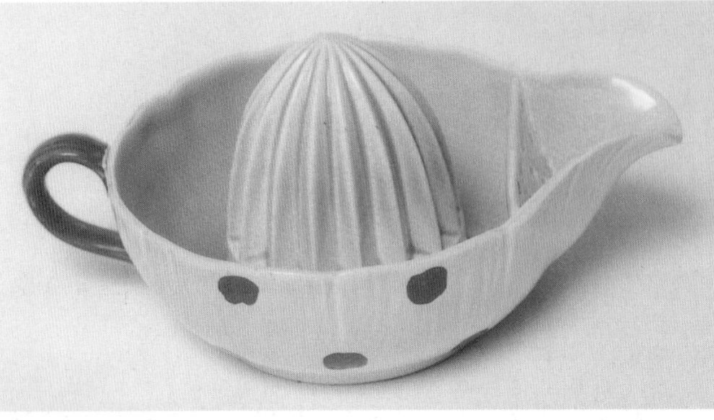

A Shelley grapefruit squeezer, designed by Mabel Lucie Attwell, c1935, 6in (15cm) long.
£175–195
$255–280 ⊞ MEM

A Shelley miniature cup and saucer, decorated with flowers, c1945, 2in (5cm) high.
£160–180
$230–260 ⊞ RH

Staffordshire

A Staffordshire figure of Hygeia, c1780, 8in (20.5cm) high.
£225–250
$325–360 ⊞ SER
In Greek mythology Hygeia was the goddess of health.

A Staffordshire spill vase, entitled Poor Maria, c1780, 7in (18cm) high.
£245–275
$350–400 ⊞ SER

A Staffordshire figure of Paul Pry, by Enoch Wood, c1820, 6in (15cm) high.
£500–550
$720–800 ⊞ JHo

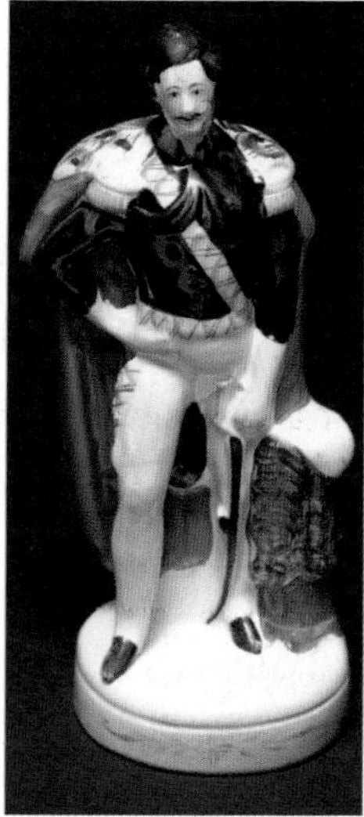

A Staffordshire figure of Prince Albert, c1845, 11in (28cm) high.
£150–200
$220–290 ⊞ ML

A Staffordshire figure of Charles Haddon Spurgeon, 1855, 12in (30.5cm) high.
£400–450
$580–650 ⊞ TUN

◀ **A Staffordshire pastille burner,** modelled as a cottage, c1840, 11½in (29cm) high.
£170–200
$250–290 ⚒ G(L)

▶ **A Staffordshire group of a musician and a dancer,** c1860, 8in (20.5cm) high.
£130–145
$190–200 ⊞ ML

A pair of Staffordshire split-leg models of dogs, with copper lustre decoration, 1860–65, 10in (25.5cm) high.
£350–400
$500–580 ⊞ ML

A pair of Staffordshire figures of the Prince and Princess of Wales, c1862, 9½in (24cm) high.
£340–380
$490–550 ⊞ SER

A pair of Staffordshire figures of a fisherman and his wife, c1880, 8in (20.5cm) high.
£150–170
$220–250 ⊞ ACO

A Staffordshire figure of a sailor, pipe missing, 19thC, 12in (30.5cm) high.
£100–120
$145–175 ⚒ G(L)

A pair of Staffordshire portrait figures of a fisherman and his wife, 19thC, 14in (35.5cm) high.
£150–180
$220–260 ⚒ G(L)

A pair of Staffordshire figures of gardeners, c1880, 11½in (29cm) high.
£250–280
$360–410 ⊞ SER

A Staffordshire group, entitled Princess Royal Heir of Prussia, damaged, c1880, 15¾in (40cm) high.
£60–80
$90–115 ⚒ SWO

A Staffordshire figure of a huntsman, c1880, 7in (18cm) high.
£165–195
$240–280 ⊞ SER

◄ A Staffordshire spill vase, modelled as a gypsy and companion, c1880, 11in (28cm) high.
£200–225
$290–325 ⊞ ACO

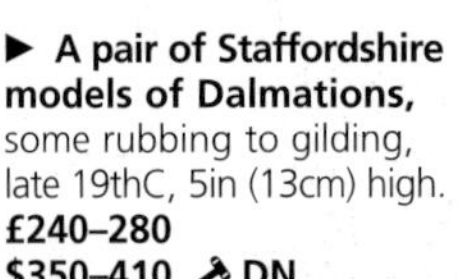

► A pair of Staffordshire models of Dalmations, some rubbing to gilding, late 19thC, 5in (13cm) high.
£240–280
$350–410 ⚒ DN

A Staffordshire group of Samson and the Lion, 19thC, 7½in (19cm) high.
£120–150
$175–220 ⚒ BWL

Studio Pottery

A Compton Pottery candle holder, c1920, 5in (12.5cm) high.
£50–60
$75–90 ⊞ DSG

A Danesby Ware stoneware jug, with stylized design around rim, c1930, 7in (18cm) high.
£75–85
$110–125 ⊞ RUSK

◄ A Winchcombe Pottery jug, c1960, 7in (18cm) high.
£65–75
$95–110 ⊞ BRU

► An Upchurch Pottery two-handled dish, c1930, 6in (15cm) diam.
£40–50
$60–75 ⊞ DSG

A Clay Pitts pottery jug, c1960, 11in (28cm) high.
£25–35
$35–50 ⊞ BSA

An Iden Pottery vase, c1970, 4in (10cm) high.
£14–16
$18–22 ⊞ PrB

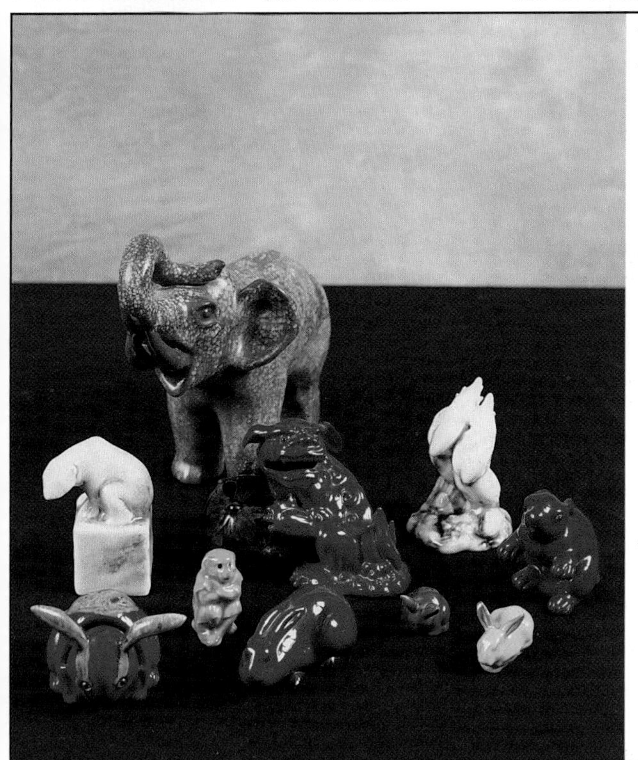

Tiles

Church floor tiles were produced in Britain from the Middle Ages but, with the dissolution of the monastaries in the 16th century, the craft disappeared. In the 17th century, blue-and-white Delft tiles were imported from Holland and English potteries began to produce similar tin-glazed tiles. Designs were hand-painted, but in 1756 John Sadler pioneered the art of transferring engraved prints onto tiles. Although this technique was to prove important in the Victorian period, tile-making again died out from the late 18th century until the 1840s, its revival coinciding with another golden age of church building. Encouraged by the celebrated Victorian Gothic architect Augustus Welby Pugin, the Minton pottery began to produce encaustic (inlaid clay) floor tiles inspired by medieval techniques and prototypes. Herbert Minton also invested in the new process of clay dust pressing (powdered clay pressed between two metal dies) which was to become the favourite means of tile-making.

The housing boom of the 1880s, the proliferation of both secular and public buildings, greater concern with hygiene and, of course, the Victorian love of decoration, all helped to fuel a massive expansion of the industry. In the home, tiles decorated hall floors, kitchen walls, bathroom surrounds and fireplaces, as well as pieces of furniture such as washstands. Shops were often tiled throughout for easy cleaning, and public buildings made extensive use of floor and wall tiles.

Numerous potteries produced tiles. Styles ranged from the fine hand-painted examples produced as individual commissions by Arts and Crafts designers such as William de Morgan, to the mass-produced tiles churned out in their thousands by major factories, and values vary accordingly today. Maker, subject, condition and rarity all affect the price. The back of a tile can be very important when it comes to identification; look out for factory stamps, design registration marks and sometimes even pencilled notes, indicating where the tile was to be placed.

A glazed terracotta tile, 16thC, 5½in (14cm) square.
£120–140
$175–200 ⊞ TRI

A set of majolica tiles, Dutch, 17thC, 5in (12.5cm) square.
£270–300
$400–440 ⊞ OLA

A tile, decorated with a rural scene, Dutch, 18thC, 5in (12.5cm) square.
£65–75
$95–110 ⊞ JHo

A tile, decorated with a lock scene, Dutch, 18thC, 5in (12.5cm) square.
£38–42
$60–65 ⊞ JHo

Two Delft tiles, one decorated with a bird, the other with a fishing boat, Dutch, 18thC, each 5in (12.5cm) square.
£15–20
$20–30 ⚒ G(L)

Twenty-eight blue and white Delft tiles, Dutch, 18thC, each 5in (12.5cm) square.
£230–280
$330–400 ⚒ SWO

A blue and white tile, London, 1760, 5in (12.5cm) square.
£90–110
$130–160 ⊞ JHo

A black and white tile, transfer-printed with a gentleman and two ladies in a landscape, Liverpool, 1765, 5in (12.5cm) square.
£180–210
$260–300 ⊞ JHo

Two Morrison & Co blue and white tiles, c1830, 5½in (14cm) square.
£30–35
$45–50 ⊞ OLA

A set of four Minton & Hollins earthenware tiles, painted by G. E. Cook with classical portrait busts within roundels, two repaired, 19thC, each, 8in (20.5cm) square.
£150–180
$220–260 ⚒ G(L)

A Victorian Wedgwood tile, entitled February, depicting a boy and girl in the snow, 6in (15cm) square.
£120–135
$175–195 ⊞ SaH

Sets/pairs

Unless otherwise stated, any description which refers to 'a set' or 'a pair' includes a guide price for the entire set or the pair, even though the illustration may show only a single item.

An encaustic floor tile, 19thC, 6in (15cm) square.
£8–10
$12–15 ⊞ OLA

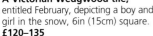

An encaustic floor tile, 19thC, 6in (15cm) square.
£8–10
$12–15 ⊞ OLA

◄ **A Victorian tile,** 6in (15cm) square.
£24–28
$35–45 ⊞ SaH

A set of eight Minton tiles, c1880, 6in (15cm) square.
£90–100
$130–145 ⊞ OLA

A Minton Pastimes series tile, depicting two men playing bowls, c1880, 6in (15cm) square.
£45–55
$65–80 ⊞ SaH

A tile, c1880, 6in (15cm) square.
£9–12
$15–17 ⊞ AL

A Wedgwood tile, depicting a fairy, c1885, 8in (20.5cm) square.
£120–135
$175–195 ⊞ SaH

◄ **A Minton tile,** c1890, 6in (15cm) square.
£12–15
$15–20 ⊞ AL

A tile, decorated with flowers, c1890, 6in (15cm) square.
£14–18
$20–30 ⊞ SaH

◄ **A Pilkington's tile,** designed by Louis F. Day, c1890, 6in (15cm) square.
£34–38
$50–60 ⊞ SaH

A Prehistoric series tile, with raised design of a dragon/dinosaur, c1880, 6in (15cm) square.
£30–35
$45–50 ⊞ SaH

Three Minton blue and white tiles, entitled Ambition, Ignorance and Idleness, c1885, 6in (15cm) square.
£130–150
$190–220 each ⊞ SaH

A Minton tile, decorated with lilies, c1860, 12 x 6in (15 x 30.5cm).
£42–48
$60–75 ⊞ SaH

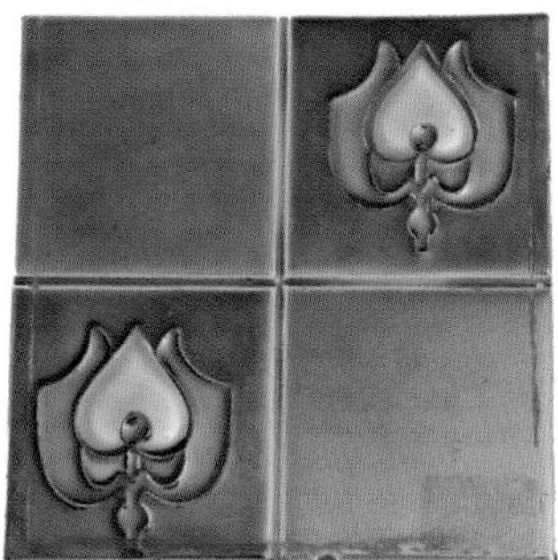

A tile, with Art Nouveau decoration, c1890, 6in (15cm) square.
£10–15
$15–20 ⊞ AL

A tile, with raised decoration, c1900, 3¼in (8cm) square.
£3–5
$4–7 ⊞ C&R

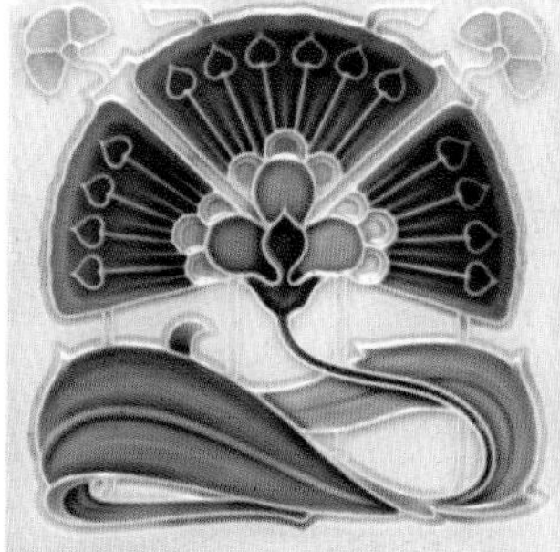

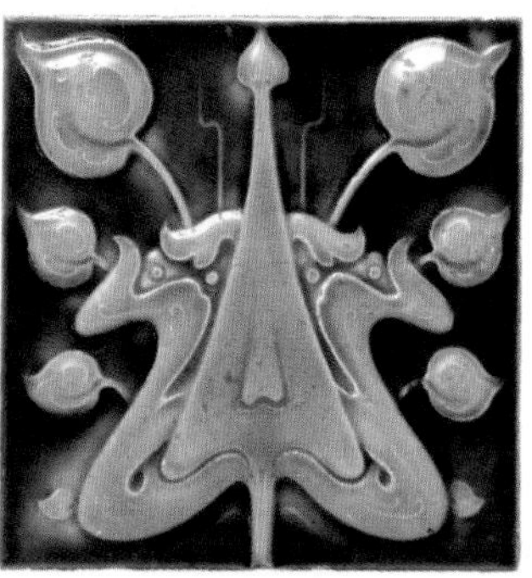

A tile, decorated with lilies, c1896, 6in (15cm) square.
£10–12
$15–17 ⊞ AL

A tile, with raised shell decoration, c1900, 3¼in (8cm) square.
£3–5
$4–7 ⊞ C&R

◄ **A tile,** with Art Nouveau decoration, c1915, 6in (15cm) square.
£34–38
$50–60 ⊞ SaH

Three Pilkington's lustre tiles, each painted with a tree, early 20thC, 6 x 3in (15 x 7.5cm), together with three floral-decorated tiles.
£620–700
$880–1,000 ⚒ S(O)

◄ **A blue tile,** with Art Nouveau decoration, c1915, 6in (15cm) square.
£40–50
$60–75 ⊞ SaH

A tile, with raised floral decoration, c1900, 6in (15cm) square.
£10–12
$15–17 ⊞ AL

A Carter & Co encaustic tile panel, decorated with foxgloves, c1902, 11¾ x 6in (30 x 15cm).
£160–180
$230–260 ⊞ DSG

A set of eight Art Nouveau Minton fireplace tiles, 6in (15cm) square.
£100–120
$145–175 ⊞ OLA

Troika

A Troika trial pot, impressed trident and St Ives mark, early 1960s, 4½in (11.5cm) high.
£300–350
$440–500 ⊞ TRO

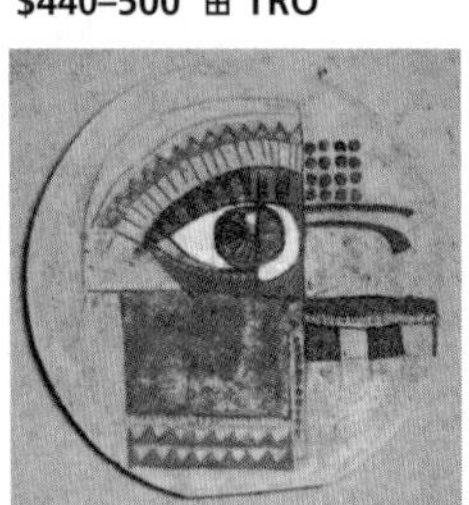

A Troika offset chimney vase, St Ives and MP mark, early 1960s, 8in (20.5cm) high.
£300–350
$440–500 ⊞ TRO

◄ A Troika wheel vase, St Ives and HC mark, mid-1960s, 12in (30.5cm) high.
£300–350
$440–500 ⊞ TRO

A Troika flask vase, impressed trident and St Ives mark, early 1960s, 6½in (16.5cm) high.
£750–850
$1,100–1,250 ⊞ TRO

A Troika globe/ball, St Ives and AB mark, early 1970s, 8in (20.5cm) high.
£675–750
$975–1,100 ⊞ TRO

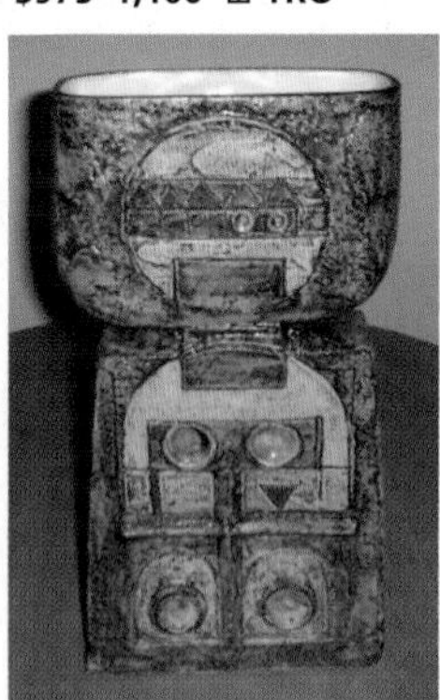

A Troika vase, with a double base, Troika and AB mark, late 1970s, 12in (30.5cm) high.
£675–750
$975–1,100 ⊞ TRO

► Two Troika vases, c1970, tallest 6¾in (17cm) high.
£100–120
$145–175 ⚒ SWO

A Troika wheel vase, 1960s, 7¾in (19.5cm) high.
£250–275
$360–400 ⊞ PrB

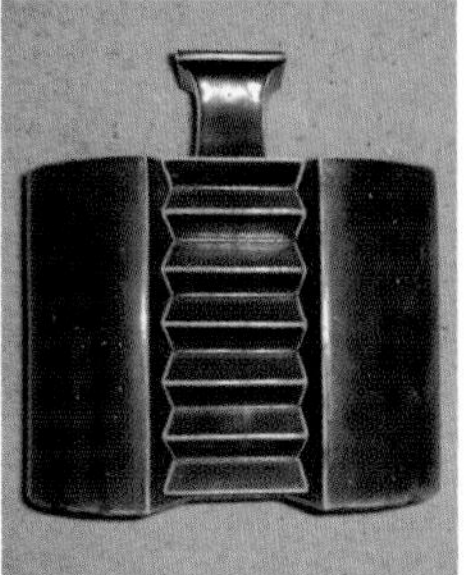

A Troika lamp base, marked AB, early 1970s, 10in (25.5cm) high.
£1,300–1,500
$1,900–2,150 ⊞ TRO
This lamp base was inspired by the abstract works of the Rumanian sculptor Constantin Brancusi (1876–1957).

History

Troika was founded in St Ives in 1963 by an artist, a potter and an architect, and ran for about 20 years. Each individual piece was conceived as a scuptural work of art, and today Troika pottery has become highly collectable.

Wade

A Wadeheath hand-painted honey pot, c1930, 4½in (11.5cm) high.
£40–45
$60–65 ⊞ CoCo

A Wadeheath jug, with Art Deco handle, c1930, 12in (30.5cm) high.
£90–100
$130–145 ⊞ RH

A Wadeheath hand-painted jug, 1930s, 8in (20.5cm) high.
£55–65
$80–95 ⊞ CoCo

A pair of Wadeheath vases, with inserts, c1930, 5½in (14cm) high.
£150–180
$220–260 ⊞ RH

► A Wade model of a rhinoceros, c1950–60, 5¼in (13.5cm) high.
£160–180
$230–160
BBR

► A Wadeheath musical jug, embossed with Snow White and the Seven Dwarfs, the handle with birds and squirrel, 1930s–40s, 8in (20.5cm) high.
£1,000–1,200
$1,500–1,750 Pott

Wedgwood

A Wedgwood blue and white coffee can, c1815, 2½in (6.5cm) high.
£70–80
$100–115 ⊞ JAY

A Wedgwood majolica two-handled dish, embossed in relief with cabbage leaves, handle repaired, foot rim chips, impressed marks, 1871, 13¾in (35cm) wide.
£180–220
$260–320 ⚒ FHF

A Wedgwood earthenware plate, with embossed vines and oak leaf trellis pattern, 1876, 9in (23cm) diam.
£30–40
$45–60 ⊞ CoCo

◄ A Wedgwood lustre bowl, decorated with Daventry pattern, c1930, 8¼in (21cm) diam.
£240–280
$350–400 ⚒ G(L)

A Wedgwood mug, designed by Keith Murray, decorated with a matt glaze, c1930, 5in (12.5cm) high.
£70–80
$100–115 ⊞ RUSK

A Wedgwood Fairyland lustre vase, decorated with Imps on a Bridge pattern, rim chips, printed marks and painted No. 25360M, c1930, 9in (23cm) high.
£750–850
$1,100–1,250 ⚒ DD
Fairyland lustre ware is extremely popular in the market place.

A Wedgwood Global vase, designed by Keith Murray, 1932–35, 7½in (19cm) high.
£250–300
$360–440 ⊞ BEV

◄ A Wedgwood coffee pot, decorated in Ashford pattern, 1950s, 9in (23cm) high.
£70–75
$100–110 ⊞ CHI

◄ **A Wedgwood Travel Series dinner service,** designed by Eric Ravilious, comprising tureen, four soup bowls and seven dinner plates, 1950s, tureen 10in (25.5cm) wide.
£450–550
$650–800 G(L)

A Wedgwood Summer Sky cruet set, 1950s, 6in (15cm) diam.
£50–55
$75–80 ⊞ CHI

A Wedgwood trio, decorated with Tigerlily pattern, 1950s, plate 7in (18cm) diam.

Cup/saucer	**£16–18**
	$20–30
Plate	**£8–10**
	$12–15 ⊞ CHI

A Wedgwood coffee pot, designed by Susie Cooper, decorated with Sunflower pattern, 1960s, 8in (20.5cm).
£85–95
$125–140 ⊞ CHI

A Wedgwood Blue Pacific coffee pot and milk jug, c1969, coffee pot 8in (20.5cm) high.

Coffee pot	**£48–50**
	$70–75
Milk jug	**£16–18**
	$20–30 ⊞ CHI

A Wedgwood teapot, designed by Susie Cooper, decorated with Keystone Gold pattern, c1969, 5in (12.5cm) high.
£70–75
$100–110 ⊞ CHI

► **A Wedgwood plate,** designed by Susie Cooper, decorated with Blue Anemone pattern, 1960s, 8in (20.5cm) diam.
£24–28
$35–45 ⊞ CHI

Worcester

A Worcester sauce boat, hand-painted, slight damage, c1770–75, 3in (7.5cm) high.
£135–155
$195–225 ⊞ WAC

A Worcester tea bowl, decorated with a floral design, c1775, 3¼in (8.5cm) diam.
£100–120
$145–175 ⊞ JAY

A Royal Worcester claret jug, with floral and gilt decoration, 1884, 8¼in (21cm) high.
£325–375
$470–570 ⊞ GRI

A pair of Royal Worcester nautilus shell vases, decorated in enamel and gilt, minor wear, with printed and impressed marks, date code for 1885, 8¾in (22cm) high.
£380–420
$560–620 ⚒ DN

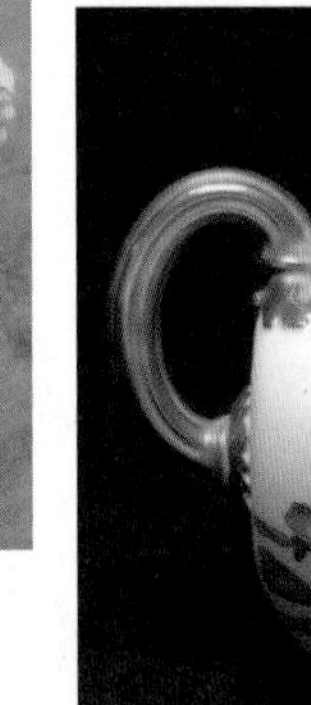

A Royal Worcester jug, c1888, 6in (15cm) high.
£160–190
$230–275 ⊞ WAC

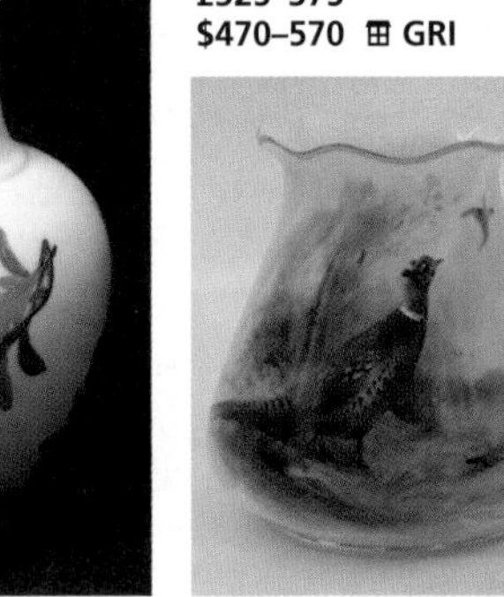

A Royal Worcester posy vase, painted by J. A. S. Stinton, signed, c1910, 3in (7.5cm) high.
£500–550
$720–800 ⊞ GRI

A pair of Royal Worcester vases, hand-painted by M. Hunt with cabbage roses , shape No. 2491, 1930, 3¼in (8.5cm) high.
£160–180
$230–260 ⚒ B(W)

Insurance values

Always insure your valuable collectables for the cost of replacing them with similar items, regardless of the original price paid. Both dealers and auctioneers can provide a valuation service for a fee.

► **A Royal Worcester coffee cup, saucer and side plate,** decorated with Royal Garden pattern, 1970s, 3½in (9cm) high.

Cup and saucer	**£28–32**
	$40–48
Side plate	**£14–16**
	$18–22 ⊞ CHI

A Worcester egg coddler, decorated with June Garland pattern, 1960s, 2in (5cm) high.
£15–20
$20–30 ⊞ CHI

Cigarette & Trade Cards

Liebig trade cards, Aïda Opera series, 1891.
£70–80
$100–115 ⊞ MUR

Lambert & Butler, Coronation Robes, set of 12, 1902.
£85–100
$125–145 ⚒ VS

British American Tobacco, Beauties, set of 25, 1903.
£85–100
$125–145 ⚒ VS

Ogden's, British Costumes from 100 BC to 1904, 40 cards, 1905.
£65–80
$100–115 ⚒ VS

Ogden's, Famous Footballers, set of 50, 1908.
£60–75
$90–110 ⚒ VS

► **Ogden's,** Boy Scouts, 5th series, set of 25, 1914.
£60–70
$90–100 ⊞ MUR

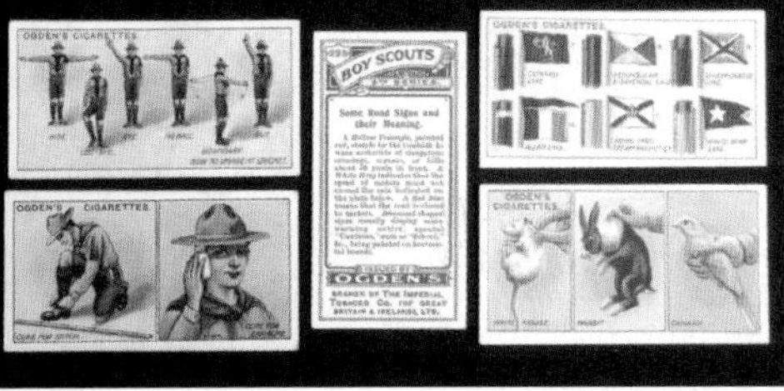

W. D. & H. O. Wills, British Birds, set of 50, 1915.
£45–50
$65–75 ⊞ MUR

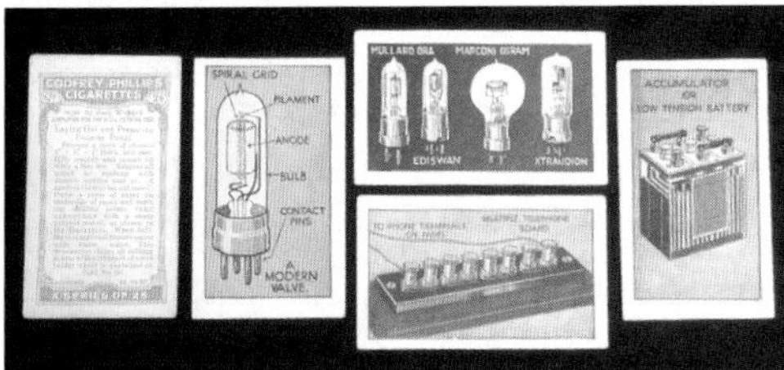

Godfrey Phillips, How to Build a Valve Amp for BDV Crystal Set, set of 25, 1922.
£65–75
$95–110 ⊞ MUR

Lambert & Butler, Motor Cars, set of 25, 1922–23.
£13–16
$15–20 ⚒ DAL

R. & J. Hill, Famous Cricketers, No. 19 missing, 39 cards, 1923.
£70–85
$100–125 VS

Major Drapkin & Co, Optical Illusion, set of 25, 1926.
£60–70
$90–100 MUR

British American Tobacco Co, Beauties, 3rd series, set of 50, 1926.
£13–16
$15–20 DAL

► **John Player & Sons,** Footballers, set of 50, 1928.
£25–30
$35–45 DAL

Ogden's, The Blue Riband of the Atlantic, set of 50, 1929.
£45–55
$65–80 VS

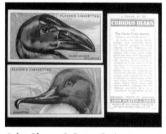

W. D. & H. O. Wills, Rugby Internationals, set of 50, 1929.
£80–90
$115–130 MUR

John Player & Sons, Curious Beaks, set of 50, 1929.
£35–40
$50–60 MUR

W. & F. Faulkner, Angling, set of 25, 1929.
£100–120
$145–175 VS

Ardath Tobacco Co, Land, Sea and Air, set of 50, 1935.
£55–65
$80–95 MUR

Ogden's, Motor Races, set of 50, 1931.
£65–75
$100–110 VS

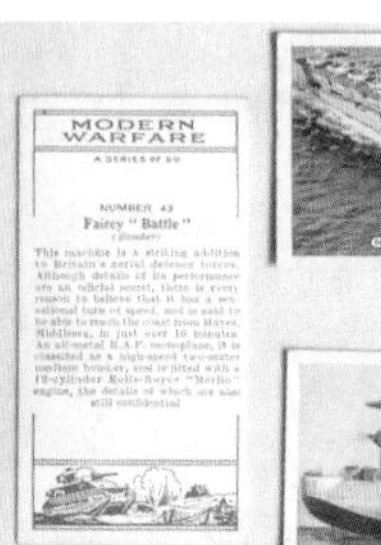

► **British American Tobacco Co,** Modern Warfare, set of 50, 1936.
£13–16
$15–20 DAL

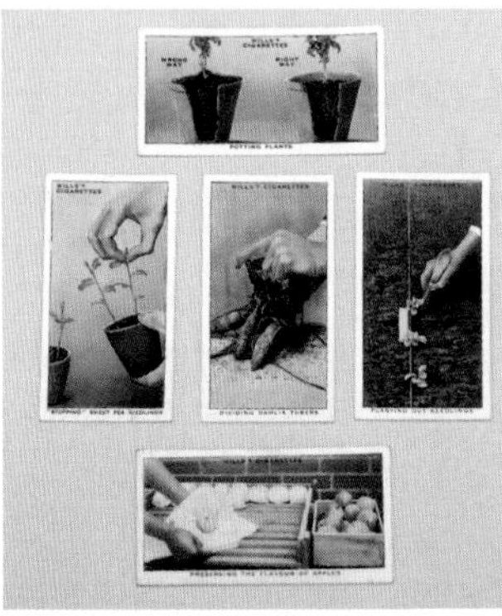

W. D. & H. O. Wills, Garden Hints, set of 50, 1938.
£8–10
$10–15 ⊞ **LCC**

John Player & Sons, Cricketers, 1938.
£45–55
$65–80 ⊞ **LCC**

W. D. & H. O. Wills, Happy Families, set of 32, 1939.
£65–75
$100–110 **VS**

◄ **A. & B. C. Gum,** Batman, set of 55, 1963.
£55–65
$80–100 ⊞ **MUR**

◄ **Primrose Confectionery,** Popeye, 4th series, set of 50, 1963.
£10–15
$15–20 ⊞ **MUR**

Barratt & Co, Captain Scarlet and The Mysterons, set of 50, 1960s, mounted in Barratt booklet.
£65–75
$100–110 **VS**

Marlow Civil Engineering, Famous Clowns, set of 25, 1990.
£25–30
$35–45 ⊞ **MUR**

W. D. & H. O. Wills, Britain's Steam Railways, Castella Panatellas series, set of 30, 1998.
£35–40
$50–60 ⊞ **LCC**

Comics & Annuals

Action Comics, No. 248, published by DC Comics, 1962.
£12–15
$15–20 ⊞ CoC

***Aquaman* comic,** No. 1, 1963.
£75–85
$110–125 ⚒ CBP

***Blade* comic,** *Wizard* Nos. 1/2, published by Marvel Comics, 1999.
£20–25
$30–35 ⊞ NOS

Adventure Comics, No. 304, 1963.
£12–15
$15–20 ⊞ CoC

The Beano Comic, No. 4, 1938.
£340–375
$500–550 ⚒ CBP

***Buffy The Vampire Slayer* comic,** No. 1, published by Dark Horse Comics, 1998.
£12–15
$15–20 ⊞ NOS

◀ ***Amazing Spider-Man* comic,** No. 1, 1963.
£500–550
$720–800 ⚒ CBP

***The Amazing Spider-Man* comic,** No. 36, pubished by Marvel Comics, December 2001.
£25–30
$35–45 ⊞ NOS

◀ ***The Beano Comic,*** No. 14, 1938.
£375–425
$550–620 ⚒ CBP

◄ ***Conan The Barbarian* comic,** No. 37, published by Marvel Comics, April 1974.
£8–10
$12–15 ⊞ NOS

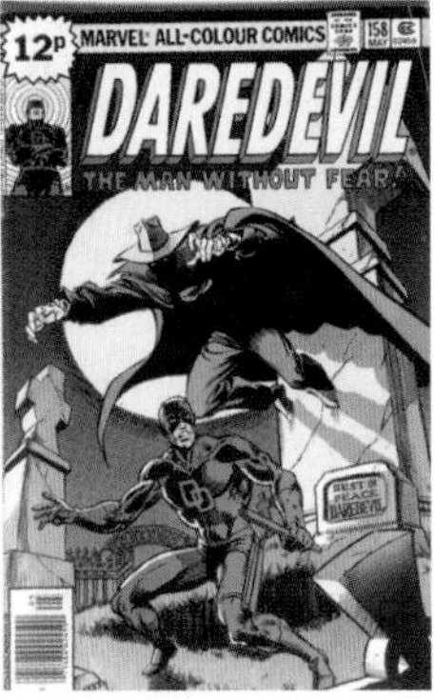

***Daredevil* comic,** No. 158, first ever Frank Miller issue, published by Marvel Comics, 1979.
£14–16
$20–25 ⊞ CoC

***Elseworlds 80-Page Giant* comic,** No. 1, published by DC Comics, August 1999.
£90–100
$130–145 ⊞ NOS
A reference to a baby in a microwave caused this comic to be pulled, hence its desirability to collectors.

***The Dandy* comic,** No. 70, second April Fool issue, 1939.
£100–110
$145–160 ⚒ CBP

***The Daredevils* comic,** No. 5, published by Marvel Comics, May 1983.
£14–15
$20–25 ⊞ NOS

***Flash Gordon* comic,** No. 1, with bondage cover, small tear, 1950.
£75–85
$110–125 ⚒ CBP

The Dandy Monster Comic, No. 2, restored, 1940.
£440–480
$650–700 ⚒ CBP

The Dandy Monster Comic, No. 5, 1943.
£325–375
$475–550 ⚒ CBP

◄ ***Dark Mysteries* comic,** No. 19, 1954.
£85–100
$125–145 ⚒ CBP

Detective Comics, No. 290, 1961.
£12–14
$15–20 ⊞ CoC

***Green Lantern* comic,** No. 13, first *Flash* crossover, 1962.
£100–120/$145–175 ⚒ CBP

► ***The Incredible Hulk* comic,** No. 180, first appearance of Wolverine, published by Marvel Comics, October 1974.
£65–75/$100–110 ⚒ CBP

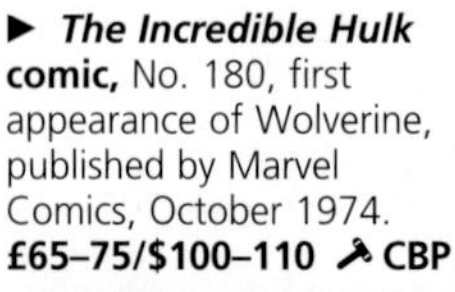

Prices

The value of comics depends on rarity and condition. The most desirable examples include first issues, special issues (for ex holiday or commemorative numbers) and comics containing the first appearance of a famous character.

***The Incredible Hulk* comic,** No. 181, published by Marvel Comics, November 1974.
£250–280
$350–400 CBP

***Justice League of America* comic,** No. 7, c1960.
£150–175
$225–255 PICC

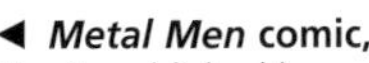

◄ *Metal Men* comic, No. 1, published by National Periodical Publications, April 1963.
£65–75
$100–110 NOS

***The Magic Comic*,** No. 1, 1939.
£1,200–1,400
$1,750–2,000 CBP
This third title from the *Beano* and *Dandy* stable only lasted for 80 issues until 1941. All issues are scarce and only seven copies of this first issue are known to exist.

***The Magic Comic*,** No. 2, 1939.
£200–220
$300–320 CBP

► *Mickey Mouse Annual*, published by Dean, 1946.
£75–85
$110–125 SDP

◀ ***A Moon, A Girl... Romance* comic,** No. 11, 1950.
£85–95
$125–140 CBP

***Oor Wullie* bi-annual,** No. 1, by Dudley Watkins, printed signature, 1941.
£750–850
$1,100–1,250 CBP

◀ ***The Silver Surfer* comic,** No. 3, artwork by Sal Buscema, published by Marvel Comics, 1968.
£45–50
$65–75 CoC

***The Spectacular Spider-Man* comic,** No. 1, published by Non Opareil, July 1968.
£65–75
$100–110 NOS

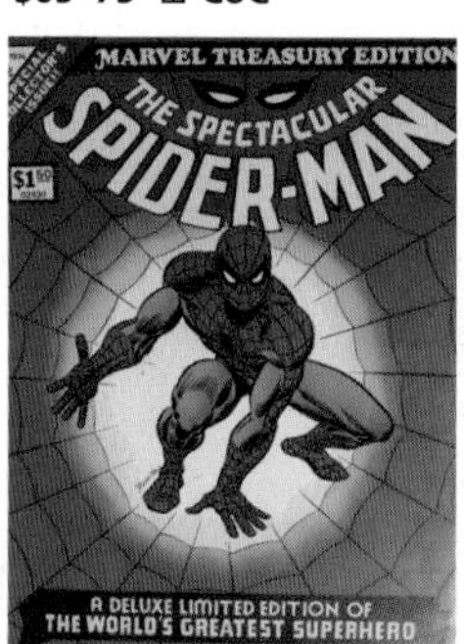

***The Spectacular Spider-Man* comic,** No. 1, Special Collector's Issue, Marvel Treasury Edition, 1974.
£25–30
$35–45 NOS

◀ ***Tales of Suspense* comic,** No. 48, 1963.
£245–285
$350–415 CBP

Cross Reference
See Sci-Fi, Film & TV (pages 331–339)

▶ ***TV Century 21* comic,** No. 1, with free gift Special Agent Decoder, 1965.
£330–360
$475–500 CBP

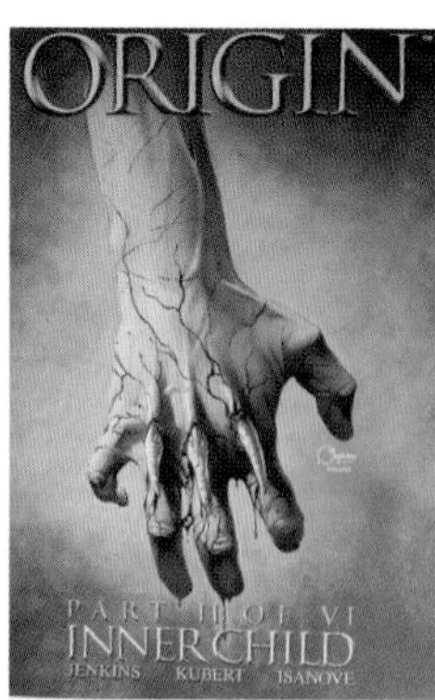

***Origin* comic,** Part II of VI Inner Child, published by Marvel Comics, December 2001.
£55–65
$80–100 NOS

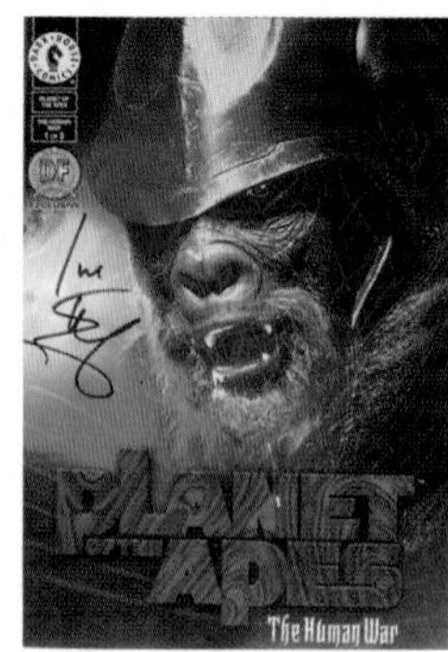

***Planet of the Apes, The Human War* comic,** No. 1, signed by the author, published by Dark Horse Comics, 2001.
£18–20
$20–30 NOS

◀ ***Simpsons Comics,*** one of four issues published a year, published by Bongo Entertainment, 1994.
£8–10
$12–15 NOS

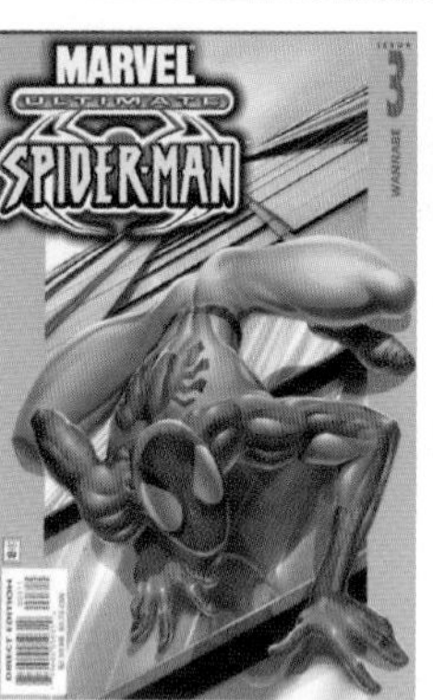

***Spider-Man* comic,** No. 3, published by Marvel Comics, 2001.
£8–10
$12–15 CoC

***Superman* comic,** No. 138, 1950s–60s.
£80–90
$115–130 PICC

LOCATE THE SOURCE

The source of each illustration in Miller's can be found by checking the code letters below each caption with the Key to Illustrations, pages 443–451.

Commemorative Ware

A porcelain commemorative jug, painted with sprays of flowers and inscribed in gilt 'Mr Thomas Knight, Fishmonger', minor crack, staining and wear, dated 1829, 7in (18cm) high.
£170–200
$250–300 ⚒ DN

► A pin dish, by Grafton, commemorating the Wembley Exhibition, 1925, 6in (15cm) wide.
£45–50
$65–75 ⊞ MURR

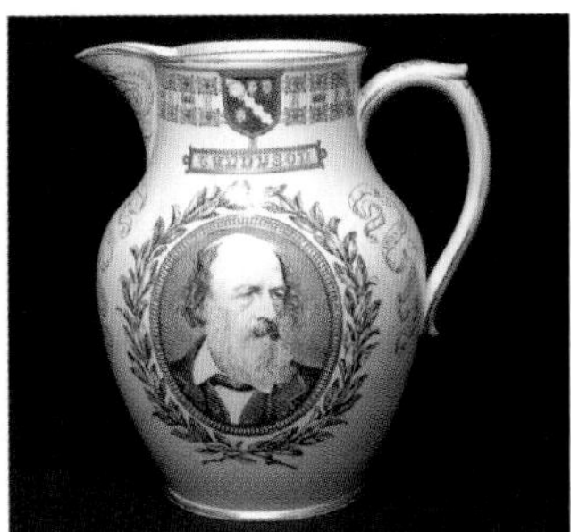

A Wedgwood mug, commemorating the death of Alfred Lord Tennyson, 1892, 10in (25.5cm) high.
£200–225
$300–325 ⊞ H&G

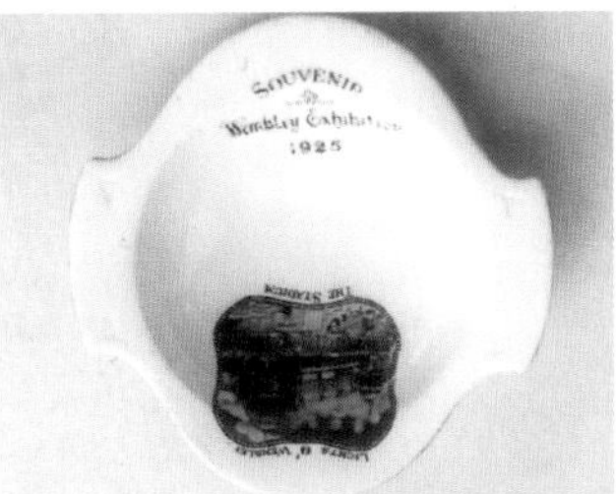

A porcelain beaker, by Grafton, commemorating the Anglo-American Exposition, London, printed in grey with views from the exhibition, flags and inscription, gilt rim, c1914, 5in (12.5cm) high.
£75–90
$110–130 ⚒ SAS

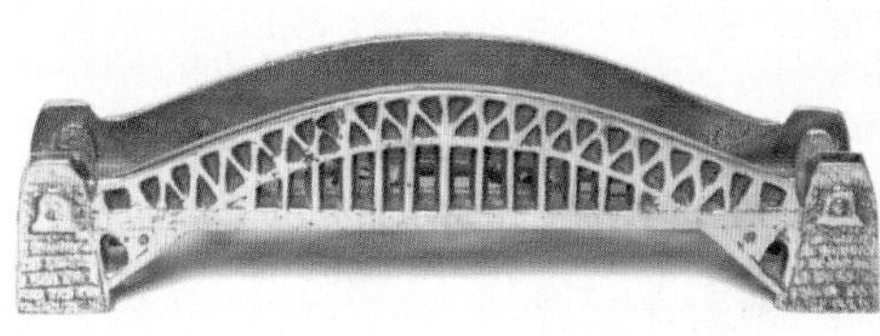

A brass souvenir, commemorating the opening for traffic of Sydney Harbour bridge, 1932, 7in (18cm) wide.
£25–30
$35–45 ⊞ RUSS

A brass souvenir cauldron, commemorating the Festival of Britain, 1951, 4in (10cm) high.
£20–25
$30–35 ⊞ MURR

A Ewenny terracotta mug, commemorating the Festival of Britain, lined in white with incised inscription, 1951, 3in (7.5cm) high.
£25–30
$35–45 ⚒ SAS

Military & Naval

A Doulton Lambeth salt-glazed stoneware jug, commemorating the death of General Gordon of Khartoum, with applied relief portrait, inscribed 'General Gordon, Hero of Heroes, Khartoum' and 'Governor General of the Soudan 1874, born Jan. 28 1833, Betrayed Jan. 26 1885', impressed mark for 1890–91, 7in (18cm) high.
£180–220
$260–320 ⚒ PF

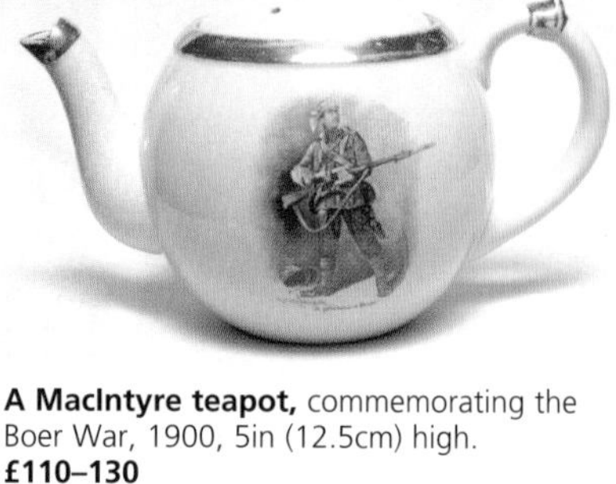

A MacIntyre teapot, commemorating the Boer War, 1900, 5in (12.5cm) high.
£110–130
$160–200 ⊞ ATK

A Carlton Ware dish, commemorating the Boer War, c1900, 4½in (11.5cm) diam.
£120–140
$175–200 ⊞ H&G

A Copeland Spode cup, decorated with a portrait of Lord Kitchener, 1914–18, 3in (7.5cm) high.
£90–100
$130–145 ⊞ ATK

A vase, commemorating WWI, with portrait of George V, the Czar, President Poincaré and the King of the Belgians, 1915–16, 8in (20.5cm) high.
£110–130
$160–200 ⊞ H&G

An Aynsley cup, inscribed 'To Commemorate Peace', 1919, 3in (7.5cm) high.
£40–45
$60–65 ⊞ ATK

Cross Reference
See Militaria & Emergency Services (pages 273–278)

► **A Crown Ducal pottery teapot,** inscribed 'War against Hitlerism', 1939, 5in (12.5cm) high.
£130–150
$200–220
⊞ H&G

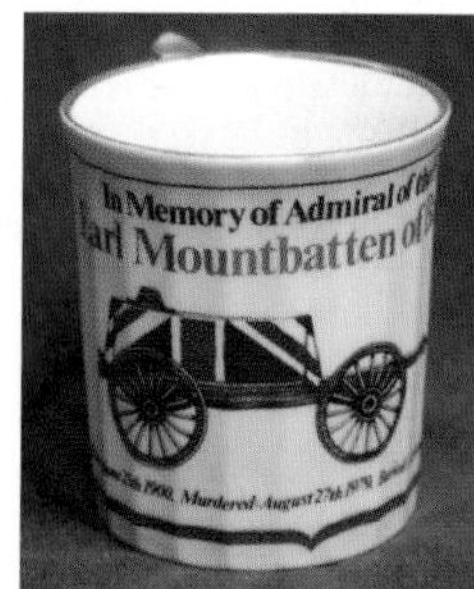

A J. & J. May mug, inscribed 'In Memory of Admiral of the Fleet, Lord Mountbatten of Burma', 1979, 3½in (9cm) high.
£75–85
$110–125 ⊞ H&G

◄ **A Crown Devon pottery chamber pot,** by Fielding, inscribed 'Have This On Old Nasty', 1941–42, 9in (23cm) wide.
£500–575
$720–850
⊞ H&G

◄ **An earthenware mug,** commemorating victory in the Falklands War, 1982, 4in (10cm) high.
£30–35
$45–50 ⊞ H&G

Politics

A bisque porcelain bust of Lord Brougham, wearing a characteristic wig, on a socle base, c1832, 4in (10cm) high.
£40–50
$60–75 SAS

► **A Doulton Lambeth stoneware tyg,** for Mortlake, commemorating the 1880 General Election, c1880, 6¼in (16cm) high.
£380–430
$575–625 SAS

LOCATE THE SOURCE
The source of each illustration in Miller's can be found by checking the code letters below each caption with the Key to Illustrations, pages 443–451.

A Wallis Gimson transfer-printed plate, commemorating Benjamin Disraeli, c1884, 10in (25.5cm) diam.
£85–95
$125–140 H&G

A child's plate, commemorating the Corn Law, c1835, 6in (15cm) diam.
£150–175
$225–255 H&G

A Royal Doulton bone china mug, commemorating Rt Hon W. E. Gladstone, 1898, 7in (18cm) high.
£170–190
$250–275 H&G

► **A mug,** transfer-printed with a portrait of Sir Robert Peel, 19thC, 4in (10cm) high.
£90–110
$130–160 POL

A glass dish, with a portrait of Henry Clay, c1850, 3½in (9cm) diam.
£50–60
$75–90 SAS
Henry Clay was the United States Secretary of State 1825–29, and a member of the Senate 1831–42. He stood unsuccessfully for President in 1832 and 1844.

A Doulton Lambeth jug, commemorating the Leeds Election, moulded with a portrait of Rt Hon W. E. Gladstone, Leeds arms and Yorkshire rose, inscribed 'Leeds Election 1880 Effort Honest ...Better than Success', with a pair of baluster mugs moulded with portraits of Herbert J. Gladstone and John Barran, jug spout restored, rim chips to beakers, 1880, jug 9½in (24cm) high.
£300–350
$450–500 DD

A Ridgway plate, commemorating Joseph Chamberlain, c1904, 10in (25.5cm) diam.
£80–90
$115–130 ⊞ H&G

A Toby jug, by Lancasters, depicting Neville Chamberlain, c1940, 3in (7.5cm) high.
£60–65
$90–100 ⊞ H&G

A Spitting Image pottery mug, commemorating the General Election, 1992, 4in (10cm) high.
£30–35
$45–50 ⊞ H&G

► **A cruet set,** modelled as Winston Churchill and Clement Attlee, 1999, 4in (10cm) high.
£20–25
$30–35 ⊞ POL

An Ashtead Pottery character jug of Stanley Baldwin, by Percy Metcalf, the underside with printed detail, signed and numbered 554 of 1,000, c1923, 7½in (19cm) high.
£100–120
$145–175 ⚒ SAS

A rubber bust of Winston Churchill, 1940s, 6in (15cm) high.
£30–35
$45–50 ⊞ COB

A silver metal brooch, depicting Winston Churchill smoking a cigar, inscribed 'Vote Conservative', c1945.
£70–85
$100–125 ⚒ SAS

A Royal Doulton bone china loving cup, commemorating Margaret Thatcher as first woman Prime Minister, 1979, 4in (10cm) high.
£40–45
$60–65 ⊞ H&G

A concrete garden gnome, modelled as John Prescott, 2001, 16in (40.5cm) high.
£50–60
$75–90 ⊞ POL

Royalty

'I should think almost every house in Britain has a royal commemorative in it,' says John Pym, manager of Hope and Glory. 'When I was a kid, Mum and Dad kept their toothbrushes in a George VI beaker in the bathroom and one of my strongest childhood memories is queuing up in the school corridor with all my mates, to pick up my Denby Elizabeth II coronation mug. Oh dear! That dates me, doesn't it? But I was so proud of it!'

Royal commemoratives are something of a British speciality. The first known commemorative ceramic was a small mug made for the coronation of Charles II and, since the restoration of the Monarchy in 1660, we haven't looked back. While hand-painted Delft pieces from the 17th and 18th centuries are comparatively rare, with the development of mass production in the 19th century, commemoratives were literally made for the masses. Cheap and cheerful patriotic china was churned out for Queen Victoria's Gold and Diamond Jubilees in 1887 and 1897, and by the time of the birth of Princess Elizabeth in 1926, the manufacture of commemoratives was a huge industry. Even though she and her sister, Margaret Rose, were not directly in line to the throne, the pretty princesses provided a perfect marketing opportunity for 1930s manufacturers. 'Much of the material from this period is extremely charming and very collectable', notes John Pym.

Following the abdication of Edward VIII on 11 December 1936, George VI became King. Potters swiftly adapted the designs intended for Edward's prospective coronation. During the war, few royal commemoratives were produced and rationing was still in force in 1947, when Princess Elizabeth married Lieutenant Philip Mountbatten (Prince Philip of Greece).

With Elizabeth II's coronation on 2 June 1953, however, all restraint was thrown to the winds. It was the dawning of a new Elizabethan age, and it was time to party. 'There was a huge outpouring of patriotic enthusiasm,' notes advertising and packaging dealer David Huxtable; '30,000 people filled the Mall, waving flags. It was also the first coronation to be televized; 25 million watched on screen. Sales of television sets boomed and if you didn't have one yourself, you went round to the neighbours and watched there, with a plate of coronation chicken on your lap. There were celebrations across the land.' Huge amounts of coronation material were produced, from mugs to tea tins, to red, white and blue coronation buttons. Throughout Queen Elizabeth's reign (as the recent Golden Jubilee celebrations have demonstrated) every notable event has been marked with commemoratives, so what should collectors be looking out for?

'Because the Queen is alive, and we are talking about what, in collectable terms, are very recent events, collectors tend to be quite specific,' advises Andrew Hilton from Special Auction Services. 'They go for rarities such as pieces produced for her marriage or for individual royal visits, and also for high-quality objects that were probably expensive at the time and therefore not produced in vast numbers'. Good manufacturers of commemorative china include Paragon, Aynsley, Crown Ducal, Coalport, Worcester and Wedgwood who produced comparatively modernist designs by artists such as Eric Ravilious and Richard Guyatt. It is not just happy events (births, marriages, jubilees) that inspire collectors. Also popular are mugs commemorating royal divorces and deaths, and the caricature egg cups depicting the royal family designed by Fluck and Law, creators of the 1980s satirical television series *Spitting Image*. 'These really are the antiques of tomorrow,' concludes John Pym. 'In my experience the majority of collectors are monarchists, rather than royalists. They believe in the monarchy, but they don't idolize it. Collecting royal commemoratives is about collecting history and satire is an important part of that history.'

◄ **A Swansea Pottery mug,** commemorating the coronation of Queen Victoria, transfer-printed and inscribed, C-scroll moulded handle, c1837, 3in (7.5cm) high.
£750–850
$1,100–1,250 ⚒ PF

◄ **A reverse intaglio crystal stickpin,** with monogram of Frederick of Prussia, c1880, 4in (10cm) high.
£1,450–1,600
$2,000–2,300 ⊞ NBL
Frederick of Prussia was the husband of Princess Vicky, Queen Victoria's eldest daughter.

A Wallis Gimson transfer-printed pottery plate, with a portrait of the Prince of Wales, flanked by flowers of the Union, c1886, 10in (25.5cm) diam.
£1,000–1,200
$1,500–1,750 SAS

A Minton mug, commemorating Queen Victoria's Golden Jubilee, 1887, 3½in (9cm) high.
£125–145
$180–200 H&G

A Royal Doulton pitcher, commemorating Queen Victoria's Diamond Jubilee, 1897, 11in (28cm) high.
£250–275
$350–400 H&G

A Balance of Payments plate, for Queen Victoria's Golden Jubilee, 1887, 10in (25.5cm) diam.
£130–150
$200–220 H&G

A pottery loving cup, commemorating the birth of Prince Edward, with incised decoration and inscription, c1894, 8in (20.5cm) high.
£350–400
$500–580 SAS

A Royal Worcester plate, commemorating Queen Victoria's Golden Jubilee, 1887, 10½in (26.5cm) diam.
£100–135
$145–200 H&G

A printed photographic portrait of Prince Edward and Princess Alexandra of Wales, 1897, 15 x 11in (38 x 28cm).
£10–12
$15–20 J&S

◄ **A Copeland pottery jug,** commemorating Queen Victoria's Diamond Jubilee, moulded with a white portrait, shield and coat-of-arms, 1897, 5¼in (13.5cm) high.
£150–180
$220–260 SAS

► **A Rowntree & Co chocolate tin,** commemorating the coronation of King Edward VII, with contents, 1902, 5½in (14cm) wide.
£75–85
$110–125 RUSS

A Crown Staffordshire jug, for Thomas Goode, commemorating the coronation of King Edward VII, limited edition of 500, c1902, 9in (23cm) high.
£675–750
$1,000–1,100 ⊞ H&G

A Fieldings beaker, 'In Memoriam' commemorating the death of Edward VII, with silver-lined rim, 1910, 5in (12.5cm) high.
£90–110
$130–160 ⚒ SAS

A Mason's jug, commemorating the Silver Jubilee of King George V, 1935, 7in (18cm) high.
£225–250
$325–350 ⊞ H&G

► **An Aller Vale jug and bowl,** incised with crossed flags and inscription, c1902, jug 2¾in (7cm) high.
£140–170
$200–250 ⚒ SAS

◄ **A pair of Royal Doulton plates,** commemorating the coronation of King Edward VII, c1902, 3in (7.5cm) wide.
£200–250
$300–350
⊞ H&G

A pair of cufflinks, commemorating the coronation of King George V and Queen Mary, with lithograph portraits, 1910, ¼in (7.5mm) diam.
£40–45
$60–65 ⊞ JBB

An Aynsley mug, commemorating the coronation of King George V, 1911, 3in (7.5cm) high.
£80–90
$115–130 ⊞ H&G

The Illustrated London News, Celebrations Number commemorating the Silver Jubilee of King George V, 1935, 14 x 10in (35.5 x 25.5cm).
£20–25
$30–35 ⊞ J&S

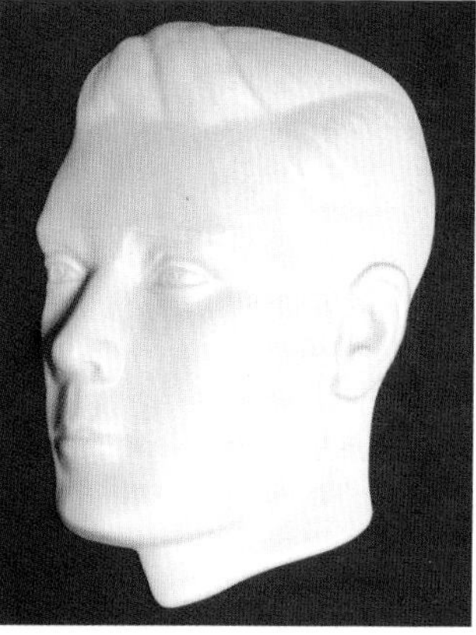

A Solian Ware wall mask of Edward VIII, 1936, 8in (20.5cm) high.
£120–140
$175–200 ⊞ H&G

A Cauldon plate, with central portrait of Edward VIII, flanked by flags, within a border detailing the Empire, 1937, 10¾in (27.5cm) diam.
£90–110
$130–160 SAS

A Coronet Ware preserve pot and cover, with black cat knop, printed with a sepia portrait of Edward VIII, 1937, 4¾in (12cm) high.
£60–70
$90–100 SAS

A box of Bryant & May Silver Jubilee matches, 1937, 3¼in (5.5cm) high.
£15–18
$20–25 ⊞ ATK

A Wedgwood beaker, commemorating the coronation of King George VI, 1937, 4½in (11.5cm) high.
£60–70
$90–100 ⊞ H&G

A pair of Royal Crown Derby nut dishes, commemorating the coronation of King George VI, 1937, 3in (7.5cm) wide.
£200–250
$300–350 ⊞ H&G

A Royal Doulton loving cup, commemorating the coronation of King George VI, 1937, 10in (25.5cm) high.
£580–650
$850–950 ⊞ H&G

A William Moorcroft mug, commemorating the coronation of King George VI, the cream ground with inscribed borders, coronet, orb, sceptre and floral decoration, incised signature, painted monogram in green, 1937, 4in (10cm) high.
£300–350
$450–500 TRM

A pair of Ringtons Maling ware tea caddies, with knopped covers and twin handles, commemorating the coronation of King George VI, c1937, 6in (15cm) high.
£60–75
$90–110 TRM

A Paragon trio, decorated with Budgies pattern, 1930s, cup 3in (7.5cm) high.
£100–120
$145–175 ⊞ ATK

This pattern was designed to commemorate the birth of Princess Margaret Rose, and is decorated with marguerites and roses to symbolize her name.

PRICE THREE SHILLINGS & SIXPENCE

THE ILLUSTRATED LONDON NEWS

IN MEMORIAM NUMBER

QUEEN MARY

The Illustrated London News, In Memoriam Number, commemorating the death of Queen Mary, 1953, 14 x 10in (35.5 x 25.5cm).
£9–10
$15–18 ⊞ J&S

A handkerchief, decorated with portraits of Princess Elizabeth and Princess Margaret, 1930s, 8in (20.5cm) square.
£14–16
$20–25 ⊞ ATK

Queen Elizabeth II and Prince Philip, a signed Christmas card, with colour photograph of the couple wearing their coronation robes and accompanied by Prince Charles and Princess Anne, gold embossed crown to cover, 1953.
£575–650
$850–950 ⚒ VS

A set of four plastic patriotic buttons, made for the coronation of Queen Elizabeth II, 1953, ¾in (2cm) diam.
£14–16
$15–20 ⊞ EV

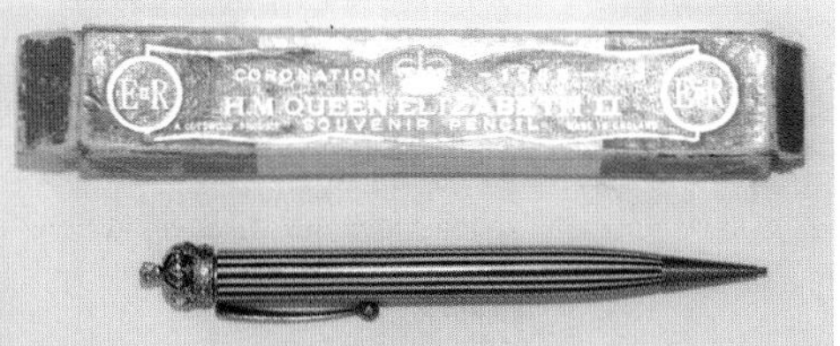

◀ **A souvenir pencil,** commemorating the coronation of Queen Elizabeth II, 1953, 5in (12.5cm) long, boxed.
£8–10
$10–15 ⊞ JUN

Queen Elizabeth The Queen Mother, a signed Christmas card, with gold embossed crown to cover, 1952.
£320–360
$475–500 ⚒ VS

Prince Philip, a signed portrait photograph of the Prince wearing dress uniform, 1953, 28¾ x 22¾in (73 x 58cm).
£150–200
$220–300 ⚒ B(Ch)

Queen Elizabeth II, a signed photograph, by Dorothy Wilding, overmounted in pale blue and burgundy, 1953, 8½ x 6in (21.5 x 15cm).
£750–800
$1,100–1,150 ⚒ VS

A Minton bowl and cover, modelled as an orb, commemorating the coronation of Queen Elizabeth II, limited edition No. 41 of 50, 1953, 5½in (14cm) high.
£1,700–2,000
$2,500–3,000 ⚒ SAS

► A Paragon mug, commemorating Prince Charles, 1953, 3in (7.5cm) high.
£70–80
$100–115 ⊞ H&G

A Copeland tyg, commemorating the coronation of Queen Elizabeth II, 1953, 6in (15cm) high.
£420–460
$620–660 ⚒ WW

A Wedgwood mug, by Richard Guyatt, commemorating Queen Elizabeth II's Silver Jubilee, 1977, 4in (10cm) high.
£20–25
$30–35 ⚒ WW

An Aynsley plate, commemorating the coronation of Queen Elizabeth II, 1953, 10in (25.5cm) diam.
£260–290
$375–425 ⊞ H&G

A Royal Crown Derby bell, commemorating the investiture of Prince Charles as Prince of Wales, limited edition of 500, 1969, 9in (23cm) high.
£425–475
$620–700 ⊞ H&G

A Royal Doulton mug, commemorating the coronation of Queen Elizabeth II, 1953, 3in (7.5cm) high.
£30–35
$45–50 ⊞ H&G

A pair of Wilson's China mugs, commemorating the wedding of Princess Anne and Captain Mark Phillips, 1973, 4in (10cm) high.
£40–50
$60–75 ⊞ H&G

A Wedgwood pint mug, commemorating Queen Elizabeth II's Silver Jubilee, 1977, 5in (12.5cm) high.
£30–35
$45–50 ⊞ H&G

◄ **A set of Waddington's Silver Jubilee playing cards,** 1977, 3½in (9cm) high.
£6–7
$8–10 ⊞ ATK

A Royal Doulton whisky container, modelled as a coronation coach, inscribed 'Royal Jubilee Scotch Malt Whisky 25 Years Old', circle mark, lion and crown, c1977, 6¾in (17cm) high.
£250–300
$350–450 ⚒ BBR

A Wedgwood pint mug, by Richard Guyatt, commemorating the birth of Prince William, limited edition of 1,000, 1982, 4½in (11.5cm) high.
£120–140
$175–200 ⊞ H&G

A Lady Gray mug, commemorating the 50th birthday of Prince Charles, limited edition of 100, 1998, 5in (12.5cm) high.
£45–50
$65–75 ⊞ H&G

A Spode mug, commemorating the wedding of Prince Charles and Lady Diana Spencer, 1981, 3½in (9cm) high.
£40–50
$60–75 ⊞ H&G

► **A set of Waddington's Royal Wedding playing cards,** commemorating the marriage of Prince Andrew and Sarah Ferguson, 1986, 5in (12.5cm) high.
£8–10
$10–15 ⊞ ATK

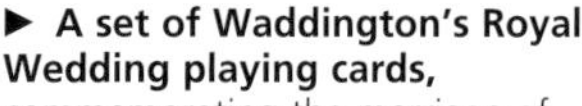

Prince Charles, a signed christmas card, with colour photograph of Prince Charles wearing a kilt, accompanied by Prince William and Prince Harry, gold embossed crest to cover, 1993.
£280–340
$400–475 ⚒ VS

A bar of soap, commemorating Queen Elizabeth II's Silver Jubilee, 1977, 3¼in (8.5cm) square, boxed.
£4–6
$6–8 ⊞ ATK

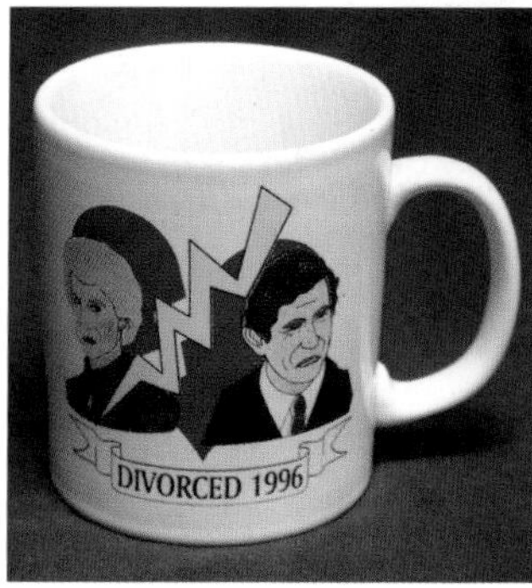

A mug, commemorating the divorce of Prince Charles and Princess Diana, 1996, 3½in (9cm) high.
£20–25
$30–35 ⊞ H&G

◄ **A mug,** commemorating the 101st birthday of Queen Elizabeth the Queen Mother, limited edition of 70, 2001, 3½in (9cm) high.
£70–80
$100–115 ⊞ H&G

Corkscrews

A silver travelling corkscrew, by Samuel Pemberton, the mother-of-pearl handle with silver bands, c1790, 3½in (9cm) long.
£170–200
$250–300 ⊞ CS

Items in the Corkscrews section have been arranged in date order.

A George III silver corkscrew, with bright-cut decoration, 3in (7.5cm) long.
£400–480
$580–700 ⚒ G(L)

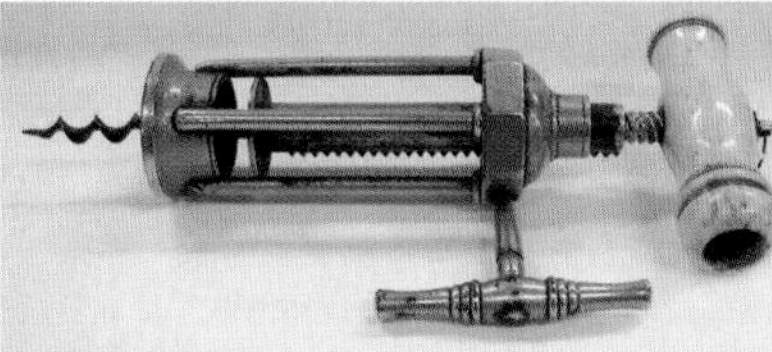

A silver-plated four-pillar 'King's Screw' double-action corkscrew, with turned bone top handle and steel side-winder handle, c1820, 9in (23cm) long.
£400–480
$580–700 ⚒ G(L)

A double-action corkscrew, the turned bone handle with dusting brush, the barrel embossed with autumnal fruits, c1820, 7¼in (18.5cm) long.
£450–550
$650–800 ⊞ CS
This type of corkscrew was patented by Sir Edward Thomason in 1802.

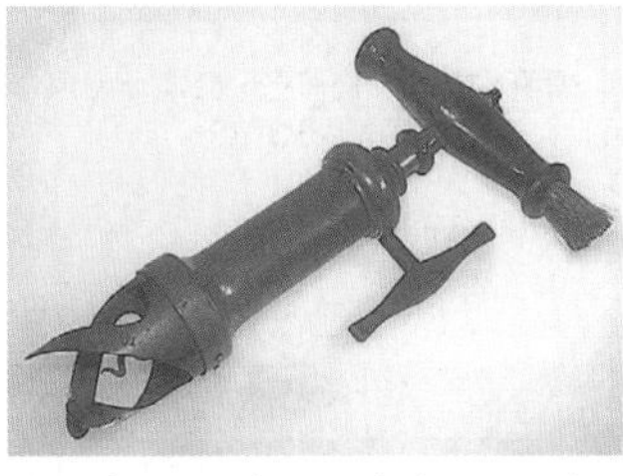

A corkscrew, by Lund, the turned wooden handle fitted with dusting brush, with side-winder handle with original steel bottle grips, c1840, 8in (20.5cm) long.
£1,250–1,750
$1,800–2,500 ⊞ CS

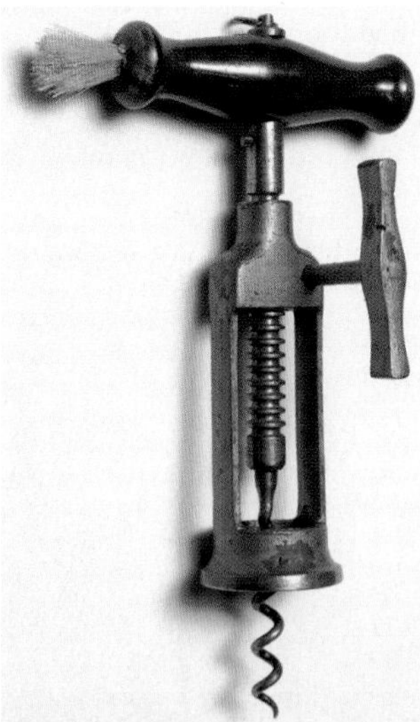

A London rack corkscrew, the turned wooden handle with dusting brush and hanging ring, side-winder handle, c1870, 7in (18cm) long.
£100–125
$145–175 ⊞ Dall

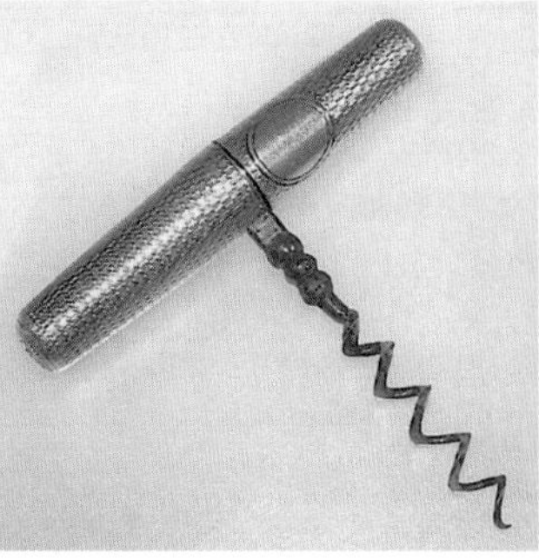

A silver Roundlet pocket corkscrew, the handle with engine-turned decoration, c1880, 3in (7.5cm) long.
£75–85
$110–125 ⊞ CS
Nickel-plated examples are more common and cost £10–15 ($15–20).

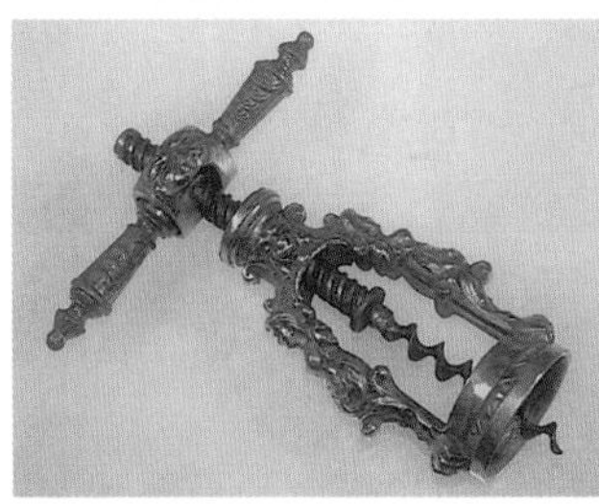

A steel lock-over-style corkscrew, with rococo design and gilded bar handle, Continental, c1880, 5½in (14cm) long.
£55–65
$80–95 ⊞ CS

► **A Holborn corkscrew,** with brass stem and wooden handle, c1880, 5¾in (14.5cm) long.
£70–80
$100–115 ⊞ Dall

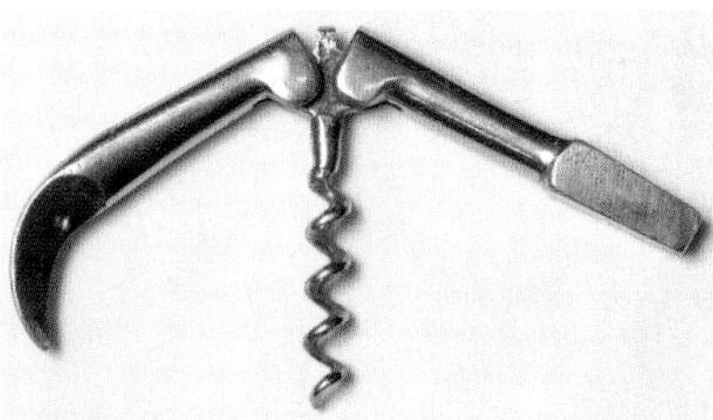

◄ **A folding pocket corkscrew,** with carriage key and foil cutter, c1880, 4in (10cm) long.
£100–120
$145–175 ⊞ Dall

A Chambers bar corkscrew, marked 'The Merritt', with replacement worm, patented 1888, 17in (43cm) long.
£170–200
$250–300 ⚒ P(B)

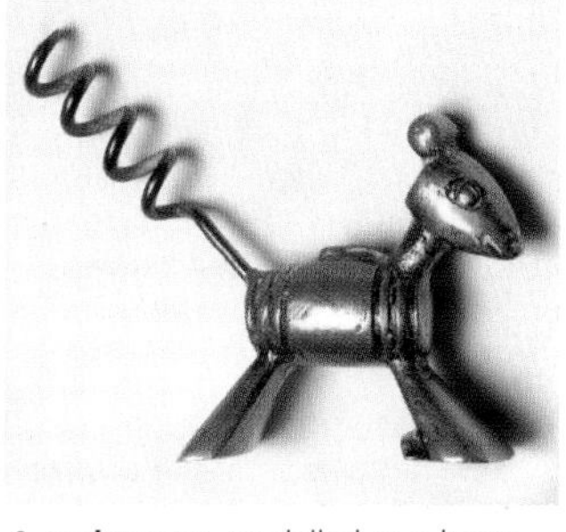

A corkscrew, modelled as a horse, c1920, 3½in (9cm) long.
£35–40
$50–60 ⊞ Dall

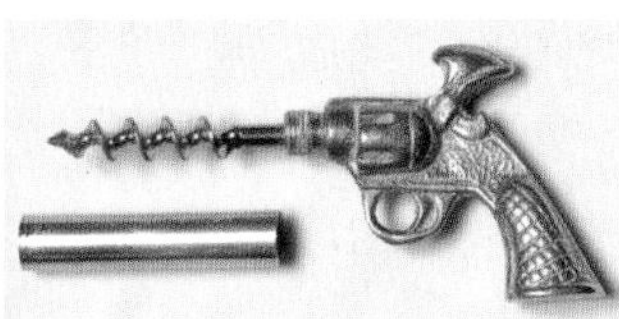

A brass corkscrew, modelled as a gun, c1930, 4¾in (12cm) long.
£35–40
$50–60 ⊞ Dall

► **A silver-plated corkscrew,** modelled as a dog, 1930, 4¼in (11cm) long.
£35–40
$50–60 ⊞ BEV

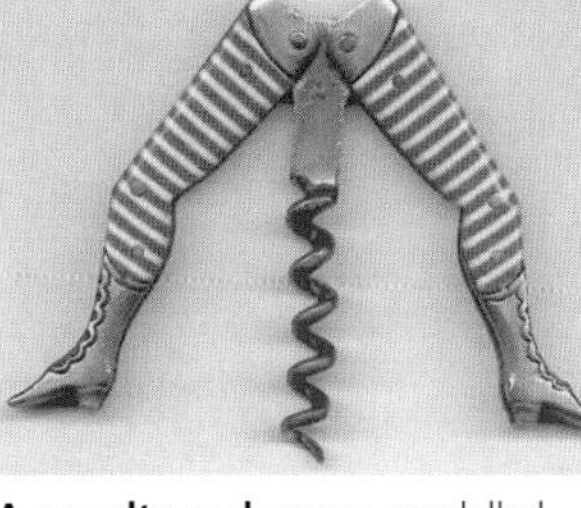

A novelty corkscrew, modelled as a pair of ladies' legs with celluloid stockings and nickel-plated lace-up boots, German, c1900, 2½in (6.5cm) long.
£120–150
$175–225 ⊞ CS

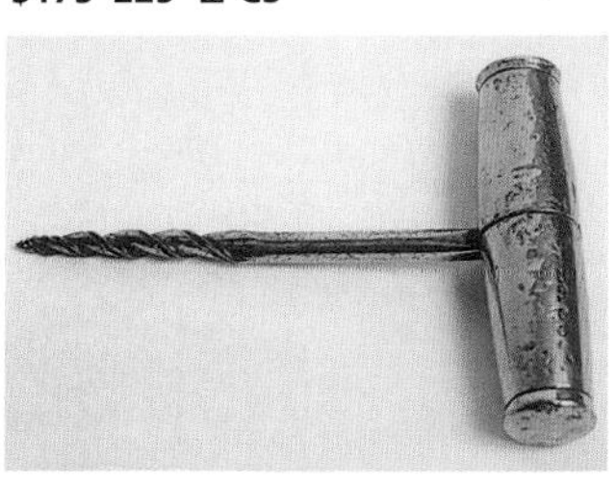

A Bass brass gimlet corkscrew, with barrel handle, 1920s, 5in (12.5cm) long.
£30–35
$45–50 ⊞ BSA

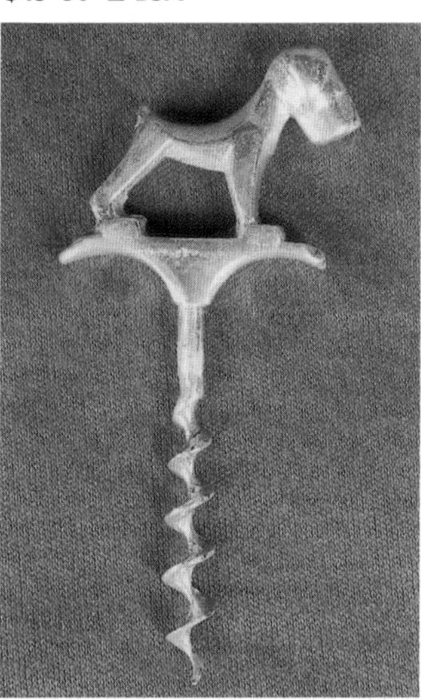

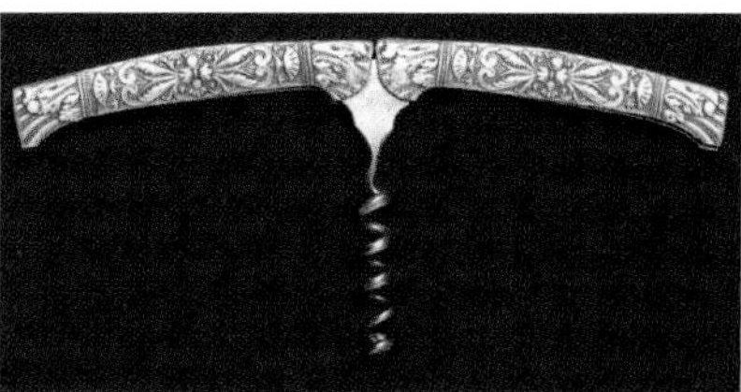

A folding corkscrew, with repoussé decoration, worm repaired, German, late 19thC, 3in (7.5cm) long folded.
£110–130
$160–200 ⚒ P(B)

An Aveze brass penknife with corkscrew, French, c1910, 3½in (9cm) long.
£18–22
$25–30 ⊞ CAL

A brass Archimedean corkscrew, early 20thC, 6in (15cm) long.
£70–80
$100–115 ⊞ CAL

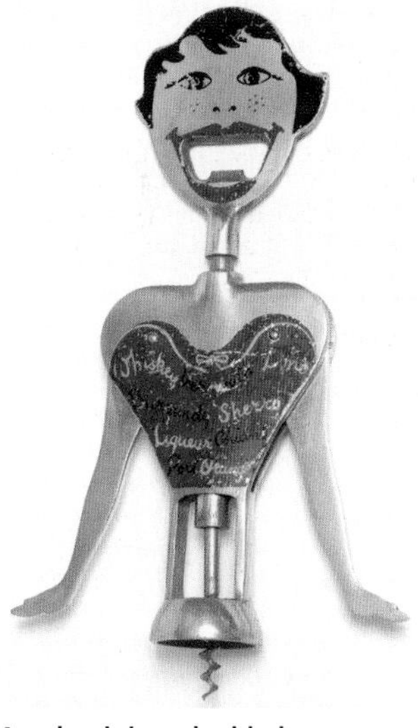

An aluminium double-lever corkscrew and bottle opener, modelled as a barmaid, Italian, c1960, 10in (25.5cm) long.
£60–70
$90–100 ⊞ CAL

Cosmetics & Hairdressing

Four advertising handbag mirrors, c1905, largest 2½in (6.5cm) diam.
£30–50
$45–75 each ⊞ HUX

A celluloid handbag mirror, by Rosie O'Neill, 1920–30s, 4in (10cm) high.
£35–45
$50–65 ⊞ MURR

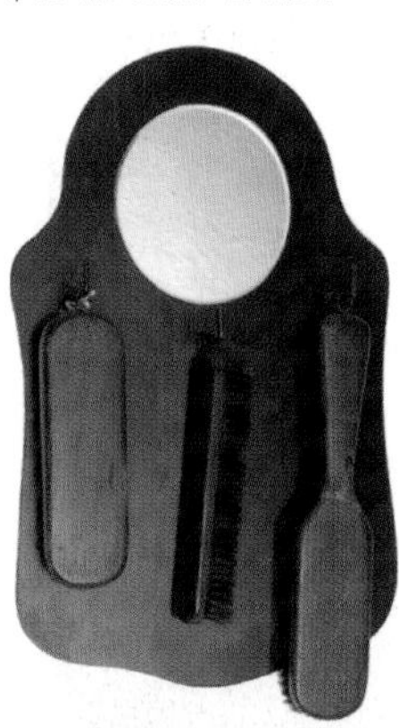

◄ A wooden brushes and mirror set, c1920, 15in (38cm) high.
£22–27/$32–38 ⊞ AL

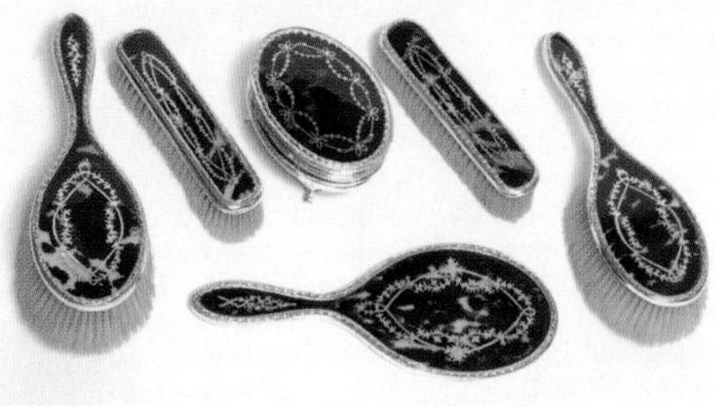

A silver and tortoiseshell dressing table set, comprising seven pieces, Chester 1908, largest 10in (25.5cm) long.
£800–900
$1,150–1,300 ⊞ BrL

A Eugene electric hair perming machine, c1930, 64in (162.5cm) high.
£250–300
$360–440 ⊞ JUN

A hairdresser's electric hair curler, c1930, 18in (45.5cm) high.
£70–80
$100–115 ⊞ JUN

► A lipstick case, with original box, c1940, 2½in (6.5cm) high.
£20–25
$30–35 ⊞ SUW

A Muholos hairdresser's hot air dryer, c1930, 12in (30.5cm) high.
£85–100
$125–145 ⊞ JUN

A box of Bourjois Evening in Paris face powder, with original tissue wrapping, c1950, 3in (7.5cm) square.
£20–30
$30–45 ⊞ LBr

◄ An Oster Airjet hair dryer, American, 1960, 8in (20.5cm) high.
£40–50
$60–75 ⊞ JUN

Compacts

Compacts became popular after WWI when, as women gained greater independence, the wearing and applying of make-up became acceptable in public. Early compacts, often imported from Paris, were small and contained blocks of dry pressed powder known as 'godets'. Such compacts were also referred to as vanity cases or vanities, although from the 1950s the term was only used for larger containers also holding lipstick, rouge and other items.

The 1920s and '30s saw many different styles, ranging from elegant Art Deco geometric designs to glowing iridescent blue patterns made from butterfly wings or coloured foil (a more affordable substitute). In the 1930s, partly reflecting the influence of Hollywood, compacts grew larger in size and novelty designs were popular, such as the 'Camera compact', a vanity case in the form of a camera, complete with 'shutter buttons' to open the lids, and 'film winder' knobs to hold lipsticks.

Production ceased during WWII, but flourished in the 1950s with the returning hunger for luxury products. American companies produced a wide range of inventive designs from the 1920s to the 1950s. Compacts are popular collectables both in Europe and the USA.

A Tango Dance finger compact, with enamelled floral design on base metal, 1925, 1½in (4cm) diam.
£65–75
$95–110 ⊞ SUW

A Bakelite hand-finished dance reticule, studded with heat-set rhinestones, with lipstick in tassle and compartments for powder and rouge, c1925, box 4in (10cm) long.
£450–500
$650–720 ⊞ SUW

An engine-turned silver compact, with fitted interior, the cover with an enamelled lakeside view, Continental, 1928, 2¼in (5.5cm) long.
£180–220
$260–320 ⚒ L

A white metal compact, with black enamel and marcasite decoration, Continental, 1920–30, 2in (5cm) square.
£60–70
$90–100 ⚒ G(L)

A Weblite white metal vanity case, with integral light, 1925–30, 3in (7.5cm) long.
£120–125
$170–180 ⊞ SUW

◄ A black suede compact bag, French, c1930, 3¼in (8.5cm) high.
£200–230
$300–330 ⊞ LaF

An Atkinson's No. 24 face powder sign and compact, c1930, sign 7 x 5in (18 x 13cm), compact 2in (5cm) diam.
Sign £165–195
$240–280
Compact £85–95
$125–140 ⊞ LBe

A souvenir compact, decorated with the World's Fair, Chicago, American, 1933–34, 3¼in (8.5cm) diam.
£80–90
$115–130 ⊞ SUW

A butterfly wing compact, 1930s, 2in (5cm) diam.
£60–70
$90–100 ⊞ LU

► **A Bakelite and rhinestone vanity case,** with compact and lipstick, French, 1930s, 22½in (57cm) long.
£475–525
$700–775 ⊞ LaF

A Gwenda compact, commemorating the coronation of George VI, 1937, 3in (7.5cm) diam.
£40–45
$60–65 ⊞ SUW

A Coty compact, perfume bottle and lipstick set, bottle contains L'Aimant perfurme, 1930s, box 5½ x 5in (14 x 12.5cm).
£150–175
$220–255 ⊞ SUW

► **An enamel compact,** in the form of a suitcase, American, 1930s, 2¾in (7cm) wide.
£60–70
$90–100 ⊞ LU

A souvenir compact, in the form of an envelope from Florida, American, 1939, 3¼in (8.5cm) wide.
£75–85
$110–125 ⊞ SUW

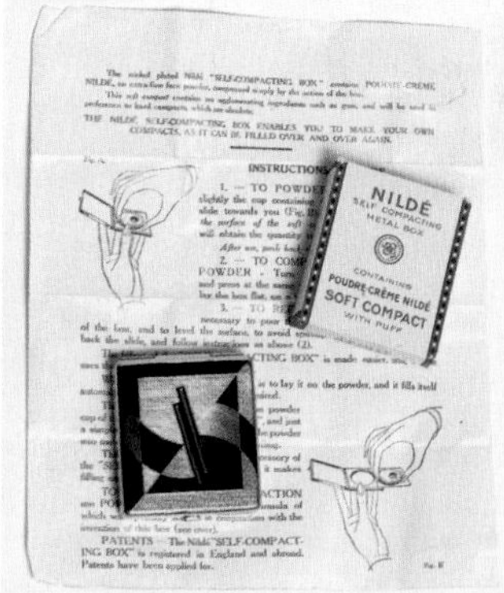

A Nildé self-compacting metal box, French, 1930s, 2½in (6.5cm) wide.
£100–120
$145–175 ⊞ LaF

A Richard Hudnut gilt metal duo compact, for powder and rouge, 1930s, 2¾in (7cm) diam.
£65–75
$95–110 ⊞ SUW

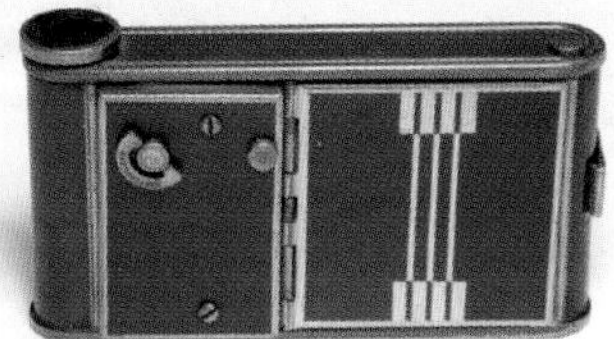

A Camera compact and musical box, with powder and lipstick, Swiss, late 1930s, 4in (10cm) wide.
£55–65
$80–95 ⊞ SUW

A metal and enamel compact, in the form of a record, 1940s, 3½in (9cm) diam.
£120–125
$170–180 ⊞ LBe

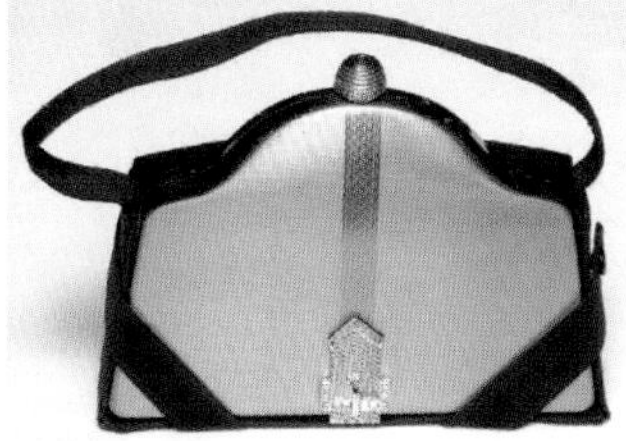

A Volupté carry-all, with powder and lipstick, in a moiré carry case, c1945–50, 6in (15cm) wide.
£110–125
$160–180 ⊞ SUW

An Alwyn compact, with enamel decoration of a Hollywood scene, American, 1950s, 3in (7.5cm) wide.
£65–75
$95–110 ⊞ LU

A celluloid Flap Jack Rex compact, American, 1940, 4¾in (12cm) diam.
£65–75
$95–110 ⊞ SUW

► **A Kotler & Kopit cigarette and compact case,** American, 1945–50, case 3¾in (9.5cm) wide.
£75–85
$110–125
⊞ SUW

An Elgin enamelled compact, American, 1950s, 2¾in (7cm) square.
£60–70
$90–100 ⊞ LU

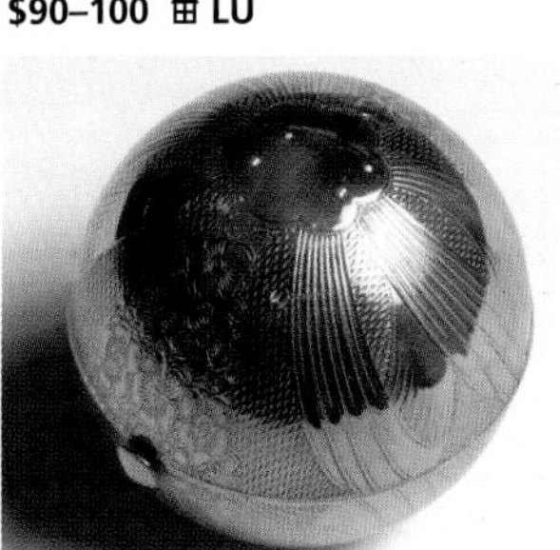

A gilt-metal compact, in the shape of a ball, 1950s, 2in (5cm) diam.
£75–85
$110–125 ⊞ SUW

► **A Mascot duo compact and cigarette case,** c1970, 3in (7.5cm) high.
£35–40
$50–60 ⊞ SBL

A Claudine Cereda compact bracelet, French, 1940s, 2½in (6.5cm) diam.
£250–300
$360–440 ⊞ LBe

A K&K jewelled compact, 1950s, 2in (5cm) square.
£85–95
$125–140 ⊞ LaF

A Rolei compact, 1950s, 3½in (9cm) wide.
£65–75
$95–110 ⊞ SUW

Mens' Hairdressing & Shaving

A Gibbs Cold Cream shaving stick, 1925–35, 3½in (9cm) high.
£12–15
$15–20 ⊞ HUX

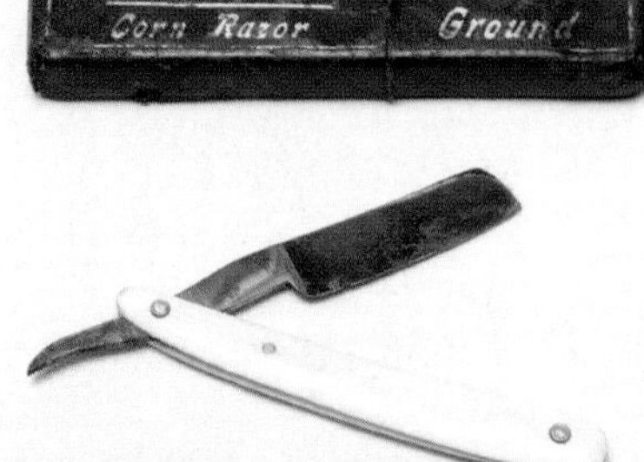

◄ **A Pall Mall corn razor,** 1930s, 4in (10cm) long.
£10–12
$15–17 ⊞ RTT

► **A Kleeneze bristle shaving brush,** 1930s, 4½in (11.5cm) high.
£8–10
$13–15 ⊞ RTT

A bottle of Oeillet Fané Brilliantine, by Grenoville, 1930s, 4¼in (11cm) high.
£10–12
$15–17 ⊞ HUX

A Gillette razor, 1930s, in original box, 2in (5cm) square.
£12–15
$17–20 ⊞ RTT

A tin of Yardley Olde English Lavender Brilliantine, 1940s, 3½in (9cm) wide.
£10–12
$15–17 ⊞ HUX

► **A bottle of Korine Brilliantine,** 1939–45, 4in (10cm) high.
£8–10
$12–15 ⊞ HUX

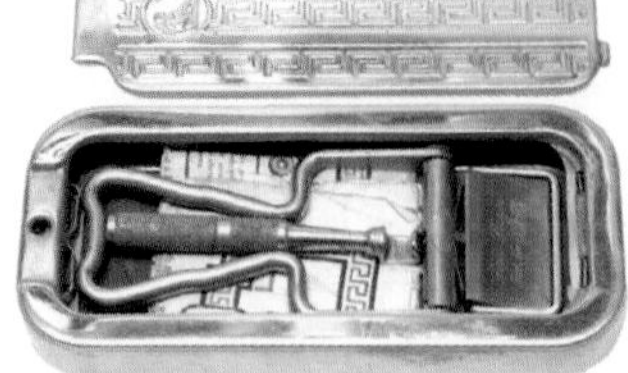

A Rolls razor, 1950s, in original box, 6in (15cm) long.
£8–10
$12–15 ⊞ RTT

◄ **A bottle of Seaforth Cologne for Men,** 1940s, in original box, 4¾in (12cm) high.
£12–15
$17–20 ⊞ RTT

A Corvette pre-electric shaving lotion and talc set, c1960, in original box, 10in (25.5cm) long.
£10–12
$15–17 ⊞ HUX

Dolls

A china dolls' house doll, with stuffed body, German, c1890, 6in (15cm) high.
£130–150
$190–220 ⊞ YC

A Hermann von Berg china-headed doll, with a soft body and original clothing, German, c1890, 16in (40.5cm) high.
£270–300
$400–440 ⊞ PSA

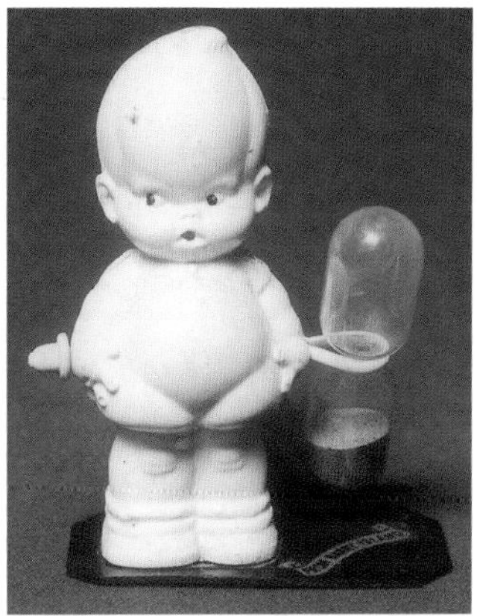

A Mabel Lucie Attwell celluloid Diddums doll, with egg timer, c1930, 4in (10cm) high.
£85–95
$125–140 ⊞ MEM

Bisque

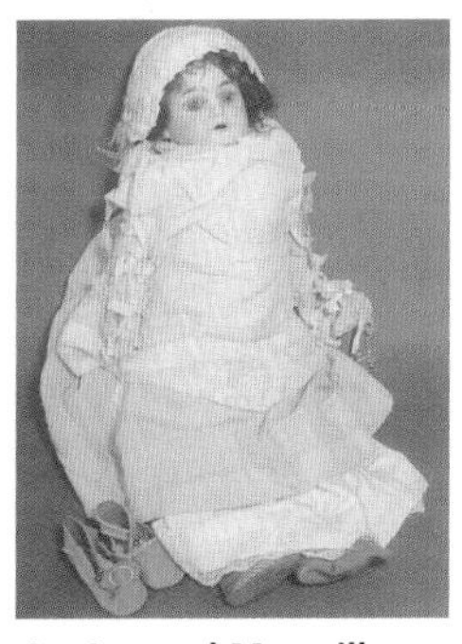

An Armand Marseille bisque-headed doll, with sleeping eyes, painted face, applied wig and over-painted pine jointed body, with original costume, German, 19thC, 19¾in (50cm) high.
£170–200
$250–290 BLH

◄ A bisque-headed miniature doll, with painted features and Alice band, bisque arms and legs and a stuffed body, original costume, c1885, 10¼in (26cm) high.
£200–250
$290–360 ⊞ YC

A glazed bisque-headed doll, with bisque arms and legs and a stuffed body, c1890, 5in (12.5cm) high.
£125–175
$180–255 ⊞ YC

► A Jumeau bisque-headed *bébé* doll, with fixed paperweight eyes, original wig and double-jointed composition body, clothes replaced, marked 'Jumeau', French, c1895, 21in (53cm) high.
£1,400–1,600
$2,000–2,300 ⊞ YC

◄ A Simon & Halbig bisque-headed doll, with fixed glass paper-weight eyes, original wig and double-jointed composition body, clothes replaced, marked S&H939, German, c1895, 19¾in (50cm) high.
£1,800–2,200
$2,600–3,200 ⊞ YC

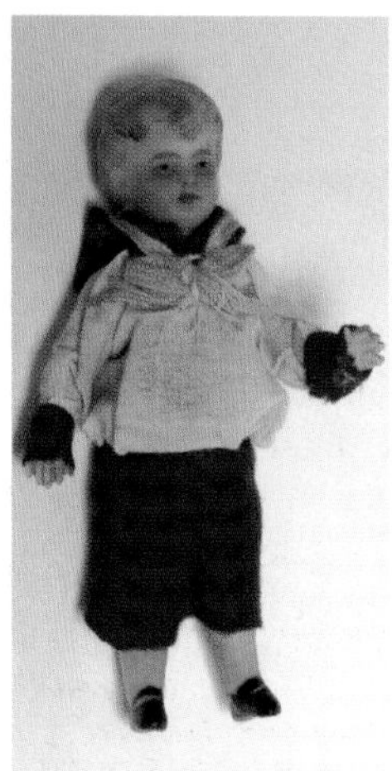

A bisque dolls' house doll, with jointed limbs, c1900, 3in (7.3cm) high.
£100–120
$145–175 ⊞ YC

► An Armand Marseille bisque-headed Dream Baby doll, No. 351/5k, with sleeping eyes and five-piece composition body, scratches to feet, German, early 20thC, 22in (56cm) high.
£100–120
$145–175 ⚒ G(L)

◄ A J. D. Kestner bisque-headed doll, No. 192, with sleeping eyes, original wig and double-jointed composition body, German, c1900, 13¼in (34cm) high.
£500–600
$720–870 ⊞ YC

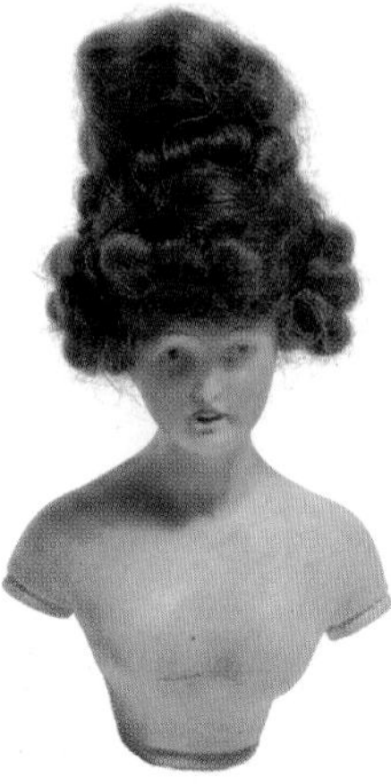

A bisque head and shoulders doll, early 20thC, 5in (12.5cm) high.
£30–50
$45–75 ⊞ YC
This doll would have been fitted with arms and attached to a tea cosy.

A bisque-headed baby doll, with sleeping eyes and five-piece composition body, marked 245/15, German, early 20thC, 9in (23cm) high.
£140–170
$200–250 ⚒ G(L)
Dolls like this would have been sold with fabric clothes. Serious collectors will research the exact type in order to match the doll to period clothes.

An Armand Marseille bisque-headed Native American doll family, with real hair wigs, five-piece composition bodies and original costumes,German, c1905, tallest 11in (28cm) high.
£800–900
$1,150–1,300 ⊞ BaN
Original costumes, multi-member family and subject matter make these dolls very collectable.

A Simon & Halbig bisque-headed mulatto doll, mould 1009, with sleeping eyes, double-jointed composition body and original dress, c1905, 17¾in (45cm) high.
£600–700
$870–1,000 ⊞ YC

A Saunier & Co bisque-headed doll, with sleeping glass eyes, original wig and double-jointed composition body, replacement clothes, marked S & C, German, c1908, 19in (48cm) high.
£400–500
$580–720 ⊞ YC

A bisque-headed miniature soldier doll, with moustache and helmet, cloth body and bisque lower arms and legs, c1910, 6in (15cm) high.
£60–75
$90–110 ⚒ Bon(C)

An Armand Marseille bisque-headed Dream Baby doll, AM 341, with weighted blue glass eyes and composition body, wearing a baby gown, German, c1910, 8in (20.5cm) high.
£80–100
$115–145 ⚒ Bon(C)

A Gerbrüder Heubach bisque-headed character doll, with painted features and composition bent-limb body, German, c1910, 8¼in (21cm) high.
£200–220
$290–320 ⊞ YC

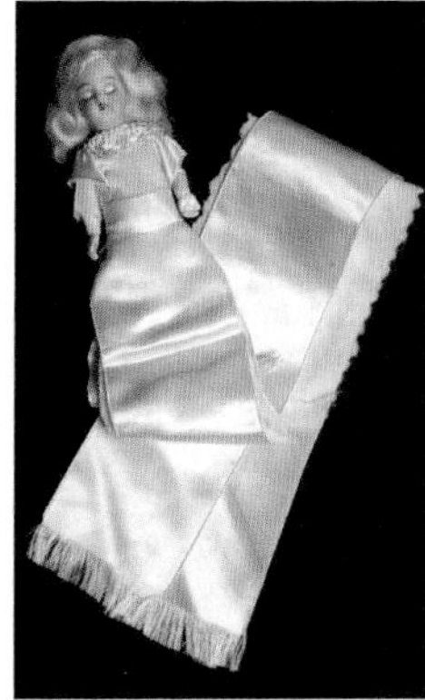

A Kämmer & Reinhardt bisque-headed sewing doll, with fixed blue eyes, blonde wig, and five-piece composition body with painted shoes and socks, German, c1910, 4½in (11.5cm) high.
£60–70
$90–100 ⚒ Bon(C)

◀ **A Recknagel bisque-headed doll,** with weighted glass eyes, brown wig and fully-jointed composition body, wearing a dress, underclothes and bonnet, c1910, 24in (61cm) high.
£90–110
$130–160 ⚒ Bon(C)

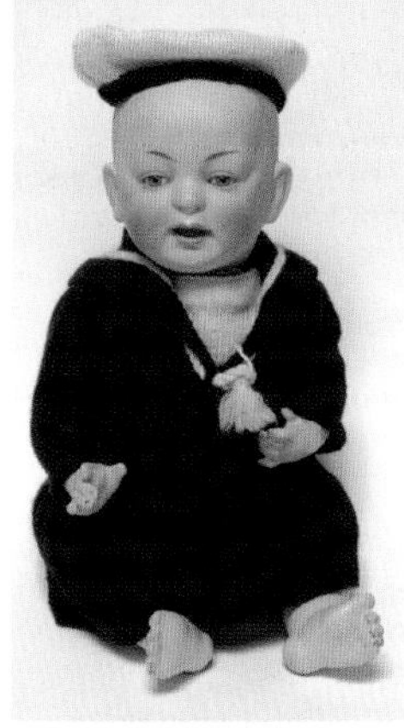

A J. D. Kestner bisque-headed sailor doll, with fixed glass eyes and a bent-limbed composition body, German, c1910, 16½in (42cm) high.
£400–450
$580–650 ⊞ YC

▶ **A Gerbrüder Heubach bisque-headed doll,** No. 8192, with sleeping eyes and a double-jointed composition body, German, c1912, 18in (46cm) high.
£300–350
$440–500 ⊞ YC

A J. D. Kestner bisque-headed doll, model 152, with sleeping eyes, original wig and double-jointed composition body, original dress, German, c1912, 15¾in (40cm) high.
£450–500
$650–720 ⊞ YC

An S.F.B.J. bisque-headed *bébé* doll, No. 301, with sleeping eyes and double-jointed composition body, French, c1912, 15¾in (40cm) high.
£200–250
$290–360 ⊞ YC

A Simon & Halbig Kämmer & Reinhardt bisque-headed doll, with sleeping eyes and jointed composition body, impressed marks to head, German, c1915, 24¾in (63cm) high.
£480–650
$700–800 ⚒ SWO

Simon & Halbig produced heads for other German and French makers including Kämmer & Reinhardt and Jumeau. Dolls usually carry the marks of both firms.

An Ernst Heubach bisque-headed doll, model No. 300, with sleeping glass eyes and jointed baby body, German, c1920, 14½in (37cm) high.
£180–220
$260–320 ⊞ YC

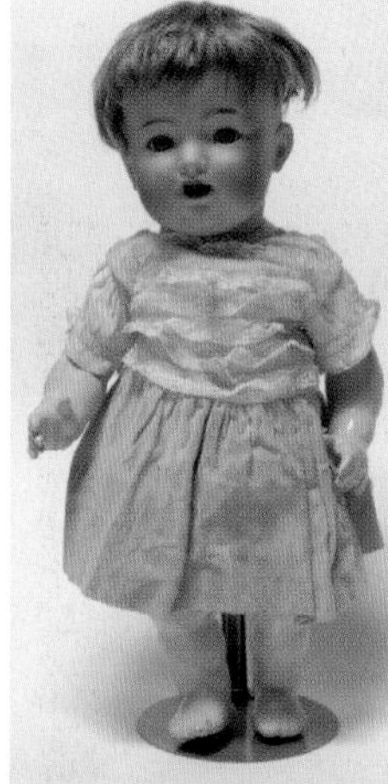

A Kämmer & Reinhardt bisque-headed doll, with sleeping eyes and original wig, on a stand-up, bent-limbed toddler body, German, c1920, 15in (38cm) high.
£225–275
$325–400 ⊞ YC

A Heubach bisque-headed fairy doll, with weighted blue glass eyes, short hair and fully-jointed composition body, wearing original costume, holding a wand, German, c1920, 14in (35.5cm) high, together with a letter from the original owner.
£300–350
$440–500 ⚒ Bon(C)

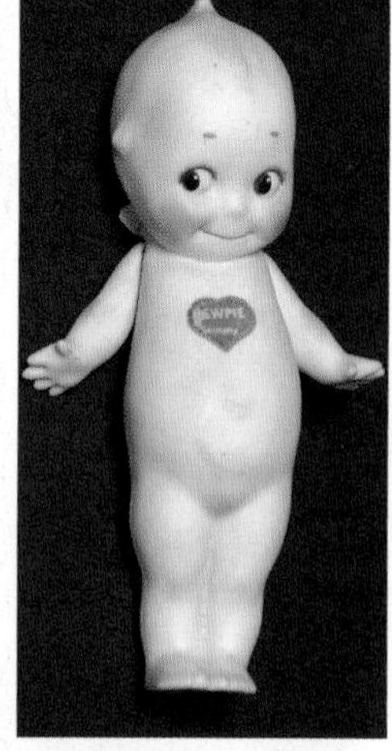

A Kestner Rose O'Neill bisque Kewpie doll, with moving arms and heart mark on chest, German, c1920, 6¼in (16cm) high.
£250–300
$360–440 ⊞ YC

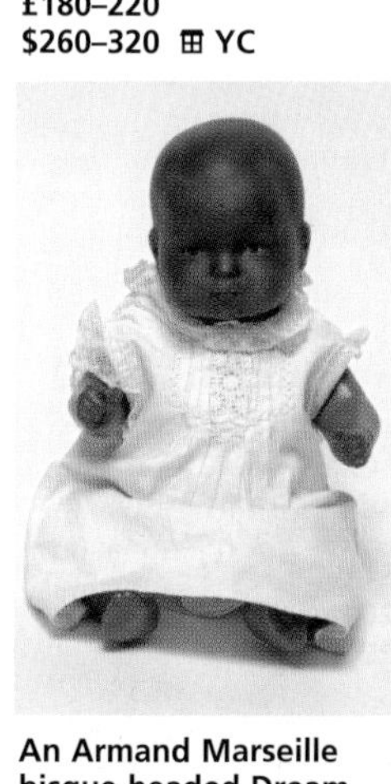

An Armand Marseille bisque-headed Dream Baby doll, with sleeping eyes and bent-limb baby body, wearing original outfit, German, c1920, 11½in (29cm) high.
£280–320
$410–470 ⊞ YC

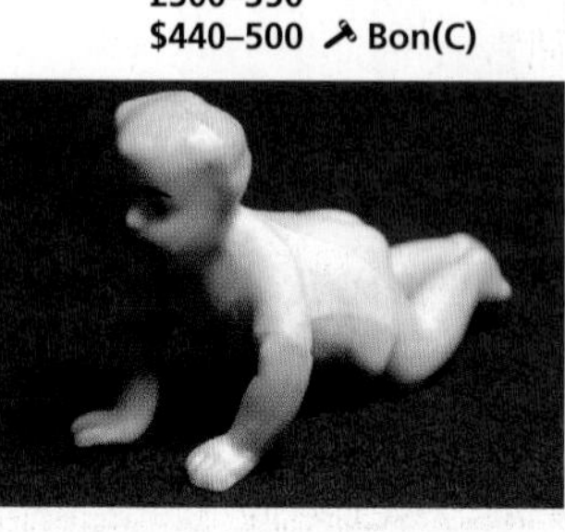

► A bisque piano baby, c1920, 3in (7.5cm) wide.
£20–30
$30–45 ⊞ YC

A set of three bisque dolls, with sleeping eyes, Japanese, c1920, 5in (12.5cm) long, in original box.
£100–150
$145–220 ⊞ YC

Cloth

A Chad Valley felt and **cloth doll,** with painted features and original outfit, c1930, 19in (48cm) high.
£200–250
$290–360 ⊞ YC

A Chad Valley painted cloth doll, with stuffed body, wearing original fairy outfit, c1930, 12½in (32cm) high.
£170–200
$250–290 ⊞ YC

LOCATE THE SOURCE

The source of each illustration in Miller's can be found by checking the code letters below each caption with the Key to Illustrations, pages 443–451.

A Dean's Rag Book cloth doll, with painted features and stuffed body, c1930, 14in (35.5cm) high, together with original swing label.
£200–250
$290–360 ⊞ YC

A Chad Valley Mabel Lucie Attwell Bambino cloth doll, c1932, 17in (43cm) high.
£325–375
$400–560 ⊞ MEM

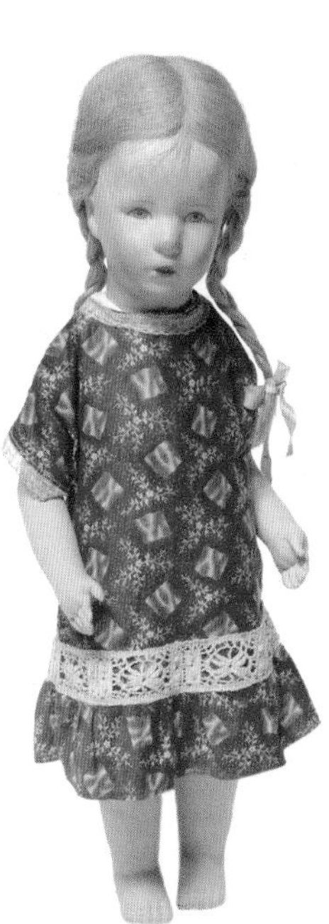

► A Käthe Kruse moulded cloth doll, German, c1938, 19¾in (50cm) high.
£1,000–1,200
$1,500–1,750 ⊞ YC
Wife of sculptor Max Kruse, the painter Käth Kruse began making dolls c1910. The mother of seven children, she was disatisfied with fragile bisque dolls and wanted to make toys that were safe, unbreakable and attractive to children. Her first doll is said to have been made from a potato and a towel filled with sand, but she soon graduated to making high-quality cloth dolls. The faces were hand-painted in oils to create a realistic effect, and the cloth bodies were designed to be washable. The dolls were marked on the left foot with a signature and number.

Composition

A Lehmann tinplate waltzing doll, with composition head and arms and a long cotton dress, on a wire frame, the clockwork action operating two spoked wheels, two casters and a bell, German, c1910, 9½in (24cm) high.
£380–420
$560–620 ⚒ AH

A composition and cloth St Trinian's doll, in a labelled outfit, c1930, 16in (40.5cm) high.
£300–350
$450–500 ⊞ Beb

Character dolls are always worth more if they have all the original accessories. If in doubt, research items in design catalogues before purchasing.

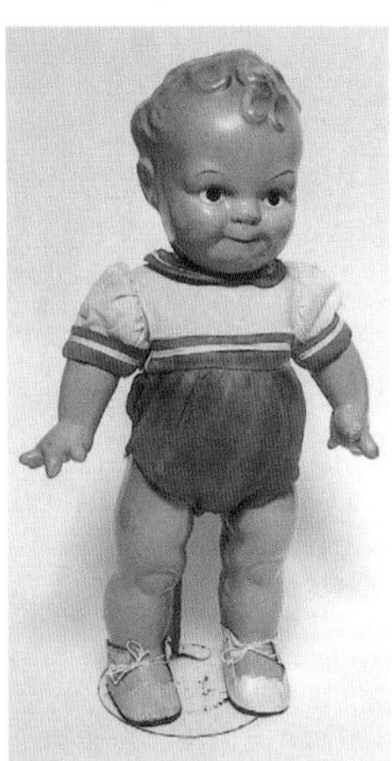

A Cameo Doll Co Rose O'Neill composition Scootles doll, with painted eyes and original clothing, c1930, 15½in (39.5cm) high.
£400–450
$580–650 ⊞ DOL

A composition musical doll, with painted features and straw-stuffed body containing a pump musical movement, c1930, 20½in (52cm) high.
£65–80
$95–115 ⊞ YC

Plastic

A Pedigree plastic walking doll, with moveable eyes, c1960, 22in (56cm) high.
£80–100
$115–145 ⊞ PAR

A Mattel Stacey doll, c1967, 11in (28cm) high.
£225–255
$325–365 ⊞ T&D

Barbie's friend Stacey was introduced c1967. Inspired by swinging London, Stacey was a British model. She also came in a talking version who, in an English accent, said 'Being a model is terribly exciting,' and 'I think mini-skirts are smashing.'

A Mattel Midge doll, with painted blue eyes, freckles and red curly hair, swivel neck, jointed at shoulders and hips, wearing a long red jumper and red and yellow striped trousers, holding a brown bag, together with a yellow plastic raincoat and hat, Japanese, 1960s, 11½in (30cm) high.
£60–70
$90–100 ⚒ Bon(C)

A Mattel Twist and Turn Barbie doll, c1967, 12½in (32cm) high, in original box.
£600–700
$870–1,000 ⊞ T&D

A Mattel Barbie doll, wearing a Made for Each Other outfit, c1967, 11½in (29cm) high.
£270–300
$390–440 ⊞ T&D

Two Mattel talking dolls, Julia and Brad, 1968–69, 11½in (29cm) high.
£280–310
$400–450 ⊞ T&D
Julia was based on Diahann Carroll's character from the popular prime-time television show Julia (1968–71). The singer was the first black female to star in her own comedy series. She also provided the voice for the doll. Brad was the boyfriend of Barbie's friend Christie, and the couple were among the first African-American dolls to be produced as girlfriend and boyfriend.

A Flair Toys Mary Quant Daisy series doll, wearing a bridal outfit, 1970, 10in (25.5cm) high, in original packaging.
£40–50
$60–75 ⊞ CTO

A Mattel Malibu Barbie doll, in a velvet outfit, c1975, 9in (23cm) high.
£150–170
$220–250
⊞ T&D

◄ A Mattel Barbie Loves Elvis doll, collector's edition, 1996, 14in (35.5cm) high, in original packaging.
£40–50
$60–75 ⊞ CTO

Dolls' Accessories

► A doll's porcelain dinner service, hand-painted, French/German, 1880–90, plate 4¾in (12cm) diam.
£200–230
$290–330 ⊞ YC

A doll's pram, with two large and two small wheels, hood damaged, c1900, 20in (51cm) long.
£110–130
$160–190 ⚒ BWL

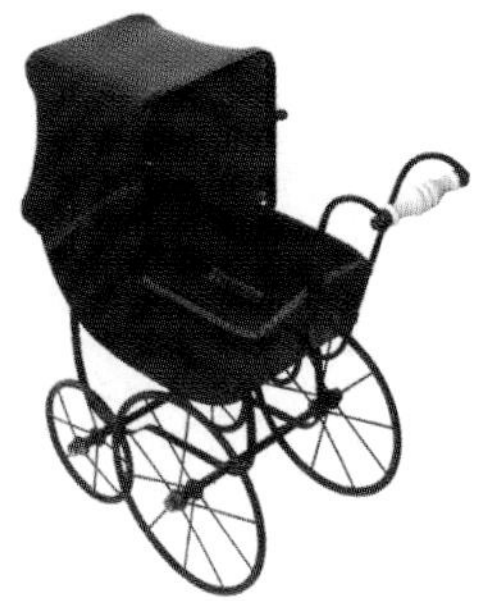

A doll's pram, with two large and two small wheels, c1900, 28in (71cm) high.
£400–450
$580–650 ⊞ JUN

◄ A doll's tin oven and set of enamel pans, with pull-out burners and oven top, German, 1890–1900, 14in (35.5cm) wide.
£500–600
$720–870 ⊞ YC

A doll's lace pillowcase, c1910, 9½in (24cm) wide.
£35–45
$50–65 ⊞ LU

A doll's porcelain tea set and tray, German, 1910–20, 5in (12.5cm) wide.
£50–60
$75–90 ⊞ YC

► **A dolls' oak longcase clock,** French, Brittany, 1930, 14in (35.5cm) high.
£80–100
$115–145 ⊞ MLL

Dolls' Clothes

A doll's dress and hat, made from 19thC fabrics, 1950s, 16in (40.5cm) long.
£300–350
$440–500 ⊞ JPr

Four outfits for Ken, Barbie's boyfriend, all in original individual packaging, c1962, largest 9in (23cm) long.
£40–45
$60–65 ⊞ T&D

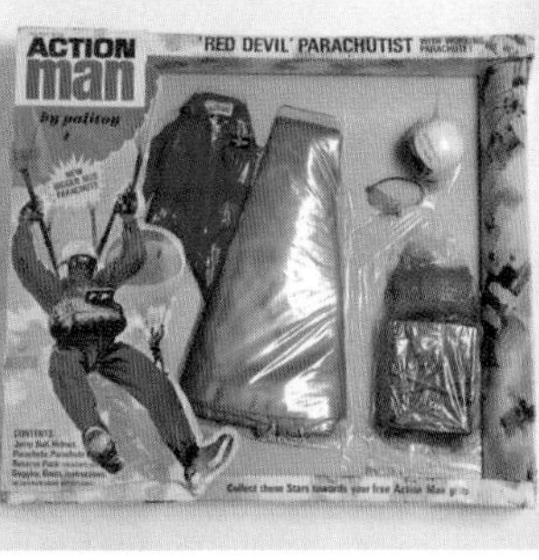

An Action Man Red Devils parachutist outfit, second issue, 1972, in original packaging, 14in (35.5cm) high.
£150–175
$220–255 ⊞ GTM

Further reading

Miller's Antiques & Collectables: The Facts At Your Fingertips, Miller's Publications, 2002

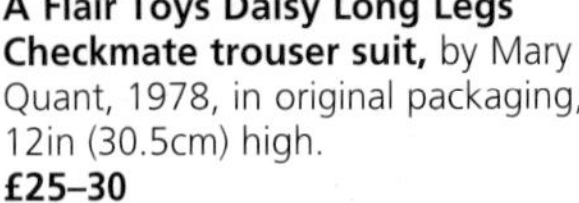

A Flair Toys Daisy Long Legs Checkmate trouser suit, by Mary Quant, 1978, in original packaging, 12in (30.5cm) high.
£25–30
$35–45 ⊞ CTO

A Flair Toys Daisy Long Legs Follies outfit, by Mary Quant, 1978, in original packaging, 14in (35.5cm) high.
£27–30
$35–45 ⊞ CTO

Five silk, feather and dried flower hats, by Suvan, 2002, largest 2in (5cm) diam.
£11–16
$15–20 each ⊞ CNM

Dolls' Houses

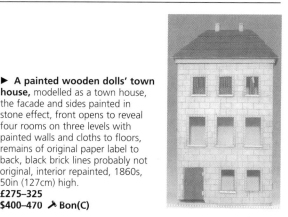

A painted wooden dolls' house, roof lifts off to reveal a single room with painted walls and floor, c1850, 26in (66cm) wide.
£275–325
$400–470 Bon(C)

► **A painted wooden dolls' town house,** modelled as a town house, the facade and sides painted in stone effect, front opens to reveal four rooms on three levels with painted walls and cloths to floors, remains of original paper label to back, black brick lines probably not original, interior repainted, 1860s, 50in (127cm) high.
£275–325
$400–470 Bon(C)

A flat-roofed dolls' house, by Lines Brothers, with four rooms, staircase, butler's sink and four fireplaces, c1910, 24in (61cm) high.
£530–630
$750–900 G(L)

A dolls' painted stable house, with a terrace and outside staircase, two stuffed pull-along horses and a tin horse-drawn roller, c1900, 20¾in (52.5cm) wide.
£520–620
$750–900 HOLL

A 'Queen Mary's Dolls' House', by Lines Brothers, Tudor-style with thatched-effect roof, on a garden plinth, with four rooms, hall, stairs, landing, two fireplaces, dresser, sink and tinplate cooker, wired for electricity, 1930s, 24in (61cm) high, including a quantity of 1930s dolls' house furniture and accessories.
£700–800
$1,000–1,150 G(L)

Dolls' House Furniture

A dolls' house pine bureau, inlaid with walnut, with four small and three large drawers, German, 1860, 5in (12.5cm) high.
£200–230
$290–330 YC

A French-style dolls' house sofa and two chairs, simulated rosewood with gold print decor, original upholstery, German, 1860–70, 2¼in (5.5cm) high.
£120–150
$175–220 YC

A French-style dolls' house writing desk, simulated rosewood and ebony, with a marble top and three drawers, German, 1860, 4in (10cm) high.
£80–100
$115–145 YC

A French-style dolls' house sewing table, simulated mahogany with printed gilt decor, with sewing accessories in drawer compartments, German, 1860–70, 3in (7.5cm) high.
£130–150
$190–220 ⊞ YC

A dolls' house rocking chair, soft white metal, gilt paint, French, 1880–1900, 2¾in (7cm) high.
£35–40
$50–60 ⊞ YC

A dolls' house sewing machine, soft white metal, painted black and gold, c1900, 2in (5cm) high.
£35–40
$50–60 ⊞ YC

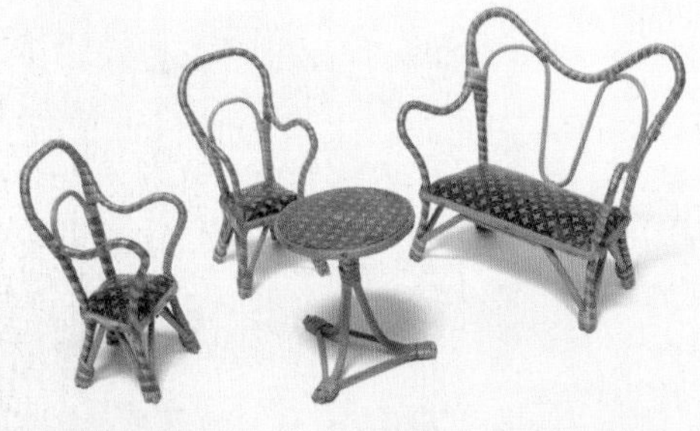

A set of dolls' house wicker chairs and a table, with leatherette papered seats, 1900–10, 7in (18cm) high.
£150–180
$220–260 ⊞ YC

A dolls' house ceramic bathroom set, Japanese, 1900–20, in original box, 4in (10cm) wide.
£45–55
$65–80 ⊞ HUM

Four pieces of dolls' house kitchen furniture, by Jane Newman, comprising dresser, two chairs and a table, 2000, dresser 7in (18cm) high.
£60–80
$90–115 each ⊞ CNM

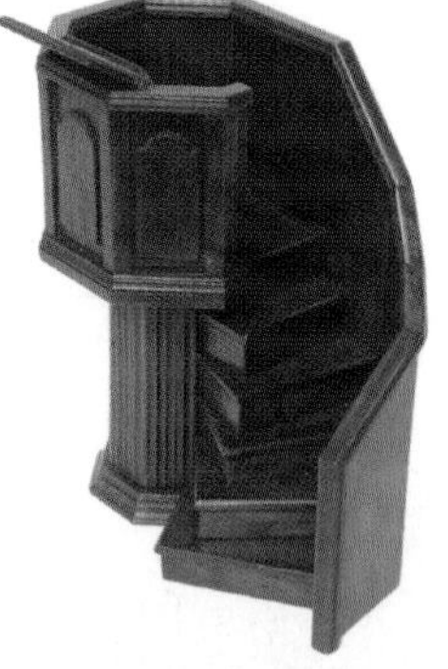

◄ A dolls' house mahogany pulpit, 2000, 8in (20.5cm) high.
£150–170
$220–250 ⊞ CNM

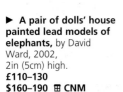

► A pair of dolls' house painted lead models of elephants, by David Ward, 2002, 2in (5cm) high.
£110–130
$160–190 ⊞ CNM

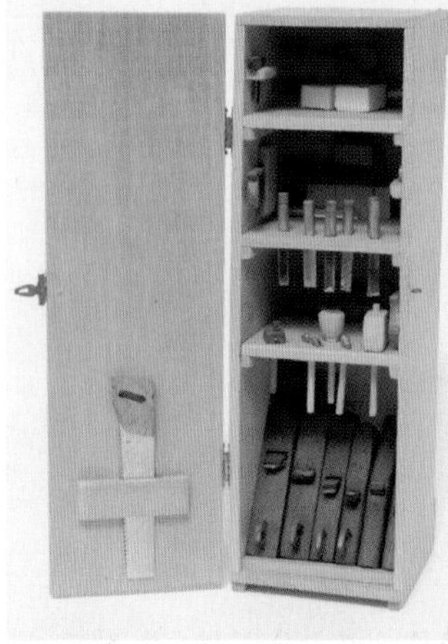

A dolls' house wooden tool cupboard, by Terry McAllister, with tools, 2002, 7in (18cm) high.
£140–160
$200–230 ⊞ CNM

Eighties

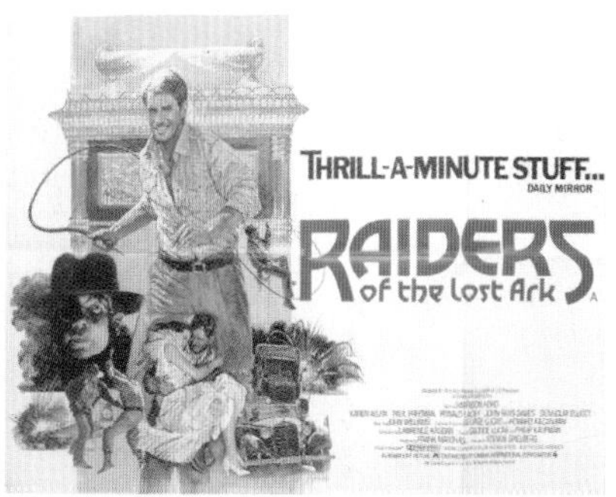

A film poster, *Raiders of the Lost Ark*, the first film in the Indiana Jones series, 1981, 40 x 30in (101.5 x 76cm).
£90–110
$130–160 ⚒ CO

A Royal Doulton coffee pot, teapot, tea cup, saucer and goblet, decorated with Tangier pattern, 1980s, coffee pot 9in (23cm) high.
Coffee pot and teapot
£44–48
$65–75 each
Cup and saucer and goblet
£12–14
$15–18 each ⊞ CHI

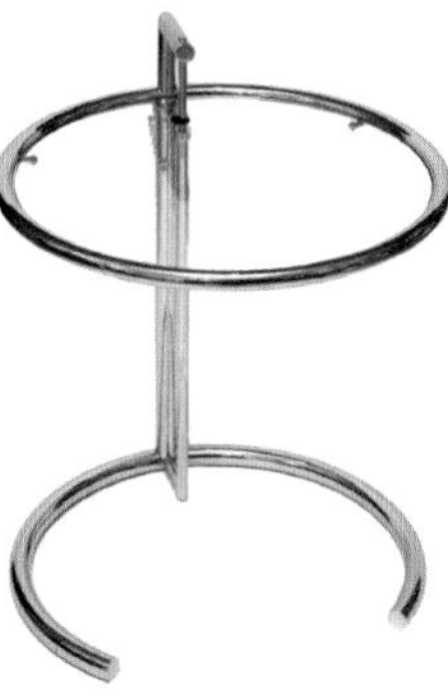

A chrome and glass side table, designed by Eileen Gray, height adjustable, designed 1930s, produced 1980s, 20in (51cm) diam.
£130–150
$190–220 ⊞ MARK

A Kenner *Star Wars* Power of Force special collectors edition, with a coin and B-wing pilot, American, 1983, 4in (10cm) high, with original packaging,
£150–160
$220–230 ⊞ SSF

A Coalport bone china General Election goblet, limited edition of 500, 1983, 5in (12.5cm) high.
£90–110
$130–160 ⊞ H&G

An Epic/Sony Michael Jackson BAD LP, Japanese pressing, 1987.
£30–35
$45–50 ⊞ BNO

A Warner Brothers Prince '1999' LP, 1983.
£27–30
$38–45 ⊞ BNO

A Denby Touchstone Falling Leaves cutlery set, comprising 5 pieces, 1984, with original box.
£35–40
$50–60 ⊞ CHI

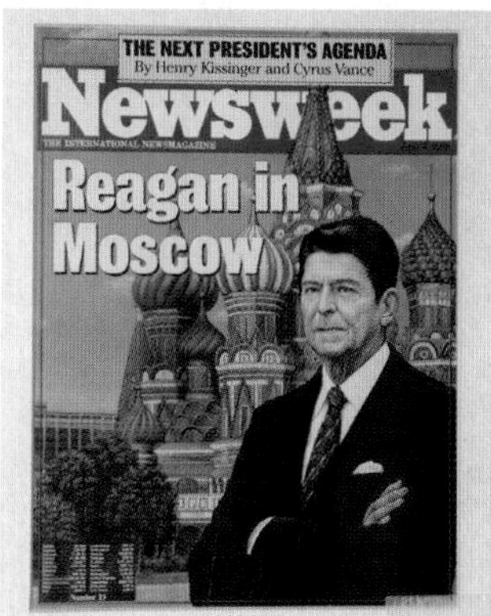

A framed *Newsweek* magazine cover, featuring Ronald Reagan in Moscow, 1988, 10 x 8in (25.5 x20.5cm).
£25–30
$35–45 ⊞ POL

Ephemera

A vellum indenture of lease, from Geoffrey Pigot to Randolph de Romundeby of York, with a pendant wax seal attached by original vellum tag, dated 1370, 5½ x 11in (14 x 28cm).
£400–450
$580–650 DW

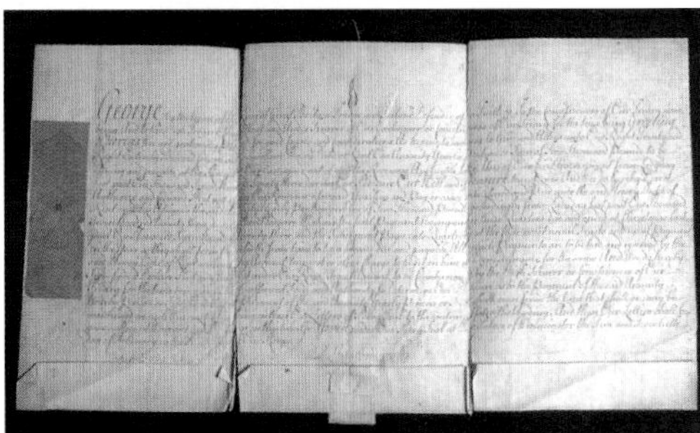

► A Royal document, Renewal of Annuity to Henry Duke of Kent, given under Privy Seal, Palace of Westminster, seal missing, worn, 1723, 11 x 20in (28 x 51cm).
£20–25
$30–35 DAL

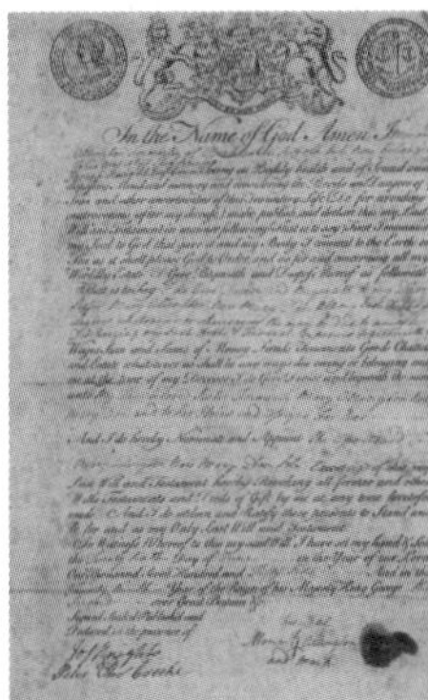

A Naval will, partially-printed with manuscript insertions and woodcut engravings showing King George II, the Royal coat-of-arms and the Insignia of the Royal Navy, with remains of wax seal, small chip, dated June 26 1756, 2°.
£180–220
$260–320 DW

Cross Reference
See Shipping (pages 342–346)

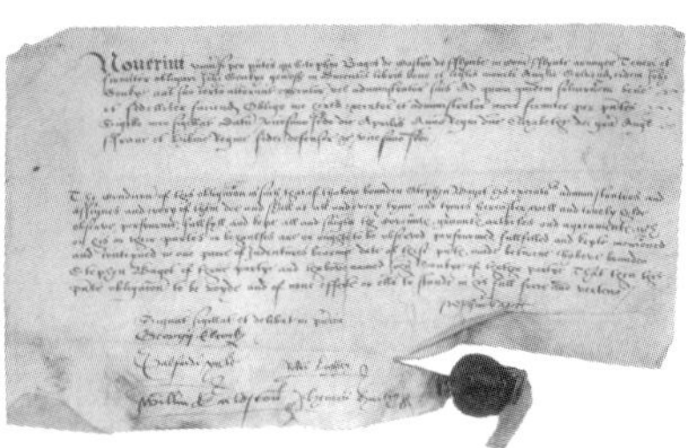

A vellum obligation bond, written in Latin and English, with wax seal attached by original vellum tag, some creasing, c1580, 10 x 5¾in (25.5 x 14.5cm).
£130–160
$190–230 DW

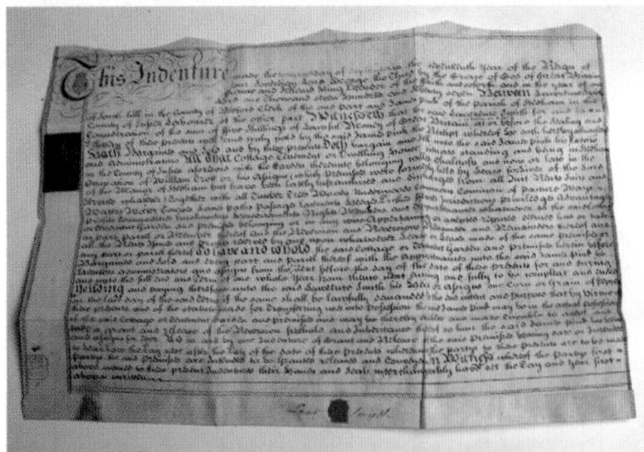

A land indenture parchment, 1777, 13 x 21in (33 x 53.5cm).
£18–20
$25–30 J&S

◄ A copy of the Freedom of London, presented to Henry John Andrew Barber, 10 March 1841, with original boxwood case.
£75–90
$110–130 SWO

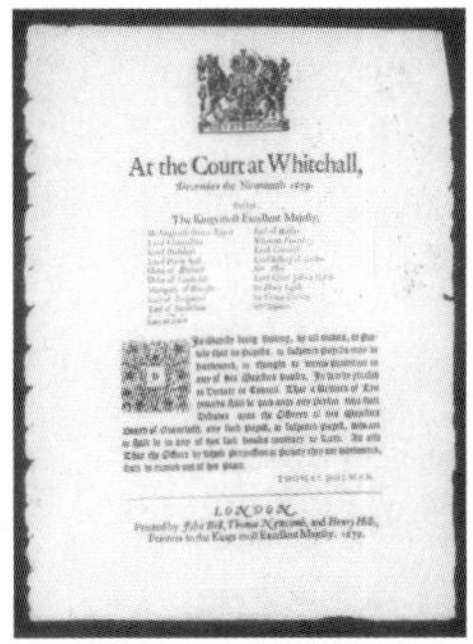

At the Court at Whitehall,

A Royal Proclamation broadside, offering a reward to 'any person who shall discover unto the officers of his majesties board of Greencloth any such papist or suspected papist who are or shall be in any of his said houses contrary to law', slight fraying to borders, dated 1679, 14¼ x 11½in (36 x 29cm).
£150–200
$220–290 DW

The reward was offered in the wake of the celebrated Popish Plot of Titus Oates – a zealous protestant who fabricated a supposed plot to kill King Charles II by a group of Catholic conspirators. The frenzy which followed resulted in many Catholics being put to death and James the Duke of York being barred from succeeding his brother. Oates was given a pension during the lifetime of Charles II, but when James eventually did succeed his brother in 1685, Oates was publicly whipped through the streets of London.

An entrance ticket to the Royal Exchange stone-laying ceremony, with the Royal coat of arms surmounting an engraved vignette view of the completed building, with wax seal, dated 7 January 1842, 10¾ x 7½in (27.5 x 19cm), with a hand-coloured steel engraving of the stone-laying event and a modern booklet providing a history of the building.
£40–50
$60–75 ⚒ DW

► **A piece of calligraphic artwork,** 'God's Saints religious verse', c1920, 13 x 10in (33 x 20.5cm).
£20–25
$30–35 ⊞ J&S

A St Patrick's Day menu, American, early 20thC, 7 x 5½in (18 x 14cm).
£45–55
$70–80 ⚒ MSB

► ***The Economic Crisis Foretold by the Daily Mail 1921–31,*** a printed booklet, 1931, 10 x 6in (25.5 x 15cm).
£8–10
$12–15 ⊞ J&S

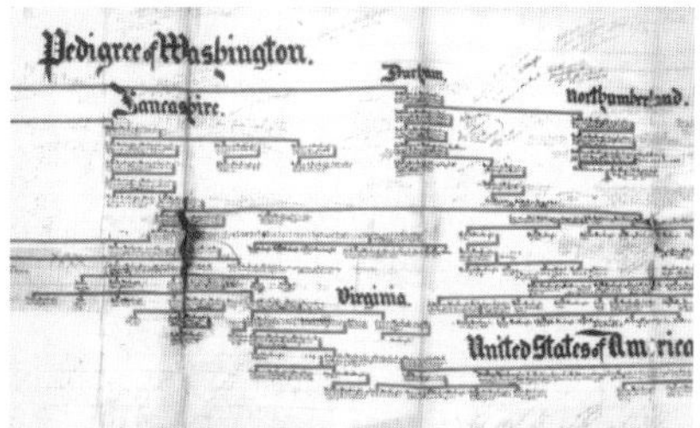

The Pedigree of Washington, giving the pedigree of George Washington, first President of the United States, some dusting and wear, mid-19thC, 204 x 24in (518 x 61cm).
£850–1,000
$1,250–1,500 ⚒ DW

This document was prepared by General Plantagenet Harrison, one of the leading genealogists of his day. He published several works on the subject – notably his history of Yorkshire – but also prepared individual pedigrees of some of the most famous men in history. In this example he traces George Washington's line back to the reign of King Stephen (1135–54) where he identifies a 'Lord of Washington' from the Richmond area of North Yorkshire.

► **A British passport,** Alexander Andrews, No. 123861, 1920s, 7 x 5in (18 x 12.5cm).
£12–15
$15–20 ⊞ J&S

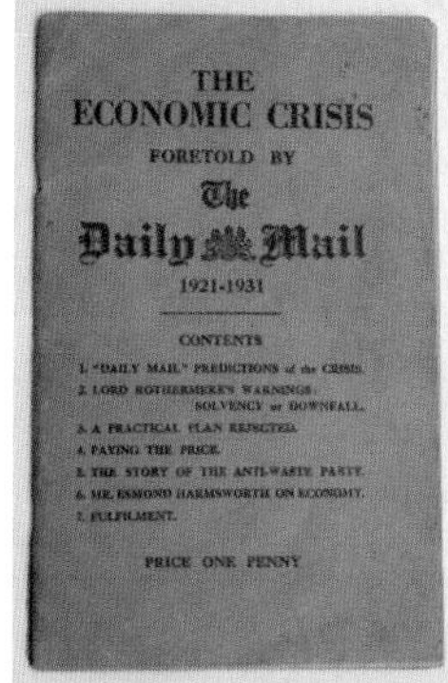

A writing book from Welchpool School, 1870s, 10 x 8in (25.5 x 20.5cm).
£20–25
$30–35 ⊞ COB

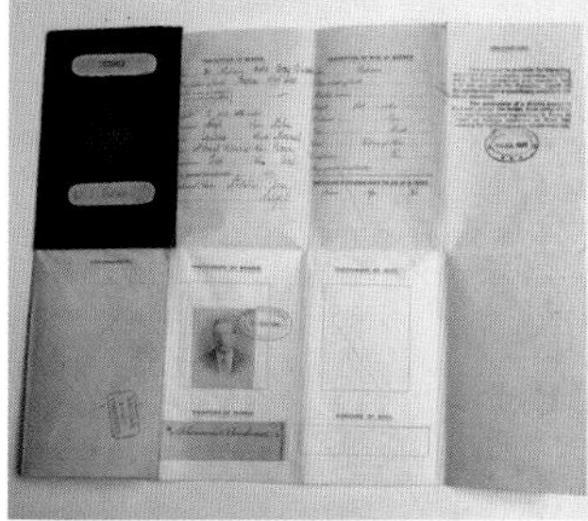

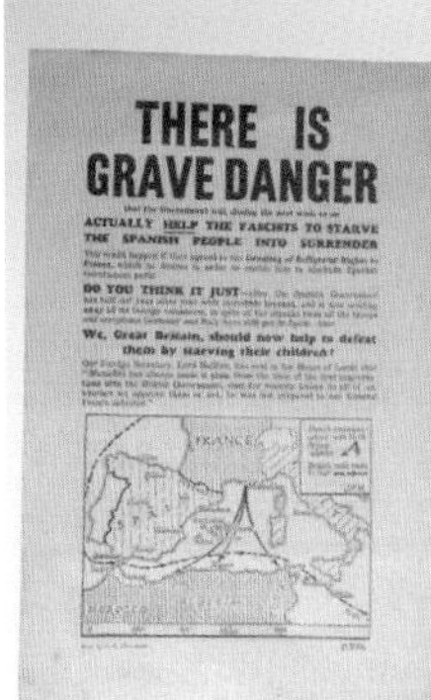

A Spanish Civil War propaganda leaflet, 1936, 10 x 7in (25.5 x 18cm).
£12–15
$15–20 ⊞ J&S

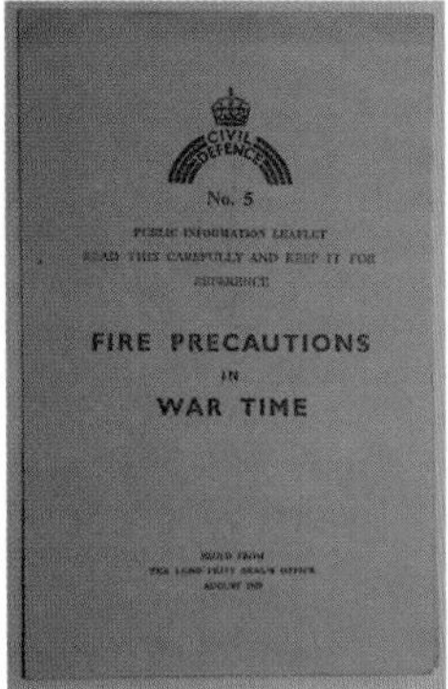

Fire Precautions in War Time, a booklet issued by the Lord Privy Seal's Office, 1939, 8¾ x 5½in (22 x 45cm).
£3–5
$5–7 ⊞ HUX

A theatre programme, for the New Theatre, Northampton, 1930s, 8 x 4in (20.5 x 10cm).
£5–10
$7–15 ⊞ COB

A Ribble Motor Services bus timetable, No. 3, East Lancs area, 1946, 7 x 4in (18 x 10cm).
£8–10
$12–15 ⊞ MRW

A Ballet calendar, 1947, 9½ x 7¾in (24 x 19.5cm).
£8–10
$12–15 ⊞ RTT

◄ **A Mabel Lucie Attwell birthday card,** Dutch, c1950, 7 x 3in (18 x 7.5cm).
£5–8
$7–10 ⊞ MEM

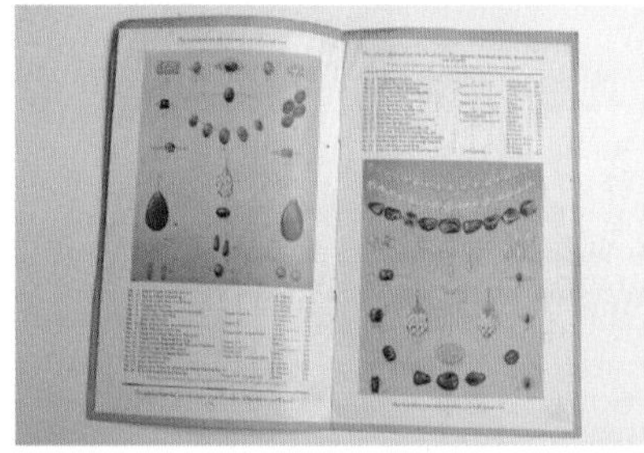

A costume jewellery catalogue, c1950, 9 x 6in (23 x 15cm).
£15–18
$20–25 ⊞ J&S

A Chipperfield's Circus programme, 1953, 9 x 5in (23 x 15cm).
£8–10
$12–15 ⊞ J&S

A Ribble coach excursions pamphlet, Lake District, 1953, 7 x 4in (18 x 10cm).
£5–10
$7–15 ⊞ COB

A Rawson calendar, 1959, 19 x 14in (48.5 x 38cm).
£1–2
$2–3 ⊞ JUN

Erotica

A Meerschaum pipe, carved with a nude woman at play with a swan, gold-mounted mouthpiece, 19thC, 4in (10cm) long, in original case.
£250–300
$350–450 G(L)

Leda, who was seduced by Jupiter in the form of a swan, provided a favourite classical excuse for portraying a nude. As a result of this union she laid eggs, from one of which hatched Helen of Troy.

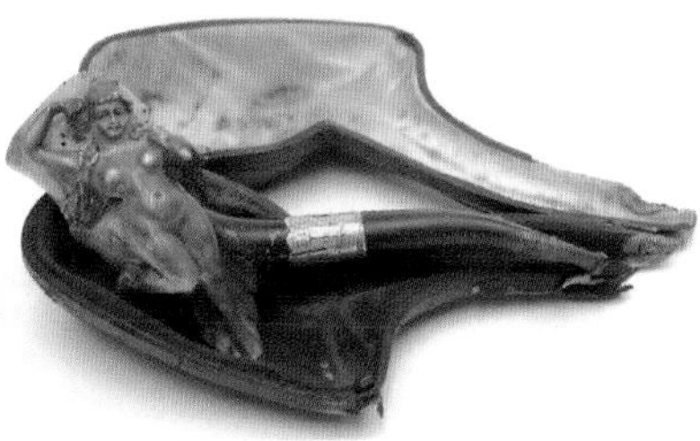

A Meerschaum pipe, carved with a nude woman, silver-mounted mouthpiece, c1910, 5in (12.5cm) long, in original case.
£130–160
$190–230 G(L)

Meerschaum (German for sea foam) is the name given to a form of magnesium silicate originally found on the shores of the Black Sea. Its insulating properties and the fact that it could be elaborately carved made it a favourite material for pipes.

Cross Reference
See Smoking (pages 361–365)

◀ **An art card,** by Walter Hempel, entitled 'Triumph of the Beauty', German, 1926, 6 x 4in (15 x 10cm).
£6–8
$7–10 ⊞ S&D

A bronze figure of a nude, signed 'Hollier', marked '178', c1894, 4½in (11.5cm) high.
£250–275
$350–400 ⊞ LBr

A coloured glamour postcard, French, 1910, 6 x 4in (15 x 10cm).
£8–10
$12-15 ⊞ S&D

A miniature painting on ivory, depicting a female nude reclining on a drapery-covered bank, 19thC, 3¼ x 4in (8.5 x 10cm).
£370–420
$550–580 TMA

A set of five miniature mirrors portraying naked women, c1905, 3in (7.5cm) long.
£20–25
$30–35 each ⊞ HUX

A calendar with glamour cover, 1940, 11½ x 9in (29 x 23cm).
£18–22
$28–32 ⊞ RTT

◀ ***Men Only* magazine,** Summer number, 1938, 7½ x 5in (19 x 12.5cm).
£3–5
$5–7 ⊞ RTT

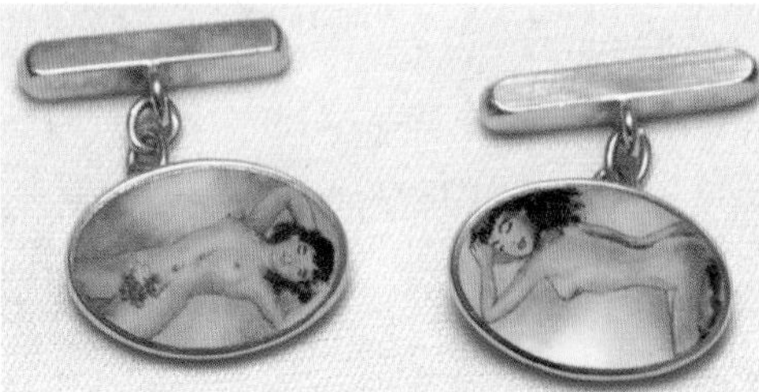

A pair of gold-plated pin-up cufflinks, hand-painted with nude women, c1940, ¼in (.75cm) diam.
£150–180
$220–260 ⊞ JBB

Three issues of *QT* magazine, 1950s, 7 x 5in (18 x 12.5cm).
£5–7
$7–10 each ⊞ RUSS

A pack of pin-up playing cards, 1950s–60s, 3½ x 2½in (9 x 6.5cm).
£12–15
$18–20 ⊞ RTT

A sheet from a pin-up calendar, August 1961, 12 x 9½in (30.5 x 24cm).
£8–10
$10–15 ⊞ RTT

◄ ***Brenda Starr* comic,** cover by Jack Kamen, American, 1948.
£450–500
$650–720 ⚒ CBP

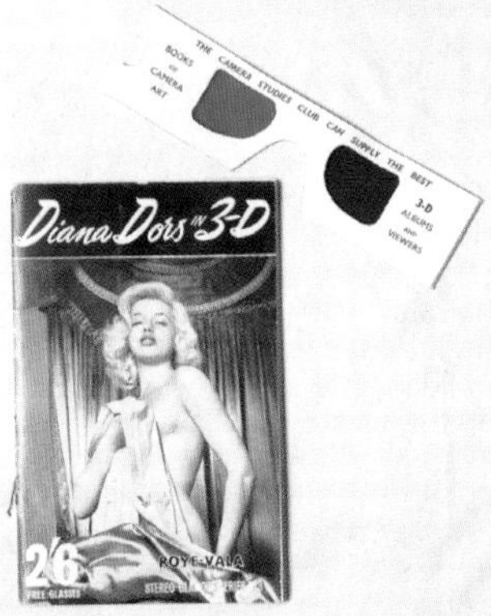

***Diana Dors 3D* booklet,** early 1950s, 6 x 5in (15 x 12.5cm), with 3D glasses.
£18–20
$25–30 ⊞ RUSS

***Tit-Bits* magazine,** 1958, 12 x 10in (30.5 x 25.5cm).
£1–2
$2–3 ⊞ JUN

► ***Playboy* magazine,** 1962, 11 x 8½in (28 x 21.5cm).
£7–9
$9–13 ⊞ RTT

***All Top* comic,** featuring Rulah, Jo-Jo, Beetle, Phantom Lady, cover by Jack Kamen, minor wear, American, 1948.
£160–200
$230–300 ⚒ CBP

***Nuff Sed* magazine,** No. 24, 1950s, 7½ x 5in (19 x 12.5cm).
£5–8
$7–10 ⊞ RTT

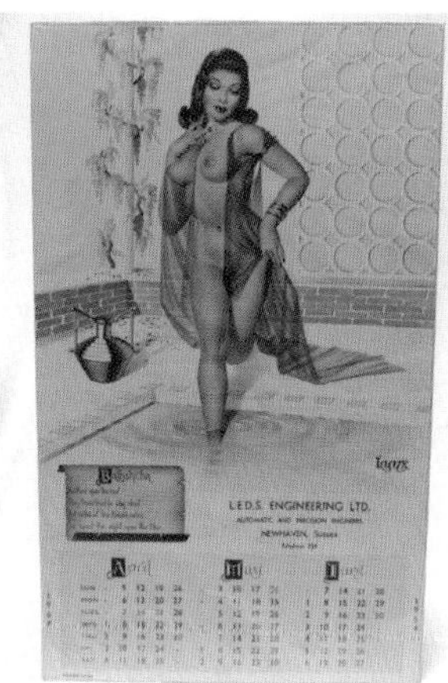

An LEDS calendar sheet, depicting a bathing beauty, April/May/June 1964, 17 x 10¼in (43 x 26cm).
£16–19
$20–30 ⊞ RTT

Invitation, an 8mm erotic film featuring Anne Walker, 1960s, box 4in (10cm) square, boxed.
£12–15
$18–20 ⊞ RTT

A Sexpo '71 poster, designed by Bernd Enzlmüller, 1971, 33 x 23¼in x (84 x 59cm)
£65–80
$95–115 ⚒ VSP

► ***Playboy* magazine,** cover by Alberto Vargas, 1965, 11 x 8½in (28 x 21.5cm).
£18–20
$28–30 ⊞ RTT
Alberto Vargas (1896–1982) was one of the most celebrated pin-up girl artists. His Vargas Girl (a painted nude) first appeared in *Esquire* magazine in 1940. The following year *Esquire* introduced the Vargas calendar, and by 1946 calendar sales had reached three million copies.

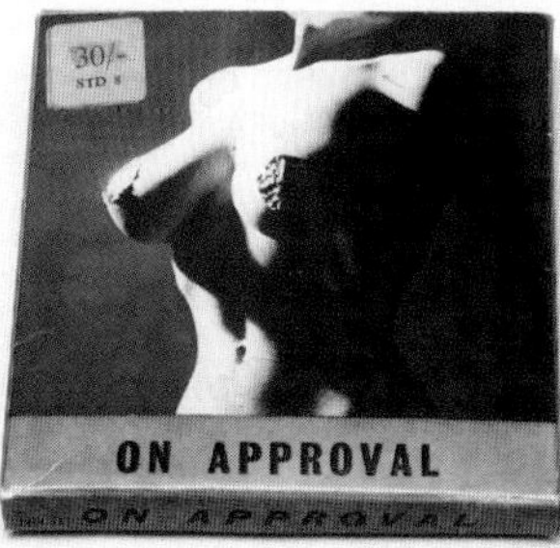

On Approval, an 8mm erotic film, 1960s, box 4in (10cm) square.
£12–15
$18–20 ⊞ RTT

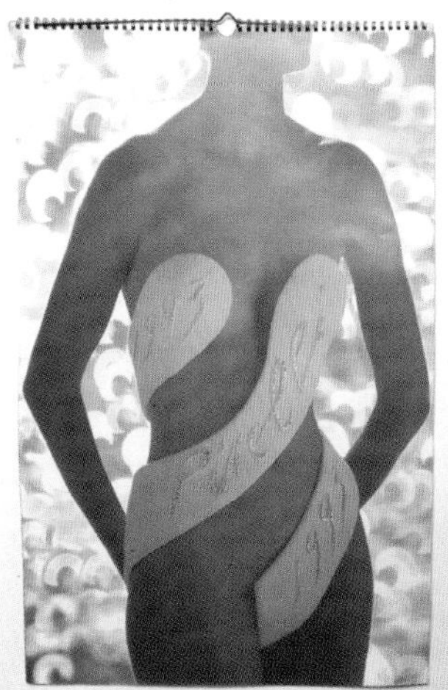

A Pirelli calendar, 1993, 24 x 17in (61 x 43cm).
£30–35
$45–50 ⊞ J&S
Probably the most famous modern European pin-up calendar, the Pirelli calendar was first issued in 1964. Distribution was intentionally limited to selected customers and associates of the Pirelli tyre company, and printing did not exceed 45,000 copies. Many famous photographers have contributed to the calendar.

***Penthouse* magazine,** 1965, 11 x 8½in (28 x 21.5cm).
£8–10
$10–15 ⊞ RTT

A Victoria Silvstedt Playmate of the Year doll, limited edition, 1997, 16in (40.5cm) high.
£55–65
$80–95 ⊞ NOS

Fans

A fan, painted with a scene from Helen of Troy, mother-of-pearl sticks carved with gilt figures, French, c1750, 10½in (26.5cm) wide.
£1,600–2,000
$2,300–3,000 ⊞ LDC

A paper and lace fan, painted with a gallant and his lady in a flowering woodland setting, the mother-of-pearl sticks partially-pierced and with trailing leaf and scroll decoration, signed 'Doneli', gilt-framed and glazed, 19thC, 13in (33cm) wide.
£360–420
$550–620 ⚒ TMA

A pair of papier mâché hand screens, painted in oils in the style of Landseer, with figures, horses and dogs, 19thC, 10½in (26.5cm) wide.
£170–200
$250–300 ⚒ G(L)

◄ **A paper and wood fan,** advertising Vichy, 1880s, 10in (25.5cm) wide.
£90–100
$130–145 ⊞ JUJ

An ostrich feather fan, with tortoiseshell handle, c1920, 18in (45.5cm) wide.
£55–65
$80–95 ⊞ Ech

A handmade lace and ivory fan, c1910, 9in (23cm) wide.
£55–65
$80–95 ⊞ Ech

A paper fan, advertising Perrier water, 1930s, 9in (23cm) wide.
£20–25
$30–35 ⊞ JUJ

► **A paper fan,** advertising Cognac Sorin, French, 1930s, 7½in (19cm) wide.
£30–40
$45–60 ⊞ JUJ

► **A paper fan,** advertising Le Curacao Picon, French, 1930s, 11in (28cm) wide.
£45–55
$65–80 ⊞ JUJ

◄ **A paper and wood fan,** advertising Gitanes cigarettes, French, 1930s, 9in (23cm) wide.
£60–70
$90–100 ⊞ JUJ

Fifties

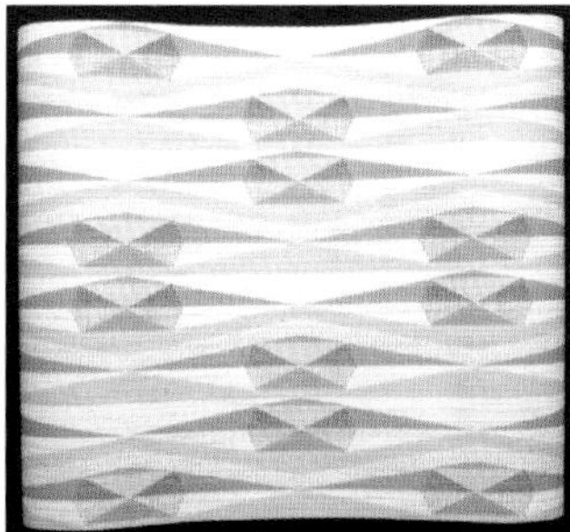

A roll of embossed wallpaper, 1950, 21in (53.5cm) wide.
£25–30
$35–45 ⊞ TWI

A set of six plastic coasters, modelled as records, 1950s, 4in (10cm) square, in original box.
£120–150
$175–220 ⊞ LBe

A Perspex ice bucket, in the shape of a top hat, 1950s, 7in (18cm) diam.
£65–75
$95–110 ⊞ LBe

A laminated bentwood armchair, in the style of Norman Cherner, with black vinyl upholstered back and seat, American, 1950s.
£230–280
$330–400 ⚒ SK

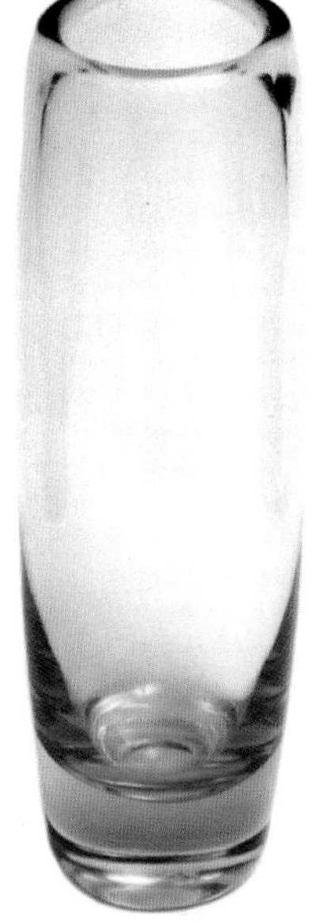

► **A Holmegaard glass vase,** by Per Lutken, 1950s–60s, 11in (28cm) high.
£80–90
$115–130 ⊞ ORI

► **A Holmegaard glass vase,** by Per Lutken, 1950s–60s, 4¼in (11.5cm) high.
£40–50
$60–75 ⊞ ORI

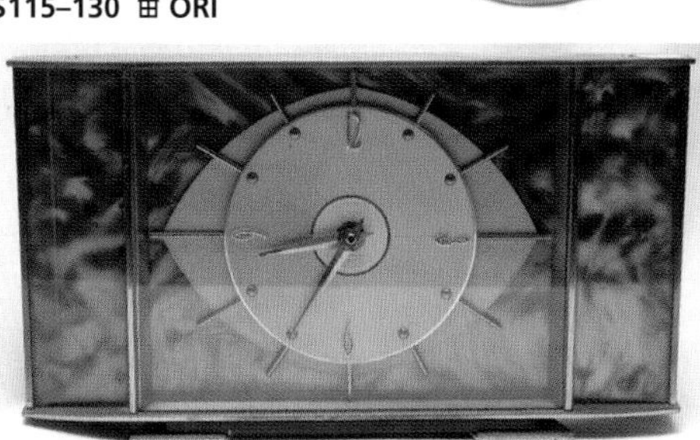

A Metamec plastic and brass clock, 1950s–60s, 11in (28cm) wide.
£18–22
$28–32 ⊞ RTT

Ceramics

A Burgess & Leigh Siesta vase, 1950, 9¾in (25cm) high.
£50–55
$75–80 ⊞ PrB

A Hornsea slipware vase, 1959, 3in (7.5cm) diam.
£15–20
$20–30 ⊞ PrB

A Beswick Teardrop vase, decorated with Zebrette pattern, c1950, 9in (23cm) high.
£40–50
$60–75 ⊞ BEV

A Midwinter plate, designed by Jessie Tait, decorated with Toadstools pattern, c1956, 9in (23cm) diam.
£45–50
$65–75 ⊞ CHI

► **A Poole teapot, milk jug, sugar basin, cup and saucer and plate,** designed by Robert Jefferson, decorated with Pebble pattern, 1959, teapot 5in (12.5cm) high.
£160–175
$230–250 ⊞ CHI

A Vallauris ceramic fish lamp, c1950, 12in (30.5cm) high.
£70–80
$100–115 ⊞ MLL

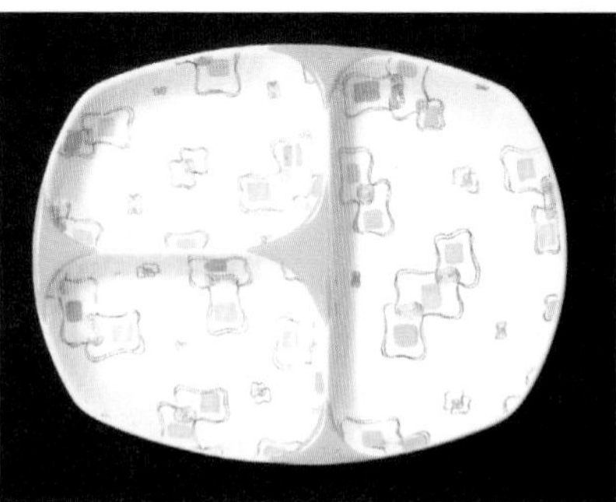

A Midwinter hors d'oeuvres dish, designed by Jessie Tait, decorated with Cuban Fantasy pattern, 1957, 10in (20.5cm) wide.
£65–70
$95–100 ⊞ CHI

A Hornsea ceramic vase, c1950, 12in (30.5cm) wide.
£55–65
$80–95 ⊞ PrB

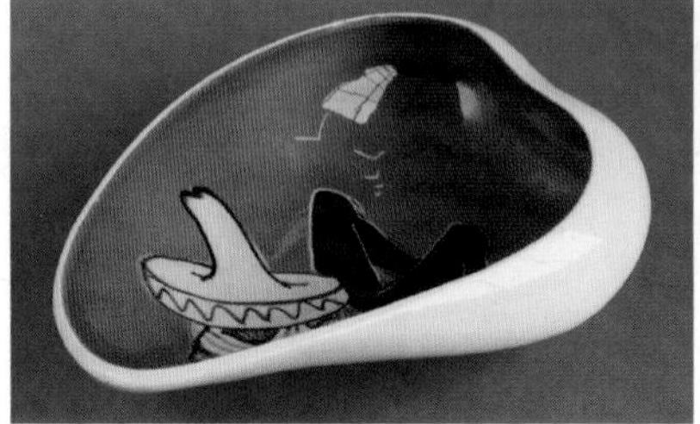

A Studio Anna bonbon dish, Australian, c1950, 7½in (19cm) wide.
£12–15
$15–20 ⊞ PrB

A set of Poole dishes, 1950s, largest 9in (23cm) diam.
£50–60
$75–90 ⊞ CHI

A Poole hors d'oeuvres dish, 1950s, 12in (30.5cm) diam.
£40–45
$60–65 ⊞ CHI

► A Wedgwood teapot, cup and saucer, decorated with Mayfield pattern, 1950s, teapot 5in (12.5cm) high.
£50–65
$75–95 ⊞ CHI

◄ A Royal Doulton sauce boat and stand, decorated with Meadow Glow pattern, 1950s, 9in (23cm) wide.
£25–30
$35–45 ⊞ CHI

A Royal Doulton coffee pot, decorated with Bamboo pattern, 1950s, 8in (20.5cm) high.
£50–55
$75–80 ⊞ CHI

► A Royal Albert TV cup and saucer, decorated with Night and Day pattern, 1950s, 9in (23cm) wide.
£30–35
$45–50 ⊞ CHI

Further reading

Miller's Collecting the 1950s, Miller's Publications, 1998

A Pountney storage jar, decorated with Long Line pattern, with lid, 1950s, 7in (18cm) high.
£40–48
£60–75 ⊞ CHI

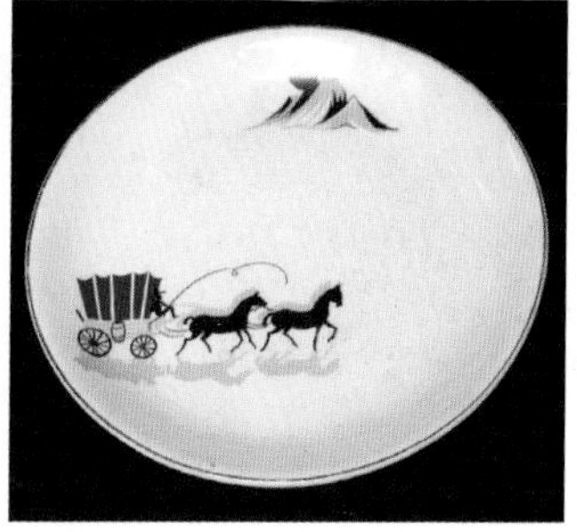

An Alfred Meakin plate, decorated with a wagon and horses, 1950s, 6¾in (17cm) diam.
£3–4
$5–8 ⊞ FLD

A Ridgways lidded tureen, decorated with Homemaker pattern, 1950s, 9in (23cm) diam.
£90–100
$130–145 ⊞ CHI

► An Alfred Meakin plate, decorated with a Mexican scene, 1950s, 9in (23cm) diam.
£3–4
$5–8 ⊞ FLD

Games

◄ **A magic set,** French, c1880, in a box 10in (25.5cm) wide.
£550–600
$800–870
⊞ AUTO

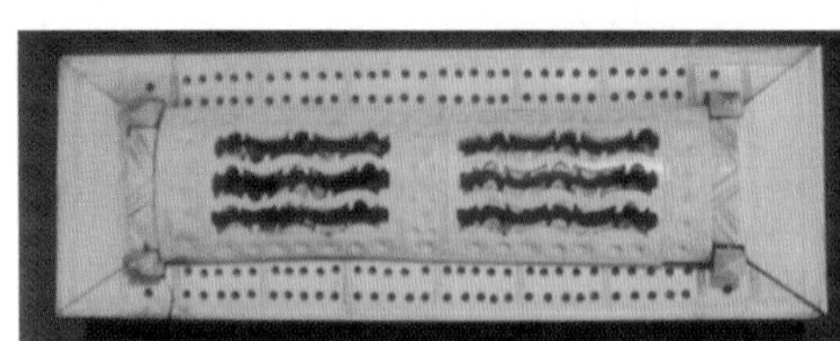

A bone cribbage board, made by Napoleonic prisoners-of-war, modelled as a casket, the domed hinged lid carved with scrolled bars, enclosing a figure of a man wearing military uniform, flanked by pierced scorers, the shaped apron on square legs, French, early 19thC, 9in (23cm) long.
£800–1,000
$1,150–1,500 ⚒ PF

A Jeu de l'Oie board game, French, c1910, 16 x 20in (40.5 x 51cm).
£20–25
$30–35 ⊞ J&J

A Snakes and Ladders board game, box missing, c1910, 10 x 20in (25.5 x 40.5cm).
£20–25
$30–35 ⊞ J&J

The Witch's Cauldron game, by Bing, German, c1920, 8 x 4in (20.5 x 10cm).
£40–45
$60–65 ⊞ J&J

A Wembley Exhibition Electrical Mah Jong set, 1924, 5 x 7in (12.5 x 18cm).
£35–40
$50–60 ⊞ COB

A Blinky Blinx Tiddledy Winks game, by Toys & All Fair Games, American, 1928, 9 x 10in (23 x 25.5cm).
£20–25
$30–35 ⊞ J&J

An Escalado horse racing game, by Chad Valley, c1930, 8 x 11in (20.5 x 28cm).
£170–200
$250–300 ⊞ RGa

A Playing for the Cup board game, by Spears Games, c1930, 7 x 10in (18 x 25.5cm).
£40–45
$60–65 ⊞ J&J

A Grand National Steeplechase board game, by Chad Valley, 1930s, 15 x 40in (38 x 101.5cm).
£80–90
$115–130 ⊞ RGa

A tinplate cat and mouse game, German, 1930s, 1½in (4cm) diam.
£20–25
$30–35 ⊞ LBe

A Wig Wam game, by Chad Valley, 1950, 19 x 15in (48.5 x 38cm).
£10–15
$15–20 ⊞ J&J

A Solitaire set, by Ilex, c1950, 7 x 10in (18 x 25.5cm).
£15–20
$20–30 ⊞ J&J

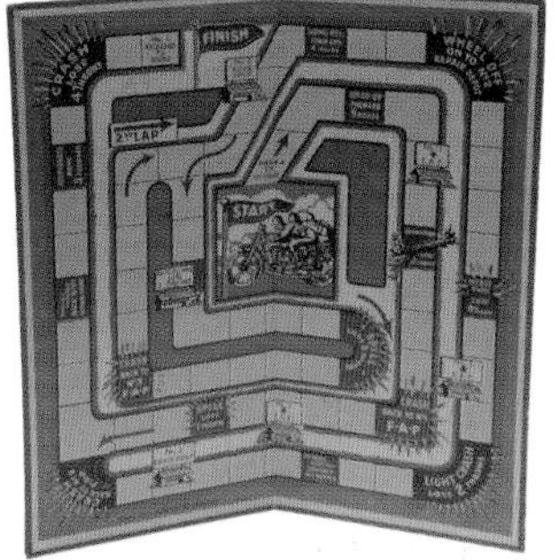

◄ A TT Race board game, incomplete, 1950s, 10in (25.5cm) square.
£7–10
$10–15 ⊞ RTT

A Table Tennis set, Reno Series, 1950, 11 x 14in (28 x 35.5cm).
£15–20
$20–30 ⊞ JUN

► A Tug of War board game, by Chad Valley, 1950s, 5 x 19in (12.5 x 48.5cm).
£20–25
$30–35 ⊞ J&J

A Speedway board game, by Ilex, c1950, 9 x 12in (23 x 30.5cm).
£30–35
$45–50 ⊞ J&J

A Touring England board game, 1950s, 14½ x 10in (37 x 25.5cm).
£15–20
$20–30 ⊞ RTT

A set of painted pine skittles, 1950, 15in (38cm) high.
£80–100
$115–145 ⊞ MLL

Walt Disney's Pinocchio board game, by Chad Valley, c1950, 14in (35.5cm) square.
£15–20
$20–30 ⊞ J&J

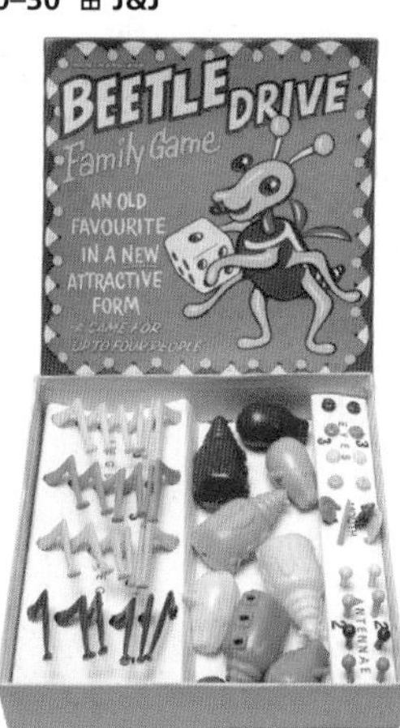

A Beetle Drive game, 1960s, 7in (18cm) square.
£8–10
$10–15 ⊞ RTT

Puzzles

The Chequers Puzzle, by Feltham & Co, c1890, 6in (15cm) square.
£40–50
$60–75 ⊞ J&J

Father Tuck's Picture-Building Puzzle, c1920, 10 x 9in (25.5 x 23cm).
£45–55
$65–80 ⊞ J&J

A Junior Jig-Saw Puzzle, by Tower Press, c1950, 7 x 6in (18 x 15cm).
£10–15
$15–20 ⊞ J&J

► **A wooden picture blocks puzzle,** 1920s, 18 x 17in (45.5 x 43cm).
£25–30
$35–40 ⊞ J&J

A Defeat of the Giant Decay jigsaw puzzle, No. 4, advertising Gibbs Dentifrice, c1930, 4 x 5in (10 x 12.5cm).
£20–25
$30–35 ⊞ J&J

A Victory jigsaw puzzle, depicting the Cunard White Star Liner *Mauretania*, 1939, 9 x 11in (23 x 28cm).
£40–45
$60–65 ⊞ J&J

A Victory wooden jigsaw puzzle, featuring pilots and their Bristol Bulldogs, c1935, 6¾ x 8¾in (17 x 22cm).
£30–35
$45–50 ⊞ HUX

A Skipper frame-tray puzzle, from the Barbie series, c1965, 14 x 11in (35.5 x 28cm).
£60–70
$90–100 ⊞ T&D

◄ **A Moonprobe jigsaw puzzle,** by Waddington's, with space exploration booklets, 1969, 13in (33cm) square.
£15–20
$20–30 ⊞ RTT

Playing Cards

Playing cards first came to Europe in the 14th century, probably from the Middle East. Various suit-marks were used by different countries. Following Islamic prototypes Italian suitmarks became Swords, Cups, Coins and Batons, with an all-male set of court cards: King, Knight, Jack. The now standard use of Hearts, Clubs, Diamonds and Spades developed in France. The simplicity of these symbols meant that while the 12 court cards (also including the Queen) had to be engraved, the others could be stencilled, making the manufacturing process far cheaper.

By the 16th century, France was Europe's leading exporter of playing cards. In order to protect themselves against foreign imports, the English manufacturers formed the Worshipful Company of Makers of Playing Cards, which was granted a Royal Charter in 1628. Thousands of packs were destroyed by the Puritans, who disapproved of gambling, but with the restoration of the monarchy in 1660, card playing was back in fashion. Recognizing that there was money to be made as well as lost on cards, the authorities levied a tax on each pack sold, which persisted until 1960. The English pack was taken by colonists to America, from where a new card emerged in the 19th century – the Joker.

The Victorian period brought many changes including the introduction in the UK of double-headed court cards (as opposed to a single figure) and from c1880 the printing of the value of the card on both top left and bottom right. With machine cutting, cards could have rounded corners which damaged less easily than square edges and, thanks to cheaper printing processes, they became more affordable and a host of different designs and games were produced. Major manufacturers included Goodall and De La Rue.

Playing cards dating from before the 19th century are very rare and most collectors focus on Victorian and 20th-century packs. Popular subjects include advertising cards (produced as promotional tools) and children's games. When buying vintage cards, check that they are in good condition without dog-eared corners or tears, and that they are complete. Packs still in their original boxes or wrappers are worth more than loose cards.

A pack of Goodalls playing cards, illustrated with Kings and Queens, c1897, 5 x 4in (12.5 x 10cm).
£70–85
$100–125 ⊞ MURR

A pack of De La Rue playing cards, depicting lady and gentleman motorists, 1900–08, 5 x 3½in (12.5 x 9.5cm).
£70–85
$100–125 ⊞ MURR

A pack of Alice in Wonderland playing cards, 1905, 5 x 3¼in (12.5 x 8.5cm).
£65–75
$95–110 ⊞ HUX

◄ A pack of French for Fun playing cards, by John Jaques & Son, 1910, 4 x 3in (10 x 7.5cm).
£12–15
$15–20 ⊞ J&J

► A pack of Lambert & Butler The Garrick playing cards, c1910, 5 x 3¼in (12.5 x 8.5cm).
£25–30
$35–45 ⊞ HUX

A pack of Florence Upton Golliwogg snap cards, 1910–20, 5 x 4in (12.5 x 10cm).
£75–100
$110–145 ⊞ MURR

► **A pack of the Round Card Game of Happy Families playing cards,** by Chad Valley, c1920, 6 x 4in (15 x 10cm).
£20–25
$30–35 ⊞ J&J

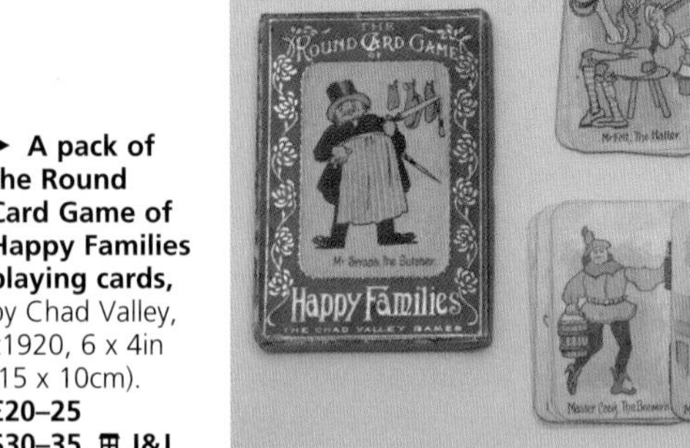

A pack of Dewar's playing cards, 1920s, 5 x 3¾in (12.5 x 9.5cm).
£20–25
$30–35 ⊞ HUX

A pack of Dewar's playing cards, 1920s, 5 x 3¾in (12.5 x 9.5cm).
£20–25
$30–35 ⊞ HUX

A pack of De La Rue playing cards, depicting a mounted jockey, 1930s, 2½ x 3in (6.5 x 7.5cm).
£12–15
$15–20 ⊞ ATK

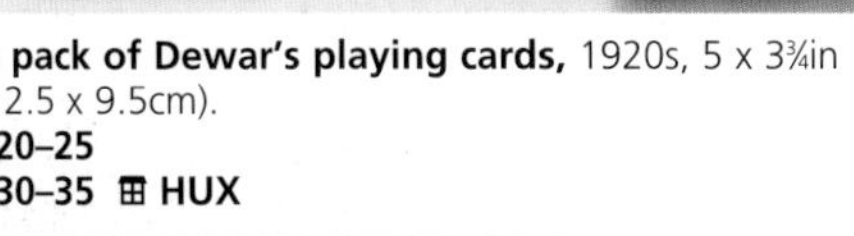

A pack of Black & White Whisky playing cards, by Waddington's, 1930s, 5 x 3¼in (12.5 x 8.5cm), in a sealed box.
£25–30
$35–45 ⊞ HUX

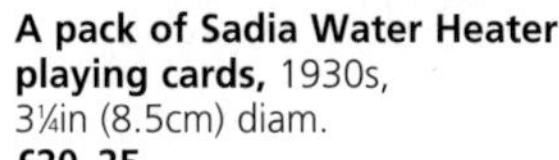

A pack of Sadia Water Heater playing cards, 1930s, 3¼in (8.5cm) diam.
£20–25
$30–35 ⊞ HUX

► **An Animal Grab card game,** 1940s, 4 x 2½in (10 x 6.5cm).
£8–10
$10–15 ⊞ RTT

A pack of Knock Knock playing cards, by Chad Valley, 1930s, 4 x 3in (10 x 7.5cm).
£15–20
$20–30 ⊞ J&J

A pack of Victory playing cards, depicting satirical portraits of WWII figures, 1939–45, 3½ x 2½in (9 x 6.5cm).
£20–25
$30–35 ⊞ HUX

A Film Fantasy card game, by Pepys, 1940s, 4 x 2½in (10 x 6.5cm).
£12–15
$15–20 ⊞ J&J

A Wizard of Oz card game, 1940s, 5 x 3¼in (12.5 x 8.5cm).
£30–35
$45–50 ⊞ HUX

An I Commit card game, by Pepys, 1940s, 3½ x 2½in (9 x 6.5cm).
£12–15
$15–20 ⊞ HUX

A Progress card game, by Castell Brothers, Pepys series, c1950, 4 x 2½in (10 x 6.5cm).
£15–20
$20–30 ⊞ J&J

► A Peter Cheyney Crime Club card game, by Pepys, c1950, 4 x 3in (10 x 7.5cm).
£12–15
$15–20 ⊞ J&J

A pack of So I Told 'Em Oldham playing cards, with Jokers, 1950s, 3½ x 2½in (9 x 6.5cm).
£24–28
$35–40 ⊞ BOB

A Disneyland Express Trainload of Walt Disney's Fantasyland Card Games, by Russell Manufacturing Co, American, 1950s, 14in (35.5cm) long.
£75–85
$110–125 ⊞ J&J

A Muffin the Mule card game, 1950s, 5 x 3¼in (12.5 x 8.5cm).
£25–30
$35–45 ⊞ HUX

A pack of Embassy Cigarettes playing cards, 1960s, 4 x 2½in (10 x 6.5cm) high.
£8–10
$10–15 ⊞ RTT

◄ A Walt Disney's Alice card game, 1960s, 5 x 3½in (12.5 x 9cm).
£23–25
$30–35 ⊞ HUX

Garden & Farm Collectables

A matched pair of staddle stones, with shaped tops, on square supports, 18th–19thC, 27½in (70cm) high.
£250–280
$350–400 🔨 DD

A cast-iron garden seat, with wooden seat and back, 19thC, 56½in (143.5cm) wide.
£650–750
$950–1,100 ⊞ PAS

A Coalbrookdale Rustic pattern cast-iron garden seat, No. 78768, c1887, 60in (152.5cm) wide.
£2,500–2,800
$3,500–4,000 ⊞ WRe

► Two half-glazed earthenware Buckley Mugs, c1890, 17in (43cm) high.
£35–45
$50–65 each ⊞ HOP
These were often used for dairy purposes, or for forcing rhubarb.

A Coalbrookdale-style blue-painted cast-iron garden seat, with Fern and Blackberry pattern, slatted wooden seat, repaired, 19thC, 61in (155cm) wide.
£550–650
$800–950 🔨 CAG

◄ A draw knife, by Gilpin, late 19thC, 15in (38cm) long.
£15–20
$20–30 ⊞ WO

A felling axe, No. 8, by Elwell, c1910, axe head 12in (30.5cm) long.
£55–65
$80–100 ⊞ WO

A cast-iron agricultural drill cog, converted for use as an umbrella stand, c1900, 18in (45.5cm) diam.
£45–50
$65–75 ⊞ HOP

A Sutton's Seeds tin, c1910, 8in (20.5cm) wide.
£70–80
$100–115 ⊞ JUN

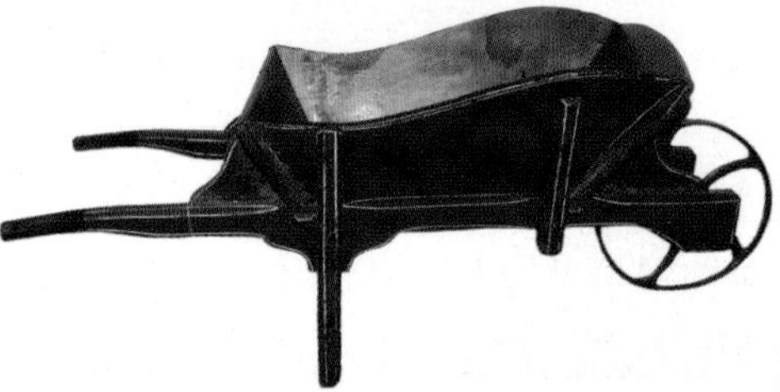

► A wheelbarrow, with original paint, c1910, 64in (162.5cm) long.
£600–700
$870–1,000
⊞ SMI

Further reading

Miller's Garden Antiques: How to Source & Identify,
Miller's Publications, 2003

A Haws tin watering can, with three attachments, c1920, 33in (84cm) long.
£50–60
$75–90 ⊞ AL

A wooden garden trug, c1920, 29in (73.5cm) long.
£65–70
$95–100 ⊞ SMI

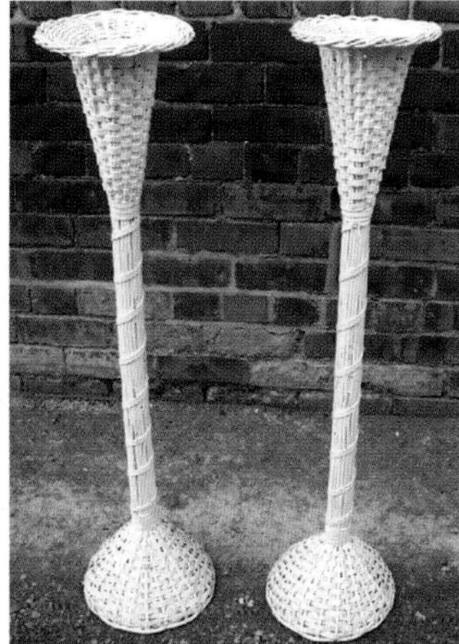

A pair of wicker florist shop stands, with metal liners, c1920, 39in (99cm) high.
£70–85
$100–125 ⊞ HOP

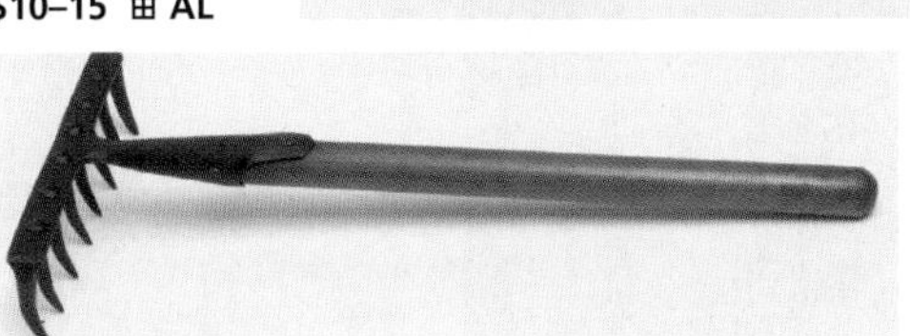

► **An iron daisy grubber,** with wooden handle, c1920, 7½in (19cm) long.
£8–10
$10–15 ⊞ AL

An iron hand rake, with wooden handle, c1920, 17in (43cm) long.
£10–12
$15–18 ⊞ AL

An iron onion hoe, with wooden handle, c1920, 19in (48.5cm) long.
£10–12
$15–18 ⊞ AL

An iron dock grubber, with wooden handle, c1920, 26in (66cm) long.
£30–35
$45–50 ⊞ AL

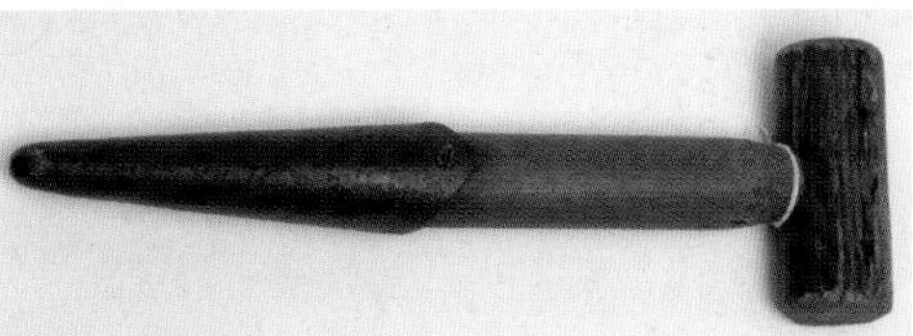

An iron dibber, with wooden handle, c1920, 12in (30.5cm) long.
£10–13
$15–20 ⊞ AL

An iron trowel, with wooden handle, c1920, 10in (25.5cm) long.
£6–8
$5–10 ⊞ AL

A Fly-Tox spray applicator, 1970s, 14in (35.5cm) long.
£10–15
$15–20 ⊞ TRA

◄ **An iron and brass cattle ear numbering punch,** 1950, box 15in (38cm) wide.
£40–45
$60–65 ⊞ GAC

Glass

A clear glass rolling pin, inscribed 'Presentat Harry Pearsall', decorated with prints of London buildings and minstrel singers, c1850, 18in (45.5cm) long.
£180–200
$250–300 ⊞ GRI

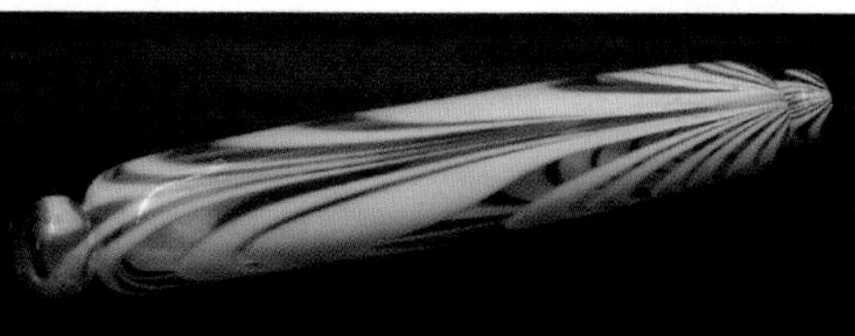

A Nailsea glass rolling pin, with white combed pattern, c1850, 13½in (34.5cm) long.
£100–115
$145–175 ⊞ GRI

Rolling pins

Glass rolling pins were made in the 18th and 19th century, often for decoration. They could also be used for practical purposes, providing a cool roller for pastry (some came with a stoppered/corked end so that they could be filled with cold water). Many were made from coloured glass, some with Nailsea-style trailed decoration. Popular gifts, particularly from sailors to their sweethearts, they were also inscribed in enamel with loving messages and portraits of ships. Another popular form of decoration was the inclusion of coloured prints inside the rolling pin. Values vary according to the colour of the glass, condition (surface enamel becomes easily worn) and extent and quality of ornamentation.

A celery vase, acid-etched with fern decoration, c1880, 9in (23cm) high.
£70–80
$100–115 ⊞ JHa

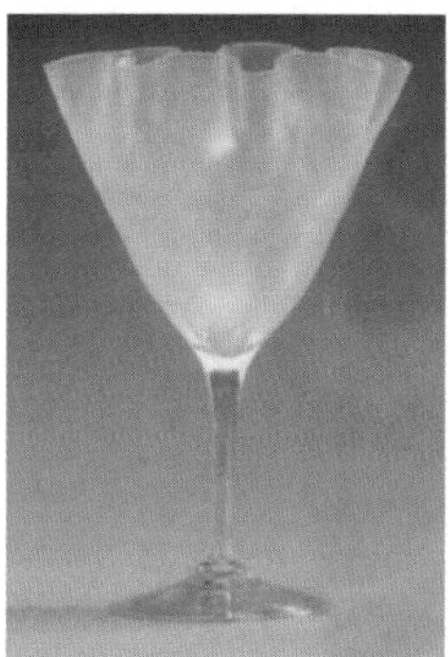

A Venetian-style glass vase, possibly by James Powell & Sons, Whitefriars, with folded rim and moulded 'peacock flower' motifs to the iridescent metal, on a plain slender stem and circular foot, c1890, 9¾in (25cm) high.
£100–120
$145–175 ⚒ TEN

◄ A facet-cut amethyst wine glass rinser, c1890, 2¾in (7cm) high.
£100–120
$145–175 ⊞ GRI

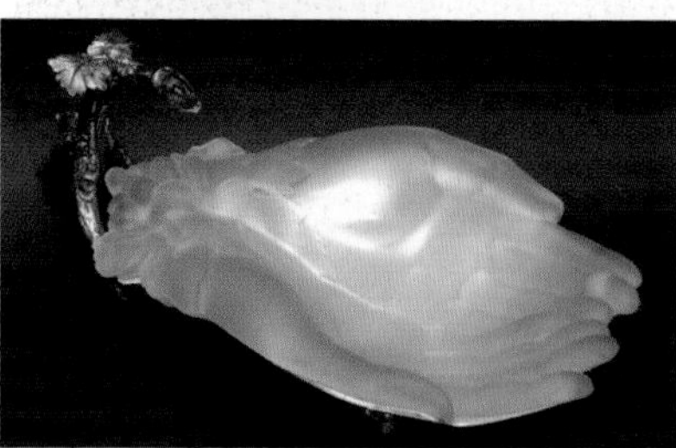

A pressed glass grape dish, modelled as a pair of hands, in a silver-plated stand, c1890, 7in (18cm) long.
£180–200
$250–300 ⊞ GRI

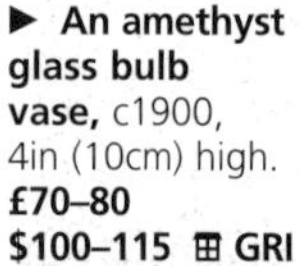

► An amethyst glass bulb vase, c1900, 4in (10cm) high.
£70–80
$100–115 ⊞ GRI

A glass *épergne*, with frilled central vase, flanked by two smaller opalescent vases with red rims, one flute missing, 19thC, 19¾in (50cm) high.
£120–140
$175–200 ⚒ BLH

A decalcomania transferred glass globe, by Doward Bros, Southport, on an ebonized stand, maker's mark to stopper, 19thC, 11¾in (30cm) high.
£200–230
$300–330 ⊞ SWO

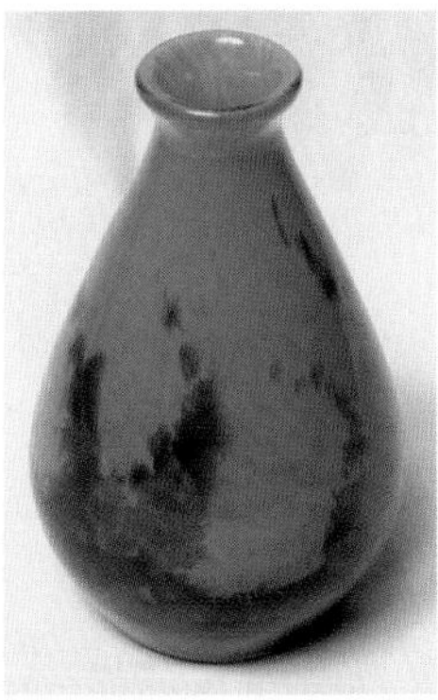

A Müller Frères glass vase, c1910, damaged, 6¾in (17cm) high.
£200–225
$300–325 ⊞ RW

A cut-glass cruet, in a silver-plated stand, c1910, 5½in (14cm) high.
£75–85
$110–125 ⊞ GRI

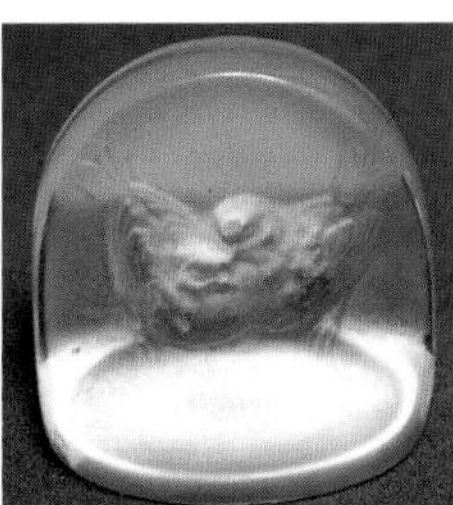

A Lalique patina rubbed glass menu holder, depicting love birds, c1920, 2in (5cm) high.
£150–180
$220–260 ⊞ LBr

A crystal glass fruit bowl, with knopped stem, on a circular base, 1920s, 10in (25.5cm) diam.
£25–30
$35–45 ⚒ BWL

A pressed glass cheese dish, c1930, 8in (20.5cm) wide.
£14–16
$20–25 ⊞ AL

A James Powell & Sons, Whitefriars, Wealdstone glass bowl, c1930, 7in (18cm) diam.
£34–38
$50–55 ⊞ RUSK

A ruby and blue splatter glass wine cooler, Continental, c1935, 9¾in (25cm) high.
£85–95
$125–140 ⊞ GRI

A Monart glass bowl, 1930s, 5in (12.5cm) diam.
£55–65
$80–100 ⊞ RW

► **A Monart glass lamp base,** 1930s, 10in (25.5cm) high.
£120–140
$175–200 ⊞ RW

A glass vase, decorated with a winter landscape, French, 1930s, 3in (7.5cm) high.
£60–75
$90–110 G(L)

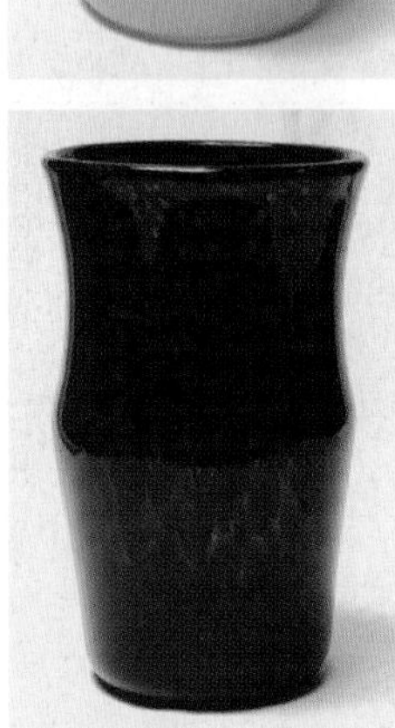

A Strathearn glass vase, 1964–75, 8¼in (21cm) high.
£75–85
$110–125 ⊞ RW
In the 1960s, the Scottish whisky distillers Teacher's became major shareholders in Vasart glass. In 1964, Teacher's invested in a new glassworks at Crieff, and Vasart's name was changed to Strathearn glass.

Three glass water jugs, c1950, 6in (15cm) high.
£6–8
$8–10 each ⊞ AL

A Murano glass ashtray, Italian, 1950s, 6in (15cm) high.
£35–40
$50–60 ⊞ HSt

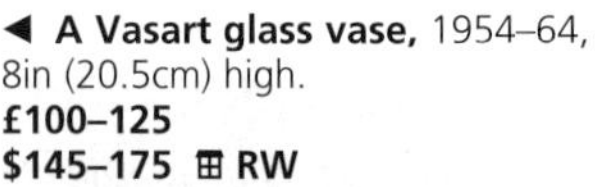

◄ A Vasart glass vase, 1954–64, 8in (20.5cm) high.
£100–125
$145–175 ⊞ RW

An Arte Vetraria Muranese basket-shaped glass vase, Italian, c1960, 5½in (14cm) high.
£125–145
$180–210 ⊞ RW

A Murano glass sweetmeat dish, 1960s, 14in (35.5cm) wide.
£25–30
$35–45 ⊞ HSt

A Vasart glass bowl, signed, 1947–54, 7½in (19cm) diam.
£60–70
$90–100 ⊞ RW
Having worked for John Moncrieff devising the Monart range, in 1947 Salvador Ysart and Augustine Vincent set up their own glassworks in Perth, Scotland, called Ysart. Vasart, their range of coloured art glass was similar in style to Monart, but more standardized. Most pieces were moulded and fine-powdered enamels were used to colour the glass rather than crushed and coarser enamel particles. In 1956 the factory's name was changed to Vasart.

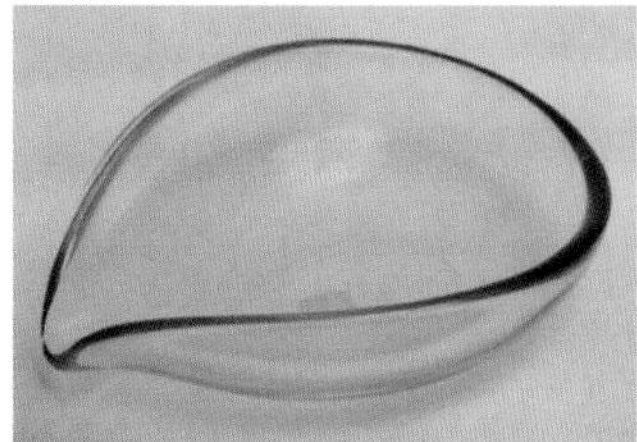

A Holmegaard Freeform glass bowl, by Per Lutken, Danish, 1950s–60s, 7in (18cm) wide.
£50–60
$75–90 ⊞ ORI

A smoky blue overlay glass vase, 1960, 7in (18cm) high.
£30–35
$45–50 ⊞ MCC

Carnival Glass

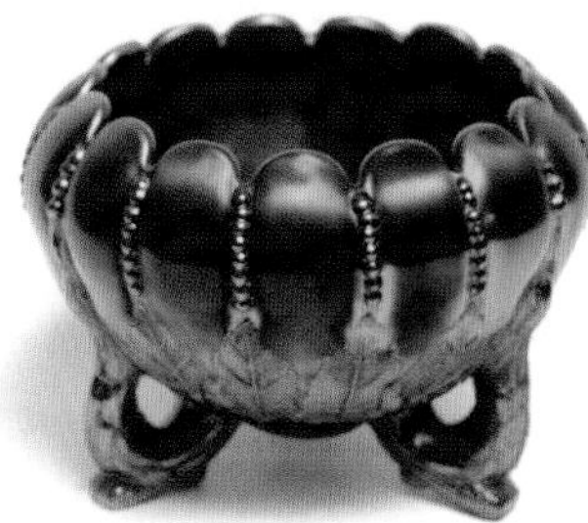

A Northwood Leaf and Beads Carnival footed glass rose bowl, American, c1910, 5in (12.5cm) diam.
£85–95
$125–140 ⊞ CAL

A Fenton Ribbed Holly Carnival glass goblet, American, c1911, 4in (10cm) high.
£25–30
$35–45 ⊞ CAL

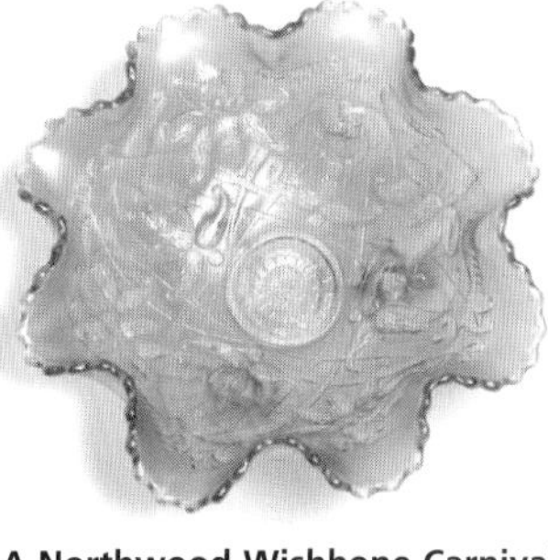

A Northwood Wishbone Carnival glass footed bowl, American, c1911, 7in (18cm) diam.
£110–125
$160–180 ⊞ CAL

◄ A Dragon and Roses Carnival glass footed sweet dish, c1920, 8in (20.5cm) diam.
£75–85
$110–125 ⊞ ML

A Bunch of Grapes Carnival glass fruit bowl, c1920, 8in(20.5cm) diam.
£34–38
$50–55 ⊞ ML

Cranberry Glass

A cranberry glass jug, with clear glass handle and frill, 19thC, 5in (12.5cm) high.
£90–100
$130–145 ⊞ BrL

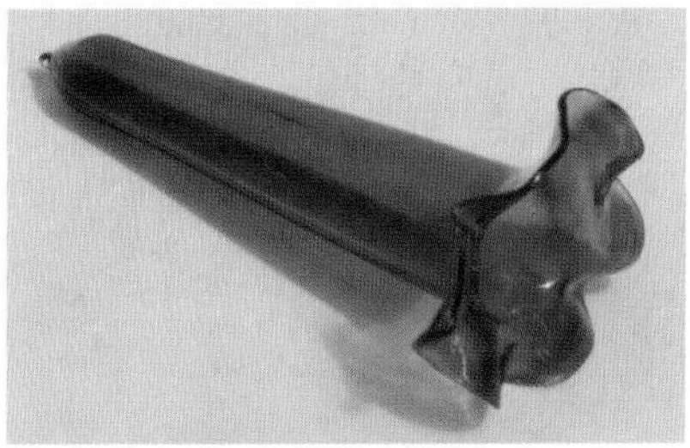

► A cranberry glass lapel posy holder, c1890, 2½in (6.5cm) high.
£25–30
$35–45 ⊞ GRI
This posy holder originally would have had a metal brooch attachment.

► A cranberry glass carafe, c1890, 6in (15cm) high.
£75–85
$110–125 ⊞ GRI

A cranberry glass custard cup, with curled clear glass handle, c1890, 3in (7.5cm) high.
£50–55
$75–80 ⊞ GRI

A cranberry-over-vaseline glass Jack-in-the-Pulpit vase, with spiral pinched frill, c1900, 10in (25.5cm) high.
£180–200
$250–300 ⊞ GRI

A ribbed cranberry glass sugar sifter, with silver-plated top, c1900, 6in (15cm) high.
£90–100
$130–145 ⊞ GRI

A cranberry glass salt, with fluted top and clear glass frill, in a silver-plated stand, c1900, stand 4in (10cm) high.
£80–90
$115–130 ⊞ GRI

► **A spiral cranberry glass vase,** c1910, 6½in (16.5cm) high.
£40–45
$60–65 ⊞ BrL

Drinking Glasses

A slice-cut port glass, 1820–30, 4in (10cm) high.
£8–10
$10–15 ⊞ JHa

A rummer, on a facet-cut stem, late 19thC, 6in (15cm) high.
£40–45
$60–65 ⊞ RUSK

A Mary Gregory champagne tumbler, c1900, 4in (10cm) high.
£70–80
$100–115 ⊞ GRI

An Orrefors smoked glass wine glass, Swedish, 1920s, 6in (15cm) high.
£25–30
$35–45 ⊞ JHa

◄ **A glass lemonade set,** comprising a jug and six glasses, with coloured and etched decoration, 1920s, jug 7in (18cm) high.
£120–140
$175–200 ⚒ SWO

► **A pair of amethyst cut-glass hock glasses,** c1930, 7¾in (19.5cm) high.
£24–28
$35–40 ⊞ GRI

Grimes House Antiques

The Antique Cranberry Glass Shop

Probably the largest selection of

OLD CRANBERRY GLASS

for sale in the country, normally over 250 pieces in stock.

Plus a very fine selection of other Victorian coloured glass

Stephen and Val Farnsworth

Est. 1978

Grimes House Antiques

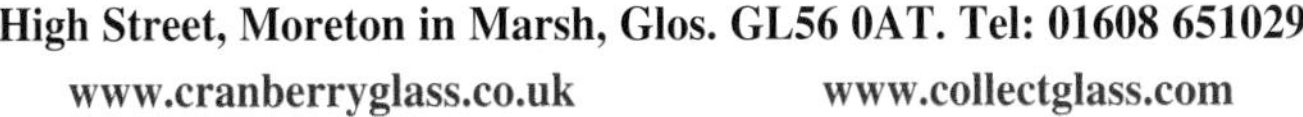

High Street, Moreton in Marsh, Glos. GL56 0AT. Tel: 01608 651029

www.cranberryglass.co.uk www.collectglass.com

Est. 1978

Paperweights & Dumps

A Bohemian glass paperweight, c1850, 2in (5cm) diam.
£230–250
$330–360 ⊞ RW

A Clichy paperweight, with white swirl, c1850, 2in (5cm) diam.
£350–400
$500–580 ⊞ RW

A glass dump, enclosing a flower and bubbles, 1860, 4in (10cm) high.
£140–180
$200–250 ⊞ JBL

A white glass paperweight, enclosing flowers and a butterfly, Chinese, c1930, 2¾in (7cm) high.
£40–50
$60–75 ⊞ SWB

A Paul Ysart Scrambled Magnum paperweight, 1930s, 4in (10cm) diam.
£1,000–1,150
$1,500–1,700 ⊞ SWB

A Murano glass paperweight, 1950–60, 3½in (9cm) diam.
£55–65
$80–100 ⊞ RW

► Three Whitefriars glass paperweights, 1960s, 3in (7.5cm) diam.
£12–15
$15–20 each ⊞ RW

A Wedgwood glass parrot paperweight, 1969–84, 8in (20.5cm) long.
£85–95
$125–140 ⊞ SWB

A Paul Ysart 'H' cane paperweight, decorated with a fish, c1970, 2½in (6.5cm) diam.
£325–365
$475–525 ⊞ SWB

A Wedgwood Silver Jubilee glass paperweight, 1977, 3½in (9cm) diam.
£15–18
$20–25 ⊞ RW

A Caithness glass paperweight, with millefiori crown decoration, 1977, 3½in (9cm) diam.
£145–165
$210–240 ⊞ RW

A 'J' glass Mini Crown paperweight, by John Deacons, 1981, 2in (5cm) diam.
£110–130
$160–200 ⊞ SWB

A Christmas Crown paperweight, by John Deacons, No. 1 of 45, 2001, 2¾in (7cm) diam.
£85–95
$125–140 ⊞ SWB

◄ A glass paperweight, Summer's Day, by Steven Lundberg, enclosing flowers and a butterfly, American, 2001, 3in (7.5cm) diam.
£200–235
$290–340 ⊞ SWB

► A Perthshire 'C' glass paperweight, 2002, 3in (7.5cm) diam.
£160–190
$230–275 ⊞ SWB
Only six of these paperweights are thought to have been produced.

Handbags

◄ **A velvet purse,** with gold-plated chain and mounts, decorated with embroidery, shells and beaded fringe, c1800, 8in (20.5cm) diam.
£240–260
$350–380 ⊞ JPr

A sovereign purse, with steel beads, early 19thC, 12in (30.5cm) long.
£40–50
$60–75 ⊞ JPr

A chain-metal purse, with blue beads, c1840, 2½in (6.5cm) long.
£65–75
$95–110 ⊞ LU

An embroidered bag, with metallic clasp and chain, c1860, 7in (18cm) wide.
£120–140
$175–200 ⊞ JPr

A Victorian beaded bag, with floral decoration and drawstring top, 10in (25.5cm) long.
£250–275
$350–400 ⊞ Ech

► **A velvet bag,** with pierced silver mount, c1880, 7in (18cm) long.
£80–90
$115–130 ⊞ JPr

A beaded finger purse, on a ring chain handle, 1890, 3in (7.5cm) square.
£40–45
$60–65 ⊞ L&L

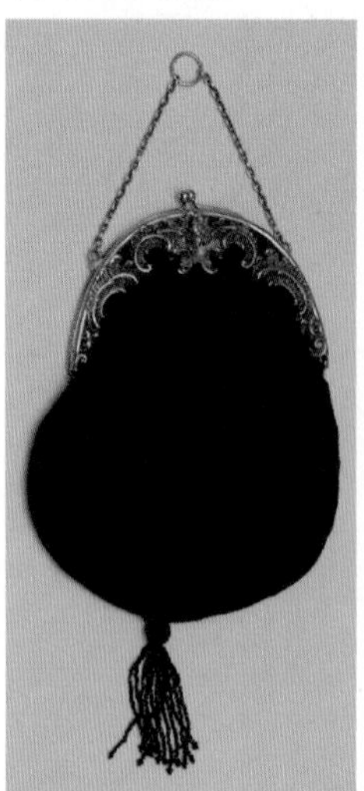

◄ **A velvet bag,** with silver mount and beaded tassel, c1910, 8in (20.5cm) long.
£120–140
$175–200 ⊞ JPr

A petit-point purse, depicting a lady and a unicorn, the reverse with a lion and a unicorn, with silver clasp, c1900, 8in (20.5cm) long.
£240–275
$350–400 ⊞ LU

An Edwardian beaded bag, 7in (18cm) long.
£110–125
$160–180 ⊞ Ech

A beaded bag, with chain handle, 1920, 7in (18cm) long.
£125–145
$180–220 ⊞ Ech

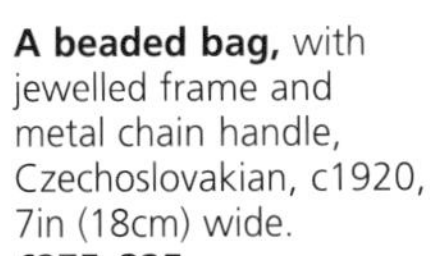

A chain-metal bag, 1920, 5in (12.5cm) square.
£40–45
$60–65 ⊞ Ech

A beaded bag, with jewelled frame and metal chain handle, Czechoslovakian, c1920, 7in (18cm) wide.
£275–325
$400–470 ⊞ LBr

◄ A beaded purse, with floral decoration and gilt-metal clasp, early 20thC, 8in (20.5cm) long.
£100–120
$145–175 ⊞ JPr

► A Bakelite and velvet bag, 1920s, 9in (23cm) diam.
£125–150
$180–220 ⊞ LBe

A glass bead bag, with blown out floral lattice frame and chain handle, Czechoslovakian, c1920, 6in (15cm) long.
£240–280
$350–400 ⊞ LBr

A petit point bag, with gilt frame, c1920, 7in (18cm) wide.
£100–120
$145–175 ⊞ JPr

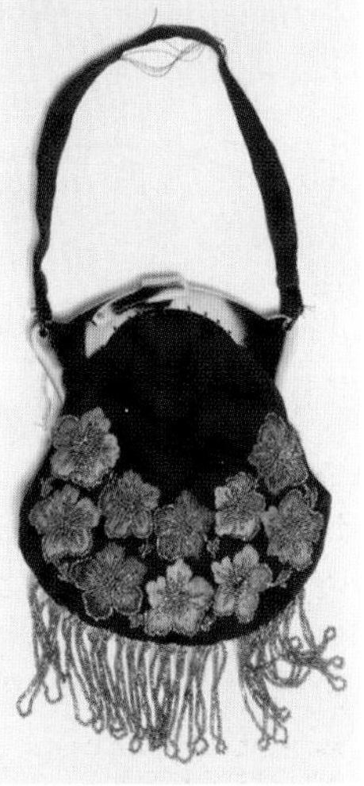

An embroidered silk handbag, with Bakelite clasp and glass and steel fringe, c1920, 9in (23cm) long.
£250–300
$350–450 ⊞ LBr

A crêpe evening bag, with petit point insert and zip top, c1930, 4in (10cm) square.
£25–30
$35–45 ⊞ SBL

A velvet evening bag, with paste trim handle, c1930, 11in (23cm) wide.
£25–30
$35–45 ⊞ SBL

A suede bag, with marcasite frame and original label, c1930, 8in (20.5cm) wide.
£160–180
$230–260 ⊞ LaF

◀ **A leather handbag,** with moiré silk lining and gilt frame, c1930, 11in (23cm) wide.
£45–50
$65–75 ⊞ SBL

A satin handbag, decorated with sequins, with chain handle and *faux* pearl clasp, 1930s, 7in (18cm) diam.
£190–220
$275–325 ⊞ LaF

A crocodile-skin clutch bag, 1930s, 11in (23cm) wide.
£55–65
$80–100 ⊞ Ech

◀ **A crocodile-skin clutch bag,** with Bakelite clasp, Argentinian, 1930s, 10in (25.5cm) wide.
£125–150
$180–225 ⊞ RGA

An antelope suede bag, with stitched decoration and a marcasite and black onyx clasp, 1930s, 6in (15cm) wide.
£750–850
$1,100–1,250 ⊞ LBe
This bag is made from a fine skin with expensive fittings and is in immaculate condition.

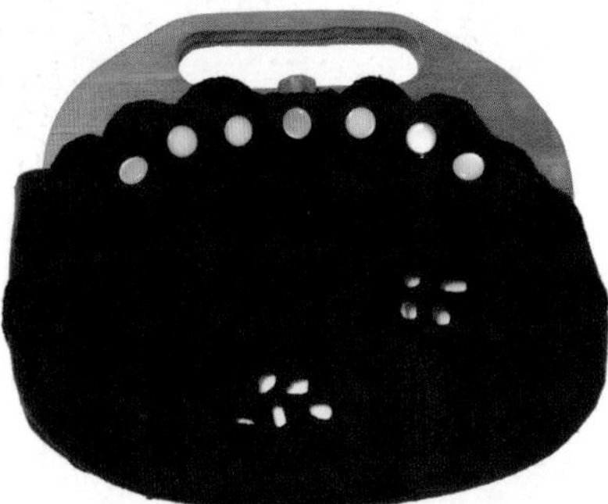

An embroidered cotton handbag, with three interchangeable covers in different colourways, with wooden handles, 1930s, 8in (20.5cm) wide.
£65–75
$100–110 ⊞ LBe

A suede compact bag, with compact and mirror inset in lid, c1938, 5in (12.5cm) long.
£220–250
$320–360 ⊞ LaF

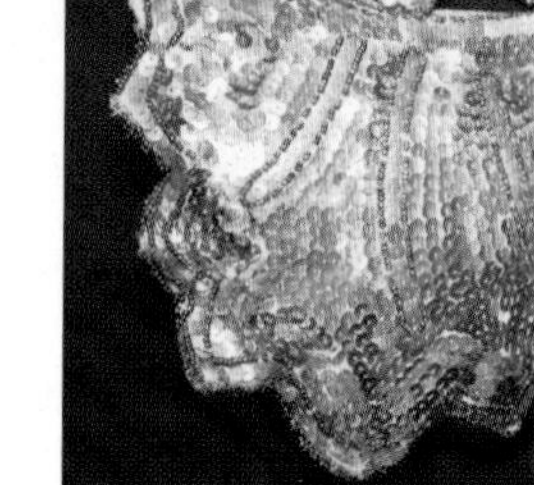

▶ **A sequined evening bag,** 1930s, 6in (15cm) square.
£25–30
$35–45 ⊞ LaF

A wicker and raffia-embroidered clutch bag, 1930s, 10½in (26.5cm) wide.
£85–95
$125–140 ⊞ LBe

◀ **A ruched and beaded silk evening bag,** with gilt clasp and chain, and matching purse, 1930s, 6½in (16.5cm) wide.
£25–35
$35–50 ⚒ G(L)

A metal-beaded purse, with Art Deco abstract pattern, gilt-metal mount and chain handle, 1930s, 9in (23cm) long.
£170–200
$250–290 ⊞ JPr

A Lucite and crystal evening bag, c1950, 10in (25.5cm) wide.
£225–250
$325–350 ⊞ LaF

A carry-all, by Majestic, with coloured glass lid and Perspex and metal fittings, 1950s, 8in (20.5cm) wide.
£165–185
$240–270 ⊞ HSt

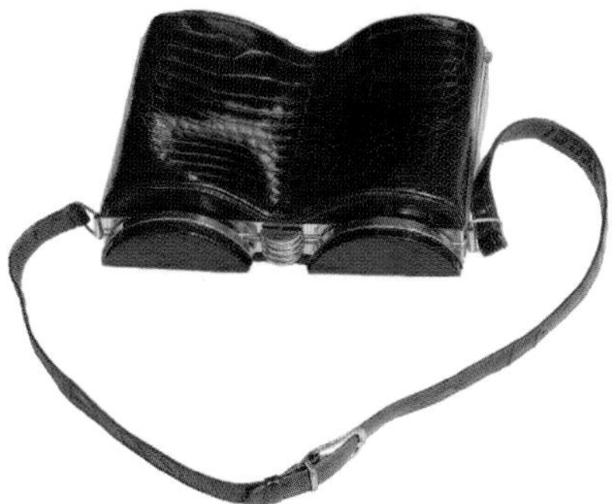

An alligator-skin handbag, in the form of a binoculars case, Mexican, 1940s, 9in (23cm) long.
£220–250
$320–360 ⊞ RGA

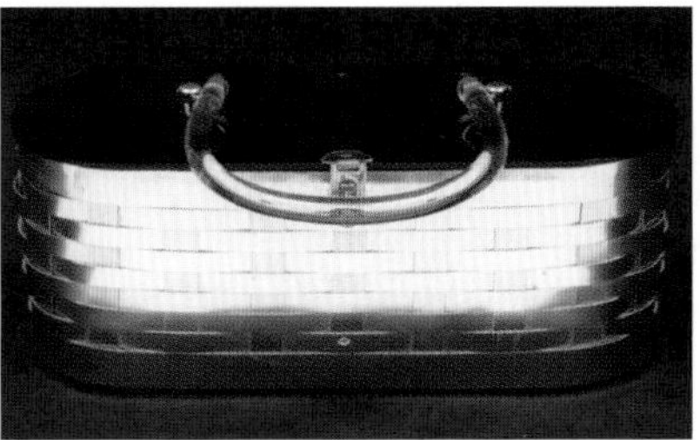

A handbag, by Majestic. with Perspex handle, 1950s, 10in (25.5cm) wide.
£125–155
$180–225 ⊞ HSt

A grosgrain bag, decorated with a satin poodle with diamanté collar and *faux* pearl lead, 1950s, 6in (15cm) wide.
£110–120
$160–175 ⊞ LBe

An alligator skin box bag, by Krumm, American, 1940s, 8½in (21.5cm) wide.
£180–200
$250–290 ⊞ RGA

A wicker bag, with appliqué butterfly decoration and Lucite handle and frame, American, c1950, 11½in (29cm) wide.
£70–80
$100–115 ⊞ SBL

A straw handbag, with hand-painted leather panel, cotton trimmings and velvet ribbon-covered handles, 1950s, 5in (12.5cm) wide.
£125–150
$180–225 ⊞ LBe

◄ **A wooden box bag,** decorated with a découpage of English country scenes, Bakelite handle, 1950s, 5½in (14cm) wide.
£175–195
$255–285 ⊞ LBe

A Gucci crocodile skin handbag, Italian, 1950s, 9½in (24cm) wide.
£225–250
$325–350 ⊞ RGA

A Barbie and Francie plastic case, c1965, 17in (43cm) wide.
£80–90
$115–130 ⊞ T&D

A snakeskin handbag, with gilt chain handle, c1970, 8in (20.5cm) wide, and matching belt with enamel buckle.
£50–60
$75–90 ⊞ SBL

► A wicker handbag, with raffia-embroidered top, American, c1970, 10in (25.5cm) wide.
£35–40
$50–60 ⊞ SBL

A box bag, by Annie Laurie Originals, Palm Beach, decorated with embossed and raised butterflies, American, c1960, 9in (23cm) wide.
£80–90
$115–130 ⊞ SBL

A leather handbag, with *faux* tortoiseshell handle and brass trim, 1960s, 10in (25.5cm) wide.
£125–150
$180–220 ⊞ LBe

A beaded bag, with lined interior and Lucite handle, American, c1960, 10in (25.5cm) wide.
£80–90
$115–130 ⊞ SBL

A tapestry handbag, by Koret, with grosgrain lining, plastic lid,chrome handle and trim, 1960s, 6½in (16.5cm) wide.
£130–150
$200–220 ⊞ LBe

◄ A snakeskin handbag, with suede lining and metal frame, c1970, 12in (30.5cm) wide.
£40–50
$60–75 ⊞ SBL

A plastic-covered silk bridal bag, by JR, embroidered with the letter B, with gilt frame, American, c1970, 10in (25.5cm) wide.
£40–50
$60–75 ⊞ SBL

Horse Collectables

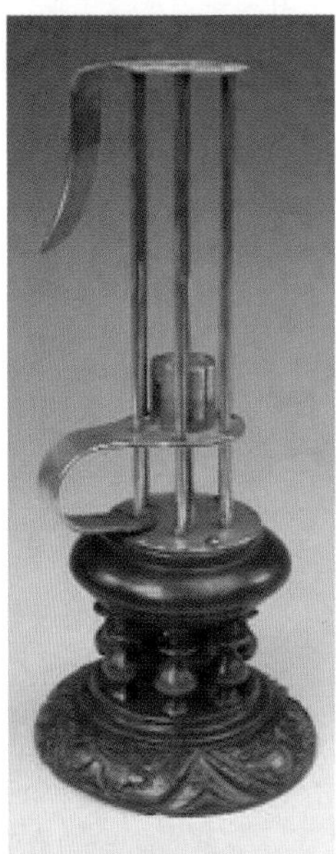

A stable candlestick, the adjustable brass candle holder with broad handle and wall clip, on a spindle-turned and carved walnut base, French, early 19thC, 11in (28cm) high.
£150–180
$220–260 ⚒ TMA

► **A wood and brass horse measuring stick,** 1920, 76in (193cm) high.
£40–45
$60–65 ⊞ RGa

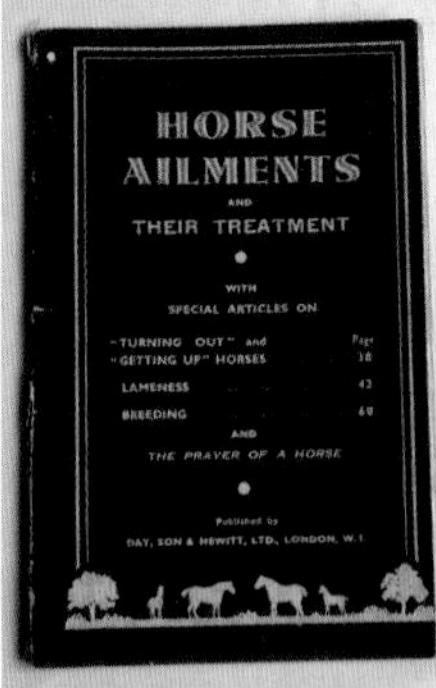

Horse Ailments and Their Treatment, published by Day, Son & Hewitt, 1937, 7½ x 5in (19 x 12.5cm).
£8–10
$10–15 ⊞ J&S

A set of oak jockey scales, the leather seat, brass scales and weight on a wooden base with barley-twist legs, 1860–70, 36in (91.5cm) square.
£7,800–8,800
$11,250–12,750 ⊞ RGa

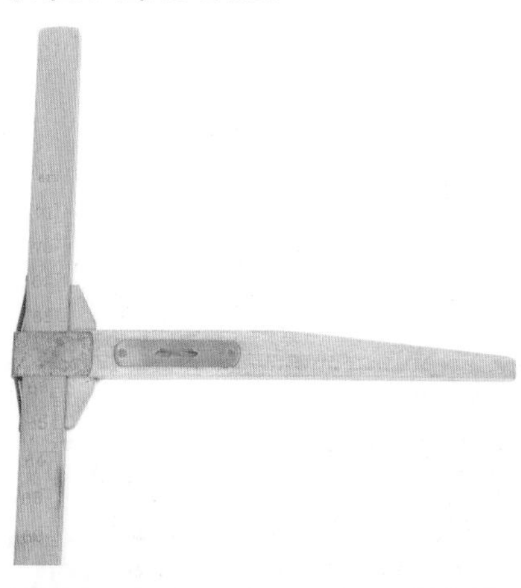

Gordon Richards, three framed photographs, two autographed and dated 1946, largest 8 x 10in (20.5 x 25.5cm), in oak frames.
£40–50
$60–75 ⚒ DA

► **A Winston Churchill horse brass,** 1940–50, 3½in (9cm) high.
£8–10
$10–15 ⊞ ATK

A wrought-iron stable fitting/harness rack, 19thC, 11in (28cm) long.
£18–20
$25–30 ⊞ RGa

An embossed leather Western-style saddle, c1900, 24in (61cm) wide.
£400–440
$580–650 ⊞ RGa

Ceramics

A Coptic hollow terracotta stylized horse, with conjoined front and hind legs, the arching neck with moulded decoration, the bridle, reins, saddle, mane and tail highlighted in red, white, cream and black slip, neck repaired, c5th–7thC AD, 4¾in (12cm) high.
£260–300
$380–440 ⚒ B(Kn)

A Carlton model of a jockey on a racehorse, with Newmarket crest, 1920s, 4½in (11.5cm) long.
£110–125
$160–180 ⊞ TWO

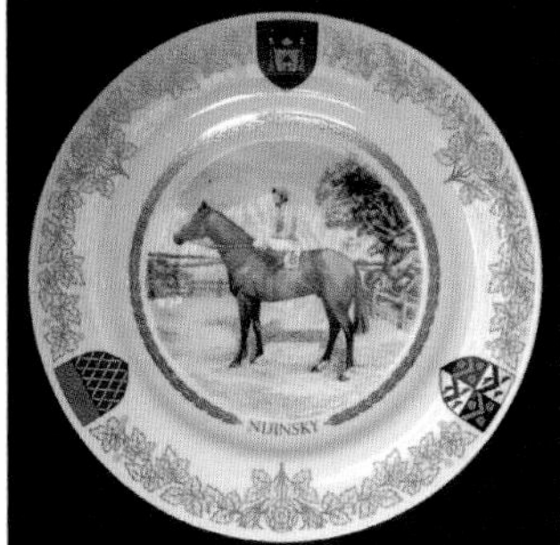

A plate, decorated with Nijinsky and mount, the border with three crests, 1970, 9½in (24cm) diam.
£40–50
$60–75 ⊞ ATK

A pair of Staffordshire spill vases, each modelled as a Shire horse with foal, c1860, 13in (33cm) high.
£1,750–2,000
$2,500–3,000 ⊞ RGa

► **A Staffordshire model of a horse,** ears and neck restored, late 19thC, 11¾in (30cm) long.
£480–580
$700–850 ⚒ SWO

A Grafton model of a Shetland pony, with Dover Ville et Portus crest, 1920s, 4in (10cm) long.
£25–30
$35–45 ⊞ TWO

A Derby tankard, commemorating the 200th running of the Derby, 1980, 4½in (11.5cm) diam.
£55–65
$80–100 ⊞ ATK

A Ridgways jasper ware mug, decorated with huntsmen and hounds, the base with basketweave banding, scroll handle, 19thC, 4¼in (11cm) high.
£100–120
$145–175 ⚒ DA

A Goebel model of a horse, c1960, 4in (10cm) high.
£18–22
$25–35 ⊞ PrB

A Beswick model of Queen Elizabeth II on Imperial, No. MN1546, 1981, 10½in (26.5cm) high.
£150–180
$220–260 ⚒ Pott

Costume & Accessories

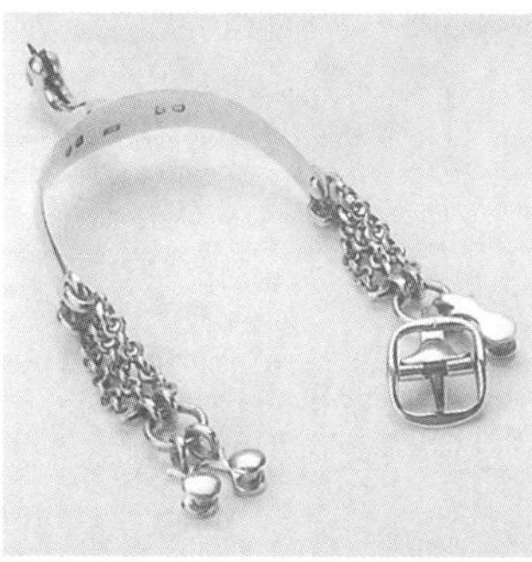

A pair of silver spurs, by Henry Vincent, with buckled securing chains and rotating five-pointed steel rowels, 1810.
£1,200–1,500
$1,750–2,150 B

A tinted brass button, depicting two saddled horses, stamped, 1880–90, 2in (5cm) diam.
£60–85
$85–125 TB

A wooden cane, with silver horse-head top, London 1888, 36in (91.5cm) long.
£1,000–1,200
$1,500–1,750 RGa

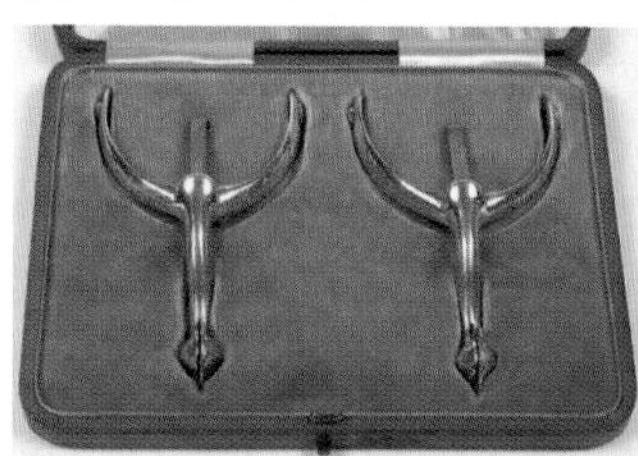

A pair of silver spurs, Birmingham 1896, in a fitted case 7in (18cm) wide.
£1,000–1,200
$1,500–1,750 RGa

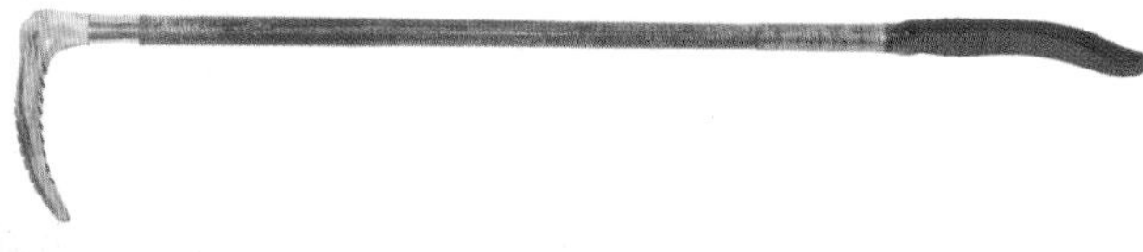

A silver-banded and plaited-leather riding crop, with horn handle, 1895, 23in (58.5cm) long.
£60–70
$90–100 RGa

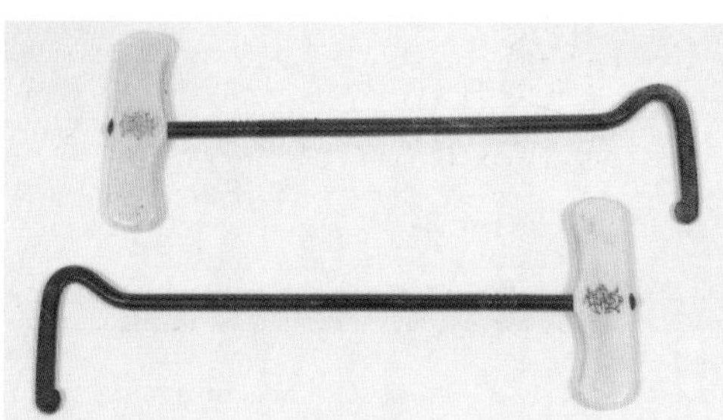

A pair of Victorian boot pullers, with ivory handles, 9in (23cm) long.
£65–75
$100–110 RGa

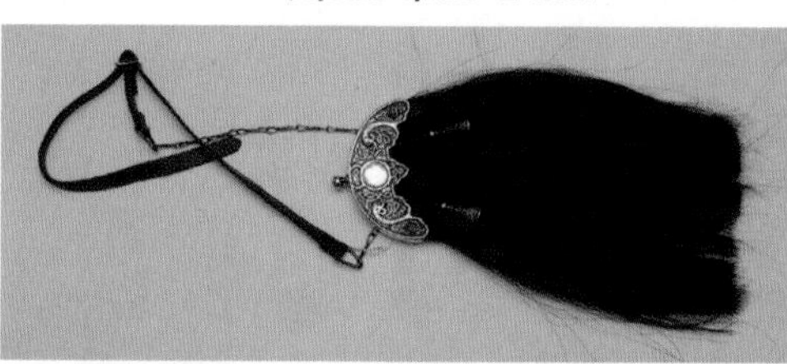

A horsehair sporran, with silver mount, late 19thC, 14in (35.5cm) long.
£90–110
$130–160 JPr

A malacca riding crop, with antler handle and leather end, c1910, 20in (51cm) long.
£40–50
$60–75 GBr

◄ **A pair of leather riding boots,** with stretchers, c1910.
£90–110
$130–160 RGa

► **A folding hunting cup,** in a watch case, c1910, 2in (5cm) high.
£30–40
$45–60 SA

A pair of Pearl & Co leather riding boots, with trees, early 20thC, 20in (51cm) high.
£230–260
$330–380 ⊞ JUN

A Coro Duette gold-coloured metal horse pin, 1940s, 2in (5cm) high.
£220–250
$320–360 ⊞ CRIS

A gold-coloured metal brooch, designed by Hattie Carnegie, modelled as Don Quixote on a horse and set with crystals, American, c1950, 2in (5cm) high.
£100–120
$145–175 ⊞ LaF

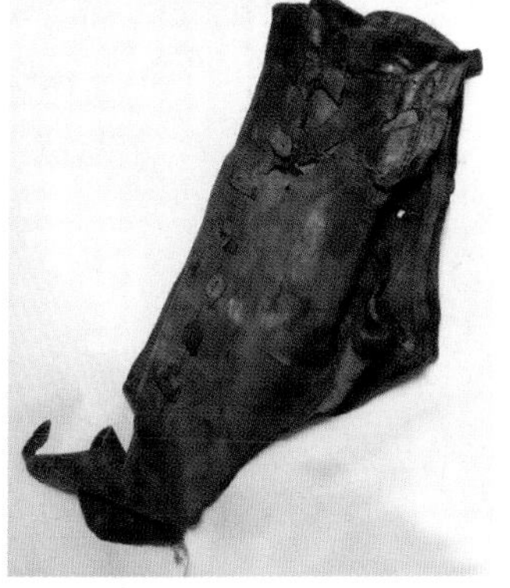

A pair of leather working chaps, American, 1950s, 38in (96.5cm) long.
£60–70
$90–100 ⊞ TRA

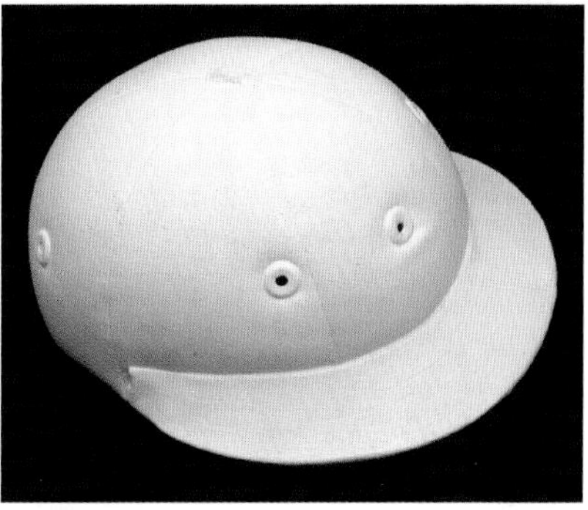

A canvas padded polo helmet, c1960, 13in (33cm) diam.
£55–65
$80–95 ⊞ SA

◄ **An ebony cane,** the silver handle modelled as a horse's head, Birmingham 1996, 35in (89cm) long.
£360–410
$500–600 ⊞ RGa

Figures & Bronzes

A cold-painted bronze model of a standing horse, by Bermann Foundry, Austrian, c1920, 7in (18cm) long.
£800–1,000
$1,150–1,500 ⊞ RGa

A silver-plated model of a horse, on a marble base, 1920s, 9in (23cm) long.
£170–200
$250–300 ⊞ BrL

A bronze model of a horse, by Apul Edouard Brierre, beside a low fence on a naturalistic cast base, early 20thC, 13in (33cm) long.
£750–850
$1,100–1,250 ⚒ DN

Household Objects

A pair of silver knife rests, modelled as two horses leaping a gate, 1853, 4in (10cm) wide.
£1,150–1,350
$1,700–2,000 ⊞ RGa

A mahogany coat rack, with horseshoe-shaped mirror and brass hooks, late 19thC, 30in (76cm) wide.
£825–925
$1,200–1,350 ⊞ RGa

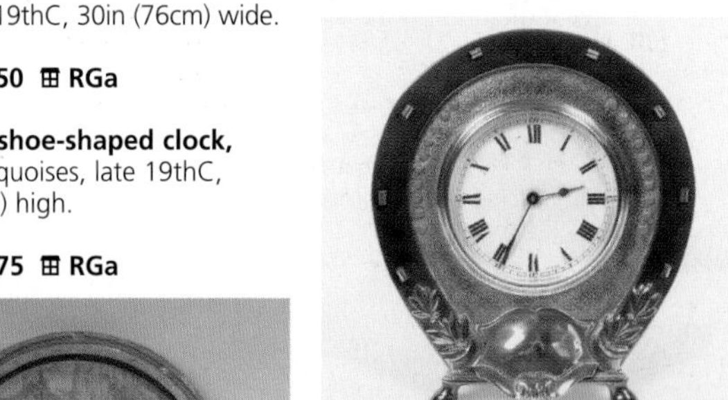

► A horseshoe-shaped clock, set with turquoises, late 19thC, 8in (20.5cm) high.
£775–875
$1,100–1,275 ⊞ RGa

A Victorian oak horseshoe-shaped tray, applied with brass horseshoes, stirrups and bits, with stirrup-shaped handles, 17in (43cm) long.
£210–250
$300–350 ⚒ SWO

A cast-iron mounted jockey doorstop, c1880, 8½in (21.5cm) long.
£170–190
$250–275 ⊞ WeA

An oak bookslide, the ends with horseshoe-shaped mounts, late 19thC, 13in (33cm) wide.
£325–360
$475–525 ⊞ RGa

A mahogany inkstand, with horseshoe-shaped pen rack, two cut-glass ink bottles with white metal hinged covers in the shape of jockeys' caps, early 20thC, 9½in (24cm) wide.
£200–240
$300–350 ⚒ TMA

A copper aspic mould, modelled as a horseshoe, c1890, 1½in (4cm) wide.
£30–35
$45–50 ⊞ WeA

A pair of silver-plated toast racks, modelled as stirrups, late 19thC, 4¾in (12cm) high.
£55–65
$80–95 ⚒ SWO

An 'Evening in Paris' perfume bottle, by Bourjois, in original horseshoe-shaped metal packaging, c1950, 3in (7.5cm) square.
£100–140
$150–200 ⊞ LBr

Toys

Equine toys are traditionally popular with children. This section opens with a wooden rocking horse, a staple fixture of the Edwardian nursery, and comes to a day-glow plastic end with My Little Pony.

Launched by Hasbro Toys, USA in 1981, My Little Pony became one of the most successful toys of the 1980s, inspiring an animated TV series and a feature film. Today these multi-coloured ponies with their rainbow manes are also attracting toy collectors both in America and across the world, many of whom originally played with the toys as children. Values depend on rarity, condition and completeness. Hooves provide vital evidence when it comes to identifying models. The underside can be marked with a range of information including maker's name, copyright date and place of manufacture (such was the international success of the ponies, that they were made all over the world). The shape of the hoof can also be a factor; for example, hooves on horses made for the American market are generally concave underneath, apart from around seven 'flat-footed' examples made in Hong Kong. Price ranges depend on rarity and condition, some horses came with accessories or as part of a play set. As with all toys, completeness is crucial to value.

A Lines rocking horse, on a safety stand, refurbished, c1900, 36in (91.5cm) long.
£2,700–3,100
$4,000–4,500 ⊞ RGa

A Jeu du Cheval Blanc board game, French, c1900, 9 x 12in (23 x 30.5cm).
£90–110
$130–160 ⊞ RGa
This is similar to the English board game of Ball and Hammer.

A toy horse, 1900–10, 12in (30.5cm) long.
£280–320
$400–475 ⊞ RGa

◄ A tin penny toy trotter, by Meier, 1920s, 5in (12.5cm) long.
£400–450
$580–650 ⊞ RGa

The Great Race Game Totopoly, by Waddington's, 1960s version of 1949 game, 14 x 20in (35.5 x 51cm).
£100–125
$145–175 ⊞ RGa

◄ A Minty My Little Pony, concave feet, 1982, 5in (12.5cm) high.
£25–30
$35–45 ⊞ RAND

Two My Little Ponies, Bubbles and Seashell, 1983, 5in (12.5cm) high.
£3–10
$5–15 each ⊞ RAND
These are the only sitting ponies ever made.

A set of three My Little Pony Ember mail order club ponies, 1983, 3in (7.5cm) high.
£2–10
$3–15 each ⊞ RAND
Ember was a character in the My Little Pony television special, and appeared as the lavender version.

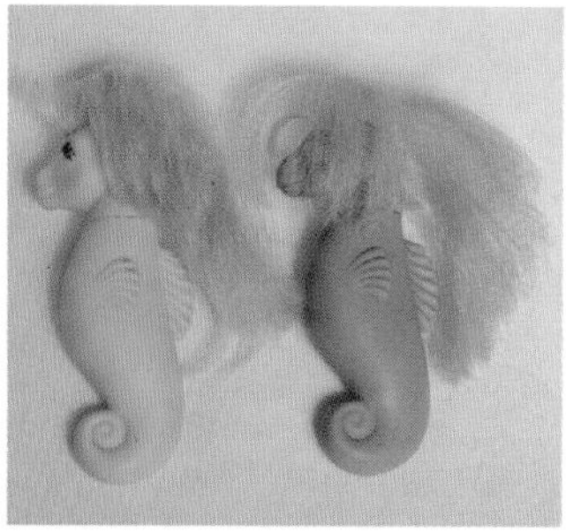

Two My Little Pony Sea Ponies, Seaspray and Wavebreaker, non-American versions, complete with standing shells, 1983, 4in (10cm) high.
£10–20
$15–30 each ⊞ RAND

A Majesty My Little Pony and Spike, part of the Dream Castle set, 1983, 2in (5cm) high.
£2–7
$3–10 each ⊞ RAND
The complete Dream Castle set would cost £70–80 ($100–115).

◄ A Baby Sea Pony My Little Pony, Surf Rider, 1984, 4in (10cm) high, with float.
£4–10
$8–15 ⊞ RAND

A Sundance My Little Pony, with Megan, 1984, 8in (20.5cm) high.
£20–25
$30–35 ⊞ RAND
Megan and Sundance were characters from the My Little Pony film.

Two Twinkle-Eyed My Little Ponies, Gingerbread and Whizzer, 1985, 5in (12.5cm) high.
£3–8
$5–12 each ⊞ RAND

LOCATE THE SOURCE

The source of each illustration in Miller's can be found by checking the code letters below each caption with the Key to Illustrations, pages 443–451.

◄ A Rollerskates My Little Pony, Melody, 1992, 6in (15cm) high.
£1–3
$2–5 ⊞ RAND

Four Flutter My Little Ponies, Peach Blossom, Honeysuckle, Rosedust and Morning Glory, 1985, 4in (10cm) high.
£4–5
$6–7 each ⊞ RAND
Flutter Ponies came with very delicate iridescent wings which were easily damaged. Examples with wings are therefore worth more £30–50 ($45–75).

Jewellery

Included below is a wide selection of Victorian and Edwardian sentimental jewellery. Jewellery was a favourite romantic gift conveying the language of love both overtly and symbolically. Popular forms include hearts, flowers, clasped hands and lovers' knots. Pieces might be inscribed with the words: *Amor*, *Mea Unica* (my only one) or *Mizpah*, a word taken from the Old Testament (31:49) and signifying: 'The Lord watch between me and thee, when we are absent from one another'. Loving messages were spelt out with the initial letters of gemstones, for example REGARD: ruby, emerald, garnet, amethyst, ruby, diamond; LOVE: lapis lazuli, opal, vermeil, emerald; and DEAREST: diamond, emerald, amethyst, ruby, emerald, sapphire and either topaz or turquoise. The language of flowers was another way of expressing feelings, with the use of roses, forget-me-nots, ivy (representing fidelity) and pansies, a reference to the French '*pensée*' and meaning 'Think of me'. Animals and birds also had symbolic values, and typical examples found on sentimental jewellery include doves, love birds, butterflies (standing for the soul) and the snake, which, with its tail in its mouth, was a symbol of eternity. Queen Victoria's betrothal ring was a gold and emerald serpent.

As well as celebrating love, jewellery also commemorated death. When Prince Albert died in 1861, Queen Victoria plunged into the deepest blackest grief, setting an example to her subjects and stimulating the fashion for mourning jewellery. The jet industry at Whitby flourished, and hair jewellery (containing locks of hair from the dear departed) was another period favourite.

Also included in this section is jewellery that in theory at least could cause death. Poison rings contain a hinged bezel that opens to reveal a secret compartment said to have once contained a deadly substance.

Bracelets

A jet bracelet, minor damage, 1860–70, 2in (5cm) wide.
£65–75
$100–110 ⊞ AM

A 15ct gold bangle, the heart-shaped mount enclosed by seed pearls, dated 1889.
£450–550
$650–800 ⊞ EXC

A 9ct gold bracelet, by Murrle Bennett, set with cabochon-cut green/turquoise matrixes, with safety chain, early 20thC.
£300–360
$450–500 ⚒ SWO

Brooches

◄ **A gold-framed mourning brooch,** the front modelled as a monument with hair tree, the back with curled locks of hair, early 19thC.
£200–250
$300–350 ⚒ GAK

A gold heart and knot brooch, set with pearls, c1850.
£345–385
$500–575 ⊞ SAY

An 18ct gold brooch, set with garnets, c1850, 1½in (4cm) wide.
£400–500
$580–720 ⊞ AMC

A gold entwined double heart brooch, set with turquoise and pearls, 1860s.
£345–385
$500–575 ⊞ SAY

A silver and gold crescent brooch, the crescent set with rubies and diamonds, on a a bar with diamonds and pearls, c1870, 2in (5cm) long.
£800–1,000
$1,150–1,500 ⊞ AMC

A gold on brass scroll brooch, set with garnets, c1870, 1½in (4cm) long.
£250–300
$350–450 ⊞ AMC

► **An 18ct gold brooch,** the hearts and three-leaf clovers set with seed pearls, 1880, 1¾in (4.5cm) wide.
£235–265
$340–380 ⊞ SPE

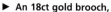

► **A silver star brooch,** 1890, 2in (5cm) diam.
£45–50
$65–75 ⊞ WAC

A silver *Mizpah* brooch, 1880, 1¾in (4.5cm) wide.
£45–55
$65–80 ⊞ SPE

A silver-plated name brooch, 'Clarie', 1890, 2in (5cm) wide.
£60–70
$90–100 ⊞ FMN

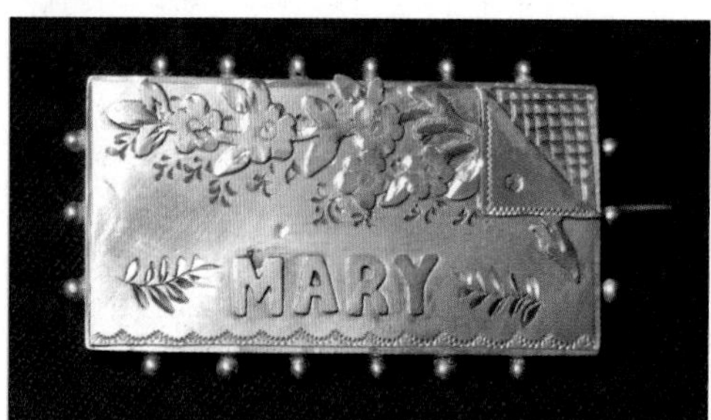

◄ **A silver name brooch,** 'Mary', 1890, 1¾in (4.5cm) wide.
£65–75
$100–110 ⊞ FMN

◄ **A gold and agate brooch,** the 8ct gold centre set with a hardstone cameo of a forget-me-not, within a 9ct gold leaf and scroll setting, c1890, 1½in (4cm) wide.
£100–125
$140–180
⊞ AMC

A silver name brooch, 'Louisa', decorated with harps and three-leaf clover, Birmingham 1891, 1in (2.5cm) wide.
£60–70
$90–100 ⊞ FMN

A silver and gold brooch, set with a basket in relief, 1897, 2in (5cm) wide.
£45–55
$65–80 ⊞ FMN

A brooch, set with a painted plaque of Justice, impressed mark, Continental, 19thC, 2in (5cm) wide.
£75–90
$110–130 ⊞ SWO

A Victorian gold pendant brooch, decorated with leaves and tendrils, set with turquoises and a diamond chip, the reverse with compartment for hair.
£75–95
$110–140 ⚒ G(L)

A gold heart brooch, with lover's knot and ivy leaves, set with a ruby and a diamond, c1900, 1in (2.5cm) wide.
£700–800
$1,000–1,150 ⊞ WIM

► **A Victorian gold brooch,** set with flat-cut garnets.
£150–180
$220–260 ⚒ G(L)

► **A Victorian gold fertility and eternity brooch,** modelled as a snake set with turquoise stones, ½in (1.5cm) wide.
£200–225
$300–325 ⊞ SPE

Two fretted and engraved mother-of-pearl brooches, modelled as birds and set with garnets, c1900, 3in (7.5cm) wide.
£18–20
$25–30 each ⊞ FMN

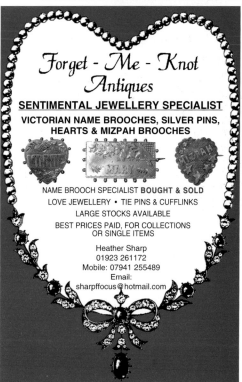

A Victorian 18ct gold brooch, with two blue and white enamel hearts inset with diamonds and surmounted by a lover's knot, 1½in (4cm) wide.
£300–330
$440–480 ⊞ SPE

An Unger Brothers .925 standard silver-gilt brooch, modelled as the man-in-the-moon and child, copyright 1904, 2in (5cm) diam.
£75–90
$110–130 ⚒ G(L)

A carved ivory brooch, modelled as a flower, c1910, 4in (10cm) diam.
£35–40
$50–60 ⊞ FMN

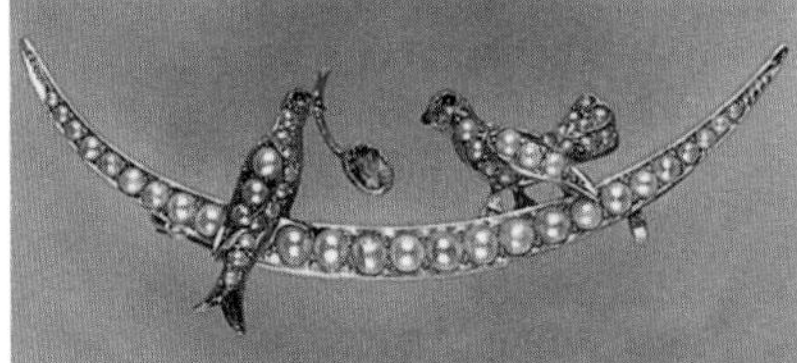

◀ An Edwardian gold brooch, set with seed pearls, depicting two birds, one holding a peridot.
£330–360
$475–525 ⚒ L

Items in the Jewellery section have been arranged in date order within each sub-section.

Cameos

A gold cameo brooch, carved with a portrait of Zeus, in a rope-twist mount, c1880, 1½in (4cm) high.
£200–225
$300–325 ⊞ AMC

A lava cameo brooch, carved with man's head and shoulders, set in silver, c1900, 1in (2.5cm) high.
£50–60
$75–90 ⊞ AMC

A Victorian shell cameo brooch, carved with a portrait of Diana the Huntress, on a pinchbeck swivel frame.
£95–115
$140–170 ⚒ G(L)

Clasps & Buckles

An enamel clasp, inset with red crystals, Czechoslovakian c1900, 4in (10cm) wide.
£35–40
$50–60 ⊞ JBB

◀ A two-piece steel clasp, c1890, 4in (10cm) wide.
£150–175
$225–255 ⊞ JBB

An enamel and silver-gilt clasp, Scandinavian, c1900, 5in (12.5cm) wide.
£90–100
$130–145 ⊞ JBB

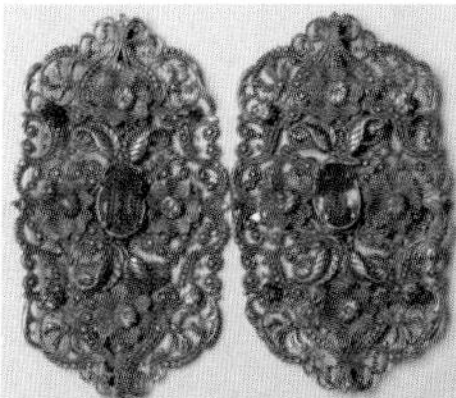

A brass and paste buckle, c1910, 3½in (9cm) high.
£35–40
$50–60 ⊞ FMN

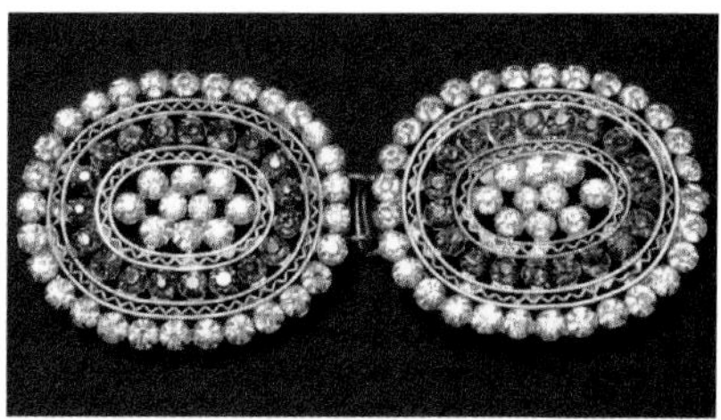

A paste clasp, 1910, 4in (10cm) wide.
£50–60
$75–100 ⊞ JBB

Earrings

◄ A pair of jet earrings, c1880, 1¼in (3cm) long.
£190–220
$275–325 ⊞ AM

A pair of jet earrings, c1885, 2in (5cm) long.
£140–160
$200–230 ⊞ AM

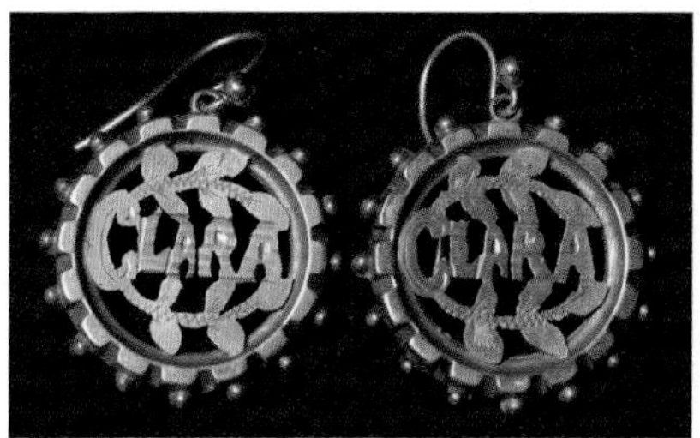

A pair of silver name earrings, 'Clara', 1890, 1in (2.5cm) diam.
£45–55
$65–80 ⊞ FMN

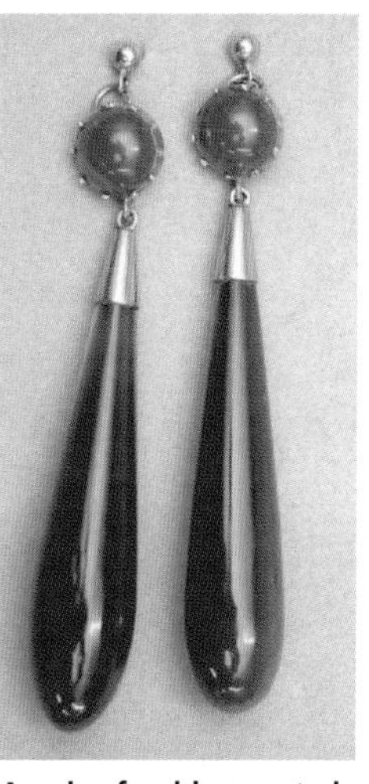

A pair of gold-mounted cornelian drop earrings, 19thC.
£160–190
$225–275 G(L)

◄ A pair of 15ct gold and enamel pansy earrings, with pearl centres, c1900, ½in (1.5cm) diam.
£875–975
$1,275–1,400 ⊞ WIM

Hat Pins

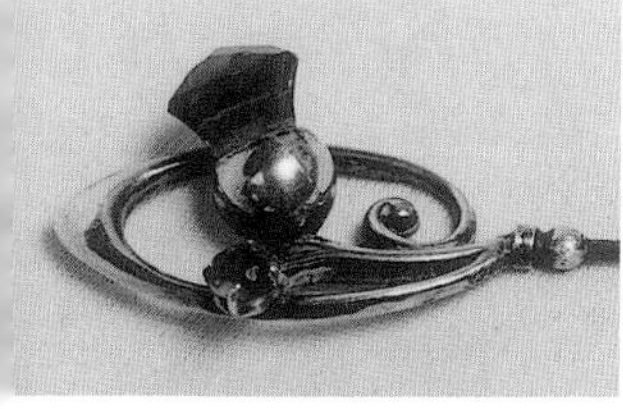

A silver hat pin, by Charles Horner, Chester 1907, 7¼in (18.5cm) long.
£50–60
$75–90 ⊞ VB

A set of Edwardian enamel and silver hat pins, with matching buckle and studs, in a fitted case.
£100–130
$150–200 ⊞ SUW

◄ A pair of enamelled hat pins, 1908, 9in (23cm) long.
£75–85
$110–125 each ⊞ VB

Men's Accessories

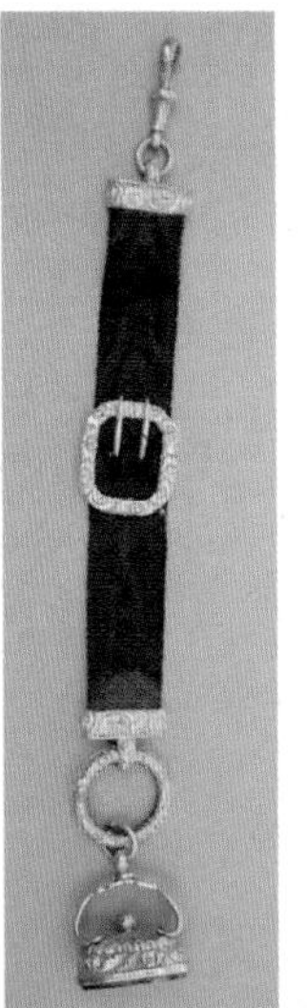

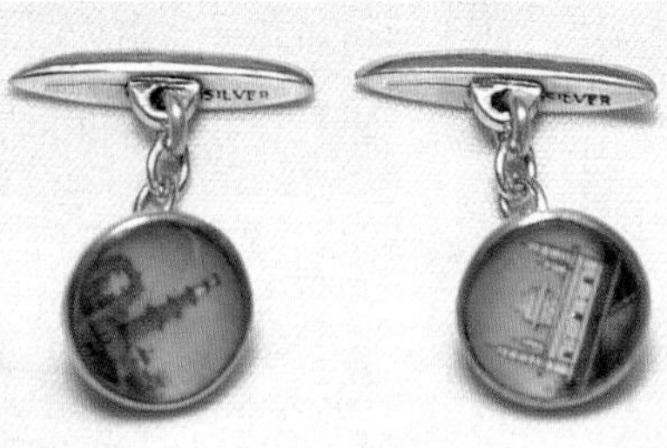

A pair of silver cufflinks, inset with ivory painted with an Indian scene, c1870.
£85–95
$125–145 ⊞ JBB

◄ **A Regency-style chased 9ct gold bloodstone fob seal,** on a silk grosgrain ribbon with gold buckle and hook, early 19thC.
£40–50
$60–75 ⚒ G(L)

A 9ct rose gold sovereign case, 1885, 1in (2.5cm) diam.
£450–550
$650–800 ⊞ EXC

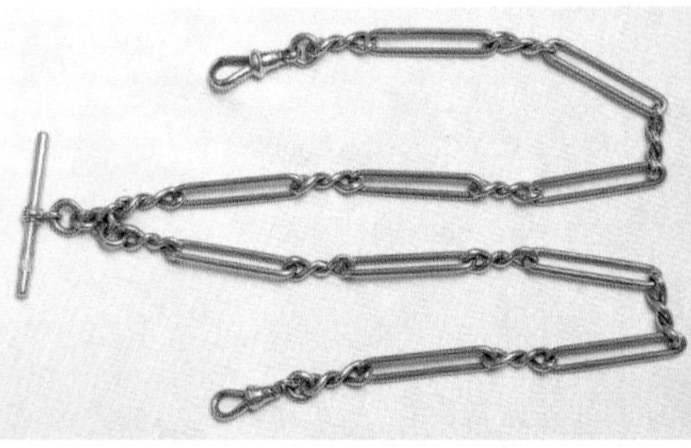

A Victorian 15ct gold watch chain, 10in (25.5cm) long.
£875–975
$1,300–1,400 ⊞ EXC

◄ **A silver name brooch,** 'Edgar', modelled as an anchor and chain, 1900, 1½in (4cm) wide.
£50–60
$75–90 ⊞ FMN

A pair of gold, mother-of-pearl and white enamel cufflinks, set with rubies, with chain connections, c1900.
£170–200
$250–300 ⚒ G(L)

A pair of brass fox cufflinks, c1900.
£28–32
$45–50 ⊞ JBB

A pair of silver scallop shell cufflinks, 1930.
£25–30
$35–45 ⊞ JBB

► **An onyx and diamond tie pin,** c1930, 2½in (6.5cm) long.
£260–325
$375–475
⚒ B(Ba)

A 14ct gold New York University fraternity ring, set with an amethyst, engraved inscription, dated 1993.
£85–95
$125–140 ⚒ SWO

◄ **A pair of silver rose cufflinks,** 1950s.
£34–38
$50–60 ⊞ JBB

Necklaces, Lockets & Pendants

A 15ct gold 'Regard' heart-shaped locket, set with emerald, garnet, amethyst, diamond and rubies, 1790–1800, ¾in (2cm) high.
£775–875
$1,175–1,275 ⊞ WIM

A Victorian 15ct gold necklace, with hearts and lovers' knots inset with garnets and pearls, 18in (45.5cm) long.
£1,000–1,250
$1,500–1,750 ⊞ SHa

A Victorian moonstone and ruby necklace, on a gold chain, 2¾in (7cm) long.
£400–450
$580–650 ⊞ BrL

A gold heart-shaped locket, c1850.
£345–385
$500–575 ⊞ SAY

An 18ct gold engraved locket, c1870, 2in (5cm) high.
£650–700
$900–1,000 ⊞ EXC

A gold and silver memorial locket, decorated with blue enamel and enclosing a portrait aperture with the glass, the reverse engraved 'Papa d June 9th 1870', within a shield-shaped cartouche, 1¼in (3cm) high.
£200–250
$300–350 ⚒ DW
This family locket commemorates the death of Charles Dickens, 1812–70.

A 15ct gold multi-locket pendant, c1890, 1in (2.5cm) diam.
£800–875
$1,150–1,275 ⊞ WIM

A jet necklace, c1900, 18in (45.5cm) long.
£275–300
$400–450 ⊞ AM

◄ **A Victorian silver locket pendant,** with floral decoration, on a decorative link collar.
£120–150
$175–225 ⚒ G(L)

Rings

An 18ct gold 'poison' ring, with snake shoulders, set with a cabochon garnet, c1820.
£450–500
$650–725 ⊞ SAY

A 15ct gold 'Regard' ring, with hand shoulders, set with a ruby, emerald, garnets, amethyst and diamond, 1860s.
£880–980
$1,275–1,500 ⊞ SAY

An 18ct gold 'poison' ring, set with a cabochon garnet, 1880.
£300–330
$440–480 ⊞ SPE

A Victorian ring, set with an old cut diamond and turquoise.
£80–100
$115–145 ⚒ SWO

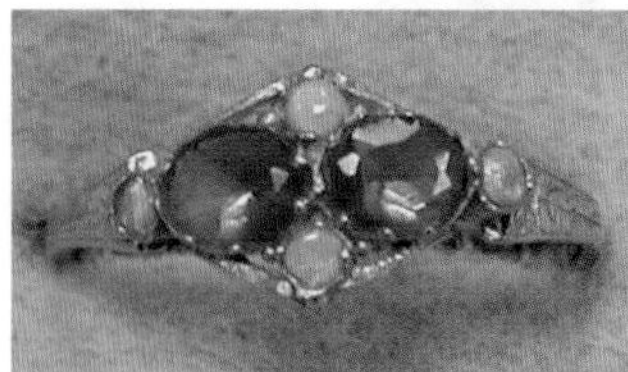

An 18ct gold enamel 'poison' ring, Swiss, 1820s.
£2,450–2,750
$3,500–4,000 ⊞ SAY

A 9ct gold 'Regard' ring, with plaited hair, 1870.
£190–220
$275–325 ⊞ SPE

A Victorian amethyst solitaire ring, with a 9ct gold engraved collet setting on a later 14ct gold shank, maker's mark W&B.
£120–150
$175–225 ⚒ SWO

A Victorian 9ct gold ring, inscribed *Mea Unica* (My Only One).
£180–220
$260–320 ⊞ SPE

◄ **A Victorian 9ct gold ring,** with engraved shoulders, set with amethysts and opals.
£50–60
$75–100 ⚒ SWO

An 18ct gold entwined double heart ring, set with a sapphire, a ruby and diamonds, 1850s.
£3,200–3,600
$4,650–5,000 ⊞ SAY

An 18ct gold memorial ring, the inner surface engraved 'b. Feby 7th 1812 d. June 9th 1870', the outer surface revealing plaited hair.
£600–700
$870–1,000 ⚒ DW
This memorial ring commemorates the death of Charles Dickens, 1812–70, and presumably contains his hair.

A Victorian *Mizpah* ring.
£130–150
$200–220 ⊞ SPE

A Victorian 18ct gold *Amor* ring.
£150–175
$225–255 ⊞ SPE

Jewellery: Costume

This section covers 20th-century costume jewellery, much of it American. The industry flourished in the USA from the 1920s, with major centres of production in the New York area and Los Angeles. Hollywood was an important influence. The sight of film stars bedecked in fabulous fakes helped costume jewellery to become acceptable to even the most elegant women – Diana Vreeland, the hugely influential editor of American *Vogue* from 1962 to 1971, and called 'the high priestess of style', formed an important costume jewellery collection. Wallis Simpson favoured Stanley Hagler and Kenneth Jay Lane. Movie actresses wore costume jewellery on as well as off the screen. Joan Crawford favoured Miriam Haskell pearls, while Joseff of Hollywood supplied everybody from Marlene Dietrich to Carole Lombard. Such was the demand for Joseff's designs for the motion pictures that he launched his own retail line around 1938 so that, he claimed, every American woman could feel like a Hollywood star.

American costume jewellery can be beautifully made. Many designers were émigrés from Europe and had often trained with 'real' jewellers. Before joining Trifari in 1930, French designer Alfred Philippe worked both for Cartier and Van Cleef & Arpels. Materials too were often of high quality, with fine paste and fake pearls and exceptional metalwork. In the 1940s, wartime restrictions actually improved the standard of jewellery when base metals, needed for the war effort, were replaced by sterling silver plated with gold.

Major manufacturers stamped their work so when buying look out for signatures (check necklace clasps, the reverse of earrings and the backs of brooches). It is also important to remember, however, that many good-quality pieces can be unsigned. Condition is important to value. Check for missing stones and any broken parts. Jewellery was often supplied in sets or 'parures' (necklace, earrings, brooch, and bracelet). A complete set will command a premium and original boxes should also be preserved.

Bracelets

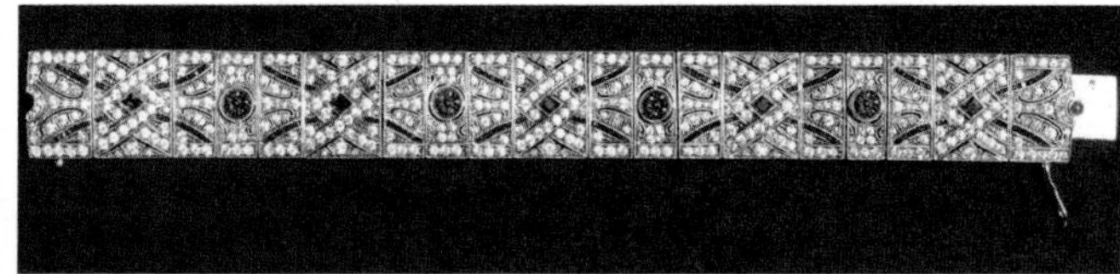

A silver and paste bracelet, set with *faux* sapphires and rubies, French, 1920s, 8in (20.5cm) long.
£400–450
$580–650 ⊞ RGA

A petit point on gilt-metal bracelet, handmade, 1950s, 1½in (4cm) wide.
£175–195
$255–285 ⊞ LBe

A chrome bracelet, set with coloured glass, c1930, 7½in (19cm) long.
£35–40
$50–60 ⊞ LaF

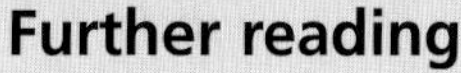

Further reading

Miller's Costume Jewellery: A Collector's Guide,
Miller's Publications, 2001

A gilt-metal and paste bracelet, 1950s, 7in (18cm) long.
£65–75
$100–110 ⊞ LaF

A gilt-metal and paste cocktail bracelet, American, 1950s, 8½in (21.5cm) long.
£70–80
$100–115 ⊞ LaF

A chinoiserie charm bracelet, by Napier, American, 1950s, 7in (18cm) long.
£100–125
$145–180 ⊞ CRIS

A gilt-metal and paste bracelet, by Weiss, American, 1950s, 7in (18cm) long.
£75–85
$110–125 ⊞ CRIS

► A gilt-metal, enamel and paste bracelet, by Kenneth J. Lane, American, c1970, 3½in (9cm) diam.
£45–50
$65–75 ⊞ SBL

Brooches

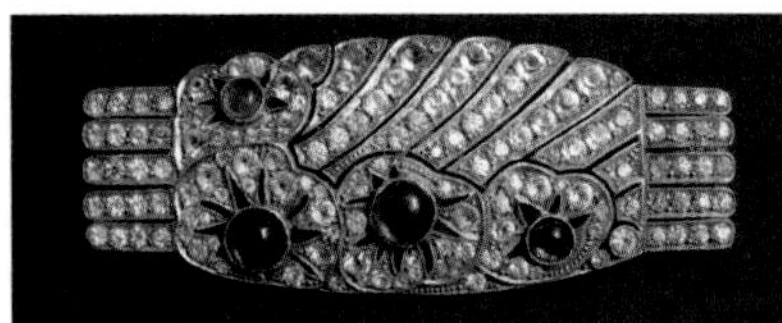

A silver and paste brooch, set with green stones, French, 1930s, 3in (7.5cm) wide.
£125–150
$180–220 ⊞ RGA

A fruit salad and wheelbarrow clip, by Trifari, American, 1930s, 2in (5cm) wide.
£175–195
$255–285 ⊞ CRIS

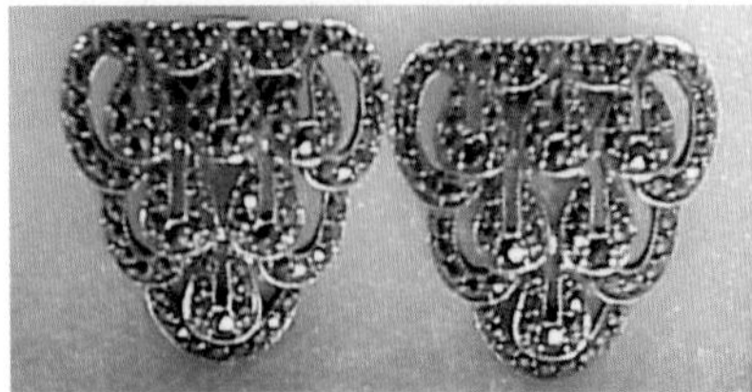

A pair of Art Deco silver and marcasite dress clips, 1in (2.5cm) wide.
£25–30
$35–45 ⊞ DEC

A rhodium-plated and paste brooch, by Marcel Boucher, American, early 1930s, 4in (10cm) long.
£125–150
$180–220 ⊞ RGA

A Royal Doulton brooch, modelled as a spaniel's head, 1930s, 1½in (4cm) high.
£190–230
$275–325 ⚒ Pott

A gilt-metal and paste flower pin, by Trifari, American, 1940s, 2¾in (7cm) diam.
£450–500
$650–720 ⊞ CRIS

◄ A gilt-metal bulldog pin, by Joseff of Hollywood, American, 1940s, 1½in (4cm) high.
£65–75
$100–110 ⊞ CRIS

A sterling silver and paste bird brooch, by Alfred Philippe for Trifari, American, 1940s, 3½in (9cm) wide.
£180–200
$250–300 ⊞ RGA

► A donkey pin, by Hattie Carnegie, American, 1950s, 3in (7.5cm) high.
£125–150
$180–220 ⊞ CRIS

A sterling silver and enamel fish brooch, by Adolpho Katz for Corocraft, American, 1940s, 2½in (6.5cm) wide.
£225–250
$325–350 ⊞ RGA

A gilt-metal and enamel frog pin, by Trifari, with paste eyes, American, 1950s, 1in (2.5cm) high.
£24–28
$35–40 ⊞ CRIS

◄ A silver basket brooch, set with glass flowers, 1950s, 2in (5cm) wide.
£85–95
$125–145 ⊞ LBe

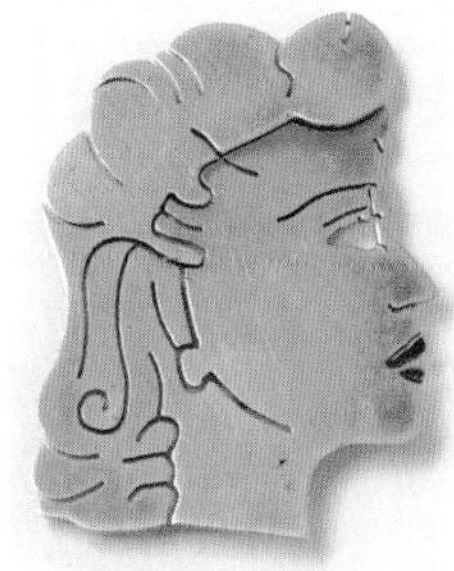

A brass brooch, modelled as a lady's head with red lips, 1940s, 2in (5cm) high.
£65–75
$100–110 ⊞ LBe

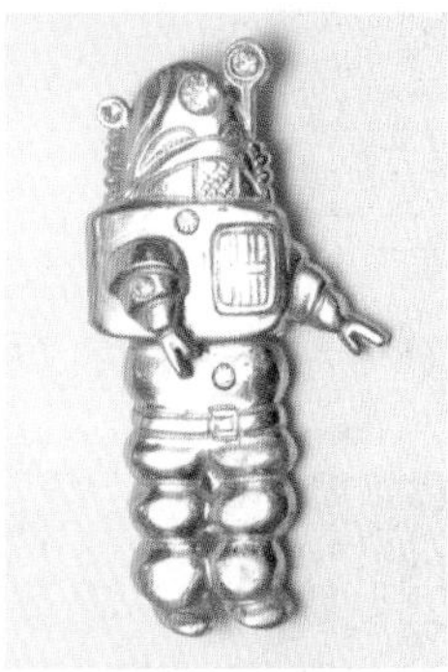

A white metal Robbie the Robot brooch, 1970s, 3in (7.5cm) high.
£12–15
$15–20 ⊞ RTT

Earrings

◄ A pair of earrings, by Alice Caviness, set with lustre stones and *faux* pearls, American, 1940s, 1¼in (3cm) diam.
£60–70
$90–100 ⊞ LaF

► A pair of teardrop earrings, encrusted with brilliant-cut rhinestones, clip/screw fastening, 1950s–60s, 1½in (4cm) long, with letter of authenticity.
£2,000–2,400
$3,000–3,500 ⚒ CO
These earrings were once owned by Marilyn Monroe and come with a letter of authenticity dated 6 March 1998 from Eleanor 'Bebe' Goddard, explaining how her foster sister Marilyn gave them to her, and this explains the price.

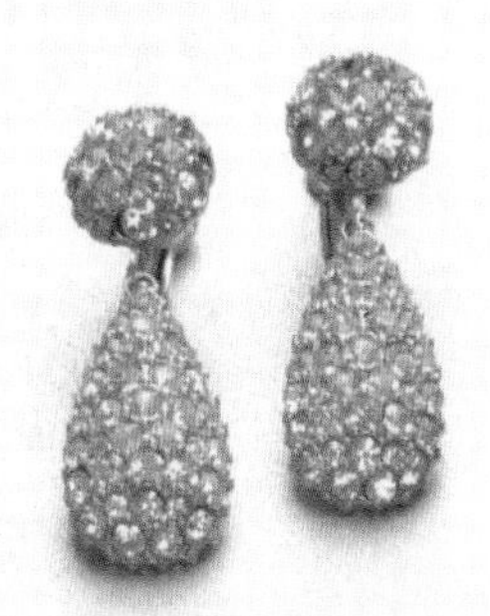

A pair of plastic earrings, modelled as flowers, c1960, 3in (7.5cm) long.
£25–30
$35–45 ⊞ SBL

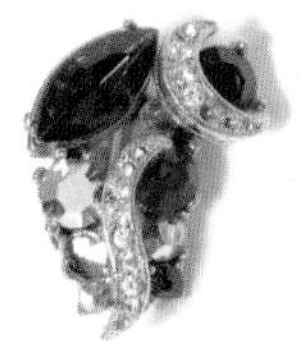

A pair of rhinestone and gilt earrings, by Spinks, with clip fastening, 1970s, 1in (2.5cm) diam.
£15–20
$20–30 ⊞ SBL

Jewellery Sets

A glass necklace, bracelet and earrings set, by Alfred Philippe for Trifari, American, 1940s, bracelet 8in (20.5cm) long, in original box.
£300–350
$450–500 ⊞ RGA

A glass and paste on gilt-metal earrings and brooch set, by Miriam Haskell, American, 1940s–50s, brooch 3in (7.5cm) high.
£350–400
$500–580 ⊞ SBT

A glass necklace and earrings set, by Stanley Haggler, American, 1950s, necklace 28in (71cm) long.
£1,450–1,650
$2,000–2,400 ⊞ LaF

LOCATE THE SOURCE
The source of each illustration in Miller's can be found by checking the code letters below each caption with the Key to Illustrations, pages 443–451.

◄ **An Austrian crystal earrings and brooch set,** by Mitchell Mayer for Christian Dior, 1951–54, brooch 2in (5cm) wide.
£270–300
$400–450 ⊞ LaF

A necklace, bracelet and earrings set, by Sarah Coventry, American, 1950s, necklace 16in (40.5cm) long.
£130–160
$200–230 ⊞ LaF

A paste brooch and earrings set, by Schreiner, American, 1950s, brooch 2½in (6.5cm) diam.
£400–450
$580–650 ⊞ CRIS

A sterling silver open-work brooch, by Georg Jensen, pattern No. 312, depicting two dolphins, seaweed and a shell, with a similar pair of earrings, c1950.
£400–480
$580–700 ⚒ G(L)

◄ **A plastic floral earrings and necklace set,** c1960, necklace 14in (35.5cm) long.
£55–60
$80–90 ⊞ SBL

► **A pendant brooch and earrings set,** by Joseph Mazer for Jomaz, American, 1960s, pendant 4in (10cm) wide.
£125–150
$180–220 ⊞ RGA

Necklaces & Pendants

A dipped and hand-carved resin necklace, with scent ball, c1930, 20in (51cm) long.
£80–90
$115–130 ⊞ FMN

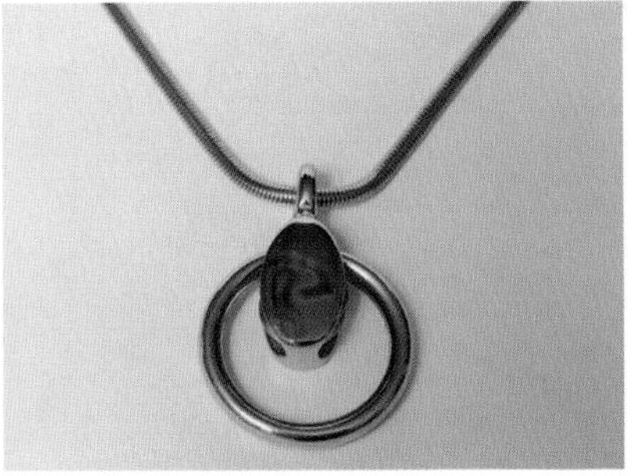

► **A cut-steel and Bakelite necklace,** 1930s, 15in (38cm) long.
£50–55
$75–80 ⊞ LaF

A gilt-brass and *faux* pearl necklace, by Miriam Haskell, American, 1940s, 15in (38cm) long.
£225–250
$325–360 ⊞ RGA

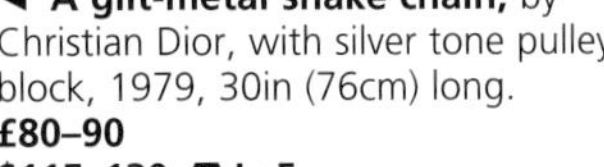

◄ **A gilt-metal snake chain,** by Christian Dior, with silver tone pulley block, 1979, 30in (76cm) long.
£80–90
$115–130 ⊞ LaF

An Austrian crystal flower drop necklace, by Norman Hartnell, c1950, 15in (38cm) long.
£225–250
$325–360 ⊞ LaF

Tiaras

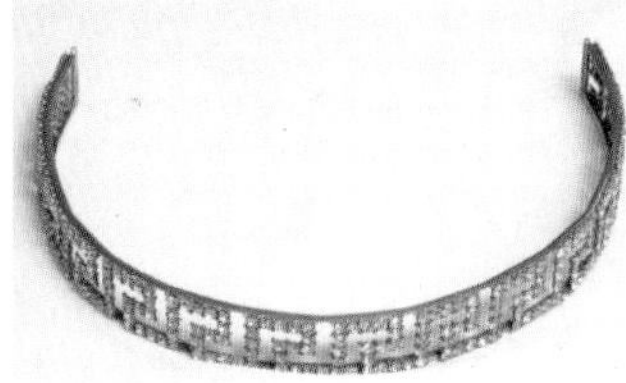

A silver-plated and paste tiara, set in Greek key pattern, 1920s, 1in (2.5cm) high.
£80–90
$115–130 ⊞ RGA

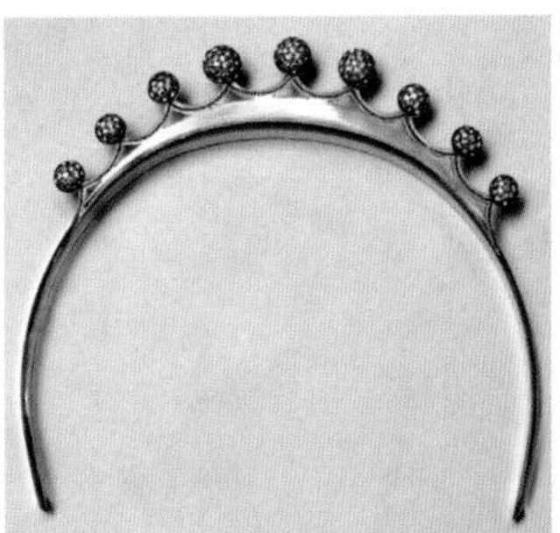

A coated metal and paste tiara, 1920s, 3in (7.5cm) high.
£550–650
$800–950 ⊞ JBB
A replica of the Russian crown jewels sold by Christies in 1924, this tiara was exhibited by them in the 1920s.

◄ **A Perspex and paste tiara,** 1930, 6in (15cm) wide.
£60–70
$90–100 ⊞ JBB

► **A beaded coronet,** 1940s, 4in (10cm) diam.
£40–45
$60–65 ⊞ JBB

A silver tiara, with carved onyx and rock crystal floral decoration, probably European, 1930s, 2½in (6.5cm) high.
£170–200
$250–300 ⊞ RGA

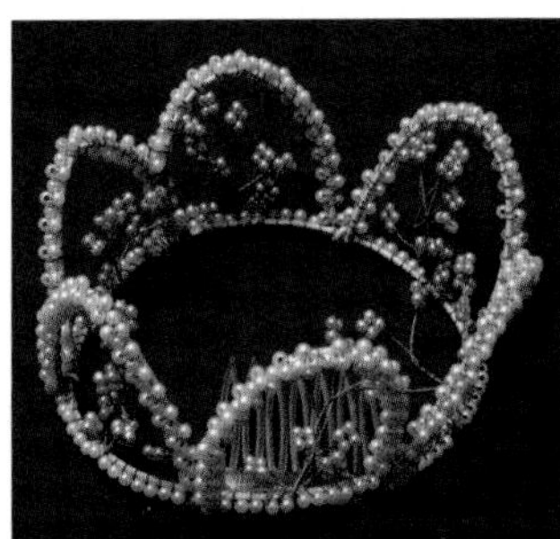

Kitchenware

A cast-iron coffee grinder, with a brass funnel, c1880, 28in (71cm) high.
£450–550
$650–800 ⊞ SMI

A cast-iron coffee mill, with a wooden handle, c1880, 6in (15cm) high.
£190–220
$275–320 ⊞ WeA

A painted tin flour bin, c1920, 21in (53.5cm) high.
£110–130
$160–190 ⊞ SMI

A brass lemon squeezer, on a wooden base, 1880, 13in (33cm) wide.
£190–220
$275–320 ⊞ SMI

A steel kettle, with a brass handle and lid, c1880, 10in (25.5cm) high.
£80–90
$115–130 ⊞ SMI

A set of tin pastry cutters, c1890, 5in (12.5cm) long, in original case.
£15–20
$20–30 ⊞ AL
This set is incomplete and slightly rusty. In better condition the value would be £35–40 ($50–60).

► An extending metal trivet, c1920, 12in (30.5cm) extended.
£15–20
$20–30 ⊞ AL

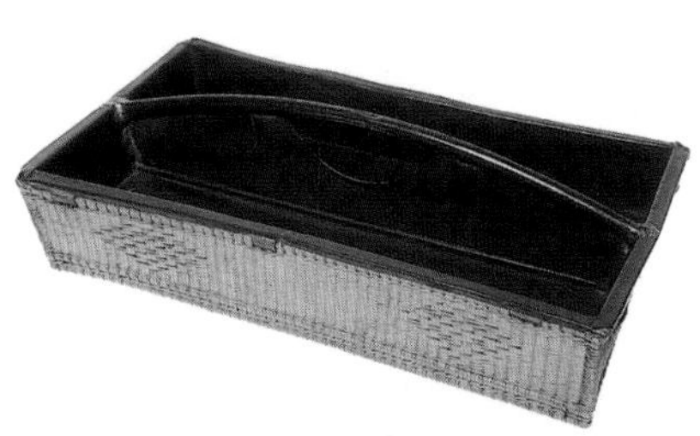

A Victorian tin-lined wicker knife tray, c1880, 16in (40.5cm) long.
£50–55
$75–80 ⊞ AL

A coffee tin, with original paint, c1880, 13in (33cm) wide.
£550–650
$800–950 ⊞ SMI

A copper, iron and ceramic *bain-marie*, with a wooden handle, c1890, 6in (15cm) high.
£175–195
$255–280 ⊞ WeA

A wire steamer basket, folds flat to make a cake tray, c1920, flat 12in (30.5cm) diam.
£12–15
$17–20 ⊞ AL

A mini oil stove, c1920, 16in (40.5cm) high.
£90–100
$130–145 ⊞ AL

A brass and steel water carrier, c1920, 20in (51cm) high.
£110–130
$160–190 ⊞ SMI

A pair of decorated tea tins, c1930, 6½in (16.5cm) high.
£10–12
$15–17 ⊞ AL

◄ A Mabel Lucie Attwell compressed card place mat/coaster, with wipe-clean finish, 1938, 5½in (14cm) diam.
£25–30
$35–45 ⊞ MEM

Cross Reference
See Advertising & Packaging (pages 11–22)

► A metalware cake icing table, c1950, 7in (18cm) high.
£35–40
$50–60 ⊞ AL

A chrome electric coffee percolator, with a plastic handle, c1950, 11in (28cm) high.
£27–30
$38–45 ⊞ JUN

Two plastic Tupperware liquid containers, with snap tops, left made in UK, right made in Belgium, 1960s, 9in (23cm) high.
£6–8
$7–12 ⊞ Mo

Cake Decorations

A porcelain wedding cake decoration, modelled as a pair of bridal slippers, decorated with a bird, c1920, 1½in (4cm) high.
£18–20
$25–30 ⊞ FMN

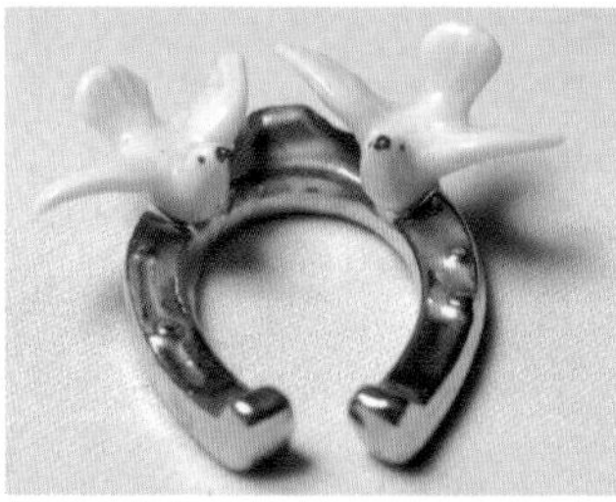

A porcelain wedding cake decoration, modelled as doves on a lucky horseshoe, 1920–40, 2in (5cm) wide.
£18–20
$27–30 ⊞ FMN

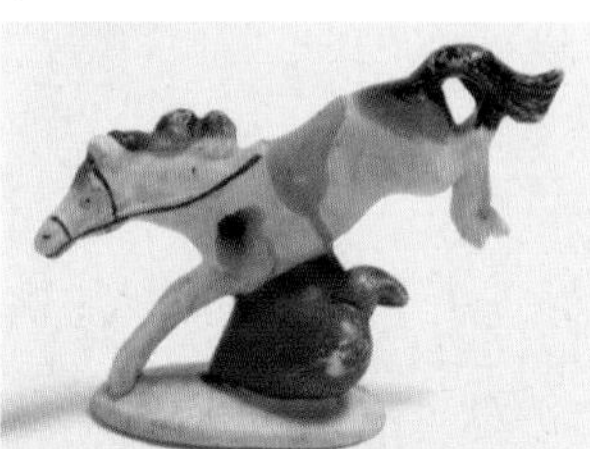

A bisque jumping horse cake decoration, c1930, 2in (5cm) high.
£60–70
$90–100 ⊞ YC

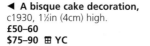

◄ **A bisque cake decoration,** c1930, 1½in (4cm) high.
£50–60
$75–90 ⊞ YC

A porcelain 21st-birthday cake decoration, modelled as a key, 1920–40, 3in (7.5cm) wide.
£15–20
$20–30 ⊞ FMN

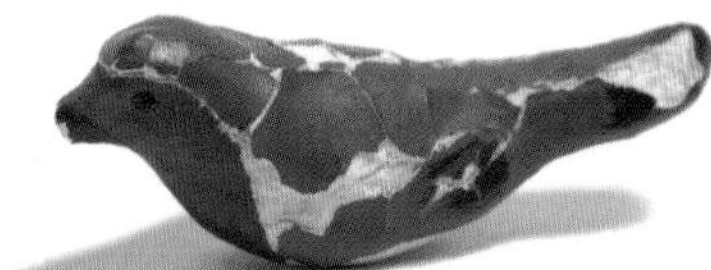

A plaster robin Christmas cake decoration, damaged, c1925, 1in (2.5cm) high.
£2–3
$3–5 ⊞ YC

A set of three bisque cake decorations, modelled as pixies, c1930, 3in (7.5cm) high.
£60–80
$90–115 ⊞ YC

Ceramics

A glazed terracotta mixing bowl, c1880, 13in (33cm) diam.
£50–55
$75–80 ⊞ AL
This bowl is called a pancheon and was used for proving bread.

An iron-glazed storage jar, late 19thC, 7in (18cm) high.
£35–45
$50–65 ⊞ IW

A Roe's ceramic pie funnel, early 20thC, 3in (7.6cm) high.
£50–55
$75–80 ⊞ B&R
Pie funnels are interesting items to collect. Prices range from £4–80, ($7–115), they do not take up much room and there are more than 300 examples from 1880–1960 to choose from.

A ceramic mixing bowl, inscribed 'Cakeoma for Cakes', early 20thC, 13in (33cm) diam.
£50–60
$75–90 ⊞ B&R

A Clarke's 'Rigid' ceramic icing bowl, shaped to tip to one side for mixing, early 20thC, 9in (23cm) diam.
£70–80
$100–115 ⊞ B&R

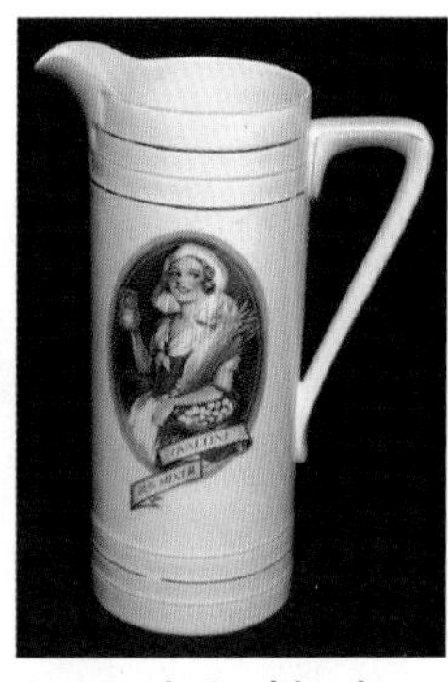

A ceramic Ovaltine jug, 1930s, 8in (20.5cm) high.
£40–45
$60–65 ⊞ SMI

A set of seven Sandland ware storage jars, with wooden lids, c1950, 4½in (11cm) high.
£110–130
$160–190 ⊞ AL

► **Two T. G. Green Church Gresley ceramic storage jars,** for Spectrum, with cork lids, 1970s, 6in (15cm) high.
£8–10
$12–15 each ⊞ CAL

Dairying

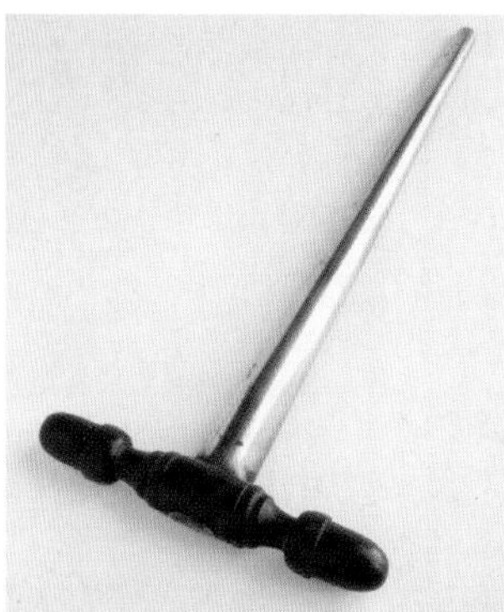

A brass butter iron, with a wooden handle, c1860, 15in (38cm) long.
£160–180
$230–260 ⊞ WeA

A wooden butter marker, carved with Prince of Wales Feather pattern, c1870, 3¾in (9.5cm) diam.
£75–85
$110–125 ⊞ WeA

A wooden butter marker, carved with a flower pattern, c1890, 1¼in (3cm) diam.
£18–22
$28–32 ⊞ WeA

A steel and brass cream can, inscribed 'B. Valentine', Scottish, c1900, 5in (12.5cm) high.
£125–150
$180–220 ⊞ SMI

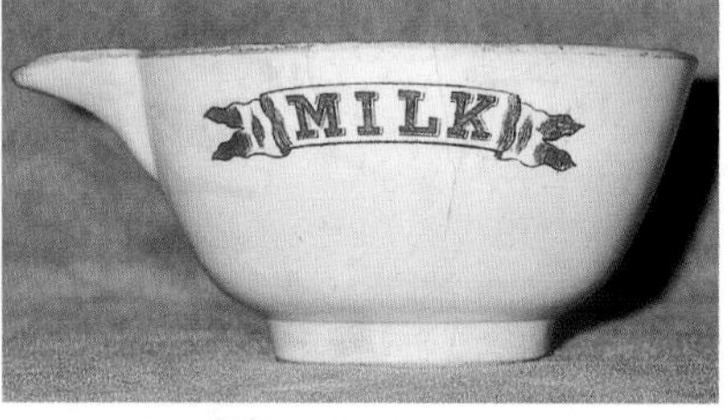

A ceramic milk bowl, rim rubbed, c1900, 7in (18cm) diam.
£50–60
$75–90 ⊞ B&R
If the rim of this bowl had been in better condition it could be worth £150–200 ($220–290).

A wooden butter roller, carved with a thistle pattern, c1900, 6½in (16.5cm) long.
£60–70
$90–100 ⊞ WeA

A steel and brass milk can, c1910, 11in (28cm) high.
£110–125
$160–180 ⊞ SMI

An Alexander cast-iron cream separator, c1910, 17in (43cm) high.
£60–70
$90–100 ⊞ JUN

A steel milk churn, 1920s, 8in (20.5cm) high.
£45–50
$65–75 ⊞ SMI

A tin cheese mould, French, c1930, 6in (15cm) high.
£8–10
$12–15 ⊞ AL

Enamel Ware

► **An enamel coffee pot,** with floral decoration, French, c1920, 13in (33cm) high.
£70–80
$100–115 ⊞ AL

► **An enamel cake tin,** c1920, 11in (28cm) diam.
£45–50
$65–75 ⊞ SMI

An enamel jug, decorated with pansies, French, c1920, 15in (38cm) high.
£50–60
$75–90 ⊞ B&R

An enamel milk can and cover, c1930, 6in (15cm) high.
£35–40
$50–60 ⊞ AL

An enamel drip tray and ladles, French, c1930, 19in (48.5cm) high.
£70–80
$100–115 ⊞ AL

An enamel urn, c1950, 15in (38cm) high.
£55–65
$80–95 ⊞ AL

Moulds

A copper ring mould, stamped 301, 19thC, 7½in (19cm) diam.
£160–190
$230–275 TMA

A tin chocolate mould, in the shape of a duck, c1890, 3½in (9cm) high.
£100–120
$145–175 ⊞ WeA

A metal chocolate mould, in the shape of a rabbit, c1910, 5in (12.5cm) high.
£75–85
$110–125 ⊞ WeA

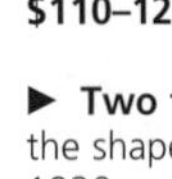

► Two tin chocolate moulds, in the shape of a gnome and an owl, 1920s, gnome 6in (15cm) high.
£65–70
$95–100 ⊞ SMI

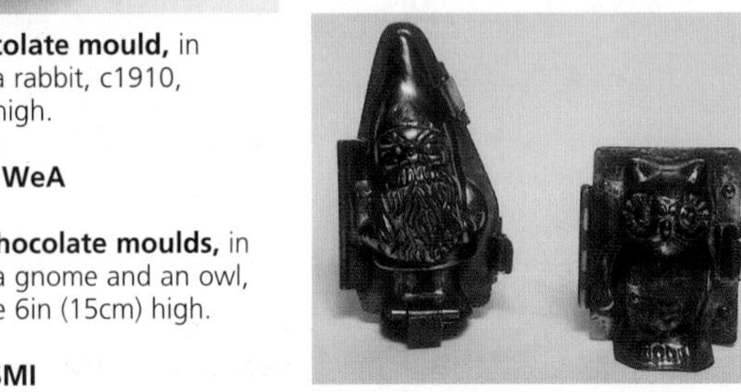

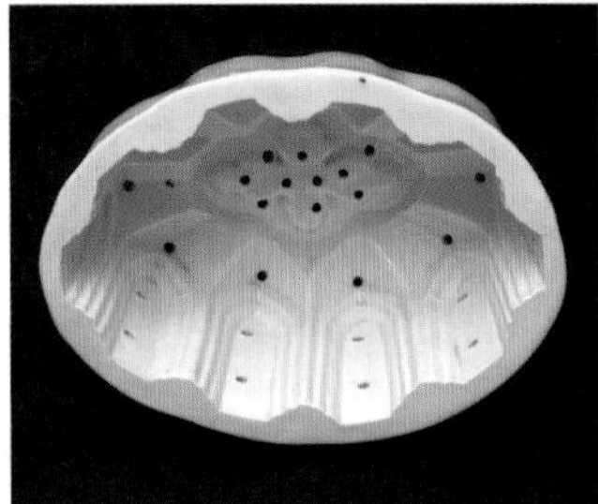

A Copeland ceramic cream cheese mould, cracked, c1870, 5in (12.5cm) high.
£50–60
$75–90 ⊞ AL

A decorated ceramic cake mould, French, Savoie, c1890, 9½in (24cm) diam.
£40–45
$60–65 ⊞ MLL

A metal chocolate mould, in the shape of a swan, c1910, 2½in (6.5cm) high.
£30–35
$45–50 ⊞ WeA

Six copper aspic moulds, c1880, fish 4½in (11.5cm) long.
£60–80
$90–115 each ⊞ SMI

A copper aspic mould, in the shape of a fish, c1890, 4½in (11.5cm) long.
£30–35
$45–50 ⊞ WeA

A metal chocolate mould, in the shape of a turkey, c1910, 4in (10cm) high.
£80–90
$115–130 ⊞ WeA

A tin chocolate mould, in the shape of two birds kissing, c1920, 11in (28cm) wide.
£85–95
$125–140 ⊞ SMI

Scales

A set of cast-iron and ceramic butter scales, c1880, 21in (53.5cm) wide.
£80–90
$115–130 ⊞ SMI

► **A set of metal scales and weights,** c1890, 14in (35.5cm) wide.
£80–90
$115–130 ⊞ AL

A set of enamel scales and weights, c1930, 10in (25.5cm) wide.
£40–50
$60–75 ⊞ AL

A set of cast-iron and brass sweet scales, c1880, 12in (30.5cm) high.
£75–85
$110–125 ⊞ SMI

A set of cast-iron and brass household scales, c1880, 18in (45.5cm) high.
£75–85
$110–125 ⊞ SMI

A metal household balance scale, c1930, 13in (33cm) high.
£50–60
$75–90 ⊞ SMI

◄ **A set of enamel scales and weights,** inscribed 'The Viking', c1930, 12in (30.5cm) wide.
£30–40
$45–60 ⊞ AL

Spice Boxes

A japanned tin spice box, c1800, 7in (18cm) high.
£130–150
$190–220 ⊞ SMI

A bent-and-turned wood spice box, lid damaged, late 19thC, 7½in (19cm) diam.
£125–145
$180–210 ⊞ B&R

A wooden spice cabinet, c1900, 3in (7.5cm) high.
£160–190
$230–275 ⊞ WeA

Toasters

Toast was a traditional part of the English diet in the 19th century, and it was the British firm Crompton & Co who invented the electric toaster in 1893. Providing an alternative to toasting forks, electric toasters soon became popular in middle-class households. 'You do not need to ring for more toast but make it yourself and eat it while it is crisp and hot,' wrote Mrs Peel, in *The Labour-Saving House* in 1917. Because they were designed for the breakfast room or dining room rather than the kitchen, designs were decorative.

Initially toasters were hand-operated and the bread had to be carefully watched, until the invention in America of the Sunbeam pop-up Toastmaster in 1926. 'Pop! Up comes the toast automatically,' boasted the advertisements. '...perfect toast every time, without watching, turning or burning.' It was not until after WWII however, that automatic toasters became commonplace. Many of the models shown here are American, reflecting the fashion for gleaming chrome and confident, bulbous shapes that characterized US kitchenware.

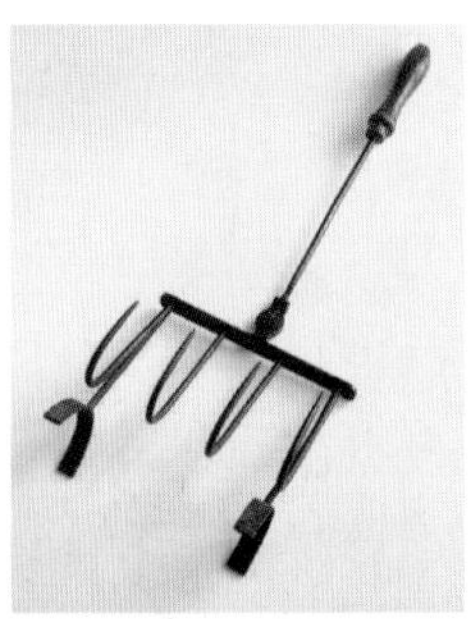

A toasting iron, with a wooden handle, c1880, 18in (45.5cm) long.
£130–150
$190–220 ⊞ WeA

A Universal Landers Ferry & Clark chrome electric toaster, American, 1920s, 7in (18cm) high.
£40–45
$60–65 ⊞ TRA

A Universal Landers Ferry & Clark chrome electric toaster, American, 1920s, 7in (18cm) high.
£50–60
$75–90 ⊞ TRA

A Sunbeam model B electric mechanical toaster, American, 1930s, 4in (10cm) high.
£40–55
$60–80 ⊞ TRA

► A Bersted chrome electric toaster, American, 1940s, 8in (20.5cm) high.
£20–25
$30–35 ⊞ TRA

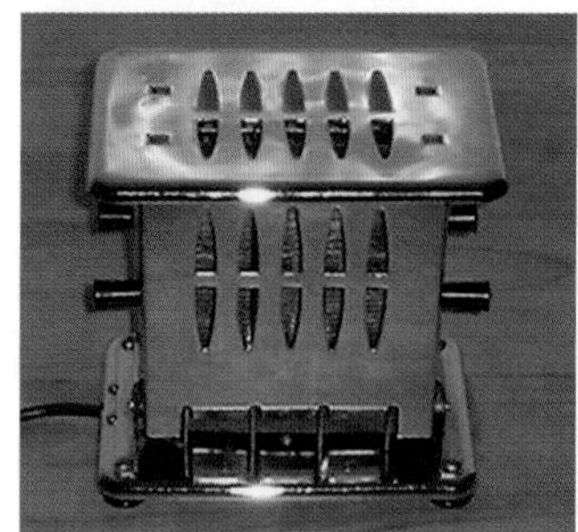

A Kenwood chrome toaster, rewired, 1950, 14in (35.5cm) wide
£65–75
$95–110 ⊞ JAZZ

◄ A Swan electric toaster, with original box, 1960, 7in (18cm) high.
£15–20
$20–30 ⊞ JUN

A Proctor Silex chrome electric toaster, Canadian, 1960s, 7in (18cm) high.
£15–20
$20–30 ⊞ TRA

Utensils

A wooden food slicer, c1860, 10½in (26.5cm) long.
£90–110
$130–160 ⊞ WeA

A steel dough knife, with a wooden handle, late 19thC, 11½in (29cm) high.
£100–120
$145–175 ⊞ WeA

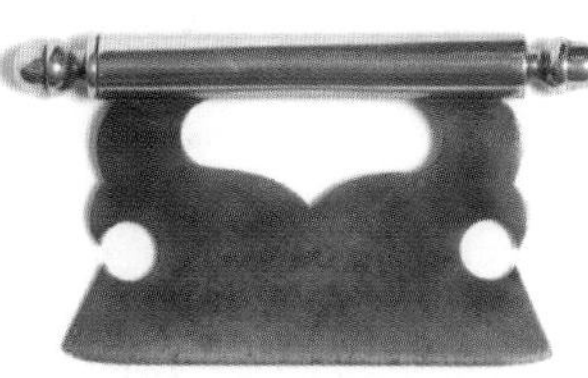

A steel herb chopper, the brass handle with acorn ends, c1880, 8in (20.5cm) wide.
£85–95
$125–140 ⊞ SMI

▶ An ice cream lick, adjusts to three sizes, c1830, 5in (12.5cm) long.
£45–55
$65–80 ⊞ AL

A tin nutmeg grater, late 19thC, 7in (18cm) long.
£60–70
$90–100 ⊞ WeA

A brass strainer, late 19thC, 18¾in (47.5cm) long.
£60–70
$90–100 ⊞ WeA

A Nutbrown kitchen saw, 1950s, 10in (25.5cm) long, in original packaging.
£3–5
$5–7 ⊞ RTT

Washing & Cleaning

A brass goffering iron, early 19thC, 11½in (29cm) high.
£270–300
$390–440 ⊞ WeA
A goffering iron is for pressing pleats into material.

A Carron's Foundry goose iron, c1850, 10in (25.5cm) long.
£25–30
$35–45 ⊞ FST
The Carron Foundry, near Falkirk, Scotland manufactured cannons from the 18th century onwards. They gave their name to the Carronade gun (chiefly used aboard ship) and to Carron oil, a liniment of linseed oil and lime water.

A Victorian lace iron, 3in (7.5cm) wide.
£70–80
$100–115 ⊞ HL

A Victorian lace iron, 2in (5cm) wide.
£70–80
$100–115 ⊞ HL

A Kenrick flat iron, 1880, 6in (15cm) wide.
£45–50
$65–75 ⊞ SMI

A brass iron trivet, c1880, 9¾in (25cm) long.
£75–85
$110–125 ⊞ WeA

► A W. Parnall & Co ceramic washing dolly, c1880, 16½in (42cm) high.
£360–400
$520–580 ⊞ WeA

A painted tin hot water jug, decorated with initials, c1900, 17½in (44.5cm) high.
£100–110
$145–160 ⊞ B&R

A Ewbank wooden carpet sweeper, c1910, 52in (132cm) high.
£55–65
$80–95 ⊞ AL

A pine shoe-cleaning stool, c1920, 12in (30.5cm) high.
£75–85
$110–125 ⊞ SMI

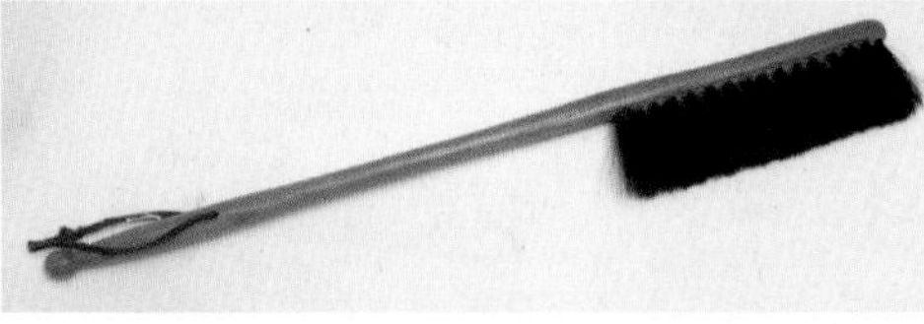

◄ A brush, with a wooden handle, c1930, 24in (61cm) long.
£6–7
$8–10 ⊞ AL

A cleaning brush, with a wooden handle, c1950, 14in (35.5cm) long.
£5–7
$7–9 ⊞ AL

► A travelling iron, with a Bakelite handle, 1950s, 4½in (11.5cm) long.
£12–15
$17–20 ⊞ RTT

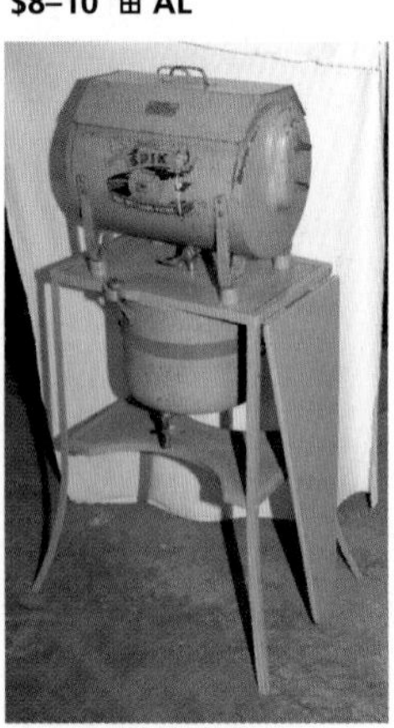

A Spik home dry-cleaning machine, c1930, 44in (112cm) high.
£130–150
$190–220 ⊞ JUN

A Swiftsure Junior copper and brass washing dolly, with a wooden handle, 1930s, 16in (40.5cm) high.
£25–30
$35–45 ⊞ SMI

Wood

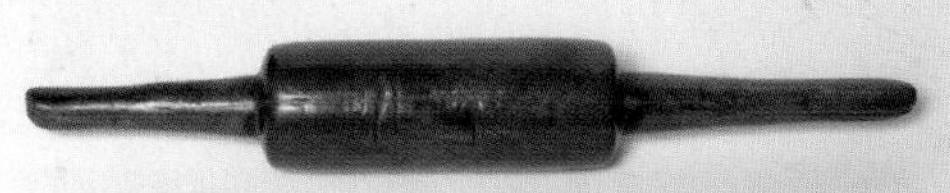

A wooden rolling pin, c1800, 12in (30.5cm) long.
£60–70
$90–100 ⊞ SDA

A sycamore dairy bowl, 19thC, 8½in (21.5cm) diam.
£325–375
$470–560 ⊞ SEA

A turned wood egg timer, late 19thC, 3in (7.5cm) high.
£65–75
$95–110 ⊞ WeA

Four wooden pastry cutters, c1900, 5in (12.5cm) long.
£12–15
$17–20 each ⊞ SDA

A pine chopping board, in the shape of a fish, 1930, 31in (78.5cm) long.
£30–40
$45–60 ⊞ MLL

A mahogany two-section cutlery tray, c1820, 16in (40.5cm) long.
£80–90
$115–130 ⊞ F&F

Two carved sycamore bread boards, c1880, 11in (28cm) diam.
£100–120
$145–175 each ⊞ SMI

Lighting

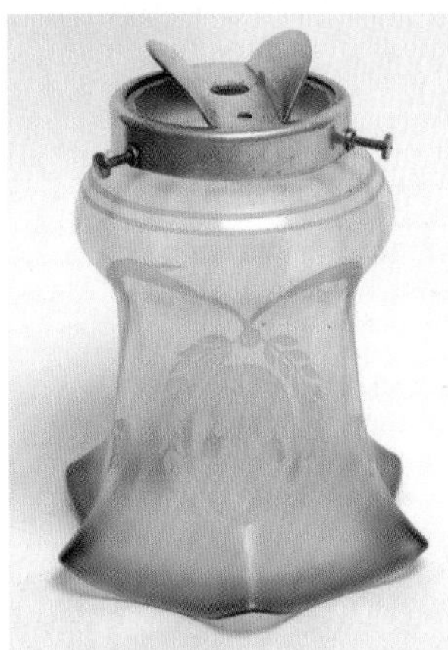

A Victorian etched glass shade, 6½in (16.5cm) high.
£60–70
$90–100 ⊞ BrL

A Victorian etched glass shade, 6¾in (17cm) high.
£65–75
$95–110 ⊞ BrL

A leaded stained glass hall lantern, 1890–1900, 12in (30.5cm) high.
£350–400
$500–580 ⊞ JeH

A metal gauze candle lantern, c1890, 11in (28cm) high.
£225–250
$325–360 ⊞ WeA

A bronze-finished Arts and Crafts lantern, with vaseline glass tube, 10in (25.5cm) high.
£375–425
$560–620 ⊞ JeH

◄ A steel and glass oil lamp, the sump decorated with flowers, 1900, 18½in (47cm) high.
£55–65
$80–95 ⊞ JAM

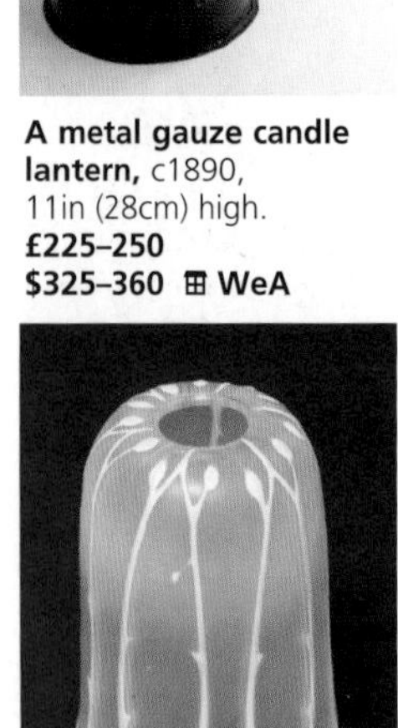

LOCATE THE SOURCE

The source of each illustration in Miller's can be found by checking the code letters below each caption with the Key to Illustrations, pages 443–451.

◄ A vaseline glass shade, c1900, 7in (18cm) high.
£150–175
$220–250 ⊞ JeH

A cranberry glass shade, with a brass gallery, c1900, 5½in (14cm) high.
£75–85
$110–125 ⊞ BrL

A brass table lamp, the adjustable shade impressed with a marine view, c1900, 23¾in (60.5cm) high.
£170–200
$250–300 ⚒ SWO

A Benson brass and copper oil lamp, with Powell opaline glass shade, marked, c1900, 22in (56cm) high.
£2,500–2,750
$3,500–4,000 ⊞ HUN

A pair of leaded light wall sconces, c1900, 13in (33cm) high.
£350–400
$500–580 ⊞ OLA

◄ A gas pole lamp, with etched glass shade, converted to electricity, c1900, 36in (91.5cm) long.
£160–190
$230–275 ⊞ JeH

A brass hanging lamp, with white glass shade, c1900, 30in (76cm) high.
£110–125
$160–180 ⊞ JAM

An Art Nouveau three-arm chandelier, with etched glass shades, 13in (33cm) diam.
£550–650
$800–950 ⊞ JeH

An Art Nouveau brass lantern, with vaseline glass tube, 14in (35.5cm) high.
£450–500
$650–720 ⊞ JeH

An Edwardian cut-glass pineapple pendant lamp, with brass gallery, 11in (28cm) high.
£170–190
$250–275 ⊞ JeH

◄ A wirework protector for an electric light bulb, French, 1920, 7in (18cm) high.
£20–25
$30–35 ⊞ TRA

A brass adjustable table, wall or ceiling lamp, with glass shade, 1910–20, 19in (48.5cm) high.
£120–150
$175–220 ⊞ JW

A cut crystal pendant lamp, with brass gallery fitting, c1910, 11in (28cm) high.
£125–150
$180–220 ⊞ JeH

A brass table lamp, with etched glass shade, c1920, 16in (40.5cm) high.
£85–95
$125–140 ⊞ JeH

A cameo glass *plaffonier*, French, 1920–30, 12in (30.5cm) high.
£300–350
$450–500 ⊞ JeH

◄ A glass hand-lamp, c1920, 14in (35.5cm) high.
£75–85
$110–125 ⊞ JAM

A brass oil lamp, 1937, 24in (61cm) high.
£400–450
$580–650 ⊞ COB
This lamp was made for, and presented to, a crew member of the liner *Queen Mary*.

A steel and brass carbide lamp, 1930, 10in (25.5cm) high.
£55–65
$80–95 ⊞ GAC

A chrome ceiling light fitting, with four glass shades, 1930s.
£225–250
$320–360 ⊞ JAZZ

A Stesco hiker's lamp, 1930s–40s, 5½in (14cm) high.
£20–22
$30–32 ⊞ RTT

A chrome ceiling light fitting, with catalan ends and glass shades, 1940s.
£110–125
$160–180 ⊞ JAZZ

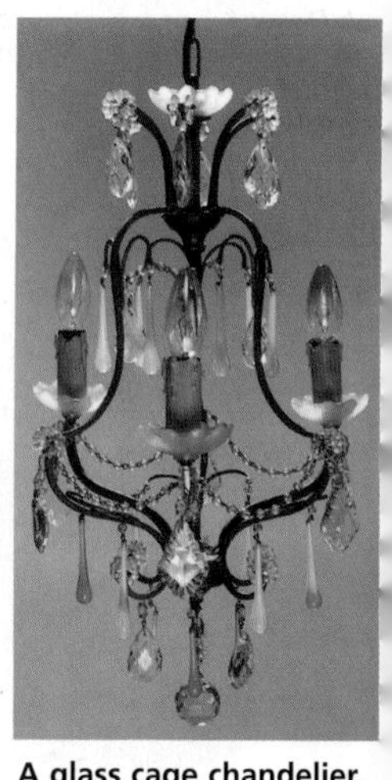

A glass cage chandelier, French, 1950s, 22in (56cm) high.
£380–420
$560–620 ⊞ JPr

Luggage

As travel improved in the 19th century with the development of the railways and shipping routes, there was an increasing need for luggage of different types. Fitted trunks, with their many compartments, served as portable wardrobes, standing as a piece of furniture in a cabin or railway compartment, thus saving their owner the labour of unpacking. Metal trunks and hatboxes were a favourite with those embarking for tropical climates as they provided added protection against insects. For those travelling light, there was the carpet bag (developed in France in the 1860s), the leather Gladstone bag, (named after the British Prime Minister) and the portmanteau, all of which paved the way for the suitcase which, by the 1900s, had become a standard travelling favourite.

Demand expanded further with the advent of the motor car. Manufacturers of luxury goods catered to the needs of wealthy tourists. In London, firms such as Asprey's and Mappin & Webb supplied handsome dressing cases with silver fixtures and fittings. On the Continent, Hermès, (who started as saddle-makers) and Gucci provided high-quality luggage to an international clientele. Another famous maker is Louis Vuitton. The company was founded in 1854, and that same year Vuitton introduced a flat-topped trunk (more space-saving than the traditional dome-topped design), covered in grey Trianon canvas. The firm produced a number of different materials in the 19th century, culminating in 1896 with the introduction of their celebrated LV monogrammed canvas. In 1914, Louis Vuitton opened their shop on the Champs Elysées in Paris, the largest travel goods store in the world. Today Vuitton is one of the most collectable names in the field, and the market is generally strong for both designer and non-designer luggage.

Look out for good quality pieces in uncracked leather with intact stitching. Leather should be 'fed' when necessary in order to avoid drying out and kept out of direct sunlight to prevent fading. Although poor condition will detract from the value of a case, signs of use such as original travel labels can add to its interest and expect to pay a premium for a smart name.

A Drew & Sons hide suitcase, with copper rivets and brass locks, c1880, 26in (66cm) wide.
£145–165
$220–240 ⊞ HO

A metal hat box, c1900, 12in (30.5cm) high.
£30–40
$45–60 ⊞ GAC

A tin trunk, monogrammed 'J. F.', c1885, 12in (30.5cm) wide.
£40–45
$60–65 ⊞ AL

A leather cartridge case, monogrammed 'A.G.D.', the interior with a label 'Charles Ingram, 18 Brenfield St. Glasgow', c1900, 23¾in (60.5cm) wide.
£350–400
$500–580 ⚒ SWO

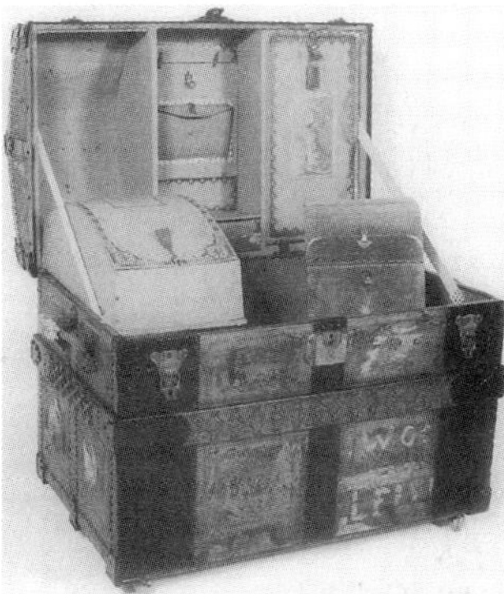

A cabin trunk, by Charles T. Wilt, the domed hinged cover enclosing a fitted interior with central recessed folding compartment flanked by two large fold-down compartments decorated with lithographic panels of young ladies, with lift-out box with jewellery compartment, American, 19thC, 36in (91.5cm) wide.
£350–400
$500–580 ⚒ LVS

A crocodile-skin case, with a gilt coronet and initial 'W', the interior fitted for bottles, mirrors and accessories, c1900, 29½in (75cm) wide.
£300–350
$450–500 SWO

A vellum hatbox, 1930s, 18in (45.5cm) wide.
£35–45
$50–65 SPT

A Vernier cardboard hatbox, 1950s, 12in (30.5cm) diam.
£8–10
$10–15 HSt

A Marshall & Snelgrove hatbox, 1960s, 12in (30.5cm) diam.
£15–18
$20–25 HSt

A gentleman's crocodile-skin case, with brass locks, 1900–10, 12½in (32cm) wide.
£200–250
$300–350 G(L)

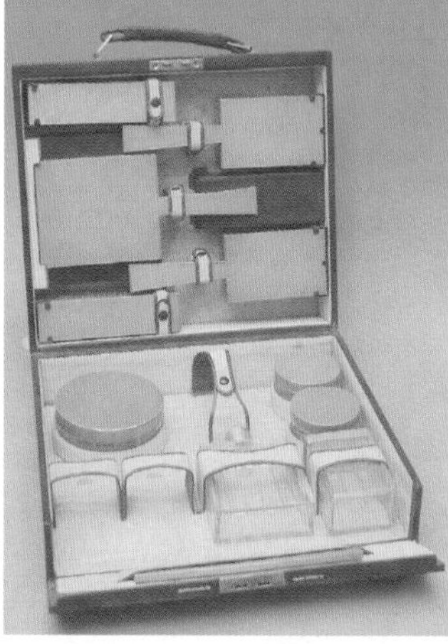

A Mappin & Webb leather vanity case, fitted with 11 silver-mounted dressing accessories, incomplete, 1933, 14in (35.5cm) wide.
£130–160
$200–230 G(L)

Two Louis Vuitton soft-sided suitcases, one stamped 'Bolkan' to the corner, French, 20thC, larger 27in (68.5cm) wide.
£850–950
$1,250–1,400 S(O)

A crocodile-skin case, by Landsdowne, Jermyn St, London, with foul-weather cover, 1920s, 20in (51cm) wide.
£300–350
$450–500 HO

A Koch three-piece fibreglass luggage set, 1950s, 25in (63.5cm) wide.
£35–40
$50–60 BB(L)

A Brexton wicker picnic hamper, with plastic containers and china plates decorated with Fiesta pattern by Barker Bros, late 1960s, 14in (35.5cm) wide.
£45–50
$65–75 PPH

Maps & Atlases

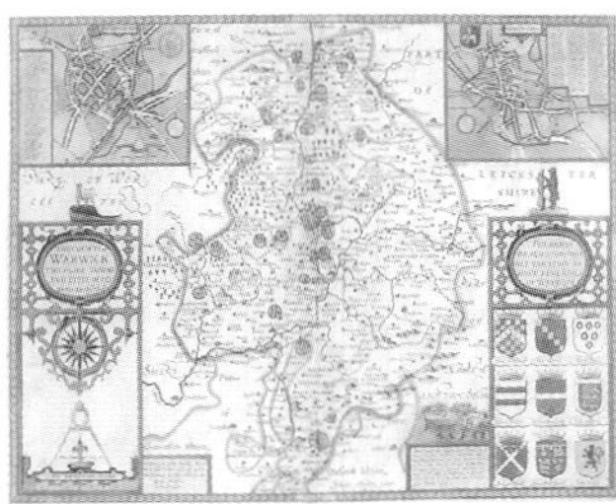

John Speed, *The counti of Warwick, the Shire Towne and Citie of Coventre Described,* double-page hand-coloured engraved map, repaired, Sudbury & Humble, 1610, 15 x 20in (38 x 51cm).
£200–250
$300–350 B(Kn)

Willem and Joannes Blaeu, *Magnae Brittanniae et Hiberniae Tabula,* engraved map with outline hand-colouring, surface dirt, light damp-staining, some creases, minor defects, Dutch, Amsterdam, c1660, 15¼ x 19¾in (38.5 x 50cm).
£340–380
$500–560 BBA

Herman Moll, *Abissina and Anian,* 1719, 8 x 11in (20.5 x 28cm).
£75–85
$110–125 MAG

► **E. Bowen**, a road map covering Sittingbourne, Kent, c1720, 7 x 5in (12.5 x 18cm).
£25–30
$35–45 MAG

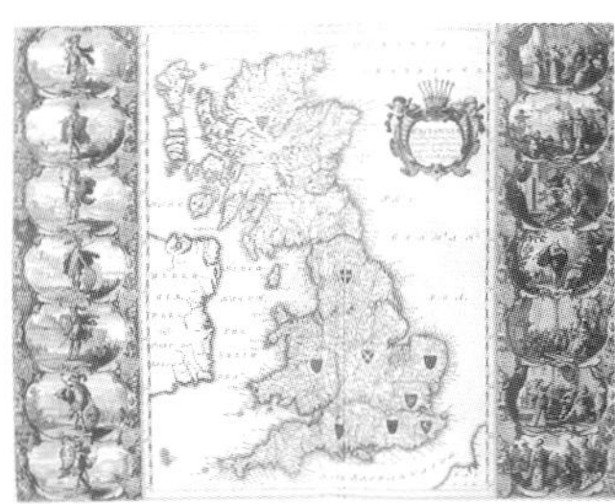

Willem Blaeu, *British Isles, Magnae Britanniae et Hiberniae tabula,* double-page engraved map, contemporary colour, Dutch text on verso, Dutch, Amsterdam, 1646, 15 x 19¼in (38 x 49cm).
£450–550
$650–800 B(Kn)

Richard Blome, *Wales, A Generall Mapp of North Wales and A Generall Mapp of South Wales,* a pair of hand-coloured engraved maps, each with ornamental title cartouche surrounded by figures, armorials and sailing ships, framed and glazed, 1670s, 13¾ x 18in (35 x 45.5cm).
£300–350
$450–500 DW

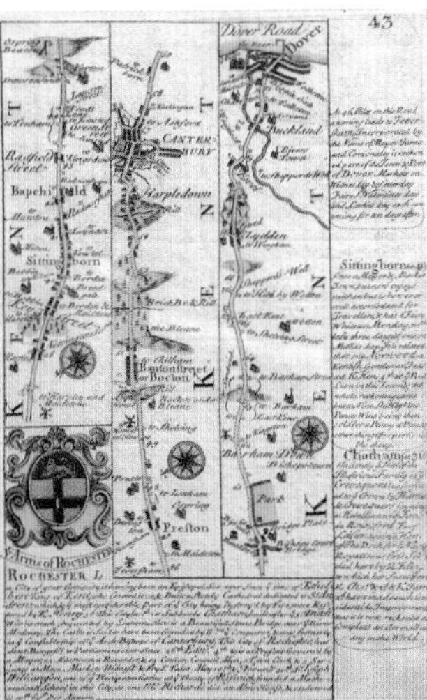

Willem and Joannes Blaeu, *Cornwall, Cornubia sive Cornwallia,* double-page engraved map, contemporary colour, Dutch text on verso, Dutch, Amsterdam, 1646, 15½ x 19¼in (39 x 49cm).
£300–350
$450–500 B(Kn)

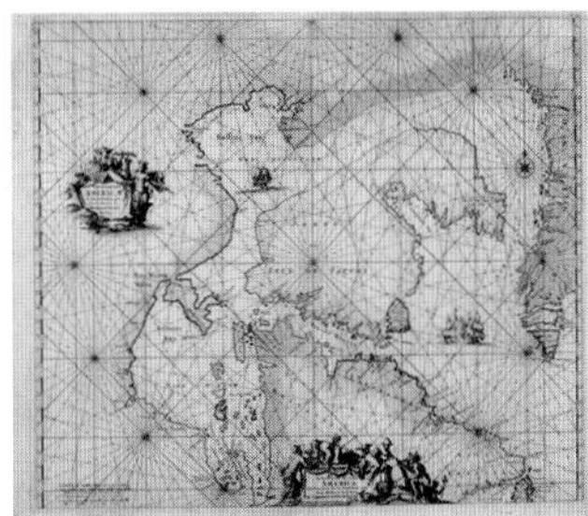

Frederick de Wit, *Septemtrionaliora Americae à Groenlandia, per Freta Davidis et Hudson ad Terram Novam,* engraved chart of the approaches to Hudson Bay and the North West Passage, tissue-backed, repairs, browning, a few spots, Dutch, Amsterdam, c1675, 19¼ x 22½in (49 x 57cm).
£450–550
$650–800 BBA

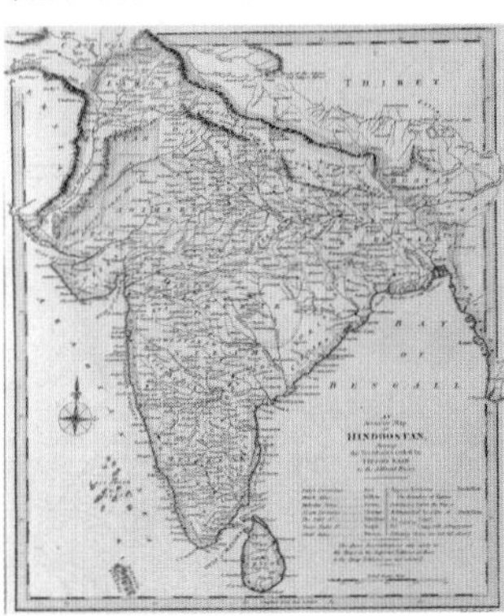

C. Cooke, *A Map of Hindoostan,* c1790, 10 x 11in (25.5 x 28cm).
£55–65
$80–100 MAG

Mostyn John Armstrong, *A Scotch Atlas or Description of the Kingdom of Scotland, divided into counties,* 1794, 4°.
£800–900
$1,150–1,300 ⚒ DW

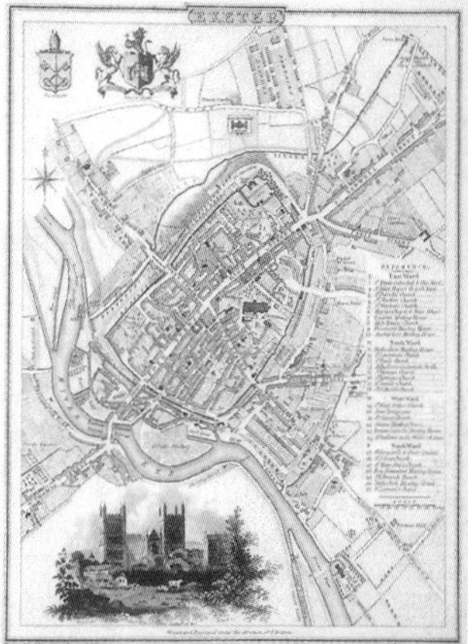

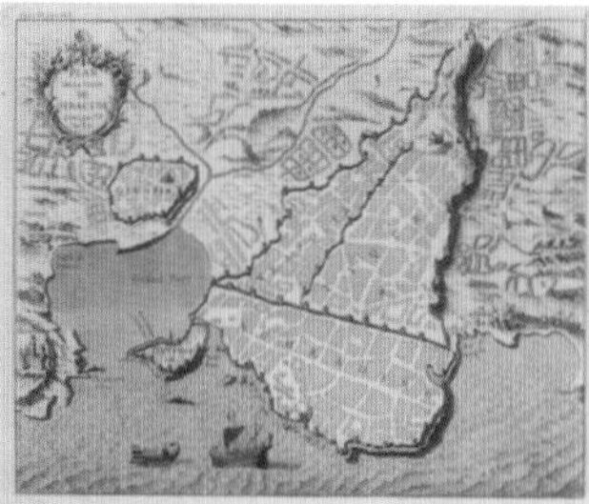

L. Barentin de Montchel, *Atlas de la Géographie Ancienne et Historique,* engraved title and 23 engraved single- and double-page maps with original outline hand-colouring, additional plate of shipping formation bound in, backstrip and two maps missing, gilt stamped 'Lycée Imperial de Paris', French, Paris, 1807, 2°.
£470–550
$700–800 ⚒ BBA

◄ **G. Cole and J. Roper,** *The British Atlas;* two hand-coloured maps including Isle of Wight, 56 county maps, plus 21 uncoloured engraved town plans, half calf, gilt-decorated spine, one plan missing, 1810, 2°.
£1,000–1,200
$1,500–1,750 ⚒ DW

J. Archer, *Oxfordshire*, steel engraved map with later colouring, 1845, 9½ x 7in (24 x 18cm).
£18–22
$25–30 ⊞ MAG

◄ **A Midland Railway map in colour on a postcard,** 1905, 6 x 4in (15 x 10cm).
£30–35
$45–50 ⊞ S&D

G. Cole and J. Roper, *Derby*, 1808, 7 x 9in (18 x 23cm).
£70–80
$100–115 ⊞ MAG

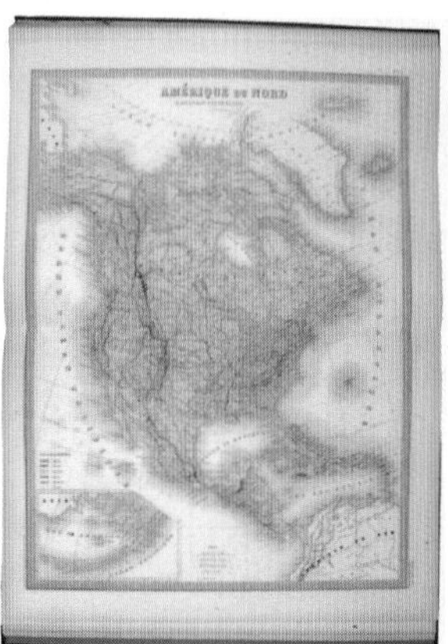

Eugène Andriveau-Goujon, *Atlas Universel de Géographie Ancienne et Moderne*, 50 double-page engraved maps, one folding, most in original hand-colouring, some colour-printed, slight damage, browning and some slight soiling, French, Paris, c1882, 2°.
£475–550
$700–800 ⚒ BBA

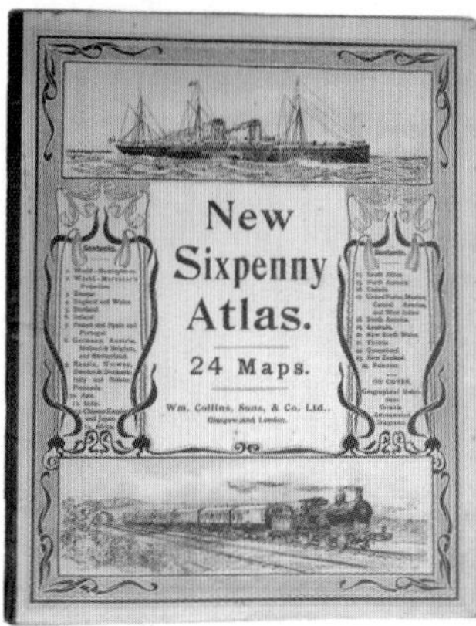

Wm Collins, Sons & Co, *New Sixpenny Atlas*, 24 maps, c1905, 11 x 9in (28 x 23cm).
£10–12
$15–20 ⊞ J&S

An Ordnance Survey District Map of Ilkley, c1920, 8 x 5in (20.5 x 12.5cm).
£4–6
$5–7 ⊞ JUN

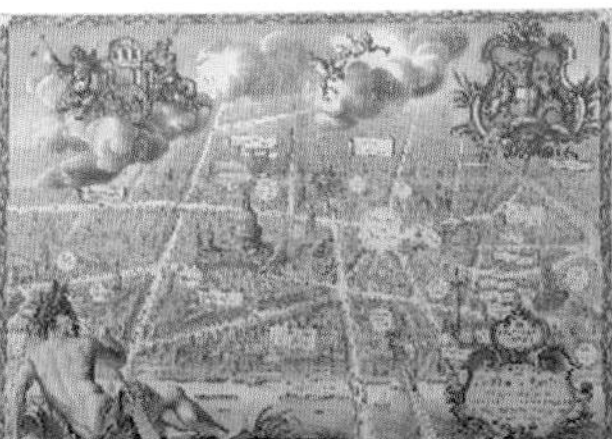

Rex Whistler, *The Prospect of the City of London, a print* from the centre of *Financial News*, 1934, 21 x 15in (53.5 x 38cm).
£270–300
$400–440 ⊞ ADD

Maps for the National Plan, a background to the Barlow, Scott and Beveridge reports, 1945, 13 x 9in (33 x 23cm).
£12–15
$15–20 ⊞ J&S

◄ **A Royal Air Force silk escape map,** showing part of China and Indo-China, 1939–45, 40 x 23in (101.5 x 58.5cm).
£20–25
$30–35 ⊞ OLD

A Motoring and Hiking Map of Great Britain, 1930s, 7½ x 5in (19 x 12.5cm).
£4–6
$5–7 ⊞ RTT

Four Bartholomew's Quarter-Inch Automobile Maps of Great Britain, Oban–Fort William, Peterborough–Norwich, Edinburgh–Berwick, Glasgow–Ayr, 1946, 9 x 4in (23 x 10cm).
£6–8
$8–12 ⊞ JUN

Cross Reference
See Automobilia (pages 47–52)

Five Esso road maps, late 1950s, 9 x 4in (23 x 10cm).
£8–10
$13–15 ⊞ JUN

World's Fair Subway Map, New York City, American, 1964, 5½ x 4in (14 x 10cm).
£4–6
$5–7 ⊞ RTT

A London Transport map and list of routes, 1970, 6 x 3in (15 x 7.5cm).
£2–4
$4–6 ⊞ RTT

Masonic Memorabilia

The Order of Freemasons is the largest secret society in the world with an estimated membership of around six million, the majority living in the USA and UK. The order evolved from the guilds of stonemasons and cathedral builders of the Middle Ages who, when major ecclesiastical building declined with the Reformation, began to accept honorary members from other professions.

Much Masonic symbolism reflects the early origins of the society, with the use of different tools, set squares, compasses, etc. The twin columns which stand at the entrance to the Masonic lodge derive from the great bronze pillars Jachin and Boaz that stood in the Temple of Solomon and were named after his sons. As with many other orders and bands, the star was a significant emblem, the number and positioning of points being given various mystic interpretations. Solomon's seal is a name given to the five-sided star or pentacle, and there is also the six-sided Star of David. It was in the 17th and 18th centuries that Freemasons began to adopt the rites and trappings of ancient religions and brotherhoods. In 1717 the first Grand Lodge was founded in London, ancestor of all subsequent lodges across the world. In the USA, the first regular lodge was founded in Boston in 1733.

Freemasons are generally divided into three major degrees: entered apprentice, fellow of the craft and master craftsman, although individual lodges also have numerous other levels, and customs vary from country to country. The combination of ceremony, symbolism and secrecy, coupled with material wealth and influence, has resulted in a host of Masonic memorabilia that can be very collectable today.

A simulated diamond-inset jewel, in the shape of a sixteen point star, for the Noble Order of the Bucks, the centre panel painted with a buck over the motto 'Honors Y Reward of Virtue', the reverse with a brass plaque inscribed 'Asyrian Lodge Holt Grand 1772', 3¼in (8cm) diam.
£270–300
$400–440 B(L)
The Noble Order of Bucks is believed to have begun c1723 and was at its height from 1750 to 1780. The last recorded meeting of the Society was 1802.

William Preston, *Illustrations of Masonry*, the first American improved edition from Strahan's tenth London edition, re-bound in leather, 1804, 7 x 5in (18 x 12.5cm).
£110–130
$160–200 B(L)

Items in the Masonic Memorabilia section have been arranged in date order.

A pearlware jug, hand-coloured with panels of Masonic symbols and inscribed 'To the Immortal Memory of William the III Prince of Orange/Success to the Orange Cause', 19thC, 6¼in (16cm) high.
£190–210
$275–300 B(L)

► **A drinking glass,** the trumpet-shaped bowl engraved with Masonic symbols and inscribed 'Lodge No. 199', on a pedestal foot, early 19thC, 5in (13cm) high.
£200–230
$300–330 B(L)

Jachin and Boaz, or An Authentic Key to the Door of Freemasonry, board bound, 1805, 4°.
£80–90
$115–130 B(L)

A firing glass, engraved with various Masonic symbols, on a heavy base, early 19thC, 4¼in (11cm) high.
£55–65
$80–100 B(L)

Firing glasses were used for toasting, their thick stem enabling them to be bumped on the table.

A porcelain box, the hinged lid painted with sun, moon and level over a set of scales and candles on a chequered floor, surrounded by knotted tassels, with moulded scrolling decoration, late 19thC, 2¼in (5.5cm) diam.
£350–390
$500–580 B(L)

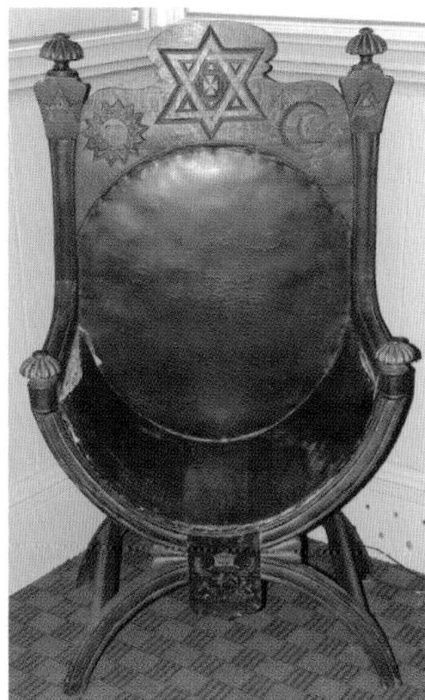

An oak throne, with reeded finials above a shaped upholstered back, carved with Masonic symbols over a dished seat forming the arms and stretchers, the reverse with a plaque inscribed 'The chair is made of the old oak and bell metal of York Minster destroyed by fire May 20th 1840'.
£2,800–3,300
$4,000–4,800 B(L)

The coat-of-arms belonged to the 2nd Earl of Zetland, who became the Grand Master of the United Grand Lodge of England in 1844, after becoming the Provincial Grand Master of Yorkshire North East Ridings from 1840 to 1844.

A pair of heavy cut-glass goblets, one engraved within a crowned shield 'Richard Scott 1844' the other 'Elizabeth Scott 1849', and with Masonic symbols, Union flowers, roses and thistles, 5¾in (14.5cm) high.
£750–850
$1,100–1,250 WAL

A *milchglass*, painted with flowers and a panel of Masonic symbols, mid-19thC, 4in (10cm) high.
£160–190
$230–275 B(L)

A silver-gilt Chapter jewel, in a watch case, 1859, 4in (10cm) long.
£150–170
$220–250 B(L)

A gold-plated half-hunter pocket watch, by Jean Pierre, the scroll-engraved cover enclosing a white dial with Masonic symbols, with 17 jewel movement, late 19thC, 2¼in (5.5cm) diam.
£90–110
$130–160 B(L)

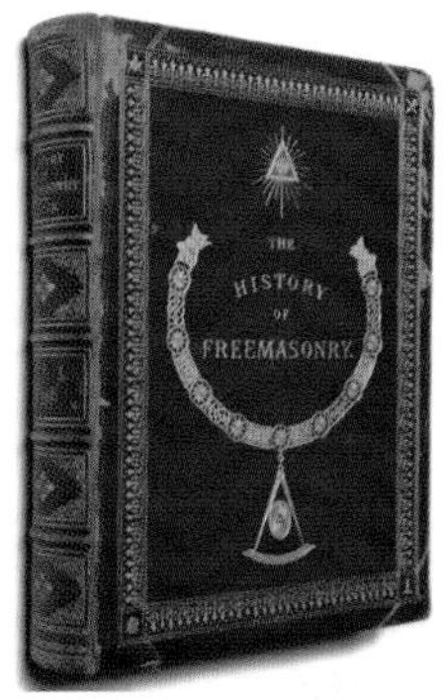

◄ **Robert Freke Gould,** *Three volumes of The History of Freemasonry*, published by Thomas C. Jack, leather bound with gilt decoration and gilt edges, 1887, 12 x 9in (30.5 x 23cm).
£110–130
$160–200 B(L)

A creamware jug, printed with a figure sitting beside the arms of the Premier Grand Lodge and surrounded by Masonic symbols above the motto 'Esit Lux et Lux Fuit', the other side printed with a poem surrounded by symbols, late 19thC, 5¼in (13cm) high.
£100–120
$145–175 B(L)

A silver and enamel cruciform jewel, with ribbon, the bar engraved 'A.O.C.F.S.E.U', the jewel with a coat-of-arms depicting a heart in a hand, the reverse inscribed 'Premier Lodge No. 1, Presented to Bro. Geo. Lawrence for past services Jan 3 1894', and a triangular silver jewel inscribed 'O.F.F.', 1894, 5in (12.5cm) high.
£30–40
$45–60 B(L)

A silver brooch, in the shape of a five-pointed star, inset with paste stones, the back inscribed 'S. Mace St Nicholas Lodge No. 1676, 5th February 1897', Birmingham 1897, 2in (5cm) diam.
£20–25
$30–35 B(L)

A silver-gilt, enamel and paste medal, by Kenning & Son, made for the Diamond Jubilee, in original box, 1897, 5in (12.5cm) long.
£250–275
$350–400 SHa

A pressed burr-wood box, the lid with Masonic and Rose Croix symbols, the base pressed with a woven pattern, c1900, 3¼in (8.5cm) diam.
£190–210
$275–300 B(L)

A glazed pottery figure of a devil, satirizing Freemasonry, seated on a set square making a secret sign of touching his nose, registration No. for 1909 on base, 7¾in (19.5cm) high.
£280–320
$410–460 WAL

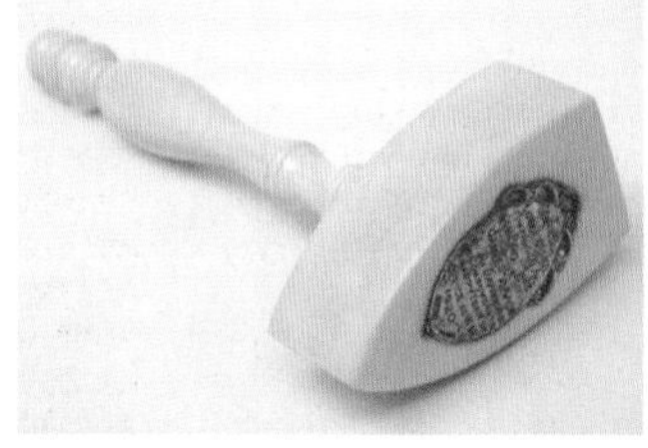

An ivory gavel, with turned handle and silver presentation plaque, 1921, 6in (15cm) long.
£275–325
$400–470 G(L)
The gavel is an object of major importance in Freemasonry, used to keep order and punctuate the activities of the Society.

◄ **A silver keyless pocket watch,** the mother-of-pearl dial with coloured symbols and inscription 'Love Your Fellow Man, Lend Him a Helping Hand', the case decorated in relief, Swiss, import marks for 1925, 2in (5cm) diam, in original box with spare glass.
£1,400–1,500
$2,000–2,150 B(L)
Associated with the Holy Trinity, along with other interpretations, the triangle is an important Masonic symbol. Triangular-timepieces were created for Freemasons and the Museum of Freemasonry in London holds a reference collection of Masonic clocks and watches.

A gold Creaton Lodge badge, 1949, 5in (12.5cm) long.
£325–365
$470–550 BrL

Medals
Commemorative

A cast-silver medal, by G. Bower, commemorating the coronation of William and Mary, 1689, 2¼in (5.5cm) diam.
£130–150
$200–220 ⊞ TML

A silver medal, for The Oak Society, inscribed '*Revirescit* 1750', 1750, 1¼in (3.5cm) diam.
£275–325
$400–470 ⊞ TML

The Jacobite Society met at the Crown and Anchor Tavern in The Strand. It is believed that on his visit to London in 1750 Prince Charles was present at a meeting of the society. The word *Revirescit* is also known to appear on drinking glasses at the time, one example bears the three feathers of the Prince of Wales badge. Members of the society were entitled to a bronze medal while presumably, those higher up the committee had the rare silver versions.

A silver medal, by W. Mossop, commemorating Baron Rokeby, Primate of Ireland, the reverse depicting the Armagh Observatory, 1789, 2in (5cm) diam.
£445–485
$650–700 ⊞ TML

A white metal medal, by P. Wyon, commemorating the death of Lord Nelson, 1805, 2in (5cm) diam.
£100–125
$145–180 ⊞ TML

A white metal medal, by P. Wyon, commemorating the death of Charles James Fox, 1806, 2¼in (5.5cm) diam.
£55–65
$80–95 ⊞ TML

► **A silver archery medallion,** by Phipps & Robinson, c1790, 2in (5cm) diam, in original sharkskin case.
£650–750
$950–1,100 ⚒ TEN

A white metal medal, by T. Halliday, commemorating the abolition of slavery, 1834, 1¾in (4.5cm) diam.
£425–485
$620–700 ⊞ TML

A white metal medal, by Bennett, with views of Stonehenge and Old Sarum, 1843, 2in (5cm) diam.
£130–150
$200–220 ⊞ TML

◄ **A bronze Services medal,** by W. Wyon, commemorating The Great Exhibition, 1851, 2in (5cm) diam.
£220–250
$320–360 ⊞ TML

A silver prize medal, by B. Wyon, for the Lanarkshire Farming Society, c1860, 2½in (6.5cm) diam.
£130–150
$200–220 ⊞ TML

A gold medal, by Mappin & Webb for the Hackney Horse Society, the reverse with a knight on horseback, c1905, 1¾in (4.5cm) diam.
£300–350
$450–500 ⚒ DNW

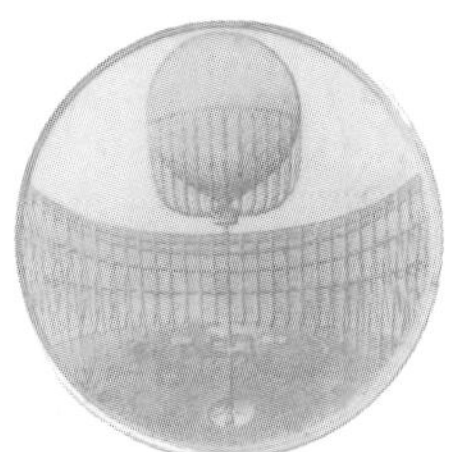

A gilt white metal medal, by Labouche, commemorating the Ascent of the Balloon Captive, 1868, 2in (5cm) diam.
£350–385
$500–570 ⊞ TML

A silvered-metal medal, from a model by Bertram Mackennal, commemorating the Olympic Games, London 1908, loose mounted with silver-coloured metal chain necklace, 2in (5cm) diam.
£80–100
$115–145 ⚒ CDC

Cross Reference
See Sport
(pages 366–378)

A silver medal, by B. Wyon after T. Landseer, commemorating the London Zoological Society, depicting a collection of birds, 1872, 3in (7.5cm) diam.
£1,000–1,250
$1,500–1,800 ⊞ TML

A medal, awarded to Mrs Fowler, owner of Honiton Lace, at the Exposition Universelle de Bruxelles, Belgium, 1910, 3in (7.5cm) diam.
£270–300
$400–440 ⊞ HL

► A Royal Automobile Club bronze medal, engraved 'Tourist Trophy Race 1928', the reverse 'R.A.C. International Tourist Trophy Race – 1919–28 Ards Circuit Ulster–Cyril Paul Class D. 64.21mph', 2in (5cm) diam.
£70–100
$100–145 ⚒ WW

A silver and enamel prize medal, by Kirkwood, for the Stockbridge Drafts Club, Edinburgh, Scotland, with integral loop for suspension, 1901, 3in (7.5cm) square.
£90–100
$130–145 ⊞ TML

A uniface cast-bronze medal, by A. Lavrillier, commemorating Auguste Rodin, French, c1920, 3¼in (8.5cm) diam.
£80–100
$115–145 ⚒ DNW

A bronze medal, by Anie Mouroux, commemorating the first French aerial crossing of the North Atlantic from West to East, depicting conjoined busts of Assollant, Lefèvre and Lotti, the reverse with aircraft in clouds above a map of the globe showing the route from the USA to Spain, 1929, 2¾in (7cm) diam.
£80–100
$115–145 ⚒ DNW
The journey from Maine, USA to Corrillas in Northern Spain covered a distance of 5,500km (3,415miles) and took 29hrs 20mins.

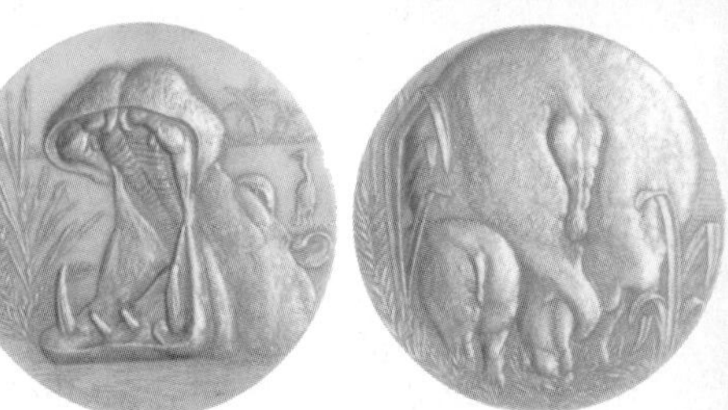

A plated-bronze medal, by P. Lécuyer, 'L'Hippopotame', edge stamped 18/100, French, 1973, 2¾in (7cm) diam.
£60–70
$90–100 ⚒ DNW

Military

► **A Crimean War Medal,** with three clasps, Alma, Balaklava and Inkermann, awarded to Lieut. Vincent Mackesy, 63rd Foot, fitted with a silver ribbon buckle, mounted inside a silver oak wreath, London 1871.
£850–950
$1,250–1,380
⚒ DNW

An Eton Volunteers silver Shooting Medal, by W. J. Taylor, swivel bar suspender, original grey ribbon attached to silver buckle clasp, edge bruise, c1860.
£100–110
$145–160 ⚒ DNW

A South African War Medal, awarded to Pte. J. Smith, 2-24th Foot, 1877–89.
£17,000–19,000
$24,650–27,500 ⚒ DNW
John Smith was present as a Private in 'B' Company at the defence of Rorke's Drift, 22–23 January 1879, and was wounded in the abdomen by an *assegai*. Material connected with the Zulu Wars is very collectable.

◄ **A group of three WWI Medals,** awarded to Pvt. Robert Smith of 10th Canadian Infantry, 1914–18.
£35–45
$50–65 ⊞ COB

► **A group of three WWI Medals,** including Military Medal for Gallantry and War and Victory Medals, awarded to 29197 Pte. Herbert Pike, 3rd Bn. Grenadier Guards, 24th January 1919.
£350–400
$500–580 ⊞ Q&C

◄ **An Indian Police Medal,** G.VI.R, awarded for gallantry, to F. J. Jude, Sergeant, Calcutta Police, with original gallantry ribbon and investiture pin brooch, with a Calcutta Police Force badge, Indian, 1946.
£650–700
$950–1,000 ⚒ DNW
The Indian Police Medal with 'Gallantry' reverse was not introduced until 1945, and only 138 awards are known to have been given, just eight of these to Europeans.

Medical

A wet drug jar, decorated with berries and leaves, inscribed 'Ollo Lavrino', the handle painted with a winged angel standing on a cloud, chips, initialled 'SM', Italian, 17thC, 5½in (14cm) high.
£500–600
$720–870 TMA

◄ **A mahogany gout stool,** late 18thC.
£140–170
$200–250 L

A ceramic Vienna eyebath, painted by Josef Pumperer, slight rim flakes, shield mark in underglaze blue and impressed mark with painters mark 'iio', 2½in (6.5cm), c1790.
£2,200–2,400
$3,200–3,500 BBR

In recent years eyebaths have become increasingly collectable. The combination of early date, artist attribution and, in this case, the royal provenance of the Princes Thurn und Taxis, Schlossmclerv, Bohemia, makes this an exceptional example.

A pair of metal cufflinks, depicting the use of an enema, 1860, in a fitted case, 2½ x 4in (6.5 x 10cm).
£300–350
$450–500 CuS

Six steel dental scaling and hygiene instruments, with bone handles, some spotting, in a fitted leather-covered case, 1820–40, 6in (15.5cm) long.
£350–400
$500–580 ET

A steel optician's sign, modelled as a pince-nez, with glass inserts, 1870, 12in (30.5cm) wide.
£400–450
$580–650 CuS

A wood and glass model of an eyeball, 1880, 7½in (19cm) diam.
£400–450
$580–650 CuS

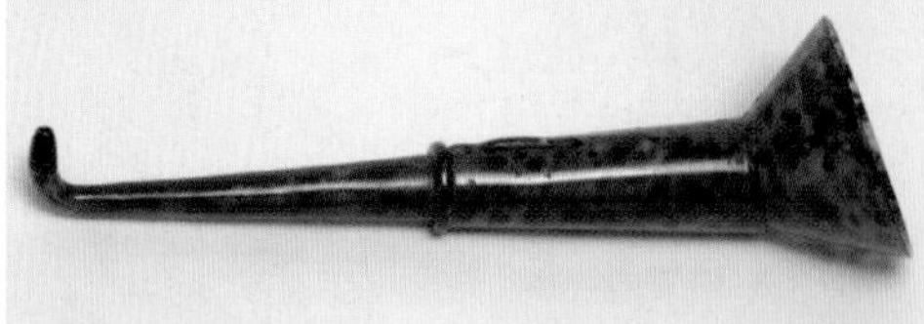

A celluloid ear trumpet, 1880, 11½in (29cm) long.
£250–275
$350–400 CuS

► **The Alexandra Inhaler,** decorated with flowers, transfer-printed with directions below, rim chip, 19thC, 5½in (14cm) high.
£90–100
$130–145 BBR

An articulated steel model of a jaw, 1890, 5in (12.5cm) long.
£400–450
$580–650 CuS

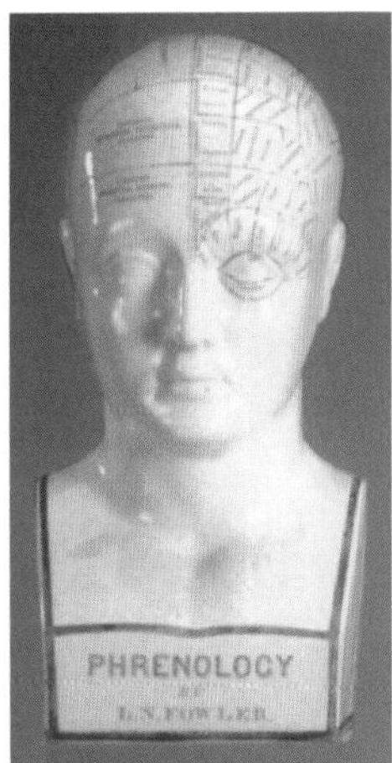

A pottery phrenology head, by L. N. Fowler, with printed details including 'For thirty years I have studied crania and living heads from all parts of the world...', 19thC, 11¼in (28.5cm) high.
£400–500
$580–720 🔨 TEN

A Mauchline ware medicinal beaker box, c1870, 3in (7.5cm) high.
£70–80
$100–115 ⊞ MB

A Sphygmomanometer (blood pressure monitor), by Down Bros, arm band and bulb missing, 1895–1905, 13in (33cm) high.
£110–125
$160–180 ⊞ WAC

A metal tooth key, with turned ebonized handle, 19thC, 5¾in (14.5cm) long.
£75–85
$110–125 🔨 FHF
First recorded in 1742, tooth keys were used to extract teeth. Initially they were straight-shafted and made from iron. As the 18th century progressed, plain handles became more decorative and were fashioned from ivory, mother-of-pearl and different woods. The introduction of a bent shaft improved the extraction process and lessened the pressure on surrounding teeth. In the second half of the 19th century, the development of dental forceps by Sir John Tomes rendered the tooth key obsolete.

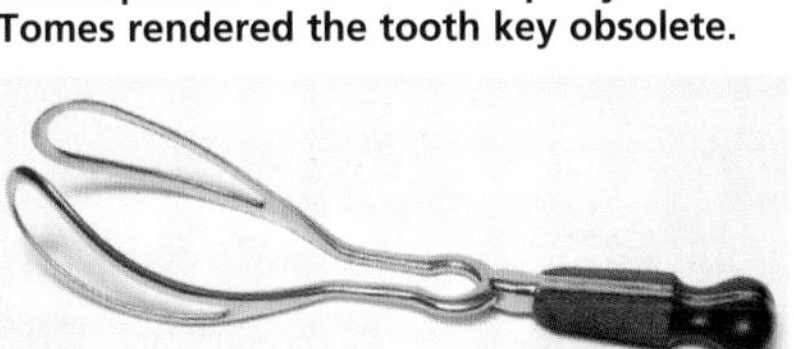

A pair of obstetric forceps, by S. Maw & Son & Thompson, London, with ebony handles, c1870, 14in (35.5cm) long.
£125–145
$180–200 ⊞ WAC

A mahogany apothecary's chest, with brass campaign handle, fitted with various glass bottles and brass scales, incomplete, ivory label inscribed 'Savory & Moore Chemists to the Queen, London', mid-19thC, 12¼in (31cm) wide.
£525–625
$750–800 🔨 AH

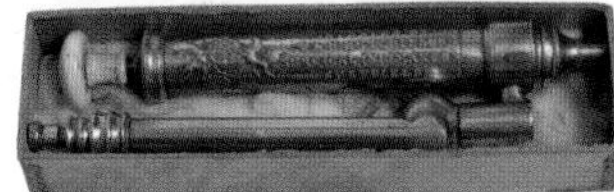

A brass enema syringe, by Garry Porter, invented by W. & H. Hutchinson, 1890s, 8in (20.5cm) long.
£80–90
$115–130 ⊞ GAC

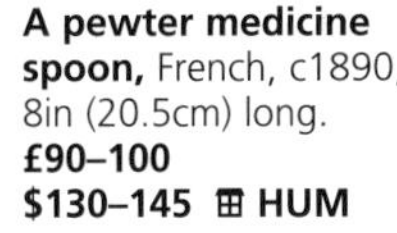

A pewter medicine spoon, French, c1890, 8in (20.5cm) long.
£90–100
$130–145 ⊞ HUM

◄ **A set of nine glass pharmacy bottles with blown stoppers,** c1890, 9in (23cm) high.
£340–380
$500–560 ⊞ BWA

► **A glass medicine bottle,** embossed 'Fishers Seaweed Extract, Manx Shrub, Registered Company, Ulverston, Quarries Patent', late 19thC, 5¼in (13.5cm) high.
£520–580
$725–850 🔨 BBR

A brass stoichiometric gas mixer, by Abbotts Birk & Co, London, late 19thC, 10in (25.5cm) long.
£30–35
$45–50 ⊞ WAC

A glass eyebath, with reservoir, c1900, 2½in (6.5cm) high.
£230–250
$330–360 ⚒ BBR

A ceramic eyebath, with floral decoration, the interior painted with an eye, 1910–20, 1¾in (4.5cm) high.
£50–60
$75–100 ⚒ BBR

A stoneware Radium Ore Revigator, the water cooler with lid, spout and printed instructions, American, c1915, 12in (30.5cm) high.
£220–250
$320–360 ⚒ SK(B)

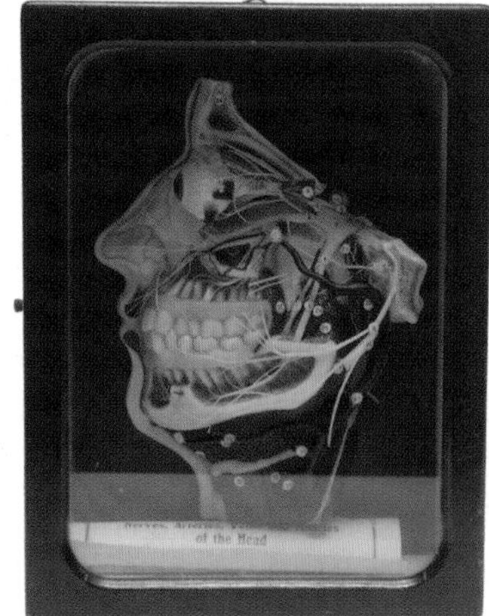

A wax model of a head, showing cross-section of nerves, arteries, veins and muscles, German, 1910, in a case 10 x 7½in (25.5 x 19cm).
£400–450
$580–650 ⊞ CuS

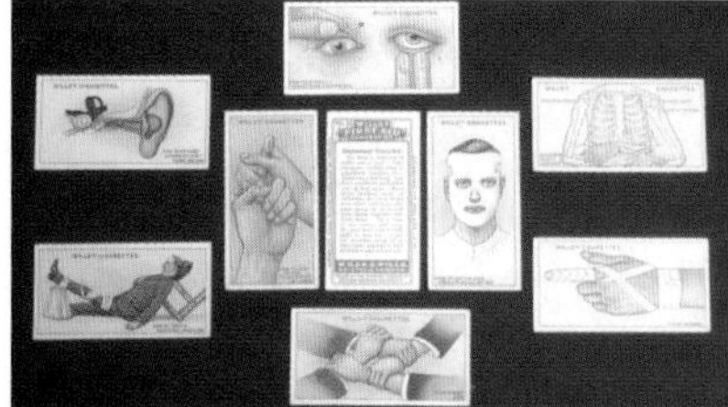

W. D. & H. O. Wills, First Aid, set of 50 cigarette cards, 1913, 3in (7.5cm) long.
£50–60
$75–100 ⊞ MUR

A Cressoline Vapo-Cresolena vaporizer inhaler, with original box, 1950s, 7in (18cm) high.
£45–50
$65–75 ⊞ GAC

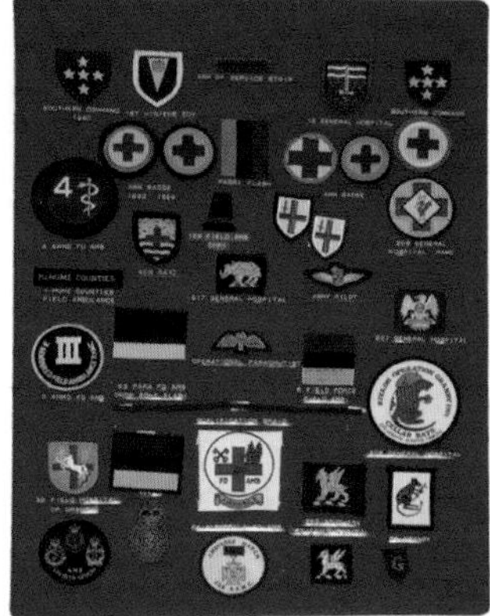

A collection of Royal Army Medical Corps badges, 1890–1924.
£270–300
$390–440 ⊞ Q&C

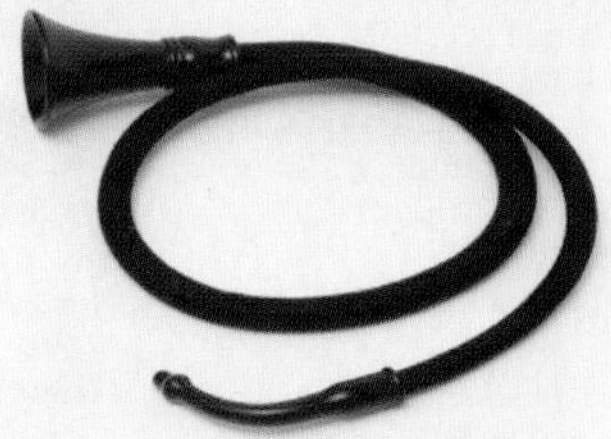

A Bakelite ear trumpet, c1910, 40in (101.5cm) long.
£120–140
$175–200 ⊞ HO

A Girl Guide's First Aid case, with contents, 1915, 4in (10cm) long.
£30–35
$45–50 ⊞ HUX

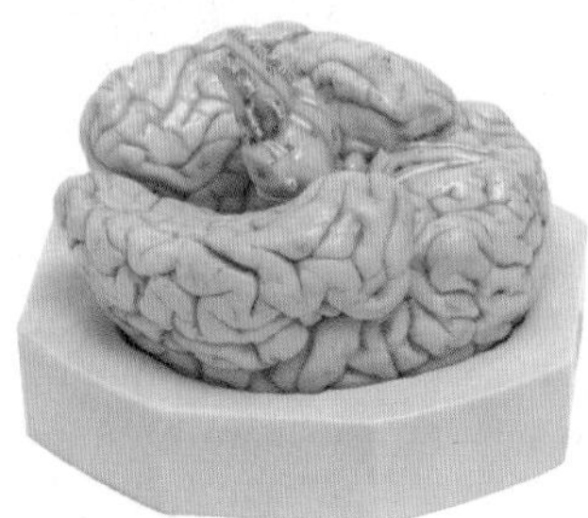

A wax model of a brain, 1950, 7in (18cm) wide.
£115–125
$170–180 ⊞ CuS

Militaria & Emergency Services

A Georgian mahogany campaign toiletry box, with brass inlay and pivoted and fitted trays, incomplete, 8½in (21.5cm) long.
£95–115
$140–170 ⚒ SWO

A WWI copper memorial plaque, 1918, 5in (12.5cm) diam.
£8–10
$10–15 ⊞ J&S
These plaques were given to the families of those killed in action.

A Longines military wristwatch, with black dial and Arabic numerals, stamped '6620335' to movement, and 'A.M 6B/159 a 5826' to dust cover, 1939–45.
£100–120
$145–175 ⚒ BLH

An Aller Vale Boer War commemorative mug, with applied rifleman, inscribed 'God Bless You Tommy Atkins' and 'Here's Your Country's Love to You', impressed mark, South African, dated 1899–1900, 3½in (9cm) high.
£100–120
$145–175 ⚒ SJH

A Royal Engineers printed silk handkerchief, with lace border, 1939–45, 8in (20.5cm) square.
£8–10
$10–15 ⊞ J&S
These handkerchiefs were presented as Christmas gifts.

An RAF aerogram, sent from the Middle East, Christmas 1943, 5 x 4in (12.5 x 10cm).
£12–15
$15–20 ⊞ OLD

A 1st Battalion Assam Rifles half shallow pattern drum, dated 1914–19, 14in (35.5cm) wide.
£225–250
$325–350 ⊞ Q&C

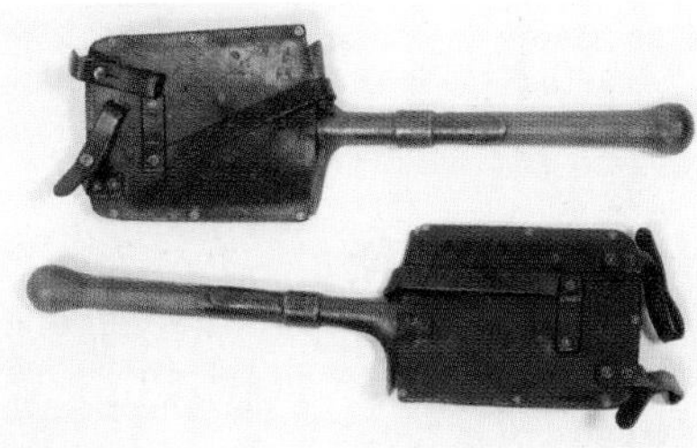

Two Swiss army steel spades, with wooden handles and leather covers, 1938–40, 32in (81.5cm) long.
£25–30
$35–45 ⊞ PICA

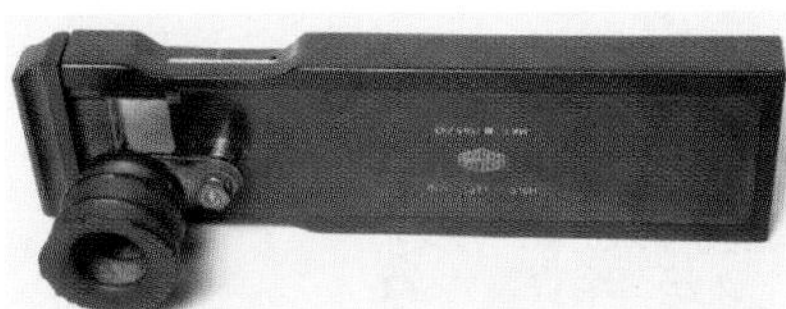

An RAF Meteorological Officer's airfield visibility gauge, by Casella, London, 1943, 10in (25.5cm) wide.
£42–48
$60–70 ⊞ OLD

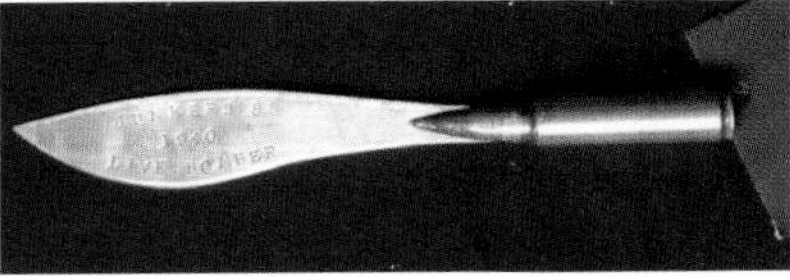

A paper knife, the handle made from a used bullet, the blade made from alloy from a bomber and inscribed 'Junkers JU88', 1940s, 7in (18cm) long.
£30–35
$45–50 ⊞ RUSS
The bomber from which the alloy was taken was shot down near Roland's Castle, Hampshire.

Edged Weapons

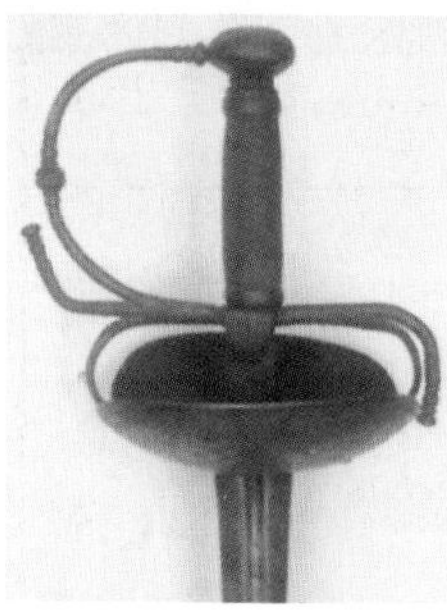

A steel rapier, stamped 'Engel Tesche Me Fecit Solingen', splayed foot cross mark, Spanish, c1700, blade 37½in (5.5cm) long.
£750–850
$1,100–1,250 WAL

LOCATE THE SOURCE
The source of each illustration in Miller's can be found by checking the code letters below each caption with the Key to Illustrations, pages 443–451.

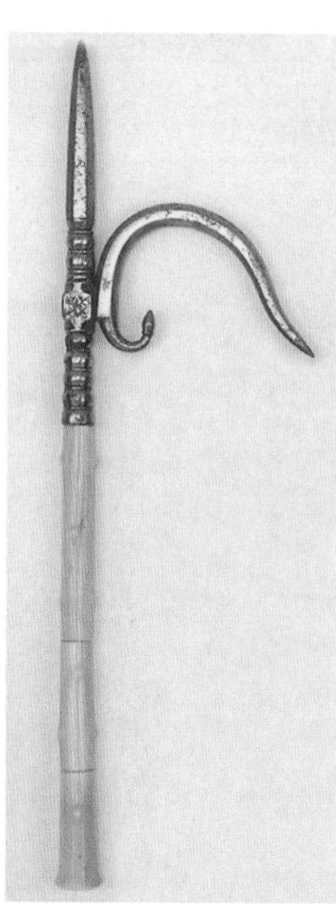

A steel-headed ankus elephant goad, with ball and ring decoration, with three-piece knobbed ivory haft, Indian, 1800, 14in (35.5cm) long.
£450–500
$650–720 WAL

A gilt-brass *shamshir*, the horn grip with engraved copper mounts, the black leather scabbard with gilt-copper fittings, early 19thC, blade 30in (76cm) long.
£320–360
$450–500 F&C

A hunting hanger, the blade etched with foliage, the brass hilt with fox's mask on shell guard, dog's head quillon finials, boar's head pommel, staghorn grip, German, 19thC, blade 19in (48.5cm) long.
£450–500
$650–720 WAL

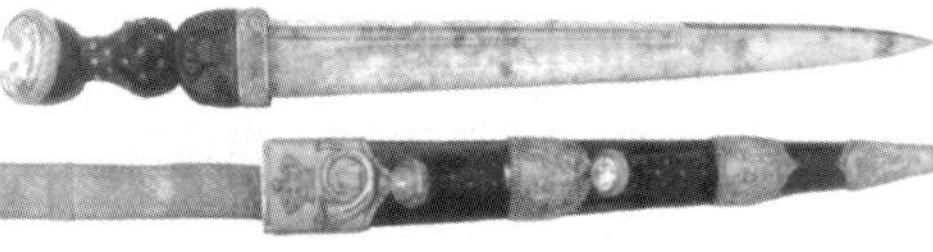

A 71st Highland Lift Infantry officer's dirk, the gilt nail-studded carved bog-oak handle with gilt ring, facet-cut stone and bonnet and broadsword/thistle panel, etched with regimental insignia, royal cypher and thistle motto, and battle honours, with later leather dirk strap, worn and pitted, 1830–37, approx 14in (35cm) long.
£1,400–1,600
$2,000–2,300 DNW

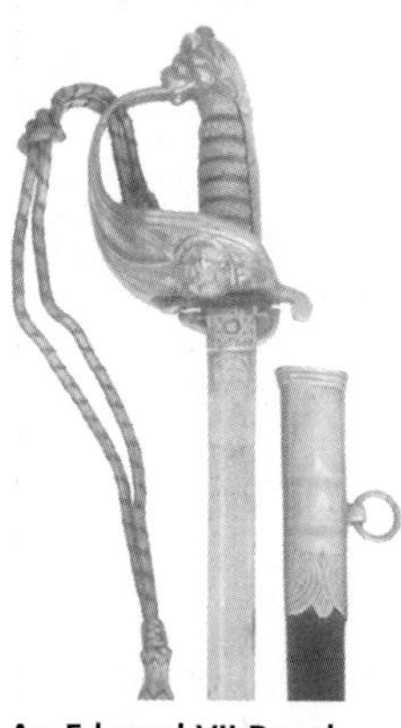

An Edward VII Royal Marine naval officer's sword, with etched pointed blade, the brass folding guard with crest and lion head pommel, wire-bound shagreen grip, with brass-mounted leather scabbard, 1901–10, blade 31in (78.5cm) long.
£250–300
$350–450 F&C

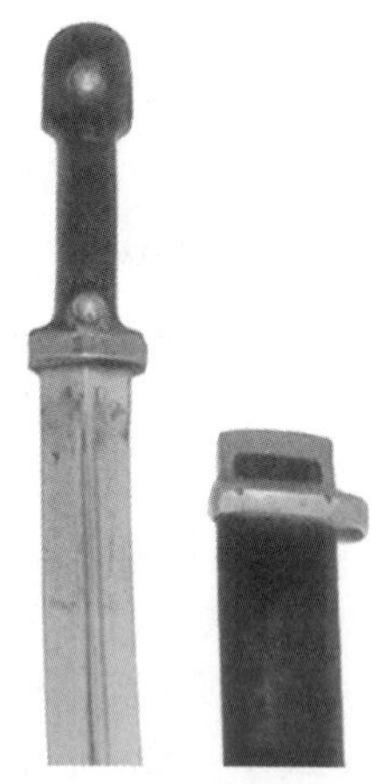

A cossack *kindjahl*, the fullered curved blade numbered and dated 1912, with brass mounts and wood grip, and brass-mounted scabbard, Russian, blade 17in (43cm) long.
£220–250
$320–350 F&C

► **An officer's presentation 1912 pattern cavalry sword,** with Rogers & Co fullered blade, etched royal cypher and 'Presented by Members of Serjeant's Mess of 9th Q R Lancers to S.S.M. P J Oxley, on his promotion to R.S.M., Feb 21/1937', with regulation guard, wire-bound fishskin grip, in leather field service scabbard with frog, 1937, blade 35in (89cm) long.
£300–350
$450–500 WAL

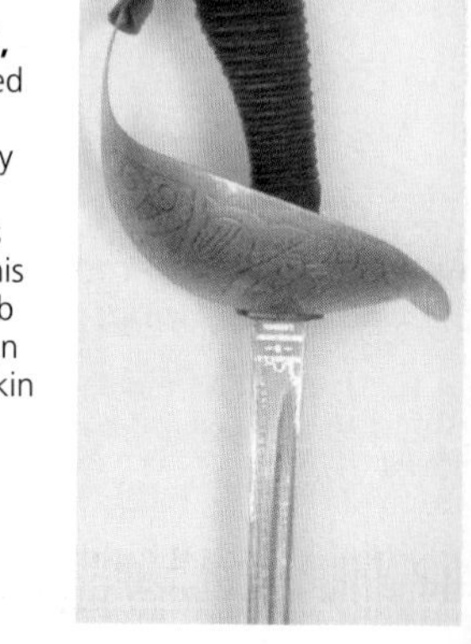

Fire & Police

Two leather fire buckets, with copper rims, one missing handle early 19thC, 12in (30.5cm) high.
£80–90
$115–130 🔨 DN

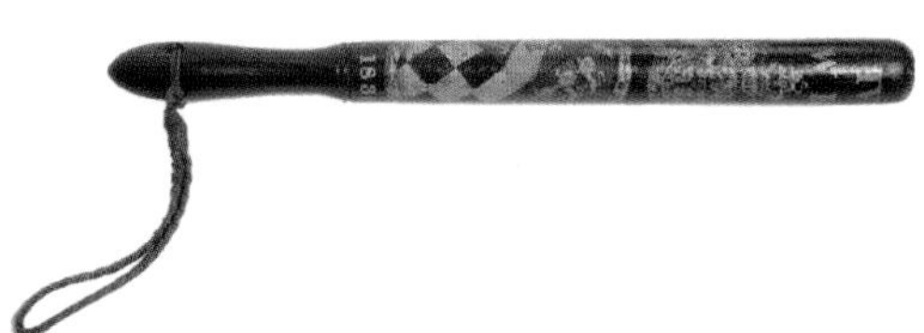

A painted wood police truncheon, 1830, 17in (43cm) long.
£180–200
$250–300 ⊞ Q&C

An inkwell, modelled as a fireman's helmet, 19thC, 3¾in (9.5cm) high.
£50–60
$75–90 🔨 SWO

◄ **A Victorian wooden police truncheon,** No. B36, with royal cypher, 17in (43cm) long.
£100–120
$145–175 ⊞ NEW

A copper and brass fire extinguisher, by Universal, American, 1920s, 24in (61cm) high.
£60–70
$90–100 ⊞ TRA

A brass and copper fire nozzle, with royal cypher, 1939, 19in (48.5cm) long.
£100–120
$145–175
⊞ Q&C

A police issue gas mask, 1939–43, in a bag 10in (25.5cm) square.
£30–35
$45–50 ⊞ J&S

◄ **A Biggin Hill Military Police Station lock-up key cover,** with master key marked 'RDL', 1940s, 14in (35.5cm) high.
£325–375
$470–560 ⊞ OLD

A leather-covered cork police motorcycle helmet, 1948, 6in (15cm) diam.
£55–65
$80–95 ⊞ UCO

Ten fire service forage cap badges, post 1952, 1½in (4cm) diam.
£6–8
$9–12 each ⊞ Q&C

A mounted division police helmet, up to 1980, 7in (18cm) diam.
£55–65
$80–95 ⊞ UCO

Firearms

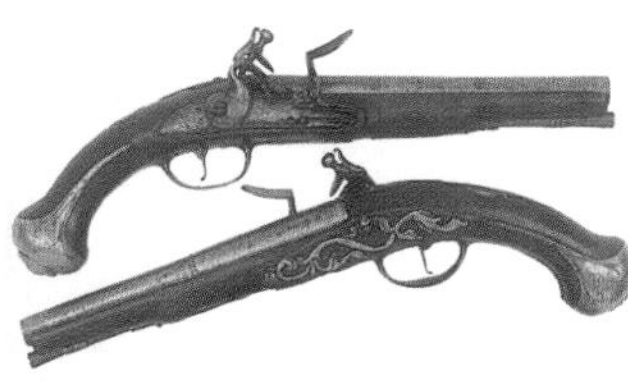

A pair of flintlock holster pistols, by T. Green, with London and maker's proofs, walnut fullstocks, brass mounts, the breeches engraved with scrolled strawberry leaves and a monster's head, and 'T Green', the escutcheon engraved with family crest, early 18thC, 15in (38cm) long.
£650–750
$950–1,100 WAL

A ¾in Cape flintlock rifle, inlaid 'Mortimer. London', plate engraved with scrolls and 'P J Botha', with German silver mounts, horn-tipped ramrod, 1820, 61in (155cm) long.
£450–500
$650–720 WAL

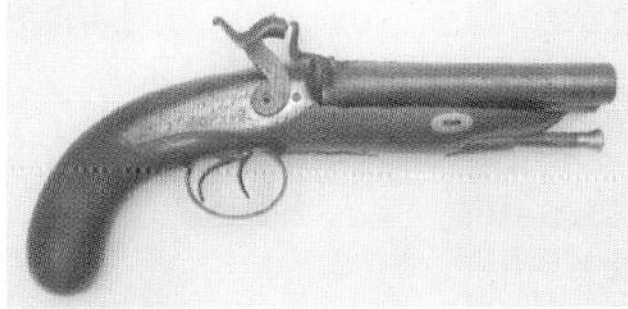

A sidelock side-by-side percussion cap pistol, the lock signed 'Wilett Lynn', 19thC, 30in (76cm) long.
£200–250
$300–350 G(L)

◄ An Adams patent five-shot double-action revolver, with engraved decoration to side plates, chequered grip, in a leather holster, mid-19thC, 9in (23cm) long.
£420–500
$620–720 G(L)

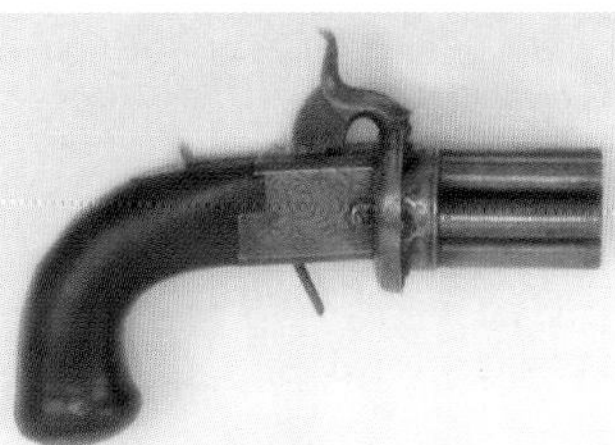

A seven-shot 160-bore hand-rotated boxlock centre hammer pepperbox turnover pistol, by Lewis & Tomes, London, with chequered walnut butt, barrels enclosing a central barrel fired by an extra nipple, hidden trigger, steel butt cap with hinged trap, 1835, 8in (20.5cm) long.
£500–600
$720–870 WAL

A 20-bore Devonport & Launceston Mail Coach flintlock holster pistol, by J. Harding & Son, with London and government proofs, walnut fullstock with plain brass military-style mounts, flat stepped lock, stamped and engraved, dated 1836, 14½in (37cm) long.
£900–1,000
$1,300–1,500 WAL

A percussion pistol, with Tower of London markings, c1850, 16in (40.5cm) long.
£250–350
$350–500 CYA

Uniform

A 2nd Somerset Militia officer's felt Albert Shako, with patent leather crown and front peaks, 1844–55, 8in (20.5cm) high.
£1,400–1,600
$2,000–2,300 ⊞ Q&C
This is known as an Albert Shako and is probably named after Prince Albert because it has the Albert patent which was taken out during his lifetime.

A King's Own Norfolk Imperial Yeomanry trooper's leather helmet, with brass fittings, chichain and rose side ornaments, quadrant spike with yellow horsehair plume, 1903–10.
£650–750
$1,000–1,100 ⚒ DNW

► A silver-plated plaid brooch, 1930s, 4½in (11.5cm) diam.
£115–125
$170–180 ⊞ Q&C

A Cameronian Foot Regiment officer's silver glengarry badge, 1874–81.
£350–400
$500–580 ⚒ DNW

A Volunteer Battalion The Queen's Regiment officer's cloth forage cap, with silver-embroidered peak and Paschal Lamb badge, 1880.
£200–240
$300–350 ⚒ WAL

A 50th Regiment of Canada officer's silver glengarry badge, by BWL, HM London 1917, worn 1913–20.
£200–250
$300–350 ⚒ DNW

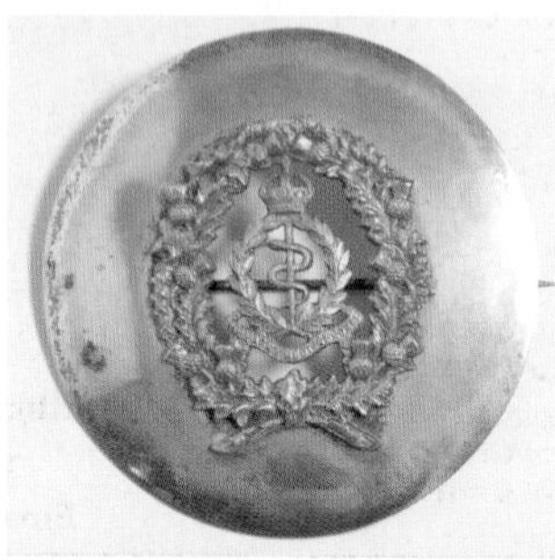

A Lanarkshire Rifles Volunteers officer's star pattern QVC helmet plate, 1878–1901.
£500–550
$720–800 ⚒ DNW

A pillbox hat, embroidered with oak leaves and acorns, monogrammed 'FL', maker's stamp 'Carl Roth Wurzburg' with plain cloth cover and card case with maker's name repeated on lid, Bavarian, 1900.
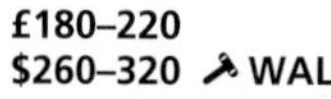
£180–220
$260–320 ⚒ WAL

A pair of Royal Signals busby badges, with horsehair plumes, King's 1920s–30s, Queen's 1960, 10in (25.5cm) high.
£150–175
$220–260 each ⊞ Q&C

Money Boxes

A steel deed/strong box, by Mordan & Co, London, 1865, 10in (25.5cm) wide.
£80–100
$115–145 ⊞ GAC

A metal Barclay's Bank Home Safe, with handle, c1930, 3½in (9cm) wide.
£15–20
$20–30 ⊞ HUX

A tin Vim advertising money box, 1930s, 2¾in (7cm) high.
£25–30
$35–45 ⊞ HUX

An Edwardian sycamore money box, modelled as a cottage, the windows and doors formed with coloured woods, 5½in (14cm) high.
£55–65
$80–100 ⚒ TMA

► A Pop Eye Dime Register Bank, 1930s, 2½in (6.5cm) square.
£70–80
$100–115 ⊞ HUX

A tinplate mechanical money box, by J. Chein & Co, modelled as the head and shoulders of a clown, American, 1940s–50s, 6in (15cm) high.
£40–45
$60–65 ⊞ HAL

Cross Reference
See Tinplate & Clockwork Toys (pages 414–416)

A Sportsman's Motor Ambulance Fund wooden charity collection box, modelled as an ambulance, c1918, 9in (23cm) long.
£45–50
$65–75 ⊞ JUN

Natural History

In this edition we include fossils, beginning with a North African trilobite, (an arthropod) that was alive approximately 500 million years ago almost undoubtedly the oldest object ever illustrated in *Miller's Collectables Price Guide*. In the 18th and 19th centuries, scientific study was a favourite amateur pursuit and it was customary for a gentleman to have in his library a natural history cabinet containing rare minerals and fossils. Today, with the development of popular science fuelled by books, magazines and television programmes, fossil collecting is once again a growing area. 'Over the past 30 years our knowledge of the prehistoric world and dinosaurs has expanded enormously, and I think this has encouraged interest,' says fossil dealer Tony Trowbridge.

Many people begin collecting as children, and the joy of fossils is that you can find them for yourself. In the UK most of our fossil sites are coastal, and what you are most likely to pick up depends on geography and the age of rock. 'The north Yorkshire coast is very good for ammonites', explains Trowbridge. 'The Isle of Wight is a great place for dinosaur fossils and more different species of dinosaur have been found there than anywhere else in Europe.' Local museums, with their specific knowledge of the area, can be a good source of knowledge for identifying fossils, and specialist advice can be sought from major natural history museums.

According to Trowbridge, generally speaking there are no restrictions about picking up fossils in the UK because they lie on the surface of beaches. 'In the USA it's a different matter, because the majority of sights are inland and finding fossils entails digging.'

Values of fossils depend on subject, aesthetic beauty and rarity. 'Vertebrate animals tend to be more expensive than invertebrates,' says Tony, 'and the more complete the remains, the higher the value.' But whether it's an iguanodon's leg, £4,500–5,000 ($6,500–7,250) or a piece of dinosaur dung, £5–10 ($10–15), all fossils represent a remarkable piece of prehistoric history.

A trilobite, from North Africa, 500 million years old, 2in (5cm) diam.
£2–3
$3–5 ⊞ FOSS

An ogygiocarella, from Llandeilo, Shropshire, Ordovician period, 450 million years old, 5in (12.5cm) wide.
£23–25
$30–35 ⊞ FOSS

An ammonite, 400 million years old, 20in (51cm) wide.
£770–850
$1,100–1,250 ⊞ DNA

An orthoceras, 400 million years old, 45in (114.5cm) high.
£2,600–2,900
$3,800–4,400 ⊞ DNA

A trilobite, 400 million years old, 9½in (24cm) long.
£450–500
$650–720 ⊞ DNA

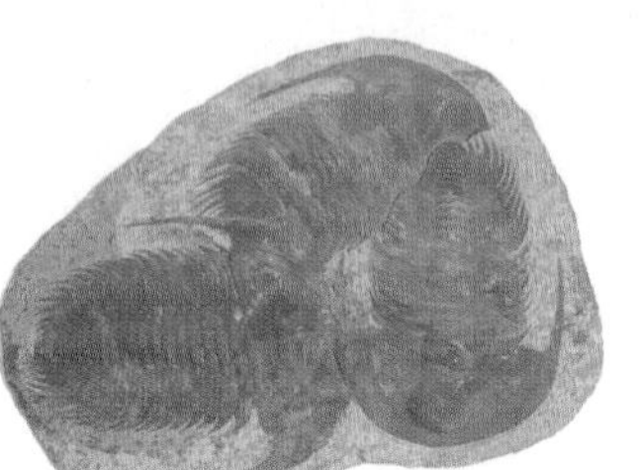

◀ **A trilobite family,** 400 million years old, 20in (51cm) long.
£1,000–1,200
$1,500–1,750 ⊞ DNA

An icthyosaur backbone column, from North Yorkshire, 180 million years old, 11in (28cm) long.
£140–160
$200–230 ⊞ FOSS

A sea urchin, clypeus ploti, from Cirencester, Gloucestershire, Jurassic period, 180 million years old, 5in (12.5cm) diam.
£23–25
$30–35 ⊞ FOSS

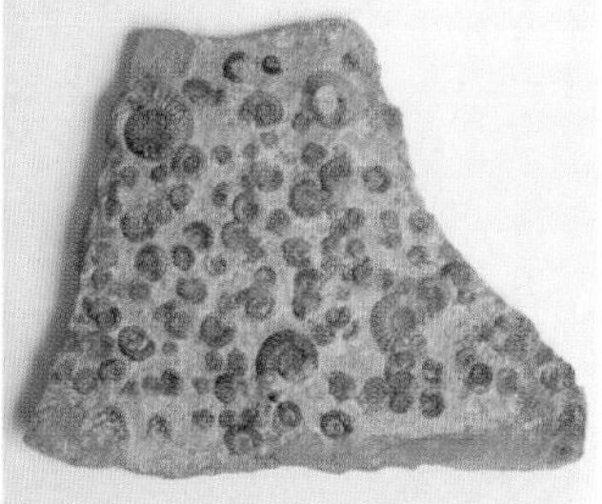

A promicroceras ammonites multiblock, from Charmouth, Dorset, 180 million years old, 12in (30.5cm) wide.
£230–260
$330–380 ⊞ FOSS

An icthyosaur jaw section, from Charmouth, Dorset, 180 million years old, 3in (7.5cm) long.
£140–160
$200–230 ⊞ FOSS

A ludwigia wigina multiblock, showing sexual dimorphism, Scottish, Isle of Skye, Jurassic period, 172 million years old, 12in (30.5cm) wide.
£450–500
$650–720 ⊞ FOSS

A dinosaur coprolite, from Sandown, Isle of Wight, Cretaceous period, 120 million years old, 3in (7.5cm) long.
£5–10
$10–15 ⊞ FOSS
Coprolite is fossilized excrement.

An iguanadon backbone vertebra, Cretaceous period, 120 million years old, 3¼in (8.5cm) long.
£70–80
$100–115 ⊞ FOSS

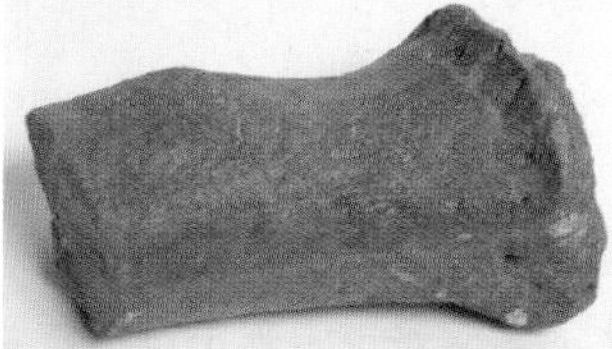

A brachiosaur metatarsal bone, from Brook, Isle of Wight, Cretaceous period, 120 million years old, 8in (20.5cm) long.
£135–150
$200–220 ⊞ FOSS

A dinosaur leg femur, from Sandown, Isle of Wight, covered in fossilized tendons and rib sections found in the Vectus formation, 120 million years old, 47in (119.5cm) long.
£4,500–5,000
$6,500–7,250 ⊞ FOSS

A hybodus (shark) spine, from the Isle of Wight, in mass mortality of bivalves, Cretaceous period, 113 million years old, 11in (28cm) long.
£90–100
$130–145 ⊞ FOSS

An asteroceras multiblock from Froddingham ironstone, from Scunthorpe, 108 million years old, 10in (25.5cm) long.
£270–300
$400–440 ⊞ FOSS

A tyrannosauridae albertasaurus canine tooth, from Montana, American, 100 million years old, 1in (2.5cm) long.
£90–100
$130–145 ⊞ FOSS

A tyrannosauridae albertasaurus canine, side of jaw, from Montana, American, 100 million years old, 1in (2.5cm) long.
£175–200
$250–300 ⊞ FOSS
This is similar to the previous example, but is from the side of the jaw.

► An iguanadon tooth, from Sandown, Isle of Wight, 100 million years old, ½in (2cm) long.
£100–120
$145–175 ⊞ FOSS

A therizinosaurus egg, Upper Cretaceous period, c75 million years old, 5¾in (14.5cm) long.
£100–120
$145–175 ⚒ SWO
The therizinosaurus was a close relative of tyrannosaurus rex.

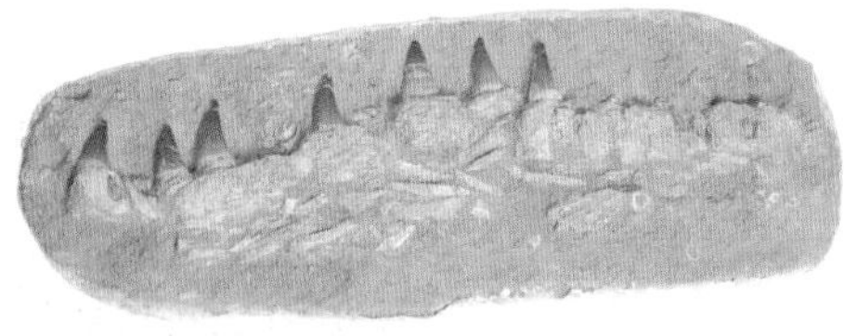

◄ A mosasaur's lower mandible, 65–95 million years old, 25in (63.5cm) long.
£3,150–3,500
$4,500–5,000
⊞ DNA

A piece of Baltic amber, from Kaliningrad, Russia, enclosing a large bug, 40 million years old, 1in (2.5cm) long.
£18–20
$25–30 ⊞ FOSS

A carcharodon megalodon (extinct great white shark) tooth, from Florida, American, 20 million years old, 4in (10cm) long.
£45–50
$65–75 ⊞ FOSS

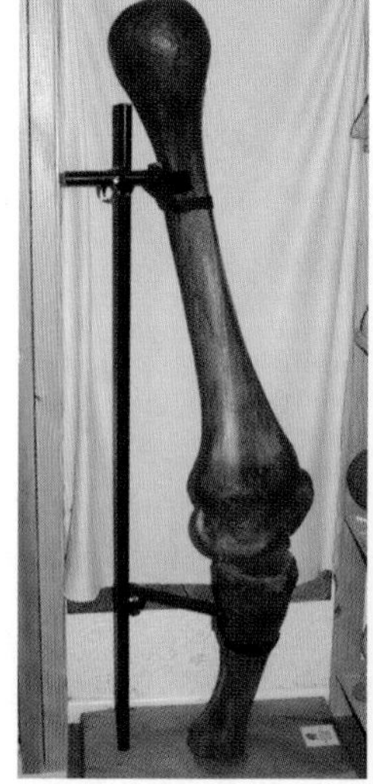

A mammuthus Primigenius femur and tibia, from the North Sea, pleistocene period, 20,000 years old, 57in (145cm) long.
£1,350–1,500
$2,000–2,200 ⊞ FOSS

A woolly rhino jaw with two teeth, from Shropham, Norfolk, Pleistocene period, 20,000 years old, 7in (18cm) long.
£135–150
$200–220 ⊞ FOSS

A mammoth tooth, from Europe or Russia, 17,000 years old, 8in (20.5cm) long.
£300–350
$450–500 ⊞ Cas

Newspapers & Magazines

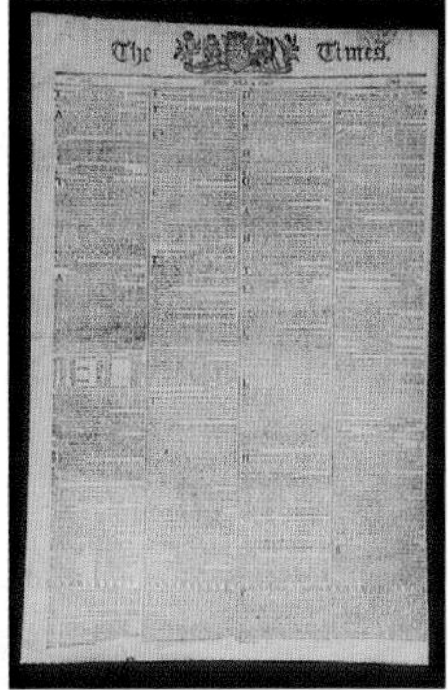
The Times

The Times, dated 4 July 1797, covering the mutiny at the Nore, 19 x 12in (48.5 x 30.5cm).
£65–80
$95–115 HaR

The Queen, the *Lady's Newspaper and Court Chronicle*, Vol. 79, in two volumes, six hand-coloured engraved plates, wood engravings, some wear, 2°, Jan–Dec 1886.
£130–150
$200–220 DW

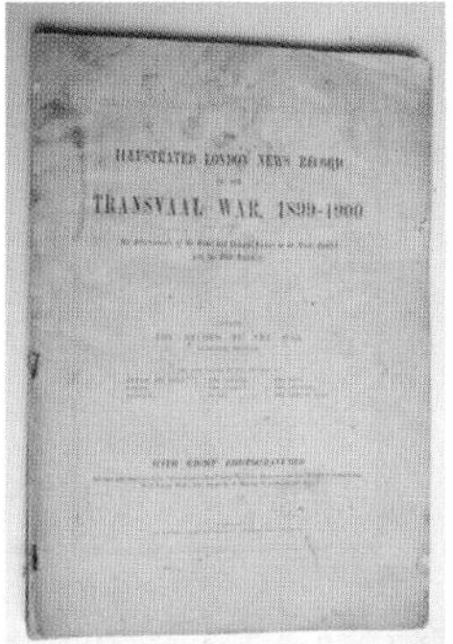
TRANSVAAL WAR, 1899-1900

(No 1)
L'ORACLE

L'Oracle, Nos. 1–365, dated 1 January–31 December 1815, two issues missing for 18th and 19th November, each a single folded printed sheet forming four pages, with postage marks to top right corner, untrimmed, slim 4°.
£450–500
$650–720 DW
***L'Oracle* was an important Brussels daily newspaper, printed in French. These issues cover the year of the Battle of Waterloo, which took place only a few miles from the place of publication.**

New York Times, *Titanic* issue, 21 April 1912, 23 x 16in (58.5 x 40.5cm).
£50–60
$75–90 COB

◄ ***The Illustrated London News,*** record of the Transvaal War, 1899–1900, c1902, 16 x 12in (40.5 x 30.5cm).
£30–35
$45–50 J&S

SUBSTANCE OF THE
Corsican Bonaparte's
HAND-BILLS;
Charming Prospect for John Bull and his Family.
BRITONS AWAKE!
Know then
Road to ENGLAND!
A true Friend to OLD ENGLAND.

Substance of the Corsican Bonaparte's Hand-Bills; or a Charming Prospect for John Bull and his family. Britons Awake!' printed broadside, 1790s, 14¼ x 8¾in (38.5 x 22cm).
£160–200
$230–300 DW

The Infants' Magazine, set of 12, 1891, 9 x 6in (23 x 15cm).
£40–50
$60–75 J&S

Boy's Own Paper, March 1920, 11¼ x 8½in (28.5 x 21.5cm).
£4–5
$6–8 RTT

The Globe

The Globe, 1809, 18 x 12in (45.5 x 30.5cm).
£20–25
$30–35 COB

Le Petit Parisien

Le Petit Parisien, with cover illustration of the execution of Mary Ansell, 1899, 18 x 12in (45.5 x 30.5cm).
£35–40
$50–60 IQ

L'Illustration, *Le Jardin des Modes*, 1922, 12 x 8in (30.5 x 20.5cm).
£8–10
$10–15 RTT

The Illustrated London News, with cover illustration of Neville Chamberlain, 1938, 14 x 10in (35.5 x 25.5cm).
£8–10
$10–15 ⊞ J&S

Man, Australian, January 1950, 12¼ x 9¼in (31 x 23.5cm).
£8–9
$12–15 ⊞ TWI

Tail-Wagger and Family Magazine, 1956, 11½ x 8½in (29 x 21.5cm).
£3–5
$5–8 ⊞ TWI

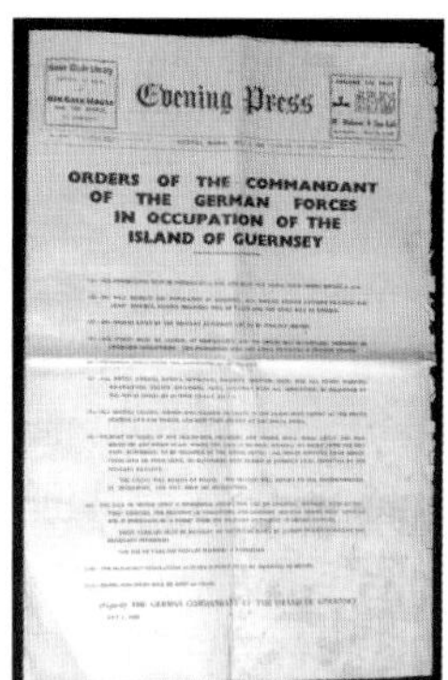

Evening Press, printed under German occupation, Channel Islands, 17 August 1940, 18 x 12in (45.5 x 30.5cm).
£8–10
$10–15 ⚒ DAL

The Times, Festival of Britain Supplement, 1951, 24 x 18in (61 x 45.5cm).
£12–15
$15–20 ⚒ RUSS

Jackie, featuring rare psychedelic posters on the cover, April 1968, 13 x 10in (33 x 25.5cm).
£8–10
$10–15 ⊞ CTO

The New Yorker, 1942, 12 x 9in (30.5 x 23cm).
£5–6
$8–10 ⊞ RTT

Vogue, 1953, 11½ x 8¾in (29 x 22cm).
£18–20
$25–30 ⊞ RTT

Cross Reference
See Sixties & Seventies (pages 355–360)

► ***Daily Planet,*** a prop newspaper from *Superman*, featuring Christopher Reeve as Superman, 1978, mounted with Superman insignia, framed and glazed, 33 x 24in (84 x 61cm).
£380–430
$575–625 ⚒ CO

Woman, 1950, 12 x 10in (30.5 x 25.5cm).
£2–3
$4–6 ⊞ FLD

Gourmet, 1955, 11½ x 8½in (29 x 21.5cm).
£3–5
$5–8 ⊞ RTT

► ***Raw,*** heavy metal magazine, No. 1 and 2, 1979, 12 x 9in (30.5 x 23cm).
£7–9
$10–15 ⊞ RUSS

Noddy

Noddy was created by Enid Mary Blyton (1897–1968), one of the most successful children's writers of the 20th century. Blyton trained as a teacher. Her first book, *Child's Whispers,* appeared in 1922 and by the time of her death she had published over 400 titles.

Blyton could produce up to 10,000 words a day and was known to complete a book in a five-day week. She was so prolific that she eventually had over 40 publishers, handling all her deals without an agent and with great success. She demanded complete control over choice of illustrator and while refusing an advance, always insisted on a minimum printing of 25,000 copies. She became well known in the 1940s for the *Famous Five* and *Secret Seven* stories but it was Noddy, conceived in 1949, that made her famous. A publisher showed Blyton some puppet drawings by the Dutch artist Harmsen van der Beek. She immediately gave the figures names and wove stories around Little Noddy, Big Ears, Mr Plod and all the characters of Toyland. Noddy was instantly and hugely successful, spawning millions of books, plays, cartoons, and a vast amount of merchandise.

A pack of Noddy snap cards, c1955, 3½ x 2in (9 x 5cm).
£12–15
$15–20 ⊞ HUX

A Noddy clock, by Smiths, 1950s, 4½in (11.5cm) diam.
£55–65
$80–95 ⊞ BBe

► **A Big Ears egg cup,** with egg cosy hat, 1950s, 4in (10cm) high.
£50–60
$75–90 ⊞ BBe

A Noddy figure, by Emco, 1950s–60s, 12in (30.5cm) high.
£45–50
$65–75 ⊞ BBe

A plastic model of Noddy, with jointed limbs and painted face, 1950s–60s, 6in (15cm) high.
£90–100
$130–145 ⊞ BBe

► **A Noddy puppet,** by Pelham Puppets, 1960s, 9in (23cm) high.
£70–80
$100–115 ⊞ BBe

A train with Noddy and Big Ears figures, by Budgie Toys, 1950s–60s, engine 4in (10cm) long.
£135–150
$200–220 ⊞ BBe

A Noddy car, by Corgi, with Noddy, Big Ears and Golly, 1950s–60s, 4in (10cm) long.
£145–165
$200–240 ⊞ BBe

A wooden Noddy egg cup, egg cosy hat and bell, 1950s–60s, 4in (10cm) high.
£25–30
$35–45 ⊞ BBe

Paper Money

A Stornaway 20 shilling note, 1823.
£90–100
$130–145 ⊞ WP

A Standard Bank Mafeking 10 shilling note, 1900.
£180–200
$250–300 ⊞ WP

A Bank of England Liverpool Branch £10 note, Nairne signature, 1914.
£450–500
$650–720 ⊞ IB

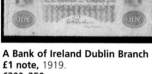

A Bank of Ireland Dublin Branch £1 note, 1919.
£300–350
$450–500 ⊞ WP

A Bank of England £5 note, Harvey signature, 1920.
£120–180
$175–250 ⊞ IB

A Munster and Leinster Bank, Ireland £1 note, 1939.
£160–190
$225–275 ⊞ WP

► **A Bank of England blue wartime £1 note,** Peppiatt signature, 1940–48.
£8–10
$12–15 ⊞ IB

◄ **A Bank of England mauve wartime 10 shilling note,** Peppiatt signature, 1940–48.
£30–35
$45–50 ⊞ IB

► **A Bank of England £1 note,** Beale signature, c1950.
£3–4
$5–7 ⊞ IB

◄ **An Irish Free State Currency Commission £20 note,** 1976.
£90–100
$130–145 ⊞ WP

Photographs

A photograph album, with a hand-painted cover, containing portrait cards, 19thC, 15¾in (40cm) high.
£110–130
$160–200 ⚒ SWO

A quarter plate ambrotype family portrait, 1860.
£40–60
$60–90 ⊞ HEG

Items in the Photographs section have been arranged in date order.

James Valentine, 12 albumen prints of the Orkney Islands, all numbered, titled and initialled, c1880, 5¼ x 8in (13 x 20.5cm), in a contemporary cloth album, oblong 8°.
£100–120
$145–175 ⚒ DW

John Edwin Mayall, a half plate daguerreotype portrait of a boy, mounted in arched tip gilt-metal surround and tan leather case, 1852–55, 5½ x 4¼in (14 x 11.5cm).
£180–220
$260–320 ⊞ APC
Named after its inventor, Louis Daguerre (1789–1851), the daguerreotype was an early photographic process introduced in 1839 in which the impression was taken on a silver plate sensitized by iodine and then developed in vapour of mercury.

A half plate ambrotype, in a gilt frame, c1865, 11¾ x 8in (30 x 20.5cm).
£90–100
$130–145 ⊞ APC
Ambrotype is the American term for an early type of glass negative that could be made to appear as a positive by backing it with black varnish or paper.

► A *carte de visite*, depicting Clifton Suspension Bridge, Bristol, c1880, 3 x 4in (7.5 x 10cm).
£5–8
$8–10 ⊞ J&S

Roger Fenton, The Falls of Lodore, albumen print, titled and numbered 183, 1850s, 11½in (29cm) square, on original card mount.
£220–250
$320–360 ⚒ BBA

Julia Margaret Cameron, Sir John Herschel, glass collodion photographic print, 1869, 5 x 3¾in (2.5 x 9.5cm), mounted on original blue card.
£500–600
$720–870 ⚒ DW
Sir J. F. W. Herschel (1792–1871), a distinguished astronomer, taught Julia Margaret Cameron the art of photography.

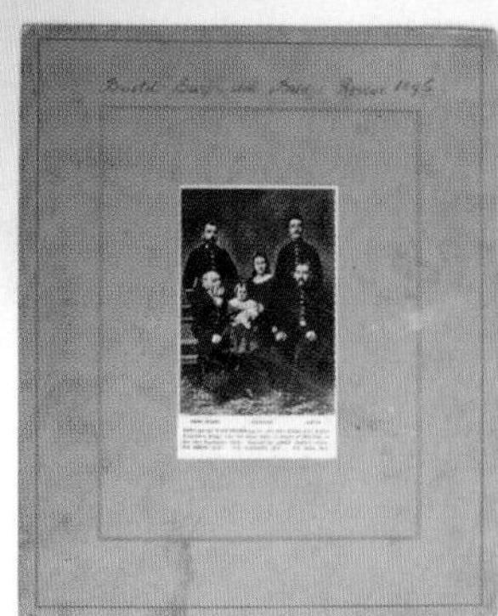

A photograph of Ruby and Elsie Brown, who were thrown from Clifton Suspension Bridge, and their rescuers, September 1896, 12 x 10in (30.5 x 15.5cm).
£15–20
$20–30 ⊞ J&S

A collection of 37 photographs, depicting military manoeuvres and scenery in Tibet, 1904, 3¼ x 4in (8.5 x 10cm).
£850–950
$1,250–1,400 ⚒ DW

A pair of photographs of King George V and Queen Mary, c1910, 9 x 6in (23 x 15cm), in original frames.
£850–950
$1,250–1,400 ⊞ SHa

A boxed set of 100 stereocards, Palestine, c1900, 8in (20.5cm) high.
£150–180
$220–260 ⊞ APC

Edward S. Curtis, 'A Baby Apsaroke', and 'Hidatsa Man', two photogravures, American, c1908, 9½ x 6in (24 x 15cm), framed.
£300–350
$450–500 ⚒ NOA

Frank Meadow Sutcliffe, three albumen prints, comprising a study of six fishermen chatting on the quayside, a group of children leaning over the harbour wall and a group of fishermen's wives standing by the quayside, c1900, 8¾ x 11in (22 x 28cm).
£1,500–1,700
$2,200–2,500 ⚒ DW

An Edwardian wedding photograph, taken in Tottenham, London, 10 x 12in (25.5 x 30.5cm).
£8–10
$12–15 ⊞ J&S

A photograph of rat catchers, 1930s, 11 x 9in (28 x 23cm).
£12–15
$15–20 ⊞ J&S

◄ **Phil Ceccola,** a set of four photographs of Bruce Springsteen, signed and numbered, limited edition of 195, 1975, 20 x 16in (51 x 40.5cm).
£320–360
$470–500 ⚒ CO

Plastic

A Bakelite electric hot water bottle, by Rothermel, c1930, 13in (33cm) long.
£25–30
$35–45 ⊞ JUN

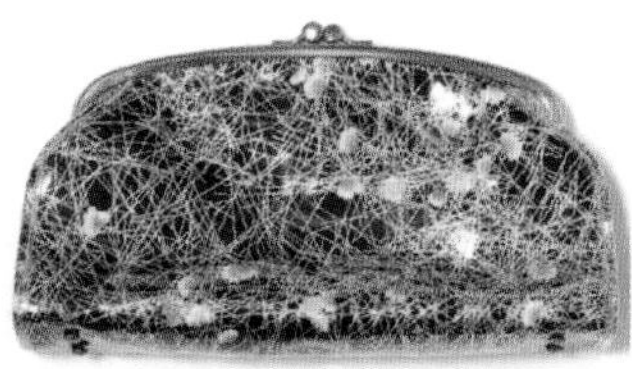

A plastic gold sparkle print bag, inset with real flowers, 1950s, 11in (28cm) wide.
£40–45
$60–65 ⊞ LBe

A clear vinyl bag, inlaid with spun gold, American, 1960s, 8in (20.5cm) long.
£35–40
$50–60 ⊞ TWI

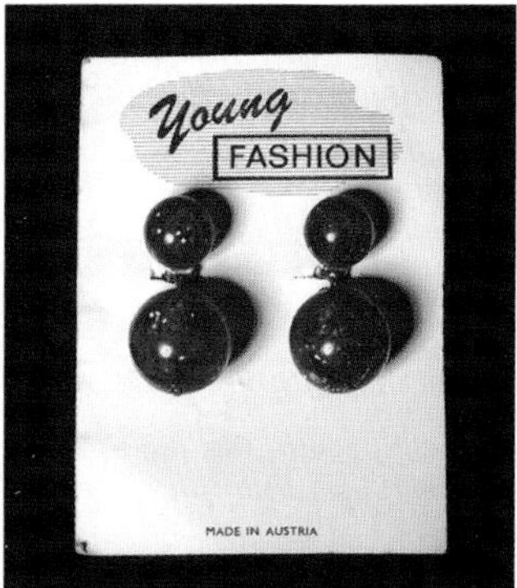

A Bakelite perpetual calendar and stationery box, 1930s, 5in (12.5cm) square.
£40–50
$60–75 ⊞ DHAR

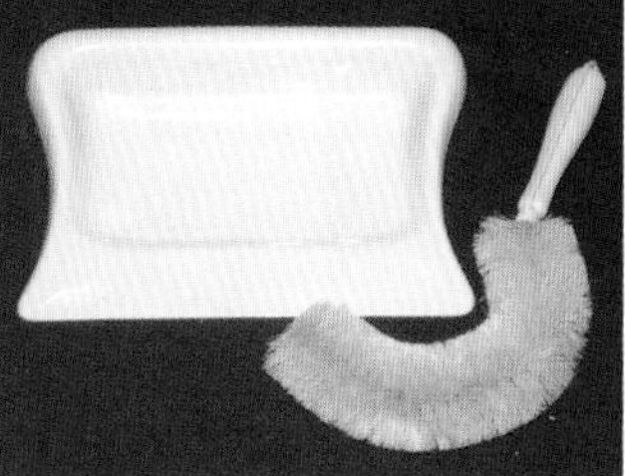

A Bakelite crumb sweeper, by Kleeneze, 1950s, 8in (20.5cm) wide.
£10–12
$15–18 ⊞ DHAR

A vinyl suitcase, inscribed 'Ken', with a picture of Ken and Barbie, c1962, 13 x 10in (33 x 25.4cm).
£40–45
$60–65 ⊞ T&D
Ken is Barbie's boyfriend.

Cross Reference
See Handbags (pages 218–222)

◄ A pair of plastic earrings, by Young Fashion, Austrian, 1960s, on a card 9¾ x 2¾in (25 x 7cm).
£8–10
$12–15 ⊞ TWI

A Bakelite electric clock, by Smith's, 1940s, 8½in (21.5cm) high.
£40–50
$60–75 ⊞ DHAR

A Bakelite television, by Bush, No. TV.12'A, 1950s, 15½in (39.5cm) high.
£140–170
$200–250 ⚒ SWO

A plastic handbag, by Princess Charming, decorated with dried flowers, American, early 1960s, 12in (30.5cm) wide.
£55–65
$80–100 ⊞ TWI

A pair of Walt Disney character plastic pez holders, Austrian, 1960–70, larger 4½in (11.5cm) high.
£8–10
$12–15 ⊞ RTT

A Perspex ice bucket, by Guzzini, with chrome handle, Italian, 1970s, 8in (20.5cm) high.
£30–35
$45–50 ⊞ TWI

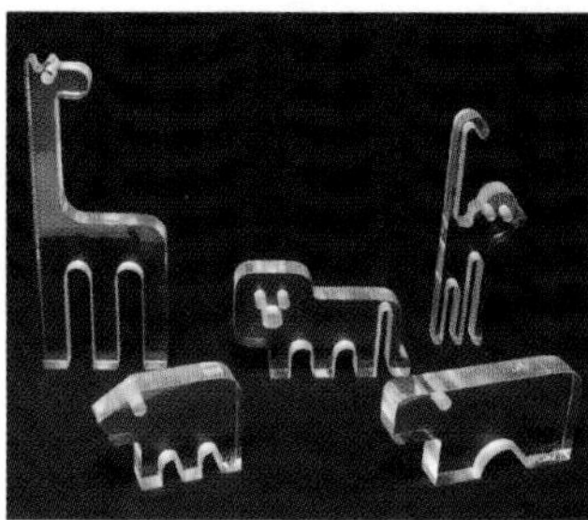

Five Perspex animals, by Guzzini, Italian, 1970s, largest 12in (30.5cm) high.
£40–50
$60–75 each ⊞ MARK

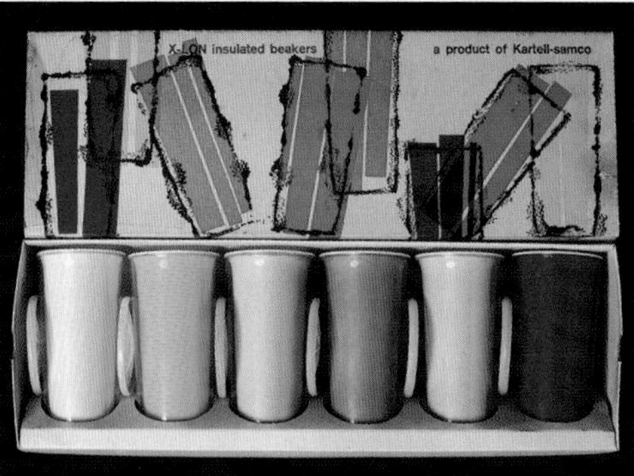

A set of plastic insulated opalescent beakers, by Kartell, 1970s, 6in (15cm) high, in original packaging.
£35–45
$50–65 ⊞ TWI

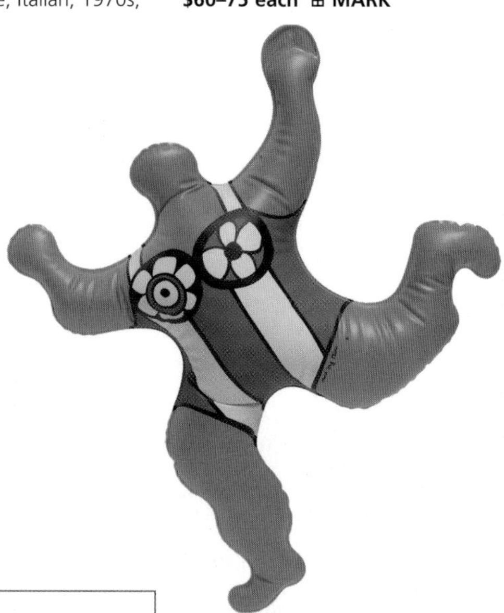

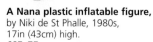

A Nana plastic inflatable figure, by Niki de St Phalle, 1980s, 17in (43cm) high.
£65–75
$100–110 ⊞ MARK

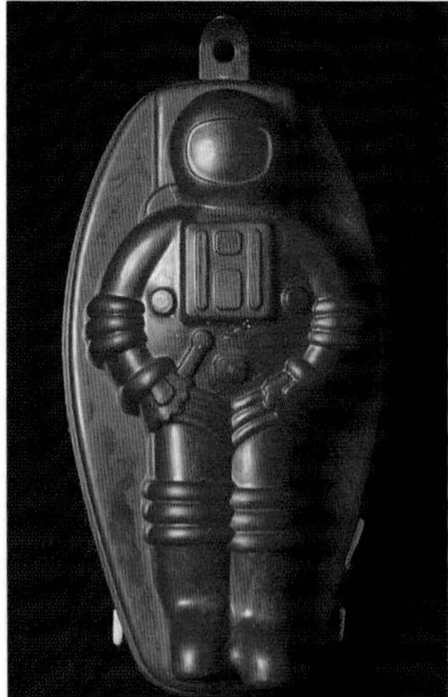

A plastic spaceman jelly mould, 1980s, 9½in (24cm) long.
£6–8
$10–12 ⊞ TWI

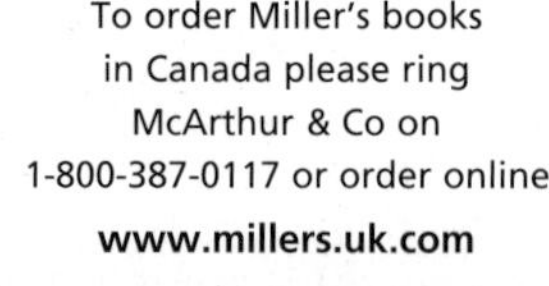

A Midland Bank plastic elephant money box, 1980s, 4½in (11.5cm) long.
£5–6
$7–10 ⊞ TWI

A Phillips plastic Discoverer colour television, with remote, 1980s, 17½in (44.5cm) high.
£250–300
$350–450 ⊞ MARK

Postcards

A chromolithographic postcard, inscribed 'Gruss aus Rolandseck', German, 1896.
£5–8
$7–12 ⊞ JMC

A photographic postcard, depicting a street scene at Castletown, Portland, 1900–10, 4 x 5in, (10 x 12.5cm).
£22–25
$32–35 ⊞ DAL

An art postcard, published by Miesmer & Buch, German, 1900, 6 x 4in (15 x 10cm).
£15–18
$20–28 ⊞ S&D

◄ A postcard, depicting the King and Queen of Norway, printed in Stockholm, 1903.
£8–10
$12–15 ⊞ S&D

A memorial postcard, inscribed 'Queen Victoria, The Mother of her Peoples', 1901, 6 x 4in (15 x 10cm).
£16–18
$22–28 ⊞ S&D

A Tucks 'Rulers of England' postcard, depicting Oliver 'Cromwell', 1901.
£10–12
$15–17 ⊞ S&D

► A set of six Art Nouveau Gem Stones postcards, published in Germany, c1905.
£140–160
$200–230
⊞ S&D

◄ A Tucks Christmas greetings postcard, 1905–10.
£25–35
$35–50
⊞ MURR

A photographic postcard, depicting a group of people and a donkey standing outside Titchfield Waterworks, 1906.
£15–20
$20–30 DAL

◄ **A glamour postcard,** by Philip Boileau, entitled 'Little Lady Demure', 1907.
£6–8
$10–12 ⊞ S&D

A patriotic souvenir postcard, entitled 'Japan', from Flags of the Nations series, published by Barribal, 1907.
£6–8
$8–10 ⊞ S&D

A colour photographic postcard, entitled 'Unser Kaiser', German, 1908.
£6–8
$8–12 ⊞ S&D

An Epps's Milenia Milk Chocolate advertising postcard, 1909.
£25–30
$35–45 ⊞ S&D

► **A Fry's Chocolate advertising postcard,** 1908–10.
£30–35
$45–50 ⊞ S&D

A humourous transportation postcard, entitled 'The Police Act', 1910.
£3–5
$5–7 ⊞ S&D

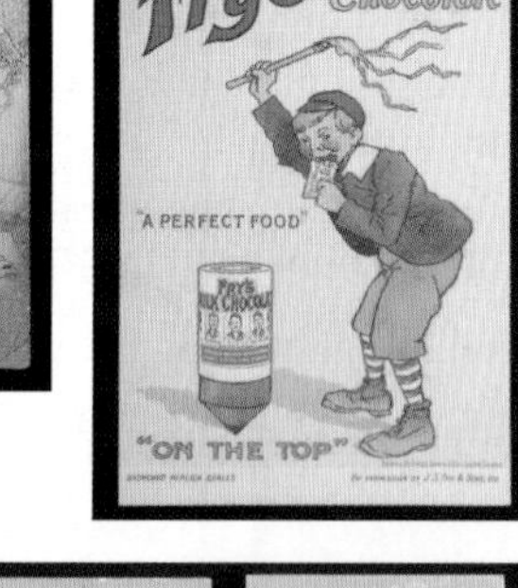

◄ **A Fry's Milk Chocolate advertising postcard,** 1908–10.
£20–25
$30–35 ⊞ S&D

A photographic postcard, depicting a Suffragettes RP Parade, c1910.
£80–100
$115–145 ⊞ VS

A pair of postcards, one depicting King George V, the other Queen Mary, c1910.
£8–10
$12–15 ⊞ S&D

A Criterion Theatre advertising postcard, for *A Little Bit of Fluff*, 1910.
£4–6
$6–8 ⊞ S&D

A Dutch Love Story postcard, entitled 'Resort to Strategy', c1911.
£2–4
$3–6 ⊞ S&D

An embroidered postcard, with a naval crest design for RND, Divisional Engineers, 1914–18.
£20–25
$30–35 ⚒ SpP

► **A colour postcard,** depicting SS *Esperia*, Italian, 1912.
£12–15
$17–20 ⊞ S&D

A Pan Yan advertising postcard, entitled 'You're in a Fine Pickle!', featuring Bonzo, 1920s.
£30–45
$45–65 ⊞ MURR

A colour postcard, depicting the Great Western Express Engine, c1930.
£2–4
$4–6 ⊞ S&D

A sepia transportation postcard, French, 1912.
£20–25
$30–35 ⊞ S&D

Posters

A stone lithographed poster, by Maxfield Parrish, designed as a promotional piece for *The Century* magazine, Midsummer Holiday Number, August, c1898, 18¾ x 12in (47.5 x 30.5cm), framed.
£650–750
$950–1,100 JDJ

◄ A WWI propaganda poster, by C. R. Macauly, 'You Buy a Liberty Bond Lest I Perish', American, 1917, 39¾ x 30in (101 x 76cm).
£140–160
$200–230 SWO

► A Paris Haute Couture poster, by Razzia, 1949, 35¾ x 23½in (90 x 60cm).
£75–85
$110–125 VSP

An A. P. I. Voghera chocolate advertising Poster, 1955, 27 x 19in (68.5 x 48.5cm).
£40–50
$60–75 RTT

A lithographic advertising poster, 'Life-Like! For Life-Like Tone Marconiphone', 1930s, 60 x 40in (152.5 x 101.5cm).
£330–370
$500–560 DW

Cross Reference
See Rock & Pop (pages 309–324)

Entertainment & Film

A *Tournées Officielles du Théâtre du Grand Guignol de Paris* poster, by Adrien Barrère, on linen, c1910, 45 x 43½in (114.5 x 110.5cm).
£2,750–3,350
$4,000–4,750 VSP

A Ringling Bros and Barnum & Bailey lithographic poster, by Bill Bailey, American, 1945, 20½ x 28¼in (52 x 72cm).
£185–225
$270–325 VSP

► A 20th Century Fox foyer poster, *Torpilles sous l'Atlantique*, 1957, 23 x 15in (58.5 x 38cm).
£100–125
$145–180 MARK

A Warner Bros poster, *Trois Marins et une Fille* Belgian, 1953, 18 x 14in (45.5 x 35.5cm).
£55–60
$80–90 RTT

LOCATE THE SOURCE
The source of each illustration in Miller's can be found by checking the code letters below each caption with the Key to Illustrations, pages 443–451.

A film poster, *Rockabilly Baby* 1950s, 40 x 27 (101.5 x 68.5cm).
£90–110
$130–160 ⊞ RTT

An Anglo-Amalgamated Productions poster, *Carry on Cleo*, 1964, 78 x 39in (198 x 99cm).
£400–450
$580–650 ⊞ MARK

A United Artists poster, *Les Joyeux Voleurs*, French, 1961, 23 x 15in (58.5 x 38cm).
£100–125
$145–180 ⊞ MARK

A Columbia Pictures poster, *Bunny Lake Ha Desaparecido*, Spanish, 1965, 39 x 27in (99 x 68.5cm).
£70–85
$100–125 ⚒ CO

A Paramount Pictures poster, *Lady Sings the Blues*, 1973, 30 x 40in (76 x 101.5cm).
£30–40
$45–60 ⊞ CTO

◄ **A United Artists** ***Raging Bull*** **film poster,** signed by Robert de Niro and Martin Scorcese, 1972, 44 x 32in (112 x 81.5cm), mounted, framed and glazed.
£380–440
$560–640 ⚒ CO

A set of 12 Walt Disney UK front of house stills, for *Mary Poppins*, 1964, each 10 x 8in (25.5 x 20.5cm).
£80–100
$115–145 ⚒ CO

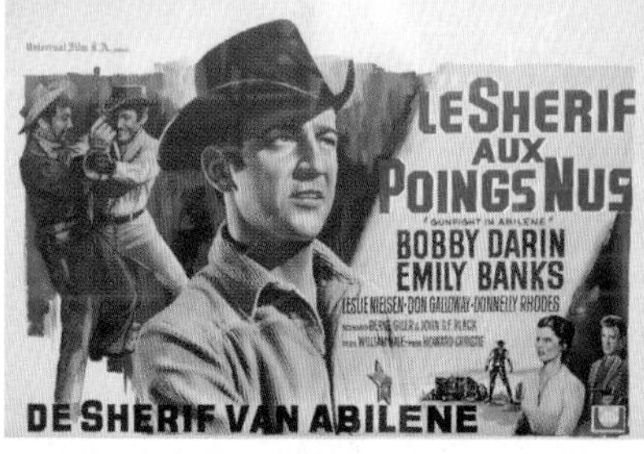

A Universal Films foyer poster, *Le Sherif Aux Poings Nus*, French, 1967, 23 x 15in (58.5 x 38cm).
£100–125
$145–180 ⊞ MARK

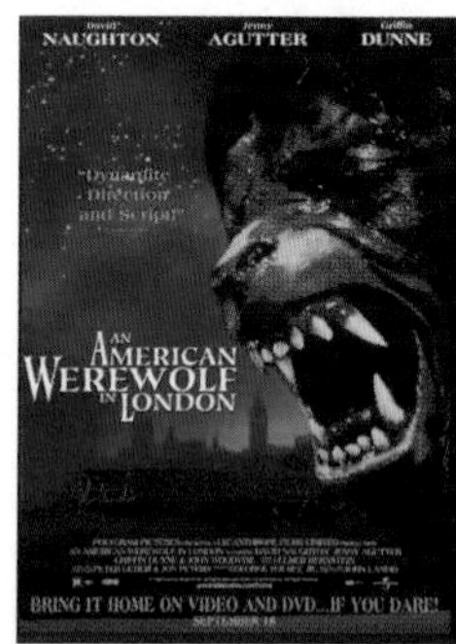

◄ **A Polygram Pictures film poster,** *American Werewolf in London,* signed by director John Landis and Griffin Dunne in black marker pen, 1981, 29 x 24in (73.5 x 61cm), framed and glazed.
£150–180
$220–260 ⚒ CO

A Warner Brothers poster, *Never Say Never Again,* 1983, 30 x 40in (76 x 101.5cm).
£30–50
$45–75 ⚒ DN

A Universal Films poster, *Monty Python's The Meaning of Life* folded, 1983, 30 x 40in (76 x 101.5cm).
£130–150
$190–220 DN

◄ **A Rank poster,** *The Terminator,* 1984, 30 x 40in (76 x 101.5cm).
£180–220
$260–320 CO

► **A Warner Brothers poster,** *The Matrix,* signed by the writers and directors Andy Wachowski and Larry Wachowski, 1999, 42 x 29in, (106.5 x 73.5cm), framed and glazed.
£200–250
$300–360 CO

◄ **A set of eight Touchstone Pictures lobby cards,** *A Nightmare Before Christmas,* by Tim Burton, 1993, 14 x 11in (35.5 x 28cm).
£90–110
$130–160 CO

Psychedelic

Psychedelic posters can command high prices in the market place. Many are associated with the underground press that flourished in the 1960s. *IT* (*The International Times*) founded in 1966 was one of the most prominent radical newspapers. 'It's in favour of soft drugs, free love, screwing the system, avant-garde Pop,' commented George Melly. *OZ,* launched in 1967, was another famous alternative magazine. In 1971, its editors were prosecuted for obscenity and the *OZ* trial became a celebrated clash between the hippy underground and the establishment.

A pair of Polypops Pinball posters, by Dave Roe, 1960s, 30 x 20in (76 x 51cm).
£65–75
$95–110 each MARK

An Acid Test poster, by Ken Kesey, textured with glitter and paint, 1965, 23 x 18in (58.5 x 45.5cm).
£650–750
$950–1,100 CO

An ***OZ*** **magazine psychedelic poster,** by Sharp and Hudford, promoting a Legalize Pot Rally, 1968, 30 x 20in (76 x 51cm).
£450–550
$650–800 CO

A promotional poster for ***International Times,*** 1960s–70s, 22 x 15in (56 x 38cm).
£375–450
$560–650 CO

Travel Posters

A partially chromolithographed Red Star Line poster, printed in Belgium, signed H. Lassiers, c1900, 34 x 24in (86.5 x 61cm).
£850–950
$1,200–1,400 JDJ

A Royal Mail Steam Packet Company 'Atlantis' Cruises poster, printed by The Baynard Press, on linen, c1930, 40 x 24¾in (101.5 x 63cm).
£350–400
$500–580 VSP

An LNER lithographed poster, East Anglia, by Frank Henry Mason, printed by Ben Johnson & Co, York, 1933, 40 x 25in (101.5 x 63.5cm).
£320–360
$470–520 B(Ch)

A British Railways poster Service to Industry Devon Trawlers, by Frank Henry Mason, printed by Waterlow, 1950s, 50 x 40in (127 x 101.5cm).
£900–1,000
$1,300–1,500 B(Ch)

A Canada by the Cunard Line poster, printed by Turner & Dunnett, c1920, 40 x 25in (101.4 x 63.5cm).
£320–380
$470–570 DW

The Electric Simplon Line poster, by Otto Baumberger, printed by Fretz Bros, on linen, 1933, 40 x 25¼in (101.5 x 64cm).
£340–380
$480–5430 VSP

A Metropole Majestic, Lugano poster, c1925, 39½ x 27½in (100.5 x 70cm).
£380–440
$560–640 VSP

A BRWS poster, Royal Albert Bridge Saltash Centenary, by Terence Cuneo, published by BRWR, printed by Waterlow, c1959, 50 x 40¼in, (127 x 102cm).
£1,000–1,200
$1,500–1,750 ONS

► **A Moscow Olympics poster,** 1979, 26 x 17½in (66 x 44.5cm).
£75–90
$110–130 VSP

Puppets

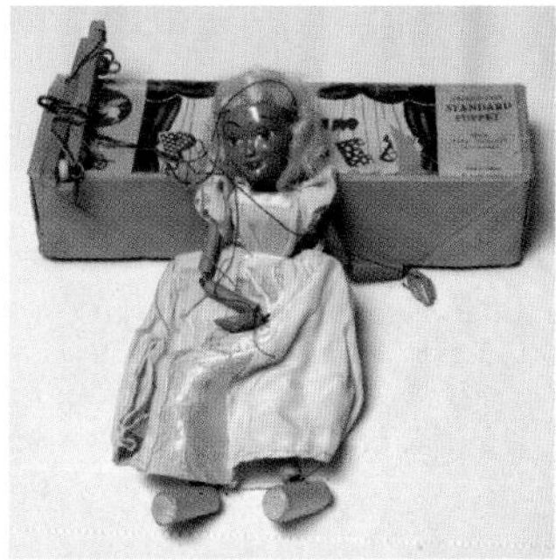

◄ **A Pelham Cinderella string puppet,** 1950s, 12in (30.5cm) high, with original brown box.
£45–50
$65–75 ⊞ J&J

A Pelham Walt Disney Donald Duck character string puppet, 1960, 10in (25.5cm) high, in original box.
£55–65
$80–95 ⊞ J&J

◄ **A Pelham Walt Disney Mickey Mouse character string puppet,** c1960, 10in (25.5cm) high, in original box.
£150–175
$220–255 ⊞ Beb

A Pelham Dopey shop display string puppet, 1960s, 18in (45.5cm) high.
£130–150
$200–220 ⊞ BBe

► **A Pelham Prince Charming string puppet,** No.122, slight damage, 1960s, 12in (30.5cm) high, in original box.
£15–20
$20–30 ⊞ J&J

A Pelham Mrs Oblige the Char string puppet, 1970s, 12in (30.5cm) high, in original window box.
£30–35
$45–50 ⊞ ARo

A Pelham Queen string puppet, 1970s, 12in (30.5cm) high, in original window box.
£40–45
$60–65 ⊞ ARo

Radios, Gramophones & Phonographs

A Burndept Ethophone No. 1 crystal set, with instruction sheet mounted in lid, 1923, 9in (23cm) wide.
£250–300
$360–440 ⊞ GM

A Gammages Super Three F three-valve radio receiver, with frame ariel mounted on a rear bracket, together with wooden horn loud speaker by S. Brown & Co, 1927–28, 13in (33cm) wide.
£350–400
$500–580 TMA

An S. G. Brown moving-iron speaker, in a mahogany case, 1929, 19in (48.5cm) wide.
£50–60
$75–90 ⊞ GM

A R. Hammond mahogany-cased crystal set, 1920s, 9in (23cm) wide.
£100–120
$145–175 SWO

A kit radio, in a mahogany-veneered case, 1930, 28in (71cm) wide.
£70–100
$100–145 ⊞ GM

An Ekco radio, model 312, in a Bakelite cabinet, 1930, 12in (30.5cm) wide.
£300–350
$450–500 ⊞ GM

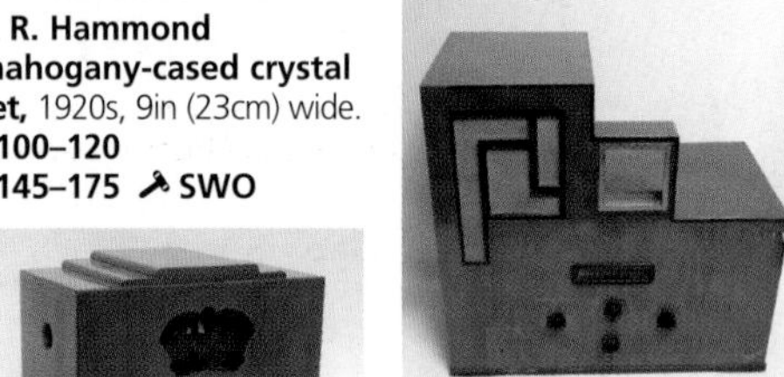

A Pye Twin Triple radio, 1930, 20in (51cm) high.
£200–250
$300–350 ⊞ GM

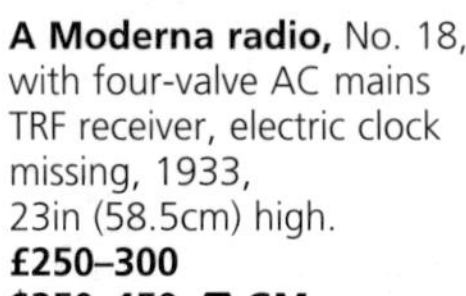

A Moderna radio, No. 18, with four-valve AC mains TRF receiver, electric clock missing, 1933, 23in (58.5cm) high.
£250–300
$350–450 ⊞ GM
This radio was probably made by Plessey for resale by another company.

A Colster Brandes two-valve mains radio, 1933, 15in (38cm) high.
£70–80
$100–115 ⊞ GM

An Ekco AD36 three-valve radio, in a Bakelite cabinet, 1935, 14in (35.5cm) diam.
£450–500
$650–720 ⊞ GM

An Ekco B37 three-valve battery TRF radio, in a Bakelite cabinet, long and medium wave, 1936, 18in (45.5cm) high.
£200–250
$300–350 ⊞ GM

A Murphy AD94 radio, designed by Eden Minns, in a Bakelite cabinet, medium wave/short wave version, 1940, 13in (33cm) high.
£175–200
$250–300 ⊞ OTA

► **A GEC BC4650 radio,** serial No. KP25918, in a Bakelite case, c1946, 15¼in (38.5cm) wide.
£30–35
$45–50 DN

A Philips 218B battery radio, in a Bakelite cabinet, 1937, 19in (48.5cm) wide.
£80–100
$115–145 ⊞ GM

An Invicta Picaninny radio, in a black-lacquered solid wood cabinet with silver-painted flutes, AC/DC chassis, 1940, 11in (28cm) wide.
£50–60
$75–100 ⊞ GM

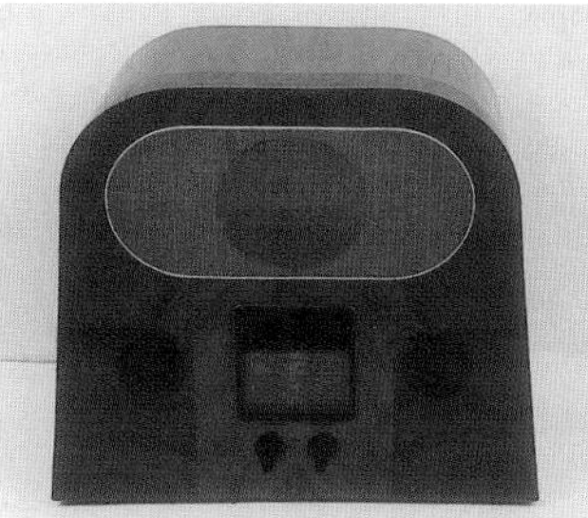

A Murphy A46 radio, designed by R. D. Russell, in veneered bent plywood cabinet, c1937, 18in (45.5cm) high.
£80–100
$115–145 ⊞ OTA

A W. & J. George WWII Resistance substitution box, 1940, 11in (28cm) wide.
£35–40
$50–60 ⊞ GM

An Ekco A28 radio, 1946, 25in (63.5cm) wide.
£40–50
$60–75 ⊞ GM
This radio was featured in the 'Britain Can Make It' exhibition in 1946.

A Philips 462A radio, in a Bakelite case, c1948, 16in (40.5cm) wide.
£125–150
$180–220 ⊞ OTA
The glass scale on this model is prone to damage, but the example here is in excellent condition.

A Bush DAC10 radio, serial No. 62/79493, in a Bakelite case, with five station/waveband push-buttons and on/off/volume and tuning knobs to the sides, 1950, 13in (33cm) wide.
£40–50
$60–75 ⚒ DN

An Ultra Bakelite AC/DC radio, with two wavebands, 1953, 12in (30.5cm) wide.
£55–65
$80–95 ⊞ CORD

A Cossor 464 Allway five-valve AC radio, in a Bakelite cabinet, c1949, 10in (25.5cm) high, with original box.
£60–100
$90–145 ⊞ OTA

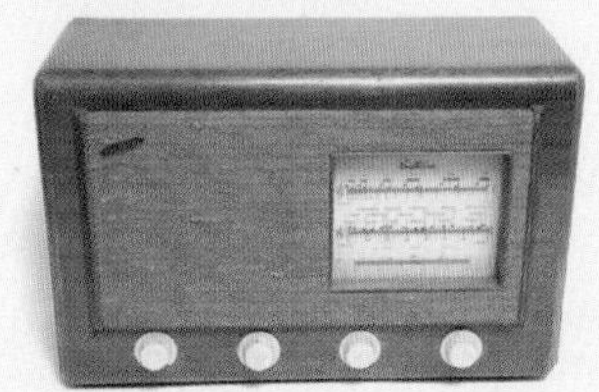

A Beethoven Electric Equipment table radio, the dial markings positioned by musical notes printed on the glass scale, 1951, 18in (45.5cm) wide.
£50–60
$75–100 ⊞ GM

◄ **A Philips 122A radio,** in a brown Bakelite cabinet, Australian, 1952, 10in (25.5cm) wide.
£50–60
$75–90 ⊞ GM

An Ekco plastic Toaster U215 AC/DC radio, 1952–53, 11in (28cm) wide.
£80–90
$115–130 ⊞ CORD
This model was also available in grey.

► **An Ultra Coronation Twin radio,** 1953, 12in (30.5cm) wide.
£50–60
$75–90 ⊞ GM

A Bush DAC 90A radio, in an ivory Bakelite case, long and medium wave, 1940–50, 12in (30.5cm) wide.
£150–175
$220–250 ⊞ DHAR
Many DAC 90s were manufactured during the 1940s and '50s, mainly in brown Bakelite; ivory is more unusual and therefore more valuable.

An Ultra R906 radio, in a simulated crocodile-skin cabinet, 1952, 15in (38cm) wide.
£80–100
$115–145 ⊞ GM

A Champion 784 radio, in a white Bakelite cabinet, 1952, 10in (25.5cm) wide.
£50–60
$75–90 ⊞ GM

A Pilot table radio, 1954, 19in (48.5cm) high.
£30–35
$45–50 ⊞ GM

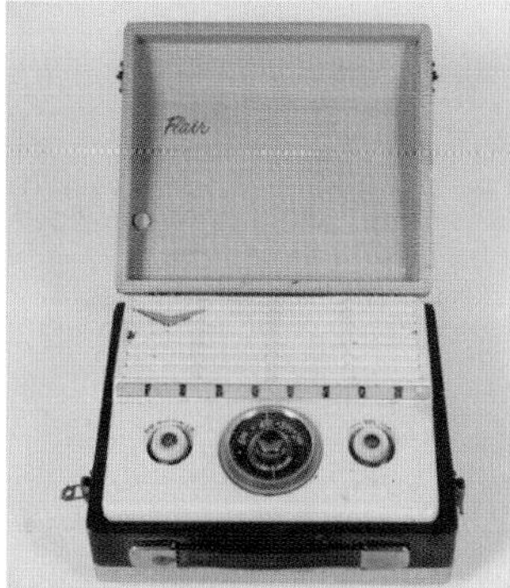

A Ferguson Flair radio, 1950s, 9½in (24cm) wide.
£10–15
$15–20 ⚒ SAF

An HMV radio, in a wooden case, 1955, 18in (45.5cm) wide.
£10–15
$15–20 ⚒ SAF

A Westminster ZA617 radio, in a Bakelite case, manufactured for Currys, with long, medium and short wavebands, 1950s, 19in (48.5cm) wide.
£150–175
$220–250 ⊞ DHAR

A Marconi T69 DA radio, in a Bakelite case, c1958, 16in (40.5cm) wide.
£5–10
$7–15 ⊞ OTA

A Hacker RP37 VHF Herald radio, with moveable station markers, in a gold-trimmed leathercloth case, 1969, 11in (28cm) wide.
£40–50
$60–75 ⊞ GM

A Grundig all-transistor Tyr transistor radio, No. RF430GB, 1970s, 20¾in (52.5cm) wide.
£60–65
$90–100 ⊞ TWI

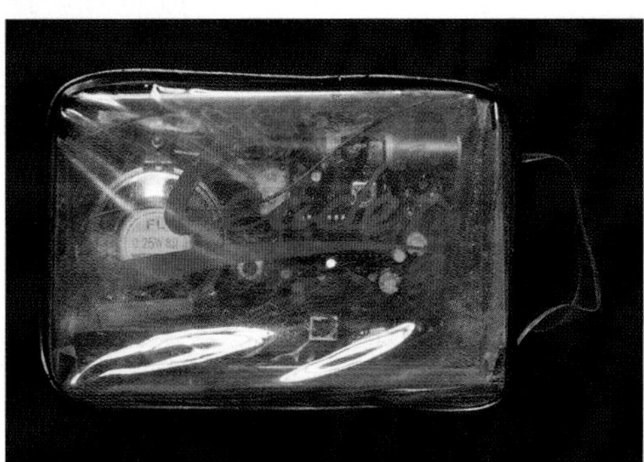

A Leader radio, 1980s, 6¾in (17cm) wide, in original plastic case.
£14–16
$18–22 ⊞ TWI

A Gramophone & Typewriter Co Dog Model gramophone, c1902, 10in (25.5cm) wide.
£1,800–2,000
$2,600–3,000 ⊞ KHW
This is the type of gramophone that was used in the famous advertisement for 'His Master's Voice' records with Nipper the dog looking into the horn.

An Edison Standard phonograph, with reproduction horn, 1908, 21in (53.5cm) wide.
£450–500
$650–720 ⊞ GM

An HMV Junior Monarch gramophone, with laminated wood horn, c1915, 13in (33cm) wide.
£1,800–2,000
$2,600–3,000 ⊞ KHW

Five phonograph cylinders, c1910, 5in (12cm) high, in original boxes.
£5–10
$7–15 each ⊞ CBGR

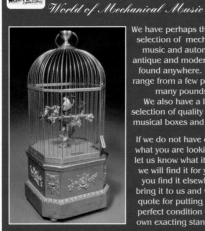

An Automatic Telephone Manufacturing Co Claritone horn speaker, with lever adjustment, BBC stamp, 1925, 19in (48.5cm) diam.
£90–100
$130–145 ⊞ GM

A Columbia Model 120 gramophone, 1926, 15in (38cm) wide.
£150–175
$220–250 ⊞ CBGR

► **An HMV record cleaner,** 1930, 2½in (6.5cm) diam.
£12–15
$15–20 ⊞ CBGR

◄ **A Liberty portable radiogram,** in a leather-covered case, the drop flaps reveal controls and ventilation, American, 1937, 13in (33cm) wide.
£100–120
$145–175
⊞ GM

◄ **An HMV nickel-plated gramophone needle container,** 1930s, 3in (7.5cm) diam.
£50–60
$75–90 ⊞ CBGR

A tin of Golden Pyramid gramophone needles, 1930s, 3in (7.5cm) high.
£20–25
$30–35 ⊞ CBGR

A Phonola portable gramophone, 1930,16in (40.5cm) wide.
£110–120
$160–175 ⊞ CBGR

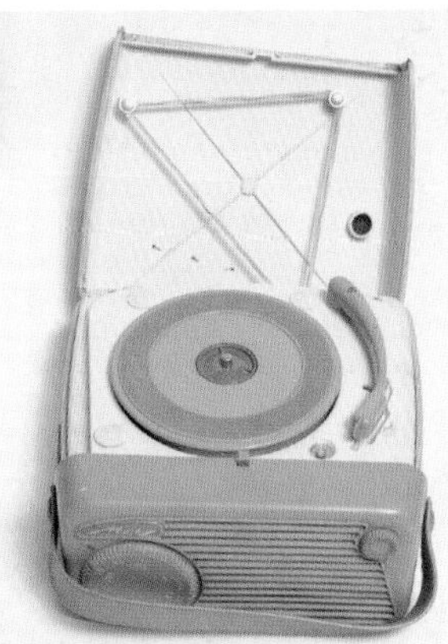

A Metz Model 102 Babyphon miniature portable radiogram, German, 1959, 9in (23cm) wide.
£65–80
$95–115 ⊞ GM

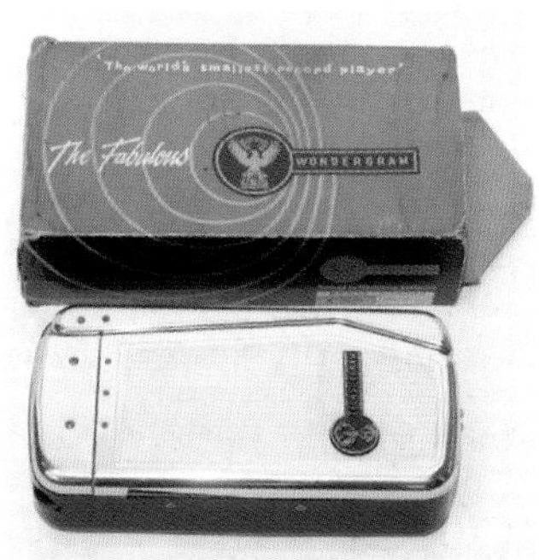

► **A Baird Wondergram portable record player,** battery-powered, 1960s, 9in (23cm) wide, in original box inscribed 'The World's Smallest Record Player'.
£45–50
$65–75 ⊞ JUN

A KB Playtime record player, battery-powered, 1961–62, 9in (23cm) wide.
£75–85
$110–125 ⊞ PPH

A Dansette Conquest Auto record player, 1962, 16in (40.5cm) wide.
£40–50
$60–75 ⊞ GM

► **A record player,** in a vinyl case, c1962, 10in (25.5cm) wide.
£175–200
$250–300
⊞ T&D

Railwayana

A BR(E) station sign, 'Thurston', some chipping and mottling, 1846, 36in (91.5cm) wide.
£900–1,100
$1,300–1,600 SRA

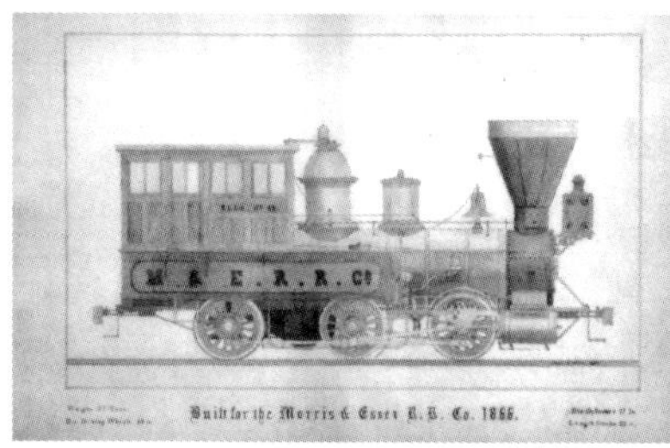

An engineer's drawing of the Morris & Essex Railroad locomotive Ella No. 44, by Charles A. Rice, built by Danforth, Cooke & Co, Patterson, New Jersey, pen and ink with water-colour, signed and dated 1867, American, 16 x 22in (40.5 x 56cm), framed and glazed.
£300–350
$440–500 SK(B)

A Waterford & Central Ireland Railway cast-iron notice, repainted, slight crack, 1868, 18½in high.
£2,200–2,400
$3,200–3,500 SRA

A cast-iron railway carriage plate, 1899, 8in (20.5cm) wide.
£150–170
$220–250 COB

Facts in brief

Station signs and totems are popular with railwayana enthusiasts. Most desirable of all, however, are locomotive nameplates, often the only identifiable relics of a scrapped train, which can fetch thousands of pounds at auction.

Three brass mirrors, from a Great Western Railway first-class carriage, c1920, 16in (40.5cm) high.
£110–140
$160–200 RUL

A Midlands Railway three-optic lamp, c1920, 11in (28cm) high.
£45–55
$65–80 GAC

An ABC Railways and Steamship Guide, for Southampton, 1929, 5 x 7in (12.5 x 18cm).
£15–20
$20–30 COB

A cast-brass nameplate, 'Zanzibar', repainted, 1936, 29in (73.5cm) long.
£17,000–19,000
$24,500–27,500 SRA

A Southern Railway brass smokebox roundel, 'Southern 1947', 26½in (67.5cm) diam.
£15,500–17,000
$22,500–24,500 SRA

Cross Reference
See Cigarette & Trade Cards (pages 155–158)

***Royal Scot, Cornish Riviera* and *The Golden Arrow*,** three train books, 1950s, 6¼ x 3¼in (16 x 8.5cm).
£8–10
$12–15 each RTT

A cast-brass nameplate, 'E. Tootal Broadhurst', face-polished and repainted, c1937, 48in (122cm) wide.
£14,200–15,000
$20,500–22,000 SRA

A BR Southern Region station totem, 'Elmstead Woods', chipped, 1950s–60s, 36in (91.5cm) long.
£220–250
$320–360 VEC

A BR Look-Out enamel arm badge, on a leather strap, 1960, 42in (106.5cm) long.
£20–25
$30–35 COB

A Southern Region enamelled destination nameboard, used at Victoria Station for the Dover to Ostend train, 1950s–1960s, 51¼ x 19¾in (130 x 50cm).
£180–200
$260–290 VEC

A BR poster for York, The Shambles, published by BR (North Eastern Region) 1/62, printed by Chorley & Pickergill Ltd, Leeds, c1965, 40 x 25in (101.5 x 63.5cm), framed and glazed.
£40–50
$60–75 MCA

Rock & Pop

Nat King Cole, signed and inscribed photograph, 1950s–60s, 7 x 5in (18 x 12.5cm), with original envelope.
£180–220
$260–320 VS

Two original material swatches, featuring *Ready Steady Goes Live*, 1966, 36 x 40in (91.5 x 101.5cm).
£125–150
$180–220 CTO

Jimi Hendrix, a modern photographic print showing Hendrix backstage in 1967, 24 x 16½in (61 x 42cm).
£240–280
$350–400 S(O)

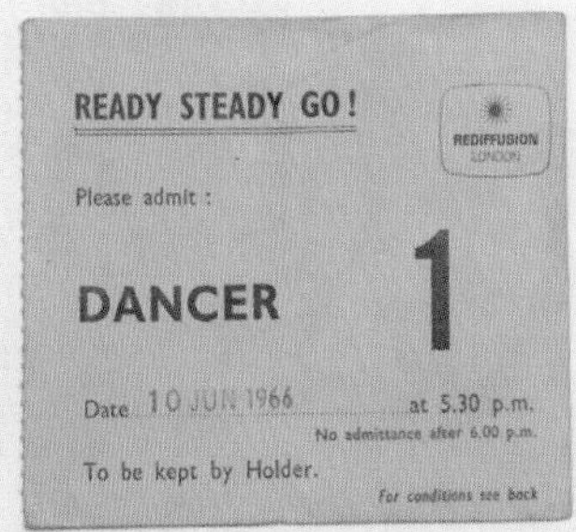

A TV studio ticket for *Ready Steady Go!*, 10 June 1966, 3 x 4in (7.5 x 10cm).
£25–30
$35–45 CTO

The Small Faces, a promotional photograph, signed in black marker pen by Stevie, Ken, Don and Ronnie, c1966, 5½ x 3½in (14 x 9cm).
£120–140
$175–200 CO

LABS in conjunction with National Blues Federation presents on Saturday February 28th at 7.30pm only
Arthur (Big Boy) Crudup
AND OTHER ARTISTS
VAUGHAN COLLEGE... st NICHOLAS CIRCLE
LEICESTER
7/- members 8/6 non-members

Arthur (Big Boy) Crudup, a signed concert ticket, c1966.
£80–100
$115–145 CO

A Lenny Bruce concert poster, designed by Wes Wilson, c1966, 20 x 14in (51 x 35.5cm).
£300–350
$450–500 CO

Cross Reference
See Psychedelic Posters (page 297)

◄ **The Who 'I Can See For Miles' promotional poster,** by Hapshash and The Coloured Coat, printed by Osiris, 1967, 30 x 20in (76 x 51cm).
£90–100
$130–145 CTO

► **A Northern California Folk-Rock Festival psychedelic poster,** by Carson-Morris Studios, featuring The Doors, 18–19 May 1968, 22 x 14¼in (56 x 36cm).
£125–150
$180–220 ASC

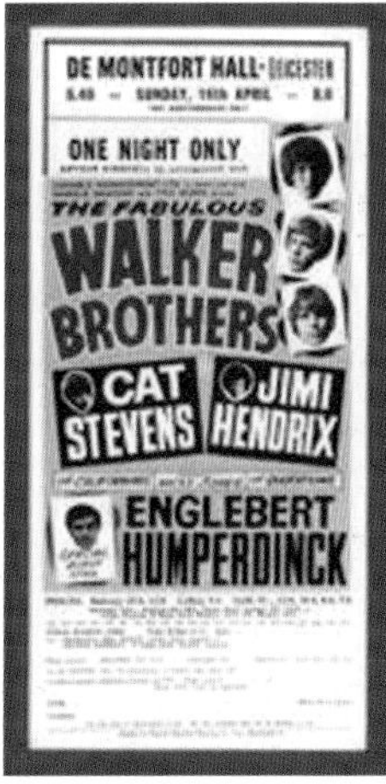

A flyer and booking form, for the Jimi Hendrix Experience and Walker Brothers show at De Montfort Hall, Leicester, 1967, 11½ x 5½in (29 x 14cm).
£600–700
$870–1,000 Bon

A Deep Purple concert poster, University of Newcastle-upon-Tyne, 22 February 1969, 30 x 20in (76 x 51cm).
£250–300
$350–450 ⚒ B(Ch)

Cliff Richard, an autographed photograph, 'To Wayne Hi! Cliff Richard' in silver ink, 1960s, 9¾ x 8in (25 x 20.5cm).
£30–40
$45–60 ⚒ B(Ch)

A Jim Morrison and The Doors 'American Poet' poster, by Bigfoot, Canadian, c1970, 35½ x 24in (90 x 61cm).
£90–100
$130–145 ⚒ VSP

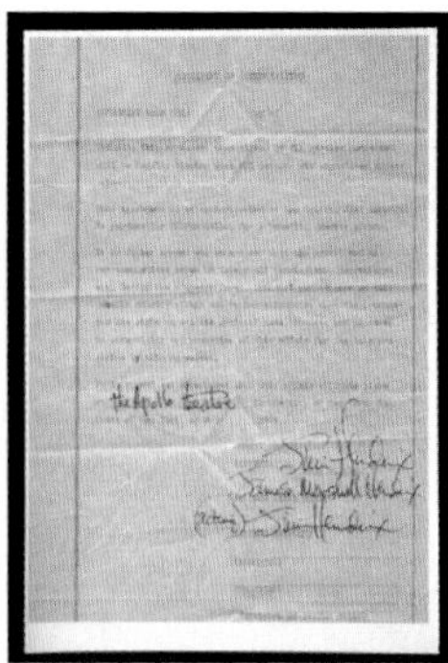

Jimi Hendrix, a signed performance contract issued by the charity Biafra Calls, for a concert at the Apollo Theatre, New York, July 1969, signed three times in blue ink 'Jimi Hendrix', 'James Marshall Hendrix' and 'Jimi Hendrix', 11 x 8in (28 x 20.5cm).
£3,000–3,500
$4,500–5,000 ⊞ ASC
The rarity of this document lies in Hendrix's use of his full signature. At his birth in November 1942, Hendrix was named Johnny Allen by his mother Lucille. His father Al, unhappy at not being consulted, renamed him James Marshall on 11 September 1946. Thus Johnny became Jimmy and eventually, following several career name changes (eg Maurice James, Jimmy James) Jimmy, at the suggestion of Chas Chandler, became Jimi. Although contracts bearing his signature as Jimi Hendrix have appeared occasionally at auction over the years, there are no records of any bearing his full signature, making this a particularly scarce and desirable item.

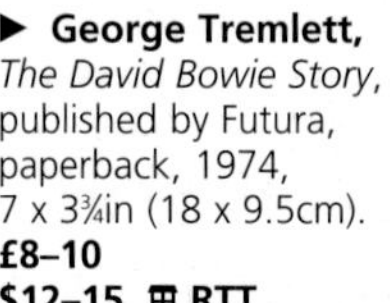

► George Tremlett, *The David Bowie Story*, published by Futura, paperback, 1974, 7 x 3¾in (18 x 9.5cm).
£8–10
$12–15 ⊞ RTT

A Bob Dylan double concert poster, The Isle of Wight Festival of Music, 29–31 August 1969, 22¾ x 34¼in (58 x 87cm).
£140–160
$200–230 ⚒ B(Ch)

A signed poster of Bob Dylan, 1960s, 33 x 24in (84 x 61cm).
£240–280
$350–400 ⚒ CO

The Rolling Stones, autographs of Keith Richard, Brian Jones, Bill Wyman and Mick Jagger, no Charlie Watts, with a colour photograph of the band, 1960s, 21 x 13in (53 x 33cm).
£280–330
$400–480 ⚒ CO

◄ 'The Yes album', signed by the band, 1971, 12in (30.5cm) square.
£250–300
$350–450 ⚒ CO

George Tremlett, *The Mark Bolan Story*, published by Futura, paperback, 1975, 7 x 4½in (18 x 11.5cm).
£7–9
$10–14 ⊞ RTT

A Louis Armstrong Jazz Greats poster, by Waldemar Swierzy, c1975, 39 x 26½in (99 x 67.5cm).
£115–130
$170–190 ⚒ VSP

Marvin Gaye, a signed souvenir programme, also signed by Rose Banks, September–October 1976, 12½ x 10in (32 x 25.5cm).
£260–300
$380–440 ⚒ VS

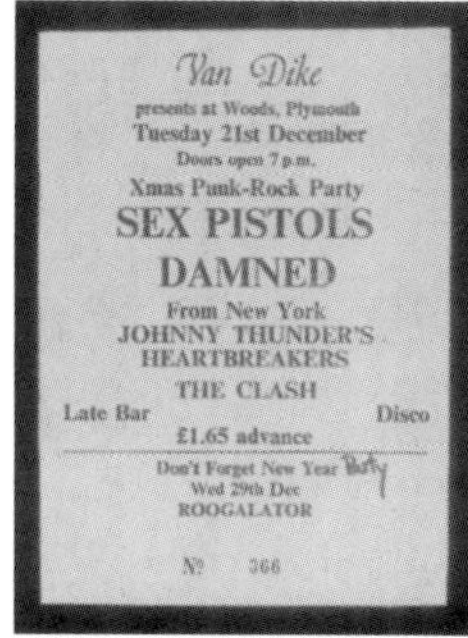
Van Dike
presents at Woods, Plymouth
Tuesday 21st December
Doors open 7 p.m.
Xmas Punk-Rock Party
SEX PISTOLS
DAMNED
From New York
JOHNNY THUNDER'S
HEARTBREAKERS
THE CLASH
Late Bar Disco
£1.65 advance
Don't Forget New Year Baby
Wed 29th Dec
ROOGALATOR
Nº 366

A Sex Pistols and The Damned concert ticket, at Woods, Plymouth, 21 December 1976, 6 x 4in (15 x 10cm).
£175–200
$250–300 ⚒ S(O)

Anarchy in the UK, No. 1, the Sex Pistols fanzine, published by Glitterbest, December 1976, tabloid newspaper format, 12pp.
£150–180
$220–260 ⊞ ASC

► **A modern photographic print of the Sex Pistols,** at EMI, Manchester Square, a take-off of the famous shot on the cover of the Beatles' album 'Please Please Me', 1976, 15½ x 24in (39. 5 x 61cm).
£350–400
$500–580 ⚒ S(O)

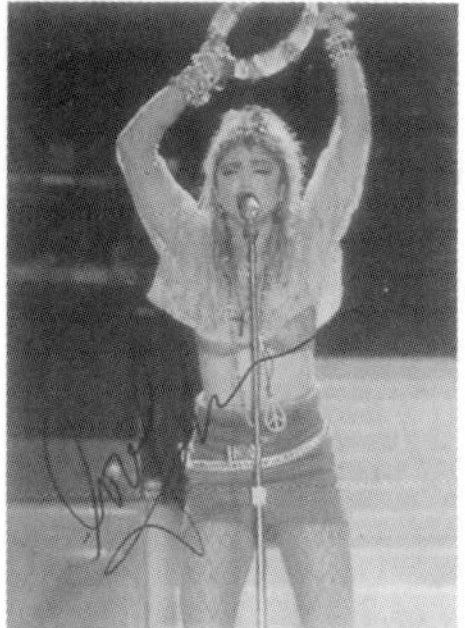

Sex Pistols Press Book, published by Glitterbest, 1976, 16pp.
£125–150
$180–220 ⊞ ASC

A Sex Pistols 'God Save The Queen' flyer, by James Reid, featuring the 'safety pin' image based on the Cecil Beaton portrait of the Queen, 1977.
£90–100
$130–145 ⊞ ASC

Elvis Presley, a Las Vegas Hilton menu, signed 'Thanks Elvis Presley', 1970s, 11¾ x 8¼in (30 x 21cm).
£350–400
$500–580 ⚒ DW

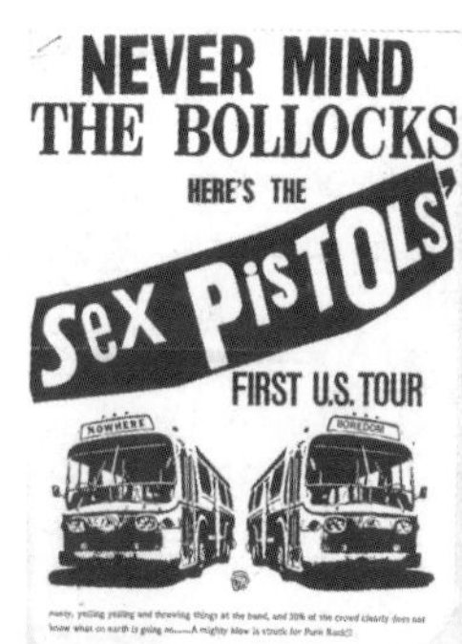

A Sex Pistols Never Mind the Bollocks tour flyer and press sheets, c1978, 10 x 8in (25.5 x 20.5cm).
£110–130
$160–190 ⚒ CO

Madonna, a signed photograph, 1980s, 10 x 8in (25.5 x 20.5cm).
£90–110
$130–160 ⚒ VS

◄ **A Freddie Mercury and Queen souvenir brochure,** for A Magic Tour, signed by all members of the band on the title page, and by Mercury across a black and white portrait photograph of himself, some loose pages, 1987.
£420–460
$625–675 ⚒ DW

Elton John, a signed photographic postcard, 1980s, 6 x 4in (15 x 10cm).
£20–25
$30–35 ⊞ S&D

John Travolta and Olivia Newton John, a signed photograph, from *Grease*, 1980s, 10 x 8in (25.5 x 20.5cm).
£75–85
$110–125 🔨 VS

The Spice Girls, a signed photograph, 1990s, 10 x 8in (25.5 x 20.5cm).
£60–75
$90–110 🔨 VS

A striped blue jacket, owned and signed by Elton John, manufactured by RPM, 20thC.
£250–300
$350–450 🔨 CO

Marianne Faithfull, a signed photograph, 1990s, 10 x 8in (25.5 x 20.5cm).
£40–45
$60–65 🔨 VS

A closed-circuit television, by RCA, from Elvis Presley's kitchen at Graceland, with plaque inscribed 'CCTV system for Graceland by mid-south Police supply', in a custom-made carved wood case, 20thC, 10 x 15in (25.5 x 38cm).
£525–625
$800–900 🔨 CO

Stereophonics, a signed Remo drumhead, wear to centre, 1990s.
£50–60
$75–90 🔨 VS

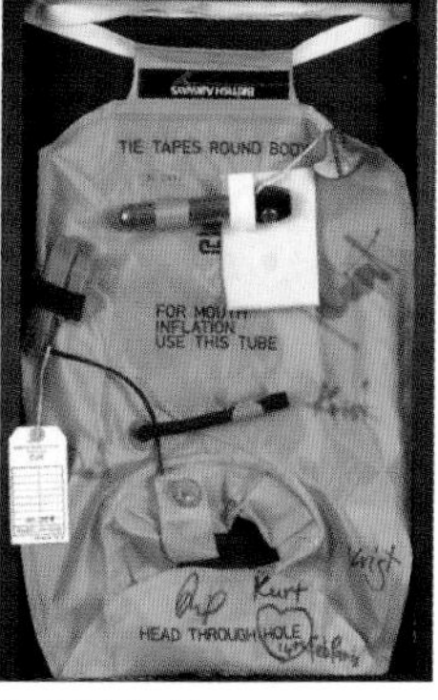

A British Airways *Concorde* life jacket, customized by Kurt Cobain, Dave Grohl and Krist Novoselic as a Valentine's Day gift for Kurt's wife Courtney Love, lead singer of Hole, mounted in a box frame, 20thC, 26½ x 16½in (67.5 x 42cm).
£500–600
$720–870 🔨 CO

Westlife, a signed photograph, c2000, 8 x 12in (20.5 x 30.5cm).
£55–65
$80–95 🔨 VS

LOCATE THE SOURCE

The source of each illustration in Miller's can be found by checking the code letters below each caption with the Key to Illustrations, pages 443–451.

► **Eric Clapton,** a signed photograph of Clapton on stage, 2002, 10 x 8in (25.5 x 20.5cm).
£180–220
$260–300 ⊞ FRa

The Beatles

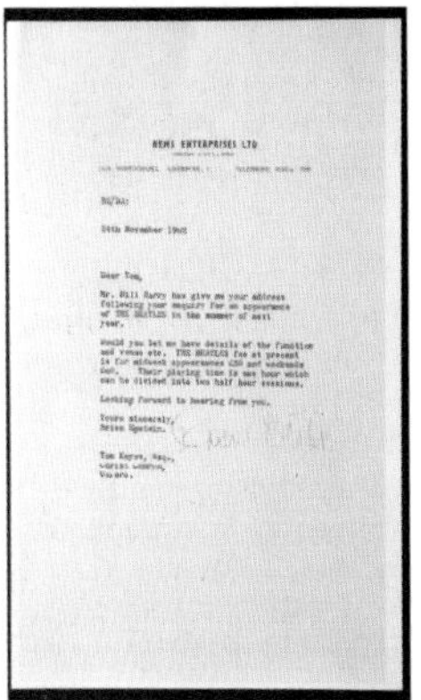

◄ **Brian Epstein,** a signed typescript letter to Thom Keyes, Christ Church, Oxford, on NEMS Enterprises headed notepaper, including the lines 'The Beatles fee at present is for midweek appearances £50 and weekends £60. Their playing time is one hour which can be divided into two half hour sessions', dated 24 November 1962, 11½ x 7¾in (29 x 19.5cm).
£350–400
$500–580 ⊞ ASC

Written soon after the Beatles' first single was released, but before their first number one three months later, the fees Epstein quotes in the letter had risen dramatically by the following summer, and not surprisingly the concert was never booked. The letter's recipient, California-born Thom Keyes, wrote *All Night Stand,* the fictitious story of a Liverpool band's rise to stardom, first published in 1966.

A Beatles poster, 'Europas Popband Nummer Ett', produced for the short tour of Sweden, October 1963, 39¼ x 27½in (99.5 x 70cm).
£700–800
$1,000–1,150 ⚒ S(O)

► **Two Beatles concert ticket stubs,** for the Gaumont Theatre, Wolverhampton, 19 November 1963, 2½ x 1½in (6.5 x 4cm).
£160–200
$230–300
⚒ B(Ch)

A Beatles plastic New Sound Guitar, by Selco, 1964, 23in (58.5cm) high.
£80–100
$115–145 ⊞ BTC

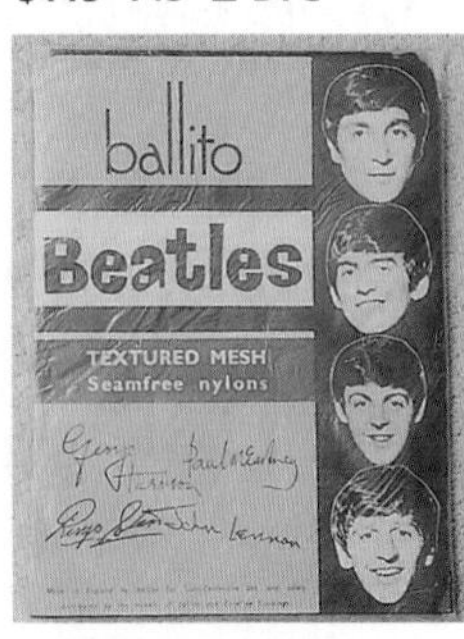

A packet of Beatles stockings, by Ballito, the tops printed with the Beatles' faces and signatures, 1964–65, 9 x 7½in (23 x 19cm).
£70–85
$100–125 ⊞ MURR

The Beatles hair pomade, by H. H. Cosmetics, with 50 packets of hair grease, in a sealed box, Philippino, 1964, 6 x 5in (15 x 12.5cm).
£75–90
$110–130 ⚒ SAF

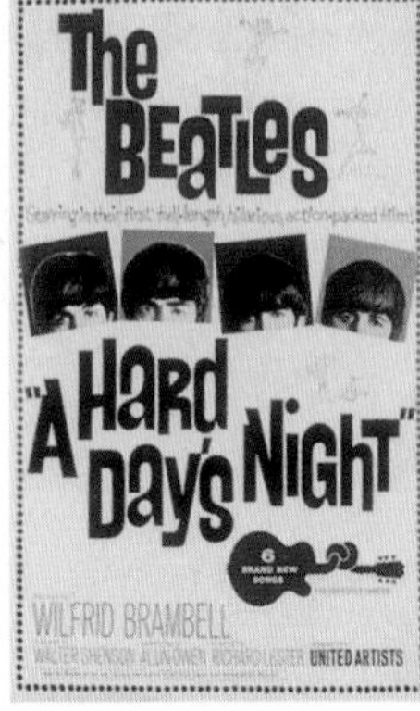

A United Artists film poster, *A Hard Day's Night,* starring the Beatles, 1964, 35½ x 24in (90 x 61cm).
£190–210
$275–300 ⚒ VSP

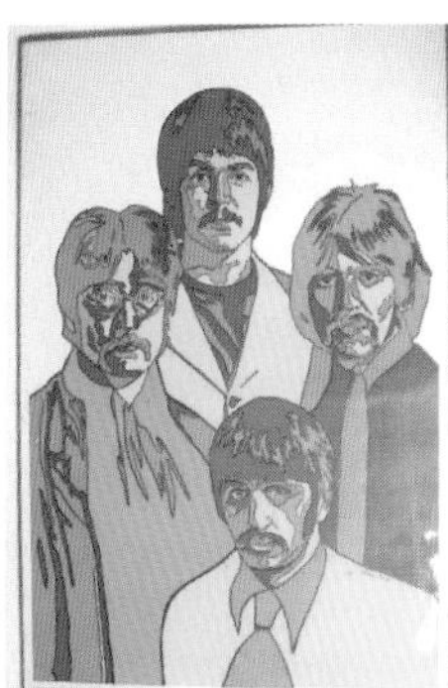

A Beatles Black Light poster, by Experimental Sensor Productions, American, 1967, 35 x 24in (89 x 61cm).
£225–250
$325–360 ⊞ CTO

aA Beatles metal tray, 1960s, 13½in (34.5cm) square.
£20–25
$30–35 ⚒ SAF

The Beatles, a photograph by Robert Freeman, taken in front of a background montage of film stars, taken at Twickenham Studios during the filming of *Help!*, limited edition, 1960s, 20 x 16in (51 x 40.5cm).
£320–380
$460–560 ⚒ CO

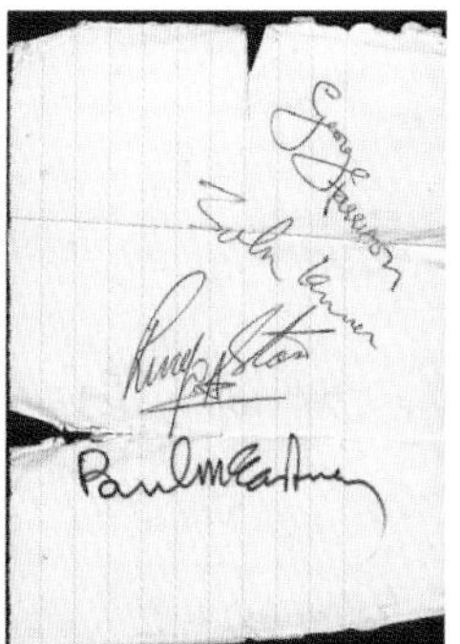

The Beatles, autographs, 1960s, 6 x 4in (15 x 10cm).
£1,400–1,600
$2,000–2,300 ⚒ CO

► A can of Beatles talc, by Margo of Mayfair, 1960s, 7½in (19cm) high.
£300–350
$400–500 ⊞ MTM

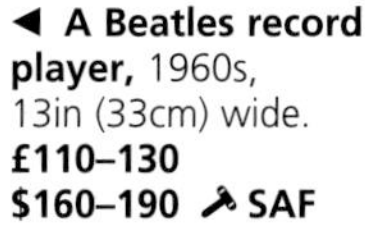

◄ A Beatles record player, 1960s, 13in (33cm) wide.
£110–130
$160–190 ⚒ SAF

A set of four 'Yellow Submarine' pin badges, 1968, 1¼in (3cm) diam.
£15–20
$20–30 ⚒ SAF

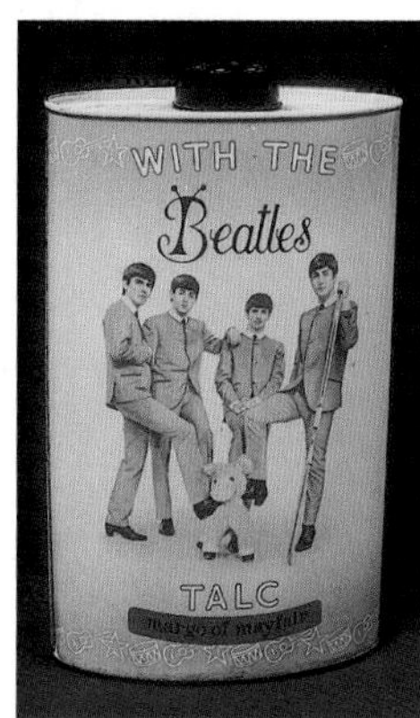

A John Lennon and Yoko Ono art exhibition programme, c1971.
£80–100
$115–145 ⚒ CO

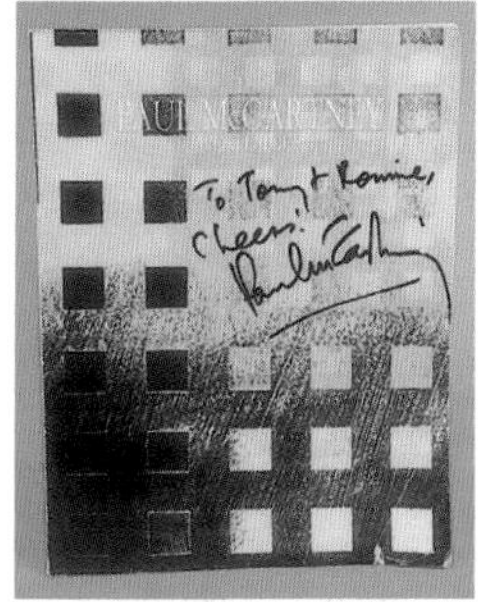

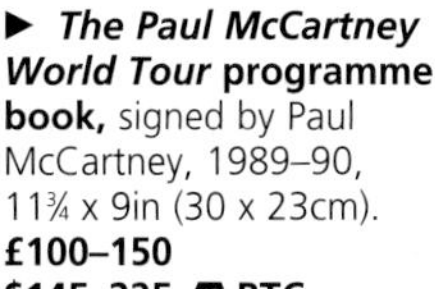

► *The Paul McCartney World Tour* programme book, signed by Paul McCartney, 1989–90, 11¾ x 9in (30 x 23cm).
£100–150
$145–225 ⊞ BTC

Guitars

Collecting vintage guitars is an expanding field. 'When rock and roll took off in the 1950s, it really changed the way we lived,' says dealer Chris Trigg. 'Suddenly children didn't have to be like their parents any more. They had their own music, their own fashions and their own identity. And also, through music, a working-class boy with a limited education could become a rich rock star and a hero. In terms of social history, vintage guitars are highly significant items, and that is one of the reasons why people collect them today.'

But it's not just romance that attracts the collectors. The models designed in the 1950s by Leo Fender, Les Paul, Gretsch and other US pioneers of the electric guitar have, in the opinion of many guitarists, never been bettered. If not classical these are certainly classic instruments. 'Like violins, these instruments are made of wood,' adds Trigg. 'Each one has its own personality and in terms of playing quality, they only improve with age.'

Prices for vintage guitars continue to rise and have not dropped in the past 25 years. 'Condition is all important to value and originality is everything,' says Trigg. 'It's getting harder and harder to find good original models today because so many are already in private collections.' The popularity and price of these early models has not only stimulated modern re-issues by the original manufacturers, but also fakes. 'If you don't know much about the subject, it can be a minefield,' warns Trigg. 'As with anything else, the more you know the better. There are very good reference books around now, but nothing beats handling the original items and when in doubt, seek advice from a reputable specialist dealer.'

A Martin 00-42 acoustic guitar, with ivory bridge, American, 1900.
£11,000–13,000
$16,000–19,000 ⊞ VRG

A Fender Music Master electric guitar, desert sand finish with anodized pick guard, American, 1957.
£800–1,000
$1,200–1,500 ⊞ VRG

A Gretsch Anniversary semi-acoustic guitar, American, 1959.
£1,600–1,800
$2,300–2,600 ⊞ VRG

A Fender Stratocaster electric guitar, sunburst finish, slab rosewood fingerboard, American, 1959, with original case.
£14,000–16,000
$20,500–23,000 ⊞ VRG

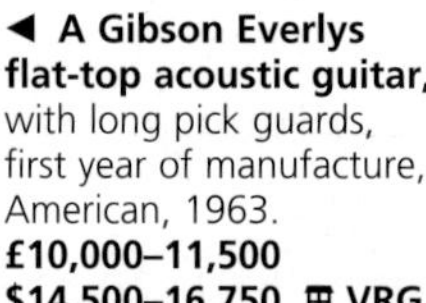

◄ **A Gibson Everlys flat-top acoustic guitar,** with long pick guards, first year of manufacture, American, 1963.
£10,000–11,500
$14,500–16,750 ⊞ VRG

Items in the Guitars section have been arranged in date order.

A Gibson Les Paul All Gold electric guitar, with P90 pick-ups, American, 1965.
£10,000–12,000
$14,500–17,500 ⊞ VRG

US guitar greats

Christian Frederick Martin (1793–1837), the son of a guitar maker, was born in Germany and emigrated to the USA in 1833. He founded the famous Martin company, producer of some of the finest flat top acoustic guitars in the world.
Leo Fender, born in California in 1909, had a childhood fascination with radios which gradually evolved into an adult interest in electronic gadgets. In the 1940s, he developed the idea of a solid body guitar and in 1950 he launched the Fender Broadcaster, the first commercially available solid body electric guitar. In 1951, he produced the Fender Precision, the world's first electric bass and, following a dispute with a rival company over names, the Broadcaster was relaunched as the Telecaster. 1954 saw the introduction of the Stratocaster, one of the most popular electric guitars of all time.
Lester William Polfus (b1916), known as 'Rhubarb Red' and the 'Wizard Waukesha', was already a successful country and R&B guitarist by the time he changed his name to Les Paul. He pioneered a number of musical inventions (including the multi-track tape recorder) and in the 1940s, like other innovators, he experimented with the solid body electric guitar. Joining forces with US manufacturers Gibson in 1952 he launched the Gibson Les Paul, known as the 'Gold Top' after its distinctive gold finish. Other models followed in the 1950s and, like Leo Fender, Les Paul is regarded as one of the seminal figures in the development of the electric guitar.
Gretsch, founded in New York in 1883, are particularly well known for their electric acoustic guitars produced in the 1950s and '60s, many of which were designed by musician Jimmie Webster.
The Gibson Company was founded in Kalamazoo, Michigan in 1902. Well known for their acoustic guitars in the late 1940s, they began to produce electric acoustics that became a favourite with many jazz and country musicians. Bands such as the Everly Brothers, who both played Gibson guitars, lent their name to specific models in general production, such as the example illustrated here. In the early 1950s, Gibson began their successful collaboration with Les Paul.

A Gibson EBO-L electric bass guitar, cherry finish, with SG-style long scale neck, American, 1974.
£600–700
$870–1,000 ⊞ VRG

A Fender Telecaster electric guitar, blond finish with maple fingerboard, American, 1974.
£1,800–2,000
$2,600–3,000 ⊞ VRG

A Music Man Sting Ray electric bass guitar, with string-through body and maple fingerboard, American, 1976.
£1,800–2,000
$2,600–3,000 ⊞ VRG

A Kramer Beretta electric guitar, designed by Eddie Van Halen, with upgraded tremolo to original Floyd Rose, possibly Korean, 1985.
£550–600
$800–870 ⊞ RAND

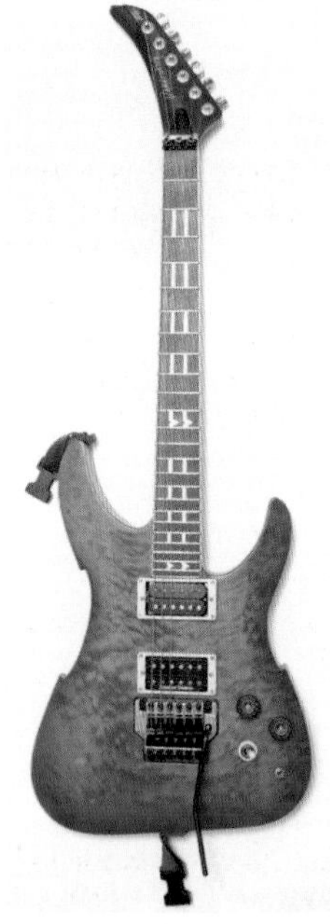

A Peavey electric guitar, with customized quilt top, owned by Adrian Vandenburg of White Snake, 1990.
£1,100–1,200
$1,600–1,750 ⊞ RAND

A Martin D28 acoustic guitar, American, 1990s.
£1,300–1,500
$2,000–2,200 ⊞ MG

Jukeboxes

A Rock-Ola 1434 Super Rocket jukebox, with 50 selections, plays 78rpm records, 1952, 58in (147.5cm) high.
£2,250–2,500
$3,250–3,600 ⊞ WAm

An AMI J120 jukebox, with 120 selections, takes American coins, rebuilt, American, 1959, 62in (157.5cm) high.
£2,500–2,750
$3,600–4,000 ⊞ WAm

An AMI Continental stereo jukebox, with 200 selections, 1961, 63in (160cm) high.
£4,250–4,750
$6,200–7,000 ⊞ MARK

Records

The advent of the CD player has left many music fans with a stack of vinyl that all too often ends up in boxes in the loft. Some records will be worth little or nothing, others will have a modest second-hand value and, if you are lucky, there might be a collectable classic lurking in your teenage collection. Record collecting is a very precise business and has stimulated a wealth of magazines and books, but for the beginner interested in either selling or forming a collection, we offer the following tips.

'With some exceptions, 78s are really not very collectable because people don't have the machines to play them on anymore,' advises Mike Chapman from Beanos record shop, 'so the market tends to focus on singles, EPs and LPs.' 'Condition is crucial to value,' adds Mike Reynolds from Memory Lane Records. 'A record might fetch £100 ($145) in mint condition, £75 ($110) if excellent, £20 ($30) if very good, and £5 ($8) if good. If a record has lost its original centre, the value can be halved. With EPs and LPs particularly, sleeves are very important to value and should be in good condition. The sleeves of 45s are less important (other than picture sleeves or a very rare label) since often single sleeves were interchangeable, and vintage single sleeves can still be purchased quite cheaply.' As Chapman notes, chart topping records were produced in vast numbers, so it is often the rarities and less successful records that are the most desirable.

It is not just the artist that is important, but also the label and serious collectors might seek to track down every single catalogue number produced by a certain company, from the greatest rock and roll classics to one-off novelty songs. Different issues of the same record can also have different values, depending sometimes on the minutest variations in the colour of the sleeve or a matrix number engraved on the vinyl. 'With less successful bands there is likely to be very little difference in value between a demo (an advance promotional copy distributed free to radio stations and journalists) and a first issue record,' says Reynolds. 'With big name artists, however, the demo can be very collectable.'

Although dominated by vinyl, the collection shown below also includes a number of CDs. 'Some CDs are already desirable. Also look out for limited edition runs on vinyl by big name artists such as Oasis or Robbie Williams. They could be a good bet for collectables of the future,' concludes Chapman.

An Animals EP record, 'In the beginning there was Early Animals ...', by Decca, 1965, in original sleeve.
£20–25
$30–35 ⊞ BNO

◀ **A John Barry LP record,** 'The Quiller Memorandum', by CBS, 1966, in original sleeve.
£20–35
$30–35 ⊞ PR

Items in the Records section have been arranged in alphabetical order according to artist.

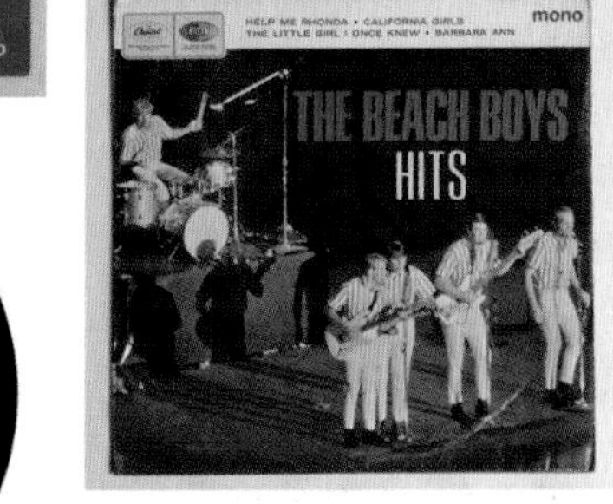

A Beach Boys EP record, 'Hits', by Capitol, 1965, in original sleeve.
£10–12
$15–18 ⊞ BNO

▶ **A Beatles one-sided 7in demo record,** 'Hello Goodbye', by Mick James Music, No. Tem. 4864, 1967.
£500–600
$720–870 ⚒ CO

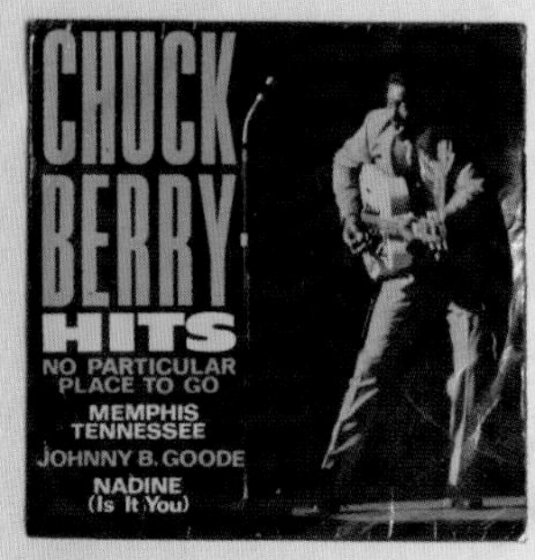

A Chuck Berry EP record, 'Hits' featuring 'No Particular Place to Go', 'Memphis Tennessee', Johnny B Goode' and 'Nadine (Is It You)', by Pye, 1964, in original sleeve.
£10–12
$15–18 ⊞ BNO

A David Bowie LP record, 'Diamond Dogs', by RCA, Japanese pressing, 1984, in original sleeve.
£35–40
$50–60 ⊞ PR

► A Freddy Cannon LP record, 'The Explosive! Freddy Cannon', by Top Rank International, 1960, in original sleeve.
£20–25
$30–35 ⊞ CTO

A Cream LP record, 'Wheels of Fire', by Polydor, 1972, in original sleeve.
£70–80
$100–115 ⊞ BNO

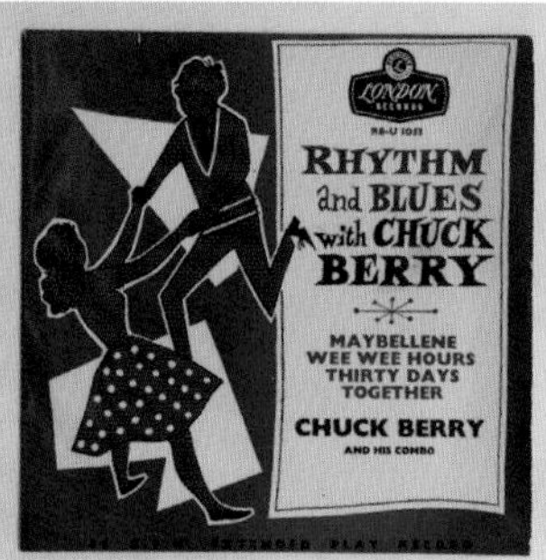

A Chuck Berry EP record, 'Maybellene', 'Wee Wee Hours', 'Thirty Days Together', by London Records, 1956, in original sleeve.
£150–170
$220–250 ⊞ BNO

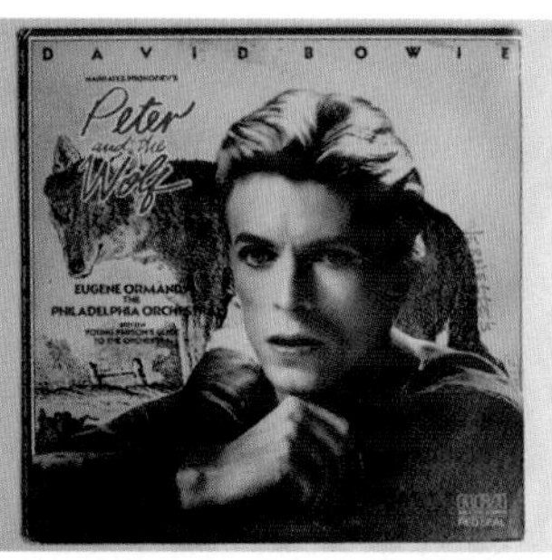

A David Bowie LP record, 'Peter and the Wolf', by RCA, American green vinyl issue, 1978, in original sleeve.
£35–40
$50–60 ⊞ BNO

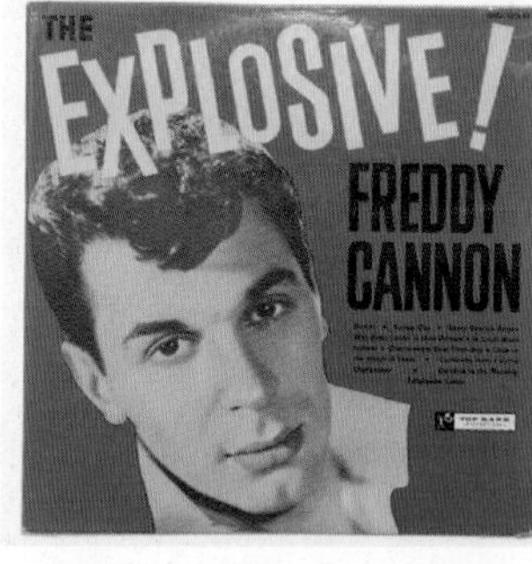

A Big Bopper EP record, 'The Big Bopper', by Mercury, 1959, with original sleeve.
£130–150
$200–220 ⊞ BNO

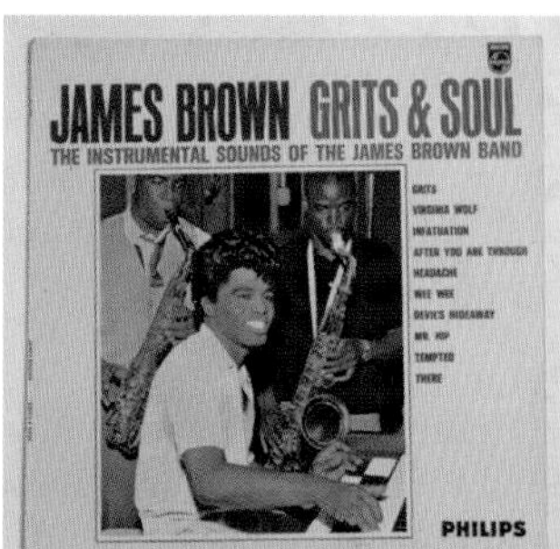

A James Brown LP record, 'Grits & Soul', by Philips, 1965, in original sleeve.
£20–25
$30–35 ⊞ PR

A Dave Clark Five EP record, 'The Dave Clark Five', by Columbia, 1963, in original sleeve.
£8–10
$12–15 ⊞ BNO

◄ A Miles Davis LP record, 'Siesta', produced in collaboration with Marcus Miller, 1987, in original cover signed by Davis and Miller.
£240–300
$350–450 ⚒ DW
This rare signature of Miles Davis is possibly the most sought-after jazz autograph of all.

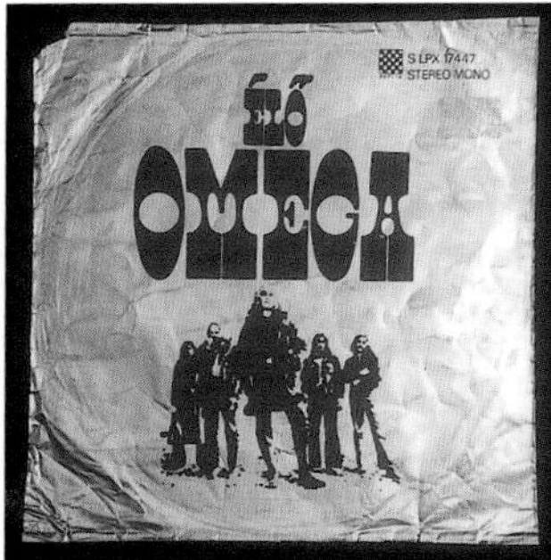

An ELO Omega LP record, 'Elo Omega', by Pepita, 1972, in original aluminium sleeve.
£15–20
$20–30 ⊞ TOT

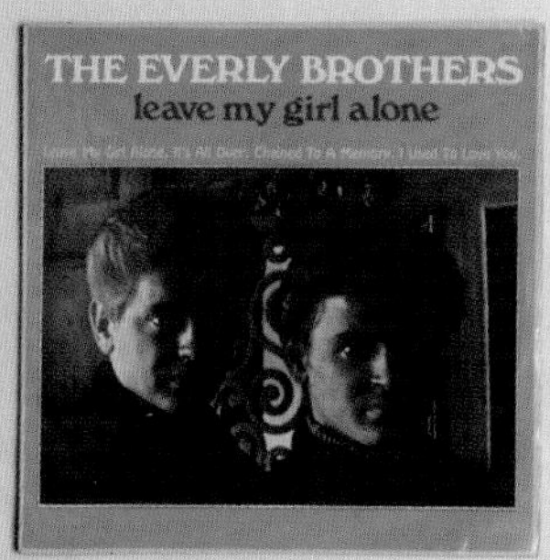

An Everly Brothers EP record, 'Leave My Girl Alone', by Warner Brothers, 1966, in original sleeve.
£35–40
$50–60 ⊞ BNO

A Georgie Fame and The Blue Flames EP record, 'Move it on Over', by Colombia, 1965, in original sleeve.
£15–20
$20–30 ⊞ BNO

◄ An Al Green LP record, 'Al Green is Love', by BMI, 1975, in original sleeve.
£15–20
$20–30 ⊞ BNO

► A Jimi Hendrix LP record, 'The Cry of Love', by Polydor, 1970, in original sleeve.
£30–35
$45–50 ⊞ BNO

A Buddy Holly 7in single record, 'Peggy Sue', by Coral, No. 9-61885, signed by Holly, disc centre missing, damage to label, 1959.
£260–300
$380–440 ⚒ CO

A Buddy Holly LP record, 'The Buddy Holly Story', by Coral, 1958, in original sleeve.
£20–25
$30–35 ⊞ CTO

► A Human League EP record, 'Tom Baker', recorded as a tribute to the actor Tom Baker when he left the television series *Dr Who*, 1981, in original sleeve.
£10–15
$15–20 ⊞ WHO

A John Keating LP record, 'Space Experience', quadrophonic pressing, by EMI, 1972, in original sleeve.
£20–25
$30–35 ⊞ PR

A Led Zeppelin box of six LP records, 'Led Zeppelin', by Atlantic Records, 1990, with 36 page booklet, in original box.
£65–75
$95–110 ⊞ BNO

A Leftfield LP record, 'Leftism', by Hard Hands, triple pressing, 1995, in original sleeve.
£20–25
$30–35 ⊞ PR

A Madonna boxed set, 'The Royal Box', by Time Warner, comprising CDs, video and poster, 1990, in original packaging.
£100–125
$145–180 ⊞ BNO

A Manfred Mann EP record, 'Groovin' with Manfred Mann', by EMI, 1964, in original sleeve.
£8–10
$12–15 ⊞ BNO

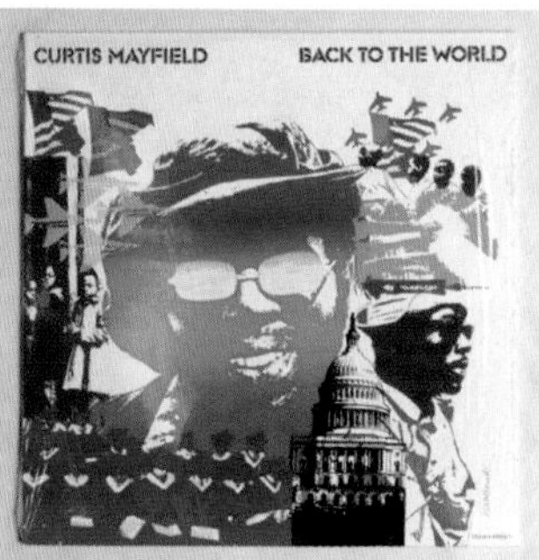

A Curtis Mayfield LP record, 'Back to the World', by Curtom Records, 1973, in original sleeve.
£10–12
$15–18 ⊞ BNO

► A Metallica CD, 'Garage Days Revisited', by Mercury, 1987.
£45–50
$65–75 ⊞ BNO

A Peter Paul and Mary EP record, 'If I Were Free', by Warner Brothers, 1966, in original sleeve.
£4–5
$6–8 ⊞ BNO

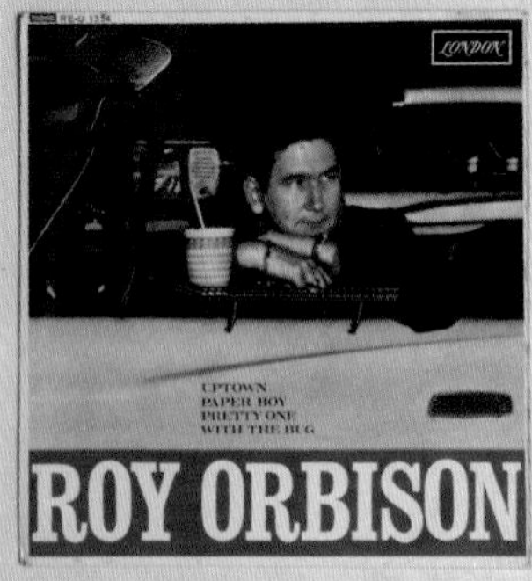

A Roy Orbison EP record, 'Uptown', 'Paper Boy', 'Pretty One', 'With the Bug', by London, 1963, in original sleeve.
£18–22
$28–32 ⊞ BNO

◄ An Elvis Presley EP record, 'Jaihouse Rock', by RCA, No. RCX 106, 1957, in original sleeve.
£12–15
$15–20 ⊞ BNO

A Queen LP record, 'A Night at the Opera', by EMI, white vinyl issue, 1975, in original sleeve.
£90–100
$130–145 ⊞ BNO

A Martha Reeves and the Vandellas LP record, 'Ridin' High', by Tamla Motown, 1967, in original sleeve.
£55–60
$80–90 ⊞ BNO

A Rolling Stones LP record, 'The Rolling Stones', by Decca, 1964, in original sleeve.
£100–120
$145–175 ⊞ BNO

◄ A Rolling Stones box of four LP records, 'The Great Years', by Decca for Reader's Digest, 1982, in original box.
£45–50
$65–75 ⊞ BNO

► A Del Shannon EP record, 'Runaway with Del Shannon', by London, 1962, in original sleeve.
£20–25
$30–35 ⊞ BNO

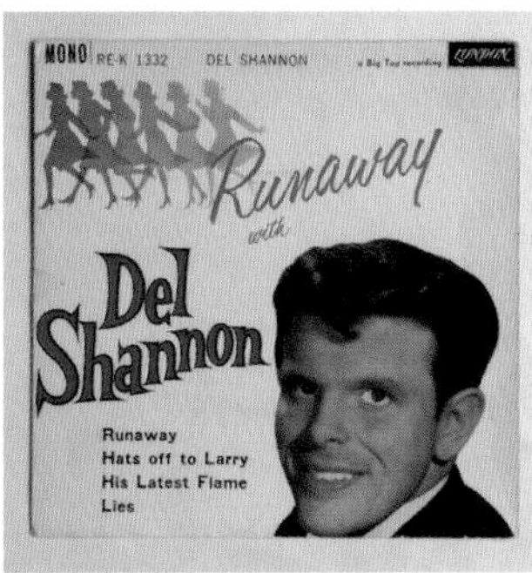

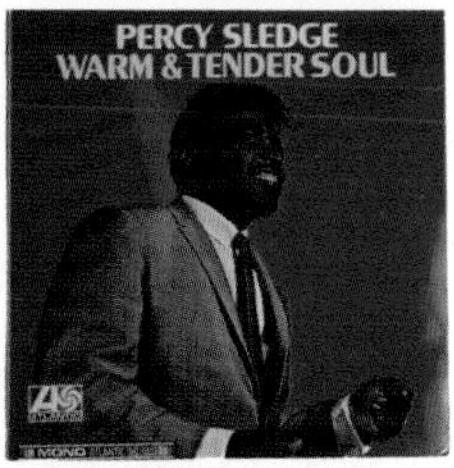

A Percy Sledge LP record, 'Warm & Tender Soul', by Atlantic, 1966, in original sleeve.
£45–50
$65–75 ⊞ BNO

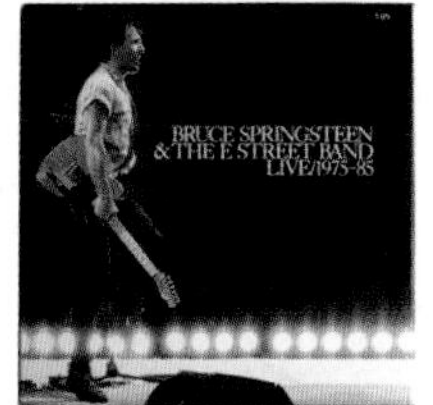

A Bruce Springsteen box of five LP records, 'Bruce Springsteen & The E Street Band Live 1975–86', by CBS, 1986, in original sleeve.
£30–35
$45–50 ⊞ BNO

A *Taxi Driver* LP record, the movie soundtrack, by Arista, 1976, in original sleeve.
£20–25
$30–35 ⊞ PR

A Temptations LP record, 'With a Lot o' Soul', by Berry Gordy, 1967, in original sleeve.
£15–18
$20–30 ⊞ BNO

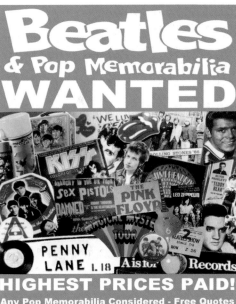

A Them LP record, 'Them Again', by Decca, 1966, in original sleeve.
£25–30
$35–45 ⊞ BNO

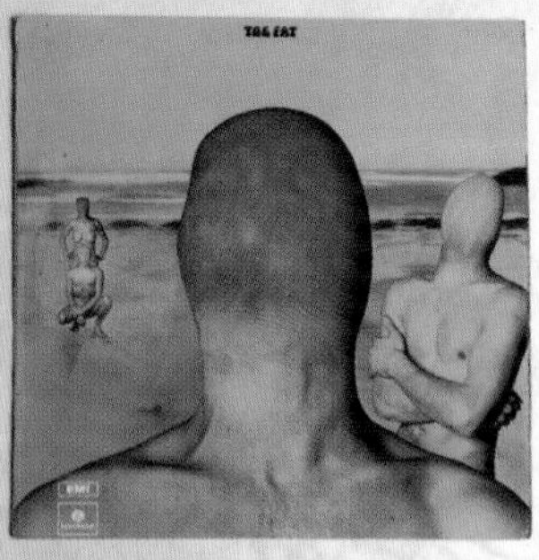

A Toe Fat LP record, 'Toe Fat', by EMI, 1970, in original sleeve.
£50–60
$75–90 ⊞ BNO

A Travelling Wilburys CD, 'The Travelling Wilburys' Vol 1, by Wilbury Records, 1988.
£50–60
$75–90 ⊞ BNO

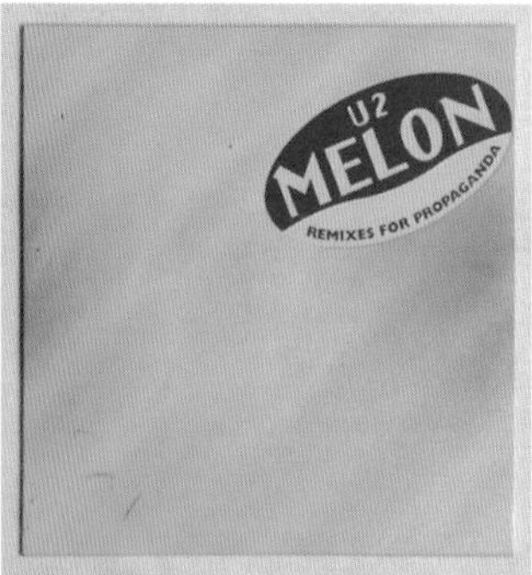

A U2 CD, 'Melon', by Island Records, produced for fan club, 1995.
£55–60
$80–90 ⊞ BNO

A Bobby Vee and the Crickets EP record, 'Bobby Vee Meets the Crickets', by EMI, 1962, in original sleeve.
£20–25
$30–35 ⊞ BNO

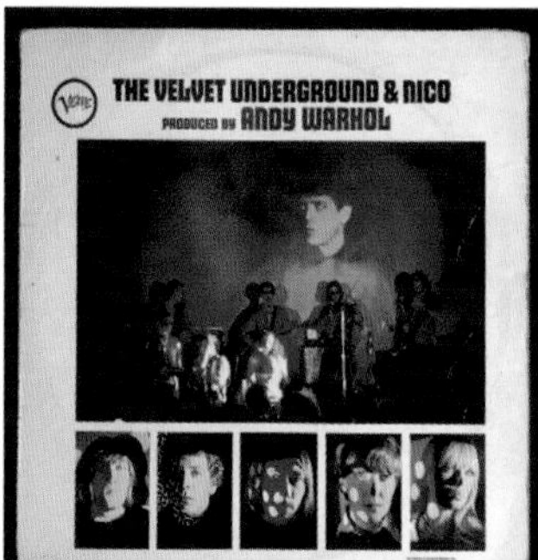

A Velvet Underground LP record, 'The Velvet Underground & Nico', by MGM, produced by Andy Warhol, 1967, in original sleeve.
£55–60
$80–90 ⊞ BNO

► A Gene Vincent EP record, 'The Crazy Beat of Gene Vincent No. 2', by Capitol, 1957, in original sleeve.
£60–70
$90–100 ⊞ BNO

A Stevie Wonder LP record, 'Down to Earth', by Tamla Motown, 1966, in original sleeve.
£50–60
$75–90 ⊞ BNO

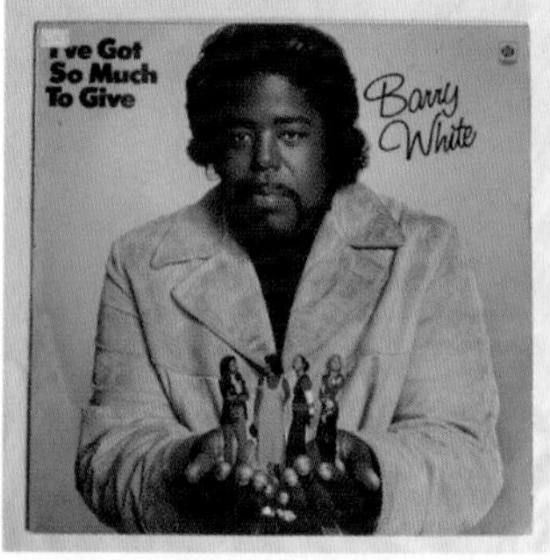

A Barry White LP record, 'I've Got So Much To Give', by Pye, 1973, in original sleeve.
£10–12
$15–18 ⊞ BNO

◄ A Johnny Zamot LP record, 'The Latin Soul of Johnny Zamot and his Latinos', by Decca, c1965, in original sleeve.
£40–50
$60–75 ⊞ TOT

Scent Bottles

A porcelain scent bottle, in the form of a lady, 18thC, 3in (7.5cm) high.
£400–450
$580–650 ⊞ LBr

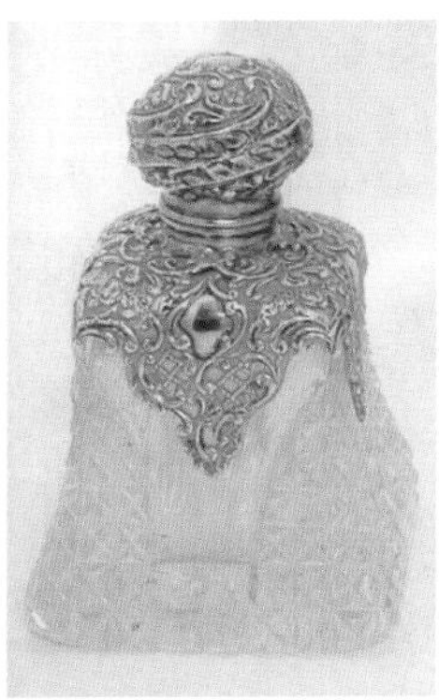

A silver-mounted cut-glass scent bottle, by H. Matthews, the mount with pierced and scroll decoration, the hinged cover with cut-glass stopper, Birmingham 1898, 4½in (11.5cm) high.
£190–220
$275–320 ⚒ B(WM)

► A Rosine Violette glass scent bottle, with gilt decoration, original label and elaborate moulded-glass scrolling stopper, 1920s, 4in (10cm) high.
£150–180
$220–260 ⊞ LBe

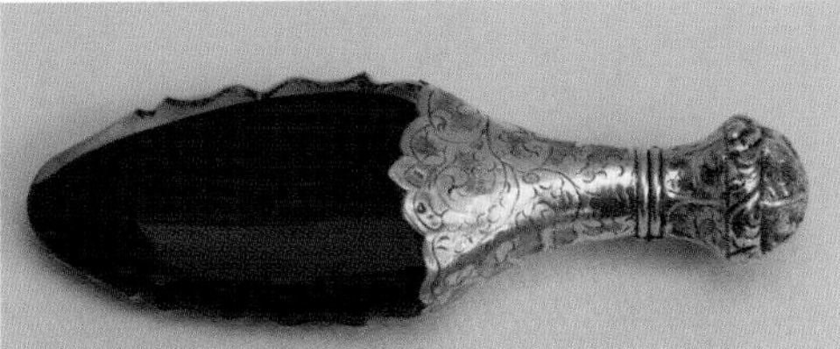

A cranberry cut-glass scent bottle, with silver collar and stopper, c1875, 3½in (9cm) long.
£350–400
$500–580 ⊞ GRI

A cut-glass double-ended scent flask, the lids with niello decoration, 19thC, 4½in (11.5cm) long.
£140–180
$200–250 ⚒ G(L)

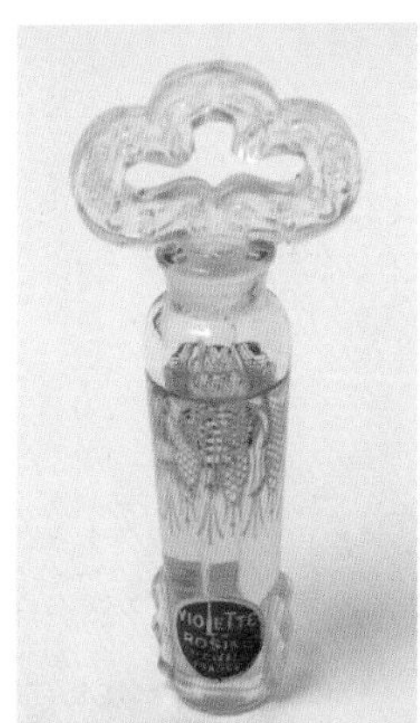

A DuBarry presentation box, with glass scent bottle, metal compact and lipstick, 1920s, box 5½in (14cm) wide.
£225–250
$325–360 ⊞ LBe

An opalescent glass scent bottle, with enamel decoration and brass fittings, c1885, 2in (5cm) long.
£80–100
$115–145 ⊞ GRI

◄ An L. T. Piver Floramye scent bottle, with faceted stopper, original label and box, c1905, 4in (10cm) high.
£40–50
$60–75 ⊞ LBr

A cardboard box for a scent bottle, modelled as a WWI shell, French, 1914–15, 6in (15cm) high.
£18–20
$25–30 ⊞ RUSS

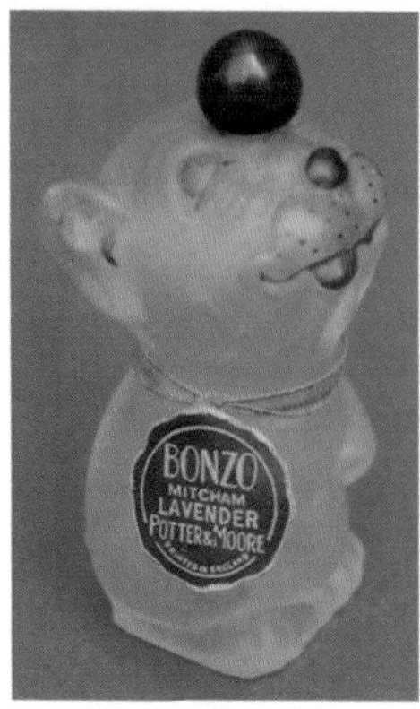

A Potter & Moore Mitcham Lavender glass scent bottle, modelled as Bonzo, the stopper forming a ball balanced on his head, with original paper tag label, c1930, 3in (7.5cm) high.
£160–180
$230–260 ⚒ BLH

◀ A Coty Paris glass scent bottle, with frosted glass stopper and original cardboard box with pull-out drawer and silk tassel, 1930s, 3½in (9cm) high.
£200–220
$300–320 ⊞ LBe

A Vigny Golli Eau de Cologne glass scent bottle, 1949–53, 6in (15cm) high.
£130–150
$190–220 ⊞ MURR

▶ A Devon Violets glass scent bottle, in the form of a poodle, with original label, 1950s, 3in (7.5cm) high.
£55–65
$80–95 ⊞ LBe

◀ A Goya 21 glass scent bottle and cologne bottle, 1950s, in original box 4 x 5in (10 x 12.5cm).
£85–95
$125–140 ⊞ LBe

A Nina Ricci L'Air du Temps glass scent bottle, engraved mark and Lalique, 12¼in (31cm) high, and a similar smaller bottle containing perfume, etched 'Nina Ricci Made in France', engraved Lalique mark, 1950s, French, 8in (20.5cm) high.
£650–750
$950–1,100 ⚒ S(O)

These famous bottles were designed for Nina Ricci in 1951 by Marc Lalique, son of the famous glass maker René Lalique. Reflecting the post-war mood, the stoppers are in the form of two doves, representing love and peace. The same design is still in production today.

An Avon Miss Lillipop plastic scent bottle, 1960s, 6in (15cm) high, in original box.
£20–25
$30–35 ⊞ LBe

An Avon glass scent bottle, in the form of a clown, 1970s, 4in (10cm) high.
£25–30
$35–45 ⊞ CoCo

◀ An Avon aftershave lotion bottle, in the shape of a guitar, 1960s–70s, 10in (25.5cm) high, in original box.
£30–35
$45–50 ⊞ LBe

Science & Technology

A gilt-brass monocular microscope, by Carpenter & Westley, London, with rack and pinion focusing, the five-drawer fitted case with a collection of eye pieces and objective lenses with accessories, in a mhogany case, 19thC, 16in (40.5cm) high.
£750–900
$1,100–1,300 ⚒ G(B)

A Victorian brass and iron scientific vacuum chamber, by Griffin, London, with a glass dome, 25in (63.5cm) high.
£100–120
$145–175 ⚒ G(L)

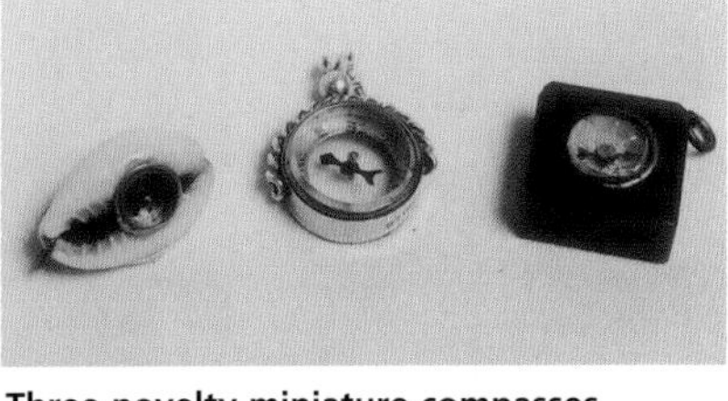

Three novelty miniature compasses, c1890, ¾in (2cm) wide.
£10–20
$15–30 each ⊞ VB

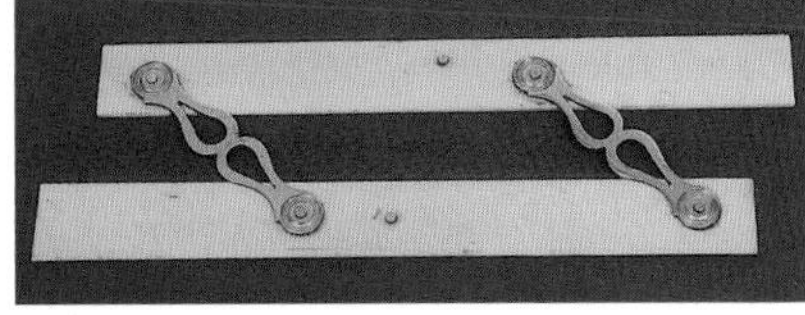

An ivory parallel rule, 1860, 6in (15cm) long.
£30–35
$45–50 ⊞ TOM

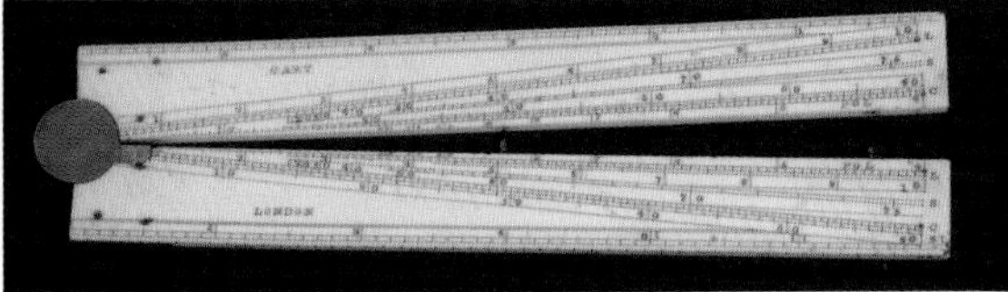

◀ **An ivory sector,** by Cary, London, c1870, 7in (18cm) long.
£60–70
$90–100 ⊞ ETO

A lacquered-brass monocular microscope, by Maw & Son & Thompson, London, c1880, 12in (30.5cm) high, in a mahogany case.
£250–285
$360–400 ⊞ WAC

A lacquered-brass marine aneroid barometer and thermometer, by M. Pillischer, London, c1880, 7in (18cm) high, in original weighted case.
£400–450
$580–650 ⊞ WAC

◀ **A metal Williams Cheque Punch,** by Peter Hooker, London, with gilt detailing, 1890, 7¾in (19.5cm) wide.
£50–60
$75–90 ⚒ Bri

A surveyor's oxidised brass compass and clinometer, by Keufel & Esser, New York, American, c1890, in a wooden case 4in (10cm) square.
£225–250
$330–360 ⊞ WAC

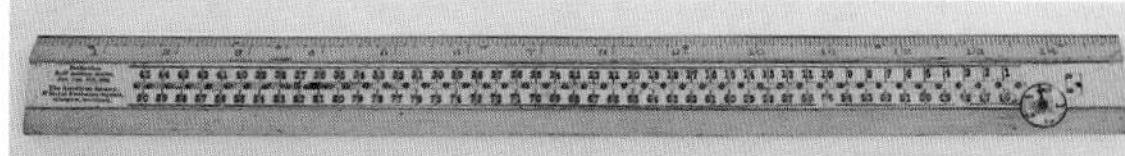

The Perfection self-adding ruler, by The American Agency, Glasgow, boxwood and ivorine, patented 1895, 15in (38cm) long.
£80–100
$115–145 ⊞ TOM

A brass clinometer, by Short & Mason, London, marked and dated 1908, 4in (10cm) diam, in a leather case.
£70–80
$100–115 ⊞ WAC

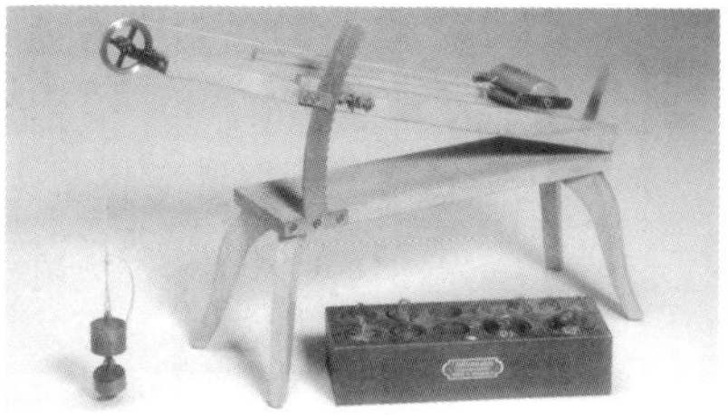

A cherrywood and brass inclined plane demonstrator, by Steflitscheck, with adjustable plane, car, pulley and set of 12 hooked weights, the arc notched for 0–18°, Austrian, c1900, 19in (48.5cm) wide.
£140–160
$200–230 ⚒ SK(B)

A Negretti & Zambra Scientific Instruments catalogue, 1900, 9 x 6in (23 x 15cm).
£250–300
$360–440 ⊞ RTW

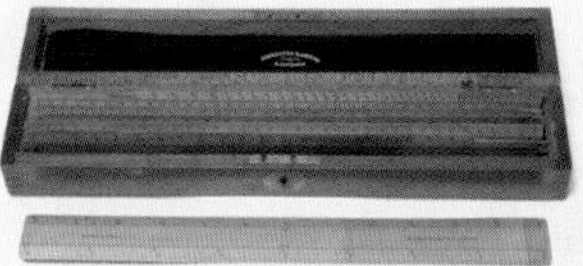

A set of rules, by Negretti & Zambra, London, c1910, in a mahogany case, 12in (30.5cm) long.
£90–100
$130–145 ⊞ WAC

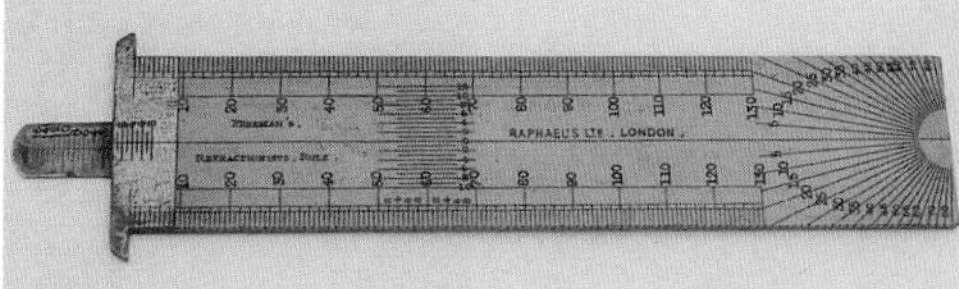

A boxwood Freeman's refractionist's rule, by Raphael's, London, 1910–20, 7in (18cm) long.
£60–70
$90–100 ⊞ TOM

A liquid-filled brass wrist compass, with leather strap and initials WBT, possibly those of instrument maker James White, pattern used both in WWI and WWII, 3in (7.5cm) diam.
£150–175
$220–250 ⊞ WAC

▶ A brass and steel binocular periscope, signed Goerz, Berlin, No. 7754, German, 1914–18, 15in (38cm) long.
£160–190
$230–275 ⚒ G(L)

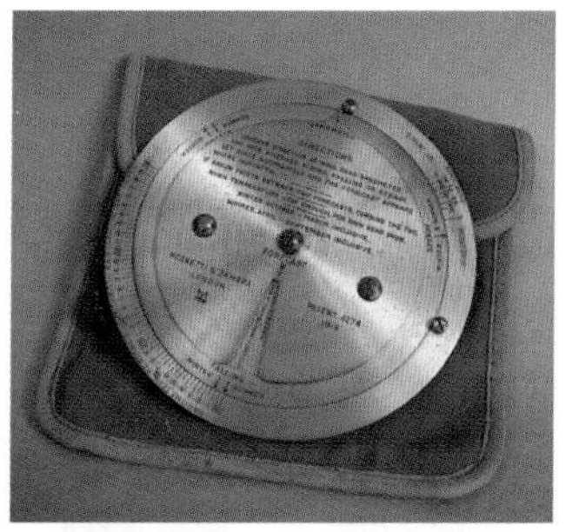

A lacquered brass patent weather forecasting dial, by Negretti & Zambra, patent No. 8276, to be used in conjuction with a barometer, inscribed with scales and instructions, dated 1915, 4¾in (12cm) diam, with original cloth pouch.
£160–190
$230–275 SWO

A brass microscope, by Husbands & Clarke, Bristol, with extra lens, accessories and slides, c1915, 14in (35.5cm) high, in a fitted wooden box.
£100–120
$145–175 G(L)

An oak barograph, by John Barker & Co, Kensington, with base drawer, c1915, 14in (35.5cm) wide.
£350–380
$500–560 G(L)

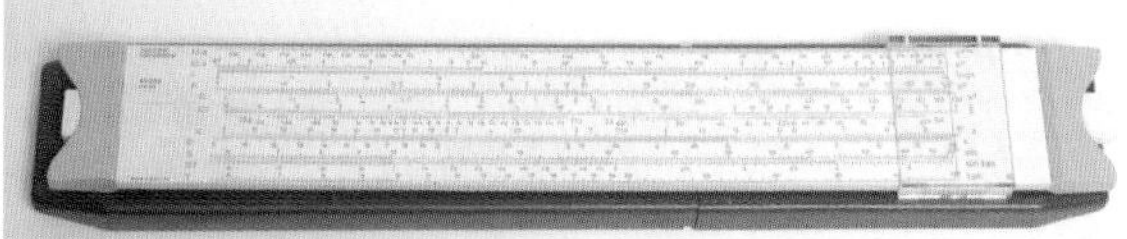

A plastic slide rule, by Thornton, c1920, 14in (35.5cm) long, in a plastic case.
£20–25
$30–35 ⊞ ETO

A sight level, by Stanley, London, 1930, 16in (40.5cm) wide.
£160–180
$230–260 ⊞ BoC

► **A Friez Standard Weather Instruments catalogue,** No. 5, with price list and original bookmark, 1937, 11 x 9in (28 x 23cm).
£90–100
$130–145
⊞ RTW

A surveyor's brass compass, by Stanley, 1930s, 3in (7.5cm) diam.
£100–120
$145–175 ⊞ GAC

A Negretti & Zambra Meteorological Instruments catalogue, 1950, 10 x 8in (25.5 x 20.5cm).
£150–180
$220–250 ⊞ RTW

A Curta calculator, German, early 1950s, 4in (10cm) high.
£225–275
$330–400 ⊞ TOM

A glass globe, with internal light, German, 1950s, 15in (38cm) high.
£350–400
$500–580 ⊞ MARK

A Sinclair ZX Spectrum, with printer, mid-1980s, 20in (51cm) wide.
£20–25
$30–35 ⊞ CGX

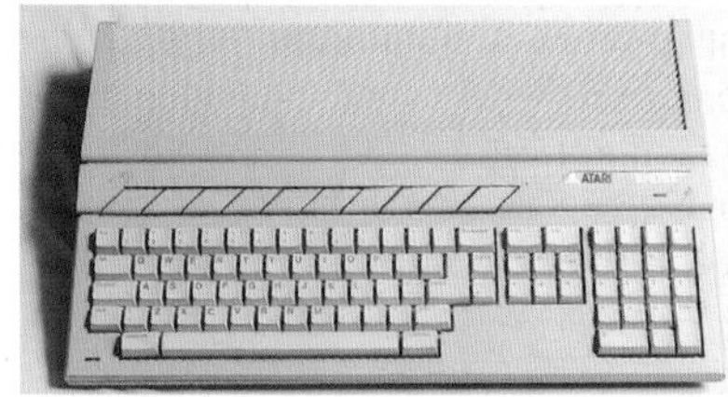

► An Atari 1040ST computer, 1988, 18in (45.5cm) wide.
£80–100
$115–145 ⊞ MEx

Binoculars & Optical Equipment

A pair of mother-of-pearl opera glasses, 19thC, 4in (10cm) wide, with original case.
£90–100
$130–145 ⊞ BrL

► Two binocular charms, 19thC, wooden charm ⅜in (1cm) high, metal charm ¼in (5mm) high.
Wood £25–30
$35–45
Metal £35–45
$50–65 ⊞ VB

◄ A pair of binoculars, by Goetz, Berlin, German, 1912, 4in (10cm) wide, with original leather case.
£40–45
$60–65 ⊞ COB

A pair of Victorian ivory and gilt opera glasses, 4in (10cm) wide, with original leather case.
£90–110
$130–160 SWO

Insurance values

Always insure your valuable collectables for the cost of replacing them with similar items, regardless of the original price paid. Both dealers and auctioneers can provide a valuation service for a fee.

A pair of Bakelite binoculars, c1930, 4in (10cm) wide, with original leather case.
£50–60
$75–90 ⊞ LaF

Sci-Fi, Film & TV

This section is devoted to memorabilia and toys relating to science fiction, film and TV. Interest in science fiction took off like a rocket from the late 1930s, pioneered by American comics. In June 1938 the No. 1 issue of *Action Comics* introduced Superman, 'The Physical Marvel who had sworn to devote his existence to helping those in need.' The following year saw the birth of *Marvel* comics, launch pad of countless superheroes and the first appearance of Batman in *Detective Comics* (No. 27). Britain had to wait till after WWII for its own space-age crusader, Dan Dare, 'Pilot of the future,' who emerged in *Eagle* No. 1 in 1950 and, like his American rivals, began to generate his own merchandise.

In the ensuing decade toys were inspired both by science fiction and real life space exploration. Tinplate robots, guns and spacecraft were produced in Japan predominantly for the US market, and examples in good condition can command high prices today. The 1960s saw a host of sci-fi-inspired children's TV programmes. American classics range from ABC's high camp interpretation of *Batman* to NCB's *Star Trek*, both premiered in 1966, although it wasn't until it was repeated in the 1970s that *Star Trek* gained its cult status and an international audience of 'Trekkies'. UK favourites include *Dr Who* (1963) and the revolutionary 'supermarionation' puppet series created by Gerry Anderson, such as *Joe 90* (1968), *Stingray* (1964), *Captain Scarlet* (1967) and, most famously, *Thunderbirds* (1965) which enjoyed a huge revival in the 1990s.

Toy companies soon recognized the potential of licensing. The British firm Corgi specialized in film- and TV-related diecasts, producing many famous and now collectable vehicles including the Batmobile, the Saint's Volvo, and a whole series of James Bond cars, beginning in 1965 with James Bond's Aston Martin DB5, which went on to sell nearly three million models. Such figures pale into insignificance, however, next to the vast amount of material created for the *Star Wars* trilogy. When the words 'Long ago in a galaxy far, far away' first appeared on US movie screens on May 25 1977 a legend was born, and by the mid-1980s US manufacturers Kenner and MPC had sold around 300 million toys worldwide. *Star Wars* remains one of the most popular sci-fi collectables.

The following section illustrates objects from the 1950s to the present day, featuring recent cult successes such as *Buffy the Vampire Slayer* alongside longer established classics. As well as toys and mass produced ephemera, it also includes film memorabilia and autographs.

Alien, original X-rated censor notice, 1979, 12 x 14in (30.5 x 35.5cm), framed and glazed.
£120–140
$175–200 CO

► ***Babylon 5,*** set of 100 trade cards, 1999, 3½ x 2½in, (9 x 6.5cm).
£125–150
$180–220
SSF

Alien Resurrection, Call figure, reissue of Hasbro Signature series, 1997, 7in (18cm) high, in original box.
£18–20
$25–30 SSF

Items in the Sci-Fi, Film & TV section have been arranged in alphabetical order according to character, film or TV series.

The A-Team, Murdock action figure, by Galoob, with accessories, 1983, 13in (33cm) high, in original packaging.
£35–40
$50–60 CTO

Batman, set of 55 bubble gum cards, by ABC, American, 1966, 3 x 2in (7.5 x 5cm).
£500–600
$720–870 ⊞ SSF

Cross Reference

See Cigarette & Trade Cards (pages 155–158), Comics & Annuals (pages 159–162) & Toys (pages 402–418)

Batman and Robin, plastic bagatelle pinball game, 1960s, 22in (56cm) high.
£40–45
$60–65 ⊞ HarC

Batman, a Riddler-style three-piece suit, comprising a double-breasted jacket, waistcoat and trousers, 1960s.
£190–220
$275–320 ⚒ CO

Batman, comic by DC, No. 194, damaged, 1967, 10 x 7in (25.5 x 18cm).
£2–4
$5–7 ⊞ CoC

Batman and Robin, a still signed by George Clooney and Chris O'Donnell, 1997, 8 x 10in (20.5 x 25.5cm).
£60–75
$90–110 ⚒ CO

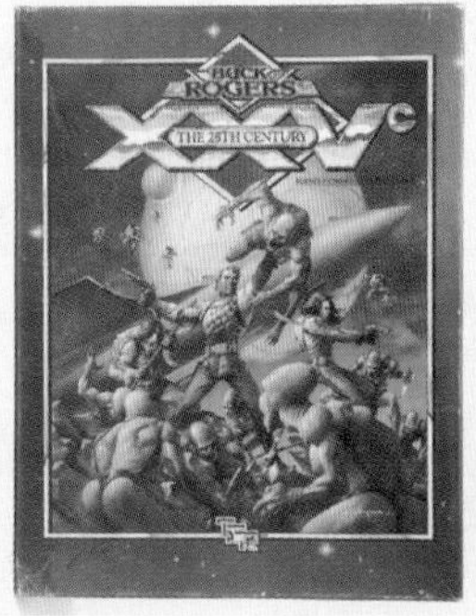

Buck Rogers in the 25th Century, role play game by TSR, American, 1990, 12 x 9in (30.5 x 23cm).
£15–20
$20–30 ⊞ SSF

Buffy the Vampire Slayer, Angelus Vampire, card from *Buffy the Vampire Slayer* card game, 2002, 3½ x 2½in (9 x 6.5cm).
£12–15
$17–20 ⊞ NOS

Doctor Who, Tardis play-house tent, by Dekker Toys, 1982, 48in 122cm) high.
£90–100
$130–145 ⊞ WHO

◄ ***Dan Dare,*** Planet Gun, by J. & L. Randell, with three spinning missiles and instructions, box worn, 1953.
£100–120
$145–175
⚒ CBP

► ***Forbidden Planet,*** C-57D Starcruiser model kit, reissue, 2001, 24in (61cm) long.
£45–50
$65–75 ⊞ SSF

Golden Heroes, super heroes role-playing game, by Games Workshop, 1984, 12 x 9in (30.5 x 23cm).
£23–25
$30–35 ⊞ SSF

James Bond, Aston Martin DB5, No. 261, with red interior and wire wheels, Bond at wheel and passenger, box contains pictorial inner car, special instructions, envelope with spare bandit and adhesive badge, 1965–69, 4in (10cm) long.
£240–280
$350–400 ⚒ B(Ch)

◄ ***James Bond,*** Toyota 2000GT, No. 336, by Corgi Toys, with two figures, in a pictorial box with inner card and unopened special instructions, 1967–69, 4in (10cm) long.
£200–250
$300–350 ⚒ B(Ch)

James Bond, Aston Martin, No. 271, by Corgi Toys, with red interior and gold bumpers and grille, Bond driving and two sealed bandits, inner card, 1:36 window tag, 1978, 4in (10cm) long.
£120–140
$175–200 ⚒ B(Ch)

Joe 90, set of 50 trade cards, by Primrose Confectionery, 1968, 1¾ x 2¾in (4.5 x 7cm).
£60–70
$90–100 ⊞ SSF

James Bond, film prop radioactive canister from the missile silo in *The World is Not Enough*, 1999, 15in (38cm) high.
£130–150
$200–220 ⊞ CoC

► ***Judge Dredd,*** a Judge Hunter gun, 1995, 46in (117cm) long.
£1,000–1,200
$1,500–1,750 ⚒ CO

James Bond, Goldfinger's Rolls-Royce set, by Solido, with Oddjob and Goldfinger, No. 008 of a limited edition of 100, with gold outer tube, c1965.
£500–550
$720–800 ⚒ VEC

James Bond, Aston Martin DB5, No. 270, by Corgi Toys, tyre slashers, unopened secret instruction pack, 1968–76, 4in (10cm) long.
£360–400
$500–580 ⚒ VEC

► ***James Bond,*** set of 270, 007 Volume 3 trade cards, by Inkworks, 1997, 3½ x 2½in (9 x 6.5cm).
£4–6
$6–8 ⊞ SSF

Joe 90, Joe's car, No. 102, by Dinky Toys, 1960s, 7in (18cm) long.
£150–175
$225–255 ⊞ GTM

King Kong, a glow-in-the-dark plastic assembly kit, by Aurora, 1960, 10in (25.5cm) square.
£180–200
$260–300 ⊞ SSF

Land of the Giants, set of 55 bubble gum cards, 1968, 3 x 2in (7.5 x 5cm).
£500–600
$720–870 ⊞ SSF

Lost in Space, a plastic lunchbox, with metal clasps, 1998, 9in (23cm) wide.
£25–30
$35–45 ⊞ SSF

The Man from U.N.C.L.E. card game photograph

The Man from U.N.C.L.E., card game, by Milton Bradley Co, American, 1960s, 6 x 10in (15 x 25.5cm).
£40–50
$60–75 ⊞ HAL

Mars Attacks!, set of 72 wide vision trade cards, by Topps, 1998, 4½ x 2½in (11.5 x 6.5cm).
£8–10
$12–15 ⊞ SSF

Masters of the Universe

Created by Mattel in 1981, Masters of the Universe was a popular and significant toy. They were the first major series of figures to incorporate action features (transforming, moving parts). Also in 1983, the Federal Communications Commission in the USA lifted a 1969 law that prohibited children's television programmes being based on children's toys. Mattel and Filmation Associates then produced the animated series *He-Man and the Masters of the Universe* – effectively an elongated advertisement – establishing a trend for product-inspired kids' TV shows, in which the merchandise is the motivating and most profitable factor.

Masters of the Universe, plastic Skeletor Lord of Destruction action figure, by Mattel, 1983, 5in (12.5cm) high, on original card.
£70–80
$100–115 ⊞ OW

Masters of the Universe, The Evil Horde Slime Pit, by Mattel, 1985, 11 x 16in (28 x 40.5cm).
£45–50
$65–75 ⊞ OW

► **Nightmare Before Christmas,** Santa Jack figure, by Jun Planning, limited edition of 800, American, 1998, 48in (122cm) high.
£80–90
$115–130 ⚒ CBP

Planet of the Apes, Taylor figure, collector's edition, Hasbro signature series, 1999, 12in (30.5cm) high.
£25–30
$35–45 ⊞ SSF

The Saint, Volvo P.1800, No. 258, by Corgi Toys, finished in white with red interior, black Saint logo to bonnet, 1965–68, 4in (10cm) long, boxed.
£140–160
$200–230 ⚒ B(Ch)

▶ ***Six Million Dollar Man,*** figure, by General Mills, Hong Kong, 1970s, 13in (33cm) high.
£35–40
$50–60 ⊞ HAL

Space 1999, a plastic bagatelle pinball game, c1970, 22in (56cm) high.
£25–30
$35–45 ⊞ HarC

▶ ***Space 1999,*** trade box of bubble gum cards, 1970s, 4 x 8in (20 x 20.5cm).
£60–70
$90–100 ⊞ HAL

◀ ***Space Precinct,*** figure of Lieutenant Brogan, 1994, in original packaging, 9 x 6in (23 x 15cm).
£4–5
$5–7 ⊞ CTO

Star Fleet, Dia-X robot, produced for the Japanese market, 1981, 7 x 6in (18 x 15cm).
£250–300
$350–450 ⊞ OW

Star Trek, A & BC, set of 55 bubble gum cards, 1969, 2 x 3in (5 x 7.5cm).
£700–800
$1,000–1,150 ⊞ SSF

Star Trek, Dr McCoy 'Bones' action figure, by Mego, American, 1974, on original card, 9 x 8in (23 x 20.5cm) carded.
£125–150
$180–220 ⊞ OW

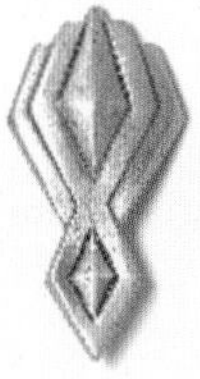

Star Trek, three Worfs medals from *Star Trek the Next Generation* TV series, 1992–93, 4in (10cm) high.
£300–350
$450–500 each ⊞ OW

▶ ***Star Trek,*** Klingon action figure, by Mego, American, 1974, 8in (20.5cm) high.
£35–40
$50–60 ⊞ OW

Star Trek The Next Generation, phaser electronic toy, by Playmates, 1993, 10in (25.5cm) long, boxed.
£40–45
$60–65 ⊞ OW

Star Trek, USS Voyager Star Ship, by Playmates, 1995, 17in (43cm) long, boxed.
£250–300
$350–450 ⊞ OW

Star Trek, General Chang action figure, by Playmates, unopened, 1995, on original card, 10 x 8in (25.5 x 20.5cm).
£25–30
$35–45 ⊞ OW

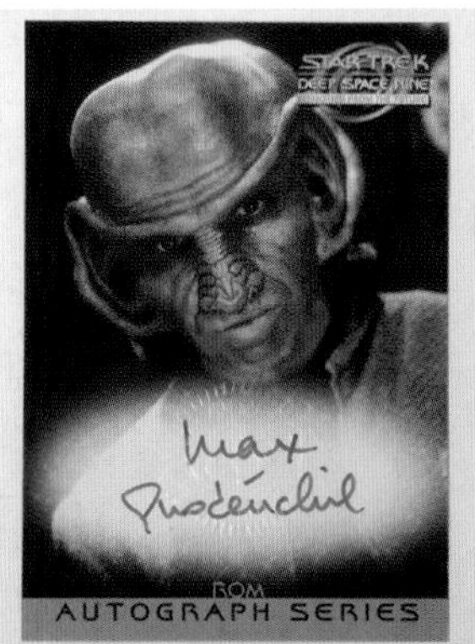

Star Trek, Max Grodenchik as Rom trading card, from Deep Space Nine Autograph Series, 1999, 4 x 2½in (10 x 6.5cm).
£30–40
$45–60 ⊞ SSF

Star Wars, Escape from Death Star board game, by Palitoy, 1977, 9 x 18in (22 x 45.5cm).
£30–35
$45–50 ⊞ SSF

► ***Star Wars,*** the first licensed poster of Luke Skywalker, by Howard Chaykin for World Con, 1976, 29 x 20in (73.5 x 51cm).
£1,300–1,500
$2,000–2,200 ⊞ OW

► ***Star Wars,*** R2D2 and C3PO figures, 1977, larger 4in (10cm) high.
£5–10
$8–15 each ⊞ SSF

Star Wars, C3PO figure, No. 12BK by Palitoy, first issue British release, 1977, on original card, 9 x 6in (23 x 15cm).
£250–300
$350–450 ⊞ OW

Star Wars, Land Speeder, by Palitoy, British, 1977, 8 x 10in (20.5 x 25.5cm), boxed.
£150–200
$220–300 ⊞ OW
The US version of this toy, made by Kenner, has a lower price range, £60–90 ($90–130), because more were produced.

◄ ***Star Wars,*** Boba Fett action figure, 1979, 12in (30.5cm) high, boxed.
£500–550
$720–800 ⊞ OW
This is a very rare figure to find mint and boxed, hence its high value.

Star Wars, a signed photograph of Dave Prower as Darth Vader, c1980, 10 x 8in (25.5 x 20.5cm).
£35–40
$50–60 ⊞ CoC

Star Wars, play mat, by Recticel Sutcliffe, 1983, 24 x 38in (61 x 96.5cm).
£200–250
$300–350 ⊞ SSF

Star Wars, *Return of the Jedi* battery-operated Millennium Falcon Vehicle, by Palitoy, 1983, 16 x 22in (40.5 x 56cm), boxed.
£125–150
$180–220 ⊞ OW

Star Wars figures

Star Wars not only took film merchandising to a new galactic stratosphere but also revolutionized the size of action figures. Previously 12in (30.5cm) figures had been the norm, but Kenner wanted figures to fit into spacecraft and realized that this measurement would entail vehicles that were enormous and prohibitively expensive. In a meeting, President Bernie Looms is reported to have held thumb and forefinger apart saying 'how about that big?' A designer measured the gap, and 3in (7.5cm) became the standard size for Luke Skywalker, with other figures and vehicles scaled to match.

Prices for *Star Wars* figures vary according to rarity and packaging. Objects will always be worth more if they are mint and carded. Among the most collectable examples are original carded figures from the first *Star Wars* film and the final set of action figures (with packaging logo *The Power of the Force*) produced in the mid-1980s after the release of *Return of the Jedi* (1983).

Star Wars, Chewbacca action figure, from *Return of the Jedi*, by Kenner, American, 1983, 4in (10cm) high, carded.
£80–100
$115–145 ⊞ SSF

Star Wars, C3PO and biker scout action figures, from *Return of the Jedi*, by Kenner, American, 1983, 4in (10cm) high, carded.
£80–100
$115–145 each ⊞ SSF

Star Wars, Luke Skywalker in battle poncho action figure, from *Return of the Jedi*, 1983, 4in (10cm) high, on a tri-logo card.
£140–160
$200–230 ⊞ SSF

Star Wars, *The Power of the Force* Lando Calrissian figure and special collectors' coin, by Kenner, American, 1984, on original card, 9 x 6in (23 x 15cm).
£85–100
$125–145 ⊞ OW

◄ ***Star Wars,*** Princess Leia action figure, from *Return of the Jedi*, by Hasbro Toys, 1984, 4in (10cm) high.
£12–15
$15–20 ⊞ CoC

Star Wars, Darth Vader costume set, by Acamas Toys, 1983, in original box.
£40–50
$60–75 ⊞ CTO

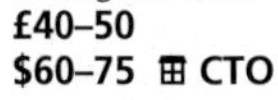

Star Wars, a card signed by Ian McDiarmid as Senator Palpatine, 2001, 2¾ x 3½in (6.5 x 9.5cm).
£350–400
$500–580 ⊞ SSF

Star Wars, set of 120 wide-screen chase cards, 1995, 2½ x 5in (6.5 x 12.5cm).
£65–75
$100–110 ⊞ SSF

Star Wars, signed photograph of Bossk and Boba Fett, 2001, 8 x 10in (20.5 x 25.5cm).
£65–75
$100–110 ⊞ SSF

► ***Star Wars,*** set of 12 Evolution cards, 2001, 3½ x 2½in (9 x 6.5cm).
£18–20
$25–30 ⊞ SSF

◄ ***Star Wars,*** Episode I, *The Phantom Menace*, Kentucky Fried Chicken plastic life-size advertising figure of Yoda, 1999, 56in (142cm) high.
£1,300–1,500
$2,000–2,200 ⊞ WAm

Star Wars, *Return of the Jedi* replica Skywalker light sabre, by Lucas Films, limited edition of 2,500, 2002, 11in (28cm) long.
£250–300
$350–450 ⊞ OW

► ***Superman,*** plastic bagatelle pinball machine, c1970, 22in (56cm) high.
£40–45
$60–65 ⊞ HarC

Star Wars, plastic model of R2D2, with holographic Princess Leia, 1999, on original card, 9 x 6in (23 x 15cm), unopened.
£30–35
$45–50 ⊞ NOS
This toy was taken off the market due to small parts and is therefore rare.

Thunderbirds, battery-operated plastic spaceship, by JR21 Toys, Hong Kong, 1960s, 11in (28cm) wide.
£225–250
$325–360 ⊞ HAL

► ***Thunderbirds,*** original Virgil Tracy puppet head on a replica body, 1960s, 21in (53.5cm) high.
£8,000–9,000
$11,500–13,000 ⊞ CO
This Virgil puppet is very rare as it is the last surviving original head complete with the old mechanism inside. The body and costume have been specially made to go with the head by Chris King, who is one of the top professional model-makers in Europe. Virgil was the pilot of Thunderbird 2 and this head is from the 1965–66 episodes.

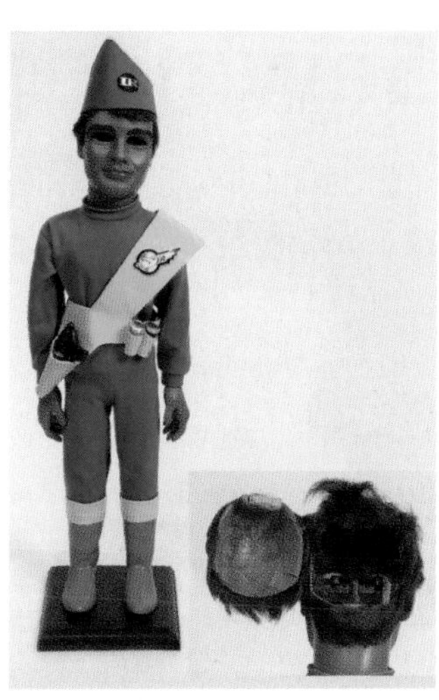

Robots & Space Vehicles

◄ **A tinplate and plastic battery-operated space capsule,** by S.H., Japanese, c1960, 15in (38cm) high.
£80–100
$115–145 ⊞ GTM

A tinplate battery-operated Rotate-O-Matic Super Astronaut robot, c1960, 12in (30.5cm) high.
£200–225
$300–325 ⊞ GTM

A tinplate battery-operated Sonicon rocket, Japanese, c1960, 13in (33cm) long.
£250–300
$350–450 ⊞ HAL

LOCATE THE SOURCE
The source of each illustration in Miller's can be found by checking the code letters below each caption with the Key to Illustrations, pages 443–451.

◄ **A plastic battery-operated robot,** 1960s, 10in (25.5cm) high.
£55–65
$80–100 ⊞ UCO

A Dinky Toys UFO Interceptor, No. 351, 1978, 9in (23cm) long.
£140–160
$200–230 ⊞ SSF

Sewing

A bone lace bobbin, decorated with stained patterns, mid-19thC, 4½in (11.5cm) long.
£15–20
$20–30 ⊞ HL

Bobbins were used for lace-making. Produced from a number of materials including wood, ivory and bone, they were variously decorated and terminated with glass beads. The different colours of the beads and the individual design of the bobbin enabled the lacemaker to identify which particular thread she was working on.

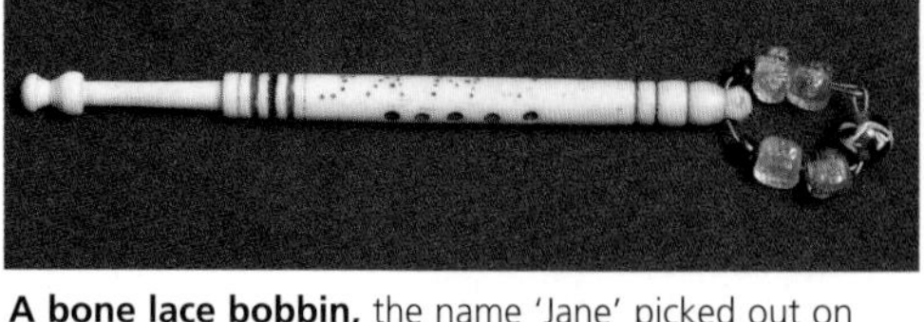

A bone lace bobbin, the name 'Jane' picked out on the shaft, mid-19thC, 4½in (11.5cm) long.
£20–25
$30–35 ⊞ HL

A wood and brass lace bobbin, mid-19thC, 4½in (11.5cm) long.
£15–20
$20–30 ⊞ HL

A wooden Downton lace bobbin, mid-19thC, 3in (7.5cm) long.
£20–25
$30–35 ⊞ HL

A Wilcox & Gibbs sewing machine, 1880, 12in (30.5cm) long.
£25–35
$35–50 ⚒ TAY

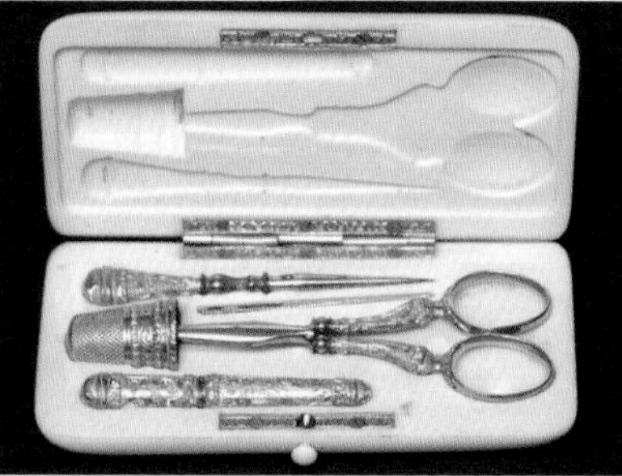

A gold and ivory *nécessaire*, French, 19thC, 4½in (11.5cm) long.
£650–750
$950–1,100 ⊞ DHA

A silver thimble, 1898, 1in (2.5cm) high.
£35–40
$50–60 ⊞ EXC

A Wanzer sewing machine, with cast-iron base, c1905, 12in (30.5cm) long.
£125–150
$180–220 ⊞ JUN

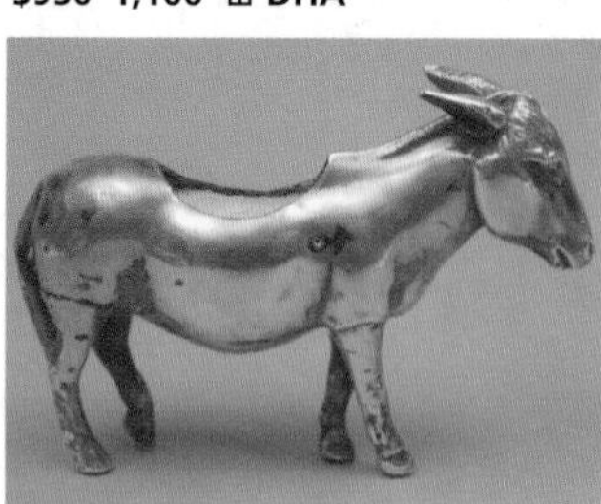

A silver novelty pincushion, modelled as a donkey, Birmingham 1905, 3in (7.5cm) long.
£260–310
$380–450 ⚒ G(L)

► A silver novelty pincushion, modelled as a hedgehog, Birmingham 1911, 2¼in (5.5cm) long.
£220–260
$320–380 ⚒ G(L)

Two silver novelty pincushions, modelled as hatching chicks, Chester 1910, largest 1¼in (3cm) long.
£260–300
$380–440 ⚒ G(L)

A china doll pincushion, with original velvet base, 1920, 4½in (11.5cm) high.
£55–65
$80–100 ⊞ VB

A Little Comfort child's hand-operated sewing machine, c1920, 7in (18cm) high.
£90–110
$130–160 ⚒ DuM

A tin novelty tape measure, modelled as a car, French, 1920s, 6in (15cm) long.
£40–50
$60–75 ⊞ JUN

A Kewpie pincushion doll, Continental, 1920s, 3in (7.5cm) high.
£175–200
$250–300 ⊞ MURR

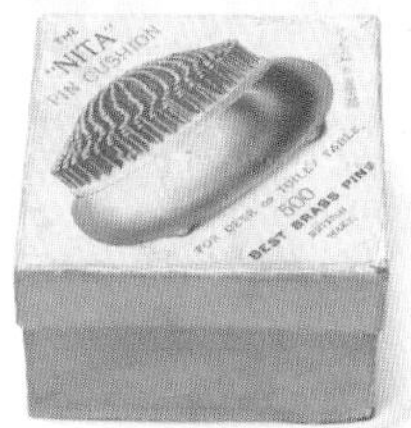

A Nita pincushion, 1920s, 3¼in (8.5cm) diam.
£8–10
$12–15 ⊞ RTT

◀ **A silver thimble,** 1924, 1in (2.5cm) high.
£34–38
$50–60 ⊞ EXC

◀ **A needle book,** the cover depicting an ocean liner, 1930s, 4 x 6in (10 x 15cm).
£20–25
$30–35 ⊞ COB

Sewing Simplified, by Singer, 1930s, 9 x 6¼in (23 x 16cm).
£7–8
$10–12 ⊞ RTT

Needlewoman and Needlecraft, 1940s, 9 x 5in (23 x 12.5cm).
£1–2
$2–4 ⊞ MRW

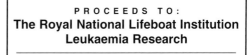

Shipping

A picture of a sailing ship in a lifebelt frame, c1900, 9in (23cm) diam.
£70–80
$100–115 ⊞ COB

A White Star Line china bowl, by Stonier, 1910–20, 12in (30.5cm) wide.
£700–800
$1,000–1,200 ⊞ MURR

► A watch case, recovered from the cargo of RMS *Lusitania*, c1915, 2in (5cm) diam.
£175–200
$250–300 ⊞ COB

A White Star Line silver-plated napkin ring, by Elkington, c1920, 2in (5cm) diam.
£35–40
$50–60 ⊞ CRN

A *Mauretania* lapel pin, 1908, ¾in (2cm) diam.
£15–20
$20–30 ⊞ COB

The *Mauretania*

The *Mauretania* (1907) was one of Cunard's most famous liners. At 31,938 tonnes, she was the largest ship in the world and held the speed record for crossing the Atlantic (four days, ten hours, 51 minutes at an average speed of 26.06 knots) for a remarkable 22 years.

A brass ship's clock, stamped 'Made for Royal Navy, London, 1920', dial 5¾in (14.5cm) diam.
£150–180
$220–260 ⚒ SWO

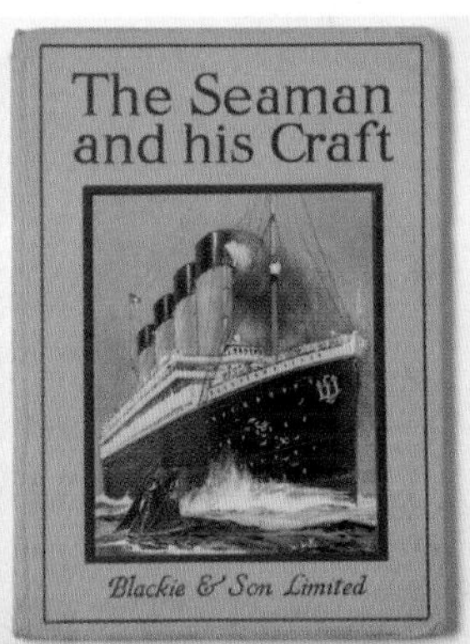

The Seaman and his Craft, published by Blackie & Son, a child's maritime book, 1910, 7 x 5in (18 x 12.5cm).
£25–30
$35–45 ⊞ COB

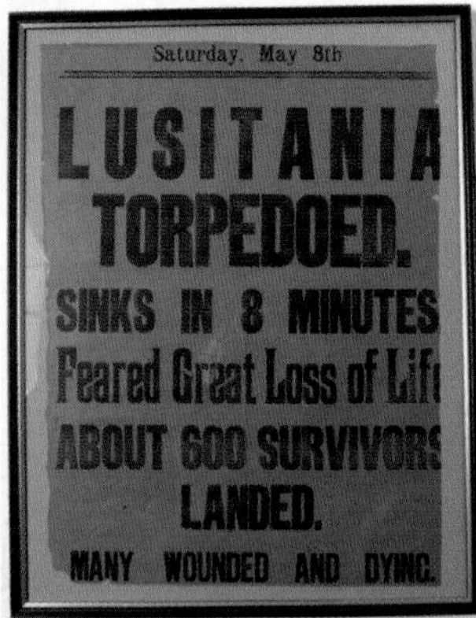

A '*Lusitania* Torpedoed' news poster, dated 8 May 1915, 24 x 18in (61 x 45.5cm).
£450–500
$650–720 ⊞ COB

Lusitania

The Cunard liner *Lusitania* was torpedoed by a German U-boat off the south coast of Ireland on 7 May 1915. She sank in 20 minutes with the loss of 1,198 lives; the millionaire Alfred Vanderbilt was among the 124 Americans who died. The tragedy influenced the USA in their decision to enter WWI in April 1917.

A brass ship's bell, inscribed '*Dilwara*, 1930, London', 8in (20.5cm) high.
£300–350
$450–720 ⊞ COB

A *Queen Mary* jigsaw puzzle, by Chad Valley, 1930s, 10 x 11in (25.5 x 28cm).
£55–65
$80–95 ⊞ MURR

Queen Mary

The White Star liner *Queen Mary* was launched in 1934. From 1938 she held the Blue Riband of the Atlantic for the fastest Atlantic round trip. Like her companion ship the *Queen Elizabeth* (1938), she was used as a troopship during WWII ferrying up to 15,000 soldiers. She again served as a luxury liner in peacetime. Sold by Cunard in 1967, she was then moored at Long Beach, California as a floating museum and hotel.

Two Cunard postcards, 1936 and 1947.
£5–8
$10–15 each ⊞ COB

A Crawford's Biscuits tin, depicting RMS *Queen Mary*, with original label, 1930s, 10in (25.5cm) square.
£55–65
$80–95 ⊞ MURR

An SS *Normandie* biscuit tin, French, 1935, 7in (18cm) wide.
£35–40
$50–60 ⊞ HUX

Normandie

Launched in 1935, the French liner *Normandie* was fitted out by the leading craftsmen of the day (lighting by Lalique, furniture by Jules Leleu, ironwork by Raymond Subes, etc). A floating monument of Art Deco style, during WWII the liner was destroyed by fire in New York. Originally costing around £33 million ($48m), the *Normandie* was sold for scrap by the US Navy for only £111,500 ($161,680).

An advertisement for SS *Normandie*, 1930s, 12 x 9in (30.5 x 23cm).
£15–20
$20–30 ⊞ COB

◄ A Mason's Ironstone Seaman's Hospital cup and saucer, 1930s, cup 2¼in (5.5cm) high.
£15–20
$20–30 ⊞ HUX

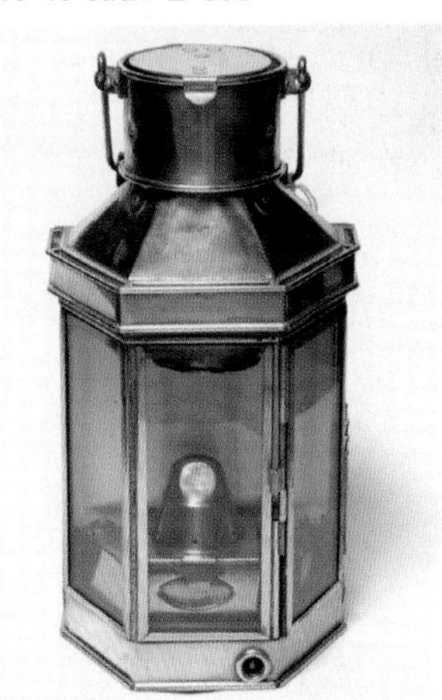

A ship's brass companionway lamp, by Bulpitt & Sons, with oil burner and enamel reflector, 1940, 17in (43cm) high.
£155–185
$225–270 ⊞ WAC

A *Stirling Castle* **advertising postcard,** 1950s.
£10–15
$15–20 ⊞ COB

A Benson's Candies tin, depicting RMS *Queen Mary*, 1950s, 8in (20.5cm) wide.
£20–25
$30–35 ⊞ HUX

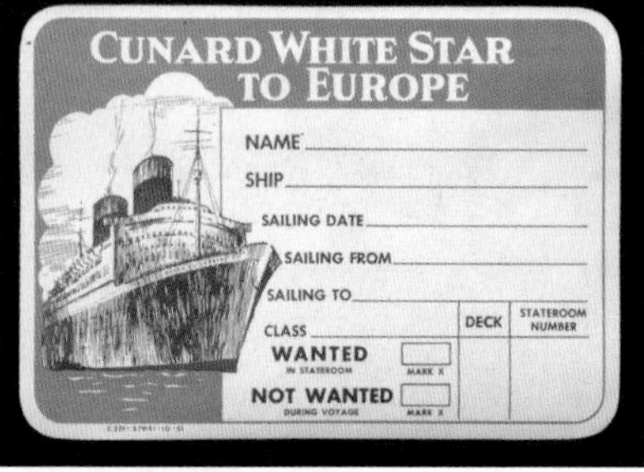

A Cunard White Star baggage sticker, 1950s, 5 x 6in (12.5 x 15cm).
£10–15
$15–20 ⊞ COB

An Orient Line cup and saucer, by Wedgwood, 1950s, cup 2in (5cm) high.
£15–20
$20–30 ⊞ HUX

Four Cunard tie-on baggage labels, 1950s, largest 7in (18cm) long.
£5–10
$7–15 each ⊞ COB

A Union Castle Line magazine holder, for *Tatler* and *Bystander* magazines, 1950s, 13 x 10in (33 x 25.5cm).
£15–18
$20–30 ⊞ COB

William A. McLeod, *Deck Games Sports & Pastimes*, 1950s, 7 x 5in (18 x 12.5cm).
£10–15
$15–20 ⊞ COB

◄ **A Royal Navy brass lifeboat binnacle,** with compass and lamp housing, 1950s, 11in (28cm) high.
£240–270
$350–400 ⊞ OLD

Six ship's matchbooks, 1950s–60s, 2in (5cm) wide.
£4–8
$6–12 each ⊞ COB

An SS ***United States*** **souvenir log,** 1962, 5 x 7in (12.5 x 18cm).
£8–10
$10–15 ⊞ COB

A Tri-ang Mini Ships model of RMS *Queen Mary*, 1960s, 7in (18cm) long.
£25–30
$35–45 ⊞ HAL

Tri-ang Minic Mini Ships model of SS *United States*, 1960s, 10in (25.5cm) long, in original box.
£45–50
$65–75 ⊞ HAL

A Tri-ang Minic tugboat trade box, 1960s, tug 1½in (4cm) long.
£6–7
$5–8 ⊞ HAL

An HM Yacht Britannia wood-mounted brass plaque, 1960s, 8 x 10in (20.5 x 25.5cm).
£150–200
$220–300 ⊞ COB

A Tri-ang Minic Mini Ships destroyers trade box, 1960s, 3in (7.5cm) long.
£5–7
$6–8 ⊞ HAL

Four shipping line souvenir spoons, with enamel decoration, 1960s, 5in (12.5cm) long.
£10–12
$15–18 each ⊞ COB

An *Ark Royal* plate, by Spode, limited edition, 1979, 10in (25.5cm) diam, in original box.
£100–120
$145–175 ⊞ COB

A screen-printed fabric panel, depicting SS *Normandie*, 1970s, 26in (66cm) square.
£60–70
$70–100 ⊞ COB

A P&O *Canberra* tie clip, with enamel insignia, 1970s, 2in (5cm) wide.
£10–15
$15–20 ⊞ COB

Titanic

The sinking of RMS *Titanic* is one of the most famous naval disasters of all time. The biggest liner ever built and branded unsinkable, she was carrying 3,000 people on her maiden voyage when she struck an iceberg on 14 April 1912. The ship went down in two hours 40 minutes, with the band still playing, and 1,513 people lost their lives. With interest repeatedly stimulated by films, exhibitions, TV programmes etc, *Titanic* memorabilia is very sought-after and relics can make record prices at auction.

A White Star Line RMS *Titanic* lettercard, written by Father F. Browne, dated 10 April 1912, 7 x 6in (18 x 15cm).
£19,000–23,000
$27,500–33,500 HAld

An RMS *Titanic* souvenir pincushion, 1912, 3½in (9cm) diam.
£19,000–23,000
$27,500–33,500 HAld

A shell wall plaque, depicting RMS *Titanic*, c1915, 6½in (16.5cm) diam.
£90–100
$130–145 HUX

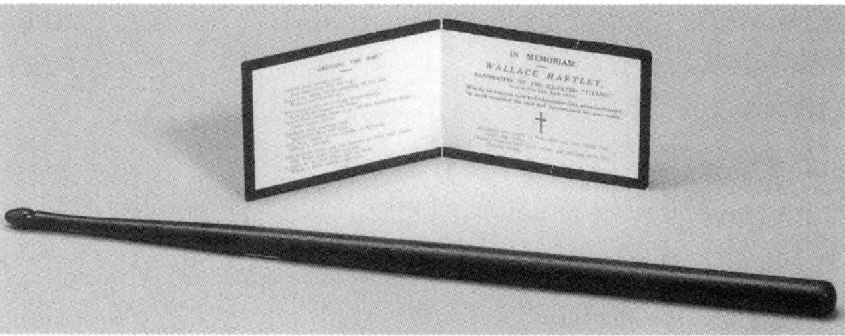

◄ **A rosewood drumstick,** used by Wallace Hartley, orchestra leader on RMS *Titanic*, c1912, together with a memorial card.
£400–500
$580–720 SK(B)

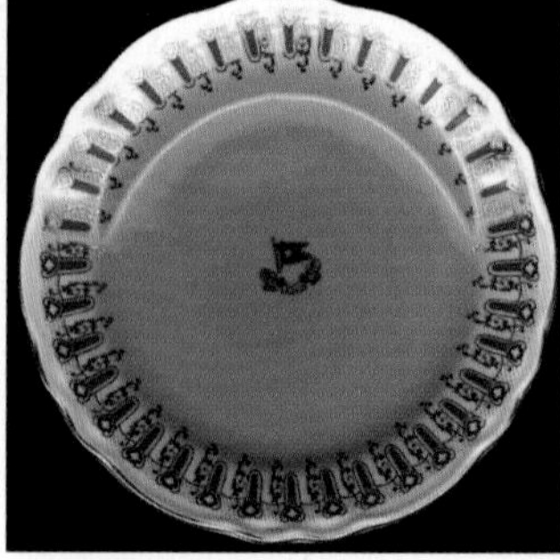

A porcelain side plate prop from the *Titanic* film, based on original design by White Star Lines, 1997, 7in (18cm) diam.
£140–170
$200–250 CO

A reprinted photograph of RMS *Titanic*, 1970s, 10 x 6in (25.5 x 15cm).
£10–15
$15–20 COB

A catalogue for the Wreck of the Titanic exhibition, held at National Maritime Museum, Greenwich, London, 1994–95, 12 x 10in (30.5 x 25.5cm).
£10–15
$15–20 COB

◄ **A glass champagne bottle prop from the *Titanic* film,** labelled 'White Star Moët & Chandon Epernay', 1997, 12in (30.5cm) high.
£150–180
$220–260 CO

Silver & Metalware

A brass and iron trivet, c1790, 11in (30cm) high.
£225–250
$325–350 ⊞ SEA

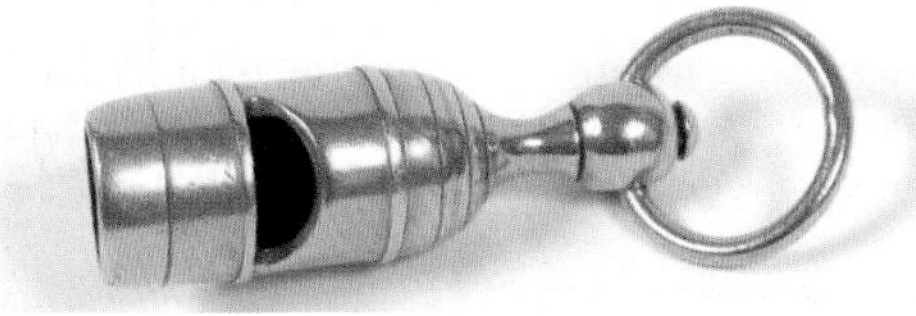

A brass whistle, c1800, 2in (5cm) long.
£65–75
$100–110 ⊞ RGe

A cast iron boot jack, in the shape of a beetle, late 19thC, 10½in (26.5cm) long.
£65–75
$100–110 ⊞ SDA

A bell metal hand bell, with rosewood handle, early 19thC, 14in (35.5cm) high.
£130–145
$190–210 ⊞ F&F

A pair of brass fire dogs, with decorative masks, foliage and pierced finials, c1890, 16in (40.5cm) high.
£200–230
$300–330 ⊞ WAC

◄ **A brass chestnut roaster,** by Peerage, c1900, 20in (51cm) long.
£125–145
$180–200
⊞ WAC

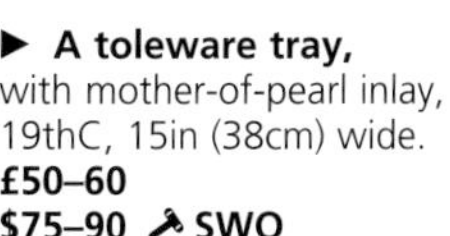

► **A toleware tray,** with mother-of-pearl inlay, 19thC, 15in (38cm) wide.
£50–60
$75–90 ⚒ SWO

An Edwardian bronze desk clip, in the shape of a duck's head, 5in (12.5cm) long.
£50–60
$75–90 ⚒ G(L)

A brass letter combination lock, c1915, 1½in (4cm) wide.
£35–40
$50–60 ⊞ HO

A tin one-gill measure, with a brass plaque, c1920, 3in (7.5cm) high.
£45–50
$65–75 ⊞ SMI

A stainless-steel 30-piece set of Viners Love Story cutlery, 1970s.
£30–40
$45–60 ⊞ RET

Copper

A copper hearth shovel, with pierced decoration, c1830, 27in (68.5cm) long.
£50–60
$75–90 ⊞ WAC

A copper tankard, c1830, 6½in (16.5cm) high.
£225–275
$325–400 ⊞ SEA

Items in the Silver & Metalware section have been arranged in date order within each sub-section.

A copper and brass coaching horn, late 18thC, 35in (89cm) long.
£85–95
$130–140
⊞ WAC

A copper kettle, c1840, 7in (18cm) high.
£165–200
$250–300 ⊞ SEA

A copper coal scuttle, with a swing handle, c1870, 15in (38cm) high.
£180–200
$250–300 ⊞ ASH

A ship's copper kettle, c1890, 11in (28cm) high.
£55–65
$80–100 ⊞ AL

◄ A copper and brass coffee pot, with wooden handle and brass finial, c1900, 10in (25.5cm) high.
£50–60
$75–90 ⊞ WAC

► A copper log/coal box, with brass handles, 1900–10, 22in (56cm) wide.
£100–125
$145–180 ⊞ WAC

A copper and brass five-gallon petrol measure, inscribed 'Stafford County Council', c1930, 18in (45.5cm) high.
£150–180
$220–250 ⊞ NoC

English Silver

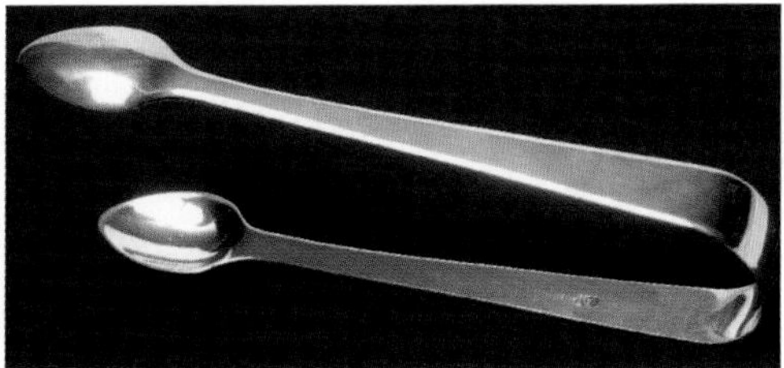

A pair of silver sugar tongs, by TD, London 1709, 5½in (14cm) long.
£25–30
$35–45 ⊞ WAC

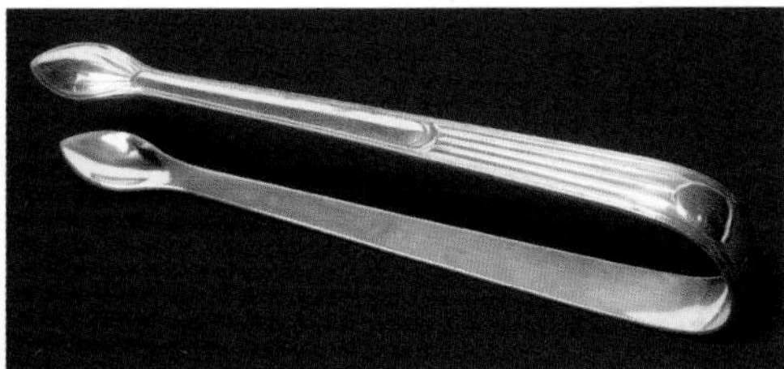

A pair of silver sugar tongs, by Charles Lias, London 1800, 5½in (15cm) long.
£50–60
$75–90 ⊞ WAC

► **A silver vinaigrette,** by John Lawrence & Co, in the shape of a handbag, Birmingham 1826, 7in (18cm) wide.
£350–400
$500–600 ⊞ LBr

A set of six silver teaspoons, by Lias, London 1831, 6in (15cm) long.
£90–100
$130–150 ⊞ WAC

A pair of silver tablespoons, by Peter and Anne Bateman, London 1796, 9in (23cm) long.
£90–100
$130–150 ⊞ WAC

A silver King's pattern fish slice, by James Hobbs, with oyster back, London 1825, 11½in (29cm) long, 6oz.
£250–275
$360–400 ⊞ GRe

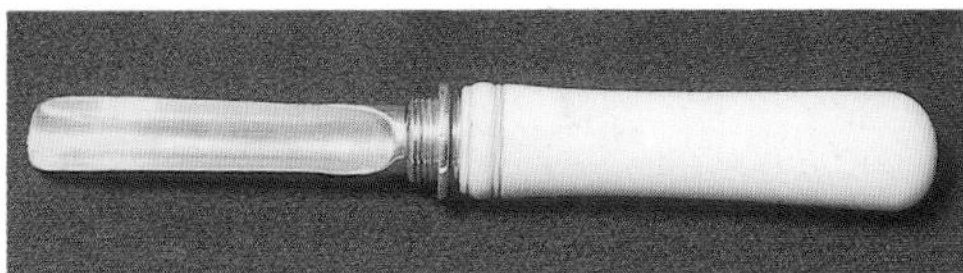

A silver travelling apple corer, probably by WM Knight II, London 1828, 6in (15cm) long.
£400–450
$580–650 ⊞ HEB

A silver 'bachelor's' teapot, by William Bateman, London 1831, 5½in (14cm) high.
£430–475
$625–700 ⊞ GRe

◄ **A set of six silver forks,** three by Chawner and three by Lias, London 1831–41, 8in (20.5cm) long.
£160–200
$230–300 ⊞ WAC

A silver vinaigrette, by Thomas Shaw, Birmingham 1834, 1½in (4cm) wide.
£350–400
$500–580 ⊞ BEX

A silver teapot, by William Moulson, decorated with panels of engraved flowers, scrolls and leaves, 1849, 5½in (14cm) high, 22½oz.
£200–230
$300–330 ⚒ L

A silver christening mug, decorated with beaded and engraved bands, 1855, 3½in (9cm) high.
£130–160
$200–230 ⚒ G(L)

A Victorian silver-gilt wine coaster, 9in (23cm) diam.
£160–200
$230–300 ⊞ BrL

► **A silver sifter,** by George Adams, London 1854, 7in (18cm) long.
£225–275
$325–400
⊞ CoHA

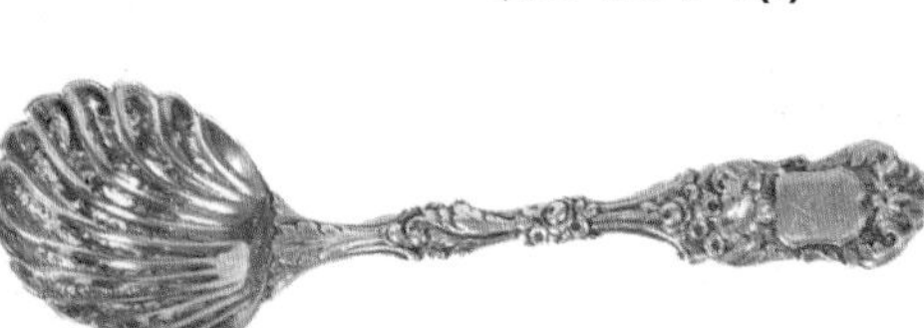

A silver three-piece tea service, Sheffield 1861, teapot 7½in (19cm) high.
£240–280
$350–400 ⚒ SWO

An engraved silver card case, 1855, 4in (10cm) wide.
£200–225
$300–325 ⊞ EXC

A silver christening set, by Hilliard & Thomason, comprising knife, spoon and fork, Birmingham 1861, 9in (23cm) long.
£200–225
$300–325 ⊞ CoHA

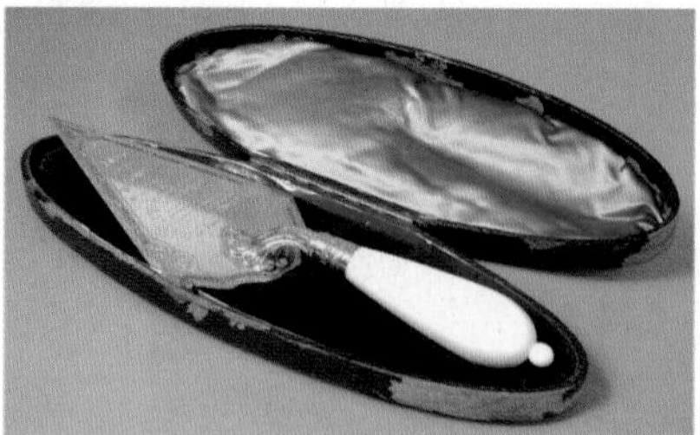

A silver trowel, with a presentation inscription and a turned ivory handle, 1877, 11in (28cm) long, in original box.
£160–190
$230–275 ⚒ SWO

A George III-style silver mug, by Messrs Lias, decorated with reeded bands, 1874, 4¾in (12cm) high, 9oz.
£190–220
$275–320 ⚒ L

► **A silver-handled bread fork,** Sheffield, 1881, 7in (18cm) long.
£35–40
$50–60 ⊞ CoCo

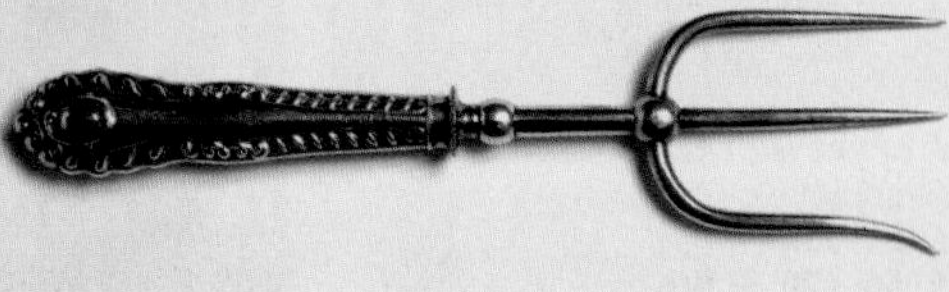

A silver card case, by George Unite, Birmingham 1895, 4in (10cm) wide.
£200–225
$300–325 ⊞ WAC

A travelling cutlery set, with horn handles, 19thC, in a hinged leather case, 5½in (14cm) high.
£160–200
$230–300 ⚒ SWO

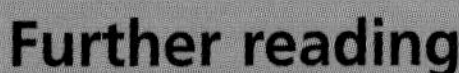

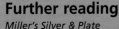

Further reading

Miller's Silver & Plate Buyer's Guide, Miller's Publications, 2002

A silver frame, Birmingham 1897, 6in (15cm) high.
£250–285
$360–420 ⊞ BrL

A silver and cut-glass decanter stopper, London 1897, 4in (10cm) high.
£80–90
$115–130 ⊞ EXC

A set of four silver egg spoons, by Jackson & Fullerton, London 1897, 4½in (11.5cm) long.
£90–100
$130–150 ⊞ GRe

A silver vesta case, Chester 1900, 2in (5cm) wide.
£40–50
$60–75 ⊞ WAC

A silver crumb brush, Chester 1890s, 7in (18cm) long.
£50–60
$75–90 ⊞ WAC

A child's silver rattle, with whistle and coral teether, slight damage, maker's mark JB, 19thC, 5in (13cm) long.
£200–240
$300–350 ⚒ SWO

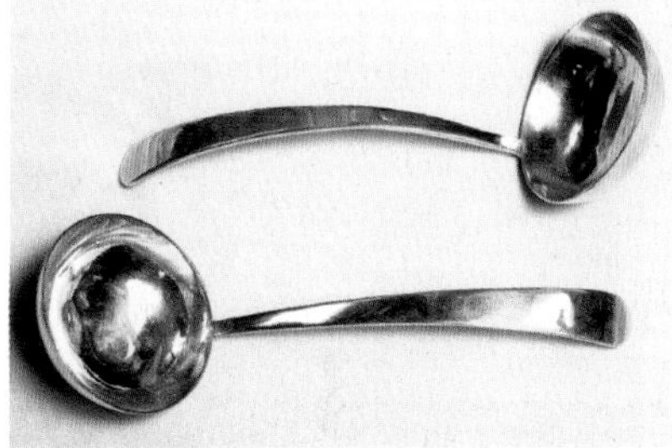

A pair of silver sauce ladles, by Aspreys, 1900, 5in (12.5cm) long.
£135–155
$200–225 ⊞ EXC

► **A 24-piece set of dessert knives and forks,** the silver-plated blades with silver pistol-grip handles, c1900, in an oak case.
£200–225
$300–325 ⊞ WAC

A silver-handled bread knife, by Oetzmann, London 1901, 13in (33cm) long.
£60–75
$90–110 ⊞ WAB

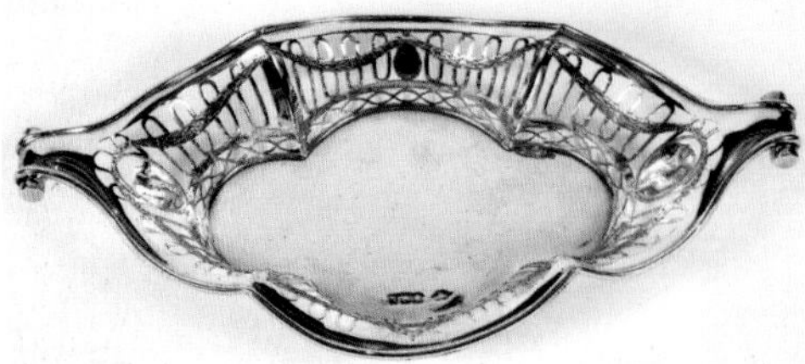

A silver bonbon dish, with pierced sides, London 1903, 6in (15cm) wide.
£425–475
$620–700 ⊞ CoHA

A silver-handled corkscrew, 1904, 5in (12.5cm) long.
£30–35
$45–50 ⊞ EXC

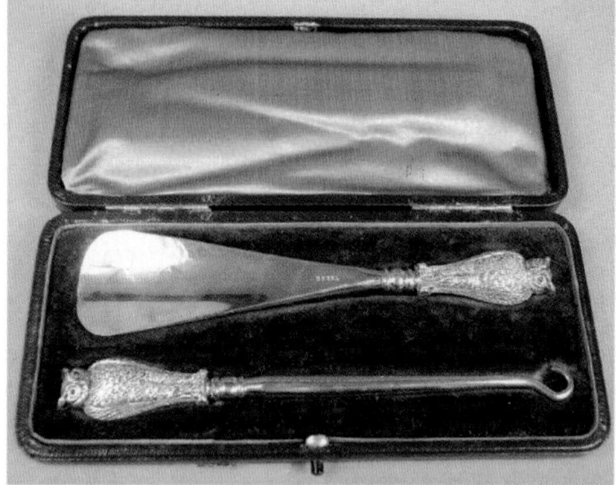

A silver shoe horn and button hook, with handles in the form of owls, 1907, 5¾in (14.5cm) long, in original case.
£160–190
$230–275 ⚒ SWO

► A silver frame, Birmingham 1908, 8in (20.5cm) high.
£245–285
$355–425 ⊞ WAC

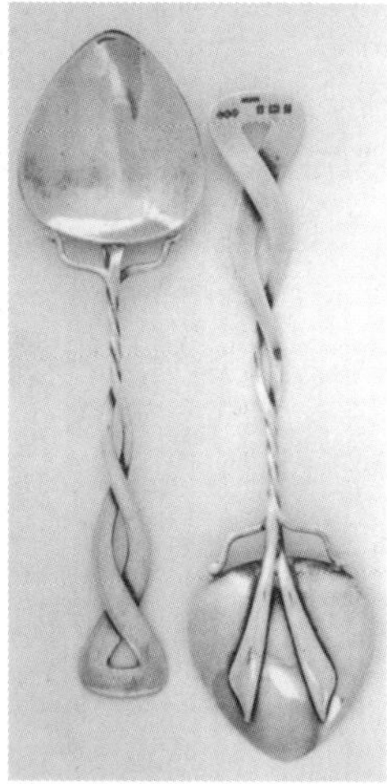

A pair of Cymric silver spoons, by Liberty & Co, with heart-shaped bowls and entwined stems, Birmingham 1902, 5oz.
£550–650
$800–1,000 ⚒ LAY

A silver vesta, in the shape of a heart, Birmingham 1904, 2in (5cm) high.
£110–130
$160–190 ⊞ BrL

A silver and crocodile-skin hip flask, by Heath & Heath, Chester 1902, 5in (12.5cm) high.
£100–150
$145–220 ⊞ STS

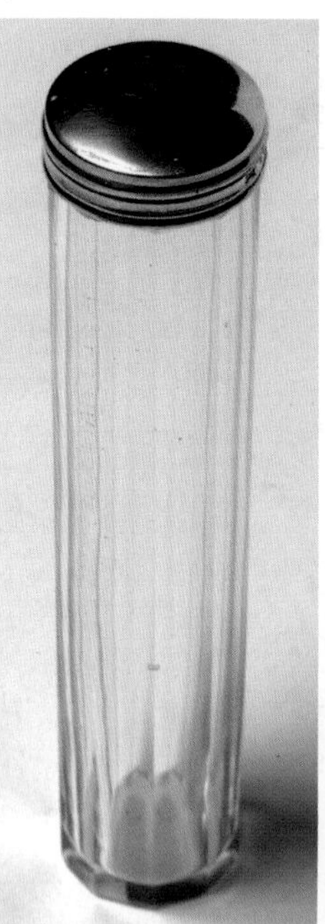

A silver-topped glass jar, by AH, London 1905, 7in (18cm) high.
£30–40
$45–60 ⊞ WAC

◄ A set of six silver teaspoons, by J. Restall, given as prizes for the Manchester & Counties Bulldog Club, bearing the profile of a bulldog, each spoon individually engraved with the name of the winning dog, 1912–15, 5½in (14cm) long.
£200–225
$300–325 ⚒ TML

A silver mustard pot, Birmingham 1913, 3in (7.5cm) high.
£70–80
$100–115 ⊞ CoCo

A pair of silver napkin rings, by Mappin & Webb, 1915, 1¼in (3cm) wide, in original case.
£75–85
$110–125 ⊞ EXC

LOCATE THE SOURCE

The source of each illustration in Miller's can be found by checking the code letters below each caption with the Key to Illustrations, pages 443–451.

► **A silver basket,** with pierced sides and cranberry glass insert, c1925, 6in (15cm) diam.
£165–200
$240–300 ⊞ EXC

► **A silver toast rack,** by Mappin & Webb, Sheffield 1941, 3½in (9cm) wide.
£95–115
$140–165 ⊞ BrL

Pewter

A pewter salt, c1800, 3in (7.5cm) diam.
£50–60
$75–90 ⊞ HO

A pewter whistle, depicting the head of a hunting dog, c1850, 2in (5cm) long.
£165–200
$240–300 ⊞ LBr

A pewter quart mug, with Staffordshire knot 'E' mark c1860 and later Glasgow marks, 6in (15cm) high.
£50–60
$75–90 ⊞ HEB

◄ **A pewter five-piece tea service,** c1910, 12in (30.5cm) diam.
£175–225
$255–325 ⊞ WAC

A pewter frame, c1900, 13in (33cm) high.
£225–250
$325–360 ⊞ WAC

► **A Tudric pewter cocktail set,** c1920, 10in (25.5cm) high.
£440–480
$650–700 ⊞ WAC

A WMF pewter chamberstick, c1910, 6in (15cm) high.
£200–225
$300–325 ⊞ WAC

Silver Plate

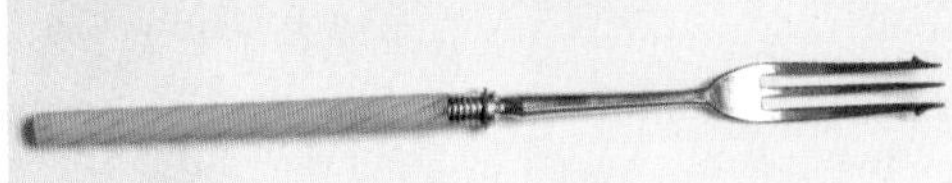

A Victorian silver-plated pickle fork, with bone handle, 9in (23cm) long.
£25–30
$35–45 ⊞ CoCo

A Victorian silver-plated hot-plate lifter, 6¼in (16cm) high.
£25–30
$35–45 ⊞ BrL

A silver-plated spoon warmer, by Henry Wilkinson & Co, c1870, 5in (12.5cm) wide.
£110–130
$160–200 ⊞ BrL

A pair of silver-plated sandwich servers, by Barker Bros, Birmingham, c1880, 9in (23cm) long.
£65–75
$95–110 ⊞ BrL

A silver-plated butter dish, by William Hutton & Sons, c1880, 7in (18cm) diam.
£110–130
$160–200 ⊞ BrL

A Sheffield plate canteen, by Akins Bros, c1880, in an oak case, 18in (45.5cm) wide.
£750–900
$1,100–1,300 ⊞ WAC

A pair of silver-plated knife rests, in the form of foxes, c1890, 4in (10cm) long.
£65–75
$95–110 ⊞ GRe

A silver-plated Guernsey milk can, with a wicker handle, c1910, 6in (15cm) high.
£50–60
$75–90 ⊞ AL

A silver-plated novelty condiment set, modelled as curling stones, 19thC, 4in (10cm) diam.
£100–120
$145–175 ⊞ GRe

► **A silver-plated three-tier cake stand,** c1930, 18in (45.5cm) high.
£70–80
$100–115 ⊞ BEV

Sixties & Seventies

Time **Magazine,** 'London: The Swinging City' issue, with 'pop art' cover, contains special 13-page feature on London by Piri Halasz, dated 15 April 1966, 11¼ x 8½in (28.5 x 21.5cm).
£20–25
$30–35 ⊞ ASC
This was the US magazine that coined the expression 'Swinging London' to describe the vibrant atmosphere of England's capital in 1966. It includes an extensive article about the people and places that were setting the swinging scene.

A compilation LP record, 'Good Time Music', by Electra, 1967.
£25–30
$35–45 ⊞ PR

Cross Reference
See Rock & Pop (pages 309–324)

► **A Haight-Ashbury Hippieville guide and map,** by Gray Line bus tours, a 'Summer of Love' souvenir sold to tourists, 1967, 22 x 17in (56 x 43cm).
£45–50
$65–75 ⊞ ASC

An LP record, 'More Music from *The Man from U.N.C.L.E.*', 1966.
£25–30
$35–45 ⊞ CTO

A Dr Timothy Leary Ph.d LP record, 'L.S.D.', by Pixie Records, American, 1966, in original sleeve.
£65–75
$100–110 ⊞ ASC
This is Timothy Leary's second LP release in which he discusses the effects of LSD on the nervous system, the determinants of set and setting and the subversive nature of the drug.

A Pop '66 concert tour programme and ticket, 1966, programme 10 x 8in (25.5 x 20.5cm).
£35–40
$50–60 ⊞ CTO

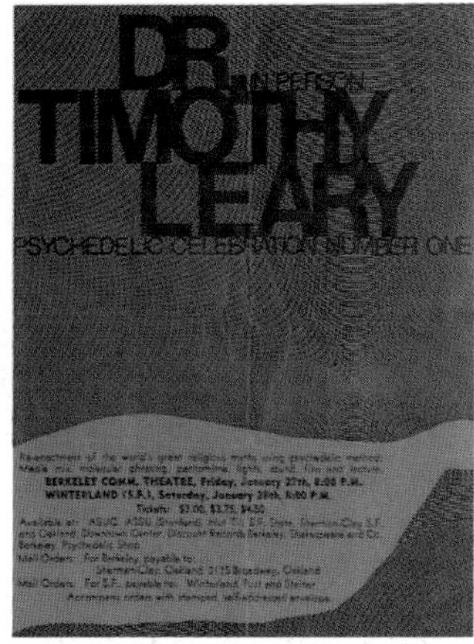

A handbill, announcing Dr Timothy Leary's 'Psychedelic Celebration Number One', American, 1967, 8 x 6in (20.5 x 15cm).
£75–85
$110–125 ⊞ ASC
Billed as a 'Re-enactment of the world's great religious myths using psychedelic method: Media mix, molecular phrasing, pantomime, lights, sound, film and lecture', the show consisted of Leary sitting on stage with Jackie Cassen and Rudi Stern's light show behind him, and a musician playing a sarod as he retold the story of the enlightenment of Gautama Buddha. Unfortunately the Grateful Dead were playing at the Avalon on the same night, and the audience at the Berkeley Community Theatre, California was disappointingly small.

A silkscreen poster, 'Legalise Cannabis – The Putting Together of the Heads', by Martin Sharp, 1967, 30 x 20in (76 x 51cm).
£135–150
$200–220 ⊞ ASC

A poster, 'Can-A-Blis', by Rick Griffin, produced by Berkeley Bonaparte, 1967, 14½ x 20in (37 x 51cm).
£85–95
$125–140 ⊞ ASC
This is a fictitious advertisment for marijuana, one of a series that Griffin produced to look like the 1920s tin and label designs he was collecting at the time. The pun works around 'can', 1960s slang for an ounce of marijuana, and 'blis', a reference to the effect of smoking the product.

A silkscreen poster, 'Luv Me', by Hapshash and The Coloured Coat, produced under the imprint Jacob & The Coloured Coat for Luv Me Film Productions, printed by Osiris Visions, 1967, 20 x 15in (51 x 38cm).
£135–165
$200–240 ⊞ ASC
Hapshash and The Coloured Coat was the name used by the psychedelic design team founded in 1967 by Nigel Weymouth and Michael English. The pair also produced their own album, which was released on red vinyl.

Hunter Davies, *The Beatles: The Authorised Biography*, first edition, published by Heinemann, jacket design by Alan Aldridge, 1968, 8¾ x 6in (22 x 15cm).
£25–30
$35–45 ⊞ ASC

***Oz* magazine,** issues 1–48, edited by Richard Neville, Felix Dennis and Jim Anderson, a complete set with all inserts and posters, January 1967 to November 1973, 11½ x 8¼in (29 x 21cm).
£1,300–1,500
$1,900–2,200 ⊞ ASC

Cross Reference
See Posters (pages 294–298)

A poster, promoting Hapshash and The Coloured Coat's record on Minit Records, designed by Hapshash and The Coloured Coat, printed by Osiris Visions, numbered OA401, c1968, 39 x 29in (99 x 73.5cm).
£600–720
$870–1,000 ⚒ CO

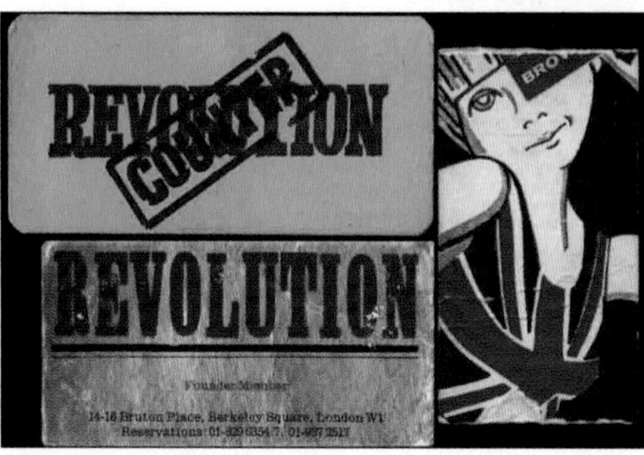

◀ Two membership cards and a free pass, to the Revolution Club, London, for the Jimi Hendrix Experience, 1968 and 1972.
£80–90
$115–130
⚒ CO

A Pierrot print, by Mariko, mid-1970s, 22 x 20in (56 x 51cm).
£15–20
$20–30 ⊞ TWI
The Pierrot became a popular decorative image in the 1970s.

◀ ***Biba,*** a promotional newspaper introducing the new Biba store in Kensington High Street, London, 1973, 17 x 13in (43 x 33cm).
£15–20
$20–30 ⊞ CTO

▶ **A silkscreen print,** by Victor Vasarely, limited edition, signed, 1970s, 20in (51cm) square.
£400–450
$580–650 ⊞ MARK
Born in 1908, Victor Vasarely was one of the pioneers of Op Art, the form of abstract painting that used optical techniques to disrupt and fragment the vision.

Tom Salter, *Carnaby Street*, first edition, published by Hobbs, with colour illustrations by Malcolm English, including one double fold-out, signed and inscribed by the author, dust jacket, 1970, 8¼ x 8in (21 x 20.5cm).
£40–45
$60–65 ⊞ ASC

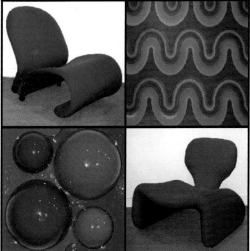

Ceramics

A Midwinter coffee pot, cup and saucer, designed by Nigel Wilde, decorated with Cherry Tree pattern, 1962–66, coffee pot 9in (23cm) high.
£55–65
$80–100 ⊞ CHI

A Denby dinner plate, decorated with Canterbury pattern, c1965, 10in (25.5cm) diam.
£12–14
$15–20 ⊞ CHI

A J. & G. Meakin coffee pot, designed by Alan Rogers, decorated with Topic pattern, 1967, 9½in (24cm) high.
£10–15
$15–20 ⊞ RET

A Barker Bros plate, decorated with Fiesta pattern, mid-1960s, 12in (30.5cm) wide.
£30–35
$45–50 ⊞ HSt

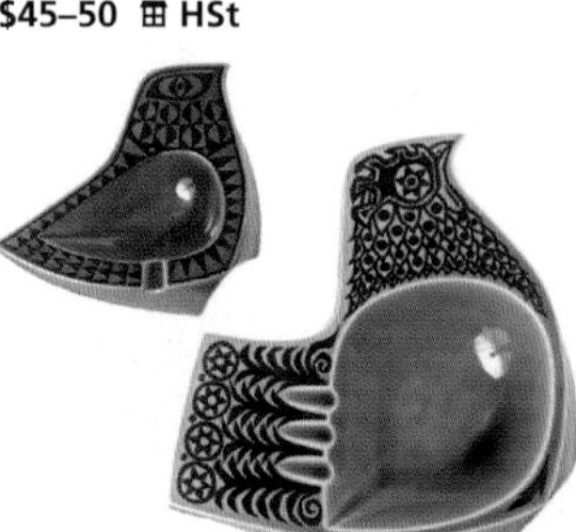
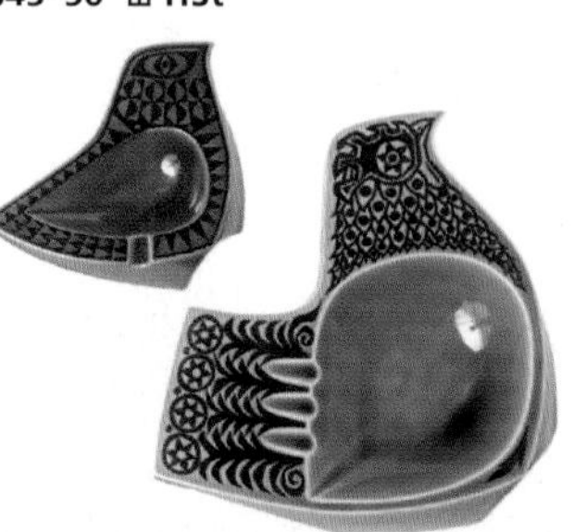

Two Hornsea Pottery Hens and Birds ashtrays, c1966, larger 8in (20.5cm) wide.
£20–30
$30–45 each ⊞ CHI

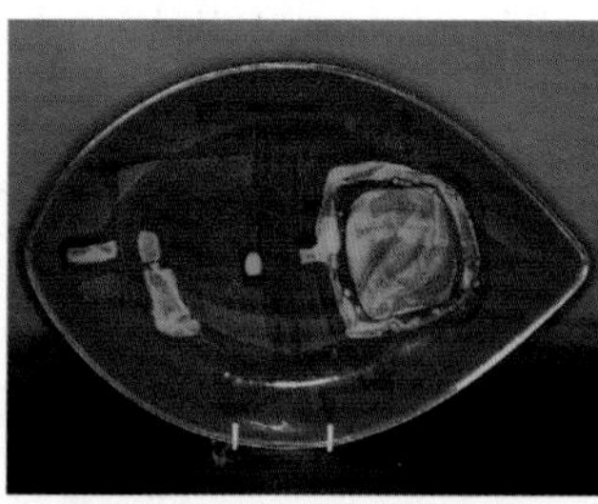

A Poole Pottery Delphis dish, shape No. 91, 1960s, 12in (30.5cm) wide.
£40–45
$60–90 ⊞ RET

A Denby vegetable dish, decorated with Chatsworth pattern, c1965, 8in (20.5cm) diam.
£25–30
$35–45 ⊞ CHI

A Hornsea Pottery mug, 1966–67, 3½in (9cm) high.
£15–20
$20–30 ⊞ CHI

A Midwinter Fine coffee pot, designed by Eve Midwinter, decorated with Tango pattern, c1969, 8in (20.5cm) high.
£30–35
$45–50 ⊞ CHI

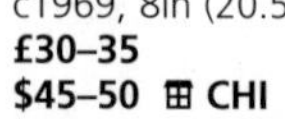

► **A coffee set,** Italian, 1960s, tray 17in (43cm) wide.
£130–160
$190–230
⊞ PrB

A Denby jug, decorated with Arabesque pattern, 1960s, 8in (20.5cm) high.
£18–20
$25–30 ⊞ CHI

A selection of Jersey pottery, 1960s, largest 5½in (14cm) high.
£6–12
$8–16 each ⊞ RET

◄ **A Hornsea Pottery coffee pot,** decorated with Heirloom pattern, 1960s, 10in (25.5cm) high.
£25–30
$35–45 ⊞ CHI

A Stavangerflint plate, Norwegian, 1960s, 8in (20.5cm) diam.
£20–25
$30–35 ⊞ PrB

A selection of Ironstone Pottery, comprising six oval plates, six side plates, six bowls and six mugs, decorated with Beefeater pattern, 1960s–70s, oval plates 11in (28cm) wide.
£20–35
$30–50 per set of six ⊞ FLD

A Denby coffee pot, decorated with Tall Trees pattern, c1970, 9in (23cm) high.
£45–55
$65–80 ⊞ CHI

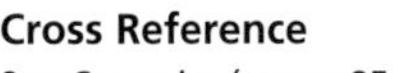

Cross Reference
See Ceramics (pages 85–154)

A Denby covered vegetable dish, decorated with Cotswold pattern, c1973, 8in (20.5cm) diam.
£40–45
$60–65 ⊞ CHI

► **A mug,** commemorating Harold Wilson and Jim Callaghan, 1976, 3½in (9cm) high.
£25–30
$35–45 ⊞ RCo

◄ **A Portmeirion tankard,** decorated with A Year to Remember pattern, 1971, 4in (10cm) high.
£25–30
$35–45 ⊞ CHI

A biscuit barrel/storage jar, decorated with Harvest pattern, manufactured for Marks & Spencer, c1979, 8in (20.5cm) high.
£20–25
$30–35 ⊞ CHI

Household Objects

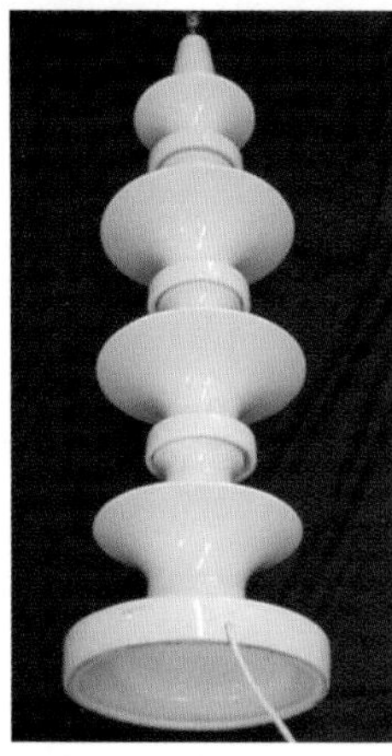

A china table lamp, with fittings, c1960, 37½in (95.5cm) high.
£60–70
$90–100 BAG

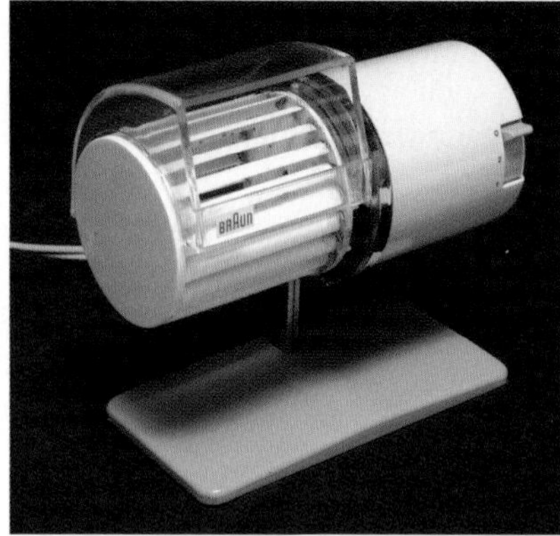

A Braun electric fan heater, designed by Dieter Rams, 1961, 6in (15cm) wide.
£85–95
$125–140 ⊞ MARK

► A Midwinter enamelled saucepan, decorated with Spanish Garden pattern, c1968, 9in (23cm) diam.
£15–20
$20–30 ⊞ CHI

A stainless steel biscuit barrel, designed by Arne Jacobsen for Stelton, Danish, c1967, 6in (15cm) diam.
£100–120
$145–175 ⊞ MARK

A roll of embossed wallpaper, 1970, 8in (20.5cm) wide.
£40–45
$60–65 ⊞ TWI

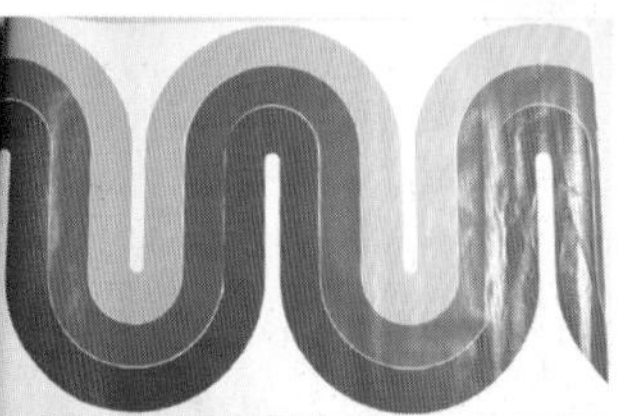

A roll of wallpaper, by UWPC, American, 1970, pattern repeat 24in (61cm).
£100–120
$145–175 ⊞ TWI

A textile, 'Bauhaus', designed by Susan Collier for Liberty, 1972, 47 x 38in (119.5 x 96.5cm).
£35–40
$50–60 ⊞ MARK

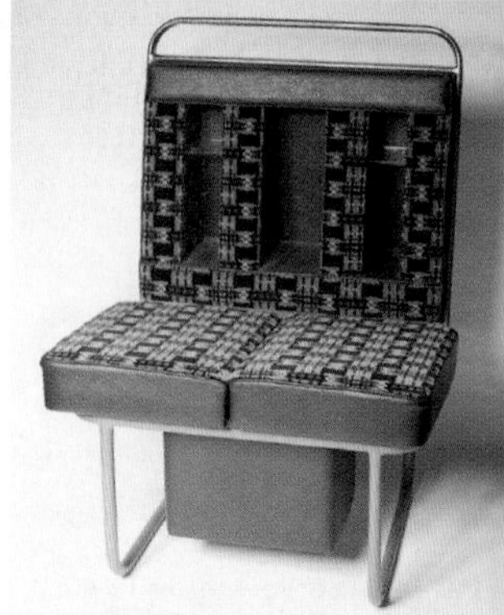

A bus seat converted into a bar, 1970s, 37in (94cm) high.
£180–200
$250–290 ⊞ TWI

A length of cotton textile, designed by Tiki, 1970s, 180in (457cm) long.
£40–50
$60–75 ⊞ HSt

◄ A plastic pineapple-shaped ice bucket, 1970s, 11in (28cm) high.
£10–12
$15–18 ⊞ REPS

Smoking

A carved and stained-wood tobacco box, modelled as the head of a boxer dog, with inset glass eyes, the base carved with foliage, 19thC, 8¼in (21cm) high.
£430–500
$625–725 Bri

A Bryant & May vesta tin/Go to Bed tin, modelled as a post box, with matches, 1885, 2½in (6.5cm) high.
£100–120
$145–175 ⊞ HUX

A Carreras Cigarettes metal vesta case, 1905, 2½in (6.5cm) wide.
£120–140
$175–200 ⊞ HUX

► **A Hignett's Golden Butterfly Cigarettes tin,** c1910, 10in (25.5cm) wide.
£80–95
$115–140 ⊞ MURR

A wooden pipe rack, modelled as a Highland terrier, c1920, 4½in (11.5cm) wide.
£18–22
$28–32 ⊞ Dall

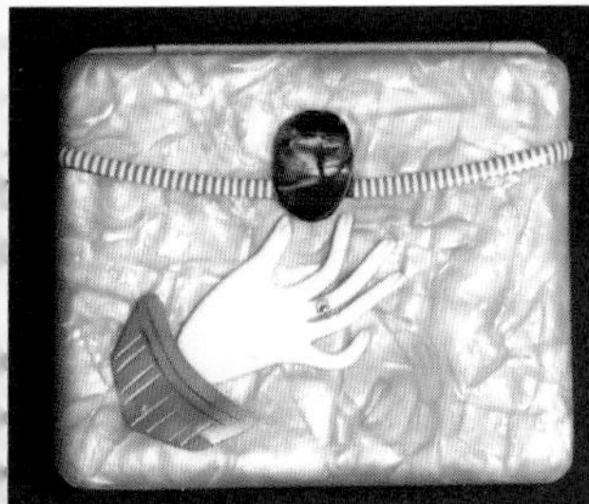

A hand-carved celluloid cigarette case, c1925, 3½in (9cm) wide.
£100–125
$145–180 ⊞ SUW

A Player's Navy Cut ceramic ashtray, 1930s, 5½in (14cm) diam.
£40–45
$60–65 ⊞ HUX

A glass ashtray, modelled as a penguin, 1950s, 5½in (14cm) long.
£30–35
$45–50 ⊞ LBe

An olivewood cigar and tobacco box, with swivelling rack, 1940–50s, 9in (23cm) wide.
£250–300
$350–450 SWO

An Afrikander Smoking Mixture tobacco tin, 1950s, 5½in (14cm) wide.
£10–12
$15–18 ⊞ RTT

► **A full pack of Alpine Light cigarettes,** 1960, 3¼in (8.5cm) high.
£4–6
$5–7 ⊞ RTT

Lighters

A silver-mounted horse's hoof cigar lighter, London 1908, 4in (10cm) high.
£1,250–1,450
$1,800–2,000 ⊞ RGa

A Rolls metal lighter, 1950–60s, 2¼in (5.5cm) in original box.
£10–12
$15–18 ⊞ RTT

► **A Marlborough Cigarettes pendant gas lighter,** on a gilt metal chain, 1970s, 3¾in (9.5cm) long.
£10–12
$15–17 ⊞ RTT

A Ronson Touch Tip cigarette lighter, modelled as a cocktail waiter shaking drinks at an Art Deco-style bar, 1930s, 6in (15cm) wide.
£50–60
$75–90 ⊞ RTT

Cross Reference
See Automobilia (pages 47–52)

A Zippo petrol lighter, for the United States Lines, 1960, 2in (5cm) high.
£35–40
$50–60 ⊞ COB

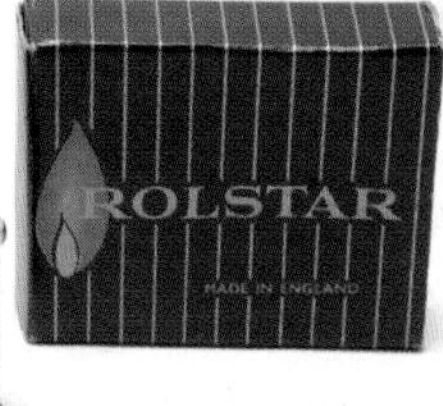

A Rolstar petrol lighter, 1950s, 2½in (6.5cm) wide, with original box.
£12–15
$17–20 ⊞ RTT

A Ronson Bakelite lighter maintenance kit, 1950, 2½in (6.5cm) high, with original box.
£20–25
$30–35 ⊞ HUX

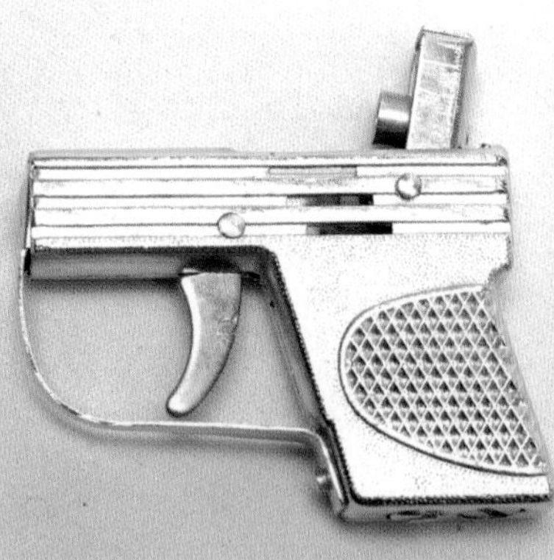

A metal lighter, modelled as a pocket pistol, 1960s, 2in (5cm) wide.
£20–22
$30–32 ⊞ RTT

LOCATE THE SOURCE
The source of each illustration in Miller's can be found by checking the code letters below each caption with the Key to Illustrations, pages 443–451.

Pipes

Though today it has fallen from grace, the former popularity of smoking has stimulated a wealth of *objets d'art*, none more decorative than the pipe. A huge variety of designs were created, and not just for novelty purposes. Asian smokers solved the problem of how to create a cool smoke by inventing the water pipe, also known as the *Nargileh* or *Hookah*. In 18th-century England, Staffordshire potters came up with another cooling system, the snake pipe, examples of which are highly collectable today. The long curling stems could extend up to 157½in (400cm) in length, so that by the time it reached your mouth, the temperature of the smoke had cooled considerably.

Clay which was cheap and a good insulator, was a favourite medium for pipes resulting in the wealth of clay pipe stems and bowls that can still be found by virtually anybody digging up their garden. Produced in Britain from the introduction of tobacco in the 16th century, these can be dated by the shape of the bowl. The 19th century saw the fashion of novelty designs, known as 'fancy clays', which came in the form of everything from famous buildings to contemporary celebrities.

Meerschaum pipes were another Victorian favourite. Meerschaum (German for sea foam) was a form of magnesium silicate originally found on the shores of the Black Sea. According to enthusiasts it is an ideal material for smokers, because the taste of tobacco comes out fully from the first draw. Manufactured in Germany, Austria and Eastern Europe meerschaum pipes were elaborately carved and waxed which improved the surface and coloration. The meerschaum was also coloured with other materials raging from nut oil to smoke itself. Values depend on quality of carving and subject matter.

Porcelain was another popular pipe material (especially in France) as was wood. Briar pipes, made from the briar root, became a particular favourite in the UK. Well-known pipe manufacturers include Alfred Dunhill, who opened a small pipe shop in the fashionable St James's area of London in 1907. Arguably the most famous British pipe smoker of all time belongs to this period: Sherlock Holmes. Created by Arthur Conan Doyle, the greatest detective of them all was famous for his curling pipe, for keeping his tobacco in a Persian slipper and for referring to a difficult case a 'a three-pipe problem.'

A Prattware puzzle pipe, with a looping stem and three circular coils, the bowl moulded with a cherub to each side, early 19thC, 12¼in (31cm) long.
£1,500–1,800
$2,200–2,600 Bri

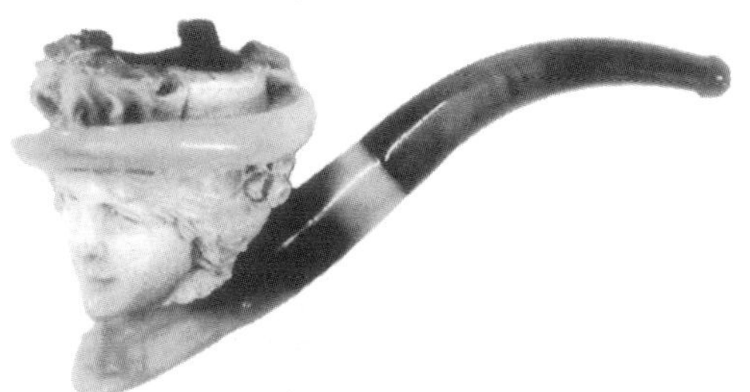

A meerschaum pipe bowl, carved as the bearded head of a Confederate soldier, 19thC, 2¼in (5.5cm) high.
£120–140
$175–200 Bri

◄ A meerschaum pipe, carved with the head of a lady wearing a bonnet, with another meerschaum pipe with a diminutive bowl supported by a hand, 19thC, larger 4¾in (12cm) long, each with original shaped case.
£80–100
$115–145 F&C

A *Nargileh*, with a decorative glass bowl and ornate brass stand with fitments and a flexible stem, Persian, 19thC, 24in (61cm) high.
£50–60
$75–90 Bri

Cross Reference
See Erotica
(pages 195–197)

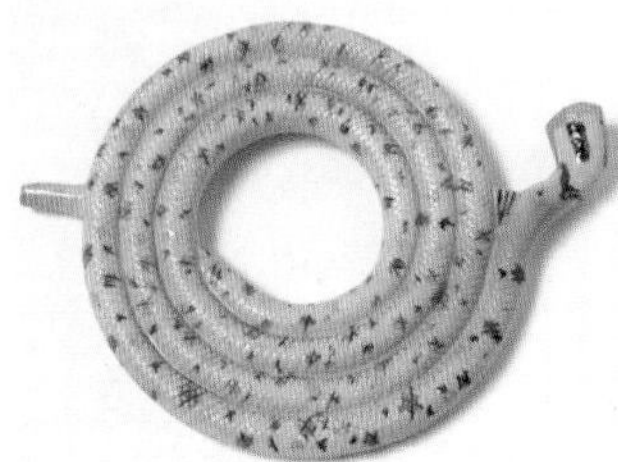

A Prattware serpent puzzle pipe, with four concentric hatched coils decorated with multicoloured dots, the bowl issuing from the serpent's mouth, early 19thC, 8¾in (22cm) long.
£550–650
$800–950 ⚒ Bri

A Wedgwood blue jasper pipe bowl, applied with a cherub scalding an insect with a torch, another with a flower garland, upper case mark, 19thC, 2¾in (7cm) high.
£260–300
$380–440 ⚒ Bri

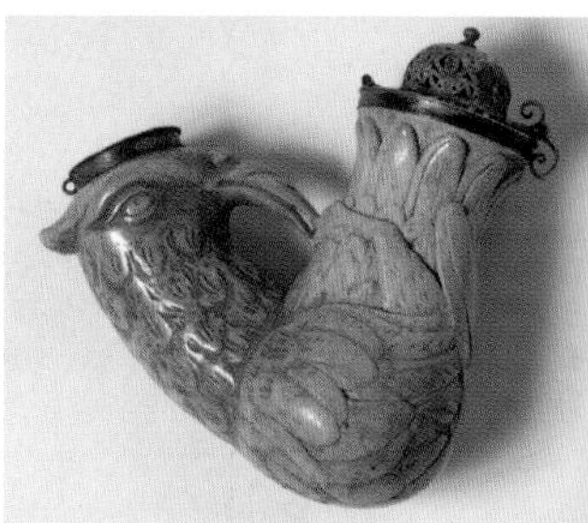

A meerschaum pipe bowl, carved as an eagle, with pierced metal lid and rim, Austro-Hungarian, 19thC, 4¾in (12cm) long.
£400–500
$580–720 ⚒ Bri

A meerschaum pipe, carved as a lady's head, her bonnet carved with flowers and ribbons, with a silver-coloured mount on an amber stem, 19thC, 7½in (19cm) long.
£300–350
$450–500 ⚒ Bri

A clay pipe bowl, carved as a bearded nobleman, marked 'Gambier/397 à Paris', together with a clay pipe, the bowl modelled with the Crystal Palace Exhibition, with part-stem, 19thC, 2½in (6.5cm) long.
£10–12
$15–18 ⚒ BBR

A meerschaum pipe, carved with a figural allegory, the bowl with a hinged white-metal cover, mouthpiece incomplete, Continental, 19thC, 6in (15cm) long.
£140–170
$200–250 ⚒ G(L)

A meerschaum pipe, carved as a bearded Arab, with copper and glass bead stem, 19thC, 6¼in (16cm) long.
£80–100
$115–145 ⚒ Bri

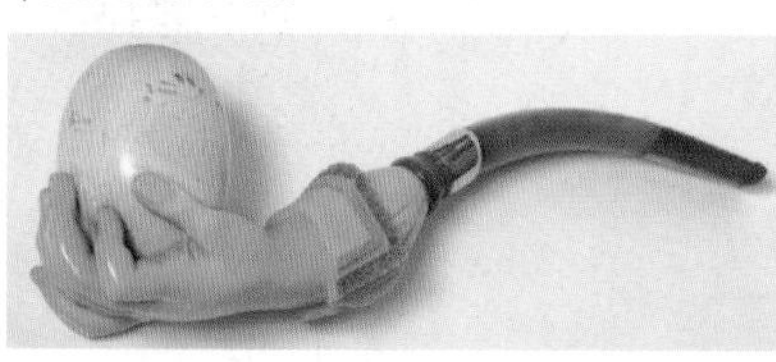

A meerschaum pipe, carved as a cupped hand holding an egg, with a silver-coloured metal band on a two-piece amber stem, 19thC, 9½in (24cm) long.
£220–260
$320–380 ⚒ Bri

► **A painted porcelain pipe,** shaped as a rabbit in full dress, the lid being the head, with a wood and horn stem, 19thC, bowl 6in (15cm) long.
£200–250
$300–360 ⚒ Bri

A clay pipe, carved as a revolver pistol, 19thC, 2¾in (7cm) long.
£40–50
$60–75 ⚒ BBR

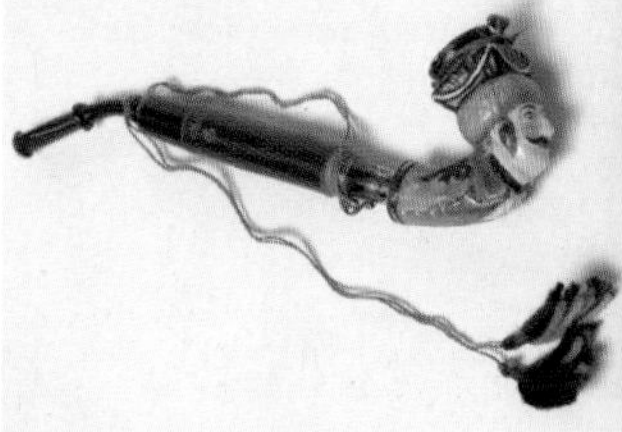

A painted porcelain pipe, the bowl moulded in the form of a soldier's head, with silver-coloured metal lid and mounts and a wooden and horn stem, German, 19thC, bowl 3in (7.5cm) long.
£400–500
$580–720 ⚒ Bri

► **A meerschaum pipe,** carved in Ragoczy style, a shell offering up the bowl, late 19thC, 5in (12.5cm) long.
£45–55
$65–80 Bri

A calabash, the wooden bowl and vulcanite stem with silver mounts, Chester 1910, 7¾in (19.5cm) long.
£85–100
$125–145 Bri

► **A water pipe,** with a ruby flash glass bowl, early 20thC, 21in (53.5cm) high.
£75–90
$110–130 Bri

A meerschaum pipe, formed as the bust of a lady in a feather hat, on a copper-based plinth, slight damage to collar, c1900, 5in (12.5cm) long.
£50–60
$75–90 Bri

Snuff

A carved ivory snuff rasp, depicting a man clutching a sack inscribed 'L'Avarice', iron rasp missing, some cracks, French, 18thC, 7¼in (18.5cm) long.
£750–900
$1,100–1,300 Bri

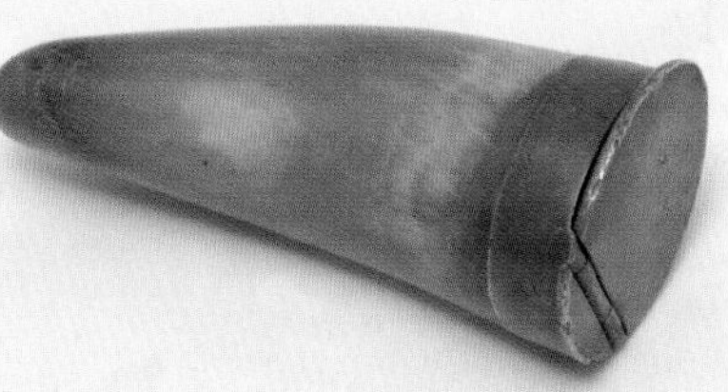

A horn and pewter snuff mull, by Durie, 1800–20, 4in (10cm) long.
£50–60
$75–90 HO

Snuff rasps

Harvested and fermented tobacco leaves were twisted into cords called 'carottes', which once dried could be either milled or grated against a tobacco rasp to produce snuff. Rasps were often produced from ivory, carved with religious, mythological and symbolic scenes. The carotte was rubbed against the grater on the back, falling into a small compartment with a sliding lid from which the powdered tobacco could be directly poured into the snuff box.

► **A miner's brass snuff box,** inscribed 'Walter Clarke 1909', 3in (7.5cm) wide.
£35–40
$50–60 BrL

A horn snuff box, the hinged chequerboard cover inlaid with bone and tortoiseshell, 19thC, 3¼in (8.5cm) wide.
£55–65
$80–95 Bri

A bloodstone snuff box, with silver-gilt mounts, Continental, 19thC, 3in (7.5cm) wide.
£150–180
$220–260 G(L)

Sport

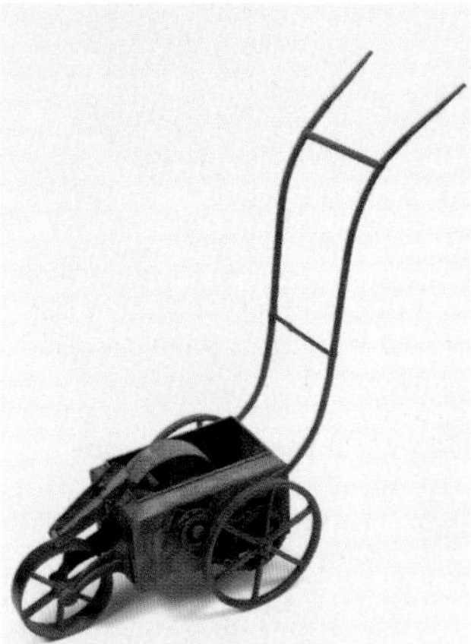

A Caxton chain-driven line marker, 1870s, 43in (109cm) long.
£550–650
$800–950 ⊞ MSh

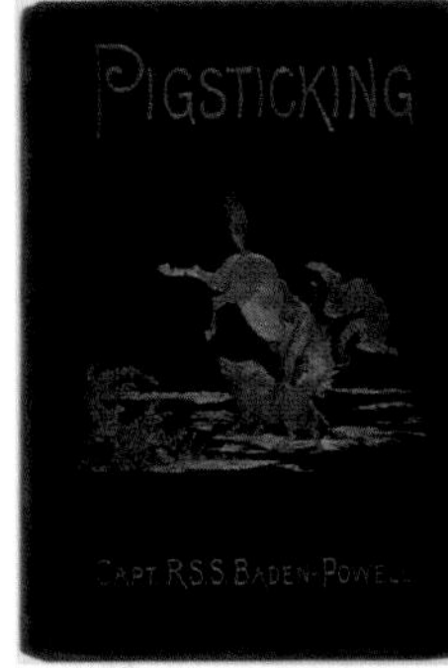

Captain R. S. S. Baden-Powell, *Pigsticking or Hoghunting. A Complete Account for Sportsmen...*, first edition, 25 plates, author's card, some staining, slightly warped, recased, 1889, 8°.
£130–150
$200–220 ⚒ BBA

A pair of oak oar blades, entitled 'Four Bumps Coxswain J Kemp', and inscribed with Cambridge Colleges, dated 1896, 33½in (85cm) long.
£130–160
$200–230 ⚒ GAK

► **A glass goblet,** acid-etched with a pair of boxers within oak branch borders, on a baluster stem, 19thC, 9in (23cm) high.
£200–230
$300–330
⚒ RBB

A wooden bowling ball, French, 1900, 7in (18cm) diam.
£30–35
$45–50 ⊞ TRA

A Spalding Bros baseball bat, No. 156. Old Hickory model, American, 1910, 32in (81.5cm) long.
£80–90
$115–130 ⊞ TRA

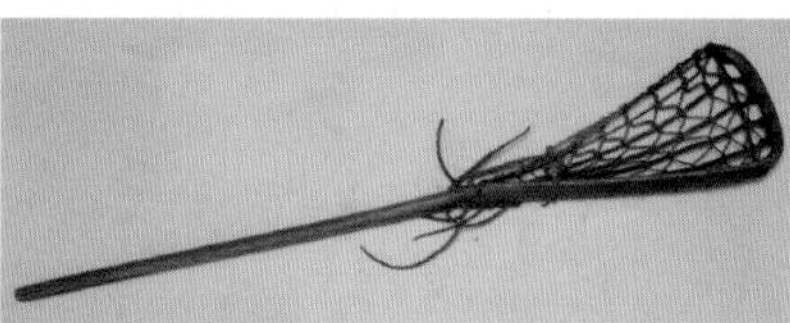

An ash and rawhide lacrosse stick, c1930, 44in (112cm) long.
£15–20
$20–30 ⊞ SA

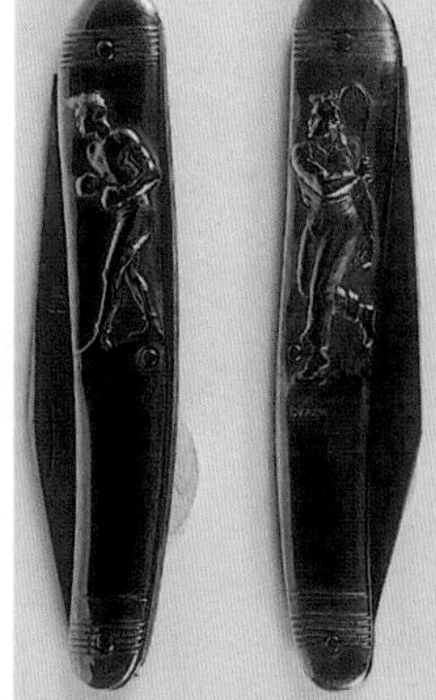

Two pen knives, decorated with a boxer and a tennis player, different image on reverse, French, 1910–20.
£15–20
$20–30 each ⊞ WAB

A pair of wood, leather and vellum ping-pong bats, c1910, 16in (40.5cm) long.
£45–50
$65–75 ⊞ SA

◄ **A pair of Ski-Rool grass skis,** French, 1950s, 34in (86.5cm) long.
£60–75
$90–110 ⊞ TRA

◄ **A leather medicine ball,** 1950s, 11in (28cm) diam.
£55–65
$80–100 ⊞ PSA
The medicine ball was used for training and exercise rather than any particular sport.

A baseball umpire's leather and metal face mask, American, 1950s, 9in (23cm) high.
£45–50
$65–75 ⊞ TRA

A pair of steel roller skates, in original leather case, 1950s, case 11in (28cm) wide.
£20–25
$30–35 ⊞ TRA

A pair of child's leather boxing gloves, 1950s, 7in (18cm) high.
£45–50
$65–75 ⊞ TRA

► **A Dartmouth tankard,** 1950s, 5½in (14cm) high.
£35–40
$50–60 ⊞ TPCS

A plastic sports bag, 'Montreal Olympics Canada 1976', 15½in (39.5cm) long.
£40–45
$60–65 ⊞ TWI
Men have been displaying a growing interest in vintage costume and accessories. Plastic sports bags from the 1970s and '80s have become fashionable along with sportswear from the same period. Objects from these decades are particularly in vogue with young collectors.

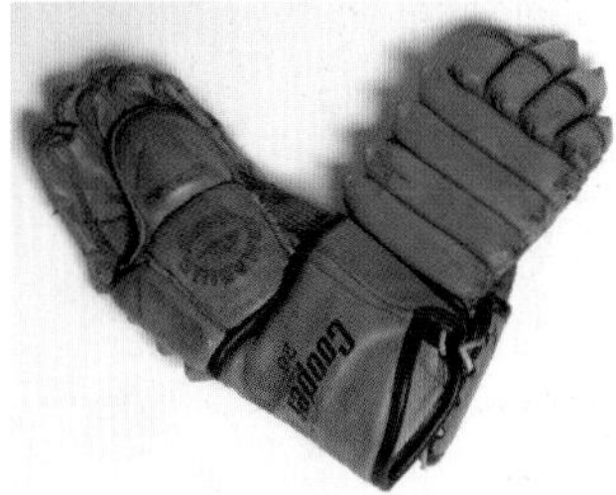

A pair of Cooper leather Ice hockey gloves, Canadian, 1970s, 14in (35.5cm) long.
£20–25
$30–35 ⊞ TRA

A pair of metal boules, in a leather case, French, 1960s, case 6in (15cm) wide.
£25–30
$35–45 ⊞ TRA

◄ **A pair of curtains,** depicting skateboarding moves, 1980s, 43in (109cm) long.
£20–25
$30–35 ⊞ TWI

An NFC Champs Super Bowl 1994 sweatshirt.
£20–25
$30–35 ⊞ TRA

Billiards & Snooker

Billiards was a favouite game in the Victorian and Edwardian periods, when country houses would have a dedicated billiard room where, after dinner, gentlemen could play, smoke and drink their port. Because it was a game for the wealthy, accessories were the best quality.

British manufacturer John Thurston (est 1799) was a leading supplier of billiard tables and revolutionized equipment design. In 1826, they supplied the first slate-bed table for White's Club in London, and as the weight of the tables increased so the legs became increasingly solid and architectural. Cushions were traditionally made of felt cloth. In the 1830s, Thurston introduced India rubber cushions which, however, lost their springiness in cold weather and had to be warmed with pans of hot water. In 1845 he took out a patent for 'frost-free' vulcanized rubber cushions. New technology also affected billiard balls, which were generally made from elephant tusk ivory until the late 19th century when the American co-inventor of celluoid, John Wesley Hyatt, pioneered the moulded plastic billiard ball. Wood remained the preferred material for cues which when not in use were stored on handsome wooden cue stands. Another accessory was the wooden scoreboard; often including marking for 'Life Pool' a game in which a player had three lives and lost one each time a game was plotted.

The game of billiards is played in many different ways but the main distinctions include billiards, played with three balls; snooker, played with 21 balls and a cue ball; and pool, played with 15 balls and a cue ball.

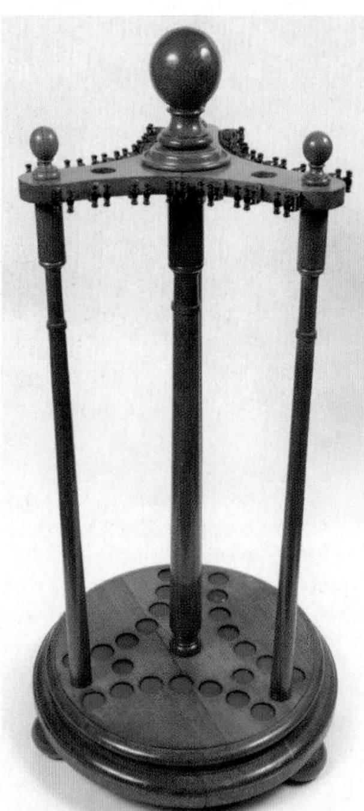

An oak revolving billiards cue stand, c1890, 45in (114.5cm) high.
£1,400–1,600
$2,000–2,300 ⊞ MSh

Items in the Sport section have been arranged in date order within each sub-section.

An E. J. Riley oak slate-bed snooker table, with rise and fall action, on four barley-twist legs, with original scoreboard, balls, cues and later cue stand, c1900, 102 x 52in (259 x 132cm).
£2,500–3,000
$3,500–4,500 ⚒ DD

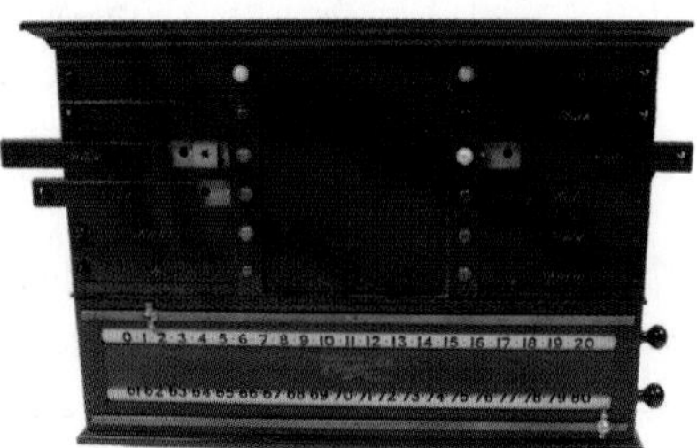

A W. Stephens & Son mahogany combined snooker and life pool scoreboard, c1900, 33in (84cm) wide.
£650–750
$950–1,100 ⊞ MSh

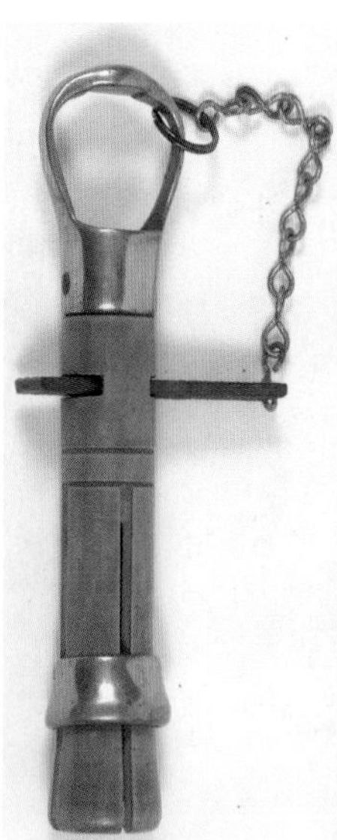

A beech and brass billiard cue tipper, c1900, 6½in (16.5cm) long.
£55–65
$80–100 ⊞ MSh

Cricket

◄ **A Haslemere Cricket Club poster,** for 'The Opening Match', 23 April 1869, 15 x 10in (38 x 25.5cm), with another poster listing the teams for a match against Shalford Institute on 29 June 1869, both stuck to board, minor damage.
£380–450
$575–650 ⚒ HAM

A Royal Doulton two-handled mug, applied in relief with a languid batsman, the reverse with a bowler, the handles of ribbon-bound trophies with hat finials, minor chips and hair crack, impressed and incised marks, 1883, 6½in (16.5cm) high.
£340–380
$500–575 ⚒ L

◄ **Two cricket caps,** 1926.
£30–35
$45–50 each ⊞ SPT

A miniature cricket bat, c1930, 15in (38cm) long.
£35–40
$50–60 ⊞ SMW

A selection of cricket spikes, c1930, 1½ x 2¾in (4 x 7cm).
£4–6
$5–7 each ⊞ HUX

► **Two leather cricket balls,** 1950s.
£4–6
$5–7 each ⊞ AL

◄ **Don Bradman,** *Farewell to Cricket*, first edition, with portrait frontispiece and black and white illustrations from photographs, signed by Bradman, dust jacket, 1950, 8°.
£75–85
$110–125 ⚒ DW

Fishing

A *pâte-sur-pâte* tile, decorated with a boy fishing from a lily pond, incised monogram, possibly by the Sèvres artist Charles Barriat, 1850–1900, 7¾in (19.5cm) square.
£300–350
$450–500 WW

A stuffed and mounted trout, in a bowfronted case, 1879, 23in (58.5cm) wide.
£750–850
$1,100–1,250 MSh

A 2in brass crank wind trout fly reel, with crank arm set inside a raised anti-foul rim, late 19thC.
£25–40
$35–60 OTB

► **A 2½in brass curved crank reel,** 19thC.
£35–40
$50–60 OLD

A Hardy's hinged accessory box, with fitted interior, 1875–1925, 7¼in (18.5cm) wide.
£80–100
$115–145 TMA

An Allcock 3in walnut Nottingham reel, c1900.
£35–40
$50–60 OLD

A Hardy 4½in gunmetal salmon fly fishing reel, c1900.
£445–485
$650–700 MSh

Cross Reference
See Ceramics – Royal Doulton (page 107)

◄ **A Royal Doulton Isaac Walton ware beaker,** with proverb, signed 'Noke', 1906, 5in (12.5cm) high.
£260–290
$380–440 MSh

A Royal Doulton Isaac Walton ware plate, with proverb, signed 'Noke', c1906, 9½in (24cm) diam.
£200–240
$300–350 ⊞ MSh

A 5¼in walnut Nottingham star-back SGA reel, with brass fittings, c1910.
£125–150
$180–220 ⊞ MSh

A Wilkes Osprey 5in brass and walnut sea reel, c1910.
£55–65
$80–100 ⊞ OLD

◀ An Edwardian watercolour trophy painting of a trout, inscribed 'caught in Monkton Pond June 2nd 1905 weight 4lb' some water damage, 16 x 30in (40.5 x 76cm).
£140–160
$200–230 SWO

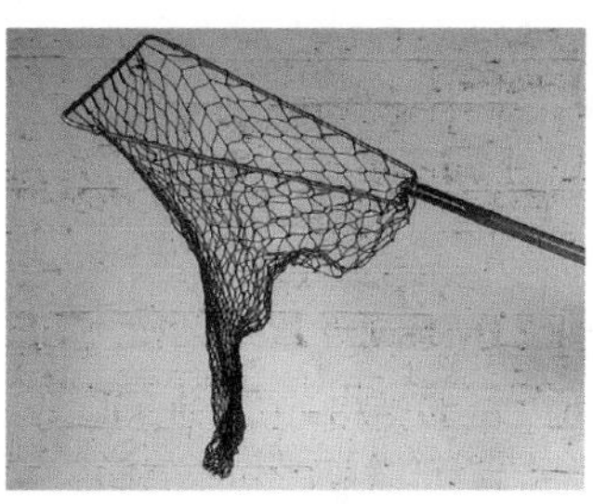

A bamboo and brass keep net, c1920, 62in (157.5cm) long.
£20–25
$30–35 ⊞ AL

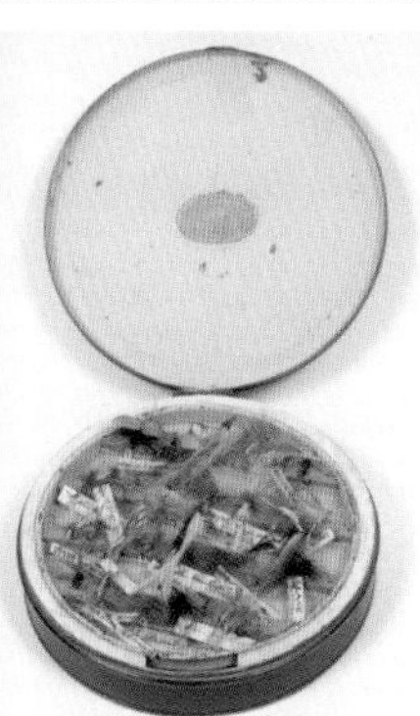

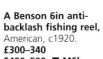

A Farlow & Son black japanned tin cast box, with lift-out fly trap and flies, 1920s, 5¼in (13.5cm) diam.
£100–120
$145–175 ⊞ MSh

A Benson 6in anti-backlash fishing reel, American, c1920.
£300–340
$450–500 ⊞ MSh

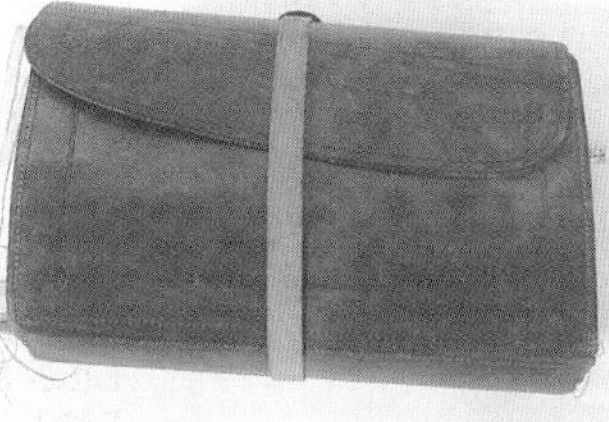

▶ A leather fly-maker's wallet and contents, including two 'Dri Fly Dressers', early 20thC, 7in (18cm) long.
£110–130
$160–190
TMA

A Hardy's Neroda fly box, containing 50 flies, c1930, 6in (15cm) wide.
£65–75
$100–110 ⊞ OLD

A Hardy Bakelite Album cast case, the lid with relief decoration of flies, maker's name stamped to base, 1930s, 4in (10cm) diam.
£30–35
$45–50 ⊞ OTB

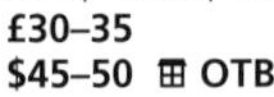

A Hardy Uniqua 3in aluminium and brass reel, 1930s.
£55–65
$80–100 ⊞ SA

◄ A Malloch of Perth 5in brass and Bakelite salmon fly fishing reel, 1930s, in a leather case.
£250–300
$350–450 ⊞ MSh

► An Alvey 9in mahogany reel, Australian, 1930s.
£60–75
$90–110 ⊞ TRA

A steel salmon gaff, with leather-bound handle, c1950, 21in (53.5cm) long.
£45–50
$65–75 ⊞ OLD

► A Hardy Perfect 3¾in salmon fly fishing reel, 1950s.
£235–265
$335–385
⊞ MSh

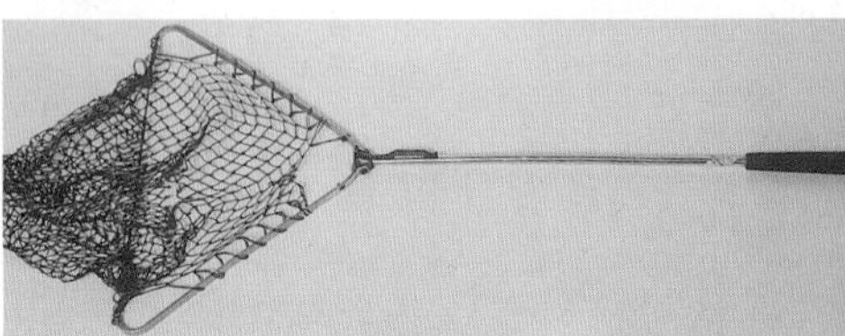

A metal folding landing net, 1950s, 35in (89cm) long.
£40–45
$60–65 ⊞ SPT

Football

Football memorabilia is a more recent entrant to the collectable league. 'It's a young market that only really got going in the 1990s,' explains Graham Budd from Sotheby's. 'But there is a lot of good football material still emerging.'

Among the most popular items with collectors are programmes and ephemera: tickets, celebration banquet menus, autographs and other paper products. 'Rarity is the principal factor and the highest prices are reserved for pre-war programmes,' says Budd. ' Examples from the 1940s and 1950s are also desirable but from c1960 onwards programmes have survived in their thousands and most are only worth pennies or a few pounds.' Condition is also an important factor. 'If a programme is damaged or has been written in, it will be regarded as substandard unless it is particularly rare,' stresses Budd.

Although every club has its supporters, the big name teams still tend to command the highest prices, most notably Manchester United, because its fan base extends beyond the UK to the USA, the Far East and across the world. 'Manchester United items can fetch twice or three times as much as other clubs,' says Budd. Some objects are of particular interest to Manchester United enthusiasts, such as material relating to Sir Matt Busby's team, 'Busby's Babes', many of whom died in the Munich air crash of February 1958, on their return from a European Cup game in Belgrade. Other subjects, such as World Cup material, transcend national club rivalry.

This section also includes modern football memorabilia, although collectors should always be cautious about buying purely for investment. 'Now that he's no longer so much in the public eye, prices for Eric Cantona material have cooled.' warns Budd. 'He might go up again, but who knows? There is no guarantee that someone who is famous at the moment will become one of football history's enduring stars.'

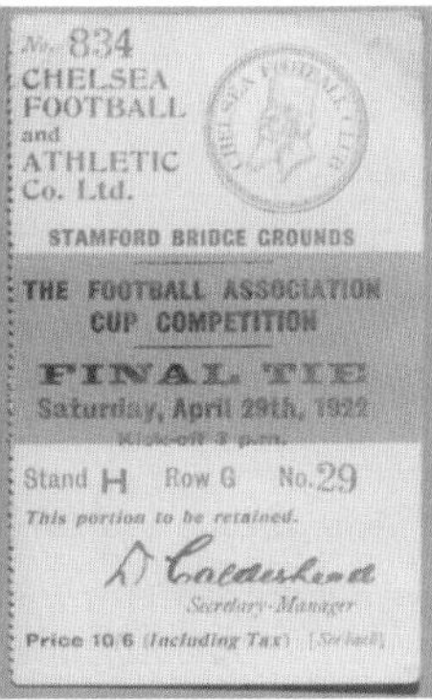

An FA Cup Final ticket stub, Huddersfield Town v. Preston North End at Stamford Bridge, with letter of issue signed by the FA Secretary F. J. Wall, 1922.
£1,800–2,000
$2,600–3,000 S(O)

A postcard, inscribed 'Ceres trying for the 5th 'Ceres' v. Nauplia July, 1928', 3 x 5in (7.5 x 12.5cm).
£40–50
$60–75 EE

Cross Reference
See Postcards (pages 291–293)

An FA Cup Final programme, Arsenal v. Huddersfield Town, 26 April 1930.
£1,000–1,200
$1,500–1,750 S(O)

► **A Scottish Championship 9ct gold medal,** inscribed 'Scottish League Championship, 1930–31, Rangers Football Club, Won by J. Simpson', in original fitted case.
£1,200–1,400
$1,750–2,000 S(O)

◄ **An FA Cup Final programme,** Portsmouth v. Manchester City, 28 April 1934.
£700–800
$1,000–1,150 S(O)

Ten Arsenal programmes, eight home and away at Brentford and Spurs, 1930s.
£530–600
$750–870 S(O)

An FA Cup Final steward's badge, 1949, 2in (5cm) wide.
£120–140
$175–200 P(NW)

A beechwood football game table, with alloy players, 1940s, 66 x 36in (167.5 x 91.5cm).
£2,700–3,000
$4,000–4,400 MSh

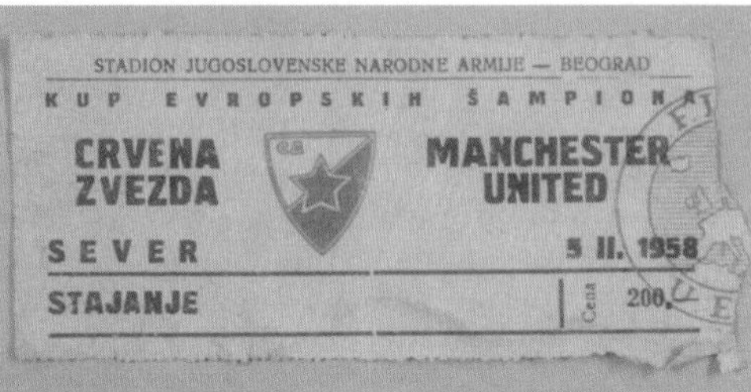

A European Cup ticket, Red Star, Belgrade v. Manchester United, 5 February 1958.
£2,800–3,200
$4,000–4,600 S(O)

David R. Jack, *Matt Busby, My Story*, c1958, 8 x 6in (20.5 x 15cm).
£40–45
$60–65 EE

Roy of the Rovers, *Super Fooball Annual*, 1959, 11 x 8in (28 x 20.5cm).
£10–15
$15–20 EE

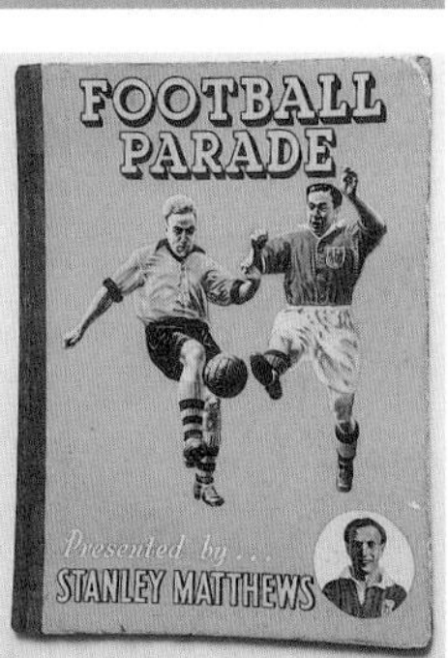

► Stanley Matthews, *Football Parade*, 1950s, 11 x 8in (28 x 20.5cm).
£20–25
$30–35 EE

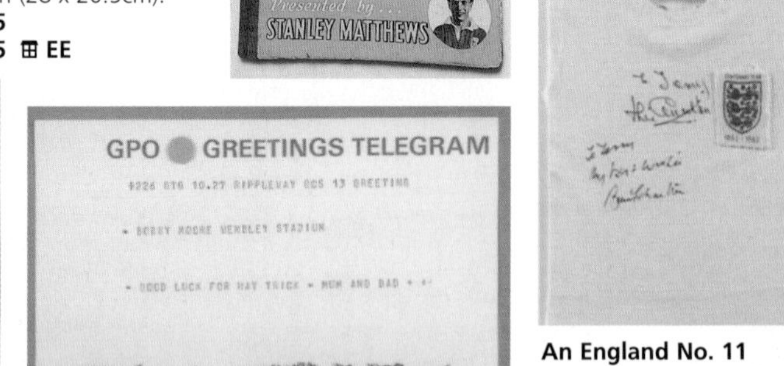

A Northern Ireland v. England and Wales International cap, 1962–63.
£950–1,150
$1,400–1,600 S(O)
This cap belonged to Terry Neill. Born in Belfast in 1942, Neill joined Arsenal in 1959 for £2,500 ($3,500). He played for the club for 11 years and managed Arsenal from July 1976 to December 1983. Neill represented Northern Ireland on 59 occasions and also managed the team.

A good luck telegram for the 1966 World Cup, sent to Bobby Moore by his parents, reading 'Bobby Moore, Wembley Stadium, Good Luck for Hat Trick, Mum and Dad', 30 July 1966.
£650–700
$950–1,000 S(O)

An England No. 11 jersey, signed by Bobby and Jackie Charlton, with cloth badge inscribed 'Centenary Year 1863–1963'.
£1,200–1,400
$1,750–2,000 S(O)
This jersey was gained as a swap after the match against England at Wembley, 20 November 1963. This was the game that England won 8–3.

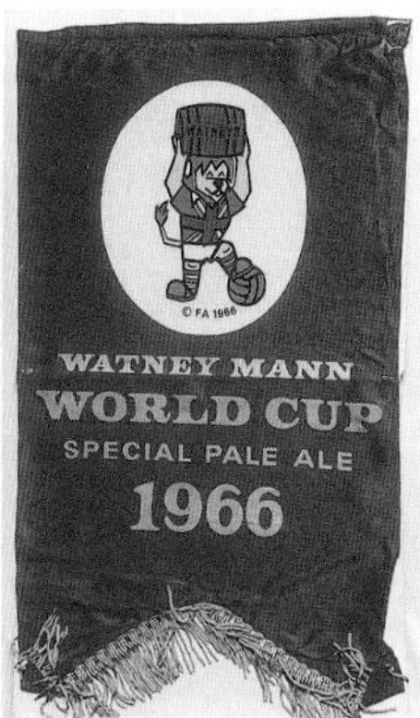

A Watney Mann Special Pale Ale World Cup pennant, featuring World Cup Willie, 1966, 18 x 9in (45.5 x 23cm).
£60–75
$90–110 ⊞ EE

A Liverpool flag, 1960s, 11 x 5in (28 x 12.5cm).
£10–15
$15–20 ⊞ EE

An England No. 8 International jersey, signed by Paul Gascoigne, c1998, with a signed letter of authenticity from Tottenham Hotspur FC.
£850–950
$1,250–1,400 ⚒ S(O)

A Cup Final programme, Everton v. Sheffield Wednesday at Wembley Stadium, 1966, 9 x 6in (23 x 15cm).
£30–35
$45–50 ⊞ J&S

A Nike practice ball, used before the 1999 Champions League final at the Nou Camp Stadium, Barcelona, Manchester United v. Bayern Munich, damaged, 1999, with a signed letter of provenance.
£375–425
$560–620 ⚒ S(O)

A Scottish League Cup 9ct gold and enamel medal, inscribed 'Scottish Football League, League Cup, Season 1967–68 Winner'.
£575–425
$850–620 ⚒ S(O)

◄ A roll of pasted vinyl wallpaper, featuring the England International team, pattern repeat, 1978.
£80–90
$115–130 per repeat
⊞ TWI

An England No. 7 jersey, signed by David Beckham and 20 England squad members, 1997, framed, 37½ x 35¾in (95.5 x 90cm).
£1,800–2,000
$2,500–3,000 ⚒ S(O)

A Soviet Union No. 3 International jersey, worn by Vladimir Kaplichni, 1969.
£450–500
$650–720 ⚒ S(O)

A Liverpool No. 9 jersey, signed 'Ian Rush, 83/84 Champions', with a photo of Ian Rush, 1983–84.
£600–650
$870–1,000 ⚒ S(O)

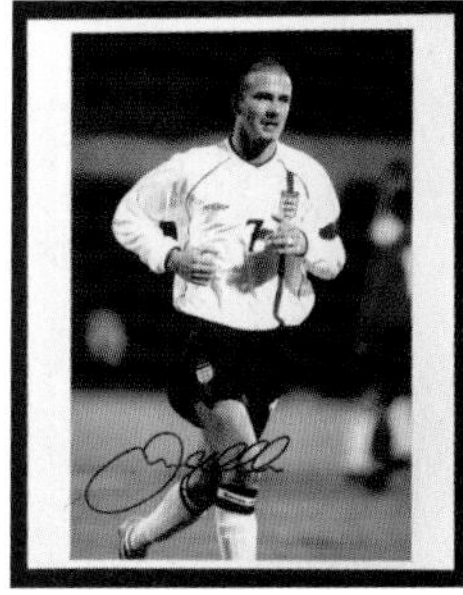

David Beckham, a signed photograph, 2001, 10 x 8in (25.5 x 20.5cm).
£150–1275
$220–250 ⊞ FRa

◄ A Nike Glasgow Ranger's jersey, with 18 players' signatures from the 1999 treble-winning side, c1999.
£180–220
$260–320 ⚒ DW

Golf

A gutta percha golf ball, handmade, 1850–56, 1½in (4cm) diam.
£800–900
$1,150–1,300 SWO

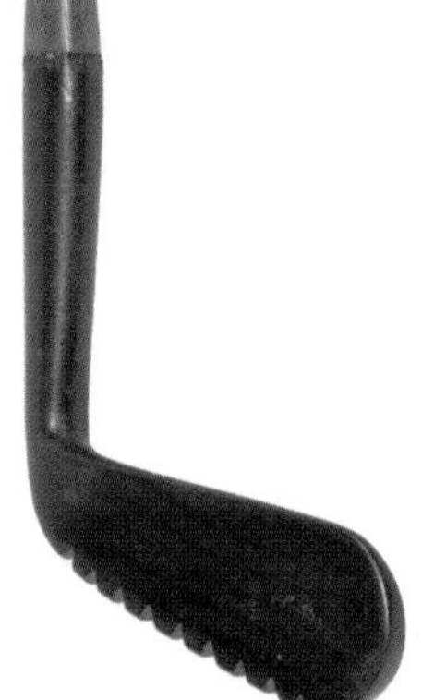

A W. Park lofting iron, with smooth face and grooved sole, 1890s.
£300–340
$450–500 MSh

◄ A gutta percha golf ball, early 20thC, 1½in (4cm) diam.
£30–35
$45–50 G(L)

A silver-plated inkstand, the inkwells in the shape of golf balls, c1900, 8in (20.5cm) wide.
£400–450
$580–650 Msh

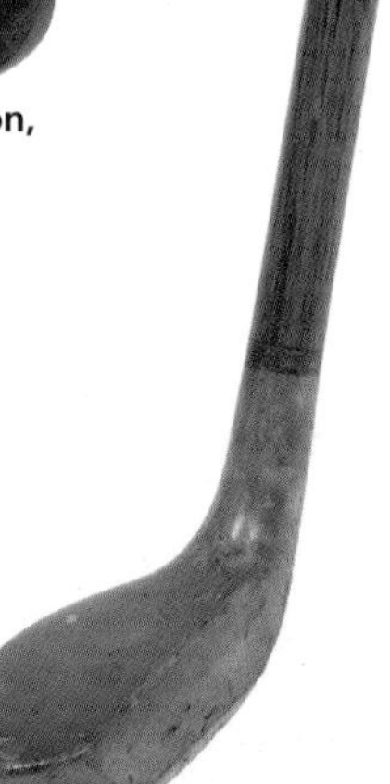

A Schenectady-style double-sided putter, with aluminium head, c1920.
£120–140
$175–200 MSh

A Sunday golf club, with beech head, lead weight and horn insert, c1900.
£300–350
$450–500 Msh

Cross Reference
See Handbags
(pages 218–222)

A Soure plastic golf handbag, American, late 1950s, 10in (25.5cm) wide.
£100–120
$145–175 TWI

A Kevin Francis character jug, 'The Golfer', No. 247 of a limited edition of 1,000, 1990s, 9in (23cm) high, boxed.
£60–70
$90–100 Pott

Rugby

A Raphanel painted spelter figure of a rugby player, c1900, 18in (45.5cm) high.
£600–700
$870–1,000 ⊞ MSh

A ceramic inkwell, in the shape of a rugby football, with brass-plated lid, c1900, 3in (7.5cm) high.
£340–380
$480–570 ⊞ MSh

► **A Staffordshire water jug,** with transfer-printed decoration of a rugby scene, c1910.
£230–260
$330–360 ⊞ MSh

A leather-covered ceramic butter dish, in the shape of a rugby ball, 1930s, 5¾in (14.5cm) wide.
£190–220
$275–320 ⊞ MSh

A Rugby Town AFC programme, 1951, 7 x 5in (18 x 12.5cm).
£5–7
$7–10 ⊞ MRW

A leather rugby ball, 1960s, 12in (30.5cm) wide.
£50–60
$75–90 ⊞ TRA

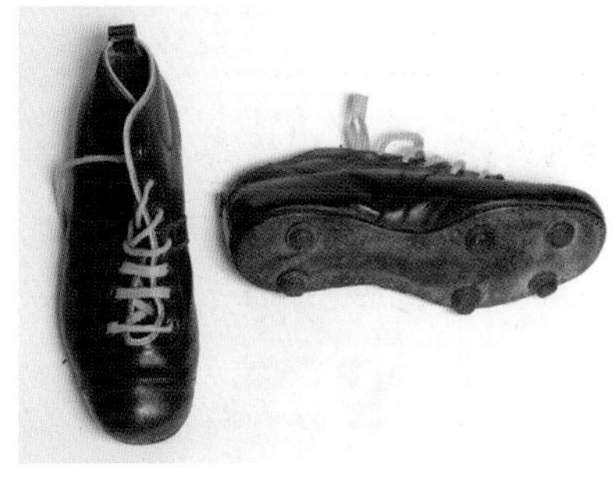

► **A pair of rugby boots,** 1960s.
£25–35
$35–50 ⊞ TRA

Tennis

◄ **A pair of chromolithographs,** each depicting a female tennis player, German, 19thC, 6¼ x 3¼in (16 x 8.5cm), framed and glazed.
£180–220
$250–320 ⚒ DW

► **A Slazenger Doherty tennis racket,** with patent shoulders, c1905.
£145–165
$200–240 ⊞ MSh

A Slazenger mahogany tennis racket press, for six rackets, with leather handle, c1910.
£220–250
$320–360 ⚒ DW

A Birmal aluminium tennis racket, with steel stringing by Birmingham Aluminium Casting, c1924.
£160–180
$230–260 ⊞ Msh

A Dayton tennis racket, with metal head, steel stringing and wooden handle, American, 1930s.
£90–100
$130–145 ⊞ Msh

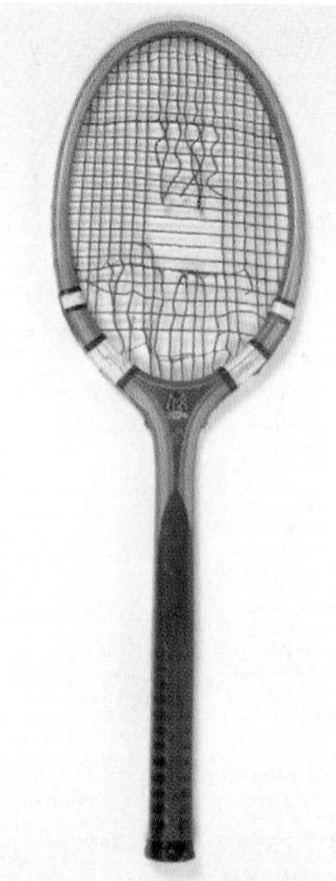

A Murray & Baldwin tennis racket, with notched grip, 1930s.
£100–120
$145–175 ⊞ Msh

A tin of Dunlop tennis balls, American, c1960, 8in (20.5cm) high.
£30–35
$45–50 ⊞ HUX

Winter Sports

► **A pair of hickory skis,** c1920, 71in (180.5cm) long.
£125–145
$180–200 ⊞ MSh

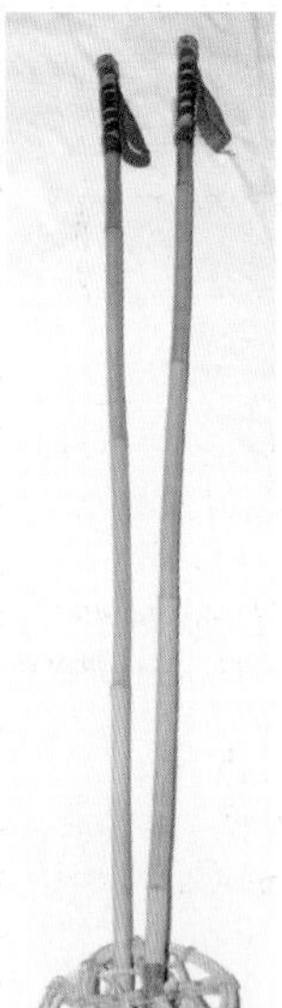

A pair of bamboo ski poles, c1910, 40in (101.5cm) long.
£30–35
$45–50 ⊞ Msh

◄ **A set of six glass tumblers,** each decorated with two skaters, 1960s, 7in (14cm) high.
£40–45
$60–65 ⊞ TWI

◄ **A granite curling stone,** mid-20thC, 11in (28cm) diam.
£90–100
$130–145 ⊞ OLA

► **A National Ski Federation supporter's badge,** 1960s, 1in (2.5cm) diam.
£3–5
$6–8 ⊞ RTT

Teddy Bears & Soft Toys

◀ **A Steiff straw-filled teddy bear,** with button eyes, hump back, worn felt pads, German, early 20thC, 10in (25.5cm) high.
£800–1,000
$1,150–1,500 AH

A Steiff cinnamon teddy bear, with unusual coloured ear button, some paw pads replaced, 1908, 16in (40.5cm) high.
£1,850–2,000
$2,700–2,900 ⊞ BBe

A mohair teddy bear, possibly by the Ideal Toy Co, with boot button eyes, felt pads, American, 1910–20, 18in (45.5cm) high.
£500–550
$720–800 ⊞ BBe

A mohair teddy bear, possibly by the Ideal Toy Co, with boot button eyes, replacement pads, American, 1910–20, 18in (45.5cm) high.
£350–400
$500–580 ⊞ BBe

◀ **A mohair teddy bear,** with glass eyes, 1920s, 18in (45.5cm) high.
£600–650
$870–1,000 ⊞ BBe

A mohair teddy bear, possibly by Schuco, with glass eyes, stitched nose and mouth and felt paw pads, swivel head and jointed at the shoulders and hips, ears missing, German, c1920, 24in (61cm) high.
£120–140
$175–200 Bon(C)

A Steiff bear on wheels, with glass eyes, stitched nose and mouth, clipped muzzle with felt-lined open mouth, stitched claws and felt pads, German, 1920s, 10in (25.5cm) high.
£180–220
$260–320 Bon(C)

A Chiltern mohair teddy bear, with glass eyes, 1920s, 24in (61cm) high.
£450–500
$650–720 BBe

A Chad Valley mohair bear, with glass eyes, stitched nose, mouth and claws, swivel head and jointed at the shoulders and hips, c1930, 13in (33cm) high.
£220–260
$320–380 Bon(C)

A Knickerbox mohair teddy bear, with glass eyes, metal nose and brushed cotton pads, American, 1930s, 18in (45.5cm) high.
£125–150
$180–220 BBe

A mohair teddy bear, possibly by Schuco, with glass eyes, separate muzzle with stitched nose and mouth, swivel head and jointed to the shoulders and hips, felt pads, 1930s, 7in (18cm) high.
£120–140
$175–200 Bon(C)

A Merrythought mohair teddy bear, with ear button, glass eyes, cotton pads and original label, 1930s, 15in (38cm) high.
£235–265
$340–380 BBe

Cross Reference
See Dolls (pages 181–190)

► **A Steiff mohair seated teddy bear,** with glass eyes, stitched nose and claws, clipped muzzle with felt-lined open mouth, down-turned paws with felt pads, swivel head and jointed shoulders, German, c1950, 10in (25.5cm) high.
£180–200
$260–300 Bon(C)

► **A Hermann Zotty teddy bear,** with glass eyes and open mouth, German, c1950, 11in (28cm) high.
£130–150
$190–220 YC

A Steiff mohair teddy baby, with glass eyes, stitched nose and claws, turned-down paws with felt pads, clipped muzzle with open felt-lined mouth, swivel head and jointed shoulders and hips, German, 1950s, 10in (25.5cm) high.
£200–240
$300–350 Bon(C)

A Pedigree mohair teddy bear, with glass eyes, stitched nose and mouth, swivel head, jointed shoulders and hips and worn Rexine paw pads, 1950s, 14in (35.5cm) high.
£60–70
$90–100 Bon(C)

A Steiff Joggi mohair hedgehog, with button eyes and original label, 1950s, 5in (12.5cm) high.
£45–50
$65–75 BBe

A teddy bear, with glass eyes and a stitched nose, 1955, 15in (38cm) high.
£100–150
$150–220 YC

A Wendy Boston teddy bear, with plastic eyes and original label on leg, late 1950s, 14in (35.5cm) high.
£55–65
$80–95 BBe

In the 1950s, Wendy Boston created the first completely machine-washable bear. The bear had plastic eyes and was made from nylon-based fabrics which, unlike other stuffings such as wool and kapok, dried easily. Wendy Boston advertised the bear on television in 1955, showing it being passed through a mangle.

► **A Steiff mohair family of cows,** with glass eyes, velvet muzzles, chests and horns, ear button to the bull, German, c1950, largest 3in (7.5cm) high.
£200–250
$300–360 Bon(C)

A mohair teddy bear, with glass eyes, stitched nose and mouth, jointed shoulders and hips and red metal heart attached to the chest, 1950s, 4in (10cm) high.
£50–60
$75–90 Bon(C)

► **A stuffed cloth lion,** with glass eyes, 1950s, 12in (30.5cm) long.
£25–30
$35–45 YC

Two Steiff wool plush and mohair poodles, the black dog with glass eyes and chest tag, the grey dog with glass eyes, chest tag and ear button, 1956–58, 4in (10cm) high.
Black dog £55–65
$80–95
Grey dog £75–85
$110–125 ⊞ BBe

A Chiltern silk plush teddy bear, on a pull-along bicycle, the bear with rubber nose and original label, 1950s–60s, 11in (28cm) high.
£100–120
$145–175 ⊞ BBe

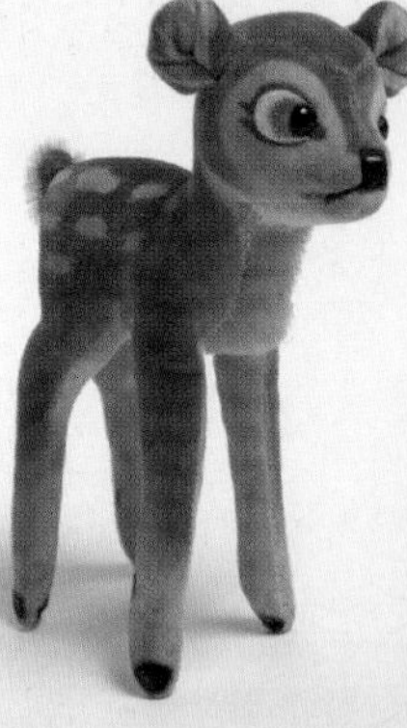

A Steiff velvet Bambi, with mohair chest and tail, button missing, 1950s–60s, 5½in (14cm) high.
£30–35
$45–50 ⊞ BBe

A Twyford mohair teddy bear, with glass eyes, Rexine pads and side label, 1960, 12in (30.5cm) high.
£150–170
$220–250 ⊞ BBe

A fur and cloth monkey, with glass eyes, c1960, 14in (35.5cm) high.
£20–25
$30–35 ⊞ YC

A Merrythought Cheeky synthetic plush teddy bear, with plastic eyes, 1960s, 14in (35.5cm) high.
£300–335
$440–475 ⊞ BBe

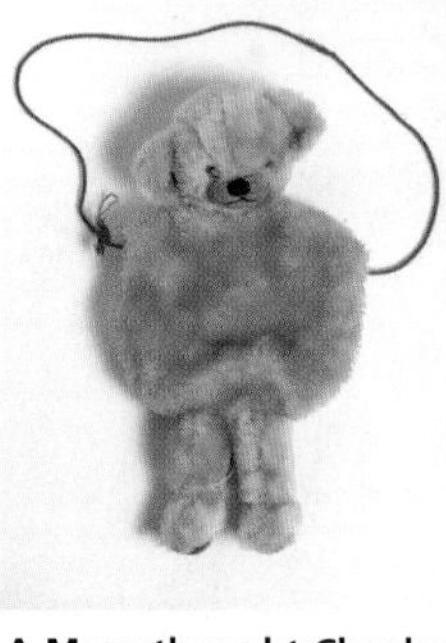

A Merrythought Cheeky Bear synthetic plush muff, with plastic eyes, velvet muzzle and stitched nose and mouth, original label, 1960s, 13in (33cm) high.
£180–220
$260–320 ⚒ Bon(C)

A Steiff Manni mohair rabbit, with glass eyes and ear button, 1960s, 4½in (11.5cm) high.
£55–65
$80–100 ⊞ BBe

A Steiff kangaroo, with ear button and chest tag, joey missing, 1960s, 6in (15cm) high.
£45–50
$65–75 ⊞ BBe

► **A mohair Paddington Bear,** with plastic eyes and nose, felt hat and coat, Wellington boots, 1970s, 18½in (47cm) high.
£80–100
$115–145
⚒ Bon(C)

Telephones

A Jydsk Magneto wooden wall telephone, with brass and chrome fittings, American, c1895, 25in (63.5cm) high.
£450–500
$650–720 ⊞ DHAR

A wooden wall-mounted telephone, with brass fittings, with battery box and writing slope, c1900, 24in (61cm) high.
£500–600
$720–870 ⊞ JUN

A cast-iron candlestick telephone, with brass and Bakelite fittings, 'The G. E. Co Ltd, Telephone Works, Coventry, England' inscribed on the transmitter mount, 1920s, 13½in (34.5cm) high.
£300–350
$440–500 ⊞ DHAR

◄ **A black metal candlestick telephone,** No. 150, 1920s, 12½in (32cm) high.
£110–130
$160–190 ⚒ G(L)

An enamel telephone sign, c1930, 29in (73.5cm) wide.
£120–140
$175–200 ⊞ JUN

Cross Reference
See Advertising & Packaging (pages 11–22)

◄ **A copper-bodied KTAS telephone,** with brass dial and Bakelite and brass handset, Danish, 1930s, 9in (23cm) high.
£150–180
$220–260
⊞ DHAR

A Bakelite telephone, wired to work, 1930s, 7in (18cm) high.
£100–120
$145–175 ⊞ TL

A Bakelite 200 series telephone, with bell box and a drawer, 1930s, 9in (23cm) wide.
£200–225
$300–325 ⊞ JAZZ

A Bakelite desk telephone, with handset, metal cradle and exposed chrome bells at the rear, Swiss, 1930s, 9in (23cm) high.
£150–175
$220–255 ⊞ DHAR

Facts in brief

Telephones with cord braid, drawer and call exchange button attract higher prices.

► **A Bakelite 'pyramid' telephone,** with drawer, 1930s, 6in (15cm) high.
£130–150
$190–220 ⊞ TL
In the UK, coloured telephones were more expensive to rent than the standard black models.

A metal wall telephone, by ATM of Liverpool and under license to Bell of Antwerp, Belgian, 1932–38, 10in (25.5cm) high.
£60–70
$90–100 ⊞ TL

A Bakelite Jukebox wall telephone, by Bell of Antwerp, Belgian, 1938–47, 10in (25.5cm) high.
£80–90
$115–130 ⊞ TL

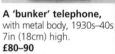

A 'bunker' telephone, with metal body, 1930s–40s 7in (18cm) high.
£80–90
$115–130 ⊞ TL

◄ **A Smiths and Phillips china plate,** decorated with two boys on the telephone and inscribed 'Hallo, who is on the line Honey', 1930–40, 6in (15cm) diam.
£50–55
$75–80 ⊞ NAW

A Bakelite 300 series telephone, with drawer, 1940s–50s, 9in (23cm) wide.
£180–200
$260–300 ⊞ JAZZ

► A cast-iron K6 telephone box, 1930s–60s, 58in (147.5cm) high.
£1,000–1,250
$1,500–1,800 ⊞ JUN
In 1924, the British General Post Office organized a competition for the design of a telephone box. It was won by Sir Giles Gilbert Scott (1880–1960), designer of Liverpool Cathedral. In addition to numerous churches, he was also responsible for Waterloo Bridge, Battersea Power Station and Bankside Power Station, now home of the Tate Modern Gallery. Known as K2 (Kiosk 2), his red cast-iron design was initially only released in London. For outside London he created the K3, made from more economical reinforced concrete, and painted cream, considered more suitable for rural areas. In 1936 he produced the K6 to celebrate the Silver Jubilee of King George V. Known as the Jubilee Kiosk, 60,000 of these red telephone boxes were introduced throughout the country and became a much-loved British landmark. In 1988, British Telecom's decision to replace these boxes created a huge outcry. Many subsequently appeared in auctions and antiques shops, but others were preserved in their original positions, protected by English Heritage.

A Western Electric payphone, the cast-metal body with a chromed finish, plastic handset and dial and cashbox at base, American, 1950s, 18in (45.5cm) high.
£360–400
$525–580 ⊞ DHAR

A Bell polished chrome telephone, 1950s, 5½in (14cm) high.
£80–90
$115–130 ⊞ TL
These original metal-bodied telephones were made in the 1950s by Bell in Antwerp and were widely exported.

◄ An Ericsson wall telephone, 1950s, 10in (25.5cm) high.
£110–130
$160–190 ⊞ TL

To order Miller's books in the USA please ring Phaidon Press toll free on 1-877-PHAIDON

A Bakelite 300 series telephone, with bell on/off option, 1950s, 9in (23cm) wide.
£115–125
$165–180 ⊞ JAZZ

A Tele 311 Bakelite wall telephone, 1950s, 10in (25.5cm) high.
£80–90
$115–130 ⊞ TL

A wall-mounted telephone, 1960s, 10in (25.5cm) high.
£20–25
$30–35 ⊞ TL
This was the last British Standard telephone, manufactured in the 1960s in either ivory or grey.

A plastic Kermit telephone, by the American Telecommunications Corporation, California, on an imitation wood base, American, 1970s, 12in (30.5cm) high.
£200–240
$300–350 ⊞ DHAR

► A Silver Jubilee plastic telephone, 1977, 9in (23cm) wide.
£55–65
$80–95 ⊞ HarC

A Kirk Bakelite telephone, Danish, 1950s, 6in (15cm) high.
£60–70
$90–100 ⊞ TL

An acrylic Ericsson Ericofon 600 telephone, of one-piece construction, the dial and the cut-off switch being in the base, 1960s, 8in (20.5cm) high.
£125–150
$180–220 ⊞ DHAR
Designed in 1954, this was the first successful single-piece telephone. Called the Erica in the USA, it was specifically targeted at housewives and manufactured in a range of colours. It is also known as the Cobra telephone.

A Bakelite telephone, 1955, 9in (23cm) high.
£325–375
$470–550 ⊞ HarC

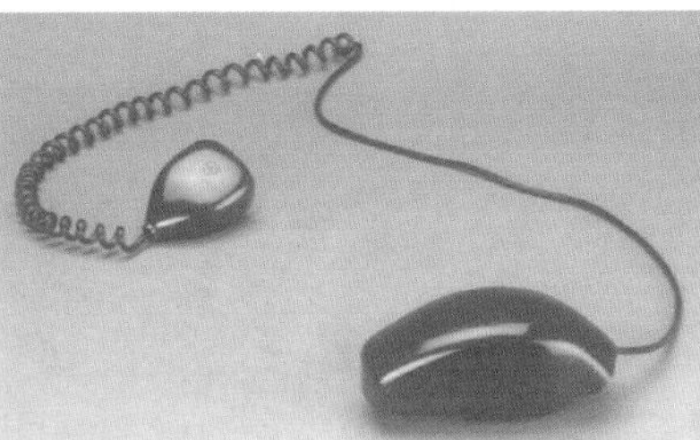

A *Grillo* telephone, by Marco Zanuso and Richard Sapper, Italian, 1965, 3in (7.5cm) high.
£180–220
$260–320 ⚒ BB(L)
***Grillo* means cricket.**

The Alexander Graham Plane telephone, by Northern Telecom, 1970s, 9in (23cm) high.
£350–400
$500–580 ⊞ DHAR
This telephone was made for the Canadian market in orange, white or camouflage. Prices vary according to the colour, between £200–400 ($300–580).

Textiles

A cotton tablecloth, some fading, 1870s, 56 x 54in (142 x 137cm).
£55–65
$80–100 ⊞ DE

A Victorian rosewood and petit point teapot stand, 9½in (24cm) square.
£40–45
$60–65 ⊞ BrL

A pair of hand-embroidered silk cuffs, Chinese, c1880, 19in (48.5cm) long.
£55–65
$80–100 ⊞ JPr

A silk bell pull, c1880, 60in (152.5cm) long.
£75–85
$110–125 ⊞ JPr

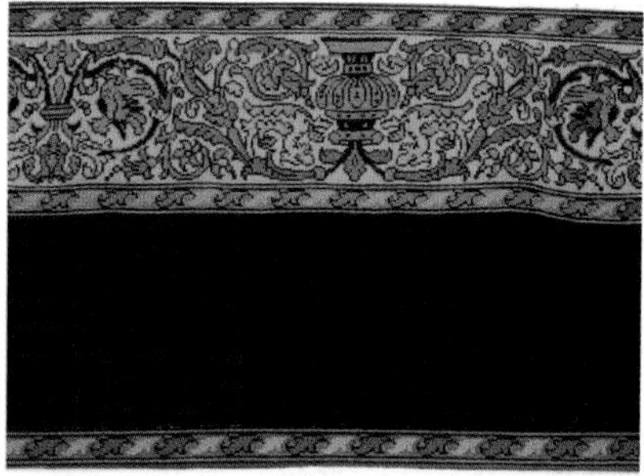
A woolwork and velvet mantelpiece cover, French, c1880, 51in (129.5cm) long.
£120–140
$175–200 ⊞ L&L

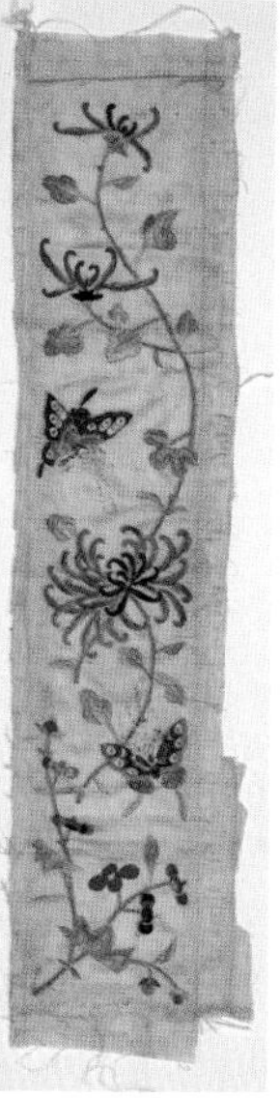
A pair of hand-embroidered silk cuffs, Chinese, c1880, 19in (48.5cm) long.
£30–35
$45–50 ⊞ JPr

A *Kashgai* cushion, c1900, 14½in (37cm) square.
£40–50
$60–75 ⊞ DNo

A silk handkerchief case, embroidered with a regimental crest and 'Souvenir From France', 1914–18, 7in (18cm) wide.
£25–30
$35–45 ⊞ L&L

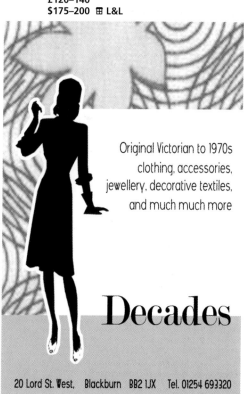

Bed Covers

A linen and hand-crocheted lace bed cover, embroidered with an Art Nouveau design, c1880, to fit a bed 54in (137cm) wide.
£260–300
$375–450 ⊞ L&L

A Victorian knitted cotton bed cover, to fit a bed 54in (137cm) wide.
£85–95
$125–140 ⊞ L&L

A child's patchwork quilt, comprising checked, floral and plain hexagonal pieces, the central panel with numbers, c1930, to fit a bed 36in (91.5cm) wide.
£70–80
$100–115 ⊞ JPr

A striped paisley quilt, with solid paisley design on reverse, Welsh, Cardiganshire, c1880, 82in (208.5cm) long.
£450–500
$650–720 ⊞ JJ

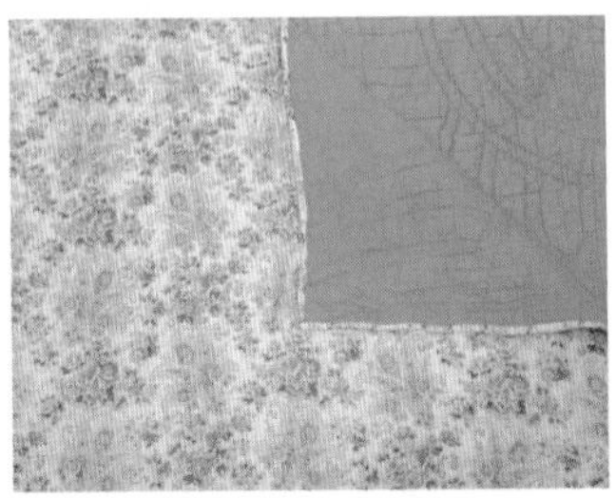

A Durham hand-stitched quilt, with floral decoration and plain reverse, 1900, 83in (211cm) long.
£135–165
$200–240 ⊞ L&L

An embroidered silk coverlet, Chinese, early 20thC, 43in (109cm) square.
£85–95
$125–140 ⊞ JPr

A North Country hand-stitched quilt, with floral decoration, c1890, 97in (246.5cm) long.
£350–400
$500–580 ⊞ JJ

A hand-stitched quilt, decorated with a fan design, Canadian, 1920s, 99in (251.5cm) long.
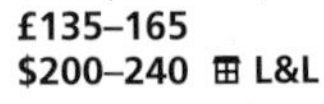
£135–165
$200–240 ⊞ L&L

A woolwork bed cover, Indian, early 20thC, 90in (228.5cm) long.
£190–220
$275–325 ⊞ JPr

◄ **A plaid wool blanket,** woven on a wide loom, Welsh, c1950, 90in (228.5cm) long.
£50–60
$75–90 ⊞ JJ

Costume

◄ **A shot silk dress,** with lace collar, 1850s.
£165–195
$240–280 ⊞ L&L

A silk dress, with bustle and apron front, 1870s.
£165–195
$240–280 ⊞ L&L

A silk dress, with leg-of-mutton sleeves and lace detail to bodice, 1890.
£180–200
$260–300 ⊞ L&L

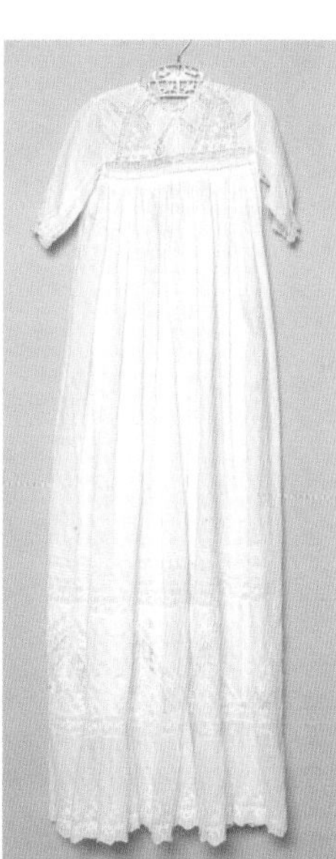

An Edwardian cotton and lace christening gown.
£55–65
$80–100 ⊞ Ech

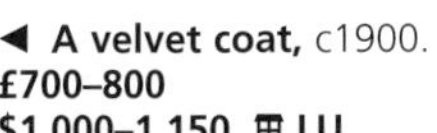

◄ **A velvet coat,** c1900.
£700–800
$1,000–1,150 ⊞ LU

A silk dress, with French jet-beaded panel, c1918.
£150–180
$220–260 ⊞ DE

◄ **A rayon dress,** unworn, 1920s.
£75–85
$110–125 ⊞ Ech

A satin drop-waisted dress, with lace trim, 1920s.
£100–125
$145–175 ⊞ Ech

A chiffon flapper dress, with clear bugle beads and handkerchief hem, 1920s.
£325–375
$470–560 ⊞ Ech

Flapper dresses

Beaded flapper dresses are very popular today, both with collectors and those who want an interesting party dress. Made from fine chiffon and often sewn with literally thousands of beads, these dresses are fragile and require careful storage. Ideally, dresses should be laid flat rather than hung as the weight of beads can cause the fabric to tear. Repairs should be carried out quickly, since if you tear the beads, they can fall off in tiny handfuls. Luckily, however, as these frocks were hand-stitched and well made in the first place, with a bit of loving attention (and a 1920s-style slip underneath, both for modesty's sake and to avoid snagging the sheer chiffon on bra straps), they can be worn with considerable pleasure today.

A crêpe dress, by Clifcella Gowns, with painted flowers, 1930.
£45–55
$65–80 ⊞ DE

A printed silk and rayon kimono, with embroidered floral decoration, 1930s.
£35–45
$50–65 ⊞ Ech

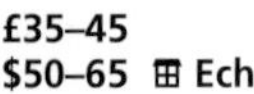

► **A silk Victory scarf,** printed with flags commemorating WWII, c1945, 35in (89cm) square.
£110–120
$160–175 ⊞ REN

◄ **A rayon crêpe dress,** printed with a floral pattern, 1940s.
£35–45
$50–65 ⊞ Ech

A child's cotton gingham dress, with smocking, 1940s–50s, 29in (73.5cm) long.
£35–40
$50–60 ⊞ Ech

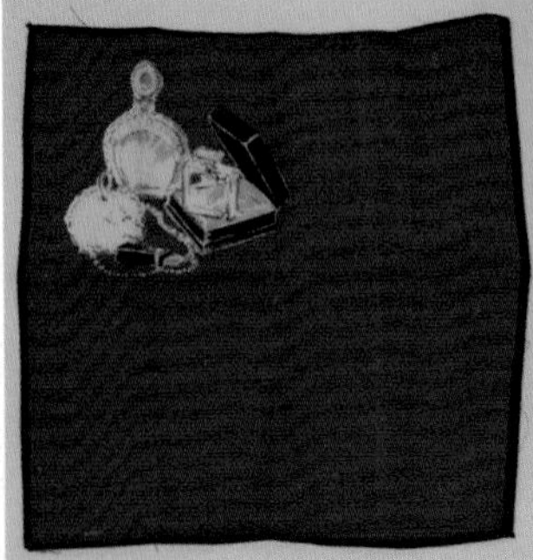

◄ **A cotton handkerchief,** printed with perfume bottles, 1950s, 9in (23cm) square.
£15–20
$20–30 ⊞ LBe

► **A cotton one-piece bathing suit,** c1950.
£15–20
$20–30 ⊞ DE

A polyester evening suit, by David Gibson, 1950s.
£40–50
$60–75 ⊞ HSt

A dress, by Pucci, 1960s.
£300–350
$450–500 ⊞ SBT

► A cotton dress, with printed decoration, 1950s.
£15–20
$20–30 ⊞ REPS

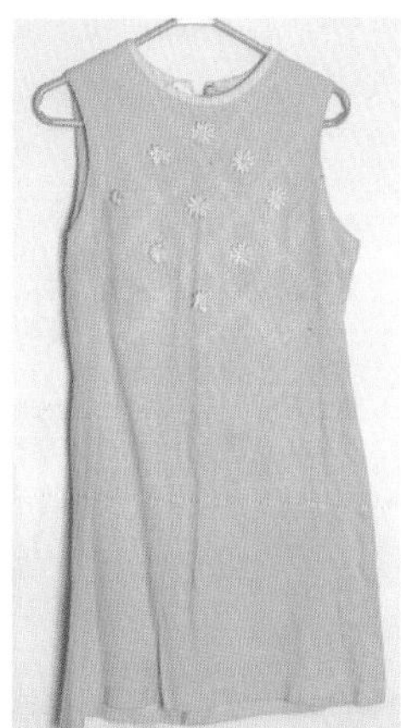

A cotton dress, with appliqué daisies, 1960.
£15–20
$20–30 ⊞ REPS

A full-length printed dress, by Miss Mouse, 1960s–70s.
£250–300
$350–450 ⊞ SBT

◄ A Vivienne Westwood Salon Collection evening gown, with embossed flocked tracery, matching fringed scarf, 1992.
£1,300–1,500
$2,000–2,200 ⚒ S(O)

A lurex dress, by Sixth Sense, 1960.
£15–20
$20–30 ⊞ DE

◄ A Vivienne Westwood Dressing Up Collection Harris tweed tartan jacket, with mini-crini 'criniscule skirt', 1991.
£550–650
$800–950 ⚒ S(O)
This is a one-off show sample.

Embroidered Pictures & Samplers

A hand-worked wool picture, depicting a still life of fruit in a bowl, early 19thC, 9½ x 7½in (24 x 19cm).
£180–210
$260–300 DA

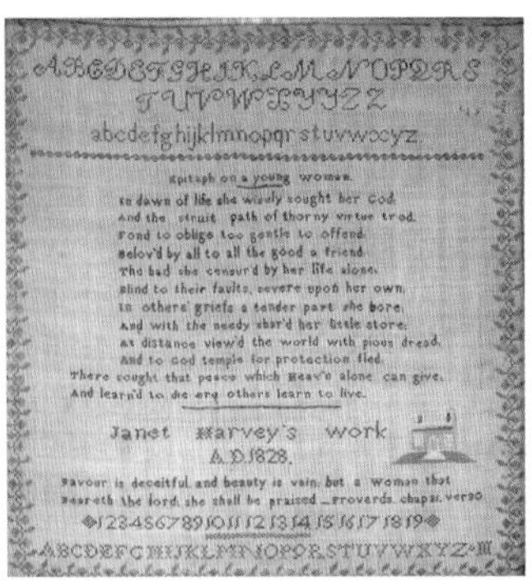

A needlework sampler, by Janet Harvey, depicting a house, with alphabet verse within a floral garland border, dated 1828, 18 x 17in (45.5 x 43cm).
£190–230
$275–335 G(L)

A sampler, by Polly Arthur, worked with alphabet, numerals and pattern bands, 1892, 17 x 16in (43 x 40.5cm).
£55–65
$80–95 G(L)

An embroidered picture, depicting a royal coat-of-arms, 1897, 19 x 28in (48.5 x 71cm).
£120–150
$175–225 ⊞ COB

A petit point picture, depicting a basket of roses and foliage, with gold mount, within a plaster moulded and painted frame, late 19thC, 8in (20.5cm) wide.
£180–200
$260–300 ⊞ JPr

A needlework sampler, by Eliza Davies, depicting a windmill and houses and a six-line verse, decorated with trees, birds and baskets of flowers, damaged, 19thC, 15 x 12in (38 x 30.5cm).
£320–370
$450–550 SWO

Items in the Textiles section have been arranged in date order within each sub-section.

A silkwork picture, depicting a garden scene, 1920s, 11 x 10in (27 x 25.5cm).
£70–80
$100–115 ⊞ JPr

A woolwork picture, embroidered with deer in a landscape, c1920, 12in (30.5cm) wide.
£100–120
$145–175 ⊞ JPr

Hats

A cotton calash, 1840, 14in (35.5cm) high.
£65–70
$95–100 ⊞ L&L

A calash or calèche was a folding bonnet with hoops made of cane or whalebone. Worn out-of-doors, particularly in the evening, it could be folded up and put in a reticule.

A lace and velvet indoor cap, 1850, 8in (20.5cm) wide.
£30–35
$45–50 ⊞ L&L

Lace caps were worn indoors in the mid-19th century, particularly by married and more elderly ladies. There were different styles for day and evening wear, the latter often more richly trimmed.

A velvet bonnet, with silk flowers and ribbon ties, 1890, 9in (23cm) high.
£70–80
$100–115 ⊞ L&L

An Edwardian straw hat, by Liberty, trimmed with velvet, decorated with silk flowers and velvet ribbon ties, 12in (30.5cm) diam.
£45–55
$65–80 ⊞ Ech

LOCATE THE SOURCE

The source of each illustration in Miller's can be found by checking the code letters below each caption with the Key to Illustrations, pages 443–451.

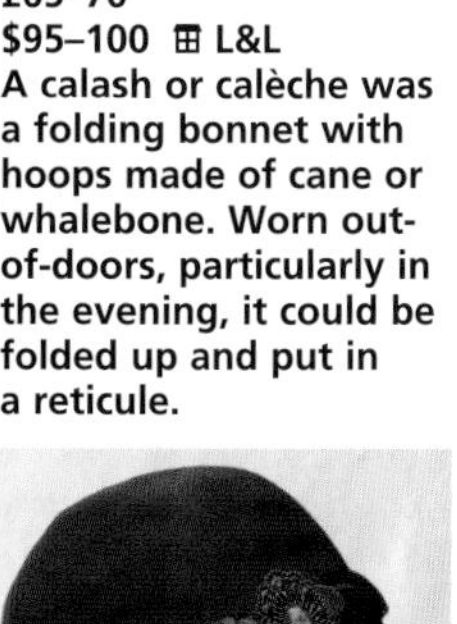

A felt cloche hat, with velvet trimmings, decorated with a brooch with red stones, 1920s.
£85–95
$125–140 ⊞ LU

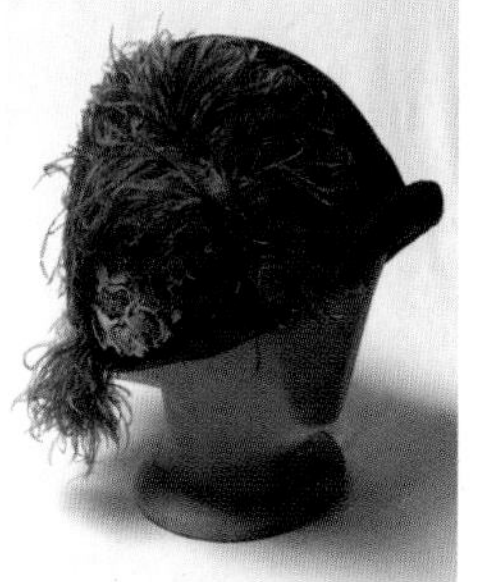

A cloche hat, trimmed with an ostrich feather and silk flowers, 1920s.
£170–200
$250–300 ⊞ LU

A straw picture hat, trimmed with net and an artificial posy, 1930, 13in (33cm) diam.
£55–65
$80–100 ⊞ Ech

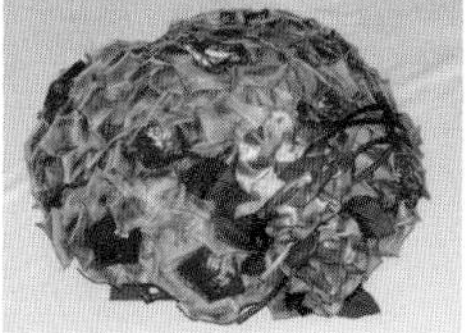

A velvet and silk hat, decorated with artificial roses, 1950s, 13in (33cm) diam.
£100–125
$145–180 ⊞ LU

Lace

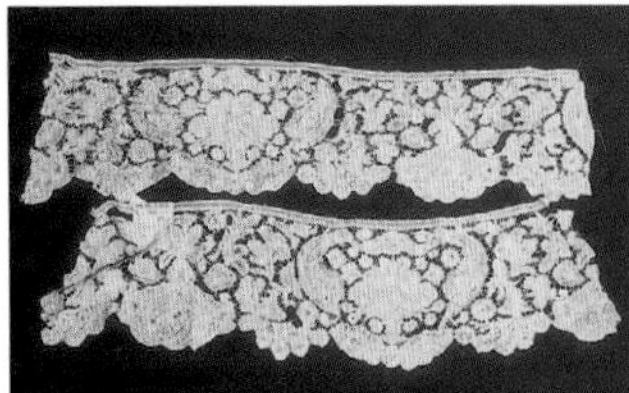

Two lengths of Flemish bobbin lace, 18thC, 7 x 25in (18 x 63.5cm).
£45–50
$65–75 ⊞ JuC

► **A panel of Brussels lace,** mid-19thC, 5 x 54in (12.5 x 137cm).
£80–90
$115–130 ⊞ HL

A Honiton lace jabot collar, late 19thC, 12in (30.5cm) long.
£100–125
$145–180 ⊞ HL

A crochet collar, probably Irish, late 19thC, 24in (61cm) long.
£50–55
$75–80 ⊞ HL

► **A Victorian hand-made lace handkerchief,** 12in (30.5cm) square.
£20–25
$30–35 ⊞ Ech

A Bruges bobbin lace handkerchief, c1880, 12in (30.5cm) square.
£40–45
$60–65 ⊞ JuC

An Edwardian Brussels lace collar, 15 x 13in (38 x 33cm).
£40–45
$60–65 ⊞ Ech

► **An Edwardian hand-made lace collar,** 5in (12.5cm) wide.
£40–45
$60–65 ⊞ Ech

A Brussels needlepoint lace handkerchief, c1850, 18in (45.5cm) square.
£45–50
$65–75 ⊞ JuC

An Edwardian tape lace collar, 7in (18cm) wide.
£25–30
$35–45 ⊞ Ech

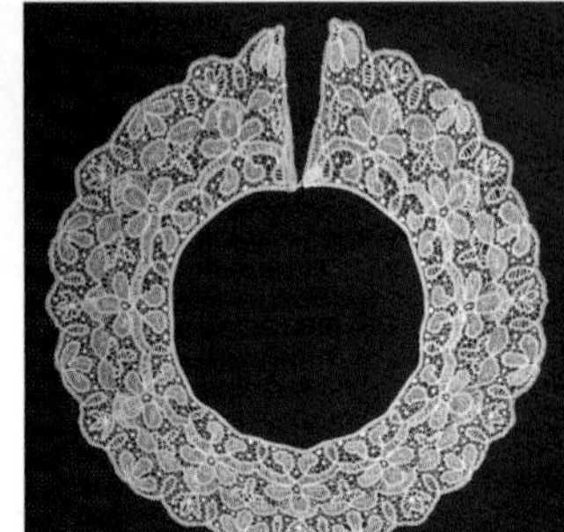

Linen

This section includes a selection of hand-embroidered linen from the 1920s and '30s. The fashion for tray cloths, decorated tea cosies and lacy doillies belongs to a more leisurely age where women stayed at home, the wireless had pride of place in the living room and everything stopped for tea. Most of these objects were home-made. Magazines and books provided step-by-step instructions, transfer patterns and even encouraging verses such as the following slightly ambiguous lines from a 1930s needlework guide: 'In fine embroidery I find/ So much of ease and gladness/ It seems to rest my tired mind/ And ease my spirit's sadness/ And friends will see the finished piece/ Admire my colour schemes/ And never know that I have stitched/ A hiding place for dreams.'

Typical decorative subjects included flowers, the English country cottage and the Victorian-style crinoline lady, a favourite romantic and escapist image that remained in popular use until the 1950s. Charming and hand-made, these objects can still be picked up for very little in charity shops, but they are also beginning to appear with dealers. Admittedly, few modern householders are likely to be in the habit of using tray cloths, runners and the other fancy linen that were part of everyday life in the inter-war years. However, on our travels, Miller's have seen these objects given other uses and transformed into patchwork quilts, fashionable handbags and even clothing, giving a new twist to an old and neglected craft.

A Victorian linen and crochet cloth, 29 x 34in (73.5 x 86.5cm).
£15–20
$20–30 ⊞ Ech

A linen table mat, embroidered with flowers, 1930s, 8½in (21.5cm) diam.
£8–10
$12–15 ⊞ HILL

► **A hand-made linen coaster,** decorated with a lady wearing a crinoline, 1930s, 6in (15cm) diam.
£4–6
$5–8 ⊞ HILL

A tablecloth, with crochet edge, c1920, 36in (91.5cm) square.
£25–30
$35–45 ⊞ AL

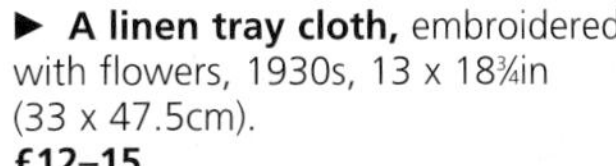

► **A linen tray cloth,** embroidered with flowers, 1930s, 13 x 18¾in (33 x 47.5cm).
£12–15
$17–20 ⊞ HILL

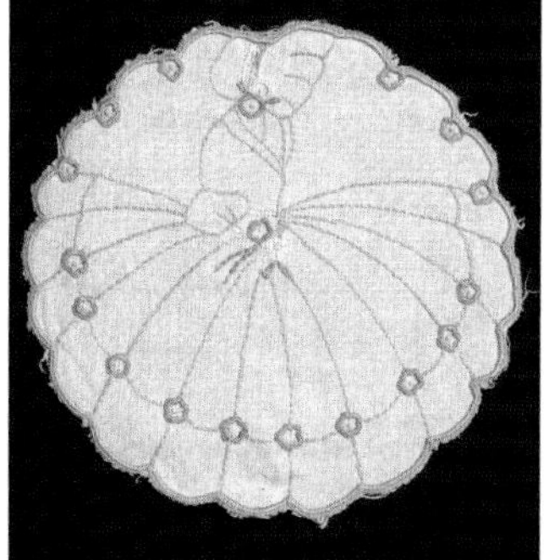

An embroidered linen tray cloth, 1920s, 10 x 14in (25.5 x 35.5cm).
£6–8
$8–12 ⊞ HILL

A Snoopy linen tea towel, 1970s, 18½ x 29 (47 x 73.5cm).
£15–20
$20–30 ⊞ TWI

Menswear

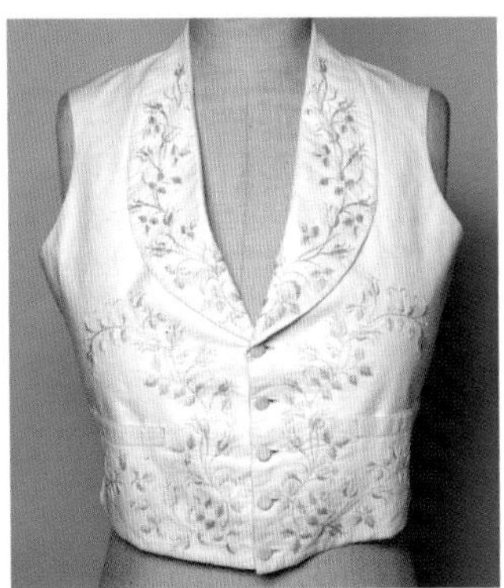

An Edwardian embroidered silk waistcoat.
£90–110
$130–160 ⊞ Ech

An Edwardian silk brocade waistcoat.
£90–110
$130–160 ⊞ Ech

A man's wool hat, labelled 'An Arbiter of Good Taste', c1930.
£20–25
$30–35 ⊞ DE

A double-breasted pinstripe jacket, by the Royal Arsenal Co-operative Society Bespoke Tailors, 1940–50.
£25–30
$35–45 ⊞ REPS

A rayon Hawaiian shirt, by Kamiauhanee, c1950.
£15–20
$20–30 ⊞ REPS

A linen collarless sports jacket, American, c1950.
£20–25
$30–35 ⊞ REPS

A cotton Hawaiian shirt, by Mr Kaitua, c1960.
£20–25
$30–35 ⊞ REPS

A linen jacket, decorated with paisley pattern, American, c1960.
£20–25
$30–35 ⊞ REPS

A Vivienne Westwood Buffalo Collection herringbone tweed suit, Buffalo Boy, with a hand-beaded jacket, c1982.
£900–1,000
$1,300–1,500 ⊞ ID
Only about 12 of these suits were made.

Shawls

Shawls became fashionable in the last quarter of the 18th century, when trading ships imported them from the East and the colonies. India was a major source, some of the finest examples coming from Kashmir. Shawls were hand-made from the wool of Tibetan goats living up high in the Himalayan mountains, whose exceptionally soft and fine woollen fleece is known as pashmina. Kashmir shawls could take 18 months to weave and were extremely expensive by the time they reached Europe.

British manufacturers began making their own shawls inspired by Indian prototypes. The main centres of production in the 19th century included Edinburgh, Norwich and Paisley, the famous textile town in Scotland which gave its name to the paisley pattern, an adaptation of a traditional Kashmiri pine cone design. Victorian fashions did much to stimulate the popularity of shawls since wide crinolines made the wearing of coats uncomfortable – Queen Victoria even lent her own original Kashmir shawls to the Paisley factory so that they could copy them. For winter there were woven shawls and for summer printed shawls, lighter and less expensive than woven examples which, even with increased mechanization and the introduction of the Jacquard loom, could still take considerable time to design and produce. By the late 19th century, the heavier paisleys had gone out of fashion in favour of richly-embroidered silk shawls, many of which were imported from Canton.

Shawls remained popular in the Edwardian period and in the 1920s, when long fringing, cut velvet and shiny lamé material provided a perfect compliment to flapper fashions and sleeveless, drop-waisted evening dresses.

Values of shawls depend on pattern, material and technique. Rare Kashmir shawls attract the highest prices and fine western paisleys are also highly collectable. As with all textiles, shawls can be damaged by light. Store in acid-free tissue paper in a cardboard box, as plastic bags can trap moisture and cause material to rot.

A fine wool paisley summer shawl, 1830–40.
£80–100
$115–145 ⊞ JPr

A woven wool paisley shawl, c1860, 60 x 120in (152.5 x 305cm).
£250–300
$350–450 ⊞ L&L

A woven silk and metal thread shawl, Indian, 19thC, 33 x 102in (84 x 259cm).
£150–175
$220–255 ⊞ CCO

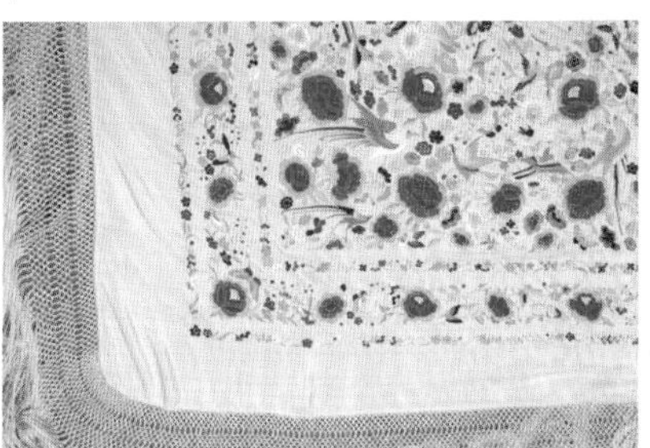

A hand-embroidered shawl, decorated with multi-coloured birds and flowers, with silk fringing, Chinese, Canton, late 19thC, 46in (117cm) square.
£200–250
$300–350 ⊞ JPr

A silk shawl, 1870, 68in (172.5cm) square.
£150–180
$220–260 ⊞ L&L

An Edwardian embroidered silk export shawl, with silk fringing, Chinese, Canton, 54in (137cm) square.
£250–300
$350–450 ⊞ Ech

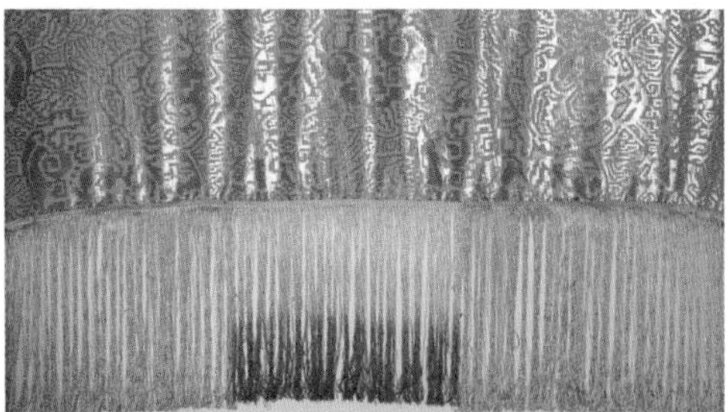

A devoré shawl, 1920s, 42in (106.5cm) square.
£125–150
$180–220 ⊞ Ech

► A silk shawl, decorated with flowers, 1920s, 42in (106.5cm) square.
£85–95
$125–140 ⊞ L&L

A lamé shawl, with silk fringe, 1930, 43in (109cm) square.
£125–150
$180–220 ⊞ JPr

Shoes

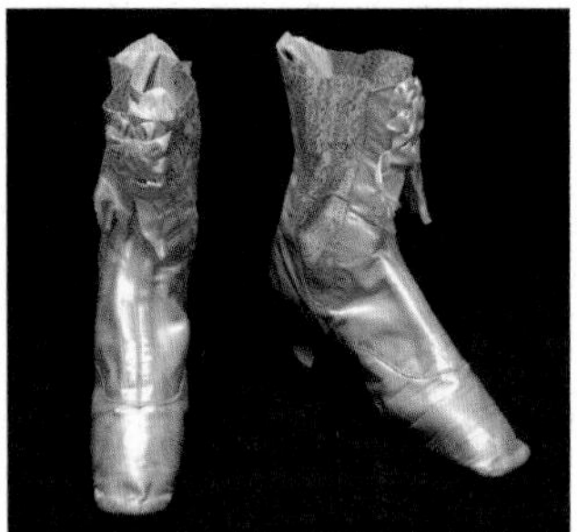

A pair of elastic-sided satin boots, 1860, 9in (23cm) high.
£90–100
$130–145 ⊞ L&L

Patented in the 1830s, the elastic-sided boot was the result of experiments with India rubber cloth. By the 1860s, they were the height of fashion. Silk boots tended to be reserved for evening wear, the colours matching the dress. Heels were again in vogue, becoming higher as the decade progressed. 'Everyone who has noticed the height to which the heels of women's boots is now carried must have marvelled much how the wearer could maintain her equilibrium,' commented *The Queen* magazine in 1871.

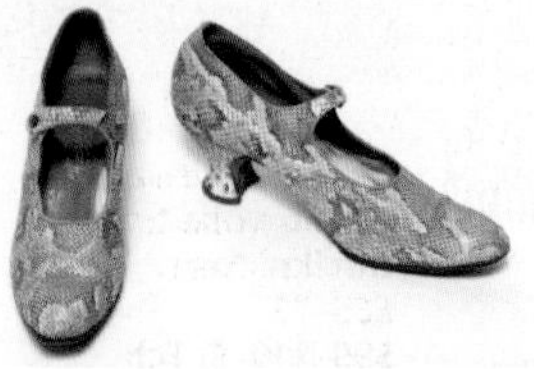

► A pair of suede and leather boots, c1880, 10in (25.5cm) high.
£85–95
$125–140 ⊞ L&L

A pair of North American Indian baby's moccasins, 1880.
£140–160
$200–230 ⊞ JPr

A pair of canvas and leather bar shoes, 1920s.
£55–65
$80–95 ⊞ Ech

◄ A pair of snakeskin shoes, retailed by Harrods, London, 1920.
£55–65
$80–95 ⊞ Ech

A pair of Clark's Horoscopes Mary Jane shoes, 1950s.
£20–25
$30–35 ⊞ TWI

Mary Jane shoes, round-toed, with a single strap, were named after a character in the *Buster Brown* comic strip that first appeared in the *New York Herald* in 1902. The classic children's party shoe, they were most famously modelled by Shirley Temple. In the 1960s Mary Janes became adult fashion. Reacting against 1950s stilettos and winklepicker toes, designers such as Mary Quant created a new and more comfortable style of footwear, inspired by tap shoes and children's sandals, they reflected the youthful look of the Swinging Sixties epitomized by Twiggy. Round-toed, low heeled, often in two-tone plastic, such shoes appeal to 'mod' enthusiasts today.

A pair of satin shoes, by Distinction, Norwich, with interchangeable diamanté buckles, 1950s.
£15–20
$20–30 ⊞ CCO

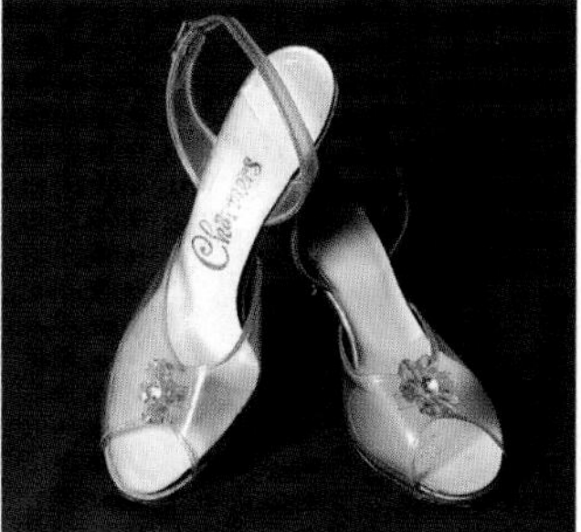

A pair of clear plastic shoes, by Charmers, American, mid-1950s.
£40–45
$60–65 ⊞ TWI

A pair of patent leather platform peep-toe sandals, 1980s, 6in (15cm) heels.
£55–65
$80–95 ⊞ MARK

Underwear & Nightwear

Movements in modern fashion certainly affect demand and prices for vintage clothing. The current taste for the corset, pioneered by designers such as Vivienne Westwood and Jean Paul Gaultier, has stimulated interest in historical corsets. The earliest recorded corset is illustrated on the sculpture of a Cretan goddess c2000 BC, but the modern corset derives from the 'cotte' a stiffened linen underbodice worn in Europe in the 14th century. As the centuries progressed, this garment became more complex and refined. Also known as a pair of 'bodies' or stays, it began to be stiffened with slats of wood or whalebone, the taste for corsets providing a major factor in the devastation of the whale population.

In 1832, a Frenchman, Jean Werly, patented the first loom-woven corsets. The 19th-century fashion for large skirts and tiny waists stimulated demand and, with the advent of the bustle in the 1870s, complex and architectural foundations, supported with bone, steel and laces, were essential to create the required S-shaped silhouette of the period.

Corsets fell from popularity after WWI until the 1940s and 1950s, when a post-war return to feminine curvaceous fashions again created a need for viciously controlling underwear – although thanks to nylon and plastic, women were spared the dangerous discomfort of metal and whalebone stays.

Corset making is a highly technical skill and corsets are collected for their structure as much as for visual appeal. Collectors are often interested in vintage lingerie from a historical point of view, although the less fragile and restrictive garments are also purchased to wear, often as outerwear rather than underwear.

A Victorian cotton and broderie anglaise camisole.
£20–25
$30–35 ⊞ Ech

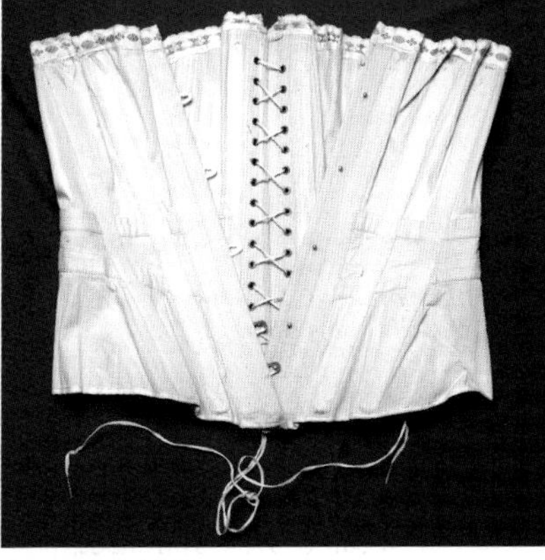

A corset, c1870.
£350–400
$500–580 ⊞ LU

A pair of Edwardian cotton voile and lace camiknickers.
£65–75
$95–110 ⊞ Ech

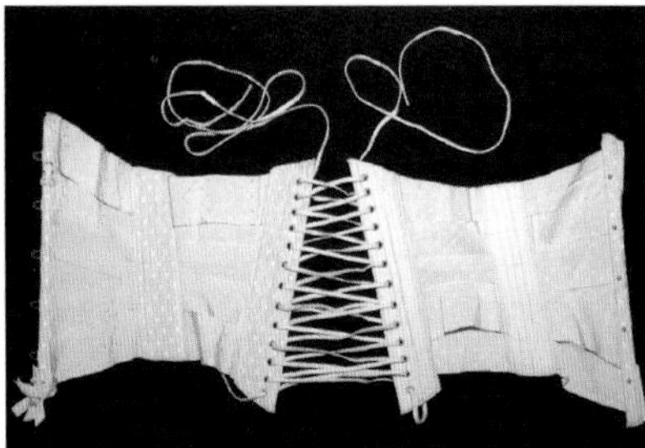

A boned silk ribbon-waist trainer corset, with back lacing, c1910.
£70–80
$100–115 ⊞ AFA

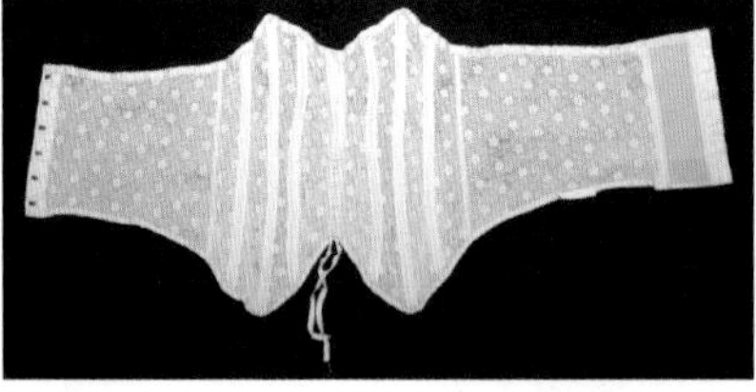

A strapless boned cotton bra/bodice, 1940s.
£25–30
$35–45 ⊞ AFA

A boned cotton corset, by C. W. S. 'Desbeau' Corsets, with stitch detailing and edging, the elastic sides held by crossover straps, with back lacing, c1910.
£125–150
$180–220 ⊞ AFA

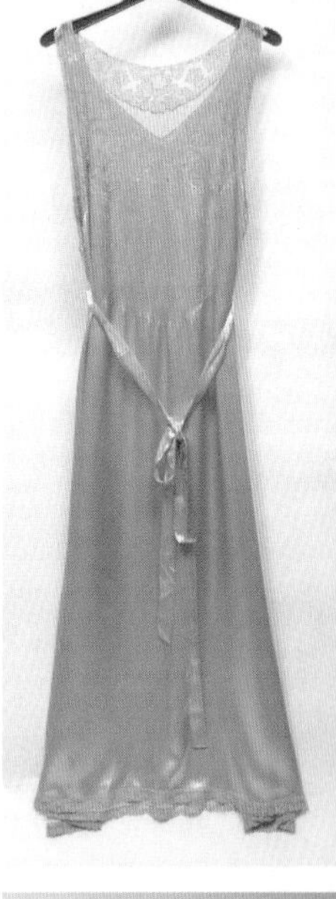

► A satin and lace nightgown, 1930s.
£40–45
$60–65 ⊞ L&L

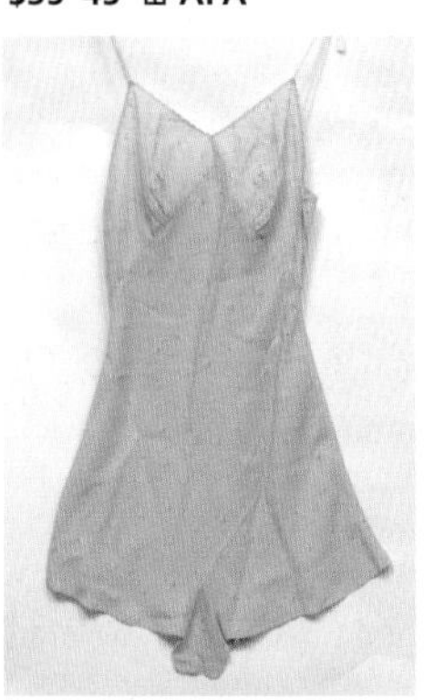

A pair of floral crepe Utility camiknickers, 1940s.
£18–22
$28–32 ⊞ L&L

A pair of satin camiknickers, 1940s.
£12–15
$17–20 ⊞ L&L

◄ A semi-boned silk corselette, by Charmis, Paris, with cotton and elastic sides, French, 1950s.
£65–75
$95–110 ⊞ AFA

A floral wincyette nightgown, 1940s.
£18–22
$28–32 ⊞ L&L

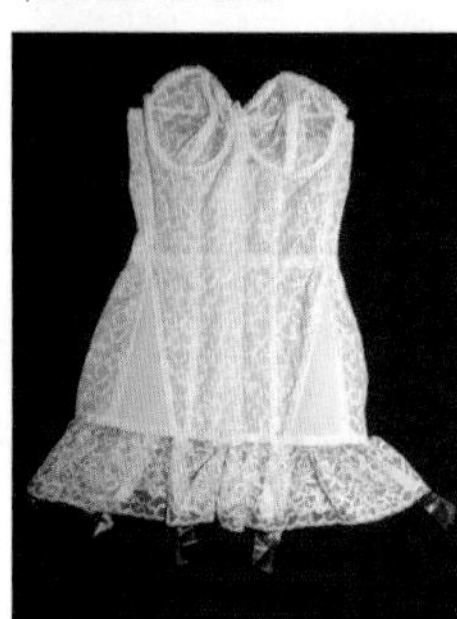

► A nylon lace corselette, with elastic inserts and frilled edge, six suspenders and suspender ribbons, 1950s.
£75–85
$110–125 ⊞ AFA

A silk and elastic girdle, by Marie Rose Lebigot, with suspenders, French, 1940s.
£35–40
$50–60 ⊞ AFA

A pair of Mary Quant footless tights, late 1960s, in original packaging 9 x 6½in (23 x16.5cm).
£10–12
$15–17 ⊞ TWI

Tools

A wooden moulding plane, by T. Phillipson, 1740–75, 10in (25.5cm) long.
£50–60
$75–90 ⊞ WO

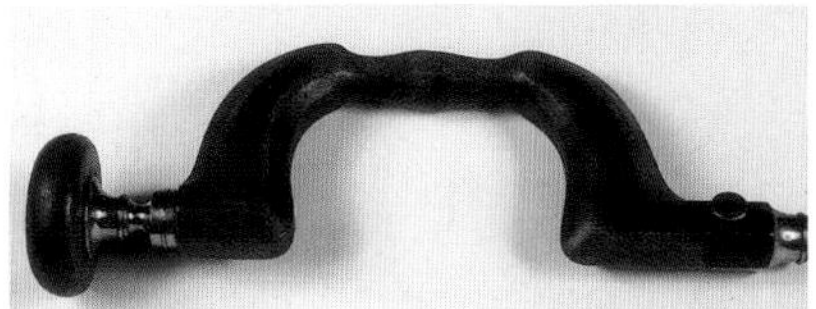

A brass-plated beech brace, by Mathieson, Glasgow, 19thC, 14in (35.5cm) long.
£90–100
$130–145 ⊞ WO

► A shipwright's wooden clamp, by BG of Paris, French, 19thC, 16in (40.5cm) long.
£25–30
$35–45 ⊞ OLD

A shipwright's wooden saw vice, 19thC, 17in (43cm) long.
£25–30
$35–45 ⊞ OLD

A shipwright's wrought-iron scribe, 19thC, 17in (43cm) long.
£30–35
$45–50 ⊞ OLD

A beech router, by Moseley, 19thC, 6in (15cm) long.
£14–18
$18–28 ⊞ WO

A set of watchmaker's tools, in a boxwood container, 19thC, 3in (7.5cm) high.
£50–60
$75–90 ⊞ MB

A wooden lead-beating tool, late 19thC, 13in (33cm) long.
£35–40
$50–60 ⊞ SDA

◄ A wooden plough plane, by Moseley, with brass and steel fittings, 1862–80, 8in (20.5cm) long.
£20–25
$30–35 ⊞ GAC

◄ A wood and steel router, by Mathieson, c1910, 7in (18cm) high.
£10–12
$15–18 ⊞ GAC

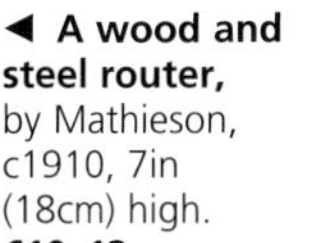

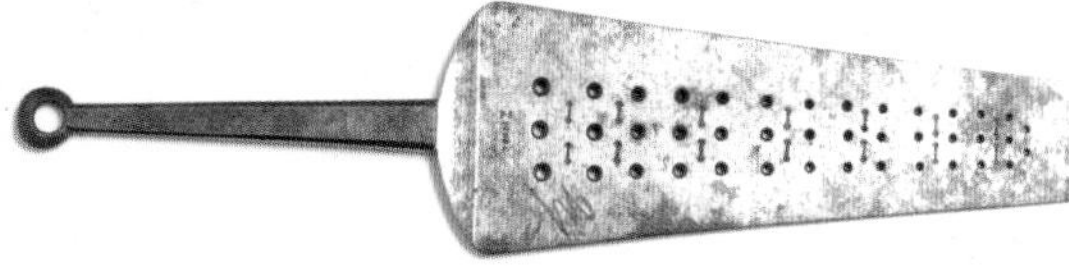

A watchmaker's steel screw plate, c1925, 6in (15cm) long.
£10–15
$15–20 ⊞ GAC

Toys

A set of child's educational blocks, printed with animals, c1880, each block 4 x 2in (10 x 5cm) square.
£250–300
$360–440 ⊞ YC

A Tri-ang child's mangle set, with buckets and washboard, 1930s, 19in (48.5cm) high.
£125–150
$180–220 ⊞ SMI

A twin cast Transformers Robot tape recorder, by Takara, Japanese, 1987, 9in (23cm) high, in original box.
£675–750
$975–1,100 ⊞ OW

A set of Anchor building blocks, German, c1890, in original box, 9 x 14in (23 x 35.5cm).
£125–150
$180–220 ⊞ YC

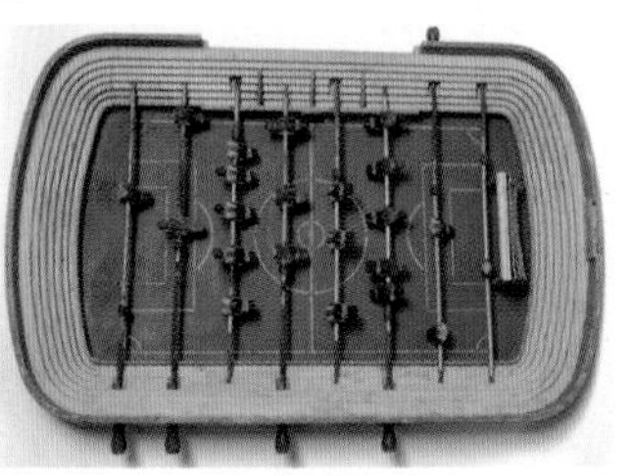

A wooden football table, with terracotta players, 1940, 38in (96.5cm) long.
£120–140
$175–200 ⊞ TRA

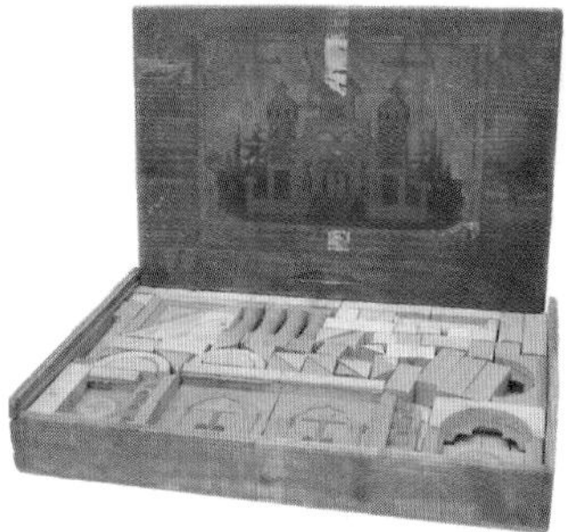

A set of French Architecture Pine building blocks, 1910, in a pine box, 12in (30.5cm) wide.
£30–35
$45–50 ⚒ G(L)

A Transformers Prowl, by M.B., French, 1985, 5in (12.5cm) high.
£90–100
$130–150 ⊞ OW

◄ **A Transformers Thrust,** by Hasbro, 1985, 8in (20.5cm) long.
£40–45
$60–65 ⊞ OW

Transformers

Transformers, one of the most successful toys of the 1980s, were launched by Hasbro, USA, in 1984. The plastic toys could be converted from robots into vehicles and demand was stimulated by an animated series, starring the 'robots in disguise', and a Marvel comic book, both launched that same year. 'The kids who originally played with them are now grown up and Transformers are becoming increasingly popular with collectors', says toy dealer Jamie Woollard. 'There are Transformers conventions in the USA and UK, and the cartoon is regarded as a classic'. Though the toys were retailed across the world, some objects, such as the tape recorder illustrated here, were only produced for the Japanese market. 'The American version was a different colour and only held one as opposed to two cassettes', explains Woollard. 'Enthusiasts always want the rarities, and that is why this toy has such a high price range.'

Aircraft

A pressed cardboard Dresden biplane, German, c1905, 3½in (9cm) wide.
£550–600
$800–870 ⊞ LEI
This is a replica of the Wright Brothers' aeroplane that took its first flight at Kittyhawk, North Carolina. Made in Germany from pressed cardboard, these early Dresden toys and ornaments are highly collectable in the USA.

► A tinplate battery-operated Super Flying Police helicopter, Japanese, 1960s, 14in (35.5cm) long.
£100–125
$145–180 ⊞ RTT

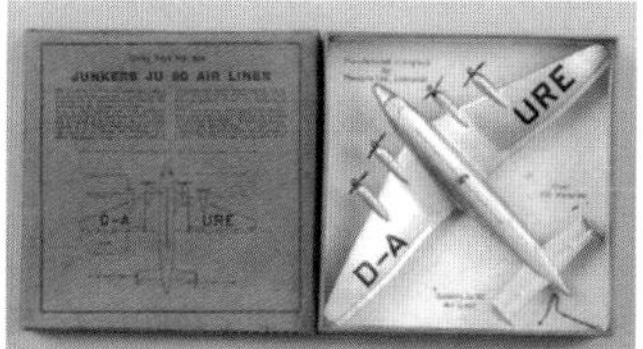

A Dinky Junkers JU90 Airliner, No. 62N, 1930s, 4¾in (12cm) wide, in original box.
£270–300
$390–440 ⚒ VEC

► A tinplate friction-driven Overseas Airlines aeroplane, 1980s, 9in (23cm) long, with original box.
£20–25
$30–35 ⊞ RTT

A Dinky Bristol Britannia airliner, No. 998, with Canadian Pacific decals, one propeller missing, 1959–64, 5½in (14cm) wide, in original box.
£110–130
$160–190 ⚒ WAL

Computer & Electronic Games

An Action Leisure Ground Grandstand Caveman electronic game, 1982, in original box, 7 x 9in (18 x 23cm).
£35–40
$50–60 ⊞ OW

◄ A Nintendo Mickey and Donald Game & Watch Multi Screen electronic game, 1982, in original box, 4 x 6in (10 x 15cm).
£80–90
$115–130 ⊞ OW

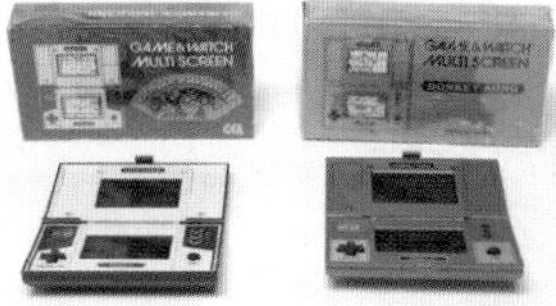

Two Nintendo Game & Watch Multi Screen electronic games, Donkey Kong and Donkey Kong II, 1982, in original boxes, 4 x 7in (10 x 18cm).
£45–50
$65–75 each ⊞ OW

Hand-held games

Nostalgia is a major factor in the collectable toy market. People tend to return to the toys of their youth and those who grew up during the 1980s were in at the birth of computer gaming. The hand-held electronic games illustrated here are the grandparents of the Game Boy. In terms of technology, these objects are the equivalent of the penny-farthing. Although they might not have much memory themselves, they are fondly remembered by those who originally played with them, hence their value today.

◄ A Tomy Tomytronic 3D stereo Skyfighters electronic game, 1984, 6 x 8in (15 x 20.5cm).
£15–20
$20–30 ⊞ OW

Diecast Vehicles

A Shackleton Foden flat truck, 1949–58, 11in (30cm) long.
£1,100–1,400
$1,600–2,000 VEC

British company Shackleton Toys (est 1948) produced a range of high-quality, large-scale diecast Foden FG lorries. Sturdily made and including a clockwork motor, Shackleton toys were more expensive than Dinky. Low sales, combined with a shortage of materials during the period of the Korean War, caused the company to close in 1952, and thanks to this short production run Shackleton toys are very collectable today.

► **A Dinky Toys Big Bedford Lorry,** No. 922, 1950–60, 5½in (14cm) long.
£125–150
$180–220 UCO

A Matchbox Moco No. 1 steam roller, early 1950s, 21in (53.5cm) long.
£30–35
$45–50 HAL

Cross Reference
See Sci-Fi, Film & TV (pages 331–339)

A Dinky Toys Golden Shred Guy van, with second-type cab and Supertoy wheels, some corrosion marks, 1957–58, 5¼in (13.5cm) long, with original box.
£200–240
$300–350 VEC

► **A Dinky Toys BBC TV roving eye vehicle,** with cameraman, camera and aerial, minor wear, c1959, 6in (15cm) long, with original box.
£100–120
$150–175
WAL

◄ **A Dinky Toys Trojan Cydrax 15cwt van,** No. 454, 1950s, 4in (10cm) long, with original box
£140–170
$200–250
HAL

► **A Dinky Toys Austin Raleigh Cycles van,** No. 472, 1950s, 3½in (9cm) long, with original box.
£150–175
$220–250
UCO

A Dinky Toys Leyland Cement wagon, No. 933, 1950s, 6in (15cm) long, with original box.
£100–120
$150–175 ⊞ HAL

A Dinky Toys Royal Mail van, No. 260, 1950s, 3in (7.5cm) long, with original box.
£90–110
$130–160 ⊞ UCO

A Dinky Toys Elevator Loader, No. 464, 1950s, 9in (23cm) long, with original box.
£45–50
$65–75 ⊞ HAL

A Dinky Supertoys Blaw Knox bulldozer, No. 561, 1950s, 5in (12.5cm) long, with original box.
£35–40
$50–60 ⊞ HAL

A Dinky Toys Ford Sedan, made in the UK for the US market, 1950s, 4in (10cm) long.
£170–200
$250–300 ⊞ HAL

A Dinky Supertoys Pompiers fire engine, 1950s, 7in (18cm) long, with original box.
£150–180
$220–260 ⊞ HAL

► **A Dinky Supertoys Coles Mobile Crane,** No. 971, 1950s, 7in (18cm) long, with original box.
£45–55
$65–80 ⊞ HAL

A Shackleton David Brown Trackmaster 30 tractor, 1950s, 11in (28cm) long, with original box.
£800–900
$1,150–1,300 ⚒ VEC
This model is extremely difficult to find and only 50 are believed to have been produced.

A Dinky Toys Ford Consul Corsair, No. 130, 1960, 5in (12.5cm) long, with original box.
£45–55
$65–80 ⊞ HAL

A Solido Fiat 850 Abarth, French, 1960, 4in (10cm) long, with original box.
£45–55
$65–80 ⊞ HAL

A Corgi Toys Massey-Ferguson combine harvester, 1960, 7in (18cm) long, with original box.
£125–150
$180–220 ⊞ HAL

A Dinky Supertoys Albion lorry-mounted cement mixer, No. 960, with revolving drum, minor chips to bumper, c1960, 4½in (11.5cm) long.
£60–70
$90–100 ⚒ WAL

A Dinky Supertoys BBC TV mobile control room, No. 967, minor wear and chips, c1960, 7in (18cm) long, with original box.
£100–120
$150–175 ⚒ WAL

A Dinky Supertoys snow plough, No. 958, some wear, c1960, 7in (18cm) long, with original box.
£100–120
$145–175 ⚒ WAL

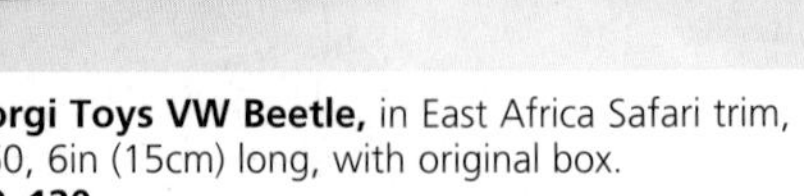

A Corgi Toys VW Beetle, in East Africa Safari trim, c1960, 6in (15cm) long, with original box.
£100–120
$145–175 ⊞ GTM

A Dinky Toys Ford Anglia, No. 155, early 1960s, 3in (7.5cm) long, with original box.
£50–55
$75–80 ⊞ HAL

A Dinky Toys RAC Patrol Mini van, No. 273, early 1960s, 3in (7.5cm) long.
£130–150
$190–220 ⊞ UCO

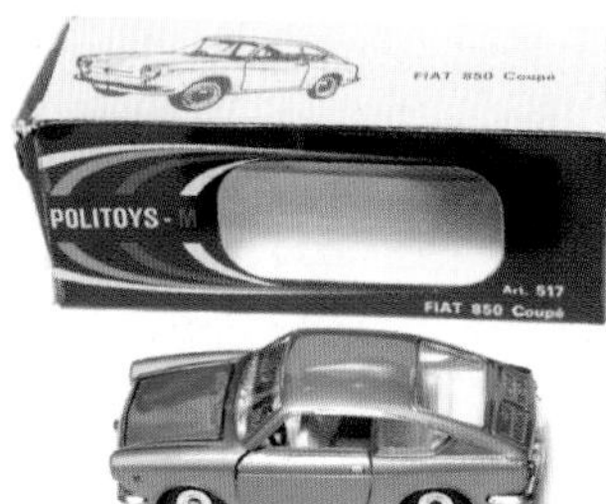

A Politoys Fiat 850 coupé, No. 517, Italian, c1960, 4in (10cm) long, with original box.
£50–55
$75–80 ⊞ HAL

A Tri-ang Spot-On gift set, No. 702, comprising Ford Zephyr 6, Morris 1100 with canoe, Austin 1800 and a dinghy and trailer, 1963, with original window box.
£230–260
$330–380 ⚒ VEC

A Corgi Toys Oldsmobile Tornado, No. 264, 1960s, 4in (10cm) long, with original box.
£30–35
$45–50 ⊞ HAL

A Matchbox King-size Foden dumper truck K-5, c1960, 5in (12.5cm) long, with original box.
£30–40
$45–60 ⊞ HAL

A Corgi Toys Rally Monte Carlo gift set, comprising Citroen DS19, Rover 2000, and a Mini Cooper-S, 1965–67, with original box.
£400–450
$580–650 ⚒ VEC

The popular series Rally Cars was produced by Corgi 1964–70. Inspired by real life races, Corgi chronicled all the major rallies until the Hillman Hunter World Cup Rally of 1970. This Monte Carlo Rally set includes a rare group of vehicles.

A Corgi Toys Plymouth station wagon, No. 219, 1960s, 4in (10cm) long, with original box.
£65–75
$95–110 ⊞ HAL

◄ **A Corgi Toys Bristol Bloodhound Guided Missile,** 1960s, 9in (23cm) long, with original box.
£100–120
$145–175 ⊞ HAL

A Matchbox King-size Hatra Tractor Shovel K3, c1960, 6in (15cm) long, with original box.
£40–45
$60–65 ⊞ HAL

A Dinky Toys Slumberland Guy van, No. 514, 1960s, 6in (15cm) long.
£150–200
$220–300 ⚒ BLH

A Matchbox Series A Lesney Drott excavator, No. 58, 1960s, 3in (7.5cm) long, with original box.
£15–20
$20–30 ⊞ HAL

A Corgi Comics Popeye Paddle Wagon, No. 802, with five figures, 1969–72, with original picture box.
£420–460
$620–670 ⚒ VEC

Model Soldiers & Figures

A Britains French Army Chasseurs à Cheval set, No. 139, minor wear and chipping, early 20thC, in Whisstock box, 15in (38cm) long.
£180–220
$260–320 WAL

A Britains Royal Sussex Regiment set, No. 36, minor chipping and wear, early 20thC, in Whisstock box,14½in (37cm) wide.
£150–180
$220–260 WAL

A Britains painted lead figure of a lady railway passenger, 1920s–30s, 2¼in (5.5cm) high.
£20–25
$30–35 HAL

A Britains painted lead figure of a farmer, cane missing, 1920s–30s, 2¼in (5.5cm) high.
£2–3
$3–5 HAL
With a cane, the price range of this figure would be £6–8 ($10–12).

A Britains mushroom, from the Garden Set, 1939, 2½in (6.5cm) high.
£130–150
$190–220 RUSS
This mushroom is a rare piece.

◄ **A Britains painted lead figure of a shepherd,** 1920s–30s, 2¼in (5.5cm) high.
£10–12
$15–18 HAL

A Britains 10th Duke of Cambridge's Own Bengal Lancers set, No. 46, minor wear, 1950s, in original box,15in (38cm) wide
£140–160
$200–230 WAL

A Britains Naval Landing Party with gun, No. 79, eight naval ratings, some wear, 1950s, with original box, 12in (30.5cm) wide.
£230–260
$330–380 ⚒ WAL

A Britains Coronation coach, dead stock, 1953, with original box, 8 x 18in (20.5 x 45.5cm).
£300–330
$440–475 ⊞ HAL

Further reading

Miller's Toys & Games Antiques Checklist, Miller's Publications, 2000

A Britains Native American plastic figure, from the Detail Range, on a metal base, 1970s–80s, 2½in (6.5cm) high.
£1–2
$2–3 ⊞ HAL

◄ **Two Britains Eyes Right sets,** Scots Guards Band and Royal Marines Band, c1970, with original boxes, 4 x 14in (10 x 35.5cm).
£70–80
$100–115 ⊞ GTM

► **A Britains French Foreign Legion plastic figure,** from the Detail Range, on a metal base, 1970s–80s, 2½in (6.5cm) high.
£4–6
$5–7 ⊞ HAL

Pedal Cars

◄ **A Tri-ang pedal tractor,** c1950, 30in (76cm) long.
£125–150
$180–220
⊞ JUN

A Giordani pedal sports car, with bullet nose, chrome brightwork and spoked wheels, electric horn and lights, dashboard with full instrumentation, restored, Italian, c1960, 45in (114.5cm) long.
£425–525
$625–750 ⚒ VEC

Rocking Horses

A Victorian carved and painted wood pull-along horse, with harness and horsehair tail, on a trolley base with iron wheels, 12in (30.5cm) high.
£225–250
$325–360 ⚒ TMA

A carved wood rocking horse, with horsehair mane and tail, remains of leather saddle and bridle, standing on wooden safety rockers, metal plaque for A. W. Gamage lmt, London, c1880, 51in (129.5cm) high.
£1,600–1,900
$2,300–2,700 ⚒ B(Ch)

A painted wood rocking horse, with glass eyes, on wooden safety rockers, late 19thC, 37in (94cm) high.
£370–450
$550–650 ⚒ RTo

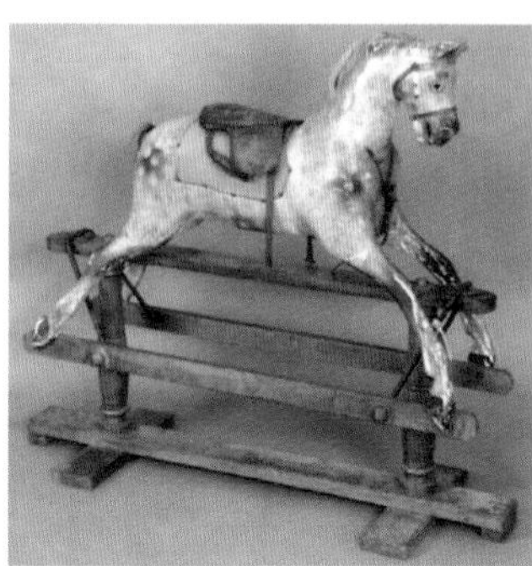

► A painted wood rocking horse, with glass eyes and leather saddle, on wooden safety rockers, late 19thC, 38¼in (97cm) high.
£300–360
$450–500 ⚒ RTo

LOCATE THE SOURCE
The source of each illustration in Miller's can be found by checking the code letters below each caption with the Key to Illustrations, pages 443–451.

A carved and painted wood rocking horse, on safety rockers, restored, late 19thC, 51in (129.5cm) high.
£550–600
$800–880 L

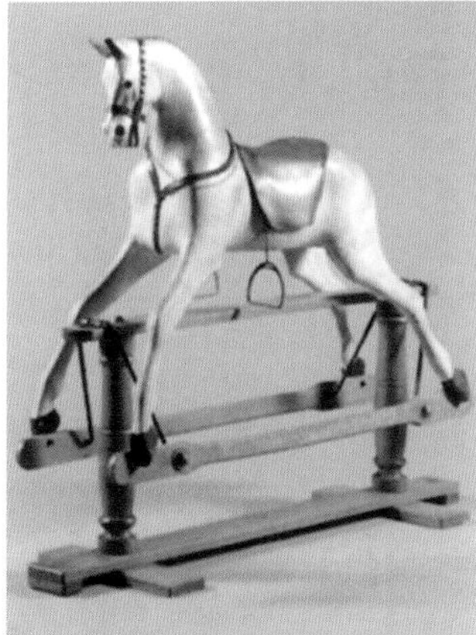

◄ **A painted rocking horse,** c1910, 48¾in (124cm) high.
£730–870
$1,000–1,250 S(O)

A carved and painted wood rocking horse, by J. Collinson & Son, real hair mane and tail, leather bridle and leather and cord saddle, on safety rockers, 1940s, 38in (96.5cm) high.
£250–300
$360–440 Bon(C)

◄ **A wood and composition rocking horse,** with saddle, bridle and stirrups, on pine safety rockers, c1950, 46in (117cm) high.
£400–480
$580–700 PF

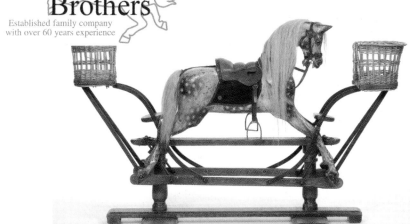

Insurance values

Always insure your valuable collectables for the cost of replacing them with similar items, regardless of the original price paid. Both dealers and auctioneers can provide a valuation service for a fee.

Tinplate & Clockwork Toys

An American Mechanical Toy Co clockwork toy, The Jubilee Dancers wearing silk and cotton dresses, on a wooden base containing the mechanism, c1890, 10in (25.5cm) high.
£600–700
$870–1,000 ⚒ B(Ch)

A Schuco tinplate clockwork monkey, wearing felt clothes, c1920, 4¼in (11cm) high.
£220–260
$150–180 ⚒ DuM

A Roullet & Descamps tin and pressed card clockwork lion, covered with skin and fur, with glass eyes, c1900, 14in (35.5cm) long.
£700–800
$1,000–1,150 ⊞ YC

A Lehmann tinplate clown on a donkey cart, German, c1905, 6in (15cm) long.
£350–400
$500–580 ⊞ JUN

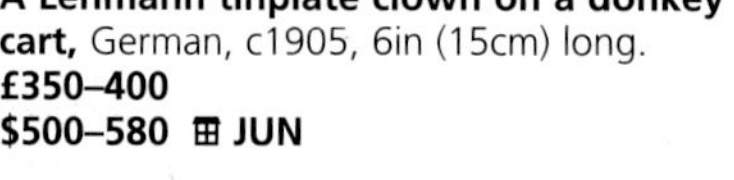

◀ **A tinplate clockwork tricycle,** the rider with lithograped face and costume, early 20thC, 8¾in (22cm) high.
£320–380
$450–575 ⚒ BLH

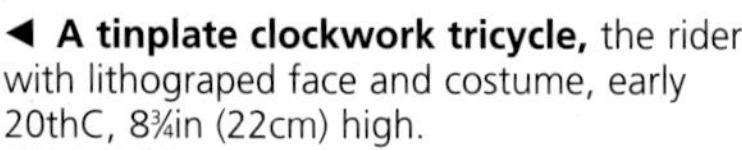

▶ **A clockwork rabbit,** wearing mohair clothes, c1920.
£450–550
$650–800 ⊞ LEI

A tinplate penny toy-style military horsedrawn communications limber, comprising a two-horse team with two French soldiers and separate limber, with camouflage finish, German, 1920, 17½in (44.5cm) long.
£100–120
$145–175 ⚒ VEC

▶ **A Louis Marx & Co tinplate clockwork Coo-Coo car,** c1920, 7½in (19cm) long.
£100–125
$150–180 ⚒ DuM

A tin and soft metal clockwork rickshaw, probably American, c1900, 6in (15cm) long.
£200–250
$300–350 ⊞ YC

A Bing tinplate raceabout roadster, 1915, 5½in (14cm) long.
£140–170
$200–250 ⚒ DuM

A DRGM tinplate clockwork railway porter, pushing an open trunk on a barrow, c1930, 6in (15cm) wide.
£275–325
$400–475 AH

While certain tinplate clockwork toys are becoming difficult to find and are consequently fetching higher prices, values have generally remained stable. This particular example has maintained its position in the market.

◄ **A tinplate cowboy clicker,** 1930s, 2½in (6.5cm) long.
£25–30
$35–45 HUX

► **A Chad Valley tinplate non-mechanical biscuit tin steam roller,** 1930s, 7in (18cm) long.
£200–250
$300–350 HAL

A Hornby Meccano copy of a shop display windmill, fully-lit, mounted on a wooden base, c1933, 30in (76cm) high.
£140–180
$200–260 VEC

A Chad Valley tinplate non-mechanical biscuit tin circus carriage, 1930s, 7in (18cm) long.
£200–250
$300–350 HAL

A tinplate peacock whistle, 1940s–50s, 1½in (4cm) high.
£10–12
$15–18 RUSS

A Schucho Examico 4001 tinplate clockwork car, manufactured in the US zone, German, 1940s, 6in (15cm) long.
£125–150
$180–220 HAL

A Mettoy tinplate clockwork tractor, 1950, 6in (15cm) long.
£65–75
$100–110 ⊞ JUN

A tinplate car, late 1950s, 4½in (11.5cm) long.
£20–25
$30–35 ⊞ RTT

A tinplate clockwork fire engine, German, 1960s, 4in (10cm) long.
£15–20
$20–30 ⊞ RTT

A tinplate and plastic jet car, Japanese, 1960s, 7in (18cm) long.
£20–25
$30–35 ⊞ RTT

► A Distler battery-operated Porsche 7500 electro matic tinplate car, German 1950s, 10in (25.5cm) long.
£300–350
$450–500
⊞ HAL

◄ An Alice in Wonderland tinplate paintbox, 1955–60, 15in (38cm) wide.
£25–30
$35–45 ⊞ HUX

An SSS Toys tinplate friction-drive Cadillac and house trailer, with picnic table, car fits inside base of caravan, Japanese, 1960, caravan 9in (23cm) long.
£160–200
$230–300 ⚒ VEC

A tinplate battery-operated Mercedes, Japanese, c1960, 9in (23cm) long.
£60–70
$90–100 ⊞ JUN

A tin bucket and spade, 1960s, 8in (20.5cm) high.
£35–40
$50–60 ⊞ JUN

◄ An Ichida tinplate battery-operated Pioneer Covered Wagon, with driver and galloping horse, Japanese, 1970, 14¼in (36cm) long.
£80–100
$115–145 ⚒ VEC

Trains

A pull-along train on a track, the train navigates around the track as the toy is pulled along, German, c1900, 8in (20.5cm) long.
£250–300
$350–450 ⊞ YC

► A Tri-ang wooden train, c1930, 26in (66cm) long.
£125–150
$180–220 ⊞ JUN

A Guntherman American Outline 4–4–0 loco and tender, No. 101, with cow catcher, 1905–10, 13¾in (35cm) long.
£500–600
$720–870 ⚒ VEC

A Hornby No. 1 gauge 0 special tank engine, c1930, 7in (18cm) long, in original box.
£200–225
$300–325 ⊞ GTM

◄ A Hornby 4–4–2 No. 3 locomotive and tender, 'Royal Scot', No. 6100, three-rail, 20v AC electric, with smoke deflectors, 1938, 12in (30.5cm) long.
£450–500
$650–720 ⚒ VEC

A Bassett-Lowke 2–6–0 live steam Mogul, No. 2945, in LMS black, only fired once or twice, with instructions and inner packing card, 1930s, 15in (38cm) long.
£550–600
$800–870 ⚒ VEC

A Hornby Dublo all-metal locomotive, 'Cardiff Castle', 1950, 11in (28cm) long, in original box.
£110–130
$160–200 ⊞ HAL

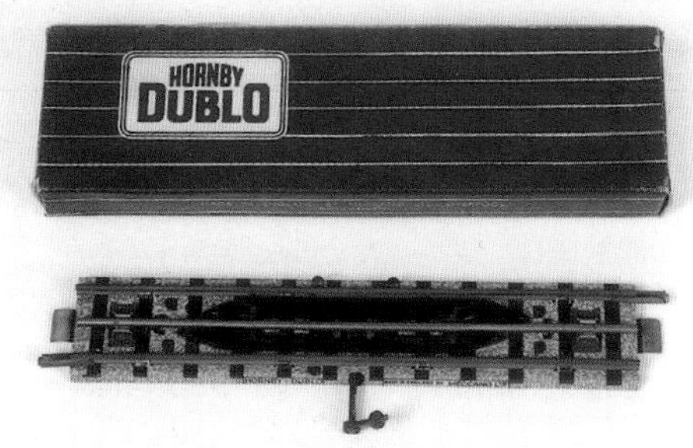

A Hornby Dublo un-coupling rail, c1952, 6½in (16.5cm) long.
£15–20
$20–30 ⊞ CWO

A Hornby Dublo tinplate restaurant car, 1950s, 9in (23cm) long, boxed.
£15–20
$20–30 ⊞ HAL

A pair of Tri-ang Emu powered and non-powered suburban motor coaches, R156 and R225, RN S1-57S and S1052S, with seats, minor wear, 1950s, 9in (23cm) long, boxed.
£100–120
$145–175 WAL

A Wrenn gauge 00 4–6–2 West Country class locomotive and tender, 'Lyme Regis', No. RN 21C109, 1973–78, 11½in (29cm) long, in original box.
£140–180
$200–260 WAL

A Wrenn gauge 00 4–6–2 City class locomotive and tender, 'City of Glasgow', No. RN 46242, 1978–91, 11½in (29cm) long, in original box with paperwork.
£110–130
$160–190 WAL

A Hornby Dublo all-metal locomotive, 'Duchess of Montrose', three-rail, 1950s, 12in (30.5cm) long, in original box.
£70–80
$100–115 HAL

A J & M Toys-style gauge 1 kit model railcar, No. RN 162, diecast bogies and steel wheels, GWR roundel transfer, 1970s–80s, 16in (40.5cm) long.
£150–180
$220–260 WAL

A Wrenn gauge 00 4–6–2 A4 class locomotive and tender, 'Sir Nigel Gresley', No. RN 7, 1979–91, 11in (28cm) long, in associated original box.
£55–65
$80–100 WAL

A Wrenn 4–6–2 streamlined locomotive and tender, 'Lamport & Holt Line', No. 35026, 1970s.
£160–200
$230–300 VEC

A Wrenn AM2 4–6–2 locomotive and tender, 'City of Carlisle', No. 46238, some paint chips and flakes, 1970s.
£180–220
$260–320 VEC

Cross Reference
See Railwayana (pages 306–308)

A Mamod Sherman's steam engine, c1980, 10in (25.5cm) long.
£80–90
$115–130 GTM

Treen

A mahogany gavel, c1830, 5¼in (13.5cm) long.
£34–38
$50–60 ⊞ SDA

► **A Penny Red stamp box,** depicting a tesserae head, c1850, 1¾in (4.5cm) long.
£80–100
$115–145 ⊞ VB

A boxwood sewing turret thimble/thread holder, 1850, 5in (12.5cm) long.
£80–100
$115–145 ⊞ MB

A boxwood bird call, c1850, 5in (12.5cm) long.
£60–70
$90–100 ⊞ F&F

A Victorian turned coquilla nut nutmeg grater, with screw top, the original grater within an ivory surround, 2½in (6.5cm) wide.
£110–130
$160–190 🔨 TMA

A Tunbridge ware box, with tumbling block inlay, 1850, 4in (10cm) wide.
£70–80
$100–115 ⊞ MB

A wooden snuff shoe, late 19thC, Belgian, 4in (10cm) long.
£50–60
$75–90 ⊞ SDA

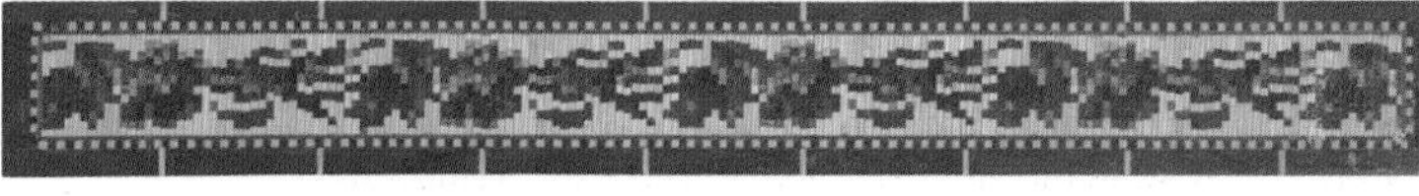

A rosewood ruler, with mosaic inlay, 1870, 9in (23cm) long.
£50–60
$75–90 ⊞ MB

A sycamore egg cup, 19thC, 3in (7.5cm) high.
£85–95
$125–140 ⊞ SEA

A lignum vitae bowl, c1880, 4½in (11.5cm) diam.
£70–80
$100–115 ⊞ SDA

► **A pair of Anri carved wood napkin rings,** surmounted by figures of a boy and a girl, Italian, c1920, 4in (10cm) high.
£34–38
$50–60 ⊞ Dall

Umbrellas & Walking Sticks

A silk parasol, embroidered with flowers, c1860, 28in (71cm) long.
£75–85
$110–125 ⊞ L&L

An umbrella, with ivory handle, c1890, 34in (86.5cm) long.
£60–70
$90–100 ⊞ GBr

A silk and lace parasol, c1860, 26in (66cm) long.
£75–85
$110–125 ⊞ L&L

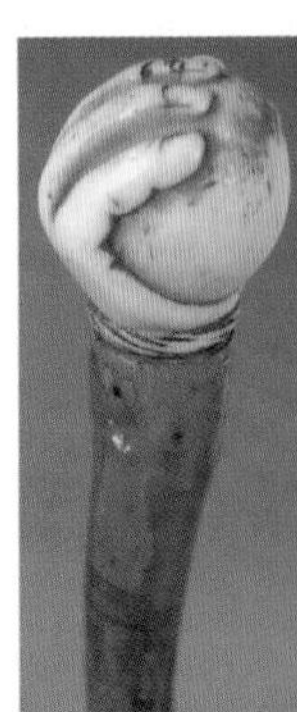

► **A walking stick,** the ivory handle carved as a hand grasping a ball, the shaft decorated with penwork figures faces and foliage, 19thC, 28¾in (73cm) long.
£150–180
$220–260
SWO

An ivory walking stick handle, carved as a bulldog's head, eyes missing, 19thC, 4½in (11.5cm) high.
£280–320
$400–450 G(L)

An ebonized walking stick, the handle carved as a walrus's head with bone tusks, c1900, 33in (84cm) long.
£230–260
$330–380 ⊞ GBr

An air cane, by E. M. Reilly, the simulated wood finish with detachable horn handle, with air pump and fitting, 1890–1910, 36in (91.5cm) long, in original oak case.
£1,100–1,300
$1,600–1,900 G(L)

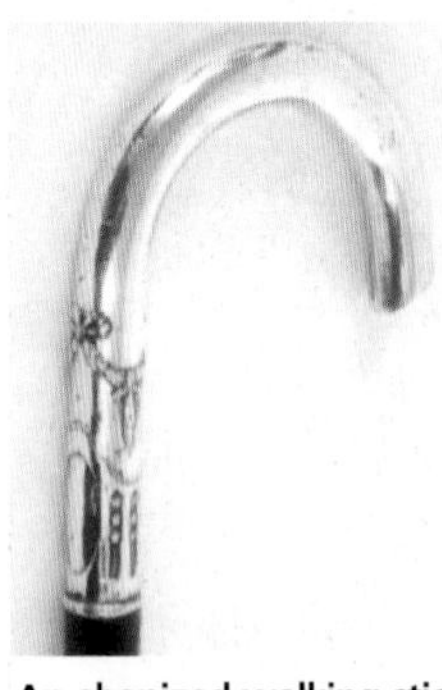

An ebonized walking stick, the silver handle with ribbon and harebell decoration, c1910, 35in (89cm) long.
£70–90
$100–130 DA

A cotton parasol, 1930, 38in (96.5cm) long.
£40–45
$60–65 ⊞ L&L

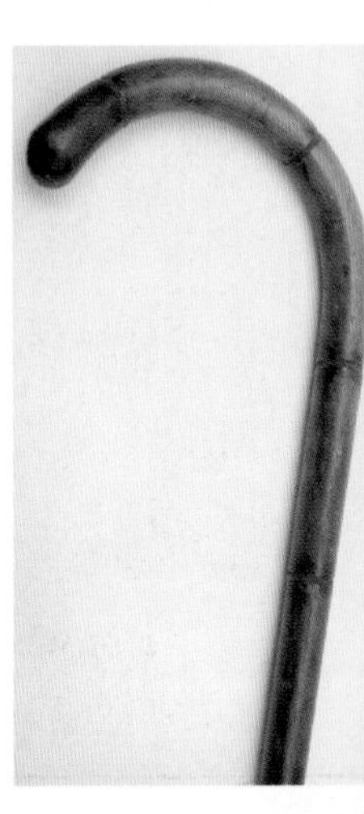

► **A bamboo-effect walking stick,** c1941, 36in (91.5cm) long.
£2,700–3,200
$3,900–4,700
G(L)

This walking stick, owned by the novelist Virginia Woolf, was found embedded in the riverbank on the day she drowned herself in March 1941. Its value reflects its literary association.

Watches & Clocks

► **A Bradley & Hubbard 30-hour parade clock,** the stamped sheet brass decorated with coloured glass roundels that glow when a candle is put inside, dial repaired, hands replaced, chain links later, maker's mark, American, c1885, 13in (33cm) high.
£480–550
$700–800 ROSc
This style of clock was carried in torchlight parades and hung outside during evening parties.

An embossed silver-cased clock, 1897, 3¼in (8.5cm) wide.
£95–115
$140–170 SWO

A silver-cased travelling clock, 1906, 4in (10cm) wide.
£135–165
$200–240 EXC

◄ **An 18ct gold pocket watch,** signed Peerless, 1909, 2in (5cm) diam.
£280–325
$400–470 GLa

► **A porcelain clock,** mounted with pigeons on a base, French, 1930s, 12in (30.5cm) wide.
£50–60
$75–90 HO

A White Star cocktail watch, set with diamonds, Swiss movement, 1930s.
£750–850
$1,100–1,250 RBB

A Longines 18ct gold bracelet watch, set with diamonds, 17 jewel nickel movement, signed, 1940s, ¾in (1.5cm) diam.
£250–300
$350–450 B

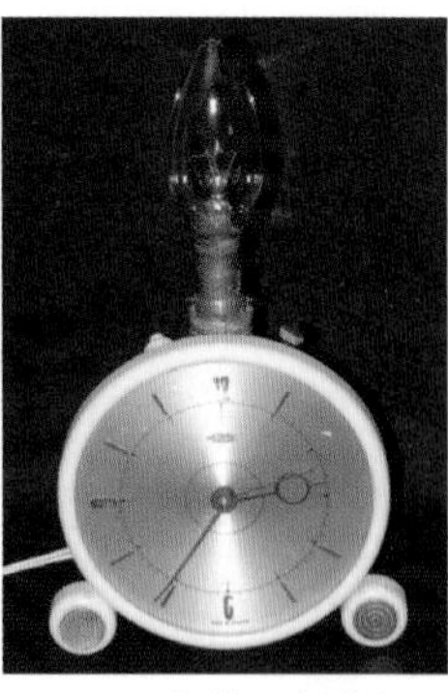

An AL Bakelite clock/ lamp, shade missing, 1940s, 9in (23cm) high.
£25–30
$35–45 DHAR

A travel alarm clock, 1960s, 3in (7.5cm) square.
£8–10
$10–15 RTT

An Omega Seamaster steel-cased wristwatch, automatic movement and date aperture, c1970, in presentation box.
£110–130
$160–190 G(L)

► **A 9ct gold watch,** c1960, ¾in (1.5cm) diam, in a fitted case.
£140–160
$200–230 EXC

A Heuer mechanical stopwatch, 1970s.
£90–100
$130–145 HARP

A JAZ clock, part manual, part battery operation, French, 1970s, 8in (20.5cm) wide.
£30–35
$45–50 TWI

A plastic digital watch, depicting the Joker from *Batman* comic, 1989, 8½ x 3½in (21.5 x 9cm), carded.
£15–20
$20–30 CTO

Writing

With increased prosperity, improved education and the development of the postal service, the manufacture of writing equipment really took off in the late 18th century. This was the period that saw the transition from the quill pen to the steel-nibbed dip pen and the birth of the fountain pen, pioneered by the American firm of Waterman in 1883.

The Victorian love of novelty expressed itself in a taste for innovative mechanical pencils (a popular collectable today) and a wide range of accessories from decorative pen wipes to inkwells, which were made from every material from metal to pottery. Basic glass ink bottles were mass-produced in their thousands, but in order to attract customers, manufacturers also produced unusual shapes such as the tea kettle and locomotive inks shown in this section. These were cheap Victorian novelties, which today, because of their rarity and the growing popularity of bottle collecting, can fetch hundreds of pounds at auction.

By the early 20th century, the fountain pen was established as the most commonly used writing instrument. Values for vintage pens depend on maker, originality and condition.

In 1943, the Hungarian hypnotist, sculptor and journalist, Lazlo Biro patented the ballpoint pen. These pens, which would not blot or be affected by changes in air pressure, were manufactured for the RAF in 1944 and the following year were put into public production in both Britain and the USA. Sales soon outsripped the fountain pen. The Bic Crystal, the first throw-away biro, was introduced to Britain from France in 1958. Priced at one shilling (a dime), 53 million were sold in 1959, approximately one for every man, woman and child in the UK.

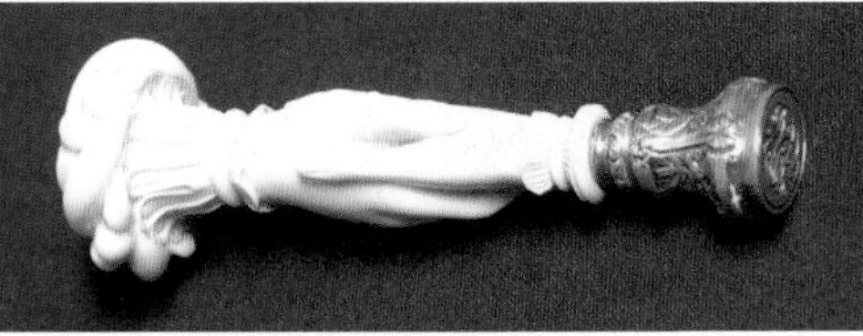

An ivory friendship seal, the shaft carved in the form of clasped hands, the silver base with a floral design, French, c1830, 4½in (11.5cm) long.
£420–460
$620–660 ⊞ LBr
Seals were used to authenticate documents, and before the introduction of the envelope to close or 'seal' letters.

► A glass tea kettle inkwell, with brass lift-up cap to spout, base chip, 1880–1900, 2¼in (5.5cm) high.
£150–200
$220–290
⚒ BBR

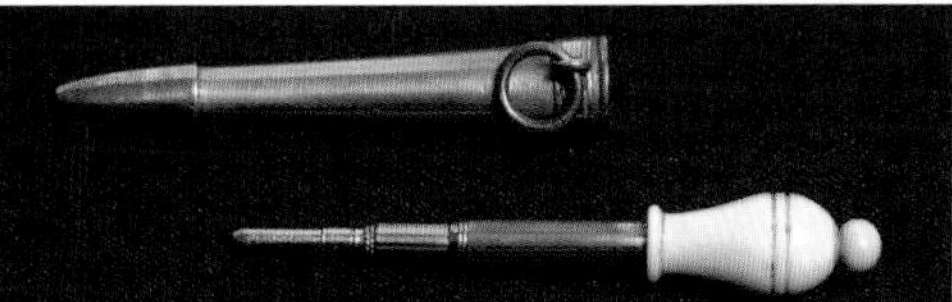

A Perry & Co base metal, ivory and gold novelty pencil, in the shape of a sheathed dagger, c1880, 2½in (6.5cm) long.
£100–120
$145–175 ⊞ PPL

A Sampson Mordan silver propelling pencil, 1830–40, 5in (12.5cm) long.
£70–80
$100–115 ⊞ PPL

► A Victorian papier mâché desk blotter, decorated with mother-of-pearl banding and a floral spray, 12¼in (31cm) wide.
£70–80
$100–115 ⚒ SWO

A Victorian brass pen wipe, in the shape of an elephant's head, with glass eyes, 3½in (9cm) wide.
£80–90
$115–130 ⊞ PPL

A travelling inkwell, leather-covered brass-coloured base metal, c1880, 2in (5cm) high.
£45–60
$65–90 ⊞ PPL

A Sampson Mordan silver desk pen and pencil set, with hand-engraved decoration, c1880, 8in (20.5cm) long, in original case.
£125–150
$180–220 ⊞ PPL

► **A glass inkwell,** in the shape of a tea kettle, with brass lift-up cap to spout, 1890–1900, 2in (5cm) high.
£320–360
$450–500
⚒ BBR

► **A glass inkwell,** in the shape of a locomotive, slight damage, 1890–1900, 2½in (6.5cm) long.
£800–1,000
$1,200–1,500 ⚒ BBR
This is one of the UK's rarest and most desirable glass ink bottles.

A glass inkwell, in the shape of a tea kettle, minor chips, 1890–1900, 2in (5cm) high.
£160–200
$230–290 ⚒ BBR

A Tunbridge ware and felt pen wipe, c1890, 4in (10cm) diam.
£50–60
$75–90 ⊞ PPL

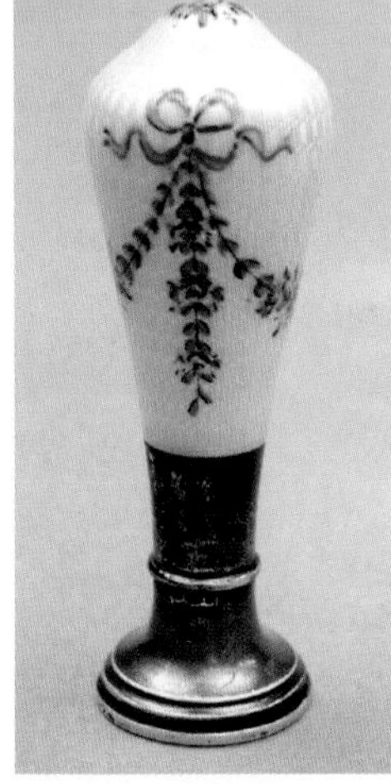

► **A silver desk seal,** with decorated enamel handle, Continental, c1900, 3in (7.5cm) high.
£180–220
$260–320 ⚒ G(L)

A novelty pencil, made from a hazelnut, c1900, 1in (2.5cm) long.
£40–45
$60–65 ⊞ PPL

A silver pencil/paper knife, Birmingham 1907, 3½in (9cm) long.
£25–30
$35–45 ⊞ Dall

An iridescent glass inkwell, with brass lion's head-decorated lid, 1920s, 4in (10cm) square.
£250–300
$360–580 ⊞ BrL

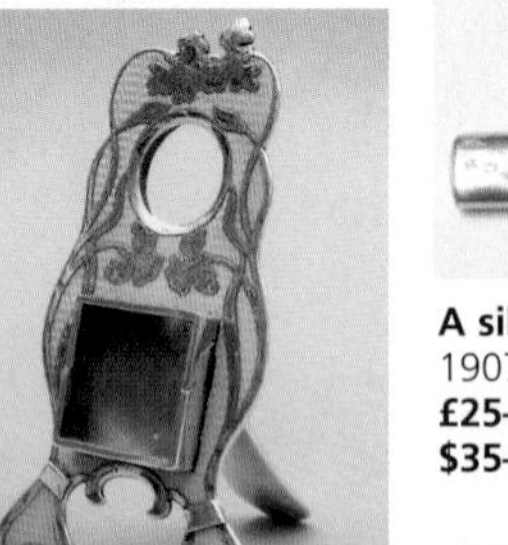

A white metal and enamel desk calendar, Continental, c1900, 5in (12.5cm) high.
£130–150
$190–220 ⚒ G(L)

An Eversharp Wahl black and pearl pen, with roller ball clip and Eversharp seal, c1930, 5in (12.5cm) long.
£270–300
$390–440 ⚒ PPL

A Eureka wood-framed writing slate, c1930, 13in (33cm) wide.
£10–15
$15–20 ⊞ AL

A Spot Ink glass bottle, 1930s, 4in (10cm) wide, with original box.
£18–20
$25–30 ⊞ RTT

A silver-mounted cut-glass inkwell, 1930s, 3in (7.5cm) square.
£80–100
$115–145 ⚒ G(L)

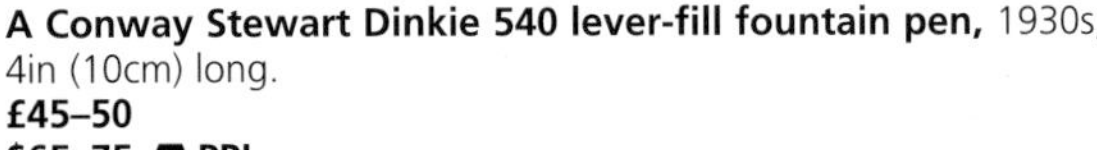

A Conway Stewart Dinkie 540 lever-fill fountain pen, 1930s, 4in (10cm) long.
£45–50
$65–75 ⊞ PPL

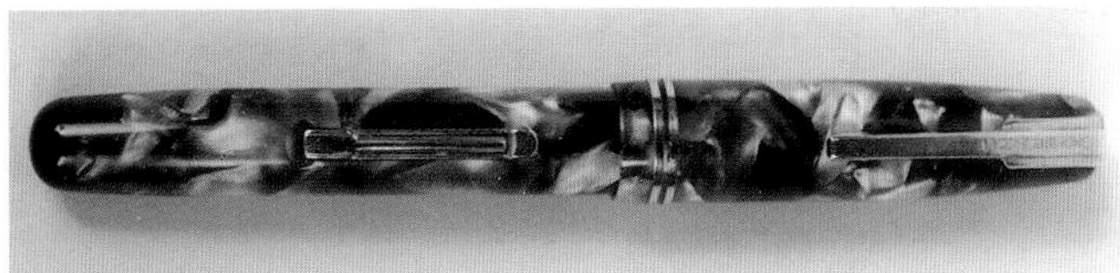

A Waterman fountain pen, 1946, 4¼in (11cm) long.
£50–60
$75–90 ⊞ RUS

◄ **A George VI wall-mounted letter box,** incomplete, 39½in (100.5cm) high.
£300–350
$450–500 ⚒ SWO

A plastic pencil sharpener, in the shape of a clock, 1950s, 1¼in (3cm) high.
£14–16
$18–22 ⚒ RUSS

An adjustable pencil sharpener, c1940, 1¼in (3cm) wide.
£15–20
$20–30 ⚒ RUSS

► **A vending machine for postage stamp books,** c1953, 16in (40.5cm) high.
£900–1,000
$1,300–1,500 ⊞ WP

A Conway Stewart 851 plastic lever-fill fountain pen, 1960s, 5in (12.5cm) long.
£70–80
$100–115 ⊞ PPL

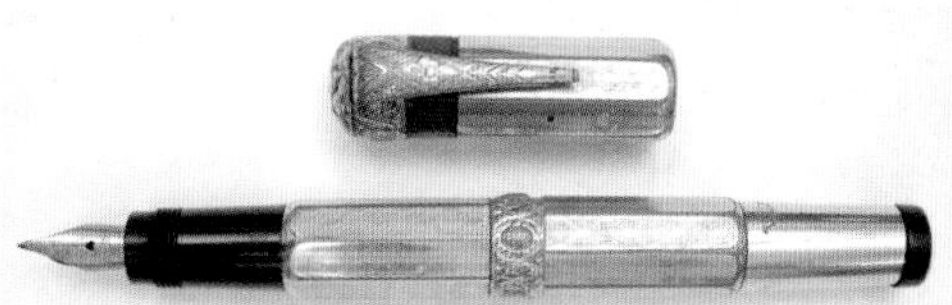

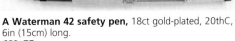

A Waterman 42 safety pen, 18ct gold-plated, 20thC, 6in (15cm) long.
£60–75
$90–110 ⚒ G(L)

Pocket Money Collectables

A Promicroceras ammonite, from Charmouth, Dorset, 180 million years old, 3in (7.5cm) diam.
£3–5
$5–7 ⊞ FOSS

A London and North Western Railway postcard, 1904.
£2–3
$3–6 ⊞ S&D

A linen fabric square, embroidered with flowers, 1920s, 13in (33cm) square.
£2–3
$3–6 ⊞ HILL

Two silver-coated moulded glass buttons, c1920, 1in (2.5cm) diam.
£2–3
$3–6 each ⊞ FMN

Four Esso road maps, 1960s, 9 x 4in (23 x 10cm).
£4–6
$6–8 each ⊞ JUN

A box of J. A. Sharwood's powdered gelatine, 1939–45, 3 x 2in (7.5 x 5cm).
£2–4
$3–7 ⊞ HUX

A Crown Jewelry shop display, containing adjustable rings, 'Makes a Teen A Queen', American, 1960s, 8½ x 7½in (21.5 x 19cm).
£3–5
$5–7 each ring ⊞ TWI

***Scorcher and Score* comic,** 1974, 11½ x 9½in (29 x 24cm).
£2–4
$3–7 ⊞ TWI

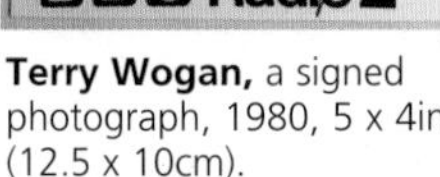

Terry Wogan, a signed photograph, 1980, 5 x 4in (12.5 x 10cm).
£3–4
$5–6 ⊞ S&D

◄ **A set of 10 Rockwell collector's cards,** Early Balloon Flight, 2002.
£4–6
$6–8 ⊞ MUR

Collectables of the Future

***The Adventures of Superman* comic,** by DC Comics, No. 596, contains reference to 11 September, American, November 2001, 10 x 7in (25.5 x 18cm).
£25–30
$35–45 ⊞ NOS

A Sutherland China beaker, commemorating the Golden Jubilee of Queen Elizabeth II, limited edition of 2,500, 2002, 5in (12.5cm) high.
£40–45
$60–65 ⊞ H&G

***Lord of the Rings*,** two foil cards, 2001, 3½ x 2½in (9 x 6.5cm).
£10–15
$15–20 each ⊞ SSF

◄ *Transformers*, new series, vol 1, issue 1, April 2002, 10 x 6½in (25.5 x 16.5cm).
£15–20
$20–30 ⊞ NOS

Kylie Minogue, a signed photograph, 2002, 10 x 8in (25.5 x 20.5cm).
£150–190
$220–275 ⊞ FRa

► A Regency-style mahogany and silk-covered dolls' house sofa, by David Booth, 2002, 6in (15cm) wide.
£110–130
$160–190 ⊞ CNM

A *The Simpsons* Convention Comic Book Guy, by Playmates Toys, with Intelli-Tronic voice activation, unopened, 2001, 7 x 6in (18 x 15cm), boxed.
£60–70
$90–100 ⊞ NOS

◄ A Bank of England £5 note, Elizabeth Fry, first prefix, first day of issue, 21 May 2002, 5¼in (13.5cm) wide.
£10–15
$15–20 ⊞ WP

Two *Star Wars* figures, by Hasbro, Clone Trooper and Saesee Tiin Jedi Master, from *Attack of the Clones*, 2002, 4in (10cm) high, carded.
£9–10
$12–15 each ⊞ CoC

Record Breakers

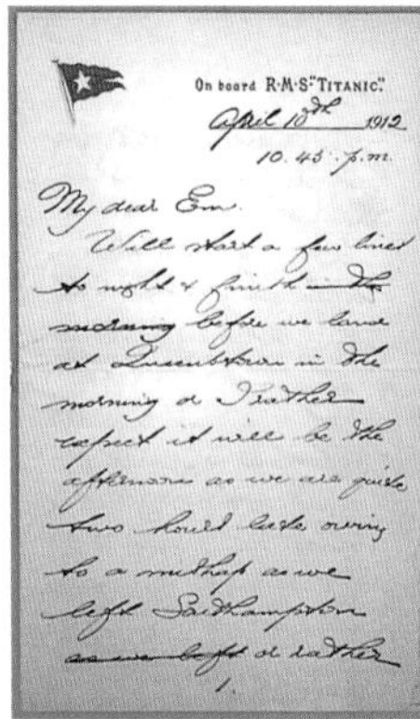
On board R.M.S. "Titanic."
April 10th 1912
10.45 p.m.
My dear Em.
Will start a few lines to night & finish in the morning before we leave at Queenstown in the morning or Thurs... expect it will be the afternoon as we are quite two hours late owing to a mishap as we left Southampton as we left at Cherbourg

An eight-page letter written on board RMS *Titanic*, by Stanley J. May, describing the train journey from Waterloo to Southampton, embarkation, arrival and departure from Cherbourg and many details of life on board ship, 10 and 11 April 1912.
World Record Price
£35,760
$52,000 HALd

► **An A. W. Buchan & Co stoneware sample ginger beer bottle,** with screw stopper, transfer-printed front and reverse, impressed to neck, impressed pottery mark, c1900, 9½in (24cm) high.
World Record Price
£2,340
$3,500 BBR
This is a very rare item and is one of the most desirable of all pottery sample ginger beer bottles.

A Shoji Hamada stoneware footed bowl, c1965, 21¾in (55.5cm) diam.
World Record Price
£57,250
$83,000 B
This is a very rare bowl.

◄ ***The Beano Comic,*** No. 1, Big Eggo, Lord Snooty and Morgyn The Mighty Start Their Adventures, 1938.
£7,540
$10,800 CBP
This is only the ninth copy known to exist of this rare first issue of *Beano*. It was owned by a man who stored it under his sofa for safe-keeping, thinking it might one day be worth about £200 ($300). The last time a first edition of *Beano* was offered for sale was in 1999, accompanied by the even rarer free Whoopee Mask. It made £6,820 ($9,800), which at that time was a world record for a British comic at auction.

A Märklin gauge 00/HO 4-4-0 three-rail electric locomotive and tender, No. E800, German, c1938, 6in (15cm) long, with original box.
World Record Price
£25,250
$37,000 VEC
This locomotive was manufactured only for export to the UK, but in 1939, as tension grew between Britain and Germany, Adolf Hitler ordered Märklin to cease exports to the UK. Very few examples are known to exist worldwide.

A six-shot 9mm double action open-frame pin-fire revolver, retailed by Crane, the octagonal barrel stamped at the breech 'E. Lefaucheux Invr Brevete', maker's marks for A. Francotte, Liège, in an ebony box with silver escutcheon on the lid engraved 'Returned to Friends at Wilbank from W. S. Churchill 1901', the interior inscribed 'Pistol employed during the escape of Winston Spencer Churchill, graciously returned to your grandfather, presented with family pride to W.O.1 K G Howard 17 Sqdn, S A A F', with a cut-glass brandy flask, the silver cup base by Asprey, hallmarked 1901 and engraved 'J.H.' and 'From W.S.C', a printed card inscribed 'To John Howard from Winston S. Churchill in recognition of the help afforded him during the South African War', all in a black japanned metal document box, the front marked 'K. G. Howard', 8in (20.5cm) long.
World Record Price
£32,000
$46,500 WAL

BACA

BRITISH ANTIQUES AND COLLECTABLES AWARDS

presented by

MILLER'S

Celebrating the Winners of BACA 2002

The third annual Awards Ceremony took place on 26 June 2002 at The Dorchester, Park Lane, London. After a champagne reception, the 320 guests enjoyed a 3 course meal and, after eagerly awaiting the presentation ceremony, learned of the winners for the first time during the evening. Eric Knowles, Chairman of BACA, presented each winner with a certificate on stage.

The evening was a tremendous occasion continuing on into the early hours with guests and winners alike sharing in the celebrations.

How to Vote for 2003

The voting process for 2003 Awards begins now and the closing date is on 28th February 2003. For a voting form, please write to Melissa Boylen at BACA or log on to the website:

BACA/Miller's
2–4 Heron Quays
London E14 4JP
www.baca-awards.co.uk

2003 AWARDS CEREMONY: TUESDAY 24 JUNE 2003

PROUDLY SPONSORED BY

2002 BACA *Winners...*

CATEGORY 1
General Antiques Dealer

LONDON (INSIDE M25)
sponsored by
Alistair Sampson Antiques Ltd
120 Mount Street

UK (OUTSIDE M25) *sponsored by*
Richard Gardner Antiques
Swan House, Market Square, Petworth, West Sussex

CATEGORY 2
Specialist Antiques Dealers

FURNITURE
sponsored by
Huntington Antiques Ltd
Church Street, Stow-on-the-Wold, Glos

MUSICAL INSTRUMENTS
Vintage & Rare Guitars
6 Denmark Street, London

ART NOUVEAU/ART DECO
The Fine Art Society plc
148 New Bond Street, London

COLLECTABLES
Manfred Schotten Antiques
The Crypt, 109 High Street, Burford, Oxon

SILVER & PLATE
Lowe & Sons
11 Bridge Street Row, Chester

SCULPTURE
Robert Bowman
8 Duke Street, St James's, London

PRINT
The O'Shea Gallery
120a Mount Street, London

WATERCOLOUR
Abbott & Holder
30 Museum Street, London

COSTUME & TEXTILES
Antique Textiles & Lighting
34 Belvedere, Lansdown Road, Bath, Somerset

POST WAR DESIGN
Target Gallery
7 Windmill St, London

CERAMICS
Andrew Dando
4 Wood Street, Bath, Somerset

CATEGORY 3
Auction Houses

LONDON (INSIDE M25)
sponsored by
Christie's South Kensington
85 Old Brompton Road, London

UK (OUTSIDE M25)
sponsored by
Gorringes incorporating Julian Dawson
15 North Street, Lewes, East Sussex

SPECIALIST DEPARTMENT WITHIN AN AUCTION HOUSE
Woolley & Wallis Ltd (Ceramics)
51–61 Castle Street, Wiltshire

CATEGORY 4
Associated Awards

FAIR OF THE YEAR
The Grosvenor House Art & Antiques Fair (June 2001)

AWARD FOR: IN-HOUSE EXHIBITION
John Walker,
The English Joined Backstool 1660–1720

JOURNALIST OF THE YEAR
Brian Sewell, Evening Standard

AUCTIONEER OF THE YEAR
Rodney Tennant
Tennant Auctioneers, The Auction Centre, Leyburn, N Yorkshire

SERVICES AWARD: THIS YEAR FEATURING ANTIQUES ON THE INTERNET
www.christies.com

AWARD FOR: FRIENDLY ANTIQUES SHOP
Megarry's
Jericho Cottage, The Duckpond Green, Blackmore, Essex

AWARD FOR: BEST ANTIQUES TOWN/VILLAGE
Saffron Walden

Directory of Specialists

If you require a valuation for an item it is advisable to check whether the dealer or specialist will carry out this service, and whether there is a charge. Please mention Miller's when making an enquiry. Having found a specialist who will carry out your valuation, it is best to send a description and photograph of the item to them, together with a stamped addressed envelope for the reply. A valuation by telephone is not possible. Most dealers are only too happy to help you with your enquiry, however, they are very busy people and consideration of the above points would be welcomed.

Bedfordshire

Offworld, 142 Market Halls, Arndale Centre, Luton LU1 2TP
Tel: 01582 736256
off_world@btconnect.com
Science fiction collectors' store for Star Wars, Star Trek, Transformers, GI Joe, He-Man, Alien, Dr Who, James Bond, Pokemon, Simpsons, Knight Rider, TY Beanies, Care Bears, hand held games etc. Open 9.30am–5.30pm Mon–Sat (closed 2pm Wed).

Berkshire

Mostly Boxes, 93 High Street, Eton, Windsor SL4 6AF Tel: 01753 858470
Antique wooden boxes.

Special Auction Services, Kennetholme, Midgham, Reading RG7 5UX
Tel: 0118 971 2949
www.invaluable.com/sas/
Commemoratives, pot lids & Prattware, Fairings, Goss & Crested, Baxter & Le Blond prints. Also toys for the collector.

Cambridgeshire

Antique Amusement Co, Mill Lane, Swaffham Bulbeck CB5 0NF
Tel/Fax: 01223 813041
Mobile: 07802 666755
www.aamag.co.uk
Vintage amusement machines also auctions of amusement machines, fairground art and other related collectables. Monthly collectors magazine.

Cloisters Antiques, 1A Lynn Road, Ely CB7 4EG Tel: 01353 668558
info@cloistersantiques.co.uk
www.cloistersantiques.co.uk
Sewing, writing, heavy horse and antiquarian books.

Cheshire

Collector's Corner, PO Box 8, Congleton CW12 4GD
Tel: 01260 270429
dave.popcorner@ukonline.co.uk
Beatles and pop memorabilia.

Dollectable, 53 Lower Bridge Street, Chester CH1 1RS
Tel: 01244 344888/679195
Antique dolls.

Moorcroft Pottery Chester
Tel: 01244 301800
Sales@Moorcroftchester.co.uk
www.Moorcroftchester.co.uk

On The Air, The Vintage Technology Centre, The Highway Hawarden, (Nr Chester), Deeside CH5 3DN
Tel/Fax: 01244 530300
Mobile: 07778 767734
www.vintageradio.co.uk
Vintage radios.

Specialist Glass Collector's Fairs Ltd
Tel: 01260 271975
dil.hier@talk21.com
'National Glass Collectors Fair' Bi-annual event at the National Motorcycle Museum – Birmingham. Off Junction 6 on the M42(A45). Quality glass from throughout the ages.

Sweetbriar Gallery Ltd, Sweetbriar House, 106 Robin Hood Lane, Helsby WA6 9NH
Tel: 01928 723851
Mobile: 07860 907532
sweetbr@globalnet.co.uk
www.sweetbriar.co.uk
Paperweights.

Charles Tomlinson
Tel/Fax: 01244 318395
charles.tomlinson@lineone.net
www.lineone.net/-charles.tomlinson
Scientific instruments.

Cleveland

Vectis Auctions Ltd/Barry Potter Auctions, Fleck Way, Thornaby, Stockton-on-Tees TS17 9JZ Tel: 01642 750616
admin@vectis.co.uk
admin@barrypotterauctions.com
www.vectis.co.uk
www.barrypotterauctions.co.uk
Toy auctions.

Cornwall

Gentry Antiques, Little Green, Polperro PL13 2RF
Tel: 01503 272 361/020 7722 1458
info@cornishwarecollector.co.uk
www.cornishwarecollector.co.uk
Cornish Ware. Also at Gray's Antique Market Mews, London W1.

Devon

The Pen and Pencil Lady
Tel: 01647 231619
penpencilady@aol.com
www.penpencilady.com

Sue Wilde at Wildewear
Tel: 01395 577966
compacts@wildewear.co.uk
www.wildewear.co.uk
Specialists in fashion accessories 1900–1950 including beaded and leather bags, purses, hats, powder compacts, buttons and jewellery. Examples from USA, France, Austria, East Germany and UK.

Dorset

Books Afloat, 66 Park Street, Weymouth DT4 7DE Tel: 01305 779774
Books on all subjects, liner and naval memorabilia, shipping company china, ships bells, old postcards, models, paintings.

Dalkeith Auctions Ltd, Dalkeith Hall, Dalkeith Steps, Rear of 81 Old Christchurch Road, Bournemouth BH1 1YL Tel: 01202 292905
how@dalkeith-auctions.co.uk
www.dalkeith-auctions.co.uk
Auctions of postcards, cigarette cards, ephemera and collectors items.

Delf Stream Gallery
Tel: 07974 926137 oastman@aol.com
www.delfstreamgallery.com
19th–20thC Art pottery.

Hardy's Collectables
Tel: 07970 613077
www.poolepotteryjohn.com
Poole pottery.

Murrays' Antiques & Collectables
Tel: 01202 309094
Shipping, motoring, railway, cycling items always required. Also advertising related items, eg showcards, enamel signs, tins and packaging and general quality collectables. Anything old and interesting. No valuations given.

Old Button Shop Antiques, Lytchett Minster, Poole BH16 6JF
Tel: 01202 622169
info@oldbuttonshop.fsnet.co.uk
Buttons & collectables.

www.collectorsworld.net, PO Box 4922, Bournemouth BH1 3WD
Tel: 01202 555223
info@collectorsworld.biz
www.collectorsworld.net
www.collectorsworld.biz
Antiques and objet d'arts including 19th and 20thC watches, clocks, cameras. Toys, Dinky, Corgi and diecast. Tinplate cars, boats, planes, dolls, memorabilia. Open 24 hours on the web.

Essex

Brandler Galleries, 1 Coptfold Road, Brentwood CM14 4BN
Tel: 01277 222269
john@brandler-galleries.com
www.brandler-galleries.com
Original artwork and production cells.

Haddon Rocking Horses Ltd, 5 Telford Road, Clacton on Sea CO15 4LP

Tel: 01255 424745
millers@haddonrockinghorses.co.uk
www.haddonrockinghorses.co.uk

Megarry's and Forever Summer, Jericho Cottage, The Duckpond Green, Blackmore CM4 0RR
Tel: 01277 821031/01277 822170
Antiques, Arts & Crafts. 11am–5pm Wed–Sun inclusive, closed Mon and Tues. Member Essex Antiques Dealers' Association.

The Old Telephone Company, The Old Granary, Battlesbridge Antiques Centre, Nr Wickford SS11 7RF
Tel: 01245 400601
gp@theoldtelephone.co.uk
www.theoldtelephone.co.uk
Period telephones.

Gloucestershire
Bourton Bears, Strathspey, Landsdowne, Bourton-on-the-Water GL54 2AR
Tel: 01451 821466
mel@strathspey-bed-fsnet.co.uk
www.bourtonbears.com
Teddy bears.

Bread & Roses, Durham House Antique Centre, Sheep Street, Stow on the Wold GL54 1AA
Tel: 01451 870404 or 01926 817342
Kitchen antiques 1800–1950s.

Gloucester Toy Mart, Ground Floor, Antique Centre, Severn Road, Old Docks, Gloucester GL1 2LE Tel: 07973 768452
Buying and selling obsolete toys and collectables.

Grimes House Antiques, High Street, Moreton-in-Marsh GL56 0AT
Tel/Fax: 01608 651029
grimes_house@cix.co.uk
www.grimeshouse.co.uk
www.cranberryglass.co.uk
www.collectglass.com
Cranberry glass.

Keith Harding's World of Mechanical Music, The Oak House, High Street, Northleach GL54 3ET
Tel: 01451 860181
keith@mechanicalmusic.co.uk
www.mechanicalmusic.co.uk
Mechanical music and automata.

Jennie Horrocks Tel: 07836 264896
gallery@aw18.fsnet.co.uk
info@artnouveaulighting.co.uk
www.artnouveaulighting.co.uk
Also at:
Top Banana Antiques Mall, 1 New Church Street, Tetbury GL8 8DS

Specialised Postcard Auctions, 25 Gloucester Street, Cirencester GL7 2DJ Tel: 01285 659057
Sales of early postcards and ephemera.

Telephone Lines Ltd, 304 High Street, Cheltenham GL50 3JF
Tel: 01242 583699
info@telephonelines.net
www.telephonelines.net
Antique telephones.

Hampshire
Classic Amusements
Tel: 01425 472164 pennyslot@aol.com
www.classicamusements.net
Vintage slot machines.

Cobwebs, 78 Northam Road, Southampton SO14 0PB
Tel/Fax: 023 8022 7458
www.cobwebs.uk.com
Ocean liner memorabilia. Also naval and aviation items.

Rick Hubbard Art Deco, 3 Tee Court, Bell Street, Romsey SO51 8GY
Tel: 01794 513133
Mobile: 07767 267607
rick@rickhubbard-artdeco.co.uk
www.rickhubbard-artdeco.co.uk
Original 20thC ceramics.

The Old Toy Shop, PO Box 4389, Ringwood BH24 1YN
Tel: 01425 470180
djwells@btinternet.com
www.TheOldToyShop.com
Clockwork, steam and electric vintage toys, memorabilia and figures.

Tickers, 37 Northam Road, Southampton SO14 0PD
Tel: 023 8023 4431
kmonckton@btopenworld.com
Clocks, watches and barometers.

Hertfordshire
Forget Me Knot Antiques, Antiques at Over the Moon, 27 High Street, St Albans AL3 4EH Tel: 01923 261172
Mobile: 07941 255489
sharpffocus@hotmail.com
Sentimental jewellery.

Tring Market Auctions, Brook Street, Tring HP23 5EF Tel: 01442 826446
sales@tringmarketauctions.co.uk
www.tringmarketauctions.co.uk

Isle of Wight
Nostalgia Toy Museum, High Street, Godshill, Ventnor PO38 3HZ
Tel: 01983 522148
toyman@nostalgiatoys.com
Diecast toys specialist and museum.

Kent
20th Century Marks, 12 Market Square, Westerham TN16 1AW Tel: 01959 562221 Mobile: 07831 778992
lambarda@btconnect.com
www.20thcenturymarks.co.uk
Original 20thC design.

Chris Baker Gramophones, All Our Yesterdays, 3 Cattle Market, Sandwich CT13 9AE Tel: 01304 375767 or 614756
cbgramophones@aol.com
Specialist dealer in gramophones and phonographs.

Beatcity, PO Box 229, Chatham ME5 8WA Tel/Fax: 01634 200444 or 07770 650890
Darrenhanks@beatcity.co.uk
www.beatcity.co.uk
Beatles and rock & roll memorabilia.

Candlestick & Bakelite, PO Box 308, Orpington BR5 1TB
Tel: 020 8467 3743
candlestick.bakelite@mac.com
www.candlestickandbakelite.co.uk
Telephones.

Dragonlee Collectables
Tel: 01622 729502
Noritake.

Stuart Heggie, 14 The Borough, Northgate, Canterbury CT1 2DR
Tel: 01227 470422
Mobile: 0783 3593344
heggie.cameras@virgin.net
Vintage cameras, optical toys and photographic images.

J & M Collectables, 64 High Street, Tenterden TN30 6AU
Tel: 01580 891657
jandmcollectables@tinyonline.co.uk
Postcards, Crested china, Osborne (Ivorex) plaques and small collectables including Doulton, Wade, etc.

Lambert & Foster, 102 High Street, Tenterden TN30 6HT Tel: 01580 762083
tenterden@lambertandfoster.co.uk
www.lambertandfoster.co.uk
Antique auctions.

The Old Tackle Box, PO Box 55, High Street, Cranbrook TN17 3ZU
Tel & Fax: 01580 713979
Mobile: 07729 278 293
tackle.box@virgin.net
Old fishing tackle.

Pretty Bizarre, 170 High Street, Deal CT14 6BQ Tel: 07973 794537
1920s–1970s ceramics and collectables.

The Neville Pundole Gallery, 8A & 9, The Friars, Canterbury CT1 2AS
Tel: 01227 453471
neville@pundole.co.uk
www.pundole.co.uk
Moorcroft and contemporary pottery and glass.

Serendipity, 125 High Street, Deal CT14 6BB Tel: 01304 369165/01304 366536 dipityantiques@aol.com
Staffordshire pottery.

Stevenson Brothers, The Workshop, Ashford Road, Bethersden, Ashford TN26 3AP Tel: 01233 820363
sales@stevensonbrothers.co.uk
www.stevensonbrothers.co.uk
Rocking horses.

Wenderton Antiques
Tel: 01227 720295 (by appt only)
Country antiques including kitchen, laundry and dairy.

Woodville Antiques, The Street, Hamstreet, Ashford TN26 2HG
Tel: 01233 732981
woodvilleantiques@yahoo.co.uk
Tools.

Wot a Racket, 250 Shepherds Lane, Dartford DA1 2PN Tel: 01322 220619
wot-a-racket@talk21.com

Lancashire

Decades, 20 Lord St West, Blackburn BB2 1JX Tel: 01254 693320
Original Victorian to 1970s clothing, accessories, jewellery, decorative textiles and more.

Tracks, PO Box 117, Chorley PR6 0UU Tel: 01257 269726 sales@tracks.co.uk
Beatles and pop memorabilia.

Leicestershire

Pooks Transport Bookshop, Fowke Street, Rothley LE7 7PJ
Tel: 0116 237 6222
pooks.motorbooks@virgin.net
Motoring books and automobilia.

Lincolnshire

Junktion, The Old Railway Station, New Bolingbroke, Boston PE22 7LB
Tel: 01205 480068/480087
Mobile: 07836 345491
Advertising and packaging, automobilia, slot machines, pedal cars, etc.

Skip & Janie Smithson Antiques
Tel & Fax: 01754 810265
Mobile: 07831 399180
Kitchenware.

London

Angling Auctions, PO Box 2095 W12 8RU Tel: 020 8749 4175/07785 281349
neil@anglingauctions.demon.co.uk

Banana Dance Ltd, 16 The Mall, Camden Passage, 359 Upper St, Islington N1 0PD
Tel: 020 8699 7728 Mobile: 07976 296987 jonathan@bananadance.com
www.bananadance.com
Decorative Arts of the 1920s and 1930s.

Barclay Samson Ltd, 65 Finlay Street SW6 6HF Tel: 020 7731 8012
richard@barclaysamson.com
Vintage posters.

Bloomsbury Book Auctions, 3 & 4 Hardwick Street, Off Rosebery Avenue EC1R 4RY
Tel: 020 7833 2636/7 & 020 7923 6940
info@bloomsbury-book-auct.com
www.bloomsbury-book-auct.com

Christie's South Kensington Ltd, 85 Old Brompton Road SW7 3LD
Tel: 020 7321 3279/020 7389 2820
mpritchard@christies.com
www.christies.com
Auctions.

The Collector, Tom Power, 4 Queens Parade Close, Friern Barnet N11 3FY
Tel: 020 8361 7787/020 8361 6111
collector@globalnet.co.uk
Contemporary collectables including Royal Doulton, Beswick, Pendelfin, Worcester, Lladro, Border Fine Art, Wade, Wedgwood, Coalport, Bossons, Lilliput Lane, David Winter, etc.

Comic Book Postal Auctions Ltd, 40–42 Osnaburgh Street NW1 3ND
Tel: 020 7424 0007
comicbook@compuserve.com
www.compalcomics.com

Dix-Noonan-Webb, 16 Bolton Street W1J 8BQ Tel: 020 7499 5022
auctions@dnw.co.uk www.dnw.co.uk
Auctioneers and valuers of orders, decorations and medals, coins, tokens and banknotes.

eBay International AG, Unit 6, Dukes Gate, Acton Lane, Chiswick W4 5DX
Tel 020 8987 6562 jhatton@ebay.com
www.ebay.co.uk

GB Military Antiques, Antiquarius Antiques Centre, 131/141 Kings Road, Chelsea SW3 4PW Tel: 020 7351 5357
info@gbmilitaria.com
www.gbmilitaria.com

Michael German Antiques Ltd, 38B Kensington Church Street W8 4BX
Tel: 020 7937 2771/020 7937 1776
info@antiquecanes.com
info@antiqueweapons.com
www.antiquecanes.com
Walking canes, arms and armour.

The Gooday Gallery, 14 Richmond Hill, Richmond TW10 6QX
Tel: 020 8940 8652
Mobile: 077101 24540
goodaygallery@aol.com
Arts & Crafts, Art Deco, Art Nouveau, Tribal, 1950s and 1960s.

Adrian Harrington, 64a Kensington Church Street W8 4DB
Tel: 020 7937 1465
rare@harringtonbooks.co.uk
www.harringtonbooks.co.uk
Antiquarian books, prints and maps.

David Huxtable, Saturdays at: Portobello Road, Basement Stall 11/12, 288 Westbourne Grove W11
Tel: 07710 132200 david@huxtins.com
Old advertising collectables.

Charles Jeffreys Posters & Graphics, 4 Vardens Road SW11 1RH
Tel: 020 7978 7976
Mobile: 07836 546150
cjeffreys@cjposters.ision.co.uk
charlie@cjposters.com
www.cjposters.com
Specialising in original, rare and collectable posters from the birth of modernism through Bauhaus to the 1960s and '70s pop art and psychedelic culture including contemporary posters.

Francis Joseph Publications, 5 Southbrook Mews SE12 8LG
Tel: 020 8318 9580
office@francisjoseph.com
www.carltonware.co.uk
Books on 20thC ceramics and glass.

Timothy Millett Ltd, Historic Medals and Works of Art, PO Box 20851 SE22 0YN
Tel: 020 8693 1111
Mobile: 07778 637 898
tim@timothymillett.demon.co.uk
Medals and works of art.

Murray Cards (International) Ltd, 51 Watford Way, Hendon Central NW4 3JH
Tel: 020 8202 5688
murraycards@ukbusiness.com
www.murraycard.com/
Cigarette & trade cards.

Colin Narbeth & Son Ltd, 20 Cecil Court, Leicester Square WC2N 4HE
Tel: 020 7379 6975
Colin.Narbeth@btinternet.com
www.colin-narbeth.com

Piccypicky.com
Tel: 0208 204 2001/0208 206 2001
www.piccypicky.com
Artwork, autographs, bubblegum cards, comics, posters, records and toys.

Rumours, 4 The Mall, Upper Street, Camden Passage, Islington N1 0PD
Tel: 020 7704 6549
Mobiles: 07836 277274 & 07831 103748 Rumdec@aol.com
Moorcroft pottery.

Totem, 168 Stoke Newington, Church Street N16 0JL Tel: 020 7275 0234
sales@totemrecords.com
www.totemrecords.com
Secondhand records, tapes, CDs bought, sold and exchanged.

Twinkled, 1st floor, Old Petrol Station, 11–17 Stockwell Street, Greenwich SE10
Tel: 0208 4880930/07940471574
info@twinkled.net www.twinkled.net
Purveyors of fine homeware from the 50s, 60s & 70s. Open Thurs/Fri 12noon–6pm, Sat & Sun 10am–6pm.

Unique Collections, 52 Greenwich Church Street SE10 9BL Tel: 020 8305 0867 glen@uniquecollections.co.uk
www.uniquecollections.co.uk
Old toys bought and sold.

Vintage & Rare Guitars (London), 6 Denmark Street WC2H 8LX
Tel: 020 7240 7500
enquiries@vintageandrareguitars.com
www.vintageandrareguitars.com

Nigel Williams Rare Books, 22 & 25 Cecil Court WC2N 4HE Tel: 020 7836 7757
Books – first editions, illustrated, childrens and detective.

Wimbledon Sewing Machine Co Ltd and The London Sewing Machine Museum, 292–312 Balham High Road, Upper Tooting SW17 7AA Tel: 020 8767 4724
wimbledonsewingmachinecoltd@btinternet.com www.sewantique.com
Antique sewing machines bought and sold. Collection of antique sewing machines.

Yesterday Child, Angel Arcade, 118 Islington High Street N1 8EG
Tel: 020 7354 1601
Fax & Tel: 01908 583403
Antique dolls and dolls house miniatures.

Middlesex

John Ives, 5 Normanhurst Drive, Twickenham TW1 1NA
Tel: 020 8892 6265 jives@btconnect.com
Reference books on antiques and collecting.

Norfolk
Roger Bradbury Antiques, Church Street, Coltishall NR12 7DJ Tel: 01603 737444
Chinese blue and white porcelain circa 1690–1820.

Cat Pottery, 1 Grammar School Road, North Walsham NR28 9JH Tel: 01692 402962
Winstanley cats.

Northamptonshire
The Old Brigade, 10A Harborough Road, Kingsthorpe, Northampton NN2 7AZ Tel: 01604 719389 theoldbrigade@easynet.co.uk www.theoldbrigade.co.uk
Military antiques.

Nottinghamshire
Sally Hawkins Tel: 01636 636666 sallytiles@aol.com
Good range of quality Victorian and Art Nouveau tiles always in stock. Display to be seen at Lady Eastwood building, Newark, NEC and Alexander Palace.

Helen Martin Tel: 01636 611171 Mobile: 07774 147197
Carlton Ware specialist.

Millennium Collectables Ltd, PO Box 146, Eastwood, Nottingham NG16 3SP Tel: 01773 769335 mail@millenniumcollectables.co.uk
Limited edition Guinness collectables.

T. Vennett-Smith, 11 Nottingham Road, Gotham NG11 0HE Tel: 0115 983 0541 info@vennett-smith.com www.vennett-smith.com
Ephemera and sporting memorabilia auctions.

Oxfordshire
Otter Antiques, 20 High Street, Wallingford OX10 0BP Tel: 01491 825544 www.antique-boxes.com fsbdial.co.uk
Sale and restoration of antique wooden boxes, always over 100 in stock.

Alvin Ross Tel: 01865 772409 vintage.games@virgin.net
Pelham puppets.

Stone Gallery, 93 The High Street, Burford OX18 4QA Tel: 01993 823302 mail@stonegallery.co.uk www.stonegallery.co.uk
Specialist dealers in antique and modern paperweights, gold and silver designer jewellery and enamel boxes.

Teddy Bears of Witney, 99 High Street, Witney OX28 6HY Tel: 01993 702616 or 706616
Teddy bears.

Pembrokeshire
Arch House Collectables, St George Street, Tenby SA70 7JB Tel: 01834 843246 archhouse@onetel.net.uk
Pen Delfins.

Republic of Ireland
Michelina & George Stacpoole, Main Street, Adare, Co Limerick Tel: 00 353 6139 6409 stacpoole@iol.ie
Pottery, ceramics, silver and prints.

Scotland
Bow Well Antiques, 103 West Bow, Edinburgh EH1 2JP Tel: 0131 225 3335
Specialists in all things Scottish.

Courtyard Antiques, 108A Causewayside, Edinburgh EH9 1PU Tel: 0131 662 9008

Rhod McEwan Golf Books, Glengarden, Ballater, Aberdeenshire AB35 5UB Tel: 013397 55429 rhodmcewan@easynet.co.uk rhodmcewan.com
Rare and out-of-print golfing books memorabilia.

Shropshire
Decorative Antiques, 47 Church Street, Bishop's Castle SY9 5AD Tel: 01588 638851 enquiries@decorative-antiques.co.uk www.decorative-antiques.co.uk
Decorative objects of the 19th and 20thC.

Mullock & Madeley, The Old Shippon, Wall-under-Heywood, Nr Church Stretton SY6 7DS Tel: 01694 771771 auctions@mullockmadeley.co.uk www.mullockmadeley.co.uk
Sporting auctions.

Somerset
Bath Antiques Online, Bartlett Street Antiques Centre, Bartlett Street, Bath BA1 2QZ Tel: 01225 311061 info@bathantiquesonline.com www.BathAntiquesOnline.com

Lynda Brine, Assembly Antiques, 6 Saville Row, Bath BA1 2QP Tel: 01225 448488 lyndabrine@yahoo.co.uk www.scentbottlesandsmalls.co.uk
Perfume bottles.

Cottage Collectibles, Pennard House, East Pennard, Shepton Mallet BA4 6TP Tel: 01749 860731 sheila@cottagecollectibles.co.uk www.cottagecollectibles.co.uk
Open Mon–Sat 10.00am–5.00pm and by appointment. English and Continental country antiques and kitchenalia. Showroom at Eccleshall, Staffordshire, open by appointment only – 01785 850210.

Julia Craig, Bartlett Street Antiques Centre, 5–10 Bartlett Street, Bath BA1 2QZ Tel: 01225 448202/310457 Mobile: 07771 786846
Textiles, linen & lace, costume.

Philip Knighton, Bush House, 17B South Street, Wellington TA21 8NR Tel: 01823 661618 philipknighton@btopenworld.com
Wireless, gramophones and all valve equipment.

The London Cigarette Card Co Ltd, Sutton Road, Somerton TA11 6QP Tel: 01458 273452 cards@londoncigcard.co.uk www.londoncigcard.co.uk
Cigarette and trade cards.

Caroline Nevill Miniatures, 22A Broad Street, Bath BA1 5LN Tel: 01225 443091 www.carolinenevillminiatures.co.uk

Joanna Proops, Antique Textiles & Lighting, 34 Belvedere, Lansdown Hill, Bath BA1 5HR Tel: 01225 310795 antiquetextiles@uk.online.co.uk www.antiquetextiles.co.uk
Antique textiles and vast selection of chandeliers and wall lights.

Richard Twort Tel/Fax: 01934 641900 Mobile: 077 11 939789
Barographs and all types of meteorological instruments.

Vintage & Rare Guitars (Bath), 7–8 Saville Row, Bath BA1 2QP Tel: 01225 330 888 enquiries@vintageandrareguitars.com www.vintageandrareguitars.com

Staffordshire
Peggy Davies Ceramics, 28 Liverpool Road, Stoke-on-Trent ST4 1VJ Tel: 01782 848002 rhys@kevinfrancis.co.uk www.kevinfrancis.co.uk
Ceramics – Limited edition Toby jugs and figures.

Keystones, PO Box 387, Stafford ST16 3FG Tel: 01785 256648 gkey@keystones.demon.co.uk www.keystones.co.uk
Denby pottery.

Gordon Litherland, 25 Stapenhill Road, Burton on Trent DE15 9AE Tel: 01283 567213 pubjugsuk@aol.com
Bottles, breweriana and pub jugs, advertising ephemera and commemoratives.

The Potteries Antique Centre, 271 Waterloo Road, Cobridge, Stoke-on-Trent ST6 3HR Tel: 01782 201455 sales@potteriesantiquecentre.com www.potteriesantiquecentre.com
Collectable ceramics.

Trevor Russell, Vintage fountain pens, PO Box 1258, Uttoxeter ST14 8XL tjrussell@onetel.net.uk
Buying, selling and repairing fountain pens.

Suffolk
Jamie Cross, PO Box 73, Newmarket CB8 8RY jamiecross@aol.com www.thirdreichmedals.com
We buy and sell, value for probate and insurance British, German and foreign war medals, badges and decorations.

W. L. Hoad, 9 St. Peter's Road, Kirkley, Lowestoft NR33 0LH Tel: 01502 587758 William@whoad.fsnet.co.uk

www.cigarettecardsplus.com
Cigarette cards.

Suffolk Sci-Fi and Fantasy, 17 Norwich Road, Ipswich Tel: 01473 400655 Mobile: 07885 298361 mick@suffolksci-fi.com www.suffolksci-fi.com
Science fiction.

Surrey

British Notes, PO Box 257, Sutton SM3 9WW Tel: 020 8641 3224 pamwestbritnotes@compuserve.com www.west-banknotes.co.uk
Banking collectables.

Collectors Choice, PO Box 99, Guildford GU1 1GA Tel/Fax: 01483 576655 louise@collectors-choice.net www.collectors-choice.net
Royal Albert, Royal Doulton, Wedgwood.

Julian Eade Tel: 01491 575059 Mobile: 07973 542971
Doulton Lambeth stoneware and signed Burslem wares.

Howard Hope, 19 Weston Park, Thames Ditton KT7 0HW Tel: 020 8398 7130 phonoking@virgin.net www.gramophones.uk.com
Specializing for 30 years in gramophones, phonographs, anything related to the history of recorded sound and other mechanical/musical items. Dealing by correspondence only, please no visits – call first. Colour pictures of any item in stock can be sent on request by email. Exporting worldwide. Shipping quotations given for any machine.

East Sussex

Tony Horsley Tel: 01273 550770
Candle extinguishers, Royal Worcester and other porcelain.

Ann Lingard, Ropewalk Antiques, Rye TN31 7NA Tel: 01797 223486 ann-lingard@ropewalkantiques.freeserve.co.uk
Antique pine furniture and kitchenware.

Rin Tin Tin, 34 North Road, Brighton BN1 1YB Tel: 01273 672424 rick@rintintin.freeserve.co.uk
Original old advertising and promotional material, magazines, early glamour, games, toys, plastics and miscellaneous 20thC collectables. Open Mon–Sat 11am–5.30pm.

Twinkled, High St Antiques Centre, 39 High Street, Hastings TN34 Tel: 01424 460068 info@twinkled.net www.twinkled.net
Purveyors of fine homeware from the 50s, 60s & 70s. Open Thurs–Tues 11am–5.30pm.

Wallis & Wallis, West Street Auction Galleries, Lewes BN7 2NJ Tel: 01273 480208 auctions@wallisandwallis.co.uk grb@wallisandwallis.co.uk www.wallisandwallis.co.uk
Specialist auctioneers of militaria, arms, armour, coins and medals. Also die-cast and tinplate toys, teddy bears, dolls, model railways, toy soldiers and models.

West Sussex

Rupert Toovey & Co Ltd, Spring Gardens, Washington RH20 3BS Tel: 01903 891955 auctions@rupert-toovey.com www.rupert-toovey.com
Auctions.

Wales

A.P.E.S. Rocking Horses, Ty Gwyn, Llannefydd, Denbigh, Denbighshire Tel: LL16 5HB Tel: 01745 540365 macphersons@apes-rocking-horses.co.uk www.apes-rocking-horses.co.uk

Michael James Tel: 01874 665487/07970 619737
Railway lamp specialist.

Jen Jones, Pontbrendu, LLanybydder, Ceredigion SA40 9UJ Tel: 01570 480610 quilts@jen-jones.com

www.jen-jones.com
Quilt expert dealing mainly in Welsh quilts and blankets. Between 200 and 300 quilts in stock with a comparable number of blankets. We buy and sell.

Warwickshire

Chinasearch, 9 Princes Drive, Kenilworth CV8 2FD Tel: 01926 512402 helen@chinasearch.uk.com jackie@chinasearch.uk.com www.chinasearch.uk.com
Discontinued dinner, tea and collectable ware bought and sold.

Chris James Medals & Militaria, Warwick Antiques Centre, 22–24 High Street, Warwick CV34 4AP Tel: 01926 495704/07710 274452 user@chrisjames.slv.co.uk www.medalsandmilitaria.co.uk
British, German, Japanese and USSR medals, swords, militaria and aviation items. For sale and purchased. 'The International', The National Motorcycle Museum, Birmingham. The U.K's largest militaria fair. A.M.&.S.E., PO Box 194, Warwick. Tel: 01926 497340

The Old Forge Antiques 29 Main Street, Stretton-under-Fosse, Nr Rugby CV23 0PE Tel: 01788 832191 Mobile: 07970 946334 vincehart@mail05.onetel.net.uk
Period furniture, collectables & soft furnishings.

Tango Art Deco & Antiques, 46 Brook Street, Warwick CV34 4BL Tel: 01926 496999/0121 704 4969 info@tango-artdeco.co.uk www.tango-artdeco.co.uk
Large Art Deco specialist shop. Open Thur–Sat 10am–5pm.

West Midlands

Antiques Magazine, H.P. Publishing, 2 Hampton Court Road, Harborne, Birmingham B17 9AE Tel: 01562 701001 subscriptions@antiquesmagazine.com www.antiquesmagazine.com
Weekly guide to buying and selling antiques.

Wiltshire

Dominic Winter Book Auctions, The Old School, Maxwell Street, Swindon SN1 5DR Tel: 01793 611340 info@dominicwinter.co.uk www.dominicwinter.co.uk
Auctions of antiquarian and general printed books and maps, sports books and memorabilia, art reference and pictures, photography and ephemera (including toys, games and other collectables).

Worcestershire

Aladdin's Cave, John Edwards, 35 Upper Tything, Worcester WR1 1JZ Tel: 01905 731737 Mobile: 07974 034313 John@royalworcester.freeserve.co.uk www.royalworcester.freeserve.co.uk
Royal Worcester, Doulton, Beswick and Wade.

Yorkshire

BBR, Elsecar Heritage Centre, Wath Road, Elsecar, Barnsley S74 8HJ Tel: 01226 745156 sales@onlinebbr.com www.onlinebbr.com
Advertising, breweriana, pot lids, bottles, Cornishware, Doulton and Beswick, etc.

Briar's C20th Decorative Arts, Skipton Antiques & Collectors Centre, The Old Foundry, Cavendish Street, Skipton BD23 2AB Tel: 01756 798641
Art Deco ceramics and furniture, specializing in Charlotte Rhead pottery.

The Camera House, Oakworth Hall, Colne Road (B6143), Oakworth, Keighley BD22 7HZ Tel: 01535 642333 (anytime) colin@the-camera-house.co.uk www.the-camera-house.co.uk
Cameras & photographic equipment from 1850. Cash purchases, part exchanges, sales and repairs. National and International mail order a speciality. Valuations for probate & insurance. Online catalogue. Please ring or email before visiting. Prop C Cox.

Country Collector, 11–12 Birdgate, Pickering YO18 7AL Tel: 01751 477481
Art Deco ceramics, blue and white, pottery and porcelain.

The Crested China Co, Highfield, Windmill Hill, Driffield YO25 5EF Tel: 01377 257042 dt@thecrestedchinacompany.com www.thecrestedchinacompany.com
Goss and crested china.

Echoes, 650a Halifax Road, Eastwood, Todmorden OL14 6DW Tel: 01706 817505
Antique costume, textiles including linen, lace and jewellery.

Gerard Haley, Hippins Farm, Black Shawhead, Nr Hebden Bridge HX7 7JG Tel: 01422 842484 Gedhaley@aol.com
Toy soldiers.

John & Simon Haley, 89 Northgate, Halifax HX1 1XF Tel: 01422 822148/360434 toysandbanks@aol.com
Old toys and money boxes.

Harpers Jewellers Ltd, 2/6 Minster Gates, York YO1 7HL Tel: 01904 632634 harpersyork@btopenworld.com www.vintage-watches.co.uk
Vintage and modern wrist and pocket watches. Sothebys.com associate dealer.

Linen & Lace, Shirley Tomlinson, Halifax Antiques Centre, Queens Road/Gibbet Street, Halifax HX1 4LR
Tel: 01484 540492/07711 763454
Antique linen, textiles, period costume and accessories.

Sheffield Railwayana Auctions, 43 Little Norton Lane, Sheffield S8 8GA
Tel: 0114 274 5085
Mobile: 07860 921519
ian@sheffrail.freeserve.co.uk
www.sheffieldrailwayana.co.uk
Railwayana, posters and models auctions.

The Troika Man Tel: 01535 273088 thetroikaman@aol.com www.troikapottery.org
Troika pottery.

USA

20th Century Vintage Telephones, 2780 Northbrook Place, Boulder, Colorado 80304 Tel: 001 44 (303) 442 3304

Antique European Linens, PO Box 789, Gulf Breeze, Florida 32562–0789
Tel: 001 850 432 4777
Cell: 850 450 463
name@antiqueeuropeanlinens.com
www.antiqueeuropeanlinens.com
Textiles including pillows and duvets.

Antiques & Art, 116 State Street, Portsmouth NH 03802
Tel: 603–431–3931

Artifacts Tel/Fax: 001 415 381 2084

Frank H. Boos Gallery, 420 Enterprise Court, Bloomfield Hills, Michigan 48302
Tel: 001 248 332 1500
Auctions.

The Calico Teddy Tel: 410 366 7011 CalicTeddy@aol.com www.calicoteddy.com

Henry T. Callan, 162 Quaker Meeting House Road, East Sandwich MA 02537–1312 Tel: 508–888–5372

Dragonflies Antiques & Decorating Center, Frank & Cathy Sykes, New England Events Mgt, PO Box 678, 24 Center Street, Wolfeboro, New Hampshire 03894
Tel: 001 603 569 0000
Dragonflies@metrocast.net
Folk Art, mahogany speed boat models, maps and antiquarian books.

Du Mouchelles, 409 East Jefferson, Detroit, Michigan 48226
Tel: 001 313 963 6255
Auctions.

The Dunlop Collection, P.O. Box 6269, Statesville NC 28687 Tel: (704) 871 2626 or Toll Free Telephone (800) 227 1996
Paperweights.

M. Finkel & Daughter, 936 Pine Street, Philadelphia, Pennsylvania 19107–6128
Tel: 001 215 627 7797
mailbox@finkelantiques.com
www.finkelantiques.com
America's leading antique sampler and needlework dealer.

Go Antiques, 2330 Aubin Lane, Baton Rouge LA 70816
Tel: US 001 877 481 5750
UK 01423 771122 AOL Keyword: GoAntiques sales@goantiques.com
www.goantiques.com
Antiques, art, collectables, etc.

Hall's Nostalgia, 389 Chatham Street, Lynn MA 01902 Tel: 001 781 595 7757 playball@hallsnostalgia.com www.hallsnostalgia.com

Harbor Bazaar, 5590 Main, Lexington MI 48450 bazaar@tias.com www.tias.com/stores/bazaar/

Hunt Auctions, 75 E. Uwchlan Avenue, Suite 130 Exton, Pennsylvania 19341
Tel: 001 610 524 0822
info@huntauctions.com
www.huntauctions.com

Randy Inman Auctions Inc., PO Box 726, Waterville, Maine 04903–0726
Tel: 001 207 872 6900
inman@inmanauctions.com
www.inmanauctions.com
Auctions specializing in advertising, coin-op, gambling devices, automata, soda pop, Coca Cola, breweriana, robots and space toys, C.I. and tin toys, Disneyana, mechanical music, mechanical and still banks, quality antiques.

J's Collectables, 5827 Encinita Avenue, Temple City CA 91780
Tel: 001 (818) 451 0010

Jackson's Auctioneers & Appraisers, 2229 Lincoln Street, Cedar Falls IA 50613 Tel: 00 1 319 277 2256

JMW Gallery, 144 Lincoln Street, Boston MA02111 Tel: 001 617 338 9097
www.jmwgallery.com
American Arts & Crafts, Decorative Arts, American Art Pottery, Mission furniture, lighting, color block prints, metalwork.

Lamps: By The Book, Inc., 514 14th, West Palm Beach, Florida 33401
Tel: 001 561 659 1723
booklamps@msn.com
www.lampsbythebook.com
Gift lamps. We also buy leather-bound books.

Joyce M. Leiby, PO Box 6048, Lancaster PA 17607 Tel: (717) 898 9113
joyclei@aol.com

Malchione Antiques & Sporting Collectibles, 110 Bancroft Road, Kennett Square PA 19348 Tel: 610–444–3509

Millicent Safro, Tender Buttons, 143 E.62nd Street, New York NY10021 Tel: (212) 758 7004 Fax: (212) 319 8474
Author of Buttons

PeterAndMark.com, Inc., 806 Sixth Avenue, Asbury Park NJ 07712
Tel: 732 776 9216
Peter@PeterAndMark.com

Right to the Moon Alice, Alice and Ron Lindholm, 240 Cooks Fall Road, Cooks Fall NY 12776 Tel: 607 498 5750

Mike Roberts, 4416 Foxfire Way, Fort Worth, Texas 76133
Tel: 001 817 294 2133

Skinner Inc., 357 Main Street, Bolton MA 01740 Tel: 001 978 779 6241
Auctions.

Skinner Inc., The Heritage On The Garden, 63 Park Plaza, Boston MA 02116 Tel: 001 617 350 5400
Auctions.

Sloan's Auctioneers & Appraisers, 4920 Wyaconda Road, North Bethesda MD 20852 Tel: 00 1 301 468 4911/800 649 5066 www.sloansauction.com

Sloan's Auctioneers & Appraisers, 2516 Ponce de Leon Boulevard, Coral Gables, Florida 33134 Tel: 305 447 0757 www.sloansauction.com

Art Smith, Antiques at Wells Union, Route 1, 1755 Post Road, Wells ME 04090 Tel: 207 646 6996

Sotheby's, 1334 York Avenue, New York NY 10021 Tel: 00 1 212 606 7000

Sotheby's, 9665 Wilshire Boulevard, Beverly Hills, California 90212
Tel: 00 1 310 274 0340

Treadway Gallery, Inc., 2029 Madison Road, Cincinnati, Ohio 45208
Tel: 001 513 321 6742
www.treadwaygallery.com
20thc art auctions.

Triple "L" Sports, P O Box 281, Winthorp, Maine 04364
Tel: 001 207 377 5787 lllsport@att.net
Winchester collectables, fishing, hunting, trapping, knives, primitives, baseball, football, golf, tennis, memorabilia and advertising.

The Unique One, 2802 Centre Street, Pennsauken NJ 08109
Tel: 001 (609) 663 2554

VintagePostcards.com, 60–C Skiff Street, Suite 116, Hamden CT 06517
Tel: 001 203 248 6621
quality@VintagePostcards.com
www.VintagePostcards.com
Postcards.

Jo Anne Welsh, PO Box 222, Riverdale MD 20738 Tel: 001 301 779 6181

Directory of Collectors' Clubs

With new Collectors' Clubs emerging every day this directory is by no means complete. If you wish to be included in next year's directory or if you have a change of address or telephone number, please inform us by 1 November 2003.

A.C.O.G.B. (Autograph Club of Great Britain) SAE to Mr R. Gregson, 47 Webb Crescent, Dawley, Telford, Shropshire TF4 3DS Tel: 01952 410332 Autographs@acogb.freeserve.co.uk www.acogb.co.uk

The Action Soldier Collectors' Club 30 New Street, Deinolen, Gwynedd, N. Wales LL55 3LH

American Toy Emergency Vehicle (ATEV) Club Jeff Hawkins President, 11415 Colfax Road, Glen Allen, Virginia 23060, USA atevclub@hotmail.com www.atevclub.org

The Antiquarian Horological Society New House, High Street, Ticehurst, East Sussex TN5 7AL Tel: 01580 200155 secretary@ahsoc.demon.co.uk www.ahsoc.demon.co.uk

Antique Wireless Association (AWA) Box E, Breesport, New York 14816, USA

Association of Bottled Beer Collectors 28 Parklands, Kidsgrove, Stoke-on-Trent, Staffordshire ST7 4US michael.peterson@ntlworld.com www.abbc.org

Association of Comic Enthusiasts: (ACE)! c/o 6 Rotherham Road, Catcliffe, Rotherham, South Yorkshire S60 5SW Tel: 0049 172 4222362 dmirfin@qsf.com

The Aviation Postcard Club Int. & USA Phil Munson, 25 Kerill Avenue, Old Coulsdon, Surrey CR5 1QB Tel: 01737 551 817

Avon Magpies Club Mrs W. A. Fowler, 15 Saunders House, Leith Avenue, Portsmouth, Hampshire PO6 4NY Tel: 023 92 380975 wendy@avonmagpies.fsnet.co.uk

B.E.A.R. Collectors' Club Linda Hartzfeld, 16901 Covello Street, Van Nuys, California 91406, USA

Badge Collectors' Circle c/o Frank Setchfield, 57 Middleton Place, Loughborough, Leicestershire LE11 2BY Tel: 01509 569270 f.setchfield@ntlworld.com www.thebadge.co.uk

Barbie Collectors' Club of Great Britain Elizabeth Lee, 17 Rosemont Road, Acton, London W3 9LU wdl@nipcus.co.uk

The Bead Society of Great Britain Carole Morris (Secretary), 1 Casburn Lane, Burwell, Cambridge CB5 0ED

Bear Buddies Susan M. Bartle, PO Box 546, North Collins, New York 14111, USA

Bearly Ours Teddy Club Linda Harris, 54 Berkinshaw Crescent, Don Mills, Ontario M3B 2T2, Canada

Belleek Collectors' Group (UK) The Hon Chairman Mr Jan Golaszewski, 5 Waterhall Avenue, Chingford, London E4 6NB jangolly@hotmail.com

The James Bond Collectors' Club PO Box 1570, Christchurch, Dorset BH23 4XS Tel: 0870 4423007 (Mon–Fri 9am–6pm) Solopublishing@firenet.uk.com

British Art Medal Society Philip Attwood, c/o Dept of Coins and Medals, The British Museum, London WC1B 3DG Tel: 020 7323 8260 pattwood@thebritishmuseum.ac.uk www.bams.org.uk/

The British Beermat Collectors' Society Hon Sec, 69 Dunnington Avenue, Kidderminster, Worcestershire DY10 2YT www.britishbeermats.org.uk

British Button Society Membership Secretary Mrs June Baron, Jersey Cottage, Parklands Road, Bower Ashton, Bristol, Gloucestershire BS3 2JR

British Compact Collectors' Society SAE to: PO Box 131, Woking, Surrey GU24 9YR www.thebccs.org.uk

British Diecast Model Collectors' Association PO Box 11, Norwich NR7 0SP www.swapmeet.freeserve.co.uk

British Doll Collectors' Club Mrs Francis Baird, Publisher & Editor, The Anchorage, Wrotham Road, Culverstone, Meopham, Kent DA13 0QW www.britishdollcollectors.com

British Equine Collectors' Forum (Model horses) Miss Kim Mason, 80 Gainsbrook Crescent, Norton Cannes, Cannock, Staffordshire WS11 3TN

British Iron Collectors 87 Wellsway Road, Bath BA2 4RU

British Model Soldier Society The Honorable Secretary, 44 Danemead, Hoddesdon, Hertfordshire EN11 9LU Tel: 01992 441078 www.model.soldiers.btinternet.co.uk

British Novelty Salt & Pepper Collectors Club Ray Dodd (Secretary), Coleshill, Clayton Road, Mold, Flintshire CH7 1SX Tel: 01352 759715

The Brooklands Automobilia & Regalia Collectors' Club (B.A.R.C.C.) Hon sec G. G. Weiner, 4–4a Chapel Terrace Mews, Kemp Town, Brighton, East Sussex BN2 1HU Tel/Fax: 01273 601960 Mobile: 07890 836734 www.barcc.biz www.brmmbrmm.com/barcc www.Brooklands-automobilia-regalia-collectors-club.co.uk

Brooklin Collectors' Club 47 Byron Avenue East, Sutton, Surrey SM1 3RB brooklincollclub@currantbun.com

Bunnykins Collectors' Club 6 Beckett Way, Lewes, East Sussex BN7 2EB Tel: 01273 479056 www.bunnykins.collectorsclub.btinternet.co.uk

The Buttonhook Society c/o Paul Moorehead, 2 Romney Place, Maidstone, Kent ME15 6LE Tel: 01622 752949 buttonhooksociety@tiscali.co.uk www.bbc.co.uk/antiques www.antiques-uk.net

The Buttonhook Society (US contact) c/o Priscilla Stoffel, White Marsh, Box 287, MD 21162–0287, USA Tel: 410 256 5541 buttonhooksociety@tiscali.co.uk www.thebuttonhooksociety.com

Caithness Glass Paperweight Collectors' Society Mrs Heather Robbie, Caithness Glass Ltd, Inveralmond, Perth, Scotland PH1 3TZ Tel: 01738 637373 collector@caithnessglass.co.uk www.caithnessglass.co.uk

Cambridge Paperweight Circle PO Box 941, Comberton, Cambridge PDO, Cambridgeshire CB3 7GQ Tel: +44 (0) 2476 386172 www.kevh.clara.net/index.htm

Carlton Ware Collectors' International Carlton Factory Shop, Carlton Works, Copeland Street, Stoke on Trent, Staffordshire ST4 1PU Tel: 01782 410504

The Carnival Glass Society (UK) Limited PO Box 14, Hayes, Middlesex UB3 5NU www.carnivalglasssociety.co.uk

The Cartophilic Society of Great Britain Ltd Membership secretary, Alan Stevens, 63 Ferndale Road, Church Crookham, Fleet, Hampshire GU52 6LN Tel: 01252 621586 www.csgb.co.uk

Cat Collectables 297 Alcester Road, Hollywood, Birmingham, West Midlands B47 5HJ Tel: 01564 826277 cat.collectables@btinternet.com

Chintz Club of America PO Box 6126, Folsom, CA 95763, USA

Chintzworld International Dancers End, Northall, Bedfordshire LU6 2EU Tel: 01525 220272 www.chintzworld-intl.com

Cigarette Case Collectors' Club 19 Woodhurst North, Raymead Road, Maidenhead, Berkshire SL6 8PH Tel: 01628 781800 colin.grey1@virgin.net

Cigarette Packet Collectors' Club of GB David C. Voaden, 56 Leeze Park, Okehampton, Devon EX20 1EE Tel: 01837 52168

Clarice Cliff Collectors' Club Fantasque House, Tennis Drive,The Park, Nottingham NG7 1AE www.claricecliff.com

The Coca-Cola Collectors' Club Membership Director, PMB 609, 4780 Ashford-Dunwoody Road, Suite A, Atlanta, Georgia 30338, USA

The Cola Club PO Box 293158, Nashville, Tennessee 37229–3158, USA

The Coleco Collectors' Club Ann Wilhite, 610 W 17th Freemont, NE 68025, USA

The Comic Journal C. J. Publications, c/o 6 Rotherham Road, Catcliffe, Rotherham, South Yorkshire S60 5SW Tel: 01724 222362 dmirfin@qsf.com

Commemorative Collectors' Society c/o Steven Jackson, Lumless House, Gainsborough Road, Winthorpe, Newark, Nottinghamshire NG24 2NR Tel: 01636 671377 commemorativecollectorssociety@hotmail.com

Corgi Collector Club c/o Corgi Classics Ltd, Meridian East, Meridian Business Park, Leicester LE19 1RL Tel: 0870 607 1204 susie@collectorsclubs.org.uk www.corgi.co.uk

The Costume Society St Paul's House, Warwick Lane, London EC4P 4BN www.costumesociety.org.uk

Cricket Memorabilia Society Steve Cashmore, 4 Stoke Park Court, Stoke Road, Bishop's Cleeve, Cheltenham, Gloucestershire GL52 8US cms87@btinternet.com www.cms.cricket.org

Crunch Club (Breakfast Cereal Collectables) John Cahill, 9 Weald Rise, Tilehurst, Reading, Berkshire RG30 6XB Tel: 0118 942 7291 crunch@jcahill99.freeserveco.uk

Deans Collectors' Club Hobby House Press, Inc, 1 Corporate Drive, Grantsville, Maryland 21536, USA

Devon Pottery Collectors' Group Mr Joyce Stonelake, 19 St Margarets Avenue, Torquay, Devon TQ1 4LW Tel: 01803 327277 Virginia.Brisco@care4free.net

Die Cast Collectors' Club c/o Jay Olins (Chairman), PO Box 670226, Los Angeles, California 90067–1126, USA jay@diecast.org www.diecast.org

Dinky Toy Club of America c/o Jerry Fralick, PO Box 11, Highland, Maryland 20777, USA www.erols.com/dinkytoy/

Dinosaur Collectors' Club Mike Howgate, 71 Hoppers Road, Winchmore Hill, London N21 3LP Tel: 020 8882 2606

The Eagle Society Keith Howard, 25a Station Road, Harrow, Middlesex HA1 2UA

Egg Cup Collectors' Club of GB Sue Wright, Subs secretary Tel: 01239 851190 Suewright@suecol.freeserve.co.uk

The English Playing Card Society c/o Major Donald Welsh, 11 Pierrepont Street, Bath, Somerset BA1 1LA Tel: 01225 465218

The Enid Blyton Society Tony Summerfield, 93 Milford Hill, Salisbury, Wiltshire SP1 2QL Tel: 01722 331 937 tony@blysoc.fsnet.co.uk

ETB Radford Collectors' Club Wendy Wright, 27 Forest Mead, Denmead, Waterlooville, Hampshire PO7 6UN Tel: 02392 267483/01275 871359 www.radfordcollect.com

The Fairing Collectors' Society Stuart Piepenstock Tel: 01895 824830

Fan Circle International Sec Mrs Joan Milligan, "Cronk-y-Voddy", Rectory Road, Coltishall, Norwich NR12 7HF

Festival of Britain Society c/o Martin Packer, 41 Lyall Gardens, Birmingham, West Midlands B45 9YW Tel: 0121 453 8245 martin@packer34.freeserve.co.uk www.packer34.freeserve.co.uk

Fieldings Crown Devon Collectors' Club Ltd PO Box 74, Corbridge, Northumberland NE45 5YP Tel: 07802 513784 www.fieldingscrowndevclub.com

Florence Collectors' Society Christine Taylor, Society Secretary, Florence (UK) Ltd, 41 Evelyn Street, Beeston, Nottingham NG9 2EU Tel: 0115 9229902 FlorenceSociety@aol.com www.florence-sculptures.it

FoF (Friends of Fred the Homepride Man) Jennifer Woodward Tel: 01925 826158

The Followers of Rupert Mrs Shirley Reeves, The Membership Sec, 31 Whiteley, Windsor, Berkshire SL4 5PJ

Football Programme Collectors' Club UKPC, 46 Milton Road, Kirkaldy, Fife, Scotland KY1 1TL

Friends of Blue Ceramic Society T. Sheppard, 45a Church Road, Bexley Heath, Kent DA7 4DD www.fob.org.uk

Friends of Broadfield House Glass Museum Broadfield House Glass Museum, Compton Drive, Kingswinford, West Midlands DY6 9NS Tel: 01384 812745

The Furniture History Society c/o Dr Brian Austen, 1 Mercedes Cottages, St. John's Road, Haywards Heath, West Sussex RH16 4EH Tel: 01444 413845 furniturehistorysociety@hotmail.com

Golly Collectors' Club Keith Wilkinson, 18 Hinton Street, Fairfield, Liverpool, Merseyside L6 3AR

Goss Collectors' Club Mrs Schofield Tel: 0115 930 0441

Goss & Crested China Club 62 Murray Road, Horndean, Hampshire PO8 9JL Tel: 023 9259 7440 info@gosschinaclub.demon.co.uk www.gosscrestedchina.co.uk

Great Britain Postcard Club 34 Harper House, St James Crescent, London SW9 7LW Tel: 020 7771 9404

The Hagen-Renaker Collectors' Club Jenny Palmer, 3651 Polish Line Road, Cheboygan, Mitchigan 49721, USA hrcc@freeway.net

The Hat Pin Society of Great Britain PO Box 110, Cheadle, Cheshire, SK8 1GG www.hatpinsociety.org.uk

Honiton Pottery Collectors' Society Robin Tinkler (Chairman), 2 Redyear Cottages, Kennington Road, Ashford, Kent TN24 0TF hpcs@moshpit.cix.co.uk www.hpcs.info

Hornby Collectors' Club PO Box 35, Royston, Hertfordshire SG8 5XR Tel/Fax: 01223 208 308 hsclubs.demon.co.uk www.hornby.co.uk

The Hornby Railway Collectors' Association 2 Ravensmore Road, Sherwood, Nottingham NG5 2AH Tel: 0115 962 5693 www.hrca.net

Hornsea Pottery Collectors' and Research Society c/o Peter Tennant, 128 Devonshire Street, Keighley, West Yorkshire BD21 2QJ hornsea@pdtennant.fsnet.co.uk www.hornseacollector.co.uk

Inn Sign Society Chairman, Mr R. P. Gatrell, Flat 19, Stamford Grange, Dunham Road, Altrincham, Cheshire WA14 4AN

International Bond and Share Society c/o Peter Duppa-Miller, Beechcroft, Combe Hay, Bath, Somerset BA2 7EG

International Bond & Share Society, American Branch Ted Robinson, Vice President, PO Box 814, Richboro, PA, USA Tel: (+1) 215 357 6820 fandr@voicenet.com

International Correspondence of Corkscrew Addicts Don MacLean, 4201 Sunflower Drive, Mississauga, Ontario L5L 2L4, Canada

The International Gnome Club Liz Spea, 22841 Kings Ct, Hayward CA 94541–4326, USA

International Golliwog Collector Club PO Box 612, Woodstock, New York 12498, USA Tel/Fax: 914 679 5769 OhGolli@aol.com

International League of Teddy Bear Collectors Pat Todd, PO Box 616, Monrovia, California 91017, USA

The International Owl Collectors' Club 54 Tiverton Road, Edgware, Middlesex HA8 6BE

International Perfume Bottle Association Details from Lynda Brine, Assembly Antique Centre, 5–8 Saville Row, Bath, Somerset BA1 2QP Tel: 01225 448488 lyndabrine@yahoo.co.uk www.scentbottlesandsmalls.co.uk

International Philatelic Golf Society Dr Eiron BE Morgan, 50 Pine Valley, Cwmavon, Port Talbot, W. Glamorgan SA12 9NF, Wales

The International Society of Meccanomen Adrian Williams, Bell House, 72a Old High Street, Headington, Oxford OX3 9HW Tel: 01865 741057 www.dircon.co.uk/meccano/

International Toy Collectors' Association – ITCA 804 West Anthony Drive, Champaign, Illinois 61822, USA

Jonathan Harris Studio Glass Ltd Woodland House, 24 Peregrine Way, Apley Castle, Telford, Shropshire TF1 6TH 01952 246381/588441 jonathan@jhstudioglass.com www.jhstudioglass.com

Just Golly! Collectors' Club SAE to Mrs A. K. Morris, 9 Wilmar Way, Seal, Sevenoaks, Kent TN15 0DN Tel: 01732 762379 quinntheeskimo@btinternet.com www.gollycorner.co.uk

King George VI Collectors' Society (Philately) 98 Albany, Manor Road, Bournemouth, Dorset BH1 3EW

The Lace Guild The Hollies, 53 Audnam, Stourbridge, West Midlands DY8 4AE

The Lewis Carroll Society Sarah Stanfield, Acorns, Dargate, Nr Faversham, Kent ME13 9HG www.lewiscarroll.org

Lighter Club of Great Britain Oliver House, 243 Selhurst Road, London SE25 6XP

Limoges Porcelain Collectors' Club, RMPC (sarl), 59 Avenue Jeanne D'Arc, 33000 Bordeaux, France Tel: 00(33) 556 938 802 Rchrdmhny@aol.com

Lock Collectors' Club Mr Richard Phillips, "Merlewood", The Loan, West Linton, Peebleshire EH46 7HE Tel: 01968 661039 rphillips52@btinternet.com

Matchbox International Collectors' Association (MICA) of North America c/o Stewart Orr and Kevin McGimpsey, PO Box 28072, Waterloo, Ontario N2L 6J8, Canada

The Matchbox Toys International Collectors' Association, Kevin McGimpsey, PO Box 120, Deeside, Flintshire CH5 3HE Tel: 01244 539414 kevin@matchboxclub.com www.matchboxclub.com

Mauchline Ware Collectors' Club Sec Mrs Christabelle Davey, PO Box 158, Leeds LS16 5WZ enquiries@mauchlineclub.org www.mauchlineclub.org

McDonald's and Fast Food Collectors' Club c/o Lawrence Yap, 110 Tithelands, Harlow, Essex CM19 5ND

Medal Society of Ireland 5 Meadow Vale, Blackrock, Co Dublin, Eire Tel: 01 2895085

Memories UK Mabel Lucie Attwell Club Abbey Antiques, 63 Great Whyte, Ramsey, Nr Huntingdon, Cambridgeshire PE26 1HL Tel: 01487 814753

Merrythought International Collectors' Club Ironbridge, Telford, Shropshire TF8 7NJ Tel: 01952 433116 contact@merrythought.co.uk www.merrythought.co.uk

Merrythought International Collectors' Club PO Box 577, Oakdale, California 95361, USA

Milk Bottle News Paul Luke, 60 Rose Valley Crescent, Stanford-le-Hope, Essex SS17 8EF Tel: 01375 679527 www.milkbottlenews.org.co.uk

Moorcroft Collectors' Club W. Moorcroft PLC, Sandbach Road, Burslem, Stoke-on-Trent, Staffordshire ST6 2DQ Tel: 01782 820510 mcc@moorcroft.com www.moorcroft.com

Muffin the Mule Collectors' Club 12 Woodland Close, Woodford Green, Essex IG8 0QH Tel/Fax: 020 8504 4943 ra@hasler.fsnet.co.uk www.Muffin-the-Mule.com

Musical Box Society of Great Britain PO Box 299, Waterbeach, Cambridgeshire CB4 8DT mbsgb@kreedman.globalnet.co.uk www.mbsgb.org.uk

New Baxter Society Membership Sec, 205 Marshalswick Lane, St Albans, Hertfordshire AL1 4XA Baxter@rpsfamily.demon.co.uk www.rpsfamily.demon.co.uk

Observers Pocket Series Collectors' Society (OPSCS) Sec Alan Sledger, 10 Villiers Road, Kenilworth, Warwickshire CV8 2JB Tel: 01926 857047

The Official Betty Boop Fan Club Bobbie West, 10550 Western Avenue #133, Stanton, CA 90680–6909, USA Tel: 00 714 816 0717 BBOOPFANS@aol.com

The Official International Wade Collectors' Club Royal Works, Westport Road, Burslem, Stoke on Trent, Staffordshire ST6 4AP Tel: 01782 255255 club@wade.co.uk www.wade.co.uk/wade

Old Bottle Club of Great Britain Alan Blakeman, c/o BBR, Elsecar Heritage Centre, Nr Barnsley, Yorkshire S74 8HJ Tel: 01226 745156 sales@onlinebbr.com www.onlinebbr.com

The Old Hall Stainless Steel Tableware Club Nigel Wiggin, Sandford House, Levedale, Stafford ST18 9AH Tel: 01785 780376 oht@gnwiggin.freeserve.co.uk www.oldhallclub.co.uk

The Old Lawnmower Club Milton Keynes Museum of Industry and Rural Life, Stacey Hill Farm, Southern Way, Wolverton, Milton Keynes, Buckinghamshire MK12 5EJ Tel: 01327 830675 olc@artizan.demon.co.uk www.artizan.demon.co.uk/olc/

On the Lighter Side (OTLS) International Lighter Collectors PO Box 1733, Quitman, TX 75783–1733, USA www.otls.com

Ophthalmic Antiques International Collectors' Club Mr R. M. Ling, 6 Grammar School Road, North Walsham, Norfolk NR28 9JH

Orders and Medals Research Society PO Box 1904, Southam CV47 2ZX Tel: 01295 690009 petedeehelmore@talk21.com www.omrs.org.uk

The Oriental Ceramic Society The Sec, 30b Torrington Square, London WC1E 7JL Tel: 020 7636 7985 ocs-london@beeb.net

Paddington's Action Club Action Research, Vincent House, North Parade, Horsham, West Sussex RH2 2DA

Pedal Car Collectors' Club (P.C.C.C.) Sec A. P. Gayler, 4/4a Chapel Terrace Mews, Kemp Town, Brighton, East Sussex BN2 1HU Tel/Fax: 01273 601960 www.brmmbrmm.com/pedalcars

Pelham Puppets Collectors' Club Sue Valentine, 46 The Grove, Bedford, MK40 3JN Tel: 01234 363 336

Pen Delfin "Family Circle" Collectors' Club Cameron Mill, Howsin Street, Burnley, Lancashire BB10 1PP Tel: 01282 432301 boswell@pendelfin.co.uk www.pendelfin.co.uk

The Family Circle of Pen Delfin Susan Beard, 230 Spring Street N.W., Suite 1238, Atlanta, Georgia 30303, USA Freephone US only 1–800 872 4876

The Pewter Society Llananant Farm, Penallt, Monmouth NP25 4AP secretary@pewtersociety.org www.pewtersociety.org

Pilkington's Lancastrian Pottery Society Wendy Stock, Sullom Side, Barnacre, Garstang, Preston, Lancashire PR3 1GH Tel: 01995 603427 Barry@pilkpotsoc.freeserve.co.uk www.pilkpotsoc.freeserve.co.uk

Pipe Club of London www.pcol.freewire.co.uk

Pocket Lighter Preservation Guild (PLPG) 380 Brookes Dr, Suite 209A, Hazelwood, MO 63042, USA Tel: 314 731 2411 www.plpg.org

Poole Pottery Collectors' Club Poole Pottery Limited, Sopers Lane, Poole, Dorset BH17 7PP Tel: 01202 666200 charlotteharvey@poolepottery.co.uk www.poolepottery.com

The Postcard Club of Great Britain c/o Mrs D Brennan, 34 Harper House, St James's Crescent, London SW9 7LW Tel: 020 7771 9404

The Pot Lid Circle c/o Ian Johnson, Collins House, 32/38 Station Road, Gerrards Cross, Buckinghamshire SL9 8EL Tel: 01487 773194/01753 279001 potlid@bpcollins.co.uk

Royal Doulton International Collectors' Club Royal Doulton, Sir Henry Doulton House, Forge Lane, Stoke-on-Trent, Staffordshire ST1 5NN Tel: 01782 404040 www.icc@royal-doulton.com

Rugby Memorabilia Society PO Box 1093, Thornbury, Bristol BS35 1DA Tel: 01454 884077 (Eves) rugby-memorabilia@blueyonder.co.uk www.rugby-memorabilia.co.uk

The Russian Doll Collectors' Club Gardener's Cottage, Hatchlands, East Clandon, Surrey GU4 7RT Tel: 01483 222789 graham@russiandolls.co.uk www.russiandolls.co.uk

Potteries of Rye Collectors' Society Membership Sec Barry Buckton, 2 Redyear Cottages, Kennington Road, Ashford, Kent TN24 0TF Tel: 01233 647898 barry.buckton@tesco.net www.potteries-of-rye-society.co.uk

James Sadler International Collectors' Club Customer Services, Churchill China PLC, High Street, Tunstall, Stoke on Trent ST6 5NZ Tel: UK (FREE) 0800 0853 581

Scientific Instrument Society Wg Cdr G. Bennett (Executive Officer), 31 High Street, Stanford in the Vale, Faringdon, Oxfordshire SN7 8LH Tel: 01367 710223 www.sis.org.uk

Scottish Exhibitions Study Group S. K. Hunter, 34 Gray Street, Glasgow G3 7TY, Scotland Tel: 0141 339 2775 stanleykhunter@compuserve.com www.biggar-net.co.uk/sesg

The Silver Spoon Club of Great Britain c/o Daniel Bexfield, 26 Burlington Arcade, Mayfair, London W1J 0PU Tel: 020 7491 1730 antiques@bexfield.co.uk

Smurf Collectors' Club International Dept 115 NR, 24 Cabot Road West, Massapeque, New York 11758, USA

The Smurf Collectors' Club The Club Sec, PO Box 2326, Bournemouth, Dorset BH11 8ZA www.globalserve.net/-astrol/bscc/british.html

Snuff Bottle Society Michael Kaynes, 1 Tollard Court, West Hill Road, Bournemouth, Dorset BH2 5EH Tel/Fax: 01202 292867 snuffbottles@tiscali.co.uk

Society for Tin Box Collectors K. Hughes, 121 Preston Drive, Brighton, East Sussex BN1 6LE Penpact@mcmail.com

Society of Tobacco Jar Collectors (USA) 19 Woodhurst North, Raymead Road, Maidenhead, Berkshire SL6 8PH Tel: 01628 781800 colin.grey1@virgin.net

The Soviet Collectors' Club PO Box 56, Saltburn by the Sea TS12 1YD collect@sovietclub.com www.deeleyhome.freeserve.co.uk

Steiff Club USA East 28th Street, 9th Floor, New York 10016, USA

Susie Cooper Collectors' Club Panorama House, 18 Oakley Mews, Aycliffe Village, Co. Durham DL5 6JP www.susiecooper.co.uk

The SylvaC Collectors' Circle 174 Portsmouth Road, Horndean, Waterlooville, Hampshire PO8 9HP Tel: 023 9259 1725 admin@sylvacclub.com www.sylvacclub.com

Teams Club – The official club for Brooke Bond Card Collectors PO Box 1, Market Harborough, Leicestershire LE16 9HT Tel: 01858 466 441

The Thimble Society c/o Bridget McConnel, Geoffrey Van Arcade, 107 Portobello Road, London W11 2QB Open Sat only antiques@thimblesociety.co.uk www.thimblesociety.co.uk

The Tool and Trades History Society Jane Rees Chairman & Membership Secretary, Barrow Mead Cottage, Rush Hill, Bath, Somerset BA2 2QP

Torquay Pottery Collectors' Society Membership Sec, c/o Torre Abbey, The Kings Drive, Torquay, Devon TQ2 5JX scandymag@aol.com www.torquaypottery.com

Totally Teapots The Novelty Teapot Collectors' Club Vince McDonald, Euxton, Chorley, Lancashire PR7 6EY Tel/Fax: 01257 450366 vince@totallyteapots.com www.totallyteapots.com

Train Collectors' Society James Day, Membership Secretary, PO Box 20340, London NW11 6ZE Tel/Fax: 020 8209 1589 tcsinformation@btinternet.com www.traincollectors.org.uk

Tremar Collectors' Club Jim Castle, 3 The Endway, Althorne, Chelmsford, Essex CM3 6DY Tel: 01621 772987

The United Kingdom Spoon Collectors' Club Miss M. Verity, 12 Briarfield Gardens, Gilder Some, Morley, Leeds LS27 7HS

The Victorian Military Society PO Box 5837, Newbury, Berkshire RG14 3FJ

The Vintage Model Yacht Group Trevor Smith, 1A Station Avenue, Epsom, Surrey KT19 9UD Tel: 020 8393 1100

The Wade Watch Carole Murdock & Valerie Moody, 8199 Pierson Ct, Arvada, CO 80005, USA Tel: (303) 421 9655 wadewatch@wadewatch.com www.wadewatch.com

The Washington Historical Autograph and Certificate Organization – Whaco! PO Box 2428, Springfield, VA 22152–2428, USA gteas@erols.com

David Winter Collectors' Club UK Helen Tallent, 11 Trinity Close, Abingdon, Oxon OX14 2QE Tel: 01235 526 259

The Writing Equipment Society c/o Mr John S. Daniels, 33 Glanville Road, Hadleigh, Ipswich, Suffolk IP7 5SQ www.wesoc.co.uk

Zippo Click Collectors' Club 33 Barbour Street, Bradford, PA 16701, USA Tel: 814 368 2725 www.zippoclick.com

Directory of Markets & Centres

Derbyshire

Alfreton Antique Centre, 11 King Street, Alfreton DE55 7AF
Tel: 01773 520781www.alfretonantiques.supanet.com
30 dealers on 2 floors. Antiques, collectables, furniture, books, militaria, postcards and silverware. Open 7 days Mon–Sat 10am–4.30pm, Sundays 11am–4.30pm.

Chappells Antiques Centre, King Street, Bakewell DE45 1DZ
Tel: 01629 812496 ask@chappellsantiquescentre.com
www.chappellsantiques centre.com
Over 30 dealers inc BADA & LAPADA members. Quality period furniture, ceramics, silver, plate, metals, treen, clocks, barometers, books, pictures, maps, prints, textiles, kitchenalia, lighting, furnishing accessories, scientific, pharmaceutical and sporting antiques from the 17th–20thC. Open Mon–Sat 12–5pm, Sun 11am–5pm. Closed Christmas Day, Boxing Day, New Years Day. Please ring for brochure.

Heanor Antiques Centre, Ilkeston Road, Heanor DE75 7AE
Tel: 01773 531181 sales@heanorantiquescentre.co.uk
www.heanorantiquescentre.co.uk
Open 7 days 10.30am–4.30pm. Now 200 independent dealers in new 3 storey extension with stylish café.

Matlock Antiques, Collectables & Riverside Café, 7 Dale Road, Matlock DE4 3LT Tel: 01629 760808
www.matlock-antiques-collectable.cwc.net
Proprietor W. Shirley. Over 70 dealers. Open 7 days 10am–5pm.

Devon

Quay Centre, Topsham, Nr Exeter EX3 0JA
Tel: 01392 874006 office@antiquesontopshamquay.co.uk
www.antiquesontopshamquay.co.uk
80 dealers on 3 floors. Antiques, collectables and traditional furnishings. Ample parking. Open 7 days, 10am–5pm. All major cards accepted.

Nightingales
89–91 High Street
West Wickham
Kent BR4 0LS
IN THE LONDON BOROUGH OF BROMLEY
BETWEEN ORPINGTON AND CROYDON
ON THE A232
Over 5,000 square feet of Antiques, Furniture and Collectors items, including CERAMICS, GLASS, SILVER, FURNITURE AND DECORATIVE WARE. THOUSANDS OF ITEMS IN STOCK!
Opposite the new Marks & Spencer with rear access from large PUBLIC CAR PARK (entry beside Woolworths)
TRADE AND TELEPHONE ENQUIRIES WELCOME
Open: Monday to Saturday 10am to 5pm
(Closed Sundays except December)
TELEPHONE: 020 8777 0335

Gloucestershire

Durham House Antiques Centre, Sheep Street, Stow-on-the-Wold GL54 1AA
Tel: 01451 870404
30+ dealers. Town and country furniture, metalware, books, ceramics, kitchenalia, sewing ephemera, silver, jewellery and samplers. Mon–Sat 10am–5pm, Sunday 11am–5pm. Stow-on-the-Wold, Cotswold home to over 40 antique shops, galleries and bookshops.

Gloucester Antiques Centre, The Historic Docks, 1 Severn Road, Gloucester GL1 2LE
Tel: 01452 529716 www.antiques.center.com
Open Mon–Sat 10am–5pm, Sun 1–5pm.

Hampshire

Dolphin Quay Antique Centre, Queen Street, Emsworth PO10 7BU Tel: 01243 379994
www.antiquesbulletin.com/dolphinquay
Open 7 days a week (including Bank Holidays) Mon–Sat 10am–5pm, Sunday 10am–4pm. Marine, naval antiques, paintings, watercolours, prints, antique clocks, decorative arts, furniture, sporting apparel, luggage, specialist period lighting, conservatory, garden antiques, fine antique/country furniture, French/antique beds.

Lymington Antiques Centre, 76 High Street, Lymington SO41 9AL Tel: 01590 670934
Open Mon–Fri 10am–5pm, Sat 9am–5pm. 30 dealers. Clocks, watches, silver, glass, jewellery, toys & dolls, books, furniture and textiles.

Hereford

The Hay Antique Market, 6 Market Street, Hay-on-Wye HR3 5AF Tel: 01497 820175
Open 6 days 10am–5pm, Sundays 11am–5pm. 17 separate units on 2 floors selling pine, country and period furniture. Rural and rustic items. China, glass, jewellery, linen and period clothes. Pictures, lighting, brass and collectables.

Kent

Castle Antiques, 1 London Road (opposite Library), Westerham TN16 1BB Tel: 01959 562492
Open 10am–5pm Mon–Sat, Sunday 11am–6pm. 4 rooms of antiques, small furniture, collectables, rural bygones, costume, glass, books, linens, jewellery, chandeliers, cat collectables. Services: advice, valuations, theatre props, house clearance, talks on antiques.

Malthouse Arcade, High Street, Hythe CT21 5BW
Tel: 01303 260103
Open Fridays, Saturdays and Bank Holiday Mondays 9.30am–5.30pm. 37 Stalls and café. Furniture, china and glass, jewellery, plated brass, picture postcards, framing, etc.

Nightingales, 89–91 High Street, West Wickham BR4 0LS Tel: 020 8777 0335
Over 5,000 sq ft of antiques, furniture and collectors' items, including ceramics, glass, silver, furniture and decorative ware. Open Mon–Sat 10am–5pm (Closed Sundays except December).

Lancashire

The Antique & Decorative Design Centre, 56 Garstang Road, Preston PR1 1NA Tel: 01772 882078
paul@paulallisonantiques.co.uk
www.paulallisonantiques.co.uk
Open 7 days a week 10am–5pm. 25,000sq.ft. of quality antiques, objets d'art, clocks, pine, silverware, porcelain, upholstery, French furniture for the home and garden.

GB Antiques Centre, Lancaster Leisure Park, (the former Hornsea Pottery), Wyresdale Road, Lancaster LA1 3LA
Tel: 01524 844734
140 dealers in 40,000 sq.ft. of space. Porcelain, pottery, Art Deco, glass, books, linen, mahogany, oak and pine furniture. Open 7 days 10am–5pm.

Kingsmill Antique Centre, Queen Street, Harle Syke, Burnley BB10 2HX Tel: 01282 431953 antiques@kingsmill.demon.co.uk www.kingsmill.demon.co.uk
Dealers, packers and shippers.

Lincolnshire

St Martins Antiques Centre, 23a High St, St Martins, Stamford PE9 2LF Tel: 01780 481158 peter@st-martins-antiques.co.uk www.st-martins-antiques.co.uk

London

Alfie's Antique Market, 13–25 Church Street NW8 8DT Tel: 020 7723 6066 post@eAlfies.com www.eAlfies.com
London's biggest and busiest antique market with over 200 dealers. Open Tues–Sat 10am–6pm.

Covent Garden Antiques Market, Jubilee Market Hall, Covent Garden WC2 Tel: 0207 240 7405
Visit the famous Covent Garden Antique Market. 150 traders selling jewellery, silver, prints, porcelain, objets d'art and numerous other collectables.

Grays Antique Markets, 1–7 Davies Mews W1K 5AB Tel: 020 7629 7034 grays@clara.net www.graysantiques.com
Over 200 specialist antique dealers selling beautiful and unusual antiques & collectables. Open Mon–Fri 10am–6pm.

Northcote Road Antique Market, 155a Northcote Road, Battersea SW11 6QB Tel: 020 7228 6850
Open 7 days. 30 dealers offering a wide variety of antiques & collectables. Open Mon–Sat 10am–6pm, Sun 12–5pm.

Palmers Green Antiques Centre, 472 Green Lanes, Palmers Green N13 5PA Tel: 020 8350 0878
Over 40 dealers. Specialising in furniture, jewellery, clocks, pictures, porcelain, china, glass, silver & plate, metalware, kitchenalia, lighting, etc. Open 6 days a week, Mon–Sat 10am–5.30pm (closed Tuesdays), Sun 11am–5pm. Open Bank Holidays. Removals & house clearances, probate valuations undertaken, quality antiques and collectables sold on commission basis. All major credit cards accepted.

Norfolk

Tombland Antique Centre, Augustine Steward House, 14 Tombland, Norwich NR3 1HF Tel: 01603 619129 or 761906 www.tomblandantiques.co.uk
Open Mon–Sat 10am–5pm. Huge selection on 3 floors. Ideally situated opposite Norwich Cathedral.

Northamptonshire

The Brackley Antique Cellar, Drayman's Walk, Brackley NN13 6BE Tel: 01280 841841
Situated under the Co-op supermarket. Very large range of antiques and collectables. 30,000 sq.ft. of showroom with up to 100 dealers. Open 7 days 10am–5pm. Disabled access.

Magpies Antiques and Collectables Centre, 1 East Grove, Rushden NN10 0AP Tel: 01933 411404
Three floor Victorian factory building 3,800 sq ft on Rectory road, A6, Rushden, Northants. 10 minutes Finedon, 15 minutes Bedford (1st left after Old Railway Station, transport museum). We have a wide selection including a superb range of glass. A bargain hunters' paradise. Opening hours Mon–Sat 10am–5pm, Sun 12–4pm. From 1st Nov–1st Mar we close at 4pm.

Oxfordshire

Antiques on High, 85 High Street, Oxford OX1 4BG Tel: 01865 251075
Open 7 days a week 10am–5pm. Sun & Bank Holidays 11am–5pm. 35 friendly dealers, wide range of quality stock.

Shropshire

Stretton Antiques Market, Sandford Avenue, Church Stretton SY6 6BH Tel: 01694 723718
60 dealers under one roof.

Staffordshire

Tutbury Mill Antiques Centre, Tutbury Mill Mews, Tutbury DE13 9LU Tel: 01283 520074 www.antiquesplus.co.uk
Open Mon–Sat 10am–5pm, Sun 12–5pm.

Surrey

Maltings Monthly Market, Bridge Square, Farnham GU9 7QR Tel: 01252 726234 FarnMalt@aol.com www.farnhammaltings.com
9.30am–4.00pm 1st Sat of the month.

East Sussex

The Brighton Lanes Antique Centre, 12 Meeting House Lane, Brighton BN1 1HB Tel: 01273 823121 peter@brightonlanes-antiquecentre.co.uk www.brightonlanes-antiquecentre.co.uk
A spacious centre in the heart of the historic lanes with a fine selection of furniture, silver, jewellery, glass, porcelain, clocks, pens, watches, lighting and decorative items. Open daily 10.00am–5.30pm, Sunday 12–4.00pm. Loading bay/parking– Lanes car park.

West Sussex

Roundabout Antiques Centre, 7 Commercial Square, Haywards Heath RH16 7DW Tel: 01444 417654
Several specialist dealers with good quality extensive stock. Open Tues–Sat 10am–5pm. Specializing in musical instruments – ring Angie 01273 835926.

Tyne & Wear

The Antique Centre, 2nd floor, 142 Northumberland St, Newcastle-upon-Tyne NE1 7DQ Tel: 0191 232 9832 time-antiques@btinternet.co.uk www.time-antiques.co.uk

Wales

Offa's Dyke Antique Centre, 4 High Street, Knighton, Powys LD7 1AT Tel: 01547 528635/520145
14 dealers. Ceramics, 18thC & 19thC earthenware, stoneware and porcelain, early 20thC industrial and studio pottery. Reference books on ceramics and general antiques. Good antique drinking glasses. Country antiques and bygones. 19thC and 20thC paintings and drawings. Antiquities. General antiques and collectables.

The Works Antiques Centre, Station Road, Llandeilo, Carmarthenshire SA19 6NH Tel: 01558 823964 storeyj@bigfoot.com www.works-antiques.co.uk
Open Tues–Sat 10am–6pm, Sun 10am–5pm. Open Bank Holiday Mondays. 5,000sq ft, 54 dealers. Ample parking. Free tea and coffee.

Warwickshire

Stratford Antiques Centre, 59–60 Ely Street, Stratford-upon-Avon CV37 6LN Tel: 01789 204180
Come and visit Stratford-upon-Avon. A one-stop collectors' experience with 2 floors and courtyard full of shops. Open 7 days a week from 10am–5pm.

West Midlands

Birmingham Antique Centre, 1407 Pershore Road, Stirchley, Birmingham B30 2JR
Tel: 0121 459 4587/0121 689 6566
Open 7 days. Cabinets available to rent.

Worcestershire

Worcester Antiques Centre, 15 Reindeer Court, Mealcheapen Street, Worcester WR1 4DF
Tel: 01905 610680 WorcsAntiques@aol.com
Open Mon–Sat 10am–5pm extending to Sundays in December. Porcelain, silver, jewellery, Art Nouveau, Arts & Crafts, leather.

Yorkshire

York Antiques Centre, 1a Lendal, York YO1 8AA
Tel: 01904 641445
15 dealers. General antiques. Open Mon–Sat 10am–5pm.

USA

Alhambra Antiques Center, 3640 Coral Way, Coral Cables, Florida Tel: 305 446 1688
4 antiques dealers selling high-quality decorative pieces from Europe.

Antique Center I, II, III at Historic Savage Mill, Savage, Maryland Tel: 410 880 0918 or 301 369 4650 antiquec@aol.com www.antique-cntr-savage.com
225 plus select quality dealers representing 15 states. Open every day plus 3 evening Sun–Wed 9.30am–6pm, Thurs, Fri and Sat 9.30am–9pm. Closed Christmas, Easter and Thanksgiving days. Open New Year's Day 12–5pm.

Antique Village, North of Richmond, Virginia, on Historic US 301, 4 miles North of 1–295 Tel: 804 746 8914
Mon, Tues, Thurs, Fri 10am–5pm, Sat 10am–6pm, Sun 12–6pm, closed Wed. 50 dealers specialising in Art Pottery, country & primitives, Civil War artifacts, paper memorabilia, African art, toys, advertising, occupied Japan, tobacco tins, glassware, china, holiday collectables, jewellery, postcards.

Antiques at Colony Mill Marketplace, 222 West Street, Keene, New Hampshire 03431
Tel: (603) 358 6343 www.antiques.colonymill.com
Open Mon–Sat 10am–9pm, Sun 11am–6pm. Over 200 booths. Period to country furniture, paintings and prints, Art Pottery, glass, china, silver, jewellery, toys, dolls, quilts, etc.

The Coffman's Antiques Markets, at Jennifer House Commons, Stockbridge Road, Route 7, PO Box 592, Great Barrington, MA 01230
Tel: (413) 528 9282/9602 www.coffmansantiques.com

Dragonflies Antiques & Decorating Center, Frank & Cathy Sykes, New England Events Mgt, PO Box 678, 24 Center Street, Wolfeboro, New Hampshire 03894 Tel: 603 569 0000 Dragonflies@metrocast.net
Also Folk Art, mahogany speed boat models, maps and antiquarian books.

Fern Eldridge & Friends, 800 First NH Turnpike (Rt. 4), Northwood, New Hampshire 03261 Tel: 603 942 5602/8131 FernEldridgeAndFriends@NHantiqueAlley.com
30 dealers on 2 levels. Shipping available in USA. Open 10am–5pm daily. Closed major holidays, please call ahead.

Goodlettsville Antique Mall, 213 N. Main St, Germantown, Tennessee Tel: 615 859 7002

The Hayloft Antique Center, 1190 First NH Turnpike (Rt. 4), Northwood, New Hampshire 03261 Tel: 603 942 5153 TheHayloftAntiqueCenter@NHantiqueAlley.com
Over 150 dealers offering Estate jewellery, sterling silver, rare books, glass, porcelain, pottery, art, primitives, furniture, toys, ephemera, linens, military, sporting collectibles and much more. Open 10am–5pm daily. Closed major holidays, please call ahead.

Hermitage Antique Mall, 4144–B Lebanon Road, Hermitage, Tennessee Tel: 615 883 5789

Madison Antique Mall, 320 Gallatin Rd, S Nashville,Tennessee Tel: 615 865 4677
18thC and 19thC English antiques and objets d'art.

Michiana Antique Mall, 2423 S. 11th Street, Niles, Michigan 49120 www.michianaantiquemall.com
Open 7 days a week 10am–6pm.

Morningside Antiques, 6443 Biscayne Blvd, Miami, Florida Tel: 305 751 2828
The city's newest antiques market specialising in English, French and American furniture and collectibles in a mall setting with many different vendors.

Nashville Wedgewood Station Antique Mall, 657 Wedgewood Ave., Nashville, Tennessee
Tel: 615 259 0939

Parker-French Antique Center, 1182 First NH Turnpike (Rt. 4), Northwood, New Hampshire 03261 Tel: 603 942 8852 ParkerFrenchAntiqueCenter@NHantiqueAlley.com
135 antique dealers all on one level offering a good mix of sterling silver, jewellery, glassware, pottery, early primitives. No crafts, reproductions or new items. Open 10am–5pm daily. Closed major holidays, please call ahead.

Showcase Antique Center, PO Box 1122, Sturbridge, MA 01566 Tel: 508 347 7190 www.showcaseantiques.com
Open Mon, Wed, Thurs, 10am–5pm, Fri, Sat 10am–5pm, Sun 12–5pm, closed Tues. 170 dealers.

Tennessee Antique Mall, 654 Wedgewood Ave, Nashville, Tennessee Tel: 615 259 4077

Key to Illustrations

Each illustration and descriptive caption is accompanied by a letter code. By referring to the following list of Auctioneers (denoted by *), Dealers (•) and Clubs (§), the source of any item may be immediately determined. Inclusion in this edition in no way constitutes or implies a contract or binding offer on the part of any of our contributors to supply or sell the goods illustrated, or similar articles, at the prices stated. Advertisers in this year's directory are denoted by (†).

If you require a valuation for an item, it is advisable to check whether the dealer or specialist will carry out this service and if there is a charge. Please mention Miller's when making an enquiry. Having found a specialist who will carry out your valuation it is best to send a photograph and description of the item to the specialist together with a stamped addressed envelope for the reply. A valuation by telephone is not possible. Most dealers are only too happy to help you with your enquiry; however, they are very busy people and consideration of the above points would be welcomed.

ACO • Angela & Clive Oliver, 68 Watergate Street, Chester CH1 2LA Tel: 01244 312306/335157

ADD • Addyman Books, 39 Lion Street, Hay-on-Wye, Herefordshire HR3 5AD Tel: 01497 821136 www.hay-on-wyebooks.com

AEL • Argyll Etkin Ltd, 1–9 Hills Place, Oxford Circus, London W1F 7SA Tel: 020 7437 7800 philatelists@argyll-etkin.com www.argyll-etkin.com

AFA • Alex Fane, Somerset

AH * Andrew Hartley, Victoria Hall Salerooms, Little Lane, Ilkley, Yorkshire LS29 8EA Tel: 01943 816363 info@andrewhartleyfinearts.co.uk www.andrewhartleyfinearts.co.uk

AL •† Ann Lingard, Ropewalk Antiques, Rye, East Sussex TN31 7NA Tel: 01797 223486 ann-lingard@ropewalkantiques.freeserve.co.uk

AM • Alison Massey, MBO 32/33 Grays Antiques, 1–7 Davies Mews, London W1K 5AB Tel: 020 7629 7034

AMC • Amelie Caswell Tel: 0117 9077960

AMH • Amherst Antiques, Monomark House, 27 Old Gloucester Street, London WC1N 3XX Tel: 01892 725552 amherstantiques@monomark.co.uk

ANG • Ancient & Gothic Tel: 01202 431721

AnS No longer trading

AOH • Antiques on High, 85 High Street, Oxford OX1 4BG Tel: 01865 251075

AOT • Annie's Old Things, PO Box 6, Camphill, Queensland 4152, Australia Tel: 0061412353099 annie@fan.net.au

APC • Antique Photographic Company Ltd Tel: 01949 842192 alpaco47@aol.com

ARB • Arbour Antiques Ltd, Poet's Arbour, Sheep Street, Stratford-on-Avon, Warwickshire CV37 6EF Tel: 01789 293453

ARo •† Alvin Ross Tel: 01865 772409 vintage.games@virgin.net

ASC • Andrew Sclanders, 32 St Paul's View, 15 Amwell Street, London EC1R 1UP Tel: 020 7278 5034 sclanders@beatbooks.com www.beatbooks.com

ASH • Adrian Ager Ltd, Great Hall, North Street, Ashburton, Devon TQ13 7QD Tel:01364 653189 afager@tinyworld.co.uk www.adrianager.co.uk

ATK • J & V R Atkins Tel: 01952 810594

AU • Auto Suggestion Tel: 01428 722933

AUTO • Automatomania, Stand 124, Grays Antique Market, 58 Davies Street, London W1K 5LP Tel: 020 7495 5259 magic@automatomania.com www.automatomania.com

AVT • Alexander von Tutschek Tel: 01225 465532

B * Bonhams, 101 New Bond Street, London W1S 1SR Tel: 020 7629 6602/7468 8233 www.bonhams.com

B(B) * Bonhams, 1 Old King Street, Bath, Somerset BA1 2JT Tel: 01225 788 988

B(Ch) * Bonhams, 65–69 Lots Road, Chelsea, London SW10 0RN Tel: 020 7393 3900 www.bonhams.com

B(Kn) * Bonhams, Montpelier Street, Knightsbridge, London SW7 1HH Tel: 020 7393 3900 www.bonhams.com

B(L) * Bonhams, 17a East Parade, Leeds, Yorkshire LS1 2BH Tel: 0113 244 8011

B(NW) * Bonhams, New House, 150 Christleton Road, Chester CH3 5TD Tel: 01244 313936

B(WM) * Bonhams, The Old House, Station Road, Knowle, Solihull, West Midlands B93 0HT Tel: 01564 776151

B&R •† Bread & Roses, Durham House Antique Centre, Sheep Street, Stow on the Wold, Gloucestershire GL54 1AA Tel: 01451 870404 or 01926 817342

BAG * Boldon Auction Galleries, 24a Front Street, East Boldon, Tyne & Wear NE36 0SJ Tel: 0191 537 2630

BAJ • Beaulieu Autojumble, Beaulieu, Hampshire

BaN • Barbara Ann Newman, London House Antiques, 4 Market Square, Westerham, Kent TN16 1AW Tel: 01959 564479

BAY • George Bayntun, Manvers Street, Bath, Somerset BA1 1JW Tel: 01225 466000 EBayntun@aol.com

BB(L) * Butterfields, 7601 Sunset Boulevard, Los Angeles CA 90046, USA Tel: 00 1 323 850 7500

BBA *† Bloomsbury Book Auctions, 3 & 4 Hardwick Street, Off Rosebery Avenue, London EC1R 4RY Tel: 020 7833 2636/7 & 020 7923 6940 info@bloomsbury-book-auct.com www.bloomsbury-book-auct.com

BBe •† Bourton Bears, Strathspey, Landsdowne, Bourton-on-the-Water, Gloucestershire GL54 2AR Tel: 01451 821466 mel@strathspey-bed-fsnet.co.uk www.bourtonbears.com

BBR *† BBR, Elsecar Heritage Centre, Wath Road, Elsecar, Barnsley, Yorkshire S74 8HJ Tel: 01226 745156 sales@onlinebbr.com www.onlinebbr.com

BCA • Bealieu Cars Automobilia, Beaulieu Garage, Brockenhurst, Hampshire SO42 7YE Tel: 01590 612999

BD • Banana Dance Ltd, 16 The Mall, Camden Passage, 359 Upper St, Islington, London N1 0PD Tel: 020 8699 7728 jonathan@bananadance.com www.bananadance.com

BDA • Briar's C20th Decorative Arts, Skipton Antiques & Collectors Centre, The Old Foundry, Cavendish Street, Skipton, Yorkshire BD23 2AB Tel: 01756 798641

Beb • Bebes et Jouets, c/o Post Office, Edinburgh EH7 6HW, Scotland Tel: 0131 332 5650 bebesetjouets@u.genie.co.uk www.you.genie.co.uk/bebesetjouets

BEV •† Beverley, 30 Church Street/Alfie's Antique Market, Marylebone, London NW8 8EP Tel: 020 7262 1576

BEX • Daniel Bexfield Antiques, 26 Burlington Arcade, London W1J 0PU Tel: 020 7491 1720

BIB • Biblion, Grays Antique Market, 1–7 Davies Mews, Mayfair, London W1Y 2LP Tel: 020 7629 1374 info@biblion.co.uk www.biblion.com

BiR • Bill Robson Tel: 01434 270206

BLH * Ambrose, Ambrose House, Old Station Road, Loughton, Essex IG10 4PE Tel: 020 8502 3951

BNO • Beanos, Middle Street, Croydon CR0 1RE Tel: 020 8680 1202 enquiries@beanos.co.uk www.beanos.co.uk

BOB • Bob's Collectables Tel: 01277 650834

BON(C) See **B(Ch)**

BoC • Bounty Antiques Centre, 76 Fore Street, Topsham, Devon EX3 0HQ Tel: 01392 875007

BR * Bracketts, Auction Hall, Pantiles, Tunbridge Wells, Kent TN2 5QL Tel: 01892 544500 www.bfaa.co.uk

Bri * Bristol Auction Rooms, St John's Place, Apsley Road, Clifton, Bristol BS8 2ST Tel: 0117 973 7201 www.bristolauctionrooms.co.uk

BRIT * British Car Auctions Ltd, Classic & Historic Automobile Division, Auction Centre, Blackbushe Airport, Blackwater, Camberley, Surrey GU17 9LG Tel: 01252 878555

BrL • The Brighton Lanes Antique Centre, 12 Meeting House Lane, Brighton, East Sussex BN1 1HB Tel: 01273 823121 peter@brightonlanes-antiquecentre.co.uk www.brightonlanes-antiquecentre.co.uk

BRU • Brunel Antiques, Bartlett Street Antiques Centre, Bath, Somerset BA1 2QZ Tel: 0117 968 1734

BSA • Bartlett Street Antique Centre, 5/10 Bartlett Street, Bath, Somerset BA1 2QZ Tel: 01225 466689 info@antiques-centre.co.uk www.antiques-centre.co.uk

BTC •† Beatcity, PO Box 229, Chatham, Kent ME5 8WA Tel: 01634 200444 Darrenhanks@beatcity.co.uk www.beatcity.co.uk

BUR • House of Burleigh Tel: 01664 454570 HousBurl@aol.com

BWA • Bow Well Antiques, 103 West Bow, Edinburgh EH1 2JP, Scotland Tel: 0131 225 3335

BWL * Brightwells Ltd, The Fine Art Saleroom, Ryelands Road, Leominster, Herefordshire HR6 8NZ Tel: 01568 611122 fineart@brightwells.com www.brightwells.com

C&R • Catchpole & Rye, Saracens Dairy, Jobbs Lane, Pluckley, Ashford, Kent TN27 0SA Tel: 01233 840457 info@crye.co.uk www.crye.co.uk

CAG * The Canterbury Auction Galleries, 40 Station Road West, Canterbury, Kent CT2 8AN Tel: 01227 763337 canterbury_auction_galleries@compuserve.com www.thecanterburyauctiongalleries.com

CAL • Cedar Antiques Ltd, High Street, Hartley Wintney, Hampshire RG27 8NY Tel: 01252 843252

Cas • Castle Antiques www.castle-antiques.com

CBGR •† Chris Baker Gramophones, All Our Yesterdays, 3 Cattle Market, Sandwich, Kent CT13 9AE Tel: 01304 375767 or 614756 cbgramophones@aol.com

CBP *† Comic Book Postal Auctions Ltd, 40–42 Osnaburgh Street, London NW1 3ND Tel: 020 7424 0007 comicbook@compuserve.com www.compalcomics.com

CCC •† The Crested China Co, Highfield, Windmill Hill, Driffield, Yorkshire YO25 5EF Tel: 01377 257042 dt@thecrestedchinacompany.com www.thecrestedchinacompany.com

CCH •† Collectors Choice, PO Box 99, Guildford, Surrey GU1 1GA Tel: 01483 576655 louise@collectors-choice.net www.collectors-choice.net

CCO • Collectable Costume Tel: 07980 623926

CDC * Capes Dunn & Co, The Auction Galleries, 38 Charles Street, Off Princess Street, Greater Manchester M1 7DB Tel: 0161 273 1911

CGC * Cheffins, Clifton House, Clifton Road, Cambridge CB1 7EA Tel: 01223 213343 www.cheffins.co.uk

CGX • Computer & Games Exchange, 65 Notting Hill Gate Road, London W11 3JS Tel: 020 7221 1123

CHI •† Chinasearch, 9 Princes Drive, Kenilworth, Warwickshire CV8 2FD Tel: 01926 512402 helen@chinasearch.uk.com jackie@chinasearch.uk.com www.chinasearch.uk.com

CNM • Caroline Nevill Miniatures, 22A Broad Street, Bath, Somerset BA1 5LN Tel: 01225 443091

CO * Cooper Owen, 10 Denmark Street, London WC2H 8LS Tel: 020 7240 4132 www.CooperOwen.com

COB •† Cobwebs, 78 Northam Road, Southampton, Hampshire SO14 0PB Tel: 023 8022 7458 www.cobwebs.uk.com

CoC • Comic Connections, 4a Parsons Street, Banbury, Oxfordshire OX16 5LW Tel: 01295 268989 comicman@freenetname.co.uk

CoCo • Country Collector, 11–12 Birdgate, Pickering, Yorkshire YO18 7AL Tel: 01751 477481

CoHA • Corner House Antiques and Ffoxe Antiques. By appointment Tel: 01793 762752 jdhis007@btopenworld.com

CORD • Corder Collectible Radios paul@pcorder.freeserve.co.uk

CrF • Crowdfree Antiques, PO Box 395, Bury St Edmunds, Suffolk IP31 2PG Tel: 0870 444 0791 info@crowdfree.com www.crowdfree.com

CRIS • Cristobal, 26 Church Street, London NW8 8EP Tel: 020 7724 7230

CRN • The Crow's Nest, 3 Hope Square, opposite Brewers Quay, Weymouth, Dorset DT4 8TR Tel: 01305 786930 peter.ledger3@btopenworld.com

CS • Christopher Sykes, The Old Parsonage, Woburn, Milton Keynes MK17 9QM Tel: 01525 290259 www.sykes-corkscrews.co.uk

CTO •† Collector's Corner, PO Box 8, Congleton, Cheshire CW12 4GD Tel: 01260 270429 dave.popcorner@ukonline.co.uk

CuS • Curious Science, 319 Lillie Road, Fulham, London SW6 7LL Tel: 020 7610 1175 curiousscience@medical-antiques.com

CWO • www.collectorsworld.net, PO Box 4922, Bournemouth, Dorset BH1 3WD Tel: 01202 555223 info@collectorsworld.biz www.collectorsworld.net www.collectorsworld.biz

CYA • Courtyard Antiques, 108A Causewayside, Edinburgh EH9 1PU, Scotland Tel: 0131 662 9008

DA * Dee, Atkinson & Harrison, The Exchange Saleroom, Driffield, Yorkshire YO25 6LD Tel: 01377 253151 exchange@dee-atkinson-harrison.co.uk www.dee-atkinson-harrison.co.uk

DAL *† Dalkeith Auctions Ltd, Dalkeith Hall, Dalkeith Steps, Rear of 81 Old Christchurch Road, Bournemouth, Dorset BH1 1YL Tel: 01202 292905 how@dalkeith-auctions.co.uk www.dalkeith-auctions.co.uk

Dall • P&R Dallimore Antique Collectibles, Cheltenham, Gloucestershire Tel: 01242 820119 rdalli5760@aol.com

DAN • Andrew Dando, 34 Market Street, Bradford on Avon, Wiltshire BA15 1LL Tel: 01225 865444 www.andrewdando.co.uk

DD * David Duggleby, The Vine St Salerooms, Scarborough, Yorkshire YO11 1XN Tel: 01723 507111 auctions@davidduggleby.freeserve.co.uk www.davidduggleby.com

DE •† Decades, 20 Lord St West, Blackburn, Lancashire BB2 1JX Tel: 01254 693320

DEC •† Decorative Antiques, 47 Church Street, Bishop's Castle, Shropshire SY9 5AD Tel: 01588 638851 enquiries@decorative-antiques.co.uk www.decorative-antiques.co.uk

DgC • Dragonlee Collectables Tel: 01622 729502

DHA • Durham House Antiques Centre, Sheep Street, Stow-on-the-Wold, Gloucestershire GL54 1AA Tel: 01451 870404

DHAR • Dave Hardman Antiques, West Street, Witheridge, Devon EX16 8AA Tel: 01884860273 dave@hardmanantiques.freeserve.co.uk

DN * Dreweatt Neate, Donnington Priory, Donnington, Newbury, Berkshire RG14 2JE Tel: 01635 553553

DNo • Desmond & Amanda North, The Orchard, 186 Hale Street, East Peckham, Kent TN12 5JB Tel: 01622 871353 Fax: 01622 872998

DNW *† Dix-Noonan-Webb, 16 Bolton Street, London W1J 8BQ Tel: 020 7499 5022 auctions@dnw.co.uk www.dnw.co.uk

DOL •† Dollectable, 53 Lower Bridge Street, Chester CH1 1RS Tel: 01244 344888/679195

DSG •† Delf Stream Gallery, Bournemouth, Dorset Tel: 07974 926137 oastman@aol.com www.delfstreamgallery.com

DUK • Dukeries Antiques Centre, Thoresby Park, Budby, Newark, Nottinghamshire NG22 9EX Tel: 01623 822252

DuM * Du Mouchelles, 409 East Jefferson, Detroit, Michigan 48226, USA Tel: 001 313 963 6255

DW *† Dominic Winter Book Auctions, The Old School, Maxwell Street, Swindon, Wiltshire SN1 5DR Tel: 01793 611340 info@dominicwinter.co.uk www.dominicwinter.co.uk

EAL • The Exeter Antique Lighting Co, Cellar 15, The Quay, Exeter, Devon EX2 4AP Tel: 01392 490848 www.antiquelightingcompany.com

Ech •† Echoes, 650a Halifax Road, Eastwood, Todmorden, Yorkshire OL14 6DW Tel: 01706 817505

EE • Empire Exchange, 1 Newton Street, Piccadilly, Manchester Tel: 0161 2364445

EMP • The Emporium Antique Centre Too, 24 High Street, Lewes, East Sussex BN7 2LU Tel: 01273 477979

ET • Early Technology, Monkton House, Old Craighall, Musselburgh, Midlothian EH21 8SF, Scotland Tel: 0131 665 5753 michael.bennett-levy@virgin.net www.earlytech.com

ETO • Eric Tombs, 62a West Street, Dorking, Surrey RH4 1BS Tel: 01306 743661

EV • Marlene Evans, Headrow Antiques Centre, Headrow Centre, Leeds, Yorkshire Tel: 0113 245 5344 also at: Red House Antiques Centre, Duncombe Place, York Tel: 01904 637000

EXC • Excalibur Antiques, Taunton Antique Centre, 27–29 Silver Street, Taunton, Somerset TA13DH Tel: 01823 289327 pauldwright@btinternet.com www.excaliburantiques.com

F&C * Finan & Co, The Square, Mere, Wiltshire BA12 6DJ Tel: 01747 861411

F&F • Fenwick & Fenwick, 88–90 High Street, Broadway, Worcestershire WR12 7AJ Tel: 01386 853227/841724

FHF * Frank H. Fellows & Sons, Augusta House, 19 Augusta Street, Hockley, Birmingham, West Midlands B18 6JA Tel: 0121 212 2131

FLD • Flying Duck, 320/322 Creek Road, Greenwich, London SE10 9SW Tel: 020 8858 1964

FMN •† Forget Me Knot Antiques, Antiques at Over the Moon, 27 High Street, St Albans, Hertfordshire AL3 4EH Tel: 01923 261172 sharpffocus@hotmail.com

FOSS • Fossil Shop, The Blue Slipper, 24 St John's Road, Sandown, Isle of Wight PO36 8ES Tel: 0778 8834586 tony@fossilshop.co.uk www.fossilshop.co.uk

FRa • Fraser's, 399 Strand, London WC2R OLX Tel: 020 7836 9325/836 8444 sales@frasersautographs.co.ul www.frasersautographs.com

FST • Curiosities and Collectables, Gloucester Antiques Centre, The Historic Docks, 1 Severn Road, Gloucester GL1 2LE Tel: 01452 529716

G(B) * Gorringes Auction Galleries, Terminus Road, Bexhill-on-Sea, East Sussex TN39 3LR Tel: 01424 212994 bexhill@gorringes.co.uk www.gorringes.co.uk

G(L) * Gorringes inc Julian Dawson, 15 North Street, Lewes, East Sussex BN7 2PD Tel: 01273 472503 auctions@gorringes.co.uk www.gorringes.co.uk

G&CC •† Goss & Crested China Centre & Museum incorporating Milestone Publications, 62 Murray Road, Horndean, Hampshire PO8 9JL Tel: (023) 9259 7440 info@gosschinaclub.demon.co.uk www.gosscrestedchina.co.uk

GAC • Gloucester Antiques Centre, The Historic Docks, 1 Severn Road, Gloucester GL1 2LE Tel: 01452 529716 www.antiques.center.com

GAK * Aylsham Salerooms, 8 Market Place, Aylsham, Norfolk NR11 6EH Tel: 01263 733195

GBr • Geoffrey Breeze Antiques, 6 George Street, Bath, Somerset BA1 2EH Tel: 01225 466499

GeN •† Gentry Antiques, Little Green, Polperro, Cornwall PL13 2RF Tel: 01503 272 361/020 7722 1458 info@cornishwarecollector.co.uk www.cornishwarecollector.co.uk

GH * Gardiner Houlgate, The Bath Auction Rooms, 9 Leafield Way, Corsham, Nr Bath, Somerset SN13 9SW Tel: 01225 812912 gardiner-houlgate.co.uk www.invaluable.com/gardiner-houlgate

GLa • Glassdrumman Antiques, 7 Union Square, The Pantiles, Tunbridge Wells, Kent TN4 8HE Tel: 01892 538615

GM •† Philip Knighton, Bush House 17B South Street, Wellington, Somerset TA21 8NR Tel: 01823 661618 philipknighton@btopenworld.com

GRI •† Grimes House Antiques, High Street, Moreton-in-Marsh, Gloucestershire GL56 0AT Tel: 01608 651029 grimes_house@cix.co.uk www.grimeshouse.co.uk www.cranberryglass.co.uk www.collectglass.com

GTM • Gloucester Toy Mart, Ground Floor, Antique Centre, Severn Road, Old Docks, Gloucester GL1 2LE Tel: 07973 768452

H&G • Hope & Glory, 131A Kensington Church Street, London W8 7LP Tel: 020 7727 8424

HAL •† John & Simon Haley, 89 Northgate, Halifax, Yorkshire HX1 1XF Tel: 01422 822148/360434 toysandbanks@aol.com

HAld * Henry Aldridge & Son, Unit 1, Bath Road Business Centre, Devizes, Wiltshire SN10 1XA Tel: 01380 729199

HAM * Hamptons International, 93 High Street, Godalming, Surrey GU7 1AL Tel: 01483 423567 fineartauctions@hamptons-int.com www.hamptons.co.uk

HaR • Mr A. Harris Tel: 020 8906 8151

HarC •† Hardy's Collectables Tel: 07970 613077 www.poolepotteryjohn.com

HARP •† Harpers Jewellers Ltd, 2/6 Minster Gates, York YO1 7HL Tel: 01904 632634 harpersyork@btopenworld.com www.vintage-watches.co.uk

HCA • Hilltop Cottage Antiques, 101 Portobello Road, London W11 Tel: 01451 844362 noswadp@AOL.com

HCJ No longer trading

HEB • Hebeco, 47 West Street, Dorking, Surrey RH4 1BU Tel: 01306 875396

HEG •† Stuart Heggie, 14 The Borough, Northgate, Canterbury, Kent CT1 2DR Tel: 01227 470422 heggie.cameras@virgin.net

HEL • Helios Gallery, 292 Westbourne Grove, London W11 2PS Tel: 077 11 955 997 heliosgallery@btinternet.com www.heliosgallery.cpm

HILL • Hillhaven Antique Linen & Lace Tel: 0121 358 4320

HL • Honiton Lace Shop, 44 High Street, Honiton, Devon EX14 1PJ Tel: 01404 42416 shop@honitonlace.com www.honitonlace.com

HO • Houghton Antiques, Houghton, Cambridgeshire Tel: 01480 461887

HOLL * Holloway's, 49 Parsons Street, Banbury, Oxfordshire OX16 5PF Tel: 01295 817777 enquiries@hollowaysauctioneers.co.uk www.hollowaysauctioneers.co.uk

HOP • The Antique Garden, Grosvenor Garden Centre, Wrexham Road, Belgrave, Chester CH4 9EB Tel: 01244 629191 info@antique-garden.co.uk www.antique-garden.co.uk

HSt • High Street Antiques, 39 High Street, Hastings, East Sussex TN34 3ER Tel: 01424 460068

HUM • Humbleyard Fine Art, Unit 32 Admiral Vernon Arcade, Portobello Road, London W11 2DY Tel: 01362 637793

HUN • The Country Seat, Huntercombe Manor Barn, Henley-on-Thames, Oxfordshire RG9 5RY Tel: 01491 641349 wclegg@the countryseat.com www.thecountryseat.com

HUX •† David Huxtable, Saturdays at: Portobello Road, Basement Stall 11/12, 288 Westbourne Grove, London W11 Tel: 07710 132200 david@huxtins.com

IB • Iain Burn, 2 Hermitage Close, Frimley, Camberley, Surrey GU16 8LP Tel: 01276 23304 iainburn@altavista.net

ID • Identity, 100 Basement Flat, Finsborough Road, London SW10 9ED Tel: 020 7244 9509

IQ • Cloud Cuckooland, 12 Fore Street, Mevagissey, Cornwall PL26 6UQ Tel: 01726 842364 inkquest@dial.pipex.com www.inkquest.dial.pipex.com/

IW • Islwyn Watkins, Offa's Dyke Antique Centre, 4 High Street, Knighton, Powys LD7 1AT, Wales Tel: 01547 520145

J&J • J & J's, Paragon Antiquities Antiques & Collectors Market, 3 Bladud Buildings, The Paragon, Bath, Somerset BA1 5LS Tel: 01225 463715

J&S • J. R. & S. J. Symes of Bristol Tel: 0117 9501074

JACK • Michael Jackson Antiques, The Quiet Woman Antiques Centre, Southcombe, Chipping Norton, Oxfordshire OX7 5QH Tel: 01608 646262 mjcig@cards.fsnet.co.uk www.our-web-site.com/cigarette-cards

JAM • Jam Jar Tel: 078896 17593

JAY • Jaycee Bee Antiques, Hampshire

JAZZ • Jazz Art Deco

JBB • Jessie's Button Box, Bartlett Street Antique Centre, Bath, Somerset BA1 5DY Tel: 0117 929 9065

JBL • Judi Bland Tel: 01276 857576

JDJ * James D. Julia, Inc., PO Box 830, Rte. 201, Skowhegan Road, Fairfield ME 04937, USA Tel: 207 453 7125 jjulia@juliaauctions.com www.juliaauctions.com

JeH • Jennie Horrocks Tel: 07836 264896 gallery@aw18.fsnet.co.uk info@artnouveaulighting.co.uk artnouveaulighting.co.uk

JHa • Jeanette Hayhurst Fine Glass, 32a Kensington Church Street, London W8 4HA Tel: 020 7938 1539

JHo • Jonathan Horne, 66 Kensington Church Street, London W8 4BY Tel: 020 7221 5658 JH@jonathanhorne.co.uk www.jonathanhorne.co.uk

JJ • Jen Jones, Pontbrendu, LLanybydder, Ceredigion SA40 9UJ, Wales Tel: 01570 480610 quilts@jen-jones.com www.jen-jones.com

JMC • J & M Collectables, 64 High Street, Tenterden, Kent TN30 6AU Tel: 01580 891657 jandmcollectables@tinyonline.co.uk

JOA •† Joan Gale Antiques Dealer, Tombland Antiques Centre, 14 Tombland, Norwich, Norfolk NR3 1HF Tel: 01603 619129 joan.gale@ukgateway.net

JON • Jonkers, 24 Hart Street, Henley on Thames, Oxfordshire RG9 2AU Tel: 01491 576427 bromlea.jonkers@bjbooks.co.uk www.bjbooks.co.uk

JPr •† Joanna Proops Antique Textiles & Lighting, 34 Belvedere, Lansdown Hill, Bath, Somerset BA1 5HR Tel: 01225 310795 antiquetextiles@uk.online.co.uk www.antiquetextiles.co.uk

JRe • John Read, 29 Lark Rise, Martlesham Heath, Ipswich, Suffolk IP5 7SA Tel: 01473 624897

JuC • Julia Craig, Bartlett Street Antiques Centre, 5–10 Bartlett Street, Bath, Somerset BA1 2QZ Tel: 01225 448202/310457

JUJ • Just Jewellery

JUN •† Junktion, The Old Railway Station, New Bolingbroke, Boston, Lincolnshire PE22 7LB Tel: 01205 480068/480087

JW • Julian Wood, Exeter Antique Lighting, Cellar 15, The Quay, Exeter, Devon EX2 4AY Tel: 01392 490848

KA • Kingston Antiques Centre, 29–31 London Road, Kingston-upon-Thames, Surrey KT2 6ND Tel: 020 8549 2004/3839 enquiries@kingstonantiquescentre.co.uk www.kingstonantiquescentre.co.uk

KES •† Keystones, PO Box 387, Stafford ST16 3FG Tel: 01785 256648 gkey@keystones.demon.co.uk www.keystones.co.uk

KHW •† Keith Harding's World of Mechanical Music, The Oak House, High Street, Northleach, Gloucestershire GL54 3ET Tel: 01451 860181 keith@mechanicalmusic.co.uk www.mechanicalmusic.co.uk

L * Lawrence Fine Art Auctioneers, South Street, Crewkerne, Somerset TA18 8AB Tel: 01460 73041

L(w) • LASSCO Warehouse, Britannia Walk, London N1 7LU Tel: 020 7490 1000 www.lassco.co.uk

L&L •† Linen & Lace, Shirley Tomlinson, Halifax Antiques Centre, Queens Road/Gibbet Street, Halifax, Yorkshire HX1 4LR Tel: 01484 540492

LaF • La Femme Tel: 07971 844279 jewels@joancorder.freeserve.co.uk

Law • Malcolm Law Collectables, Greenways Garden Centre, Bethersden, Kent Tel: 0777 3211603

LAY * David Lay (ASVA), Auction House, Alverton, Penzance, Cornwall TR18 4RE Tel: 01736 361414

LBe • Linda Bee Art Deco, Stand L18–21, Grays Antique Market, 1–7 Davies Mews, London W1Y 1AR Tel: 020 7629 5921

LBr • Lynda Brine, Assembly Antiques, 6 Saville Row, Bath, Somerset BA1 2QP Tel: 01225 448488 lyndabrine@yahoo.co.uk www.scentbottlesandsmalls.co.uk

LCC •† The London Cigarette Card Co Ltd, Sutton Road, Somerton, Somerset TA11 6QP Tel: 01458 273452 cards@londoncigcard.co.uk www.londoncigcard.co.uk

LDC • L & D Collins Tel: 020 7584 0712

LEI • Joyce M. Leiby, PO Box 6048, Lancaster PA 17607, USA Tel: (717) 898 9113 joyclei@aol.com

LU • Lucia Collectables, Stalls 57–58 Admiral Vernon Antique Arcade, Portobello Road, London Tel: 01793 790607 sallie_ead@lycos.com

LVS * Loves Auction Rooms, 52 Canal Street, Perth PH2 8LF, Scotland Tel: 01738 633337

MAG • Magna Gallery Tel: 01285 750753 info@magna-gallery.com

MARK •† 20th Century Marks, 12 Market Square, Westerham, Kent TN16 1AW Tel: 01959 562221 lambarda@btconnect.com www.20thcenturymarks.co.uk

MB •† Mostly Boxes, 93 High Street, Eton, Windsor, Berkshire SL4 6AF Tel: 01753 858470

MCA * Mervyn Carey, Twysden Cottage, Scullsgate, Benenden, Cranbrook, Kent TN17 4LD Tel: 01580 240283

MCC • M.C. Chapman Antiques, Bell Hill, Finedon, Northamptonshire NN9 5NB Tel: 01933 681260

MED * Medway Auctions, Fagins, 23 High Street, Rochester, Kent ME1 1LN Tel: 01634 847444 medauc@dircon.co.uk www.medwayauctions.co.uk

MEM § Memories UK Mabel Lucie Attwell Club, Abbey Antiques, 63 Great Whyte, Ramsey, Nr Huntingdon, Cambridgeshire PE26 1HL Tel: 01487 814753

MEx • Music Exchange, 21 Broad Street, Bath, Somerset BA1 5LN Tel: 01225 333963/339789

MF • Maurice Flinton Tel: 01723 863215

MG • Music Ground, 51 Hallgate, Doncaster, Yorkshire DN1 3PB Tel: 01302 320186

MIN • Ministry of Pine, The Ministry,St James Hall, Union Street, Trowbridge, Wiltshire BA14 8RU Tel: 01225 719500 ministryofpine.uk@virgin.net

ML • Memory Lane, Bartlett Street Antiques Centre, 5/10 Bartlett Street, Bath, Somerset BA1 2QZ Tel: 01225 466689

MLa • Marion Langham Tel: 020 7730 1002 mlangham@globalnet.co.uk ladymarion@btinternet.co.uk

MLL • Millers Antiques Ltd, Netherbrook House, 86 Christchurch Road, Ringwood, Hampshire BH24 1DR Tel: 01425 472062 mail@millers-antiques.co.uk www.millers-antiques.co.uk

Mo • Mr Moore

MPC •† Moorcroft Pottery Chester Tel: 01244 301800 sales@Moorcroftchester.co.uk www.Moorcroftchester.co.uk

MRW • Malcolm Welch Antiques, Wild Jebbett, Pudding Bag Lane, Thurlaston, Nr. Rugby, Warwickshire CV23 9JZ Tel: 01788 810 616 www.rb33.co.uk

MSB • Marilynn and Sheila Brass, PO Box 380503, Cambridge MA 02238–0503, USA Tel: 617 491 6064

MSh • Manfred Schotten, 109 High Street, Burford, Oxfordshire OX18 4RG Tel: 01993 822302 www.antiques@£schotten.com

MTM • More than Music, PO Box 2809, Eastbourne, East Sussex BN21 2EA Tel: 01323 649778 morethnmus@aol.com www.mtmglobal.com

MUR •† Murray Cards (International) Ltd, 51 Watford Way, Hendon Central, London NW4 3JH Tel: 020 8202 5688 murraycards@ukbusiness.com www.murraycard.com/

MURR • Murrays' Antiques & Collectables Tel: 01202 309094

NAW • Newark Antiques Warehouse, Old Kelham Road, Newark, Nottinghamshire NG24 1BX Tel: 01636 674869 enquiries@newarkantiques.co.uk

NBL • N. Bloom & Son (1912) Ltd, 12 Piccadilly Arcade, London SW1Y 6NH Tel: 020 7629 5060 nbloom@nbloom.com www.nbloom.com

NEW • Newsum Antiques, 2 High Street, Winchcombe, Gloucestershire GL54 5HT Tel: 01242 603446

NOA * New Orleans Auction Galleries, Inc, 801 Magazine Street, AT 510 Julia, New Orleans, Louisiana 70130, USA Tel: 00 1 504 566 1849

NoC • No.1 Castlegate Antiques, 1–3 Castlegate, Newark, Nottinghamshire NG24 1AZ Tel: 01636 701877

NOS • Nostalgia and Comics, 14–16 Smallbrook Queensway, City Centre, Birmingham, West Midlands B5 4EN Tel: 0121 643 0143

NW • Nigel Williams Rare Books, 22 & 25 Cecil Court, London WC2N 4HE Tel: 020 7836 7757

OLA • Olliff's Architectural Antiques, 19–21 Lower Redland Road, Redland, Bristol, Gloucestershire BS6 6TB Tel: 0117 923 9232 marcus@olliffs.com www.olliffs.com

OLD • Oldnautibits, PO Box 67, Langport, Somerset TA10 9WJ Tel: 01458 241816 geoff.pringle@oldnautibits.com www.oldnautibits.com

ONS * Onslow's Auctions Ltd, The Coach House, Manor Road, Stourpaine, Dorset DT8 8TQ Tel: 01258 488838
ORI • Origin 101 Gateway Arcade, Islington High Street, London N1 Tel: 07769 686146/ 07747 758852 David @origin101.co.uk www.naturalmodern.com www.origin101.co.uk
OTA •† On The Air, The Vintage Technology Centre, The Highway, Hawarden (Nr Chester), Deeside, Cheshire CH5 3DN Tel: 01244 530300 www.vintageradio.co.uk
OTB •† The Old Tackle Box, PO Box 55, High Street, Cranbrook, Kent TN17 3ZU Tel: 01580 713979 tackle.box@virgin.net
OW • Offworld, 142 Market Halls, Arndale Center, Luton, Bedfordshire LU1 2TP Tel: 01582 736256 off_world@btconnect.com
P(B) See **B(B)**
P(NW) See **B(NW)**
PAR • Park House Antiques & Toy Museum, Park Street, Stow-on-the-Wold, Gloucestershire GL54 1AQ Tel: 01451 830159 info@thetoymuseum.co.uk www.thetoymuseum.co.uk
PAS • Tina Pasco,Waterlock House, Wingham, Nr Canterbury, Kent CT3 1BH Tel: 01227 722151 tinapasco@tinapasco.com www.tinapasco.com
Penn • Penny Fair Antiques Tel: 07860 825456
PF * Peter Francis, Curiosity Sale Room, 19 King Street, Carmarthen SA31 1BH, South Wales Tel: 01267 233456 Peterfrancis@valuers.fsnet.co.uk www.peterfrancis.co.uk
PIC • David & Susan Pickles Tel: 01282 707673
PICA • Piccadilly Antiques, 280 High Street, Batheaston, Bath BA1 7RA Tel: 01225 851494 piccadillyantiques@ukonline.co.uk
PICC •† Piccypicky.com Tel: 020 8204 2001/020 8206 2001 www.piccypicky.com
PIL • Pilgrim Antique Centre, 7 West Street, Dorking, Surrey RH4 1BL Tel: 01306 875028
PLB • Planet Bazaar, 149 Drummond Street, London NW1 2PB Tel: 0207 387 8326 info@planetbazaar.co.uk www.planetbazaar.co.uk
POL • Politico Book Shop, 8 Artillery Row, London SW1 Tel: 020 7828 0010
Pott * Potteries Specialist Auctions, 271 Waterloo Road, Cobridge, Stoke on Trent, Staffordshire ST6 3HR Tel: 01782 286622
PPH • Period Picnic Hampers Tel: 0115 937 2934
PPL • The Pen and Pencil Lady Tel: 01647 231619 penpencilady@aol.com www.penpencilady.com
PR • Prime Cuts, 85 Gloucester Road, Bishopston, Bristol BS7 8AS Tel: 0117 9830007
PrB •† Pretty Bizarre, 170 High Street, Deal, Kent CT14 6BQ Tel: 07973 794537
PSA • Pantiles Spa Antiques, 4, 5, 6 Union House, The Pantiles, Tunbridge Wells, Kent TN4 8HE Tel: 01892 541377
Q&C • Q&C Militaria, 22 Suffolk Road, Cheltenham, Gloucestershire GL50 2AQ Tel: 01242 519815 john@qc-militaria.freeserve.co.uk www.qcmilitaria.com
RAND • Becky Randall, c/o 36 Highfield Road, Wilmslow, Buckinghamshire MK18 3DU Tel: 07979 848440
RBB See **BWL**
RCo • Royal Commemorative China Tel: 0208 863 0625 royalcommemorative@hotmail.com
RdeR • Rogers de Rin, 76 Royal Hospital Road, London SW3 4HN Tel: 020 7352 9007
RDG • Richard Dennis Gallery, 144 Kensington Church Street, London W8 4BN Tel: 020 7727 2061
REN • Paul & Karen Rennie, 13 Rugby Street, London, WC1N 3QT Tel: 020 7405 0220 info@rennart.co.uk www.rennart.co.uk
REPS • Repsycho, 85 Gloucester Road, Bishopston, Bristol BS7 8AS Tel: 0117 9830007
RET • Retro-Spective Tel: 07989 984659 fineart692hotmail.com
RGa • Richard Gardner Antiques, Swanhouse Market Square, Petworth, West Sussex GU28 0AN Tel: 01798 343411
RGA • Richard Gibbon, Shop 4 34/34a Islington Green, London N1 8DU Tel: 020 7354 2852 neljeweluk@aol.com
RGe • Rupert Gentle Antiques, The Manor House, Milton Lilbourne, Nr Pewsey, Wiltshire SN9 5LQ Tel: 01672 563344
RH •† Rick Hubbard Art Deco, 3 Tee Court, Bell Street, Romsey, Hampshire SO51 8GY Tel: 01794 513133 rick@rickhubbard-artdeco.co.uk www.rickhubbard-artdeco.co.uk
RIA • Riverside Antiques, 60 Ely Street, Stratford-upon-Avon, Warwickshire Tel: 01789 262090
ROSc * R. O. Schmitt Fine Art, Box 1941, Salem, New Hampshire 03079, USA Tel: 603 893 5915 bob@roschmittfinearts.com www.antiqueclockauction.com
RTo * Rupert Toovey & Co Ltd, Spring Gardens, Washington, West Sussex RH20 3BS Tel: 01903 891955 auctions@rupert-toovey.com www.rupert-toovey.com
RTT • Rin Tin Tin, 34 North Road, Brighton, East Sussex BN1 1YB Tel: 01273 672424 rick@rintintin.freeserve.co.uk
RTW •† Richard Twort Tel: 01934 641900
RUL • Rules Antiques, 62 St Leonards Road, Windsor, Berkshire SL4 3BY Tel: 01753 833210/01491 642062
RUSK • Ruskin Decorative Arts, 5 Talbot Court, Stow-on-the-Wold, Cheltenham, Gloucestershire GL54 1DP Tel: 01451 832254 william.anne@ruskindecarts.co.uk
RUSS • Russells Tel: 023 8061 6664
RW • Robin Wareham

RWA • Ray Walker Antiques, Burton Arcade, 296 Westbourne Grove, London W11 2PS Tel: 020 8464 7981 rw.antiques@btinternet.com

S * Sotheby's, 34–35 New Bond Street, London W1A 2AA Tel: 020 7293 5000/020 72935205 www.sothebys.com

S(O) * Sotheby's Olympia, Hammersmith Road, London W14 8UX Tel: 020 7293 5000

S&D • S&D Postcards, Bartlett Street Antique Centre, 5–10 Bartlett Street, Bath, Somerset BA1 2QZ winstampok@netscapeonline.co.uk

SA • Sporting Antiques, St Ives, Cambridgeshire Tel: 01480 463891 john.lambden@virgin.net

SAF * Saffron Walden Auctions, 1 Market Street, Saffron Walden, Essex CB10 1JB Tel: 01799 513281

SaH • Sally Hawkins Tel: 01636 636666 sallytiles@aol.com

SAS *† Special Auction Services, Kennetholme, Midgham, Reading, Berkshire RG7 5UX Tel: 0118 971 2949 www.invaluable.com/sas/

SAY • Charlotte Sayers, 360 Grays Antique Market, 58 Davies St, London W1K 5LP Tel: 020 7499 5478

SBL • Twentieth Century Style Tel: 01822 614831

SBT • Steinberg & Tolkien Vintage & Designer Clothing, 193 Kings Road, London SW3 5EB Tel: 020 7376 3660

SDA • Stephanie Davison Antiques, Bakewell Antiques Centre, King Street, Bakewell, Derbyshire DE45 1DZ Tel: 01629 812496 bacc@chappells-antiques.co.uk www.chappells-antiques.co.uk

SDP • Stage Door Prints, 9 Cecil Court, London WC2N 4EZ Tel: 020 7240 1683

SEA • Mark Seabrook Antiques, PO Box 396, Huntingdon, Cambridgeshire PE28 0ZA Tel: 01480 861935 enquiries@markseabrook.com www.markseabrook.com

SER •† Serendipity, 125 High Street, Deal, Kent CT14 6BB Tel: 01304 369165/01304 366536 dipityantiques@aol.com

SHa • Shapiro & Co, Stand 380, Grays Antique Market, 58 Davies Street, London W1Y 5LP Tel: 020 7491 2710

SJH * S.J. Hales, 87 Fore Street, Bovey Tracey, Devon TQ13 9AB Tel: 01626 836684

SK * Skinner Inc, The Heritage On The Garden, 63 Park Plaza, Boston MA 02116, USA Tel: 001 617 350 5400

SK(B) * Skinner Inc, 357 Main Street, Bolton MA 01740, USA Tel: 001 978 779 6241

SMI •† Skip & Janie Smithson Antiques Tel: 01754 810265

SMW • Sporting Memorabilia of Warwick, 13 Market Place, Warwick CV34 4FS Tel: 01926 410600 sales@sportantiques.com sportsantiques.com

SPE • Sylvie Spectrum, Stand 372, Grays Market, 58 Davies Street, London W1Y 2LB Tel: 020 7629 3501

SpP *† Specialised Postcard Auctions, 25 Gloucester Street, Cirencester, Gloucestershire GL7 2DJ Tel: 01285 659057

SPT • Sporting Times Gone By Tel: 01903 885656 www.sportingtimes.co.uk

SRA *† Sheffield Railwayana Auctions, 43 Little Norton Lane, Sheffield, Yorkshire S8 8GA Tel: 0114 274 5085 ian@sheffrail.freeserve.co.uk www.sheffieldrailwayana.co.uk

SSF • Suffolk Sci-Fi and Fantasy, 17 Norwich Road, Ipswich, Suffolk Tel: 01473 400655 mick@suffolksci-fi.com www.suffolksci-fi.com

SSL • Star Signings Ltd, Unit E16/E17 Grays in the Mews, 1–7 Davies Mews, London W1K 5AB Tel: 020 7491 1010

SSM • Sue Scott Motoring Memorabilia Tel: 01525 372757

StC • Carlton Factory Shop, Carlton Works, Copeland Street, Stoke-on-Trent, Staffordshire ST4 1PU Tel: 01782 410504

STS • Shaw to Shore, Church Street Antiques Centre, Stow-on-the-Wold, Gloucestershire GL54 1BB Tel: 01451 870186

SUW • Sue Wilde at Wildewear Tel: 01395 577966 compacts@wildewear.co.uk www.wildewear.co.uk

SWB •† Sweetbriar Gallery Ltd, Sweetbriar House, 106 Robin Hood Lane, Helsby, Cheshire WA6 9NH Tel: 01928 723851 sweetbr@globalnet.co.uk www.sweetbriar.co.uk

SWO * Sworders, 14 Cambridge Road, Stansted Mountfitchet, Essex CM24 8BZ Tel: 01279 817778 www.sworder.co.uk

T&D • Toys & Dolls, 367 Fore Street, Edmonton, London N9 0NR Tel: 020 8807 3301

TAC • Tenterden Antiques Centre, 66–66A High Street, Tenterden, Kent TN30 6AU Tel: 01580 765655/765885

TAY * Taylors, Honiton Galleries, 205 High Street, Honiton, Devon EX14 8LF Tel: 01404 42404

TB • Millicent Safro Tender Buttons, 143 E.62nd Street, New York NY10021, USA Tel: (212) 758 7004

TEN * Tennants, The Auction Centre, Harmby Road, Leyburn, Yorkshire DL8 5SG Tel: 01969 623780 enquiry@tennants-ltd.co.uk www.tennants.co.uk

TH •† Tony Horsley Tel: 01273 550770

TL •† Telephone Lines Ltd, 304 High Street, Cheltenham, Gloucestershire GL50 3JF Tel: 01242 583699 info@telephonelines.net www.telephonelines.net

TMA *† Tring Market Auctions, Brook Street, Tring, Hertfordshire HP23 5EF Tel: 01442 826446 sales@tringmarketauctions.co.uk www.tringmarketauctions.co.uk

TMa • Tin Man, St Ives, Cambridgeshire Tel: 01480 463891 john.lambden@virgin.net

TML • Timothy Millett Ltd, Historic Medals and Works of Art, PO Box 20851, London SE22 0YN Tel: 020 8693 1111 tim@timothymillett.demon.co.uk

TOM •† Charles Tomlinson, Chester
Tel: 01244 318395
charles.tomlinson@lineone.net
www.lineone.net/-charles.tomlinson

TOT •† Totem, 168 Stoke Newington, Church Street, London N16 0JL Tel: 020 7275 0234
sales@totemrecords.com
www.totemrecords.com

TPCS § Torquay Pottery Collectors' Society, Membership Secretary, c/o Torre Abbey, The Kings Drive, Torquay, Devon TQ2 5JX
scandymag@aol.com
www.torquaypottery.com

TRA • Tramps, Tuxford Hall, Lincoln Road, Tuxford, Newark, Nottinghamshire NG22 0HR
Tel: 01777 872 543 info@trampsuk.com

TRI • Trident Antiques, 2 Foundry House, Hall Street, Long Melford, Suffolk CO10 9JR
Tel: 01787 883388 tridentoak@aol.com

TRM * Thomson, Roddick & Medcalf, 60 Whitesands, Dumfries DG1 2RS, Scotland
Tel: 01387 255366

TRO •† The Troika Man Tel: 01535 273088
thetroikaman@aol.com www.troikapottery.org

TWAC • Talbot Walk Antiques Centre, The Talbot Hotel, High Street, Ripley, Surrey GU23 6BB
Tel: 01483 211724

TWI • Twinkled, 1st floor, Old Petrol Station, 11–17 Stockwell Street, Greenwich, London SE10 Tel: 020 84880930 info@twinkled.net
www.twinkled.net
also at: High St Antiques Centre, 39 High Street, Hastings, East Sussex TN34
Tel: 01424 460068

TWO • Two P'S Tel: 01252 647965
twops@ntlworld.com

TWr • Tim Wright Antiques, Richmond Chambers, 147 Bath Street, Glasgow G2 4SQ, Scotland
Tel: 0141 221 0364

UCO •† Unique Collections, 52 Greenwich Church Street, London SE10 9BL Tel: 020 8305 0867
glen@uniquecollections.co.uk
www.uniquecollections.co.uk

VB • Variety Box Tel: 01892 531868

VBo • Vernon Bowden, Bournemouth, Dorset
Tel: 01202 763806

VCL • Vintage Cameras Ltd, 256 Kirkdale, Sydenham, London SE26 4NL
Tel: 020 8778 5416
info@vintagecameras.co.uk
www.vintagecameras.co.uk

VEC *† Vectis Auctions Ltd/Barry Potter Auctions, Fleck Way, Thornaby, Stockton-on-Tees, Cleveland TS17 9JZ Tel: 01642 750616
admin@vectis.co.uk
admin@barrypotterauctions.com
www.vectis.co.uk
www.barrypotterauctions.co.uk

VH • Valerie Howard, 4 Campden Street, Off Kensington Church Street, London W8 7EP
Tel: 020 7792 9702

VJ • Ventnor Junction, 48 High Street, Ventnor, Isle of Wight PO38 1LT Tel: 01983 853996
shop@ventjunc.freeserve.co.uk

VRG •† Vintage & Rare Guitars, 7–8 Saville Row, Bath, Somerset BA1 2QP Tel: 01225 330 888
enquiries@vintageandrareguitars.com
www.vintageandrareguitars.com
also at: 6 Denmark Street, London WC2H 8LX
Tel: 020 7240 7500

VS *† T. Vennett-Smith, 11 Nottingham Road, Gotham, Nottinghamshire NG11 0HE
Tel: 0115 983 0541 info@vennett-smith.com
www.vennett-smith.com

VSP * Van Sabben Poster Auctions, PO Box 2065, 1620 EB Hoorn, Netherlands
Tel: 31 229 268203
uboersma@sabbenposterauctions.nl
www.vsabbenposterauctions.nl

WAB • Warboys Antiques, St Ives, Cambridgeshire
Tel: 01480 463891 john.lambden@virgin.net

WAC • Worcester Antiques Centre, 15 Reindeer Court, Mealcheapen Street, Worcester WR1 4DF Tel: 01905 610680
WorcsAntiques@aol.com

WAL *† Wallis & Wallis, West Street Auction Galleries, Lewes, East Sussex BN7 2NJ
Tel: 01273 480208
auctions@wallisandwallis.co.uk
grb@wallisandwallis.co.uk
www.wallisandwallis.co.uk

WAm • Williams Amusements Ltd, Bluebird House, Povey Cross Road, Horley, Surrey RH6 0AG
Tel: 01293 782222
adrian@williams-amusements.co.uk
www.williams-amusements.co.uk

WeA • Wenderton Antiques Tel: 01227 720295

WHO • The Who Shop International Ltd, 4 Station Parade, High Street North, East Ham, London E6 1JD Tel: 020 8471 2356
whoshop@hilly.com www.thewhoshop.com

WilP * W&H Peacock, 26 Newnham Street, Bedford MK40 3JR Tel: 01234 266366

WIM • Wimpole Antiques, Stand 349, Grays Antique Market, 58 Davies Street, London W1Y 2LP
Tel: 020 7499 2889
wimpoleantiques@compuserve.com

WO • Woodville Antiques, The Street, Hamstreet, Ashford, Kent TN26 2HG Tel: 01233 732981
woodvilleantiques@yahoo.co.uk

WP •† British Notes, PO Box 257, Sutton, Surrey SM3 9WW Tel: 020 8641 3224
pamwestbritnotes@compuserve.com
www.west-banknotes.co.uk

WRe • Walcot Reclamations, 108 Walcot Street, Bath, Somerset BA1 5BG Tel: 01225 444404

WW * Woolley & Wallis, 51–61 Castle Street, Salisbury, Wiltshire SP1 3SU
Tel: 01722 424500/01722 411854

YC •† Yesterday Child, Angel Arcade, 118 Islington High Street, London N1 8EG
Tel: 020 7354 1601/01908 583403

YEST • Yesterdays, V.O.F. Yesterdays, Maaseikerweg 202, 6006 AD Weert, The Netherlands
Tel: 0475 531207

ZOOM No longer trading

Index to Advertisers

Index

Bold numbers refer to information and pointer boxes

C